Truth or Economics

On the Definition, Prediction, and Relevance of Economic Efficiency

Richard S. Markovits

Yale University Press

New Haven and London

Published with assistance from the Kingsley Trust Association Publication Fund established by the Scroll and Key Society of Yale College.

Printed in the United States of America.

Library of Congress Control Number: 2007930444
ISBN: 978-0-300-11459-1

A catalogue record for this book is available from the British Library.

The paper in this book meets the guidelines for permanence and durability of the Committee on Production Guidelines for Book Longevity of the Council on Library Resources.

10 9 8 7 6 5 4 3 2 1

To Daniel, Stefanie, Benjamin, Julia, and Rebecca, Inga's and my children, who are also our friends, for providing us with both satisfaction and pleasure.

Contents

Acknowledgments

I would like to begin by thanking my personal assistant Judy Dodson for typing various drafts of this difficult manuscript skillfully and with good humor. I would also like to thank my son Daniel S. Markovits of the Yale Law School and my daughter Julia E. Markovits of the Harvard Society of Fellows for useful conversations about Parts I and III. Finally, I would like to thank the participants in various colloquia I have given over the years at different institutions on the material this book develops. The relevant institutions include Bath University (England), Bremen University (Germany), Brooklyn Law School, Brunel University (England), the Centre for Socio-Legal Studies (Oxford University, England), Columbia University, University of Connecticut, Emory University, Fordham University, George Washington University, The Institute for Competition and Industry (Institut für Wettbewerb und Industrie, Berlin, Germany), The Institute of Advanced Study, Berlin (Wissenschafts Kolleg zu Berlin), Hamburg University (Germany), University of Konstanz (Germany), London School of Economics (England),

Stanford University, Technical University (Berlin) (Technische Universität, Berlin), University of Texas, Tulane University, United States Department of Justice (Antitrust Division), and University College, London (England).

Truth or Economics

Introduction

Both economists in general and law and economics scholars of all backgrounds devote a great deal of attention to economic efficiency. Some studies executed by such scholars focus exclusively on the economic efficiency of the private choice or government policy they analyze. And others that primarily investigate the impact of some choice or policy on price, unit output, investment, seller profits, and/or relevant consumer equivalent-dollar[1] gains or losses conclude with a section that purports to establish the implications of their findings for the economic efficiency (and allegedly derivatively, the "social optimality") of the choice or policy in question. This book is a constructive critique of the way in which economists and law and economics scholars define, predict, and assess the moral and legal relevance of the impact of private choices or government policies on economic efficiency.

The book has three parts, which are respectively concerned with these three issues. Each part has two chapters. The first chapter of each part delineates the way in which I think the relevant issue should be resolved. The second states, illustrates, and criticizes the ways in which economists and law and economics scholars have handled these issues and demonstrates the importance of the errors it reveals.

Part I addresses the definition of the concept of the impact of a choice on economic efficiency. Chapter 1 focuses on the "correct" definition of this concept. It begins by arguing against the general position that there is no correct way to define this type of concept. In particular, it argues that definitions of concepts of this type should be evaluated by two criteria: (1) the conformity of the definition with professional and (where relevant) popular understanding, and (2) the usefulness of the concept the definition creates. It then delineates a monetized definition of the concept that satisfies these criteria. According to this definition, a choice's economic efficiency equals the difference between the number of dollars its beneficiaries would have to receive to be left as well off as the choice would leave them and the number of dollars its victims would have to lose to be left as poorly off as the choice would leave them, where the dollar figures in question are calculated on the following three assumptions:

1. A. the relevant winners did not voluntarily agree to exchange the policy for the transfers in question and were not aware of the linkage between their receipt of this money and the policy's rejection, and
   B. the relevant losers did not voluntarily agree to pay money to prevent the policy's adoption and were not aware of the connection between the policy's rejection and the withdrawal of money from them;
2. the relevant winners and losers had no attitudes toward government, nonparochial distributive preferences, or defensible normative commitments that would lead them to prefer the transfer to the choice or policy or vice versa; and
3. the transfers in question would not affect the relevant individual winners and losers by changing the behavior of others by changing their income or wealth positions.

Chapter 1 concludes by addressing the more specific argument of many non-economist critics[2] of economics and (surprisingly) some economists[3] that there is no non-arbitrary ("correct") way to define the concept of the impact of a choice on economic efficiency because there is no non-arbitrary way to resolve the so-called offer/asking problem—that is, to decide between measuring

1. each sovereign, maximizing winner's equivalent-dollar gain by the number of dollars he would be indifferent to offering to secure a policy that would benefit him but would otherwise be rejected or the number of dollars he

would be indifferent to accepting in exchange for (the minimum number of dollars he would ask for) his critical acquiescence to its rejection and
2. each sovereign, maximizing loser's equivalent-dollar loss by the number of dollars he would be indifferent to accepting for (the minimum number of dollars he would ask for) his critical acquiescence to the relevant policy's adoption or the number of dollars he would be indifferent to paying to prevent the adoption of a policy (that he would offer to secure the policy's rejection when it would otherwise be adopted).

Chapter 2 states and criticizes the various definitions of (tests for) economic efficiency that economists use—the Pareto-superior/Pareto-inferior definition, the Kaldor-Hicks test,[4] the Scitovsky test,[5] and the potentially-Pareto-superior definition. In addition to explaining why these definitions are wrong, Chapter 2 points out why these errors matter—why they tend to cause both those who make them and the policy audience to reach policy conclusions that disserve their values.

Both Chapter 1's definitional proposal and Chapter 2's critique of most of the contrary definitions explicitly or implicitly used by others are based on two central points. The first is that the equivalent-dollar gain a choice or policy confers on each of its beneficiaries and the equivalent-dollar loss it imposes on each of its victims equal what economists call the "equivalent variation" in each relevant individual's wealth, not what economists term the "compensating variation" in his wealth. Broadly speaking (see the second point discussed below), this position asserts that

1. a choice's beneficiary's equivalent-dollar gain equals the number of dollars he would have to be given instead of the choice to be made as well off as the choice would make him, not the number of dollars whose withdrawal from him would perfectly offset the choice's effect on him—that is, on the equivalent variation in his wealth, not on the compensating (perfectly offsetting) variation in his wealth—and
2. a choices' victim's equivalent-dollar loss equals the number of dollars that would have to be withdrawn from him to make him as poorly off as the choice would make him (would be equivalent to the choice in question), not the number of dollars whose transfer to him would perfectly offset (fully compensate him for) the policy's impact on him.

My conclusion that this position is correct has two factual premises. The first is that these operationalizations capture what the general public and economists mean by "the (equivalent-) dollar gain a private choice or public policy confers on its beneficiaries" and "the (equivalent-) dollar loss it imposes on its victims"—that is, is consistent with both popular and professional intuitive understanding and usage. The second premise is that these operationalizations maximize the contribution that these concepts and the concept of economic efficiency that incorporates them can make to the normative evaluation (in particular, to the utilitarian evaluation) of the choices in question. More specifically, this position is correct because—to the extent that the concept of economic efficiency can play a useful role in the utilitarian evaluation of a private choice or government policy—it can do so because the most utility-promoting way to evaluate a policy from a utilitarian perspective is to predict the equivalent-dollar gains and losses the choice or policy would generate (defined in equivalent-variation terms), weight those monetized gains and losses by the average utility-value of the dollars gained and lost, and compare the weighted equivalent-dollar gains with the weighted equivalent-dollar losses.

The second point (actually, set of points) that is central to Part I's argument relates to the assumptions one should make when determining the money transfer to a choice's winner that would leave him as well off as the choice would leave him (would be equivalent to the choice) and the money withdrawal from a choice's loser that would leave him as poorly off as the choice would leave him (would be equivalent to the choice). In particular,

1. since (A) no winner would actually be voluntarily exchanging the choice for the money transfer and no loser would actually be voluntarily paying money to prevent the choice from being made, and (B) in some circumstances, individuals place a positive or negative value on engaging in such voluntary transactions, the equivalent variations should be determined on the assumption that the relevant winners did not voluntarily agree to accept the equivalent transfers as payment for foregoing the choice and the losers did not voluntarily agree to pay the equivalent sum to prevent the choice from being made;
2. since (A) no money transfer would actually be made, (B) some individual winners might value or disvalue in itself the substitution of a money transfer to them (and to the policy's other beneficiaries) for the policy even when they did not consent to this switch, and (C) some individual losers might value or disvalue in itself the substitution of a money withdrawal from them (and from the policy's other victims) for the policy

even when they did not consent to this switch, the equivalent variations should be determined on the assumption that the relevant individuals would be intrinsically indifferent to the switches in question or unaware of the linkage between the policy's rejection and the transfer to or from them;

3. since the relevant money transfers are purely hypothetical, they should be calculated on the assumption that the winners and losers in question have no distributive attitudes toward such transfers in themselves (for example, toward the government's engaging in such activities), no non-parochial distributive preferences, and no normative distributive commitments that would give them a reason to prefer the transfer or withdrawal to the choice/policy or vice versa; and
4. since the equivalent money transfers in question are purely hypothetical and could be financed in a large number of different ways that would have different impacts on the income or wealth positions of others, they should be measured on the assumption that their execution would not have an equivalent-dollar impact on any individual winner or loser by changing the conduct of others by altering their income or wealth positions.

Part I's conclusion that there is a correct way to resolve both the equivalent-versus-compensating variation issue and the other issues with which the second set of points just discussed are concerned underlies both my rejection of the claim that there is no non-arbitrary way to resolve the offer/asking problem and my critiques of several of the tests for or definitions of the impact of a choice on economic efficiency that many economists use. Thus, the conclusion that there is a correct way to define the impact of a choice on economic efficiency obviously implies that there is a correct way to respond to the offer/asking problem. And my critiques of the Kaldor-Hicks, Scitovsky, and potentially-Pareto-superior tests for or definitions of the impact of a choice on economic efficiency focus on the fact that they implicitly measure the relevant effects either exclusively or partially by the compensating rather than the equivalent variations in question and fail to respond appropriately to the issues with which the second set of points is concerned.

Part II focuses on the proper way to assess the economic efficiency of any choice in the monetized sense in which Part I defines this concept. Part II argues that, to be acceptably cost-effective, any approach to economic-efficiency assessment that does not proceed by identifying a random sample of the relevant choice's winners and losers and estimating the equivalent-dollar gains and losses it would confer or impose on them must take appropriate account of The General Theory of Second Best.[6] According to this general theory, given a series of conditions whose fulfillment guarantees the achievement of an optimum, if one or more of these conditions cannot or will not be fulfilled, there is no general reason to suppose that a choice that reduces the number or magnitude of the departures from these conditions (hereinafter, the number or magnitude of the imperfections in the system) will even tend to bring one closer to the optimum. In crude terms, this conclusion reflects the fact that, in general, the imperfections one could reduce or eliminate will be as likely to counteract as to exacerbate the effects of the remaining imperfections. In the context of this book, the relevant optimum is maximum economic efficiency, and the relevant optimal conditions are the so-called Pareto-optimal conditions—perfect competition among sellers, perfect competition among buyers, no externalities, no taxes on the margin of income, individual sovereignty, individual maximization, and no misallocation-causing buyer surplus.[7]

Even at this juncture, two points should be emphasized about The General Theory of Second Best's implications for economic-efficiency assessment. First, on the down side, contrary to the claims of many economists, The General Theory of Second Best implies far more than that policies that reduce the number and/or magnitude of the Pareto imperfections in our inevitably Pareto-imperfect world *may possibly* (that is, in exceptional circumstances) *decrease economic efficiency* on that account; it implies that, unless one can make an appropriate argument to the contrary, one must assume that such policies *will not even tend to increase economic efficiency.* Second, on the up side, contrary to the fears of many economists, The General Theory of Second Best does not counsel despair—does not imply that it will always or even usually be impossible to contribute to efforts to increase economic efficiency by making economic-efficiency assessments on which one can justifiably rely. Second-best theory does imply that, to be sound, economic-efficiency assessments must be based on an analysis that

1. takes appropriate account of the various types of economic inefficiency the choice under consideration may increase or decrease, the various Pareto imperfections that could individually cause each such type of resource misallocation in an otherwise-Pareto-perfect world, and the various ways in which these imperfections interact to cause the various types of resource misallocation each would cause on its own; and
2. does an appropriate job of collecting and assessing data on the Pareto imperfections and other parameters whose relevance theoretical analysis

establishes (that is, on both their pre-choice magnitudes and the effect that the choice or policy in question would have on them).

However, second-best theory does not imply that, to be sound, economic-efficiency assessments must be generated by (economically inefficient) analyses whose theoretical and empirical components are perfect. Nothing in second-best theory disfavors an analyst's deciding not to think through some theoretical possibility or not to collect some additional data when it would be *ex ante* economically inefficient for him to do the theoretical or empirical work in question. In fact, second-best theory can be used to identify those shortcuts that would be *ex ante* economically efficient—that is, can provide the basis for developing what I call "third-best economic-efficiency analysis," the approach to economic-efficiency analysis that is economically efficient, given the cost, probable deficiencies, and possible value of theoretical analyses and the cost, inevitable inaccuracy, and possible value of data.

Chapter 3 (the first chapter of Part II) presents and illustrates an approach to economic-efficiency analysis that I think is third-best economically efficient. This distortion-analysis approach focuses on the impact of the private choice or public policy under consideration on the difference between the profitability and economic efficiency (the "distortion" in the profitability) of the least profitable but not unprofitable (in that sense, marginal) "choices of each type" that would be affected by the decision under scrutiny. The choices to which the previous sentence refers are choices about how to use resources, such as choices to use one production process rather than another to produce a given product, to produce an additional unit of some good, or to develop and introduce a new product variant. More specifically, this approach derives its economic-efficiency predictions from conclusions about the impact of the private choice or public policy under scrutiny on the weighted-average value and weighted-average absolute deviation of the distribution of positive percentage distortions in the profits yielded by the marginal resource uses of all types in the economy where the phrase "percentage profit distortion" stands for the ratio of the distortion in the profits yielded by the relevant resource use to its allocative cost and the weight assigned to each percentage-profit-distortion figure equals the ratio of the marginal allocative cost of the resource use to which it relates to the sum of the marginal allocative costs of all resource uses in the distribution.

Chapter 3 outlines this approach and concretizes it in two ways:

1. by developing formulas for the distortions in the profits yielded by the least profitable but not unprofitable actual resource uses of particular types

that would be generated by imperfections in seller price competition, by externalities, by the combination of imperfections in seller price competition and externalities, or by all extant Pareto imperfections and
2. by executing partial and preliminary distortion analyses of the economic efficiency of prohibiting price-fixing, of providing tax breaks for investments of all types, of shifting from a negligence *plus* contributory-negligence tort-law regime to a strict-liability *plus* contributory-negligence tort-law system, and of requiring marine rescuees to pay various amounts of compensation to successful marine rescuers who have not been able to negotiate binding prices for their services.

As just described, Chapter 3 focuses on "what's right"—on what I take to be the economically efficient way to assess the economic efficiency of any policy. However, Chapter 3 does make two assertions about "what's wrong"—about the quality of the economic-efficiency analyses to be found in the economics and law and economics literatures. First, Chapter 3 asserts that the overwhelming majority of published economic-efficiency analyses are first-best economic-efficiency analyses, which proceed on an implicit, unrealistic assumption that enables their authors to ignore The General Theory of Second Best: the relevant assumption, which implies that any policy that reduces or eliminates the imperfection it targets will tend to increase economic efficiency of that account, is that the only (relevant) Pareto imperfection in the system is the target imperfection the policy under consideration is designed to reduce or eliminate. Second, Chapter 3 asserts that even the small but thankfully growing number of exceptions to this general rule, which do take some account of second-best theory by examining the implications of a second Pareto imperfection that will not be controlled for the ability of a policy that will reduce or eliminate the target Pareto imperfection to decrease one or perhaps two types of resource misallocation, still do not respond appropriately to second-best theory: they ignore the fact that the impact of the policies they are scrutinizing on the types of economic inefficiency they do consider is also affected by a number of Pareto imperfections their analyses do not take into account, ignore as well many of the types of economic inefficiency whose magnitudes will be affected by the policies they recommend, fail to offer any third-best economic-efficiency justification for these omissions in circumstances in which such justifications seem unlikely to be available, and generate conclusions whose accuracy the relevant omissions call into question.

Chapter 4 follows up on these negative assertions. In particular, Section 1 of Chapter 4 justifies these claims by executing constructive critiques of the standard analysis of nine economic-efficiency issues:

1. the "deadweight loss of monopoly,"[8]
2. the overall economic efficiency of horizontal mergers that simultaneously reduce marginal costs and increase prices,[9]
3. the economic efficiency of R&D,[10]
4. the so-called social costs of monopoly,[11]
5. the economic efficiency of internalizing pollution costs or accident costs,[12]
6. the economic efficiency of the alleged common law practice of making the members of an industry strictly liable in tort during its infancy but liable in tort only for the consequences of their negligence after the industry has matured,[13]
7. the economic efficiency of making scope-of-liability decisions in tort cases depend on the standard of liability that will be applied to the defendant,[14]
8. the economic efficiency of ideal housing codes, and
9. the economic efficiency of marine-salvage law[15] and of so-called judge-made law in general.[16]

Section 2 of Chapter 4 then criticizes the arguments that those economists who have some knowledge of second-best theory use to justify ignoring it.[17] As it shows, these arguments are not just wrong, but obviously wrong.

Part II concludes by explaining why the failure of economists to respond appropriately to second-best theory is socially costly. In an era in which many public choices are based exclusively or substantially on their predicted economic efficiency, the economics profession's relentless commitment to an approach to making economic-efficiency predictions that yields highly inaccurate conclusions will cause the government to make many decisions that are economically inefficient and, in part on that account, undesirable.

Part III analyzes the relevance of a choice's or policy's economic efficiency to its justness and moral desirability, moral-rights considerations aside, and the relevance of the economic efficiency of an interpretation or application of the law to its correctness as a matter of law. Part III contains a lengthy introduction, which defines various components of and positions on prescriptive-moral analysis and the analysis of the answer to a legal-rights question that is correct as a matter of law (the internally right answer to a legal-rights question).

The introduction to Part III begins by defining and distinguishing four moral types of societies—immoral societies, amoral societies, goal-based societies, and rights-based societies (the last being societies whose members and governments draw a strong distinction between the just and the good—between moral-rights discourse and moral-ought discourse—and are committed to instantiating its conception of the just even when the good as defensibly conceived must be sacrificed to do so). Next, the introduction elaborates on and illustrates the difference between moral-rights discourse (about the just) and moral-ought discourse (about the good) in rights-based societies—*inter alia,* by pointing out that moral-rights discourse is grounded on a moral norm (which I denominate the society's basic moral principle) that is societally chosen and that the individual members, participants, and governments of the society in question are bound by this norm regardless of whether they personally subscribe to it. After that, the introduction to Part III delineates the different types of approaches that various scholars take to the analysis of justice:

1. purely conceptual (so-called Foundationalist) approaches, which try to derive an objectively true and therefore universally applicable conception of justice from the concept of the moral, of human freedom, of human flourishing, or of human nature;
2. philosophically uninformed, empirical (so-called conventionalist) approaches, which report uncritically the self-styled moral practices of a given society; and
3. the philosophically informed, empirical approach to a given society's prescriptive-moral practices that I think is appropriate.

After asserting that the societies for which the scholars on whose work this book focuses are making policy recommendations are liberal, rights-based societies, the introduction delineates some of the concrete corollaries of a liberal, rights-based society's basic moral commitment to treating all moral-rights bearers for whom it is responsible with appropriate, equal respect and to showing appropriate (in the case of individuals) or appropriate, equal (in the case of government) concern for them as well—in part for their welfare or utility as economists understand these concepts but preeminently for their actualizing their morally defining potential to lead lives of moral integrity by taking their moral obligations seriously and by taking seriously as well the dialectical task of developing a personal conception of the good (choosing what I call their "personal ultimate value") and living a life that fulfills their personally chosen commitments. The introduction to Part III moves on to delineate some of the ultimate values to which members of contemporary liberal, rights-based societies are personally committed (as contrasted with the liberal basic moral principle the society commits them to instantiating when making choices that affect moral rights): classical and modern utilitarianism, equal-utility egalitarianism, equal-resource egalitarianism, equal-opportunity egalitarianism, and libertarianism (which may not be a [defensible] moral norm). The introduction to Part III closes its discussion of prescriptive-moral discourse by delineating the structure of the moral-rights argument and two different types of moral-ought arguments (those in which utility considerations respectively do and do not play a role) that can legitimately be made in liberal, rights-based societies.

The introduction to Part III then turns its attention to the following two issues: (1) are there answers to any, some, or all legal-rights questions that are uniquely correct as a matter of law (as opposed to being morally required or desirable) in liberal, rights-based societies, and (2) if there are answers to at least some legal-rights question that are uniquely correct as a matter of law and some answers to legal-rights question that are wrong as a matter of law, how does one identify these answers? The introduction to Part III begins its discussion of these issues by distinguishing three types of legal rights that exist in liberal, rights-based societies: legal rights that derive from moral rights, legal rights that were created by legislative acts that were designed to secure some legitimate conception of the good (to achieve some legitimate social goal or goals), and legal rights that were created by legislative acts that were designed to serve the parochial interests of their beneficiaries.

Next, the introduction to Part III defines and distinguishes legitimate legal arguments—arguments whose use is consistent with the moral commitments of the society in which they are made—and valid legal arguments—arguments that affect the answers to legal-rights questions that are correct as a matter of law in the societies in question. The introduction concludes by delineating (1) my own conclusions about legitimate and valid legal argument and the structure of legitimate and valid argument about different types of legal rights in liberal, rights-based societies and (2) the contrary positions on these issues taken by members of the two jurisprudential or arguably jurisprudential schools that probably have the most adherents in the contemporary American legal academy—the legal positivists and the legal realists. As the introduction points out, my own position is distinguished by two related conclusions. First, in my judgment, the basic moral principle to which a rights-based society is committed not only is generically inside its law but also forms the basis of a type of legal argument (arguments of moral principle) that are the dominant mode of legal argument in such societies in that such arguments operate both directly and indirectly by controlling the legitimacy, presumptive validity, and argumentative force of all variants of the other types of argument used in such societies to determine the answer to individual legal-rights questions that is correct as a matter of law (textual, structural, historical, precedent-related or other type of legal-practice-related, and prudential arguments). Second, in part because I believe that arguments of moral principle dominate legal argument in rights-based societies, I think that answers that are uniquely correct as a matter of law can be given to all legal-rights questions in such societies.

With this background, Chapter 5 proceeds to analyze the relevance of the economic efficiency of a choice to its justness and moral desirability, moral-rights considerations aside, and the relevance of the economic efficiency of a legal interpretation or application to its correctness as a matter of law. The first topic it addresses is the connection between a choice's economic efficiency and its justness in a liberal, rights-based society. It begins by pointing out that economic-efficiency analysis cannot contribute to the analysis of various issues that justice (moral-rights) analyses must resolve. It then argues that economic-efficiency analysis is insensitive to various distinctions that play a significant role in the analysis of many justice (moral-rights) claims: in particular, that economic-efficiency analysis cannot contribute to the identification of those creatures that are moral-rights holders, is insensitive to the distinction between preferences that are licit and illicit from a liberal perspective, cannot adequately capture the importance of the distinction between effects on mere utility and effects that prevent or enable individuals to lead lives of moral integrity (or perhaps give them or deprive them of a meaningful opportunity to lead such lives), is insensitive to the distinction between providing assistance to someone and not injuring someone (between the negative and positive rights of moral-rights holders in liberal, rights-based societies), and (somewhat overlappingly) is insensitive to the distinction between an individual's psychological or material-welfare interest in some matter and his entitlement interest in that matter.

Chapter 5 then proceeds to illustrate the conclusion that the economic efficiency of a rights-related choice is not a necessary or sufficient condition for its justness in a liberal, rights-based society by analyzing the connection between economic efficiency and the following rights of members of and participants in a liberal, rights-based society: the right to

1. those resources and educational experiences that will substantially contribute to their opportunity to lead a life of moral integrity,
2. privacy,
3. make choices of different kinds (the relevant individuals' liberty rights),
4. not be the target of actively-illicitly-motivated choices of others that are against their interests,
5. not have the mere-utility losses a person confronts *ex ante* because of the possibility of becoming the victim of an accident or pollution event increased by the potential injurer's rejection of an avoidance move he should have perceived *ex ante* would be economically efficient,
6. not have the probability that a person would be deprived of a meaningful opportunity to lead a life of moral integrity by an accident or pollution event increased by a relevant potential injurer's rejection of an avoidance move he should have perceived *ex ante* would have served the interest of the relevant population in having such an opportunity, and
7. the positive assistance (for example, rescue services) of others.

Next, Chapter 5 turns its attention to the connection between the economic efficiency of a choice and its moral desirability, moral-rights considerations aside. Chapter 5 begins this discussion by pointing out that, even if the relevant evaluation is to be utilitarian in character, the economic efficiency of the choice under consideration will be neither a necessary nor a sufficient condition for its desirability and that, although—from a utilitarian perspective—it probably is desirable to generate estimates of the economic efficiency of a choice (more precisely, of the total equivalent-dollar gains and total equivalent-dollar losses it caused or should be predicted to cause) when evaluating it, even this conclusion is empirically contingent. More specifically, this latter conclusion is empirically contingent because it depends on the utility of generating utilitarian conclusions circuitously by calculating the relevant equivalent-dollar gains and losses, estimating the average utility-values of the equivalent-dollars respectively gained and lost, weighting the equivalent-dollar gains and losses by the estimated average utility-values in question, and comparing the weighted equivalent-dollar gains with the weighted equivalent-dollar losses rather than by calculating and comparing the utility gains and losses directly. Chapter 5 then argues that information on the economic efficiency of a choice will have absolutely no bearing on its moral desirability, moral-rights considerations aside, if it is to be evaluated from a purely non-utilitarian perspective.

After that, Chapter 5 analyzes the relevance of the economic efficiency of a legal interpretation or application to its correctness as a matter of law in a liberal, rights-based society on the assumption that my conclusions about legitimate and valid legal argument in such societies are correct. Chapter 5 argues that the conclusion that the economic efficiency of a choice is not a necessary or sufficient condition for its justness implies that the economic efficiency of a decision about a moral-rights-related legal right is also not a necessary or sufficient condition for its correctness as a matter of law. Relatedly, Chapter 5 argues that the conclusion that the economic efficiency of a choice is not a necessary or sufficient condition for its moral desirability, moral-rights considerations aside, from either a utilitarian or a nonutilitarian perspective implies that the economic efficiency of a decision about a legal right that derives from a legislative choice that was designed to promote a personal ultimate value or secure one or more morally defensible social goals is also not a necessary or sufficient condition for its correctness as a matter of law. Not surprisingly, since there is every reason to believe that legislation that was designed to promote the parochial interest of its beneficiaries will not be economically efficient, Chapter 5 argues that the economic efficiency of a decision about a legal right allegedly created by such parochial legislation is not a necessary or sufficient condition for its correctness as a matter of law.

Chapter 5 concludes by analyzing the implications of legal realism and legal positivism for the relevance of the economic efficiency of an interpretation or application of the law to its correctness as a matter of law. It points out that the legal realists do not attempt to provide a comprehensive account of legitimate and valid legal argument in the societies they study and differ both about the frequency with which internally right answers can be given to questions about the existence of legal rights of all sorts and about the values on which legal-rights conclusions should be based when the answer to a legal-rights question is either contestable or essentially contestable. Therefore, there is no reason to conclude that legal realists believe that the answers to legal-rights questions that are internally correct or that morally ought to be given will be economically efficient. In fact, the equal-utility egalitarian value that early legal realists seem to have supported and the more communitarian values that later legal realists or their critical legal studies progeny came to support do not support making all decisions that are economically efficient.

Chapter 5 then analyzes the implications of legal positivism for the relevance of the economic efficiency of a legal interpretation or application to its correctness as a matter of law and to whether it morally ought to be given when no unique, internally correct answer exists for the legal-rights question under consideration. The legal positivists believe that a legal-rights question will have an answer that is uniquely correct as a matter of law if and only if one and only one answer to the relevant question is favored by all variants of textual, structural, historical, precedent-related and other legal-practice-related, and prudential arguments that have been validated by their use. Chapter 5 points out that, on this legal positivist account, the uniquely correct answer to many legal-rights questions that have such answers will often be economically inefficient, regardless of the type of legal right at issue and that the answer that morally ought to be given to legal-rights questions for which no answer is uniquely correct as a matter of law (questions that have more than one answer that is favored by at least one variant of validated legal argument) will not always be economically efficient, regardless of the personal ultimate value the relevant legal positivist thinks morally ought to be used to resolve such cases.

Chapter 6 delineates and criticizes (1) various arguments that economists and law and economics scholars have made about prescriptive-moral and legal analysis as well as (2) more specific arguments they have made about the connection between the economic efficiency of a choice and its justness, the connection between the economic efficiency of a choice and its moral desirability (rights considerations aside), and the connection between the economic efficiency of a legal interpretation or application and its correctness as a matter of law. Chapter 6 begins by articulating and criticizing various positions to which many economists subscribe on prescriptive-moral and legal analysis—for example, the position that for a moral norm to be coherent (to have any substantive meaning), its extensions must be deductively or at least uncontestably derivable from its abstract formulation. Chapter 6 then proceeds to criticize three arguments that academicians have made about the relevance of a choice's economic efficiency to its justness:

1. a utilitarian argument that is based on the alleged impossibility of making interpersonal comparisons of utility;
2. a nonutilitarian ("envelope conception of justice") argument that assumes that justice can be operationalized as an increasing function of such *desiderata* as utility, autonomy, and equality; and
3. an autonomy-based hypothetical-consent argument.[18]

After that, Chapter 6 states and criticizes an argument that economists have made about the relevance of a choice's economic efficiency to its moral desirability, moral-rights considerations aside: an argument of general application that assumes (1) that a universally-accurately-applied decision-protocol to make all economically efficient choices and reject all economically inefficient choices would bring the economy to a Pareto-superior position in the long run and (2) that it will always be morally desirable to bring the economy to a Pareto-superior position.[19] Next, Chapter 6 considers two types of argument that law and economics scholars have used to establish their conclusion that the decisions judges make when (allegedly) creating judge-made law can best be predicted from the relative economic efficiency of the options available to them—that judges in common-law and constitutional-law cases overwhelmingly and increasingly make the decisions that are the most-economically-efficient decisions they could make.[20] Chapter 6 concludes by using an American-antitrust-law example to illustrate my claim that law and economics scholars and economists tend to exaggerate the frequency with which legislation is designed to increase economic efficiency.[21]

The book's Conclusion has four sections. The first summarizes (1) its conclusions about the correct way to define the impact of a choice on economic efficiency, the allocatively efficient way to assess the economic efficiency of a choice, the relevance of a choice's economic efficiency to its justness and moral desirability, moral-rights considerations aside, and the relevance of the economic efficiency of a legal interpretation or application to its correctness as a matter of law and (2) its criticisms of the positions that economists and law and economics scholars have taken on these issues.

The second section illustrates its critique of the standard economics approach to economic-efficiency analysis by criticizing a highly regarded law and economics analysis of the economic efficiency of protecting commercial and personal privacy: Richard Posner's argument that it is economically efficient to protect commercial privacy—that is, discovered information and the right of an individual to control the commercial use of his likeness and endorsements—because doing so will increase economic efficiency by providing potential discoverers with appropriate incentives to make and use commercially valuable discoveries and by enabling individuals to maximize the private value of their likenesses and endorsements to those who put them to commercial use but that it is economically inefficient to protect personal privacy since protecting the ability of individuals to preserve the secrecy of information about themselves will decrease economic efficiency by enabling them to defraud others.[22]

The third section of the Conclusion reviews the evidence that the book provides for its subtheme that the economists and law and economics scholars who commit the errors it demonstrates either knew or should have known that they were making the mistakes in question and speculates on the possible causes of this pattern of conduct. And the fourth section comments on the relevance of the book's positive and negative conclusions not just for economists but also for members of the policy audience more generally and for university administrators.

I close this Introduction with two comments. The Introduction gives something of a false impression of the percentages of the book devoted to philosophical and jurisprudential as opposed to economic analysis. Although the Introduction allocates more space to summarizing the various philosophical and legal points the book makes than to outlining its economic arguments, the book devotes far more pages to economic analysis than to philosophical and legal analysis—for example, Part II is far longer than Parts I and III combined. I have written the Introduction this way because I hope that a substantial percentage of the readers of the book will be economists and I think it important to remind them that the value of their economic-efficiency analyses depends on their relevance to prescriptive-moral and legal analysis.

The second comment relates to some of the vocabulary used in the Introduction—more particularly, to the fact that the rest of the book will not consistently use the language the Introduction employs. Thus, in order to combat any tendency readers may have to assume that economic efficiency is more relevant to moral and legal analysis than it really is, the text that follows will often substitute the seemingly more technical (less normatively charged) expression "allocative efficiency" for "economic efficiency." (Admittedly, this usage conflicts with the practice of some economists of using "allocative inefficiency" to refer to a particular type of economic inefficiency, most often the type I call "relative-unit-output misallocation.") For simplicity and to avoid any confusion between the expressions "equivalent-dollar gain or loss" and "equivalent variation," the text that follows will also sometimes substitute the expressions "dollar gain" or "dollar loss" for the expressions "equivalent-dollar gain" or "equivalent-dollar loss."

Part One **The Definition of Economic Efficiency**

Economists have defined the central concept of welfare economics—the impact of a choice on economic efficiency—in a number of different ways. None of these definitions is satisfactory. Part I focuses on the definition of this concept. It contains two chapters. Chapter 1 delineates a monetized definition of the impact of a choice on economic (allocative) efficiency that is correct in that it creates a concept that is useful and conforms with both professional and popular understanding. Chapter 2 criticizes the various different definitions of and tests for allocative efficiency that economists and law and economics scholars of various backgrounds continue to use.

Chapter 1 The Correct Definition of the Impact of a Choice on Economic (Allocative) Efficiency

Chapter 1 has four sections. The first articulates the monetized definition of the impact of a choice on economic efficiency that I think is correct, explores its critical features, and explains why it is correct. The second elaborates on this definition by analyzing whether those equivalent-dollar effects of a choice that reflect the external or bad preferences of the individual who experiences them should be ignored when calculating the choice's allocative efficiency. The third points out that my argument for the correctness of my monetized definition of the impact of a choice on allocative efficiency defeats the claim that there is no non-arbitrary way to resolve the offer/asking problem. And the fourth considers various additional moral issues that the definition or operationalization of economic efficiency implicates.

SECTION 1. THE CORRECT DEFINITION OF THE ECONOMIC EFFICIENCY OF A CHOICE

As the Introduction to this book indicates, I believe that, correctly defined, the impact of a choice on economic efficiency equals the difference between the equivalent-dollar gains the choice confers on its beneficiaries (the winners) and the equivalent-dollar losses it imposes on its victims (the losers). Although most economists would not find this definition controversial, many would find my operationalizations of the winners' equivalent-dollar gains and losers' equivalent-dollar losses problematic. I argue that a winner's equivalent-dollar gain should be defined to equal the number of dollars that would have to be transferred to him to leave him as well off as the choice would leave him if

1. he did not agree to the transfer;
2. he either was intrinsically indifferent to the substitution of the transfer for the policy in question or was unaware of the linkage between the transfer and the policy's rejection;
3. his distributive attitude toward such transfers, non-parochial distributive preferences, or normative distributive commitments gave him no reason to prefer the transfer to the choice or vice versa; and
4. the transfer would not benefit or harm him indirectly by changing the conduct of others by altering their incomes and/or wealth.

Similarly, I argue that a loser's equivalent-dollar loss should be defined to equal the number of dollars that would have to be withdrawn from him to leave him as poorly off as the choice would leave him under the four assumptions just delineated.

The preceding operationalizations measure the relevant dollar gains and losses by the equivalent variations in the relevant winners' and losers' wealths and then elaborate on the definitions of the equivalent variations in question. This section explains why the relevant equivalent variations differ from the compensating variations that I think are incorrect operationalizations of the dollar effects of an event, public policy, or private choice on its individual beneficiaries and victims. It also discusses the reasons why the equivalent variations should be calculated on the assumptions the preceding two sentences specified and referenced.

I have already explained why the dollar impacts that are components of the impact of an event, public policy, or private choice on monetized economic efficiency should be measured by the equivalent rather than by the compensating variations in the relevant winners' and losers' wealths: the equivalent variation captures both the professional and popular (intuitive) understanding of the relevant dollar gains and losses—that is, correctly operationalizes the meaning of these expressions in professional and popular understanding—

and, relatedly, defines these concepts in the way that maximizes their contribution to the evaluation of any private choice or public policy. I now want to explain how and why the relevant equivalent variations differ from the relevant compensating variations and what my resolution of these issues implies for the accuracy and bias of estimates of the impact of a private choice or public policy on monetized economic efficiency that are based on compensating-variation estimates of the relevant dollar gains and losses.

Equivalent variations differ from compensating variations for two reasons. The first is that money has diminishing marginal value, regardless of whether the individual in question values money for the utility it enables him to secure or for some other reason. The diminishing marginal value of money causes the number of dollars that a choice's winners would have to be given to be left as well off as the choice would leave them (the total of the equivalent variations in their respective wealths) to exceed the number of dollars that would have to be withdrawn from them to leave them as poorly off as the choice would leave them (the compensating variations in their wealths). Assume, for example, that (1) a relevant winner values both money and the policy for the utility they will give him, (2) the relevant winner possesses $50,000 in the initial position, and (3) the policy will give him 300 units of utility (utils) regardless of whether his wealth is increased or decreased over the relevant range prior to the policy's implementation, (4) the average utility-value of the dollars that would raise his wealth from $50,000 to $50,300 is one util, and (5) the average utility-value of the dollars that would raise his wealth from $49,750 to $50,000 (or lower his wealth from $50,000 to $49,750) is 1.2 utils (where the utility-value of each dollar above $49,750—indeed, above $1—is lower than the utility-value of its predecessor). On these facts, the variation in the relevant winner's wealth that would be equivalent to the policy would be $300 (since 300[1 util] = 300 utils), while the compensating variation to the policy would be $250 (since 250[1.2 utils] = 300 utils). Hence, if money has diminishing marginal value, a policy's compensating variation will tend to be lower than its equivalent variation on that account, and any analysis of a policy's economic efficiency that incorporates a compensating-variation definition of the dollar gains it generates will tend on that account to underestimate the policy's economic efficiency.

The diminishing marginal value of money will also cause the number of dollars that would have to be withdrawn from a policy's losers to leave them as poorly off as the policy would leave them (the equivalent variations in their wealths) to be lower than the number of dollars that would have to be transferred to them to perfectly offset the policy's impact on them (the compensating variations in their wealths). Once again, if we assume that the utility cost of the policy to its victims will not be affected by relevant variations in their wealths, this conclusion that the equivalent variations in the losers' wealths will be lower than the compensating variations in their wealths will reflect the fact that—since the average marginal utility of any given number of dollars transferred to them will be lower than the average marginal utility of that number of dollars when withdrawn from them—the number of dollars that would have to be given to them to offset a given utility loss will exceed the number of dollars that would have to be taken from them to reduce their utility by the same amount that the policy would reduce their utility. Therefore, since the diminishing marginal value of money will cause the compensating variation in the wealth of each of a policy's losers to be higher than the equivalent variations in his wealth, (1) any analysis of the dollar losses that a policy would impose on its victims that measures those losses by the total of the compensating variations in the wealth of each loser will tend on that account to overestimate those losses, and (2) any operationalization of a policy's economic efficiency that measures the losses it generates by the total of the compensating variations in the wealth of each of its victims will tend on that account to underestimate its allocative efficiency to the extent that the marginal value of money diminishes.

In short, if money has diminishing marginal value, any analysis of a private choice's or public policy's economic efficiency that incorporates the compensating-variation definitions of its winners' equivalent-dollar gains and losers' equivalent-dollar losses will tend on that account to underestimate those gains and overestimate those losses. Clearly, these conclusions imply that the diminishing marginal value of money will render any operationalization of economic efficiency that incorporates compensating-variation definitions of the dollar gains of a policy's winners and the dollar losses of a policy's losers not only inaccurate but also biased against its economic efficiency. If I am right in assuming that money virtually always has diminishing marginal value for a given possessor, this conclusion will virtually always be applicable, regardless of the way in which the choice or policy being analyzed affects its winners and losers.

Although the second reason equivalent variations may differ from compensating variations will also apply when the marginal value of money is not declining, it has a far more limited domain of applicability than the first reason (that is, the diminishing marginal value of money). Specifically, this second reason applies only when the private choice or public policy affects the beneficiary or victim by lowering or raising the price he must pay for a good. The second reason is the non-zero wealth-elasticity of the demand for goods. To the extent that the demand that a policy victim or policy beneficiary has for a good whose price the policy will change is wealth-elastic, the compensating variation will differ from the equivalent variation because the relevant compensating and equivalent variations are calculated respectively on a counterfactual and accurate assumption about the wealth the relevant individual will possess when the policy is adopted. In particular, the compensating variation in the wealth of a policy's beneficiary equals the positive dollar value the policy would have for the beneficiary if (counterfactually) his wealth were reduced by the compensating variation before the policy's adoption, and the compensating variation in the wealth of a policy's victim equals the negative dollar value the policy would have for the victim if (counterfactually) his wealth were increased by the compensating variation prior to the policy's adoption.

I will now discuss some examples that illustrate the difference between the compensating and equivalent variations to policies that change the price some of their beneficiaries or victims must pay for some good. Assume that the policy is an antitrust-exemption policy or a pollution tax that would harm a particular victim by increasing the price of some good he purchased—the good whose producers the policy would exempt from antitrust regulation or the good whose production would be subjected to a pollution tax. If the relevant victim's demand for the good is positively wealth-elastic (that is, if, given the price of the good, the number of units this individual will purchase will increase with his wealth), as is typically the case, then the dollar cost of the policy to him (the sum of [the product of the number of units of the good that he will continue to buy at the higher price the policy causes to be charged and the price increase the policy would generate] and [the buyer surplus he originally realized by purchasing the units at the lower, pre-policy price that he did not buy at the higher, post-policy price]) will be higher if his wealth is increased prior to the policy's adoption by the amount that would constitute the compensating variation to the policy's adoption (since in this case the number of units he will purchase at the higher, post-policy price [and at the lower, pre-policy price]—the number of units for which the policy would cause him to pay a higher per-unit price—will be higher). Hence, when the relevant victim's demand for the good in question is positively wealth-elastic, the compensating-variation measure of the dollar loss the policy will inflict on him will be higher than the equivalent variation—that is, will overestimate the loss the policy will inflict on the victim in question—and hence any approach to economic-efficiency assessment that incorporates a compensating-variation measure of the dollar losses in question will tend on that account to underestimate the allocative efficiency of the policy in question. On the other hand, if the relevant victim's demand for the good is negatively wealth-elastic (if, given the price of the good, the number of units this individual will purchase will decrease as his wealth increases), as is sometimes the case, then for analogous reasons the dollar cost of the policy to him will be lower if his wealth is increased prior to the policy's adoption by the amount that will constitute the compensating variation to the policy's adoption. In this case, the compensating variation will be lower than the equivalent variation—will underestimate the loss the policy will inflict on the victim—and hence any approach to economic-efficiency assessment that incorporates a compensating-variation measure of the dollar losses will tend on that account to overestimate the allocative efficiency of the policy.

Obviously, analogous arguments would establish analogous conclusions in cases in which the relevant policies were pro-price-competition policies or policies that remove pollution taxes. The compensating-variation measure of the gains that such policies confer on those of their beneficiaries who purchase the goods whose prices they reduce will overestimate the dollar gains such policies confer on those buyers whose demands for the goods in question are negatively wealth-elastic and would underestimate the dollar gains they confer on those buyers whose demands for the goods are positively wealth-elastic. It is worth noting that the preceding results imply that any approach to allocative-efficiency assessment that adopts the compensating-variation measure of the dollar gains and losses a choice or policy generates will underestimate its allocative efficiency in what I take to be the typical case in which the relevant wealth-elasticities of demand are positive.

Of course, precisely the opposite conclusions will be warranted when the relevant winners' and losers' demands for the products whose prices the policies will affect are negatively wealth-elastic. In such cases, the compensating-variation measures of the relevant losers' dollar losses and relevant winners' dollar gains will tend to underestimate those dollar losses and overestimate those dollar gains, and any approach to allocative-efficiency assessment that incorporates compensating-variation measures of the dollar gains and losses in question will tend to overestimate the economic efficiency of the policy in question on that account.

Admittedly, the fact that the compensating-variation measure of the equivalent-dollar losses and gains a policy generates may be wrong for two reasons does not guarantee that allocative-efficiency assessments that are based on this measure of those gains and losses will always be inaccurate on that account. Conceivably, in some cases, the non-zero wealth-elasticity of demand-related error of the compensating-variation measure approach to dollar gain and loss assessment will perfectly offset the diminishing marginal value of money-related error it makes. Since the latter error will always tend to cause approaches to allocative-efficiency assessment that incorporate the compensating-variation measure of the dollar gains and losses the policy generates to underestimate its allocative efficiency, this outcome will be conceivable only when the policy in question

1. A. harms some victims by increasing the price of one or more goods they purchase and
   B. the relevant victims' demands for those goods are negatively wealth-elastic or
2. A. benefits some winners by reducing the price of goods they purchase and
   B. the relevant winners' demands for those goods are negatively wealth-elastic.

However, even in what I take to be the unusual circumstances in which the relevant demands are negatively wealth-elastic, the error associated with the non-zero wealth-elasticity of demand will perfectly offset the error associated with the diminishing marginal value of money only rarely and fortuitously. In any event, because I believe that the relevant wealth-elasticities of demand are usually positive, I suspect that, in most cases, the former error will usually compound the tendency of the latter error to cause any allocative-efficiency analysis that adopts the compensating-variation measures of the dollar gains and losses a policy generates to underestimate its allocative efficiency.

I will now explain the four assumptions on which equivalent-variation estimates should be based. The first such assumption is that the policy's winners did not voluntarily agree to accept money in exchange for their essential consent to the policy's rejection and that the policy's losers did not voluntarily agree to sell for money their essential consent to the policy's adoption. The following two facts make these assumptions necessary: (1) in practice, the policy's winners and losers will not have engaged in such voluntary market transactions, and (2) in some relevant instances, some such winners and losers would find engaging in such voluntary market transactions intrinsically costly or valuable. Take, for example, a policy that would benefit a parent by preventing his child from being injured or becoming ill. To the extent that, for self-definitional reasons, the parent would place a negative value on voluntarily exchanging the policy for a money payment, any operationalization of the parent's equivalent-dollar gain that equated that gain with the number of dollars for which he or she would be indifferent to voluntarily surrendering the policy when in fact no such consensual exchange would occur would underestimate the dollar gain the policy would confer on him even if he were a sovereign maximizer. Such an operationalization would also yield underestimates of the dollar gains that would be generated by policies that would protect a winner's own health or a family heirloom when the winner did not actually trade the policy for money to the extent that, for self-definitional reasons, the winner respectively (1) would disvalue voluntarily selling his health (endangering his health for a money payment) and (2) identified with his family and found it costly to sell its heritage. I hasten to add, however, that the counterfactual, voluntary-market-transaction operationalization of a winner's dollar gain could also overestimate the dollar gain the policy actually conferred on its beneficiaries—would overestimate that gain when the beneficiary would positively value voluntarily trading the policy for money. This outcome would occur, for example, in a case in which the policy would protect a beneficiary's health if the beneficiary (1) valued being a good family provider or valued the welfare of his wife and children and (2) believed that the money he could obtain by trading a policy that would protect his health would benefit his family more than family members would be harmed by the pain, worsened health, and reduction in future earning power he would experience if the policy were rejected instead of implemented.

Obviously, a counterfactual, voluntary-market-transaction operationalization of the dollar loss a policy would impose on its victims will also mismeasure that loss when the victim would find agreeing to make a payment to prevent the policy's adoption either costly or beneficial in itself (independent of its material impact on him). Thus, such an operationalization would underestimate the equivalent-dollar loss a policy would impose on its victims to the extent that the amount that they should be indifferent to paying to block the policy would be reduced by their placement of a negative value on making such voluntary payments—as they might if they thought that the government (private actor) ought to and/or was morally obligated to reject the policy (choice) without such a transfer's being made. Particularly when the transfer would go to the perceived wrongdoer (the person who or organization that would otherwise make the harmful choice in question), its potential victim may disvalue making any payment to prevent it because he disvalues rewarding wrongdoers or believes that making such a payment would amount to giving in to extortion and disvalues doing so.

Second, the relevant money transfers should be calculated on the assumption that the policy's winners and losers would perceive no linkage between its rejection and any related transfers that one would imagine being made respectively to them and from them. Even if the relevant operationalizations did not assume that the policy's winners (losers) voluntarily agreed to accept (make) the payments in question to forego (prevent) the relevant policy, operationalizations would mismeasure the dollar gains and losses the policy would generate to the extent that some winners or losers would find the relevant nonconsensual transfers intrinsically valuable or distasteful. Thus, an operationalization of the dollar gains that would be generated by a policy that would prevent a child's being injured (or would reduce the probability that a child would be injured) that assumed that the child's parents would be aware of the linkage between any transfer to them and the policy's rejection would overestimate the dollar gain the policy would confer on the parents to the extent that the parents would find it intrinsically costly to accept "blood money" *ex post* as compensation for exposing their child to injury or a greater risk of injury (for the policy's rejection) even if they did not agree *ex ante* to trade the policy for the money payment.

Third, the relevant money transfers should be measured on the assumption that the winners and losers in question would not find them valuable or costly because they approved or disapproved of their government's executing such transfers for reasons that do not relate to their direct parochial interests or their distributive preferences or values. Since the money transfer that is being said to be equivalent to the relevant party's equivalent-dollar gain or loss is purely hypothetical, its calculation should not be affected by any such attitudes, distributive preferences, or distributive moral commitments.

Fourth, since (1) the relevant money transfers are purely hypothetical and could be financed in different ways that would have different distributive impacts and hence have different effects on the choices that people make by altering their income/wealth positions and (2) the indirect behavioral consequences of the transfer's distributive impact not only (A) could benefit or harm the individual winners and losers of the policy or choice but (B) could also produce a net equivalent-dollar impact on all such individuals combined, the dollar gains and losses the policy or choice would generate should be measured on the assumption that it would not produce any net dollar effects on its winners and losers in this indirect way.

Points (2A) and (2B) in the preceding sentence require some explanation. I will use two illustrations to explain the former point. Assume first that

1. the beneficiary of a particular policy owns a business;
2. the business in question faces imperfect price competition;
3. the hypothetical money transfer to him would be financed in a way that reduces the wealth of one of his customers; and
4. this reduction in his customer's wealth would reduce the latter's demand for the beneficiary's product or services.

In this case, the transfer would hurt its direct beneficiary indirectly by reducing the profits his business earned. Assume, alternatively, that

1. the victim of a particular policy was different from the victim of the hypothetical dollar transfer that the policy's beneficiary would find equivalent to the policy;
2. unlike the victim of the actual policy, the victim of the hypothetical transfer would in any event drive his car by the residence of the policy's beneficiary;
3. the equivalent-dollar loss the hypothetical transfer would impose on its victim would induce him to (make it profitable for him to) purchase and operate a more polluting and breakdown-prone car (make it personally attractive for him to buy a cheaper car, which was more externality-prone); and
4. the actual policy would not affect its beneficiary by generating such secondary-feedback effects.

In this case, unlike the actual policy, the hypothetical money transfer would hurt its direct beneficiary indirectly by increasing the equivalent-dollar loss its direct victim imposed on him by driving in his neighborhood.

Point (2B) in the relevant sentence—namely, that the indirect effect of the hypothetical money transfers on the policy's winners and losers may not offset each other perfectly (may not produce the same net total dollar effect on the policy's winners as on the policy's losers)—requires a more abstract explanation. Admittedly, in an otherwise-Pareto-perfect world, allocative-transaction-costless money transfers will not produce any net equivalent-dollar effects—that is, the economy will be maximally allocatively efficient (will contain no resource misallocation) regardless of the initial endowments of its participants. However, for two reasons, this proposition does not imply that the relevant money transfers will have no net equivalent-dollar impact on the policy's winners and losers. First, in our actual, Pareto-imperfect world, the amount of allocative inefficiency will often be affected by the distribution of initial endowments—that is, in a Pareto-imperfect world, allocative-transaction-costless money transfers can either increase or decrease allocative efficiency and hence can affect the difference between the policy's winners' equivalent-dollar gains and losers' equivalent-dollar losses even if they do not have any net equivalent-dollar impact on other individuals. Second, even when the money transfers in question do not affect allocative efficiency, the net equivalent-dollar impact of the combination of the policy and transfers on the policy's winners and losers will be different from that of the policy when the transfers have a net equivalent-dollar impact on people who would neither gain nor lose from the policy.

I anticipate that—at least at this juncture—some readers will wonder why I have bothered to discuss the four assumptions on which I think the equivalent variations that are components of an event's, private choice's, or public policy's allocative efficiency should be calculated. Chapter 2 makes my reasons for discussing these issues apparent. As it shows, several of the tests for or definitions of economic efficiency that economists and law and economics scholars continue to use are wrong not only (1) because they incorporate compensating-variation measures of relevant dollar gains and losses, but also (2) because they measure such variations and any equivalent variations they also consider on assumptions that the preceding discussion shows to be inappropriate, and sometimes (3) because they incorporate other features or ploys whose inappropriateness the preceding discussion reveals.

SECTION 2. THE CORRECTNESS OF EXCLUDING EXTERNAL-PREFERENCE-DERIVED AND BAD-PREFERENCE-DERIVED EQUIVALENT-DOLLAR EFFECTS FROM ECONOMIC-EFFICIENCY CALCULATIONS

According to my definition of the impact of a choice on economic efficiency, all of a choice's equivalent-dollar effects count equally in the economic-efficiency calculation. In this conception, for purposes of measuring the economic efficiency of a choice, equivalent-dollar effects that derive either from an individual's external preferences[1] for others' welfare (such as for the welfare of family members, friends, or members of particular racial, ethnic, or religious groups or for the instantiation of some non-parochial distributive norm) or from bad tastes (such as sadistic tastes or prejudices) count the same as equivalent-dollar effects that derive from any other kind of preference (such as for breathing less-polluted air oneself).

For one or both of two reasons, some economists have reached a different conclusion about the appropriateness of counting equivalent-dollar effects that derive from external or bad preferences in economic-efficiency calculations. In particular, some advocate excluding external- or bad-preference-derived equivalent-dollar effects from economic-efficiency calculations because they believe that such effects cannot be measured acceptably accurately or cheaply. And others support such exclusions because they believe that it would be immoral to let the effects in question influence the choices or policies under review. I do not find either of these arguments persuasive.

Thus, although it will be difficult to estimate the magnitude of external-preference-derived equivalent-dollar gains and losses when relevant actors do not have to put their money where their avowals are, I do not think that economic-efficiency calculations that are based on the assumption that external-preference-derived net equivalent-dollar effects are zero will be more accurate than ones that incorporate regrettably crude calculations of such net equivalent-dollar effects.[2] Economists who disagree with this conclusion sometimes try to bolster their position by suggesting that it will be more costly and less feasible to estimate a choice's external-preference-derived net equivalent-dollar effects acceptably accurately than to generate acceptably accurate estimates of the other, conventional components of its economic efficiency. I have two responses to this suggestion. First, even if one could estimate the conventional components of a choice's economic efficiency more accurately and cheaply than one can estimate the choice's external-preference-derived net equivalent-dollar effects, that fact would not imply the infeasibility, economic inefficiency, or moral unattractiveness of taking the choice's external-preference-derived effects into account when estimating its economic efficiency. Second, because the economists in question all ignore The General Theory of Second Best, they massively underestimate the cost of generating acceptably accurate estimates of the economic efficiency of a choice, external-preference-derived consequences aside, and concomitantly the extent to which it is relatively cheaper to estimate acceptably accurately the net non-external-preference-derived equivalent-dollar effect of a choice as opposed to its net external-preference-derived equivalent-dollar impact.

However, there are at least three "nondefinitional" reasons why this information-provision response is superior to excluding external-preference-derived equivalent-dollar gains and losses from economic-efficiency calculations (in effect, to giving a zero weight to such gains and losses). First, in some instances, a protocol that gives zero weight to such dollar gains does not produce the appropriate overall evaluation of the choice that generates them. Thus, in those instances in which a morally bad external preference critically affected the choice that was made, the morally bad preference in question will render the relevant choice unjust (moral-rights-violative) as opposed to "not more attractive" than it would be in its absence (as the exclusion would imply). In other circumstances, the appropriate way to deal with bad-preference-derived equivalent-dollar gains is to attach a negative rather than a zero weight to them. Second, in my judgment, the concept of economic efficiency should not be defined to exclude bad-preference-derived equivalent-dollar effects because economists are not trained to make and are inept at making the moral judgments such a definition would require them to make.[4] Third, even if economists would do as good a job of determining the moral status of relevant preferences as would the people who are authorized to make the choices under consideration or the agents to whom these principals delegated this authority, economists should not exclude bad-preference-derived effects from economic-efficiency calculations because doing so allocates to them decision-making power that has been assigned elsewhere. Although the "costs" of the usurpation of power that an unauthorized decision to exclude external-preference-derived equivalent-dollar effects entails will be mitigated to the extent that the economists who make "economic-efficiency" calculations that reflect such exclusions reveal what they have done, any definition of "economic efficiency" that excludes external-preference-derived and bad-preference-derived equivalent-dollar effects will tend to be undesirable because it will tend to increase the extent to which economists exercise unauthorized power (which is bad in itself in liberal, rights-based societies).

SECTION 3. THE UNSOLVABILITY OF THE OFFER/ASKING PROBLEM

As the Introduction indicates, at least some non-economist critics of economics and some economics and law and economics scholars believe that economic-efficiency estimates are inevitably arbitrary because there is no non-arbitrary way to resolve the so-called offer/asking problem. This section begins by explaining why the number of dollars that a choice's sovereign, maximizing beneficiary would be indifferent to offering to secure it is different from the number of dollars he would be indifferent to asking (to be paid) for his critical acquiescence to its rejection (if he had to make good on any such accepted offer) and why the number of dollars a choice's sovereign, maximizing victim would be indifferent to offering to prevent its adoption is different from the number of dollars he would be indifferent to asking to be paid for his critical consent to it. Next, it explains why an analyst's decisions about whether to measure a choice's equivalent-dollar effect on its beneficiaries' and victims' offer prices or asking prices could affect not just his conclusion about the amount by which the choice will increase or decrease economic efficiency but also his conclusion about whether it will increase or decrease economic efficiency. Finally, this section examines the implications of the first section's discussion of the correct way to define the impact of a choice on economic efficiency for the existence of a correct (non-arbitrary) resolution of the offer/asking problem (or at least for the existence of such a resolution if no problems are generated by the voluntariness and hypothetical character of the offers or demands the offer/asking approaches contemplate).

I will initiate the analysis of these issues by recalling four facts that Section 1 established:

1. a choice's or policy's beneficiary's offer price is a distorted measure of the variation in his wealth that would compensate him for the policy (perfectly offset the effect of the policy on him)—distorted by the fact that any use of the offer price presumes counterfactually that the beneficiary was voluntarily offering to pay to secure the policy's adoption;
2. a choice's or policy's beneficiary's asking price is a distorted measure of the variation in his wealth that would be equivalent to the policy's adoption—distorted once more by the fact that the use of the asking price presumes counterfactually that the beneficiary was voluntarily asking to be paid for granting his critical assent to the policy's rejection;
3. a choice's or policy's victim's offer price is a distorted measure of the variation in his wealth that would be equivalent to the policy's adoption—distorted yet again by the fact that the use of the offer price presumes counterfactually that the victim was voluntarily offering to pay to secure the policy's rejection; and
4. a choice's or policy's victim's asking price is a distorted measure of the variation in his wealth that would compensate him for the policy's adoption—distorted as well by the fact that the use of the asking price presumes counterfactually that the victim was voluntarily asking to be paid for granting his critical acquiescence to the policy's adoption.

Given these facts,

1. Section 1's discussion of why—in a world in which money has a diminishing marginal value and individual demand curves for particular products may have non-zero wealth-elasticities—compensating variations will virtually always differ from the associated equivalent variations should serve to demonstrate that in such a world (almost certainly in our world) the relevant offer prices will differ from the associated asking prices;
2. Section 1's demonstrations that—in a world in which money has diminishing marginal value and relevant demand curves have non-zero wealth-elasticities—the compensating-variation measure of a policy's beneficiaries' dollar gains will usually underestimate those gains and the compensating-variation measure of a policy's victims' dollar losses will usually overestimate those losses should establish that an analyst's decision about whether to measure the dollar gains and losses a policy generates by the relevant individuals' asking prices or offer prices may affect not only his conclusion about the amount by which the policy would increase or decrease (has increased or decreased) allocative efficiency but also his conclusion about whether the policy would increase or decrease (has increased or decreased) allocative efficiency; and
3. Section 1's explanations both of why the correct measure of the relevant dollar gains and losses is the total of the equivalent variations in the wealths of each winner and each loser respectively and of why those equivalent variations should be calculated on the assumption that the relevant individuals did not voluntarily agree to exchange the policy for the transfers in question—indeed, were unaware of the linkage between the money transfers and the policy's adoption—should serve to establish that the offer/asking problem does not imply the impossibility of defining the impact of a choice on allocative efficiency non-arbitrarily.

In short, the discussions in Section 1 of Chapter 1 demonstrate that the offer/asking problem is not unsolvable and that the argument that this problem implies the impossibility of defining the impact of a choice or policy on allocative efficiency non-arbitrarily is a red herring. The correct measures of the relevant dollar gains and losses are the relevant offer prices if the individuals in question (1) neither valued nor disvalued participating in the associated counterfactual transactions, (2) would be indifferent to or ignorant of the linkage between the policy and the transfers, (3) had no relevant attitudes toward government, distributive preferences, or distributive values, and (4) estimated their offer prices not only accurately but also on the assumptions that the payments in question would not affect them indirectly by altering the income or wealth positions and derivatively the conduct of others.

SECTION 4. THE CORRECT ANSWERS TO VARIOUS QUESTIONS RAISED BY THE DEFINITION OF THE IMPACT OF A CHOICE ON ECONOMIC EFFICIENCY THAT IMPLICATE MORAL ISSUES

Although all of the preceding discussions were guided by my belief that the definition and operationalization of the impact of a choice on economic efficiency that is correct is the one that creates a concept that can contribute most to the moral evaluation of private choices or public policies, moral analysis has so far played only a background role in this chapter. This section addresses four issues related to the definition and operationalization of economic efficiency in which moral analysis moves to the foreground.

The Boundary Condition for Economic-Efficiency Analysis

Neither economists in general nor law and economics scholars in particular have paid any attention to the following issue: what attributes must a creature possess for a choice's equivalent-dollar impact on the creature to count directly[5] for the choice's allocative efficiency? Economists with whom I have raised this issue have almost always responded by claiming that the relevant creatures are those who could provide estimates of their equivalent-dollar gains and losses. This response is clearly unsatisfactory: the fact that an economic-efficiency calculation must directly count the equivalent-dollar impact of a choice on even those infants who will not survive long enough to be able to estimate the choice's impact on them refutes the claim that the defining attribute of those creatures whose equivalent-dollar welfare is directly relevant to economic-efficiency calculations is their ability to understand the concept or estimate the equivalent-dollar impact of a choice on them.

I would respond to this boundary-condition issue in the following way: Since the point of calculating the economic efficiency of a choice is to provide information that can contribute to the choice's prescriptive-moral evaluation, the attributes that make the impact of a choice on a particular creature's equivalent-dollar welfare a component of its impact on allocative efficiency in a given society are the same as the creature-attributes that make the impact of a choice on some creature relevant to its prescriptive-moral evaluation in that society. I believe that, in a rights-based society such as the United States, those are the attributes that make a creature rights-bearing in the society in question (though I admit that some members of such societies might believe that one morally ought to take account of the effects of choices on some creatures they would admit are not moral-rights holders in the society in question).

In my judgment, one should determine the attributes that make a creature rights-bearing in a rights-based society by executing a philosophically informed empirical analysis of the relevant rights-based society's relevant practices to identify the moral-status-defining-attributes conclusion that best discounted-fits both the substance of the moral rights one has concluded the society's moral-rights bearers have and the conclusions the society's members and governments have reached about the identifying attributes of moral-rights bearers (where the relevant discount is applied to non-fits whose existence is explicable in ways that reduce the damage they do to the "candidacy" of the relevant attribute-conclusion for the "title" of "identifying attribute of moral-rights bearers" in the society in question). In my admittedly contestable judgment, in liberal, rights-based societies such as the United States, this protocol will yield the conclusion that the attribute of a creature that makes it moral-rights-bearing (and that therefore makes the equivalent-dollar gains or losses any choice confers or imposes on the creature a component of the choice's allocative efficiency) is its possession of the neurological prerequisites for taking its life morally seriously (for taking its moral obligations seriously and for taking seriously as well the dialectical task of forming a conception of the good and living a life that is consonant with that conception). Thus, this conclusion discounted-fits what I take to be the social consensuses that newborns, individuals who are asleep, and individuals who are in reversible comas are moral-rights bearers as well as the consensus that animals that do not have the capacity to take their lives morally seriously are not moral-rights bearers.[6] Similarly, this boundary-condition conclusion is most closely aligned to my conclusion that liberal, rights-based societies place a lexically highest value on individuals' having and seizing the opportunity to lead a life of moral integrity.

The Relevance of Any Tendency of a Choice to Affect the Number of Relevant Creatures That Are Born or the Length of Their Lives

Policies may affect the number of creatures whose equivalent-dollar gains and losses are components of their allocative efficiency. Some will do so by changing the number of such creatures who are born by affecting the survival, health, material welfare, general education, procreation preferences, or birth-control information and equipment that is available to potential biological parents. Others will do so by affecting the length of the lives of relevant creatures who are born by changing the general material welfare and health care of the individuals in question, the external preferences of the society's members and participants (*inter alia,* the extent to which they like or dislike injuring or killing others), the profitability to them of committing acts that impose mortal risks on others (relevant external preferences aside), and so on.

Although economists have never explicitly considered the boundary condition for economic-efficiency calculations, they do recognize that the allocative efficiency of a policy that alters the number of creatures that are created whose experiences count in any such calculation and/or the longevity of any such creatures depends not only on the externalities that the relevant creatures or days of life would generate[7] but also on the positive or negative equivalent-dollar value that each creature whose life would be created, prevented, prolonged, or shortened would place or would have placed on the life or days of life in question, given his or her conception of the good.[8]

Unfortunately, it is far from easy to make the required adjustments. Clearly, one should avoid the mistake (made by some economists) of discounting the equivalent-dollar gains or losses that would be (would have been) experienced by the persons the policy would cause to be (prevent from being) created and the equivalent-dollar gains or losses that would be (would have been) experienced during the days in question by the persons whose lives the policy would lengthen (shorten) on the ground that these gains or losses will be experienced in the future. Still, in many cases, it will be very difficult to measure the effects in question. When the issue is the value to someone of having his life prolonged or shortened, it may be appropriate to rely on the relevant individual's assessments. However, it may not be acceptably reliable to base economic-efficiency conclusions on the equivalent-dollar value assigned to his life by an individual whose life the relevant policy has created and will not be possible to use such "self-assessments" when the policy prevents a life from being created.

How should one proceed if one cannot rely on the life-valuations of the individuals who will lead, did lead, or would have led the lives in question? At least one respected philosopher, John Broome, has argued that the analyst should be able to determine a range of well-being that is neutral in the sense that causing a person to be born who would experience a level of well-being in that range would be neither good nor bad[9] (apparently from a utilitarian perspective). Although Broome does not make the following point, if it were possible to estimate such a range, it might also be possible to determine the equivalent-dollar value of the life (or of the days of life) a policy would create to the individual who would experience it (them) by determining the income/wealth position that would enable the individual in question to lead a life in this neutral range of well-being (given his conception of the good) and then value his actual life by the difference between his actual income or wealth position and the position that would place his life in the middle of the relevant neutral range.

I hasten to add that the word *might* played an important role in the preceding protocol. To execute it, one would have to devise a conception of an individual's income/wealth position that would be appropriate to use in this context and deal with the complexities caused by the following facts:

1. an individual's well-being may vary substantially during his life;
2. an individual's (or his parents') income/wealth position in his early years may affect the level of income and wealth that will enable him to experience well-being that is neutral on the average throughout his lifetime by affecting his conception of the good, his preferences, and his capacities; and
3. the difficulty of this task will be increased when the policy in question prevents a relevant life from being created since the analyst will have to speculate on the neutral zone of well-being for the average person whose creation the policy would prevent.

I want to conclude this section with two observations. First, unlike John Broome (who was admittedly focusing on cost-benefit analysis as opposed to allocative-efficiency analysis), I do not think that the analyst's inability to determine whether the lives (or days of life) whose creation a policy would induce or prevent were good or bad for the individuals who led them or would have led them preclude him from generating a determinate allocative-efficiency conclusion. If the analyst's weighted-average estimate of the equivalent-dollar value of the lives or days of life a policy creates to the individuals who will lead them is zero, this effect of the policy should be valued at zero in his allocative-efficiency calculation. If the analyst has no idea how to value such lives or days of life, he should say so, but this admission does not reduce the importance of his other allocative-efficiency calculations. Second, I want to discuss the point of this section. I have included it not because I believe that I know the correct way to respond to the problem it raises; in fact, I regard my proposals as tentative at best. I have included it because I believe that this problem will at least sometimes be important and hope that, by calling attention to it, I will induce others to address it more successfully.

Changes in the Preferences That Underlie the Equivalent-Dollar Effects of a Policy or Choice

Tastes change, sometimes spontaneously and sometimes because the individual in question has obtained new information or has reconsidered his nonmoral preferences without obtaining additional data. Personally selected values change for the same sorts of reasons, as do an individual's perception of his societally imposed moral obligations and the equivalent-dollar value he places on choices or policies (controlling for his income/wealth position) because he approves or disapproves of them for moral reasons. Sometimes the policy or choice whose allocative efficiency is to be assessed has nothing to do with the relevant preference changes. And sometimes such changes occur because the choice or policy in question induces the relevant individual (1) to try a new product (by altering the relative prices of goods or his income/wealth position), (2) to observe or interact with people with different tastes, conceptions of the good, or lifestyles (by inducing him to change his residence or job or to travel), (3) to obtain more formal education or read more widely on his own, or (4) to reconsider his own tastes, conception of the good, or perception of his society's moral commitments (by exposing him to different advertising, giving him more leisure time, exposing him to more information about the lives of others or the prescriptive-moral perceptions and conduct of his society's members and governments, or generating a change in his income/wealth position that induces him to reflect on the justness or desirability of the society's economic and social institutions). In any event, particularly when, but not only when, the choice or policy under consideration has engendered some such change, it will require the allocative-efficiency analyst to resolve a number of tricky issues.

The first such issue is the allocative efficiency of the changes themselves. Changes in taste can increase or decrease allocative efficiency for a variety of reasons. Take, for example, a change in taste that involves an individual's learning to appreciate more expensive goods (fine wines or higher-quality sound-reproduction systems). If this change in the relevant individual's ability to discern and appreciate quality-differences generates a reduction in the absolute amount of pleasure the individual can obtain by consuming or using the cheaper good (by drinking the less expensive wine with which he was originally completely satisfied or listening to music on an inexpensive stereo system that originally served his purposes perfectly well), it may actually inflict an equivalent-dollar loss on the individual in question and tend to reduce economic efficiency on that account. In particular, this outcome will obtain whenever the change in taste reduces the satisfaction he obtains by consuming a good he continues to purchase or whenever the difference between the equivalent-dollar benefits the individual in question originally obtained from the cheaper good and the equivalent-dollar benefits he secured from the more expensive good he consumes after the change in his tastes is smaller than the difference between the allocative cost of the cheaper and more expensive products in question. Of course, such a change in an individual's ability to discern and appreciate quality-differences could also benefit the individual who experienced it and increase allocative efficiency on that account as well. In particular, this latter outcome would obtain if the increase in the individual's ability to discern quality-differences led him to purchase the more expensive good without reducing the pleasure he could obtain from the cheaper good and the allocative cost of his consuming the more expensive rather than the less expensive product was smaller than the amount by which post-change the value to him of the more expensive good exceeded the value to him of the less expensive good. Moreover, regardless of whether the change in question increases or decreases the value of some good to the relevant individual, it can also increase allocative efficiency because other Pareto imperfections critically distort the private cost to the relevant individual of shifting to the more expensive good whose value to him has been enhanced by his change in taste (or critically distort the private cost-savings he secures by shifting to a cheaper good when the change in taste involves his placing a higher value on a cheaper good than he originally placed on that product). Take, for example, the case of someone who learns to enjoy fast driving. If this change in taste causes him to purchase and drive a more expensive, racy sports car rather than a staid station wagon, it might decrease allocative efficiency if his post-taste-change driving generates more external pollution and accident costs or if the difference between the prices of the sports car and station wagon and the gas they consume is lower than the difference in the allocative costs of their production and use.

Changes in an individual's personal "value" commitments, in his perception of his society's value commitments, or in the equivalent-dollar value he assigns to fulfilling his personal value commitments or societally imposed moral commitments can also either increase or decrease allocative efficiency. I have quoted the word *value* in its first use in the preceding sentence because, for current purposes, it does not matter whether the decision standard to which the individual perceives himself to be committed is morally defensible.

I will illustrate the claim made in the first sentence of this paragraph with one example of a change in values that will increase economic efficiency and one example of a change in values that will decrease economic efficiency.

Assume that the policy under consideration induced some of the society's members to value the impact of their choices on others—indeed, to internalize to themselves the net equivalent-dollar impact of their choices on others and hence to make those choices and only those choices they would have found profitable had they themselves experienced the net equivalent-dollar impact their choices had on others (rather than, say, making the choices that would be profitable for them to make if they were indifferent to the impact of their choices on others). Some policies might be specially designed to produce this effect; some might do so by manifesting the State's concern for members' and participants' welfare; and some might do so by causing those they affect to have experiences that make them more conscious of the consequences of injuries that others sustain or that persuade them that interpersonal differences in real income do not primarily or even substantially reflect differences in the choices the relevant individuals made for which these others were morally responsible.

This change in values could increase allocative efficiency in two ways. First, it may deter the relevant individuals from making external-cost-imposing choices they would have found attractive (profitable) had they been indifferent to the choices' impact on others but were rendered allocatively inefficient by the losses the choices would have imposed on others or induce the relevant individuals to make external-benefit-conferring choices (for example, to execute rescues) they would not have found profitable had they been indifferent to the choices' impact on others but were rendered allocatively efficient by the choices' impact on others. Second, it may enable the actors in question to obtain the equivalent-dollar benefits they secured because the choices they made were ones their values implied they should make (where the choices in question would have been allocatively efficient in any event). I should add that, although the relevant society might be able to induce its members and participants to make allocatively-efficient-avoidance decisions and rescue decisions by promulgating and enforcing an allocatively-efficient-tort law, an appropriate system of civil fines and subsidies, and/or an appropriate body of criminal law, allocative efficiency will clearly be increased if the State does not have to rely on legal incentives to induce the conduct in question. The latter conclusion reflects the allocative transaction cost of the legal approach, the reality that its execution will be hampered by imperfections in the information available to legal decision makers, and the private or allocative equivalent-dollar gains people secure or generate by acting the way they think they should act when it is not conventionally profitable for them to do so. The preceding argument will also apply when the policy in question causes some of the society's members and participants to fulfill their societally imposed (liberal) moral obligations by informing them of their society's (liberal) justice commitments and/or persuading them of the value of their society's justice commitments and fulfilling their moral obligations (though the equivalent-dollar gains people get from fulfilling their societally imposed moral obligations may be different from the gains they secure from fulfilling their personally chosen commitments).

Assume next that the policy in question induces individuals to adopt libertarian "values"[10] that imply that individuals have no duty to rescue others whose imperilment was not their fault and have a moral right to choose whether to provide or not provide rescue services (to be guided by their own preferences on such matters). A State's policies could induce its members to adopt such values by manifesting indifference toward people in need of help, by calling attention to evildoing criminals without revealing information about their histories that might account for their conduct, or by calling attention to "the undeserving poor" who commit welfare or unemployment-insurance fraud. To the extent that such policies deter some of the society's members and participants from making rescue attempts that would be allocatively efficient even if the rescue attempters did not gain satisfaction from helping others (rescue attempts that were originally rendered even more allocatively efficient by the satisfaction they gave the rescue attempters because they valued living up to their personally chosen or perceived societally imposed commitments) by inducing them to substitute libertarian social commitment perceptions and personal commitments for their pre-policy altruistic counterparts, they will reduce allocative efficiency on that account.

In one sense, this section has said both too little and too much. Too little because, in a world in which time and space were free goods, it would be useful both to refine and extend the preceding comments. And too much because (I fear) my discussion of these possibilities may tempt readers to reject my conclusion that some effort should be made to measure and count any external-preference-derived and bad-preference-derived equivalent-dollar gains and losses a choice generates when calculating its allocative efficiency.

Actor Mistakes about the Equivalent-Dollar Value of Particular Goods or Bads That the Relevant Policy Generated

In my experience, economic-efficiency analysts give two justifications for their practice of assuming that (1) the individuals who believe that they have won or lost (or will win or lose) from a private choice or public policy are actual or prospective winners and losers and (2) the relevant self-perceived or actual winners and losers accurately estimate the gains and losses the policy will confer or impose on them as well as the value to them of other things from whose value the policy's impact on them might be inferred.[11] First, these scholars argue that these assumptions are justified by the difficulty of determining whether someone has misvalued a policy or a related choice from his own perspective and substituting a more accurate estimate of the policy's or choice's impact on someone for the relevant party's erroneous estimate of that impact. Second, they argue that these assumptions are justified by the autonomy interest such individuals have in their evaluations' being accepted, regardless of whether those valuations are correct or incorrect from their own perspectives.

I will start by analyzing the second supposed justification for the economists' assumption that all parties are sovereign maximizers. I have two responses to this argument of principle. First, I do not think that members of a liberal, rights-based society have an autonomy interest in having private or public choices be influenced by the mistakes they make in valuing them from their own perspectives. Liberalism places great weight on the autonomy interests individuals have in choosing their own conception of the good, but, with an important practical qualification to be discussed below, I do not see why the members of a liberal, rights-based society have an autonomy interest in private or public choices' being influenced by their mistakes in valuing outcomes or processes from their own perspectives. Indeed, one could argue that a liberal, rights-based society's duty to show appropriate concern for such parties obligates its governments to base their decisions on correct as opposed to mistaken estimates of the value of the relevant choices to the parties in question. Second, even if one assumes *ad arguendo* that those who actually are affected by a policy or choice may have an interest in the choice's being based on their mistaken valuations of the policy or something else whose value to them affects the economists' economic-efficiency calculations, the economists should not simply accept these individuals' evaluations without reporting

Economists also argue that all external-preference-derived equivalent-dollar gains and losses should be excluded from economic-efficiency calculations because it is immoral to take morally bad external preferences into consideration when generating economic-efficiency conclusions.[3] This argument fails on two accounts.

First, it fails because it assumes inaccurately that all external preferences are morally bad. External preferences that manifest their holder's commitment to his society's morally defensible conception of justice or to his own morally defensible personal convictions about how resources and opportunities should be distributed are clearly not "morally bad." Nor, I would argue, are external preferences that reflect their holder's love for, friendship for, sympathy with, or empathy with particular others.

Second, even if all external preferences were morally bad, the claim that external-preference-derived equivalent-dollar gains and losses should be excluded from economic-efficiency calculations would fail because it is inconsistent with the nature of economic efficiency. Economic efficiency is not a moral concept, is not a good in itself. Moreover, the economic efficiency of a choice is totally irrelevant to its moral desirability from many normative perspectives and has only limited relevance to its desirability from those (utilitarian) perspectives from which it is somewhat salient. I want to emphasize that this objection to excluding external-preference-derived equivalent-dollar gains and losses from economic-efficiency calculations is not sterilely definitional. The alleged moral justification for excluding such gains and losses is objectionable because it sends the wrong message about the moral relevance of economic-efficiency conclusions—a message that confirms the false assumptions of many economists and law and economics scholars that either (1) economic efficiency is a value itself or (2) economically efficient choices are always just and morally desirable, justice-considerations aside.

I hasten to add that it would be very useful for economic-efficiency analysts to report to the prescriptive-moral evaluators to whom they are supplying information any data they have not just on the magnitude of the external-preference-derived effects that their economic-efficiency calculations incorporate but also on the substance of the preferences that underlie each of the effects in question. Such information would put the prescriptive-moral evaluators in a position to adjust their conclusions in the way that the moral status of the external preferences in question warrants (from the normative perspective from which the evaluator is operating).

their suspicions that the winners and losers in question have made relevant errors: economic-efficiency calculators should inform the decision makers they are advising that their calculations substituted the affected parties' estimates of the equivalent-dollar value to them of the policy or something related to the policy's economic efficiency for the economists' own estimates of the equivalent-dollar sums in question (should put the decision maker in a position to base his choice on all possibly relevant information).

I am more sympathetic to the "practical" justification for economists' assuming that a policy's winners and losers have correctly estimated the value of the policy or some related choice-option to them—namely, the concern that the economists' estimates of the equivalent-dollar value of the policy or some relevant good, service, or option to the policy's winners and losers is unlikely to be more accurate than their own. Even analysts who have a sophisticated grasp of the different tastes people may have, the full range of the conceptions of the good to which members of the relevant society may subscribe, the different conceptions various people may have of the justice-commitments of the relevant society, and the different extents to which different members of the relevant society value their living up to their respective commitments may find it difficult to discern whether an individual's surprising valuation of a choice or policy reflects his making an error from his own perspective or his having unusual tastes, an unusual conception of the good, an unusual understanding of his society's moral commitments, or an unusual "preference" for his and his society's fulfilling their respective commitments. And, in my experience, economists do not have a sophisticated grasp of these matters—for example, doubt that individuals have altruistic preferences and suspect that moral-rights discourse and all values that focus on something other than total utility and perhaps the distribution of utility are incoherent (indeed, in many instances, think that, deep down, everyone is really a utilitarian). To the extent that these shortcomings would lead economists to substitute valuations that reflect their own values and preferences for valuations that reflect the values and preferences of those who would actually be affected by a choice or policy, instructing economic-efficiency analysts to correct what they perceive to be the valuation-mistakes of those who have been (will be) or who believe that they have been (will be) affected by a choice or policy may (1) decrease rather than increase the accuracy of their economic-efficiency conclusions and (2) disserve the autonomy interests of the affected parties. However, my preferred response to this problem would be to instruct economic-efficiency analysts to make such corrections but require them to accompany their conclusions with a clear and full statement of the corrections they made and their reasons for making them rather than to instruct them to assume the accuracy of the policy's winners' and losers' valuations of the policy and various things whose value to the winners and losers bears on the policy's economic efficiency.

Chapter 2 A Critique of the Definitions of and Tests for Economic Efficiency That Economists and Law and Economics Scholars Use

Economists and law and economics scholars use one or more of the following four definitions of or tests for economic efficiency—the Pareto-superior/Pareto-inferior definition, the Kaldor-Hicks test, the Scitovsky test, and the potentially-Pareto-superior definition. This chapter delineates, comments on, and criticizes each.

SECTION 1. THE PARETO-SUPERIOR (PARETO-INFERIOR) DEFINITION OF AN INCREASE (DECREASE) IN ECONOMIC EFFICIENCY

According to this definition, a choice or policy is said to increase allocative efficiency if and only if it brings the economy to a Pareto-superior position—that is, if and only if it makes one or more individuals better off and no one worse off. Relatedly, on this definition, a choice or policy is said to decrease allocative efficiency if and only if it brings the economy to a Pareto-inferior position—that is, if and only if it makes one or more individuals worse off and no one better off.

I have four observations. First, this definition is stipulative (perhaps "technical" would be a friendlier word) in that it is inconsistent with both popular understanding and (as I will indicate next) professional usage. Although everyone would agree that all Pareto-superior choices are economically efficient and all Pareto-inferior choices are economically inefficient, on common understanding (1) choices that confer total equivalent-dollar gains on their beneficiaries that exceed the total equivalent-dollar losses they impose on their victims are deemed economically efficient despite the fact that they are not Pareto-superior, and (2) choices that impose total equivalent-dollar losses on their victims that exceed the total equivalent-dollar gains they confer on their beneficiaries are deemed economically inefficient despite the fact that they are not Pareto-inferior.

Second, in practice, when actually analyzing the allocative efficiency of particular government policies, no economist ever uses "economic efficiency" in this Pareto-superior/Pareto-inferior sense. In my experience, all articles that begin by defining economic efficiency in the Pareto-superior/Pareto-inferior sense end up implicitly defining the concept in the correct monetized sense Chapter 1 delineated.

Third, the Pareto-superior/Pareto-inferior definition of economic efficiency is disfavored not only by its inconsistency with popular and professional understanding and usage but also by the fact that the concept it creates would be completely or virtually useless. Since in our actual, highly-Pareto-imperfect world virtually all private choices and (I would submit) all public policies benefit some and harm others, the economic efficiency of all or virtually all choices whose economic efficiency economists investigate would be indeterminate if the concept were defined in the Pareto-superior/Pareto-inferior sense. Such a definition would therefore prevent the concept from making the contribution Part III will argue it can make if defined in the monetized sense Chapter 1 articulates to the utilitarian evaluation of choices and policies.

Fourth, for two reasons, the Pareto-superior/Pareto-inferior definition of the impact of a choice on economic efficiency will not enable economists to achieve the goal that led them to propose it—namely, to increase their social contribution by increasing the moral significance of the economic-efficiency conclusions their expertise enables them to generate. I have already explained the first reason, which is empirically more important: on this definition, the economic efficiency of all or virtually all choices will be indeterminate. The second reason (which is admittedly less empirically important) may be somewhat more surprising. Contrary to the assumption of most economists, not all Pareto-superior (Pareto-inferior) choices are morally desirable (morally undesirable) from all defensible moral perspectives.

The following example illustrates this second point. Assume that a prosecutor who has discovered a previously undetected 50-year-old murder and has identified its perpetrator must decide whether to charge and try the killer. Assume in addition that the following conditions are fulfilled:

1. the prosecutor himself is indifferent to charging and trying the killer;
2. at this stage in his life, the murderer is a productive member of the society who is loved by family and friends and poses no risk to the community;
3. the trial and conviction of the murderer would not secure any general-deterrence benefits (because the revelation that the perpetrator had escaped trial for 50 years would disserve general deterrence by at least as much as his trial, conviction, and punishment would secure it);
4. the individuals other than the prosecutor who would arrest, prosecute, defend, judge, and incarcerate the perpetrator would not profit from doing so;
5. the trial and punishment of the murderer would not benefit his economic competitors or his employer's economic competitors;
6. the prosecution of the murderer would provide no one with an equivalent-dollar gain by avenging the victim's death or securing justice (because the victim could not be identified or no living person would know the victim and those who value criminal justice's being served would be as upset by the revelation that the perpetrator escaped justice for 50 years as they would be pleased by his belated trial, conviction, and punishment); and
7. a decision to prosecute the perpetrator would harm him, those who would have gained from the productive labor his trial and punishment would prevent him from supplying, his family and friends, and those who would have benefited from the goods and services the resources that would be consumed by his trial and punishment would have produced had they been devoted to other uses.

On these facts, a decision to not call attention to the crime and identify and prosecute its perpetrator would be Pareto-superior—it would impose an equivalent-dollar loss on no one and would benefit all those that a decision to prosecute the perpetrator would harm, including all those individuals mentioned in item (7) of the preceding list.

Nevertheless, from a variety of nonutilitarian moral perspectives, the prosecutor morally ought to make the Pareto-inferior choice to prosecute the murderer in question. This conclusion would be favored not only by retributivist moral norms but also by a variety of other moral norms that value the resources or welfare that individuals possess or experience matching their moral merits (their deserts).[1]

In short, the Pareto-superior/Pareto-inferior definition of the impact of a choice on economic efficiency is inconsistent with popular and professional understanding and usage, produces a concept that will result in the economic efficiency of virtually all choices being determined to be indeterminate, and in part for this latter reason will not enable economists to achieve the goal they hoped to secure by adopting it—namely, increasing the social value of their expertise in analyzing the economic efficiency of private choices and public policies.

SECTION 2. THE KALDOR-HICKS TEST FOR ECONOMIC EFFICIENCY

The Kaldor-Hicks test[2] for economic efficiency was designed to overcome the basic deficiency of the Pareto-superior/Pareto-inferior definition—more positively, to create a concept that would enable its employer to say something determinate about the economic efficiency of all choices, including the overwhelming majority of choices that have both beneficiaries and victims. According to the Kaldor-Hicks operationalization, a choice or policy is said to increase economic efficiency not only if it brings the economy to a Pareto-superior position but also if, in the absence of transaction costs, the number of dollars its beneficiaries could pay its victims to secure their essential consent to it and remain equally well-off *exceeds* the number of dollars for which its victims could sell their essential consent to the choice or policy to its beneficiaries and remain equally well-off—if in the absence of transaction costs the choice's or policy's winners could profitably bribe its losers to provide their essential acquiescence to the policy's adoption. This hypothetical-compensation test implicitly measures a policy's winners' equivalent-dollar gains by the number of dollars they should be indifferent to voluntarily paying its losers to secure their critical acquiescence to its adoption, implicitly measures a policy's losers' equivalent-dollar losses by the number of dollars they should be indifferent to voluntarily accepting in exchange for their critical acquiescence to its adoption, and implicitly measures the impact of a private choice or public policy on economic efficiency by the difference between the bribe its winners should (in their own interest, broadly defined) be indifferent to paying its victims to secure the policy (if the alternative were the policy's rejection) and the bribe the policy's victims should be indifferent to accepting from the beneficiaries in exchange for granting their critical consent to its adoption. Virtually all law and economics scholars and most economists who set out to analyze the allocative efficiency of some private choice or public policy claim to be defining the impact of a choice or policy on economic efficiency in the way that the Kaldor-Hicks test implicitly operationalizes this concept.

The analysis in Section 1 of Chapter 1 reveals that the Kaldor-Hicks test for a policy's economic efficiency is wrong for four reasons. First, since the bribes it seeks to identify are purely hypothetical, the Kaldor-Hicks test will misestimate the winners' equivalent-dollar gains and the losers' equivalent-dollar losses to the extent that the individuals in question find it intrinsically valuable or costly to engage in the voluntary market transactions the test tries to identify—that is, to the extent that the policy's winners' and losers' accurate answers to the question to which the Kaldor-Hicks test implicitly asks them to respond (How much should you, the winners, be indifferent to paying the losers to secure the policy and how much should you, the losers, be indifferent to accepting from the winners in exchange for your agreeing not to block the policy?) would be affected by their finding it intrinsically valuable or costly to engage in the relevant voluntary market transactions, the Kaldor-Hicks test will on this account tend to incorporate inaccurate measures of the equivalent-dollar gains and losses the policy in question will generate.

Second, *ceteris paribus,* even if the Kaldor-Hicks test's voluntary-market-transaction error is eliminated, its assessment of the dollar gains, dollar losses, and change in economic efficiency a policy will generate will be inaccurate to the extent that the positive or negative dollar value that the policy's winners and losers place on the policy because of their attitudes toward governments' adopting the policy after requiring the hypothetical transfers to be made, because of their distributive preferences, and/or because of their distributive values differs from the positive or negative value these individuals would place on the policy itself on these accounts.

Third, the Kaldor-Hicks test is deficient and at least potentially inaccurate because the questions it implicitly seeks to answer do not indicate that the withdrawal from the winners that would perfectly offset the impact of the policy on them should be calculated on the assumption that it would not affect them indirectly by changing the wealth and derivatively the conduct of others and that the transfer to the losers that would perfectly offset the impact of the policy on them should be calculated on a counterpart assumption.

Fourth, the Kaldor-Hicks test is deficient in that—even if the preceding faults were remedied—it would measure a policy's winners' dollar gains and losers' dollar losses by the respective total compensating variations in their wealths rather than by the respective total equivalent variations in their wealths. As we have seen, this fourth deficiency of the Kaldor-Hicks test will almost certainly tend to cause it to be biased against the allocative efficiency of the private choices and public policies whose allocative efficiency it is used to assess. Although in individual cases this bias could be perfectly offset by the biases introduced by the other errors just delineated, this outcome would be fortuitous and, I believe, exceedingly rare. Indeed, I suspect that across all cases the voluntary-market-transaction error of the Kaldor-Hicks test will compound the tendency of its compensating-variation versus equivalent-variation error to cause it to yield underestimates of the allocative efficiency of the choices and policies to which it is applied.

SECTION 3. THE SCITOVSKY TEST FOR ECONOMIC EFFICIENCY

In 1941, Tibor Scitovsky proved something that implies that the Kaldor-Hicks test must be wrong.[3] Specifically, Scitovsky demonstrated that in some circumstances both a policy and its immediate reversal will pass the Kaldor-Hicks test. This Scitovsky Paradox invalidates the Kaldor-Hicks test because it implies that, if that test were accurate and a Scitovsky Paradox arose, both the policy and its reversal would be economically efficient and, hence, the policy would simultaneously be economically efficient and economically inefficient. Economists responded to this bad news by proposing that a choice or policy should be deemed economically efficient if and only if two conditions are fulfilled: (1) it passes the Kaldor-Hicks test, and (2) its reversal does not pass the Kaldor-Hicks test. This section provides an ordinarily meaningful account of the circumstances in which the Scitovsky Paradox will arise (something Scitovsky never did), relates the occurrence of the Scitovsky Paradox to the compensating-variation versus equivalent-variation error the Kaldor-Hicks test makes, and demonstrates that the Scitovsky test is also incorrect (that its substitution for the Kaldor-Hicks test is not an appropriate response to the deficiency of the Kaldor-Hicks test that the Scitovsky Paradox manifests).

In one sense, the incorrectness of the Scitovsky test should not be surprising: rather than trying to understand the problem that underlies the

Scitovsky Paradox and responding to it by taking care of that problem, Scitovsky's contemporaries tried to circumvent his work by altering the Kaldor-Hicks test to create a new, patched-up test that would not produce internally inconsistent conclusions. I should add that, if anything, Scitovsky's contemporaries' unsatisfactory response to his paradox is superior to their successors': most contemporary economists ignore the Scitovsky Paradox altogether—in particular, continue to use the unsupplemented Kaldor-Hicks test that Scitovsky showed could not possibly be right.

To reveal in everyday terms why Scitovsky Paradoxes can arise, I will focus on a monetized example that is based on the following seven assumptions:

1. the relevant policy's beneficiaries and victims do not value or disvalue in itself participating in the voluntary market transactions in which the Kaldor-Hicks test hypothesizes they will engage;
2. those individuals have no attitudes toward government, distributive preferences, or distributive values that would tend to make the Kaldor-Hicks test inaccurate, *ceteris paribus*;
3. the transactions the Kaldor-Hicks test hypothesizes will not affect any relevant individual indirectly by changing the income/wealth position and derivatively the conduct of someone else (will generate no relevant secondary-feedback effects);
4. the policy's beneficiaries should be indifferent to securing it by paying its victims $200 to obtain their essential consent to it (that the total of the winners' compensating variations would be $200 if paying the losers $200 rather than having that money withdrawn from them produced no special, relevant effects);
5. the policy's victims should be indifferent to accepting an offer from its beneficiaries to pay them $180 to forego blocking the policy when it would then be adopted (that, on the counterpart assumption to the one delineated in the preceding item, the total of the victims' compensating variations was $180);
6. once the policy was adopted without any cross-payments having been made, its original victims (the beneficiaries of its reversal) would be indifferent to paying its original beneficiaries $210 to secure its reversal (that, on the same assumption, the total of the original policy's victims' equivalent variations for the original policy was $210); and
7. once the policy was adopted, its original beneficiaries (the victims of its reversal) should be indifferent to accepting $205 in exchange for their

agreement to allow the policy to be reversed (that, on the same assumption, the total of the original policy's beneficiaries' equivalent variations for the original policy was $205).

In this case, the Scitovsky Paradox would arise because both the policy—compare assumptions (4) and (5)—and its reversal—compare assumptions (6) and (7)—would pass the Kaldor-Hicks test.

But how could these facts obtain? There is nothing unusual about the conjunction of assumptions (4) and (7): the assumption that the policy's winners' total "asking price" (for foregoing the policy [asked of its victims, hence the quotation marks]) of $205 is higher than their total "offer price" (to secure the policy) of $200 is consistent with my expectation that in most cases the policy's beneficiaries' equivalent-dollar valuation of the policy will be positively wealth-elastic. Admittedly, there is something unusual about the conjunction of assumptions (5) and (6), which jointly give rise to the Scitovsky Paradox: the assumption that the original policy's victims' "asking price" (for their consent to the policy [asked of its beneficiaries]) of $180 is lower than their "offer price" (to secure the policy's rejection [offered to its beneficiaries]) of $210 deviates from what I take to be the typical state of affairs in which a policy's victims' negative (absolute) dollar-valuation of the policy will be positively wealth-elastic—that is, with my assumption that the amount that a policy's victims should be indifferent to paying to block a policy will typically be lower than the amount they should be indifferent to accepting for allowing the policy to be adopted. To see why the current example assumes that the policy's victims' negative (absolute) dollar-valuation of the policy is negatively wealth-elastic, note that it assumes that the number of dollars that the policy will cost them ($210) when they are poorer (when they had to pay to block it) *exceeds* the number of dollars it would cost them ($180) when they were richer (when they would be paid for permitting it to be adopted).

However, although I do not think such negative-wealth-elasticity cases arise that often, they clearly will sometimes occur. For example, assume that the policy in question is an antitrust-exemption policy or a pollution-tax policy that would impose an equivalent-dollar loss on its victims by raising the price they have to pay for the goods whose producers would be exempted from antitrust regulation or whose production would be taxed. If these victims' demands for the goods in question are negatively wealth-elastic—that is, if (at least for this policy's victims) the goods in question are what economists call "inferior goods" (if, controlling for the goods' prices, the original policy's victims' quantity demands for them increase with reductions in their wealth over the relevant range)—the price increases that the policies would generate would cost the victims more if the victims were poorer (since then their quantity demands for the goods in question would be higher) than if they were richer (since then their quantity demands for the goods in question would be lower), and the number of dollars the policies' victims should be indifferent to paying to block or reverse the policies would be higher than the number of dollars they should be indifferent to accepting to allow the policies' adoption (at least given the first three assumptions I built into the preceding example).

In this case, then, the Scitovsky Paradox will arise because the (\$210 − \$180 = \$30) dollar-valuation effect of the negative wealth-elasticity of the victims' valuations of the policy *exceeds* (the \$20 by which the Kaldor-Hicks test would conclude the original policy would increase economic efficiency) *plus* (the \$5 dollar-valuation effect of the positive wealth-elasticity of the original policy's beneficiaries' dollar-valuations of the policy). In the case in which the original policy's beneficiaries' dollar-valuations of the policy are negatively wealth-elastic and the original policy's victims' dollar-valuations of the policy are positively wealth-elastic, the Scitovsky Paradox will arise whenever the dollar-valuation effect of the negative wealth-elasticity of the beneficiaries' valuation of the policy *exceeds* the sum of the Kaldor-Hicks assessment of its economic efficiency and the dollar-valuation effect of the positive wealth-elasticity of the original policy's victims' negative dollar-valuations of the policy. Finally, in the case in which the dollar-valuations of the policy by both its beneficiaries and its victims are negatively wealth-elastic, the Scitovsky Paradox will arise whenever the sum of the dollar-valuation effects of the policy's winners' and losers' relevant negative wealth-elasticities *exceeds* the amount by which the Kaldor-Hicks test would imply the policy would increase economic efficiency.

It should now be possible to relate Scitovsky's critique of the Kaldor-Hicks test to the preceding section's discussion of that test's errors. Basically, both a policy and its reversal can pass the Kaldor-Hicks test because a policy's passing the Kaldor-Hicks test is neither a necessary nor a sufficient condition for its being economically efficient in the correct sense of that expression. This conclusion reflects the fact that—even if one ignores the error the Kaldor-Hicks test makes by accepting the voluntary-market-transaction paradigm, its failure to deal with affected parties' attitudes toward government and distributive preferences and values, and its secondary-feedback error—it would be undermined by its compensating-variation versus equivalent-variation error.

The correct response to the Scitovsky Paradox is not to supplement the Kaldor-Hicks test by adding a requirement that the policy's reversal not pass the test but to reject the Kaldor-Hicks test altogether. The replacement that is warranted, the test that Chapter 1 proposed, is a cleaned-up version of the second condition of the Scitovsky test for economic efficiency—namely, that the relevant choice's or policy's reversal would not pass the Kaldor-Hicks test. In essence, the non-cleaned-up version of this response would correct the Kaldor-Hicks test's compensating-variation versus equivalent-variation error since the Scitovsky-Paradox-induced add-on (1) implicitly measures the equivalent-dollar gains of the original policy's winners (the equivalent-dollar losses of the policy reversal's victims) by the total of the original policy's equivalent variations for them (by the total of their asking prices for granting their essential consent to the original policy's rejection or reversal) rather than by the total of the compensating variations for them for the original policy (by the total of their offer prices for securing that policy) and (2) implicitly measures the equivalent-dollar losses of the original policy's victims (the equivalent-dollar gains the policy's reversal would confer on the reversal's beneficiaries) by the total of the equivalent variations for the victims of the original policy (by the total of their offer prices for the original policy's rejection or reversal) rather than by the total of the variations in the original policy's victims' wealths that would compensate them for the original policy (by the total of their asking prices for granting their essential acquiescence to its adoption).

Of course, although the Scitovsky-Paradox-induced add-on to the Kaldor-Hicks test correctly resolves the compensating-variation versus equivalent-variation issue, it still is not correct. To be correct, it would have to be cleaned up in three ways. First, one would have to eliminate any suggestion that the relevant equivalent-dollar gains and losses were respectively the amount of dollars the reversal's winners would be willing to pay its losers in a voluntary market transaction to secure the policy's reversal and the amount of dollars the reversal's losers would be willing to accept from its winners in a voluntary market transaction in exchange for their essential acquiescence to its reversal. Second, one would have to make clear that the test's estimates of the equivalent-dollar gains and losses the policy would generate would ignore the relevant winners' and losers' attitudes toward government and potentially relevant distributive preferences and values. And third, one would have to make clear that the test would ignore any secondary-feedback effects that the cross-payments it hypothesizes would have on the policy's beneficiaries and victims.

In short, the Scitovsky test for economic efficiency is incorrect for two reasons. First, its requirement that the policy pass the Kaldor-Hicks test brings with it all the mistakes the Kaldor-Hicks test makes and causes it to be under-inclusive (causes it to classify as not economically efficient choices or policies that are economically efficient but fail the Kaldor-Hicks test for economic efficiency). Second, the Scitovsky test's second requirement—that the reversal of the relevant choice or policy fail the Kaldor-Hicks test—is mis-specified in that it needs to be cleaned up to eliminate the errors the traditional Kaldor-Hicks test's formulation commits in addition to its compensating-variation versus equivalent-variation error.

SECTION 4. THE POTENTIALLY-PARETO-SUPERIOR DEFINITION OF AN INCREASE IN ECONOMIC EFFICIENCY

The potentially-Pareto-superior definition of the impact of a choice or policy on economic efficiency is directed exclusively at determining whether choices or policies increase economic efficiency. According to this definition, a choice or policy that is not Pareto-superior is said to increase economic efficiency if and only if the combination of the policy and an allocative-transaction-costless government-arranged money transfer to its victims that would not be financed in a way that caused any misallocative choices to be made among market-labor, do-it-yourself-labor, and leisure or among saving, consumption, and gift- or bequest-giving[4] would be Pareto-superior (would leave somebody better off and no one worse off). Although virtually all law and economics scholars still claim to be using the Kaldor-Hicks test for the economic efficiency of a choice or policy, a substantial and increasing percentage of economists in general have adopted the potentially-Pareto-superior definition just articulated.

Those economists who have shifted to this potentially-Pareto-superior definition seem to have done so for both positive and negative reasons. The positive motivation is the one that led many economists to adopt the Pareto-superior definition—the desire to make their expertise at assessing the economic efficiency of a choice or policy more valuable (a desire made relevant by their belief that Pareto-superior choices will always be morally desirable from all legitimate normative perspectives and their apparent failure to recognize that even if, contrary to fact, this belief were correct it would not imply the moral desirability of potentially-Pareto-superior policies that were not Pareto-superior by themselves). The negative motivation appears to be their felt uneasiness with the Kaldor-Hicks test, an uneasiness that may be associated with their recollection that Scitovsky established the invalidity of that test.

Admittedly, the potentially-Pareto-superior definition of a choice that increases economic efficiency does have two advantages over the Kaldor-Hicks operationalization of this concept. First, it does not make the compensating-variation versus equivalent-variation error. Second, its formulation leaves open the possibility that it could take account of any equivalent-dollar gains or losses that affected individuals experience because for nonmaterial reasons they value or disvalue the money transfer whose combination with the policy under review would or might create a Pareto-superior policy package. Unfortunately, the potentially-Pareto-superior definition does make an error that is a counterpart to the Kaldor-Hicks operationalization's secondary-feedback-related error.

Proponents of the potentially-Pareto-superior definition believe that it is accurate because they implicitly assume that any allocative-transaction-costless money transfer that would be the second component of any Pareto-superior policy package that could be identified would have no effect whatsoever on economic efficiency properly understood if it would generate no allocative transaction costs, no misallocative choices among market-labor, do-it-yourself-labor, and leisure, and no misallocative choices among saving, consumption, and gift- or bequest-giving.[5] If this assumption were correct, the fact that the combination of the policy under investigation and such a money transfer would move the economy to a Pareto-superior position would guarantee that the policy under consideration would increase economic efficiency: if economic efficiency would be increased by $X by the combination of the policy under investigation and a money transfer that had no effect on economic efficiency, the policy must increase economic efficiency by $X. However, although the assumption that such money transfers will not affect economic efficiency might be deemed acceptably accurate in an otherwise-Pareto-perfect economy,[6] it is not acceptable in our actual, highly-Pareto-imperfect economy. Even if no one has external preferences for or against the money transfer whose combination with the policy under investigation would (or would otherwise) create a Pareto-superior policy package, in a world that does or may contain other Pareto imperfections, a transaction-costless money transfer that caused no labor/leisure or savings/consumption misallocation can still either increase or decrease resource misallocations of other sorts by changing the wealth and derivatively the conduct of various affected individuals (for the same reason that the bribe the Kaldor-Hicks test contemplates may generate secondary-feedback effects on the relevant payors or payees that would cause their answers to the questions the Kaldor-Hicks test implicitly poses to misrepresent the equivalent-dollar impact on them of the choice or policy whose economic efficiency the Kaldor-Hicks test is being used to assess).

More specifically, in our actual, Pareto-imperfect world, such a money transfer to the basic policy's victims would tend to decrease economic efficiency if, for example, it made it personally attractive for the victims to make misallocative decisions to buy and to drive more expensive, more pollution-generating sports cars in more accident-prone and more polluting ways instead of driving less expensive, less pollution-generating station wagons in less accident-prone and less polluting ways. In the other direction, such a money transfer to the basic policy's victims would tend to increase economic efficiency if it made it personally attractive for them to make economically efficient decisions to buy and operate more expensive, less pollution-generating, less breakdown-prone cars instead of less expensive, more pollution-generating, more breakdown-prone cars. The type of money transfer that the potentially-Pareto-superior definition requires its applier to identify may also decrease or increase economic efficiency by changing the wealth and derivatively the conduct of those beneficiaries of the policy who would be harmed by the money transfer in question (who would, in effect, finance the money transfer to the policy's victims either directly by paying taxes or requisitions or indirectly by suffering losses that the government transfer generated by causing inflation or inducing the government to forego other expenditures). Indeed, the money transfer in question could also decrease or increase economic efficiency by altering the choices of anyone else whose real income or wealth it increased or decreased by altering the choices of the winners and losers of the policy under scrutiny by altering the wealth of each of these latter individuals.

In any event, the possibility that the type of money transfer whose combination with the policy under investigation would create a Pareto-superior policy package might increase economic efficiency on its own if the policy were enacted implies that a policy's potential-Pareto-superiority is not a sufficient condition for its economic efficiency in the correct monetized sense of that expression. The relevant choice would be economically inefficient despite the fact that it was a component of a Pareto-superior policy package that also included an appropriate money transfer if the money transfer component of that policy package increased economic efficiency by more than the policy decreased it.[7] Similarly, the possibility that the money transfer that generated no allocative transaction costs, no labor/leisure misallocation, and no savings/consumption misallocation that would otherwise be part of a relevant Pareto-superior policy package might decrease economic efficiency in other ways implies that the fact that no such transfer's combination with the policy whose economic efficiency is to be assessed would create a Pareto-superior policy package is not a sufficient condition for the policy's economic inefficiency (or neutral impact on economic efficiency). It might not be possible to create a Pareto-superior policy package by combining the policy under consideration with such a money transfer because all such money transfers that would otherwise be suitable might decrease economic efficiency by more than the policy to be investigated increased economic efficiency.[8]

In short, although the potentially-Pareto-superior definition of choices or policies that increase economic efficiency does not make or need not make two of the errors that render the Kaldor-Hicks test inaccurate, it does make an error that is a counterpart of the Kaldor-Hicks test's secondary-feedback-related error—it does ignore the fact that in our actual, Pareto-imperfect world the money transfers it seeks to identify (those whose combination with the policy under investigation would otherwise create a Pareto-superior policy package if they generated no allocative transaction costs, no labor/leisure misallocation, and no savings/consumption misallocation) could increase or decrease economic efficiency. This error renders the potentially-Pareto-superior test for economic efficiency inaccurate: policies that are not potentially-Pareto-superior may be economically efficient, and policies that are potentially-Pareto-superior may be economically inefficient.

Moreover, even if the potentially-Pareto-superior definition of economic efficiency were accurate, there are two reasons why its adoption would not result in the economic-efficiency conclusions it generated having the prescriptive-moral significance its proponents want them to have. First, as we have seen, even Pareto-superior choices will sometimes not be morally desirable from all legitimate moral perspectives. Second, choices that are only *potentially*-Pareto-superior (that are not *actually*-Pareto-superior, that produce losers as well as winners) may not be morally desirable even if some policy package to which the choices in question could belong would be both Pareto-superior and morally desirable. Like the Kaldor-Hicks bribe, the potentially-Pareto-superior policy package is purely hypothetical. Indeed, not only the relevant political realities but also the allocative-transaction-costliness of money transfers and their tendency to cause misallocation both among market-labor, do-it-yourself-labor, and leisure and among saving, consumption, and gifting or bequesting probably make it even less likely that the money transfer this definition seeks to identify will be executed than that the bribe the Kaldor-Hicks test hypothesizes will be paid.

Conclusion to Part I

Part I has delineated the criteria by which definitions of such concepts as the impact of a choice on economic efficiency should be evaluated, proposed the definition that these criteria warrant, and explained why the various definitions of this concept that economists and law and economics scholars have proposed and continue to use are incorrect—namely, they are inconsistent with both popular understanding and professional usage, and they create concepts that are not useful.

Part I's analysis is valuable for at least seven reasons. First, from a purely academic perspective (hopefully in the nonpejorative sense of this adjective), it is important to define the basic concepts of a field clearly and correctly.

Second and relatedly, as Part III will explain in some detail, the use of what I am denominating the correct definition of the impact of a choice or policy on economic efficiency will maximize the contribution that predictions or postdictions of a choice's or policy's economic efficiency will make to its prescriptive-moral evaluation and, on some occasions on which the decision to be made is an application of the law, to the identification of the legal conclusion that is correct as a matter of law.

Third, in the course of discussing the correct and incorrect definitions of economic efficiency, Part I revealed that economists at least sometimes make philosophical or prescriptive-moral claims that cannot bear scrutiny—a reality that will receive considerable attention in Part III because it underlies various false claims that economists make for the relevance of economic-efficiency conclusions.

Fourth, at some points of Chapter 1, throughout Chapter 2, and particularly when discussing the way in which the economics profession reacted to the Scitovsky Paradox, Part I reveals not just that (like everyone else, including me) economists make technical mistakes but that economists also sometimes react to demonstrations that they have made such mistakes in a way that is disappointing—not by trying to understand and correct their mistake but by thoughtlessly patching up their position to circumvent a particular objection to it, thoughtlessly shifting to a significantly different position that has some of the same deficiencies as the position they have abandoned, or ignoring the critique altogether. This proclivity is also manifest in the profession's reaction to (refusal to adjust appropriately to) The General Theory of Second Best when executing economic-efficiency analyses (the subject of Part II).

Fifth, the practical value of Chapter 2's critique of the Kaldor-Hicks test and Chapter 1's delineation of the correct definition of the impact of a choice or policy on economic efficiency has recently been substantially enhanced by decisions by various governments to base social-overhead-capital decisions (for example, about whether to construct a particular dam or where to locate an additional airport in a particular metropolitan area) at least in part on the answers the decision's prospective beneficiaries give to the question "How many dollars would you be willing to pay to secure the policy?" and the answers the decision's prospective victims give to the question "How much would you be willing to accept in exchange for granting your critical acquiescence to the policy or pay to prevent the policy?" Admittedly, the importance of this point depends on the way in which the errors the relevant misspecifications yield interact with the other errors this protocol involves (errors related to the possibilities that the respondents may not be sovereign maximizers or may be lying to promote their own interests). I hasten to point out that The General Theory of Second Best, which will play a dominant role in Part II's analysis of the correct way to assess the economic efficiency of a choice, also provides a structure for dealing with this complication—that is, for analyzing the impact of one type of analytic error on the erroneousness of the conclusions that the analysis of any issue generates in situations in which the error in question is not the only error the analysis makes.

Sixth, Chapter 2's critique of the Kaldor-Hicks test is also important because it applies equally forcefully to the Coase Theorem, which (as I will show below) implicitly adopts the Kaldor-Hicks test for economic efficiency.

Seventh, Part I's discussion of the compensating-variation versus equivalent-variation issue is significant because it implies that, contrary to the generally held view, the fact that the sovereign, maximizing beneficiaries of some free government service would not have found it profitable to purchase that service from the government at a price equal to its marginal allocative cost does not imply the allocative inefficiency of the government's supplying the service without charge. I have placed the sixth and seventh members of this list last because they require some elucidation.

In 1960, Ronald Coase wrote a famous article[1] that purported to demonstrate *inter alia* that if there were no transaction costs[2] the rule of liability (say, in the law of torts) would not matter in the sense that the rule would not affect the extent to which resources were misallocated. Coase's argument was deceptively simple. He contended that, in a transaction-costless world, the rule of liability would not matter in the above sense because, if a liability rule were adopted that failed to make it privately profitable for a relevant party to engage in allocatively efficient avoidance, those who would benefit from such avoidance would bribe the relevant potential avoider to engage in it. Unfortunately, this argument would be persuasive only if the Kaldor-Hicks definition of an increase in allocative efficiency (which it implicitly adopts) were correct and the other Pareto imperfections the economy contains could for some reason be ignored.[3] The text will focus on the first of these possibilities.

To see that Coase has implicitly adopted the Kaldor-Hicks definition of an increase in allocative efficiency, note that his argument assumes that if the winners from an avoidance choice (the potential tort victims if the relevant avoidance is injurer avoidance) cannot bribe the losers (the potential injurers in the above case) to avoid—that is, if the avoidance move fails the Kaldor-Hicks test—the avoidance cannot be allocatively efficient. To see why this assumption is incorrect, recall that the diminishing value of money implies that the total of the number of dollars that each of the avoidance move's beneficiaries would be indifferent to paying to secure its execution (the total of the compensating variations in their wealths) will be lower than the total of the number of dollars that each of the avoidance move's beneficiaries would have to receive to be left as well off as the avoidance move would make him *ex ante* (the total of the equivalent variations in their wealths). Clearly, this conclusion implies that (if we assume away any voluntary-market-transaction and secondary-feedback complications), the fact that the highest sum potential tort victims could profit *ex ante* by paying their potential injurer to induce him to avoid is less than the cost of avoidance to the potential injurer is compatible with the potential injurer's avoidance's yielding his potential victims *ex ante* equivalent-dollar gains that exceed the cost of avoidance to the potential injurer when the potential victims do not have to pay the injurer to induce him to avoid.

In the preceding example, only the avoidance move's beneficiaries' equivalent variation and compensating variation were different. The two variations were the same for the avoidance move's victim (the potential injurer) because the cost to him of avoiding was assumed to be a purely monetary cost. It may be instructive to explore an example in which the equivalent and compensating variations are different for both the conventional potential injurer and the conventional potential victim.

For simplicity, I will continue to assume that the relevant individuals place no intrinsic value on paying each other or being paid by each other and that the cross-payments under consideration would generate no relevant secondary-feedback effects. For the same reason, I will also assume that the affected parties are interested solely in utility as economists would understand that concept. Assume that two neighbors—Mr. Planter and Mr. Sneezer—are both interested solely in their own utility and that Mr. Planter is choosing between planting roses and planting grass. Assume as well that—externalities aside—there is no difference in either the private or the allocative cost of Mr. Planter's planting roses or grass. Assume next that, in the initial position, Mr. Planter prefers roses to grass by $100—that the variation in his wealth that would be equivalent to the loss he would sustain if he planted grass instead of roses was $100. Assume in addition that Mr. Sneezer is allergic to roses but not to grass. In particular, assume that Mr. Planter's decision to plant grass would confer $105 in external benefits on Mr. Sneezer—that the variation in Mr. Sneezer's wealth that would be equivalent to Mr. Planter's choosing to plant grass rather than roses would be $105. On these assumptions, it would be economically efficient for Mr. Planter to plant grass if Mr. Sneezer did not have to compensate him and did not compensate him for doing so. Mr. Planter's decision to plant grass rather than roses would generate $105 in allocative benefits (Mr. Sneezer's gain) and $100 in allocative costs (Mr. Planter's loss). Hence, a liability rule that entitled Mr. Sneezer to compensation if Mr. Planter planted roses would be economically efficient in this situation—that is, it would increase allocative efficiency by inducing Mr. Planter to plant grass rather than roses since he would rather suffer the equivalent-dollar loss of $100 his planting grass rather than roses would impose on him than pay Mr. Sneezer the $105 in damages he would have to pay him if he planted roses.

Now assume that the opposite liability rule is in force—that Mr. Sneezer is not entitled to be compensated by Mr. Planter for the loss Mr. Sneezer would sustain if Mr. Planter planted roses. Coase assumes that, in this case, no economic inefficiency will result in the absence of transaction costs (and any other Pareto imperfections) because in this type of situation Mr. Sneezer will always find it profitable to bribe Mr. Planter to plant grass instead of roses. But in some instances of these cases (in some situations in which the above conditions are fulfilled), this assumption will not be correct. Assume, for example, that—although Mr. Sneezer would gain the equivalent of $105 if Mr. Planter planted grass instead of roses without Mr. Sneezer's having to compensate him to do so—Mr. Sneezer would find it unprofitable to pay Mr. Planter anything more than $101 to plant grass rather than roses. This possibility simply reflects the diminishing marginal utility of money: even if the util value to Mr. Sneezer of Mr. Planter's planting grass rather than roses would not be affected by changes in Mr. Sneezer's wealth over the relevant range, the util value of the $105 whose transfer to him would be equivalent to Mr. Planter's decision to plant grass might equal the util value to him of the $101 we are assuming he would be indifferent to paying Mr. Planter to plant grass rather than roses.

Moreover, something similar may be going on with Mr. Planter. We have assumed that planting grass rather than roses would cost Mr. Planter the same amount of utility that a $100 reduction in his wealth would cost him. However, this does not mean that Mr. Planter should be indifferent to foregoing his right to plant grass for a $100 payment. Since the marginal utility of each dollar of any $100 he would be paid would be lower than the marginal utility of each of the dollars whose withdrawal from him would *in toto* be equivalent to an uncompensated decision to plant grass instead of roses, the number of dollars that Mr. Planter would have to be offered in exchange for agreeing to plant grass rather than roses would be higher than $100—might, for example, be $102 if the utility-value of a $102 gain equaled the utility-value of the $100 loss that would be equivalent to the loss he would sustain if he planted grass rather than roses without being compensated for doing so. Assume this is the case.

But if these are the facts, the rule of liability will matter even if there are no transaction costs and no other relevant Pareto imperfections. Although in the initial situation it would be allocatively efficient for Mr. Planter to plant grass rather than roses if he were not compensated for doing so—although such a decision would cost Mr. Planter the equivalent of $100 and would confer on Mr. Sneezer a gain whose dollar-equivalent was $105, the highest sum that Mr. Sneezer could pay Mr. Planter for planting grass rather than roses without incurring a loss on the deal—$101—is lower than the lowest sum Mr. Planter could accept for foregoing his right to plant grass without making a loss on the deal—$102. If the rule of liability does not make Mr. Planter liable, Mr. Sneezer will not be able to profit by bribing Mr. Planter in effect to accept liability—to avoid inflicting harm on Mr. Sneezer.

In short, the Coase Theorem is "wrong"—that is, must be significantly qualified. The rule of liability will sometimes matter in the sense of affecting the extent of resource misallocation even when there are no traditional transaction costs or relevant Pareto imperfections. The rule of liability will sometimes matter because of the difference between one or more affected parties' compensating and equivalent variations—because this difference will sometimes create situations in which potential victims are not able to profit *ex ante* by bribing their potential injurer to engage in avoidance that would be allocatively efficient if its beneficiaries did not have to compensate its victims for engaging in it.

I now will elaborate on the seventh and final point in the preceding list. The difference between the compensating and equivalent variation in an individual's wealth that undermines both the Kaldor-Hicks test for economic efficiency and the Coase Theorem also undermines the conventional economic assumption that, absent transaction costs of contracting or any (other) relevant Pareto imperfections, a law that requires a seller or the government to give (sovereign, maximizing) consumers a good that would not be profitable for the consumers to buy at a price equal to its allocative cost will always be allocatively inefficient even if such a law could itself be devised, passed, and enforced without generating any transaction costs. To see why this is so, let us examine the possible allocative efficiency of a law that would require the producer of a good whose marginal allocative cost was $50 to supply it cost-free to someone who could not profitably pay more than $49 for it in a situation in which all the various Pareto-optimal conditions were fulfilled.

Assume that the relevant recipient's valuation of the good or service in question is positively wealth-elastic. As we saw, in this case the fact that the highest price the recipient could profitably pay for it was less than $50 (was $49) is perfectly compatible with the good's being worth more than $50 (say, $51) to him if the individual receives it without having to pay for it (is perfectly compatible with monetized allocative efficiency's being increased by a law that would—without generating any transaction costs—require the relevant seller or the government to supply the relevant buyer with the good cost-free). Thus, if the relevant buyer's original wealth is $50,000, the fact that he could profitably pay no more than $49 for the good in question indicates only that the buyer would be indifferent between having (1) $49,951 and the good or (2) $50,000—that after his wealth was reduced to $49,951 by the $49 payment he made to the supplier of the good, the value of the good to him would be $49. Obviously, this fact is perfectly compatible with the good's being worth $51 to him if he receives it free of charge—that is, with his being indifferent between (1) possessing $50,051 and not having the good and (2) possessing $50,000 and the good. As we have seen, results like these will be compatible whenever the relevant consumer's valuation of the good in question is positively wealth-elastic. To summarize: the conventional wisdom is that it will always be economically inefficient for the government to supply someone with a good for free that the recipient would not have profited from buying at a price equal to its marginal allocative cost; this conclusion is sometimes wrong[4] because it ignores the fact that the value of a good to someone who receives it without having to pay for it equals the equivalent variation in his wealth, not the compensating variation in his wealth—the amount he could pay for it and remain equally well off if he did not place any intrinsic value or disvalue on making the payment and the payment would not have any secondary-feedback impact on him.

My analysis of the definition of the impact of a private choice or public policy on economic efficiency is now complete. However, before proceeding to Part II, I want to describe and comment on the reaction that many economists have had to Part I's argument when I have presented it to them orally at various colloquia. A fair account of this reaction is "Well, I guess you're right. But why are you bothering with this? Theoretical studies show that the difference between the compensating and equivalent variation is small: we would guess that, at most, it is 2 percent to 3 percent. External preferences are empirically unimportant, and the equivalent-dollar gains and losses that derive from them should not be counted in any event. Moreover, the feedback effects you are talking about are second-order (too small to merit consideration)."

I always respond to this argument in four ways (admittedly without much effect). First, I retort, "Even if you are right—even if (contrary to my own belief) the change in definition I am proposing would increase accuracy by only 2 to 3 percent—why not get it right? With a possible exception related to the counting of external-preference-derived and bad-preference-derived equivalent-dollar gains and losses, it is no more difficult to understand and apply the correct definition of the impact of a choice or policy on economic efficiency than the incorrect ones you are using. What justification can there possibly be to continuing to use a definition (of such a central concept) that you admit is wrong? If you observed a natural scientist persisting in using a wrong formula when there is no advantage for doing so other than the benefits he obtains by giving in to his laziness or indulging his preference for not changing, would you not criticize him for doing so?"

Second, I argue, "Why do you think that a 2 to 3 percent difference is not worth bothering about? If the error in question critically affects a billion-dollar decision to build an airport or construct a dam, even a 2 to 3 percent error could well cause $20 to $30 million dollars in economic inefficiency. For that matter, if the 2 to 3 percent error critically affects a thousand million-dollar decisions, it could also cause $20 to $30 million dollars in economic inefficiency on this account."

Third, I respond, "Your estimate that the error that will be generated by the mistakes I am pointing out will be only a 2 to 3 percent error strikes me as wildly optimistic. The most recent scholarship has challenged the older studies' conclusions that the difference between the compensating and equivalent variation is always small; this scholarship suggests that, at least when public investments are concerned, the difference in question may be quite substantial.[5] Moreover, the vast amount of charitable contributions that people make,[6] lab experiments that try to measure their participants' altruism or related external preferences,[7] and the frequency with which Americans make rescue attempts that put them at significant risk[8] all suggest that you vastly underestimate the incidence and magnitude of external preferences, which give rise to equivalent-dollar effects that will not in general cancel each other out and that (contrary to your view) should in principle always be counted in economic-efficiency calculations and will usually be relevant to prescriptive-moral evaluations as well."

Fourth, and finally, I respond, "Your conclusion that the relevant secondary-feedback effects or the impact of independent Pareto imperfections on the economic efficiency of policies or money transfers are of second-order importance is almost certainly wrong[9] and is clearly based on no argument that can bear the slightest scrutiny."

Perhaps this last point provides an appropriate segue to Part II's discussion of the correct way to analyze the economic efficiency of a choice or policy in our highly-Pareto-imperfect economy and the failure of economists to adjust their economic-efficiency analyses to take appropriate account of The General Theory of Second Best.

Part Two The Assessment of Economic Efficiency

Part I argued that, on its correct definition, the impact of a private choice or public policy on economic efficiency equals the difference between the equivalent-dollar gains it confers on its beneficiaries and the equivalent-dollar losses it imposes on its victims. However, economists have never tried to assess a choice's or policy's impact on economic efficiency by identifying all or a random sample of its winners and losers and estimating their respective equivalent-dollar gains and losses. In part, this fact reflects the unreliability of the responses that a policy's actual winners and losers would give to questions about its impact on them. Since a policy's winners will want it to be adopted, they will tend to exaggerate their equivalent-dollar gains to increase the likelihood that the policy will be found economically efficient and desirable; and since a policy's losers will want it to be rejected, they will tend to exaggerate their equivalent-dollar losses for an analogous reason. And in part, it reflects the prohibitive cost and difficulty of estimating the gains and losses that individuals experience through any method that does not rely on their testimony. The impracticability of this approach to assessing a policy's allocative efficiency has led economists to base their economic-efficiency assessments on welfare economics propositions that relate the impact of a private choice or public policy on economic efficiency to its impact on the Pareto imperfections in the economy. Although this general approach is almost certainly best, the particular welfare economics propositions on which economists have relied and continue to rely are wrong.

The vast majority of economists base their approach to economic-efficiency assessment on the assumption that the fact that the economy will contain no economic inefficiency if it contains no Pareto imperfections[1] implies that any choice or policy that reduces (increases) the number or magnitude of the Pareto imperfections in the economy will tend on that account to reduce (increase) the amount of economic inefficiency in the economy. As the Introduction indicated, The General Theory of Second Best demonstrates the invalidity of this argument and suggests that its conclusion is almost certainly incorrect. Since in general the imperfections one can eliminate will be as likely to counteract as to exacerbate the effects of any imperfections that remain, there is no general reason to believe that the fact that a choice or policy will reduce the number or magnitude of the Pareto imperfections in the economy will even tend on that account to increase economic efficiency if it will not eliminate all Pareto imperfections in the economy.[2] Of course, in some (perhaps many) situations, policies that reduce the number or magnitude of the Pareto imperfections in the economy will increase economic efficiency. However, in each instance, one will have to establish this conclusion through an argument that takes appropriate account of (1) the various ways in which different Pareto imperfections interact to cause the various types of misallocation whose magnitudes the policy under scrutiny will or may affect, (2) the number and extent of the Pareto imperfections that would be present in the economy if the choice or policy in question would be rejected, and (3) the impact that the relevant choice or policy would have on those imperfections.

Economists recognize that policies that reduce the Pareto-imperfectness of the economy may be economically inefficient if they (1) are sufficiently transaction costly,[3] (2) misallocate resources sufficiently by preventing firms from taking advantage of allocative economies of scale, and/or (3) misallocate resources sufficiently by preventing firms from achieving various types of allocative efficiencies by combining assets that are complementary for nonscale reasons. However, the overwhelming majority of economists proceed on the incorrect assumption that any policy that reduces the Pareto-imperfectness of the economy will tend on that account to increase economic efficiency—that is, ignore The General Theory of Second Best altogether.

Admittedly, a small but growing percentage of economic-efficiency analyses do take some account of second-best theory. Typically, these studies analyze the way in which a policy that would reduce or eliminate one Pareto imperfection will affect one or two kinds of resource misallocation in an economy that also contains another Pareto imperfection either of the same type as the one the policy targets or of a different type that will not be removed by the policy or anything else and that would also on its own cause one or both of the types of misallocation on which the relevant analysis focuses. However, although these studies represent an important step in the right direction, they still are deficient in that they

1. ignore many of the types of Pareto imperfections that affect the extent of the types of misallocation they do consider,
2. ignore many types of economic inefficiency whose magnitudes the choices or policies they consider seem likely to affect,
3. make no argument to justify these omissions, and, relatedly,
4. announce conclusions that they do not justify and that generally are highly inaccurate.

Before proceeding, I want to delineate some vocabulary and related acronyms that I will use in the following text and to summarize some of the most important concrete implications of second-best theory. The vocabulary and acronyms relate to three different approaches to allocative-efficiency analysis that are worth distinguishing. The text uses the expression "first-best-allocative-efficiency analysis" to refer to the approach to economic-efficiency analysis (used by the overwhelming majority of economists and law and economics scholars) that proceeds on the assumption that any choice or policy that decreases the number or magnitude of Pareto imperfections will tend on that account to improve resource allocation. Relatedly, the text uses the acronym FBLE to stand for "first-best-allocative-efficiency." In part, this acronym seems appropriate because FBLE resembles the word *fable*, and FBLE analyses are based on the fable that a decrease in a particular Pareto imperfection necessarily increases economic (allocative) efficiency (or that the imperfection on which the analyst is focusing is the only imperfection in the system).[4]

The text that follows uses the expression "second-best-allocative-efficiency analysis" to refer to the approach to economic-efficiency analysis that would be perfectly accurate and economically efficient if perfect theoretical analyses could be costlessly executed and perfect data could be costlessly collected. Second-best-allocative-efficiency analyses take perfect account of all the types of resource misallocation whose magnitudes the relevant choices or policies might affect, develop perfect formulas relating the extent of each such type of resource misallocation to the various Pareto imperfections that interact to cause it, and collect and perfectly analyze the implications of perfect data on (1) the magnitude these imperfections would have if the choice or policy under scrutiny were rejected, (2) the impact that the choice or policy in question would have on them, and (3) the pre-policy and post-policy magnitudes of any other parameters whose relevance the theoretical analysis reveals. In what follows, the acronym SBLE is used to signify "second-best-allocative-efficiency." SBLE is an appropriate acronym for this modifier because it resembles the word *sable*, which signifies a beautiful object that is prohibitively expensive, and SBLE analysis would be prohibitively expensive even if it were doable, given the imperfectness of the economy, the multiplicity of resource uses, and the inevitable cost and inaccuracy of both data and analysis.

The text that follows uses the expression "third-best-allocative-efficiency analysis" to refer to the approach to economic-efficiency assessment that is allocatively efficient, given the fact that in our actual, worse-than-second-best world Pareto imperfections are pervasive, choices or policies affect the magnitudes of large numbers of types of resource misallocation, and data and analysis are costly and inaccurate. Third-best-allocative-efficiency analysis differs from SBLE analysis in that it incorporates only those theoretical and empirical research projects whose predicted allocative benefits exceed their predicted allocative cost. The text uses the acronym TBLE to stand for "third-best-allocative-efficiency." TBLE is an appropriate acronym for this modifier because it resembles the world *table* and TBLE analysis is the type one should bring to the policy evaluation table.[5]

I now want to delineate those implications of second-best theory that I suspect will be most salient to both economists and law and economics scholars. The General Theory of Second Best justifies the following conclusions:

1. the fact that perfect competition among sellers and buyers is a Pareto-optimal condition does not imply that policies that increase competition will tend to increase economic efficiency on that account in a still-Pareto-imperfect world;

2. the fact that no externalities is a Pareto-optimal condition does not imply that policies that internalize externalities will tend to increase economic efficiency on that account in a still-Pareto-imperfect world;
3. the fact that no taxes on the margin of income is a Pareto-optimal condition does not imply that policies that reduce taxes on the margin of income will tend to increase economic efficiency on that account in a still-Pareto-imperfect world;
4. the fact that individual sovereignty and maximization (no human errors) are Pareto-optimal conditions does not imply that policies that reduce human errors by increasing the information available to human actors (such as by indicating the contents and nutritional value of food products) or reducing the probability that they will do their math wrong (such as by indicating the price per ounce of food products) will tend on those accounts to increase economic efficiency in a still-Pareto-imperfect world; and
5. the fact that no buyer surplus is a Pareto-optimal condition does not imply that policies that allow sellers to convert buyer surplus into seller surplus or that government grants that internalize such surplus to the producer who generated it will tend on that account to increase economic efficiency in a still-Pareto-imperfect world.

Put somewhat more constructively, The General Theory of Second Best demonstrates that, unless one can generate an appropriate, mixed theoretical/empirical argument to the contrary, one cannot assume that policies of any of the above sorts that reduce the Pareto-imperfectness of the economy will even tend on that account to increase economic efficiency.

Part II focuses on the implications of second-best theory for economic-efficiency analysis. Chapter 3 delineates a distortion-analysis approach to economic-efficiency assessment that I think responds appropriately to second-best theory and illustrates this approach by providing examples of some if its components and by using simplified versions to examine a number of economic-efficiency issues that economists have analyzed. Chapter 4 delineates some canonical economic-efficiency analyses that pay no attention to or respond inappropriately to second-best theory, explains why they are deficient, and demonstrates that the conclusions their authors reach seem likely to be highly inaccurate. Chapter 4 also presents and criticizes the various justifications that economists who are aware of The General Theory of Second Best have offered for ignoring it.

Chapter 3 The Distortion-Analysis Approach to Economic-Efficiency Assessment

Chapter 3 has four sections. Section 1 sets the stage for its successors by (1) delineating the three major stages of the resource-allocation process, the major category of economic inefficiency that can be generated at each, and the various subtypes of each major category of economic inefficiency, (2) explaining in general the ways in which each Pareto imperfection can misallocate resources in an otherwise-Pareto-perfect economy, and (3) illustrating the way in which the various types of Pareto imperfections interact to cause one kind of economic inefficiency—the economic inefficiency that results when a worker makes an economically inefficient marginal choice between performing an additional unit of unit-output-producing market labor and consuming an additional unit of leisure. Section 2 (1) delineates and develops symbols for the key concepts that the distortion-analysis approach to economic-efficiency assessment employs, (2) explains the relationships from which the distortion-analysis approach derives, and (3) outlines the distortion-analysis approach. Section 3 explains the ways in which individual Pareto imperfections or various combinations of Pareto imperfections cause various private figures to be distorted.

More specifically, the first subsection of Section 3 analyzes the way in which certain individual Pareto imperfections or combinations of Pareto imperfections distort the private benefits, private costs, and profits yielded by the production of marginal units of output of a given product. This subsection sometimes proceeds on the unrealistic assumption that the resources consumed by the production of the respective marginal units of output of one good are withdrawn exclusively from the production of other products not including leisure and sometimes proceeds on the realistic assumption that some of the resources that the production of the marginal unit of each of the economy's products consumes may be withdrawn not just from the production of other products not including leisure but also from the creation of marginal QV (quality-or-variety-increasing) investments, the execution of marginal PPR (production-process-research) projects, and the production of marginal units of leisure. The second and third subsections of Section 3 execute analogous analyses of the distortions in the private benefits, private costs, and profits yielded respectively by the creation and/or use of a marginal QV investment and the execution and/or use of a marginal PPR project. The fourth subsection of Section 3 then analyzes the monopoly distortion in the private benefits, cost, and profits yielded by a producer's break-even decision to reduce the accident and pollution losses he generates by shifting to a less-accident-loss-prone and/or less-pollution-loss-prone production process that is otherwise more expensive.

Section 4 illustrates the distortion-analysis approach somewhat differently by carrying out distortion-analysis assessments of (1) antitrust policies designed to increase price competition, (2) antitrust policies, tax policies, and intellectual-property policies designed to reduce the amount of misallocation the economy generates because it devotes the wrong amount of resources to product R&D and PPR from the perspective of economic efficiency, and (3) tort-law policies designed to increase economic efficiency by reducing the sum of the allocative accident and pollution losses that are generated and the allocative cost of the avoidance moves potential injurers and victims make to prevent them. All three of these analyses will be more crude and less encompassing than would be third-best allocatively efficient (hereinafter, TBLE will stand for "third-best allocatively efficient" as well as "third-best-allocative-efficiency") in that they fail to address some theoretical issues whose consideration would be TBLE if the policy choice did not have to be made immediately and do not contain any empirical work, much less the empirical work that would be TBLE to do in different circumstances.

SECTION 1. THREE PRELIMINARY ISSUES

The Three Major Categories of Resource Allocation and Misallocation and the Various Specific Types of Economic Inefficiency That Are Worth Distinguishing

THE THREE MAJOR CATEGORIES OF RESOURCE ALLOCATION AND MISALLOCATION

The expression "allocation of resources" refers to the pattern in which an economy's basic resources are distributed among their various possible users and uses and the way in which an economy's output is distributed among its possible consumers. Conventionally, welfare economists somewhat artificially distinguish three stages of the resource-allocation process and three related major categories of resource misallocation. At the first, so-called production-optimum stage, basic resources are allocated among alternative producers, and resources are said to be misallocated (that is, production-optimum misallocation is said to be present) to the extent that an allocative-transaction-costless shift to some alternative allocation would yield more units of some good without yielding fewer units of any other good.

At the second, so-called top-level-optimum stage, the economy's producers take the resources that have been allocated to them and choose to use them to design and create product and distributive variants (where product is defined to reflect *inter alia* average speed of delivery throughout a fluctuating-demand cycle) or to produce physical units of the products that have been created (including leisure). Traditionally, economic inefficiency is said to have been generated at this top-level-optimum stage if an allocative-transaction-costless shift in the allocation of resources between or among the production of different products that are in production or between the production of those products and the creation of superior or different product variants could make somebody better off without making anyone else worse off.

At the third, so-called consumption-optimum stage, the units of various goods, services, and leisure that have been produced are allocated among their potential consumers. Resources are said to have been misallocated at this consumption-optimum stage to the extent that—if it could be executed without generating any allocative transaction costs—a reallocation of the economy's output among its alternative potential consumers could have made somebody better off without having made anyone else worse off.

I want to make two comments on this traditional typology of resource-allocation stages and major types of economic inefficiency. The first relates to the definition of economic inefficiency that the traditional analysis implicitly adopts: obviously, there is no reason why the traditional account should not be altered by substituting the monetized definition I think is most useful for the traditional Pareto-inferiority definition. The second comment relates to the artificiality of the traditional typology. To the extent that the traditional account implies that the decisions made at the three stages of the allocative process it distinguishes are independent, that implication is clearly false. The consumer choices that affect the allocation at the third, consumption-optimum stage and the producer choices that affect the allocation at the second, top-level-optimum stage obviously affect the identity of the producers to whom particular resources are allocated at the "first," production-optimum stage. If resources were allocated among producers through some nonmarket procedure at the production-optimum stage, that allocation would affect both the top-level allocations that would be made and the identities of the consumers who would end up with the goods that were produced, and so on and so forth. However, I do not think that this interdependence of the relevant allocations undercuts the analytic usefulness of the traditional three-stage description. In fact, as the text that follows manifests, I also find it analytically useful to focus on similarly artificially defined types of allocative inefficiency. For example, normally, a producer's decision to create a new product variant or distributive outlet involves the withdrawal of some resources from the creation of other new product variants and distributive outlets, some resources from the production of units of existing products, some resources from the production of leisure, and some resources from the execution of production-process-research projects. Nevertheless, at times, I will focus on the factors that would cause the allocation of resources to discovering or designing a particular new product variant to be economically inefficient on the unrealistic assumption that all the resources that would be used for this purpose would be withdrawn either exclusively from the creation of new product variants that would not rival the product variant in question or exclusively from the production of additional units of existing products.

THE SUBTYPES OF ECONOMIC INEFFICIENCY: DEFINITIONS, NAMES, AND SYMBOLS

This subsection defines various subtypes of the three major categories of resource misallocation its predecessor distinguished. It begins by identifying various subtypes of top-level misallocation, then (after noting one type of misallocation that relates to the allocation of resources between top-level and production-optimum-related uses) identifies various subtypes of production-optimum misallocation, and concludes by identifying various subtypes of consumption-optimum misallocation.

Antitrust policy analysts have focused almost exclusively on the first subtype of top-level-optimum misallocation I will distinguish—unit-output to unit-output (henceforth UO-to-UO or relative-unit-output [RUO]) misallocation. On my definition, UO-to-UO misallocation is present to the extent that the equivalent-dollar gains that an allocative-transaction-costless shift in the proportions in which the different goods or services that are in production are produced would confer on its beneficiaries would exceed the equivalent-dollar losses it would confer on its victims—to the extent that, controlling for the amount of resources devoted to the production and distribution of units of goods and services that have been designed and for which production facilities already exist and the amount of consumption-optimum and production-optimum misallocation that is generated, economic efficiency in my monetized sense would have been increased had the output of some goods been higher and the output of others been lower. In some situations, I find it useful to distinguish two subtypes of UO-to-UO misallocation: intra-industry UO-to-UO misallocation and inter-industry UO-to-UO misallocation.[1] Intra-industry UO-to-UO misallocation occurs when goods that are often competitive for the patronage of the same buyers are produced in allocatively inefficient proportions. Inter-industry UO-to-UO misallocation occurs when goods that are rarely competitive for the patronage of the same buyers are produced in the wrong proportion to each other.[2] I should also point out that the set of products that may be produced in allocatively inefficient proportions to each other includes present and future products and leisure and do-it-yourself labor. Thus, the expression "UO-to-UO misallocation" analysis includes the analysis of the trade-offs an economy makes between future and current production and the analysis of the choices that individuals make when allocating their time among market labor, do-it-yourself labor, and leisure.

The second major category of top-level-optimum misallocation I distinguish is QV-to-QV misallocation. In my terminology, a QV (quality- or-variety-increasing) investment is an investment that creates and develops an additional or superior product variant, an additional or superior distributive outlet, or additional capacity and inventory (which enable the investor to reduce his average speed of supply throughout a fluctuating-demand cycle). QV-to-QV misallocation is present to the extent that, given the total amount of resources the economy devotes to creating QV investments and the amount of production-optimum and consumption-optimum misallocation that is generated, the equivalent-dollar gains that would have been generated had a different set of QV investments been executed would exceed the equivalent-dollar losses that the creation of that different set of QV investments would have generated. In some situations, I find if useful to distinguish two types of QV-to-QV misallocation—intra-industry QV-to-QV misallocation and inter-industry QV-to-QV misallocation. Intra-industry QV-to-QV misallocation is present to the extent that, given the amount of resources devoted to QV investment in a given industry—that is, in an area of product-space that contains products that are atypically competitive with each other—economic efficiency would have been increased had a different set of product variants been created and produced by the industry. Inter-industry QV-to-QV misallocation is present to the extent that economic efficiency could be increased by an allocative-transaction-costless choice to eliminate an existing QV investment and substitute a QV investment that would create a product variant that was distantly competitive or non-competitive with the eliminated product variant.

The third significant subtype of top-level misallocation is UO-to-QV misallocation. This type of misallocation is present to the extent that an allocative-transaction-costless shift of resources from the production of units of existing products to the creation of a superior or more numerous set of product and distributive variants or vice versa could increase allocative efficiency in the monetized sense in which I think that expression should be defined. As already indicated (for reasons the next subsection will explain), I believe that the American economy and almost certainly all basically capitalist economies currently devote too many resources to generating quality and variety and not enough to producing units of a lower-quality, less varied, less conveniently-and-attractively-distributed, and less quickly delivered set of products.

The next three specific subtypes of economic inefficiency are top-level-optimum/production-optimum hybrids. All three relate to the amount of resources devoted to production-process research (research that is designed to discover a privately and/or allocatively cheaper way to produce a relevant quantity of an existing product). UO-to-PPR misallocation is present to the extent that an allocative-transaction-costless reallocation of resources from UO production to PPR or vice versa would increase allocative efficiency. QV-to-PPR misallocation is present to the extent that an allocative-transaction-costless reallocation of resources from QV-investment creation to PPR or vice versa would increase economic efficiency. And (UO + QV)-to-PPR misallocation is present to the extent that an allocative-transaction-costless reallocation of resources from all types of top-level uses to PPR or vice versa would increase economic efficiency. Sometimes, I find it analytically or expositionally useful to refer to total-UO/total-QV/total-PPR misallocation rather than to the separate types of UO-to-QV, UO-to-PPR, and QV-to-PPR misallocation just distinguished.

In some circumstances, it is also useful to distinguish a number of types of pure production-optimum misallocation, though unlike the types of top-level-optimum misallocation (which were defined by the types of resource-use choices they involved), most of the types of production-optimum (and consumption-optimum) misallocation I will be distinguishing are defined by their causes. More specifically, I think that in some contexts it will be useful to distinguish at least ten types of production-optimum misallocation.

The first type of production-optimum misallocation is generated when too few or too many resources are devoted to PPR from the perspective of economic efficiency (though this type of production-optimum misallocation necessarily affects top-level allocations as well).

A second type of production-optimum misallocation is generated when, controlling for the total amount of resources devoted to PPR, economic efficiency would have been enhanced if a different set of PPR projects had been executed. This type of production-optimum economic inefficiency can be termed PPR-to-PPR misallocation (though one might want to distinguish PPR-to-PPR misallocations that relate to the projects executed to discover a cheaper way to produce a given product from PPR-to-PPR misallocation that results because, given the total amount of resources devoted to PPR, too many are devoted to discovering cheaper ways to produce some products and not enough to discovering cheaper ways to produce other products).

A third type of production-optimum misallocation is generated when a more economically efficient production process that has been discovered is not used to the extent that would be economically efficient either because its discoverer has patent protection and the transaction cost of the price discrimination that would prevent this outcome makes it profitable for him to price licenses to use the discovery in a way that deters some economically efficient uses or because the cost of securing patent protection and the imperfectness of that protection makes it most profitable for a production-process discoverer to keep his discovery secret and use it exclusively himself when it would be economically efficient for others to use it as well.

A fourth type of production-optimum misallocation results when producers of the same product variant fail to take full advantage of economies of scale in its production, promotion, distribution, or financing. These failures may reflect human error, but they are most likely to be caused by antitrust laws (which may be allocatively efficient on balance).

Human errors and antitrust regulations may also cause a fifth type of production-optimum misallocation that is worth distinguishing—namely, the type that results when firms fail to combine assets that are complementary for nonscale reasons (such as when a firm with unused capacity in its production division fails to merge with another firm with unused capacity in its distribution division when the managers and staff in question have developed some firm-specific capital).

A sixth type of production-optimum misallocation occurs when a buyer purchases a product from a supplier whose marginal allocative costs are higher rather than from a supplier whose marginal allocative costs are lower. This outcome is most likely to occur when the producer making the sale has higher private marginal costs but has beaten his privately-better-placed rival's oligopolistic or nonoligopolistic offer (in the latter case because the seller who made the sale had engaged in retaliatory or predatory pricing). However, this type of production-optimum misallocation can also result when a sale is made by a seller whose private marginal costs are lower if his marginal allocative costs are higher (most likely because his production of the marginal unit generated more external costs than would have been generated by the production of a marginal unit of the product by his privately-worse-placed but allocatively-better-placed rival).

A seventh type of production-optimum misallocation results when the legal system increases the allocative transaction costs businesses have to generate to engage in various kinds of behavior—such as when the antitrust laws require companies that want to engage in a merger of a certain type that would not reduce competition in comparison with the status quo ante to demonstrate that they made reasonable efforts to identify more-pro-competitive mergers of the relevant type that would also have been profitable and had failed to discover any such option.

An eighth type of production-optimum misallocation is generated when the relative cost to producers of a given product of two or more inputs they use to produce that product are different. A sovereign, maximizing producer will produce his output with the combination of inputs that equates the ratio of each input's marginal physical product (MPP) to the marginal cost he has to incur to purchase a marginal unit of the input in question (MK)—that is, that equates the physical product he produces with the last penny he spends on each input he uses. (Throughout, MK will stand for the marginal cost of buying something, and MC for the marginal cost of producing something.) If the inputs are A and B, a sovereign, maximizing producer will choose an input package that equates MPP_A/MK_A with MPP_B/MK_B. If MK_A/MK_B is higher for one producer of a given product (say X1) than for another producer of that product (say, X2), MPP_A/MPP_B will be higher for X1 than for X2 in equilibrium, and more units of the final product D could be produced with the same inputs if X1 used more A and less B while X2 used more B and less A. Thus, if MPP_A/MPP_B for X1 was 10/5 (because the price of A[$P_A = MK_A$] for X1 was $6, while the price of B[$P_B = MK_B$] for X1 was $3) while MPP_A/MPP_B for X2 was 5/10 (because $P_A = MK_A$ for X2 was $3 and $P_B = MK_B$ for X2 was $6), both a transfer of a unit of A from X2 to X1 and a transfer of a unit of B from X1 to X2 would increase the output of D by 5 units. This type of production-optimum misallocation is most likely to be caused by price discrimination.

A ninth type of production-optimum misallocation occurs when the use by different producers of the same unit of a given input generates different amounts of externalities (perhaps because the plants of the different producers are not equally proximate to population centers or ecologically sensitive areas).[3]

Finally, a tenth type of production-optimum misallocation is caused by public-utility (fair rate-of-return) price regulation. Fair-rate-of-return public-utility-pricing regulation constrains the public utility to charge a price that is calculated to yield a fair rate of return on its capital investment (the rate base). Usually, that fair rate of return is supernormal. This type of regulation tends to cause public utilities whose regulated price would otherwise be lower than the price they would find profit-maximizing to generate production-optimum misallocation by choosing a higher-private-cost and presumptively higher-allocative-cost, more-capital-intensive production process whose use increases their rate base and hence increases the price they will be allowed to charge (the price that will yield them the fair rate of return on the higher rate base). (Fair-rate-of-return public-utility-pricing regulation also tends to cause PPR-to-PPR production-optimum misallocation by inducing production-process researchers to direct their research at discovering more-capital-intensive production processes when efforts to discover less-capital-intensive production processes would be more allocatively efficient.)

Finally, I want to distinguish six types of consumption-optimum misallocation (again distinguished primarily by their causes). The first three are counterparts to types of production-optimum misallocation that have already been discussed. Consumption-optimum misallocation can result from (1) human error, (2) differences in the relative MK of two products to their different potential buyers, and (3) inter-consumer differences in the amount of externalities that will be generated by the consumption of a given unit of a given product.[4]

The next three types of consumption-optimum misallocation all relate to some economic-efficiency consequence of the distribution of income associated with the extant allocation of final goods among consumers. Thus, consumption-optimum misallocation will be generated to the extent that the equivalent-dollar gains that a shift to an alternative allocation of final goods among consumers would confer on those who have external preferences that would lead them to value it for nonmaterial reasons exceed the equivalent-dollar losses that the shift in question would impose on those who have external preferences that would lead them to disvalue it for nonmaterial reasons. Next, consumption-optimum misallocation will be generated to the extent that an alternative allocation of the goods that have been produced would increase economic efficiency by reducing the extent to which we underinvest from the perspective of economic efficiency in human capital (particularly in the human capital of the children of the poor). Underinvestment in the children of the poor has at least three possible causes: because (1) parents and guardians may not give economically efficient weight to the children's equivalent-dollar welfare, (2) children cannot be legally obligated to pay back loans contracted on their behalf, and (3) some of the increase in any individual's allocative product that results from investment in his human capital may redound not to him but to his employer and his employer's customers and to the State (in the form of the higher taxes the person in whom the investment has been made pays and the lower transfers he receives when the investment increases his earned and unearned income). Finally, consumption-optimum misallocation will also be present to the extent that some alternative allocation of final goods that would be associated with a different distribution of income would reduce the misallocation caused not only by criminal behavior but also by noncriminal choices that generate external costs (choices to purchase polluting, breakdown-prone cars or to rent disease- and fire-spreading housing) as well as by choices that are simply mistaken from the chooser's own perspective.

The Distorting Impact of Each Pareto Imperfection

In my usage, the private benefits (PB) a chooser can obtain by making a particular choice are distorted to the extent that they diverge from the allocative benefits (LB) the choice will yield; the private cost of a choice (PC) to the chooser is distorted to the extent that it diverges from the allocative cost (LC) of the choice—the allocative value that the resources the choice "consumes" (in the sense of using up) would yield in the alternative use from which they were withdrawn; and the (private) profits (Pπ) a choice confers on the chooser are distorted to the extent that they diverge from the choice's allocative efficiency (LE). Obviously, since Pπ = PB − PC and LE = LB − LC, Pπ will be distorted when either PB or PC is distorted unless both are distorted and the two distortions perfectly offset each other. Somewhat more specifically, in my terminology, a PB, PC, or a Pπ figure is said to be not just distorted but also inflated if it exceeds its allocative counterpart and deflated if it is lower than its allocative counterpart.

Having established this vocabulary, I can now explain how in an otherwise-Pareto-perfect economy individual exemplars of the various types of Pareto imperfections will tend to cause misallocation (1) by distorting the PB and/or PC and thereby the Pπ of various choices and/or (2) by leading individuals to make choices that are not in their individual interest. For expositional reasons, it will sometimes be useful to begin the relevant discussions by explaining how the fulfillment of the relevant Pareto-optimal condition (the absence of the Pareto imperfection in question) would eliminate resource misallocation in an otherwise-Pareto-perfect economy.

IMPERFECTIONS IN SELLER COMPETITION

I will start by examining the way in which an individual imperfection in seller competition (sometimes inaccurately denominated "monopoly") will distort various PB, PC, and Pπ figures. Competition among sellers has two dimensions—price competition and QV-investment competition. Price competition is the process through which rival sellers compete away their potential profits by driving their prices down to their marginal costs (MC)—the additional cost they have to incur to produce their last unit of output. QV-investment competition is the process through which rival sellers compete away their potential supernormal profits by introducing additional QV investments until even the most profitable project in the relevant area of product space generates just a normal rate of return.

(i) Imperfections in Seller Price Competition

A group of competitors are said to face perfect price competition[5] if each faces a demand curve—a curve constructed in a diagram in which dollars are measured along the vertical axis and quantity is measured along the horizontal axis that portrays the relationship between the quantity of a product someone can sell and the price he is charging for that product—that is horizontal over the relevant range[6] (at a height [price] that equals both the seller's marginal cost at the output he can sell at that price[7] and his minimum average total cost).

Perfect seller price competition is a Pareto-optimal condition for two reasons. First, in an otherwise-Pareto-perfect economy, the fact that a seller faces perfect price competition guarantees (*inter alia*) that the private benefits he can secure by producing a marginal unit of output ($PB_{\Delta UO}$, where Δ stands for last and UO stands for unit of output) will equal the allocative benefits his production of that unit will generate ($LB_{\Delta UO}$). Second, in an otherwise-Pareto-perfect economy, the fact that the producers from whom he is withdrawing the resources his production of his marginal unit of output consumes face perfect price competition guarantees (*inter alia*) that the private cost he must incur to produce his marginal unit of output ($PC_{\Delta UO}$) equals the allocative cost his production of that unit generates ($LC_{\Delta UO}$), which in turn equals the net allocative benefits the resources would have generated in their alternative uses.

I will first explain why the fact that perfect price competitors face horizontal demand curves guarantees that $PB_{\Delta UO} = LB_{\Delta UO}$ for all perfect price competitors in an otherwise Pareto-perfect economy and then explain the related reason why it guarantees that $PC_{\Delta UO} = LC_{\Delta UO}$ in such an economy. The key point is that, since a seller who faces a horizontal demand curve can sell additional units of his product for the same price he can obtain for his intramarginal units, the pre-sales-tax price he receives for marginal units of his product equals the additional revenue he obtains by selling a marginal unit of his product—MR or (somewhat redundantly) $MR_{\Delta UO}$.[8] Therefore, to show that $PB_{\Delta UO} = MR_{\Delta UO} =$ (the pre-sales-tax price the seller obtains for his marginal unit), I need to show only that, in an otherwise Pareto-perfect economy, (1) the pre-sales-tax price the seller obtains equals the after-sales-tax price the buyer pays ($P_{\Delta UO}$) and (2) $P_{\Delta UO} = LB_{\Delta UO}$. Since all sales taxes (as well as all consumption taxes, excise taxes, and value-added taxes) are ruled out by the otherwise-Pareto-perfect assumption that there are no taxes on the margin of income, the pre-sales-tax price the seller of a marginal unit of output receives will always equal the after-sales-tax price its buyer pays ($P_{\Delta UO}$). $P_{\Delta UO}$ will equal $LB_{\Delta UO}$ in an otherwise-Pareto-perfect economy because the facts that in such an economy there will be no externalities of consumption, all buyers will be sovereign maximizers, and purchases of the marginal unit of any product will generate no critical buyer surplus (henceforth, for simplicity, no buyer surplus at all) jointly guarantee this result. Thus, the fact that the purchase and consumption of marginal units of output generate no externalities guarantees that $LB_{\Delta UO}$ for any marginal unit of output will equal the private benefits that the consumption of that marginal unit confers on its consumer; the combination of the fact that the buyer is a sovereign maximizer and the fact that the consumption of the marginal unit of the relevant good generates no buyer surplus guarantees that the dollar value of the relevant marginal unit to its buyer equals its dollar cost to him; and the fact that the buyer is not a monopsonist guarantees that the cost he must incur to purchase the marginal unit at any given price equals that price. Since, then, for each product in an otherwise-Pareto-perfect economy, $LB_{\Delta UO}$ equals the relevant unit's private value to its buyer, the relevant unit's private value to its buyer equals its private cost to him, and that private cost equals the after-sales-tax price the buyer had to pay for the unit in question, $LB_{\Delta UO} = P_{\Delta UO}$ in such an economy. Hence, in an otherwise-Pareto-perfect economy, the fact that a seller faces perfect price competition will guarantee not only that $PB_{\Delta UO}$ equals $P_{\Delta UO}$ but also that $PB_{\Delta UO}$ equals $LB_{\Delta UO}$.

At least if I simplify (as we will eventually see, noncritically) by assuming that all the resources that the production of the marginal unit of any product consumes will be withdrawn from the production of other goods or services already in production, the preceding proof also implies that, in an otherwise-Pareto-perfect economy, $PC_{\Delta UO}$ will equal $LC_{\Delta UO}$ for each product if sellers face perfect price competition. To see why, note that the private cost a producer must incur to purchase a resource equals (infinitesimally exceeds) the private benefits that resource would yield its alternative employer, while the allocative cost a producer's use of a given resource will generate if (as we are now assuming) his use of it does not generate any externalities will equal the allocative benefits it would generate in its alternative use. Given these relationships, the preceding proof that in an otherwise-Pareto-perfect economy the private benefits that the factor rivals Y1 . . . of each seller X would obtain by using the resources X would use to produce his marginal unit of output to produce units of their own products would equal the allocative benefits these resources would generate in X's input rivals' employ if they faced perfect price competition implies that, in an otherwise-Pareto-perfect economy in which all sellers face perfect price competition, the private cost of the resources any seller uses to produce his marginal unit of output will equal the allocative cost of his using these resources—that $PC_{\Delta UOX} = LC_{\Delta UOX}$ for each product X.

In the other direction, with two empirically insignificant qualifications,[9] in an otherwise-Pareto-perfect economy, imperfections in the price competition a seller faces will deflate the private benefits he can secure by producing a marginal unit of output and derivatively the private cost that others would have to incur to bid away from him the resources he would use to produce a marginal unit of output. Assume, as is usually the case, that the imperfection in the price competition that the relevant seller faces reflects the fact that he enjoys competitive advantages when dealing for the patronage of particular buyers and/or can obtain oligopolistic margins from them and that both individually and jointly these competitive advantages and oligopolistic margins vary among the buyers he is privately best placed to supply (can profitably supply by making an offer that no one else would find inherently profitable to match even if the matching offer would be accepted). In these circumstances, the seller who faces such nonperfect competition will face a downward-sloping demand curve—that is, will be able to sell successive units of his product only at progressively lower prices. If a seller who faces such a downward-sloping demand curve must incur pricing costs to charge a lower price for his marginal unit without reducing the price or prices he is charging for his intramarginal units, the net marginal revenue he will obtain by selling his marginal unit will be less than the price for which he sells it, regardless of whether he charges a discriminatory price for it (for example, charges a lower price for his marginal unit than for his intramarginal units). Assume, for example, that a seller can sell 10 units of his product at a price of $10 but must reduce the price of the eleventh unit to $9.50 to sell it (because the eleventh-highest valuation of his product by any potential buyer is \$9.50). If such a seller would find it prohibitively expensive to charge \$9.50 for his eleventh unit while continuing to charge higher prices for his first 10 units (say, continuing to sell them for \$10 per unit)—that is, if he would have to incur more than \$5 in additional pricing costs to price his product this way rather than to reduce his price for all 11 units to \$9.50—the marginal revenue (MR) he would obtain by selling his eleventh unit for a price of \$9.50 would be \$4.50 since, in order to sell the eleventh unit for \$9.50, he would take \$.50 less for each of his first 10 units. In this situation, both $PB_{\Delta UO}$ and concomitantly $P\pi_{\Delta UO}$ will be deflated for the seller in question since, on our otherwise-Pareto-perfect assumptions that the marginal unit's buyer is a sovereign, maximizing nonmonopsonist and that his purchase and consumption of the unit in question would generate no buyer surplus or externalities, $LB_{\Delta UO}$ equals the price the buyer paid for the unit in question ($P_{\Delta UO} = \$9.50$), not the MR its sale would have generated ($MR_{\Delta UO} = 11(\$9.50) - 10(\$10) = \$104.50 - \$100 = \$4.50$) even if no sales tax had been levied on it. Derivatively, in this situation, in an otherwise-Pareto-perfect economy, the imperfection in the price competition the relevant seller faced would deflate (to $\$4.51 < \$9.50$) the cost to his input rivals of bidding away from him the resources he would use to produce his eleventh unit of output and hence would inflate the profitability of the alternative uses to which his relevant input rivals would devote the resources he would have used to produce an eleventh unit of his product.

(ii) Imperfections in QV-Investment Competition

The second dimension of perfect competition is perfect QV-investment competition. QV-investment competition is perfect in some area of product-space when in equilibrium the most profitable QV investment in that area of profit-space yields a (lifetime) normal rate of return. QV-investment competition can be imperfect for one or more of the following four reasons:

1. the existence of profit-differential and risk barriers to entry and expansion—the fact that one or more of the QV investments that would have to be executed by an expanding established firm or entering potential competitor to bring total QV investment in the relevant area of product-space to the level that would preclude even the most profitable project(s) in that area of product-space from yielding supernormal profits (given the actual extent to which prices would be supra-competitive at different QV-investment levels) will be less privately profitable and hence (presumptively) less allocatively efficient than the most profitable project in the relevant area of product-space;

2. the existence of scale barriers to entry and expansion—the fact that QV investments are lumpy (there are economies of scale in their execution) so that the (supernormal) rate of return that will be generated by the $(n+1)$th QV investment in a given area of product-space will on this account be lower than the rate of return its n predecessors would generate when there were only n QV investments in the relevant area of product-space even if the $(n+1)$th QV investment would yield the same rate of return as its predecessors at any total QV-investment level in the relevant area of product-space;
3. the investor(s) who would have to make one or more QV investments that would have to be executed in the relevant area of product-space for QV-investment competition to be perfect would face retaliation barriers to expansion or entry on the investment(s) in question (see below); and/or
4. the investor(s) who would have to make one or more of the QV investments in question would face what I call "monopolistic or natural oligopolistic QV-investment disincentives" on the investments in question (see below).[10]

The first two of these causes of imperfect QV-investment competition will not directly distort the profitability of any QV investment in an otherwise-Pareto-perfect economy (though they may distort the profitability of a wide variety of decisions including QV-investment decisions in such an economy by increasing the supra-competitiveness of the prices charged in the relevant area of product-space by deterring QV investments whose introduction would have reduced prices by reducing competitive advantages and possibly oligopolistic margins as well and, derivatively, by inflating the private value to potential QV investors of the resources they would use to create QV investments in it). This conclusion reflects the fact that the first two sources of imperfect QV-investment competition just listed reduce the allocative efficiency of the QV investments whose execution they deter (roughly speaking) by as much as they reduce their profitability.

However, both the relevant retaliation barriers and the relevant QV-investment disincentives will deflate the private benefits and hence the profits yielded by the QV investments to which they apply. A prospective QV investor faces a retaliation barrier to the extent that he anticipates that the amount by which the investment in question will increase his whole organization's operating-profit yield will be decreased by one or more rivals' responding to his QV investment by making inherently unprofitable, retaliatory moves to deter him and his future counterparts from making future QV investments in their areas of product-space or other types of competitive moves against them in the future. By definition, retaliatory responses are inherently unprofitable in that they would not be profitable but for their tendency to increase the retaliator's long-run profits by deterring his target and others from competing against him. The relevant retaliatory responses would usually be inherently unprofitable price cuts to the potential customers of the target's new and preexisting projects, inherently unprofitable advertising campaigns directed at potential purchasers of the target's new and old products, possibly inherently unprofitable decisions by the retaliator to relocate his existing QV investments (say, distributive outlets) closer to the target investor's projects, and conceivably decisions by the retaliator to make an additional QV investment that would compete against the target's new and old projects. Even though it would be incorrect to claim that such (misallocative) responses would distort the private benefits and profit yields of the QV investments at which they would be directed if they would reduce economic efficiency by the same amount that they would reduce the contribution the target's new investment would make to his organization's overall operating profits, in practice such responses certainly distort and probably deflate the private benefits of the QV investments at which they are directed. Primarily, the preceding deflation-conclusion reflects my perception that retaliation primarily takes the form of retaliatory price cuts, that many retaliatory price cuts result in their target's making sales at lower prices rather than losing customers, and that the losses that retaliatory price cuts that reduce their target's prices and profits without causing the target to lose customers to the retaliator impose on the target far exceed the allocative inefficiency the price cuts directly generate—the allocative transaction costs the retaliator generates when making his price cuts *plus* the allocative transaction costs the target generates when responding to the retaliator's price cuts by reducing his prices *plus* any increase or *minus* any decrease in UO-to-UO and other sorts of misallocation that results from the target's price cuts.[11]

The monopolistic and natural oligopolistic QV-investment disincentives that can cause QV-investment competition to be imperfect also deflate the private benefits and profits that one or more QV investments generate. In my vocabulary, a prospective QV investor is said to face a monopolistic QV-investment disincentive in relation to a particular QV investment if that investment would reduce the profit yields of his preexisting projects by more than those profit yields would otherwise have been reduced by any rival QV investment the QV investment in question would deter. If a new QV investment by someone who already has one or more projects in the area of product-space in which the new QV investment will be located does not deter a rival from making a QV investment in that area of product-space, the new QV investment will reduce the profit yields of the investor's preexisting projects by taking sales away from those projects directly[12] and by inducing rivals to make nonretaliatory responses (say, nonretaliatory price cuts) that also reduce the profit yields of the investor's preexisting projects. A QV investor will face a monopolistic QV-investment disincentive on this account if the new QV investment in question will not deter any rival from adding a QV investment to the relevant area of product-space or if the amount by which the new QV investment would reduce the investor's preexisting projects' profit yields in the above ways in comparison with the *status quo ante* exceeds the amount by which the deterred rival QV investment would have done so.[13]

In some situations, a prospective QV investor will realize that his new QV investment will reduce his preexisting projects' profit yields in comparison with the *status quo ante* not only in the ways just described but also by inducing a rival to make a new QV investment the rival would not otherwise have made (because the rival would otherwise have concluded that his new QV investment would induce the investor on whom we are focusing to make a QV investment this latter investor would not otherwise have made). In my vocabulary, a prospective QV investor in this type of situation is said to face a natural oligopolistic QV-investment disincentive equal to the sum of the amount by which the QV investment in question and the rival QV investment it induces to be made would reduce the profit yields of his preexisting projects and the amount by which the induced rival QV investment would reduce the profit yield of the new QV investment.

Two points need to be made about these disincentives. First, although prospective investors can face monopolistic and natural oligopolistic QV-investment disincentives when the economy is otherwise-Pareto-perfect, such disincentives will be much higher when price competition is imperfect in the area of product-space in which the investment in question would be made. This is because in such circumstances the sales that the new QV investment cannibalizes will have been more profitable and the nonretaliatory, non-QV-investment rival responses it induces will be likely to be more damaging to the investor. Second, monopolistic QV-investment disincentives and at least the first component of natural oligopolistic QV-investment disincentives listed above not only reduce but also deflate the private benefits and profits that will be generated by the QV investment to which they relate. The reduction in the investor's original projects' profit yields that result from his new project's taking sales away from his old projects (cannibalizing the sales of his old projects) are purely private losses that have no allocative counterpart. So too are the losses the investor sustains because his new project induces his rivals to respond to his new project by making nonretaliatory price cuts: indeed, as we shall see, those price cuts probably increase allocative efficiency (by reducing total-UO/total-QV/total-PPR misallocation) at the same time they reduce his preexisting projects' profit yields. The amount by which any rival QV investment the QV investment in question induces to be made reduces the profit yields of the relevant investor's preexisting projects also represents a private loss that has no direct economic-efficiency counterpart, though the magnitude of the negative distortion in the private benefits yielded by a QV investment that induces a rival to make a QV investment will be decreased by the economic inefficiency of the rival QV investment whose execution it induces.

In short, although two of the causes of imperfections in QV-investment competition—namely, (1) profit-differential and risk barriers to entry and expansion and (2) scale barriers to entry and expansion—do not directly distort the private benefits or profits yielded by any QV investment, two such causes—namely, (1) retaliation barriers to making QV investments and (2) monopolistic and natural oligopolistic QV-investment disincentives—do deflate the private benefits and profits yielded by QV investments. Moreover, the first two sources of price-competition imperfections will cause misallocation in an otherwise-Pareto-prefect economy by making prices supra-competitive and by inflating the private value to potential QV investors of the resources they use to create QV investments in the relevant area of product-space.

IMPERFECTIONS IN BUYER COMPETITION

The second Pareto-optimal condition I will discuss is perfect competition among buyers (no monopsony). By definition, buyers who are perfect competitors when buying some good (who are not monopsonists of the relevant good) can purchase as many units of the good in question at the same per-unit price over the relevant range. Supply curves (SS) are curves constructed in a diagram whose vertical axis measures money and whose horizontal axis measures the quantity of the good in question that represents the way in which the quantity of the good that will be supplied varies with the price that buyers offer to pay for it. Thus, buyers who are perfect competitors are buyers who face supply curves that are horizontal over the relevant range. Since such buyers can purchase an additional unit of the good in question at the going price (without paying more for any intramarginal unit), the price they must pay for the marginal unit will equal the marginal cost of that unit to the buyer in question (MK). Moreover, since in an otherwise-Pareto-perfect economy the price of the good in question will equal its marginal allocative cost (MLC)—given that the fulfillment of the other Pareto-optimal conditions will guarantee that producers will have to pay a price for each input they purchase that equals the allocative cost of their using it and will have to purchase all inputs they use, MK for any resource or unit of output will equal not only its price but also the allocative cost of the relevant buyer's consuming or using it.

In the other direction, by definition, a buyer who faces imperfect competition (who is a monopsonist) will have to pay progressively higher prices for each successive unit of the good in question he purchases—that is, he will face an upward-sloping supply curve for the good in question. This fact implies that the private cost to a monopsonist of all units of a product or resource he purchases beyond the first unit he purchases (MK) will exceed the price he pays for those units (P) if he cannot engage in price discrimination when purchasing the marginal unit in question without incurring any costs—for example, if when he buys an $(n + 1)$th unit he pays the higher price he must pay to purchase that unit for the n units he would otherwise have bought more cheaply. Thus, the MK to a nondiscriminating monopsonist of purchasing a second unit of the product in question when he can purchase one unit for $2 but must offer $2.10 to elicit the supply of a second unit will be $2.20—the $2.10 he pays for the second unit *plus* the $.10 extra he pays for the first unit when he chooses to pay $2.10 for each of two units rather than $2 for one unit. Assume that the object being purchased is a marginal unit of a final good. Since the otherwise-Pareto-perfect assumption guarantees that $P_{\Delta UO} = MLC_{\Delta UO}$, the fact that $MK_{\Delta UO} > P_{\Delta UO}$ guarantees that $MK_{\Delta UO} > MLC_{\Delta UO}$ for a monopsonist who does not engage in relevant price discrimination—that is, for all or virtually all monopsonists. Hence, in an otherwise-Pareto-perfect world, monopsony will (1) inflate the private cost to a buyer of purchasing a marginal unit of the good in question and hence deflate the profits he can earn by making such a purchase, (2) deflate the private benefits the good's producer can realize by producing the good in question (by deflating the price for which he can sell it) and hence deflate the profits he can realize by producing the relevant unit, and (3) deflate the private cost to their alternative possible users of the resources the monopsonized good's producers would use to produce marginal units of the good (by deflating the private benefits the monopsonized good's producers can secure by selling the units of output the relevant resources would enable them to produce) and thereby inflate the profits yielded by the alternative uses to which the resources in question could be devoted.

EXTERNALITIES

A choice is said to generate external costs if the chooser does not have to pay anything for some of the resources the choice "consumes." A choice is said to generate external benefits if the equivalent-dollar benefits it confers on others who enjoy observing it or sensing it or profit from its physical consequences are not fully internalized to the chooser. In an otherwise-Pareto-perfect economy, externalities of both consumption and production can distort the PC, PB, and thereby the Pπ of various choices and hence cause economic inefficiency.

(i) Externalities of Consumption

In an otherwise-Pareto-perfect economy, externalities of consumption can cause consumption-optimum misallocation by distorting the private benefits that consumers can obtain by consuming a unit of a particular good when the amount of externalities the consumption of a particular unit will generate will vary with the identity of the individual who consumes the unit in question. Thus, although the fact that Buyer I has outbid Buyer II by $5 for (places a $5 higher value on) a particular unit of a particular product with which each can be supplied at the same marginal allocative production cost will result in the good's being allocated to Buyer I in a market economy, it does not guarantee that that allocation will be economically efficient if consumption can generate externalities. If Buyer I's consumption of the unit in question generates $6 in external costs while Buyer II's consumption of that unit would generate no externalities, the allocation of the unit to Buyer I rather than to Buyer II will have caused $1 in consumption-optimum misallocation. Externalities of consumption can also cause top-level-optimum misallocation. Thus, even if the externalities that the consumption of a unit of some good generates do not depend on the identity of the individual who consumes the unit, in an otherwise-Pareto-perfect economy, externalities of consumption can also cause UO-to-UO misallocation by distorting the private benefits and private profits that the producer of the good can realize by producing his marginal and intramarginal units of the relevant product. Moreover, to the extent that the amount of consumption externalities (as a percentage of total cost) generated by all units of particular goods varies among products that have been or might be introduced, such externalities will tend to cause QV-to-QV misallocation in an otherwise-Pareto-perfect economy—for example, in such an economy, would cause such misallocation between QV investments whose creation and use would consume an equal amount of resources valued by their allocative cost if (1) the amount by which the supernormal profits that were or would be yielded by the more-profitable QV investment *exceeded* their counterpart for the less-profitable QV investment *was lower than* (2) the amount by which the external costs that were or would be generated by the consumption of the output of the product that the more-profitable investment created *exceeded* the external costs that would be generated by the consumption of the output of the product that the less-profitable QV investment did or would create.

Externalities of consumption can also cause PPR-to-PPR production-optimum misallocation in an otherwise-Pareto-perfect economy. In particular, externalities that would be yielded by the consumption of the units of output that would be sacrificed if the relevant different PPR projects were executed and the externalities that would be generated by the consumption of any additional units of output those projects would cause to be produced by yielding production-process discoveries whose use would reduce the marginal cost of producing the goods to whose production process they related can also cause PPR-to-PPR misallocation by generating different distortions respectively in the private cost of executing and private benefits yielded by alternative PPR projects where the differences in the private cost and private benefit distortions in question are not perfectly offsetting.

Finally, externalities of consumption can cause total – UO/total – QV/total – PPR misallocation by producing different distortions in the rates of return yielded by marginal expenditures of each of these types. The relevant analysis is complex. For example, external costs of consumption will deflate (inflate) the profitability of a marginal QV investment that creates a new product by the amount by which the externalities generated by the consumption of the good it creates are lower (higher) than the external costs that would otherwise be generated by the units of existing projects that will not be produced and consumed when the new product is created and produced. The distorting impact of externalities of consumption on the profits yielded by a QV investment that creates an additional distributive outlet will be affected as well by the impact of the outlet's operation on the amount of externalities buyers generate when traveling to do their shopping or perhaps when traveling for any purpose—amounts whose analysis is complicated by the possibility that the construction of a new distributive outlet might alter some parties' residential-location, employment-location, and business-location decisions.

(ii) Externalities of Production

Externalities of production will cause or tend to cause the same or analogous types of misallocation in an otherwise-Pareto-perfect economy. First, to the extent that the amount of externalities that the use of an input generates varies with the identity of the producer who employs it to produce a given product, the externality in question will cause production-optimum misallocation by causing the producers whose use of the input generates higher external costs to produce too high proportions of the units of output that are produced and the producers whose use of the input generates lower external costs to produce too low proportions of the output in question (by deflating the private costs of the former producers by more than they deflate the private costs of the latter producers). Second, externalities of production can also cause production-optimum misallocation even if their magnitude does not vary among producers of a given product by distorting the private cost of shifting from a known, more-externality-prone production process to a known, less-externality-prone production process and by deflating the profitability of production-process research that was designed to discover less-externality-prone production processes. Moreover, in an otherwise-Pareto-perfect economy, marginal external costs of production will also cause UO-to-UO misallocation to the extent that they constitute different percentages of the private marginal costs of producing different goods—to the extent that they deflate $PC_{\Delta UO}$ of different goods by different percentages. Externalities (say, external costs) of production will also tend to cause QV-to-QV misallocation if they constitute different percentages of the total private cost of creating and producing actual units of different products—that is, if they deflate the total private cost of creating and using different QV investments by different percentages. Finally, externalities (say, external costs) of production may cause total-UO/total-QV/total-PPR misallocation if, for example, the percentage that they constitute of the total private cost of creating and using a marginal, intramarginal, or extramarginal QV investment is different from the percentage they constitute of producing marginal, intramarginal, or extramarginal units of output and/or of executing and using marginal, intramarginal, or extramarginal PPR projects.

TAXES ON THE MARGIN OF INCOME

The condition that no taxes be levied on the margin of income requires no taxes to be levied that vary with any individual taxpayer's marginal earned income, marginal unearned (investment-generated) income, marginal wealth (which increases with earned and unearned income), or marginal consumption (which also increase with earned and unearned income) or with any business taxpayer's marginal sales or profits. Hence, for this condition to be fulfilled, there must be no individual or business income taxes, no wealth taxes or estate taxes, and no consumption, sales, excise, value-added, or property taxes.[14] *Ceteris paribus,* taxes on the margin of income distort the PB, PC, and derivatively the Pπ of various resource-use choices because tax payments are private costs that have no allocative counterpart.

Public-finance experts and welfare economists more generally conventionally claim that, in an otherwise-Pareto-perfect economy, taxes on the margin of income will always cause economic inefficiency. However, although they may not have worked out the precise circumstances in which the following qualification to the preceding conclusion would be important, I do not think they would be surprised by, much less reject (even initially), the claim that one can imagine sets of taxes on the margin of income that would not be misallocative in an otherwise-Pareto-perfect economy. Collectively, the members of each such set would not distort or would not critically distort the profitability of any choice because they would counteract each other either perfectly or well enough for misallocation to be avoided. The set of taxes on the margin of income that would not be misallocative that is easiest to identify would be taxes that apply the same effective tax rate to each unit of real income generated by the consumption of leisure, the purchase of any other good, the performance of each unit of do-it-yourself or market labor, the sale of land or other natural resources, the sale of any intermediate or final product, or the provision of capital—more specifically, that would apply to each unit of real income generated in any of these ways an effective tax rate that does not critically affect the profitability of the choices that yielded the real income in question (that is not higher than 100 percent [that does not render an otherwise profitable choice unprofitable] and is not sufficiently below zero percent to render an otherwise unprofitable choice profitable). Sets of taxes that do not satisfy these conditions may (probably fortuitously) not critically distort the profitability of particular types of choices if the distortions created by the various imperfections in the system of taxes on the margin of income from the above perspective perfectly offset each other.

For example, assume the following facts:

1. an entrepreneur must decide between making one of two QV investments (A and B);
2. the tax system is progressive—imposes a higher effective tax rate on each increment of a taxpayer's income;

3. the sales tax that is imposed on raw materials is lower than the income tax that is levied on marginal income;
4. for simplicity, the suppliers of the relevant raw materials need incur no labor costs to supply these resources—say, the buyers supply all the relevant labor;
5. the labor that would be consumed by the creation and use of QV investment A is more skilled and better paid than the labor that would be consumed by the creation and use of QV investment B so that the (average) effective tax rate that would be levied on the wages paid to the workers who would execute and use QV investment A would be higher than the average effective tax rate that would be levied on the wages paid to the workers who would create and use QV investment B; but
6. wage costs would constitute a lower percentage of the private cost of creating and using QV investment A than of the private cost of creating and using QV investment B, while raw-material costs would constitute a higher percentage of the private cost of creating and using QV investment A than of the private cost of creating and using QV investment B.

In these circumstances, the distortion generated by the progressivity imperfection (the fact that different units of wage income are subjected to different effective tax rates) could perfectly offset the distortion generated by the imperfection associated with the difference in the effective tax rates applied respectively to raw-material sales and (in effect) labor sales—that is, could leave undistorted the profitability of choosing to create and use QV investment A rather than B or vice versa. Of course, this outcome is unlikely to occur in practice. Indeed, there are good reasons to believe both that all extant systems that tax marginal income have imperfections that would cause them to generate various types of misallocation in an otherwise-Pareto-perfect economy and that the imperfections will not be and, in some instances, cannot be or should not be removed.

I offer three illustrations of these claims. First, all extant regimes of taxes on the margin of income are imperfect in that no such regime taxes all types of real income generated by taxpayer choices. In particular, no current regime taxes the value of the leisure the taxpayer consumed, the real income he derived from do-it-yourself labor, the nonmonetary income the taxpayer secured by working because he found the labor in question intrinsically pleasant or unpleasant, given the working environment in which he performed it, or the buyer surplus he obtained by purchasing goods. Admittedly, this feature of the relevant tax regimes is not ineliminable—most of these omissions are not justified by the impossibility or allocative-transaction-costliness of estimating these types of real income. However, even if these formal tax-base omissions were eliminated and all taxes could be levied without generating any allocative transaction costs, the difficulty of estimating these types of real income would cause regimes that tax marginal income to be misallocative in an otherwise-Pareto-perfect economy to the extent that the mean errors that would be made in estimating these various types of income (1) would be non-zero, (2) would vary from type of income to type of income or from taxpayer to taxpayer, and (3) could be anticipated by the relevant taxpayers before they made the choices whose after-tax profitability these errors would affect.

Second, all extant regimes of taxes on the margin of income are imperfect in that they apply different effective tax rates to the marginal incomes of different taxpayers. This reality reflects two facts. First, all contemporary tax systems are progressive over at least some ranges in the sense of making the effective tax rate applied to a taxpayer's marginal taxable income increase with his taxable income within some relevant range. Second, taxable income varies considerably from taxpayer to taxpayer in all contemporary societies. Although flat taxes could eliminate this imperfection, they are probably not politically viable and could not be adopted in any event without sacrificing the pure distributive benefits that progressive taxes generate from many normative perspectives (and, if we relax our otherwise-Pareto-perfect assumption, the allocative-efficiency gains they generate in the real world as well).

Third, many, if not all, contemporary tax systems are imperfect in that they contain investment-credit, investment-expensing, and accelerated-depreciation provisions for certain types of investments (such as in R&D) and/or provisions specifying that reduced tax rates be applied to the income generated by the sale of certain types of natural resources (such as oil and trees) that either individually or in combination reduce the effective tax rate applied to the profits (or losses) generated by the business choices in question sufficiently below zero to render otherwise unprofitable investments profitable. Relatedly, in practice, at least some contemporary tax regimes include protocols for evaluating the cost of capital withdrawn from retained earnings that sufficiently underestimate the normal rate of return on risky projects to raise the effective *ex ante* tax rate applied to expected profits above 100 percent—that is, to render unprofitable *ex ante* investments that would otherwise be profitable *ex ante*. Although these imperfection-generating provisions are not ineliminable, the longevity of at least the former sorts of provisions suggests that, given extant distributions of political power, in the real world they are unlikely to be removed.

I will now list and explain some of the specific types of resource misallocation that the tax imperfections I have just delineated can cause. I start by delineating some of the types of resource misallocation that would be caused in an otherwise-Pareto-perfect economy if the tax base did not include some of the types of real income a taxpayer can obtain by making particular choices. First, if the equivalent-dollar value to the taxpayer of the leisure he consumes or the do-it-yourself labor he performs is not included in his tax base while the monetary income he obtains by performing market labor is taxed, the system will cause economic inefficiency in an otherwise-Pareto-perfect economy by rendering it profitable for individuals to make economically inefficient substitutions of leisure and/or do-it-yourself labor for market labor by deflating the private cost of their foregoing market labor to produce leisure or do-it-yourself labor (by reducing the net wage the worker obtains from performing a marginal unit of market labor below the gross wage, which as we shall see in the next subsection of this chapter will equal the marginal allocative product of the worker's marginal unit of market labor in an otherwise-Pareto-perfect economy). Second, if the tax base does not reflect the dollar value of the pleasure workers derive from performing the labor they perform in the physical working environment in which they perform it with their actual coworkers but does reflect the monetary income they receive for working and the dollar value to them of the health care and other conventional fringe benefits they receive, the tax system will cause economic inefficiency in an otherwise-Pareto-perfect economy by rendering it profitable for workers to make economically inefficient substitutions of more attractive work, bigger offices, more attractive shop floors, more attractive or compatible workmates (such as workmates against whom they are not prejudiced), and conventional fringe benefits for the goods and services they would purchase with the higher wages they are foregoing to secure such benefits by deflating the net monetary-wage cost to them of these untaxed benefits.[15] Third, if the benefits individuals obtain by consuming today rather than tomorrow are not taxed while the unearned income they realize by investing (delaying their consumption) is taxed, the taxes on the margin of income that are levied will cause UO-to-UO misallocation by rendering it profitable for individuals to make economically inefficient substitutions of current goods for future goods in an otherwise-Pareto-perfect economy by deflating the private cost of current consumption (by taxing the unearned income that the individuals could realize by foregoing current consumption).

The following five examples illustrate the fact that taxes on the margin of income will tend to generate economic inefficiency in an otherwise-Pareto-perfect economy if there are intertaxpayer differences in the effective tax rate applied to taxpayer marginal income (say, taxpayer marginal wages). First, in an otherwise-Pareto-perfect economy, taxes on the margin of income will tend to cause production-optimum misallocation if the tax rate levied on marginal wages varies with the taxpayer's income (for example, if the tax system is progressive), the production processes among which the producer must choose employ labor in different tax brackets, and labor costs would constitute the same percentage of the alternative production processes' total costs if no taxes were levied. More specifically, in these circumstances, in an otherwise-Pareto-perfect economy, a tax system that employs taxes on the margin of income that increase with that taxpayer's income will tend to render it profitable for producers to make economically inefficient substitutions of production processes that employ less skilled, lower-paid, lower-taxed labor for production processes that employ more skilled, higher-paid, more-highly-taxed labor by inflating the private benefits of this substitution by inflating the total gross wages the producer will have to pay the higher-paid workers the latter production process uses by more than it inflates the total gross wages the producer will have to pay the lower-paid workers whom the former production process uses.[16]

Second, in an otherwise-Pareto-perfect-economy, taxes on the margin of income will cause UO-to-UO misallocation if the tax rate levied on marginal wages increases with the taxpayer's income if, in a world without taxes, wage costs would constitute the same percentage of the marginal cost of producing marginal units of all products and the production of some products consumes the labor of more skilled, more-highly-paid workers whose marginal income is taxed at a higher rate while the production of other products consumes the labor of less-skilled, less-highly-paid workers whose marginal income is taxed at a lower rate. In particular, in these circumstances, the applicable taxes on the margin of income will cause UO-to-UO misallocation by inflating the former products' marginal costs and prices by a higher percentage than the percentage by which they inflate the marginal costs and prices of the latter products—that is, by rendering it profitable for consumers to make economically inefficient substitutions of the latter products for the former by making the rate at which they can substitute the latter products for the former at the margin higher than the rate at which the economy can transform (so to speak) the latter products into the former at the margin.

Third, in two situations, in an otherwise-Pareto-perfect economy, taxes on the margin of income will cause QV-to-QV misallocation if the effective tax rate levied on marginal income varies with the taxpayer's income and this variation causes the total tax distortion of the wage cost of creating and using different QV investments to differ. In the first such situation, (1) only one of two potentially rivalrous QV investments, each of which would be profitable if it were the only one made, can be profitable, (2) the effective tax rate applied to the earned income of the more-allocatively-efficient and otherwise-more-profitable project is higher than its counterpart for the less-allocatively-efficient and otherwise-less-profitable project, and (3) this difference in the effective tax rates applied to the earned income of the workers whose labor the two projects will employ causes the positive difference between the tax-related inflation of the cost of creating and operating the more-allocatively-efficient and otherwise-more-profitable project to exceed the tax-related inflation of the cost of creating and operating the less-allocatively-efficient and otherwise-less-profitable project by more than the allocative efficiency of the former project exceeds the allocative efficiency of the latter project—that is, causes the more-allocatively-efficient project to be less profitable. In the second such situation, the tax system imposes a positive effective tax rate on the income earned by the labor an allocatively efficient QV-investment project consumes that renders that project unprofitable and a negative effective tax rate on the income earned by the labor an allocatively inefficient QV-investment project consumes that renders that project profitable.

Fourth, if I assume for simplicity that (1) labor costs would represent the same percentage of the private cost of different PPR projects if no taxes were levied, (2) some such projects use more-skilled, more-highly-paid workers who face higher effective tax rates on their marginal income than do the workers other PPR projects employ, (3) no taxes are levied on the purchase of any other inputs the relevant PPR projects would consume, and (4) the suppliers of those other inputs do not incur any labor costs, then a system of taxes on the margin of earned income that is progressive will tend to cause PPR-to-PPR misallocation whenever the following condition is satisfied: (the amount by which the allocative efficiency of a PPR project that uses more-highly-paid workers *exceeds* the allocative efficiency of a project that uses less-highly-paid workers) *is less than* (the amount by which the applicable taxes on labor income inflate the labor costs of the former, more-allocatively-efficient project *exceeds* the amount by which the applicable taxes on labor income inflate the labor costs of the latter, less-allocatively-efficient project).

Fifth, if I assume for simplicity that (1) in a world without taxes, wages and salaries would constitute the same percentage of the total cost of making marginal QV investments, of executing marginal PPR projects, and of producing marginal units of output of existing products, (2) no taxes are levied on the purchase of the nonlabor inputs the relevant marginal resource uses consume, and (3) the suppliers of these various other inputs do not incur any labor costs, then differences in the effective tax rates applied to the marginal income of different taxpayers (say, progressive income taxation) will cause total-UO/total-QV/total-PPR misallocation in an otherwise-Pareto-perfect economy to the extent that, on average, unit output production, QV-investment creation and use, and PPR execution and use consume the labor of workers in different tax brackets. If I had to guess, I would assume that the average wage paid to PPR-executing-and-using workers was highest, to QV-investment-creating-and-using workers was second highest, and to unit-output-producing workers was lowest. If so, in an otherwise-Pareto-perfect economy, progressive taxation would tend to cause too many resources to be allocated to unit output production relative to the amount allocated to PPR and QV-investment creation and use, and too many resources to be allocated to QV-investment creation and use relative to PPR execution and use because such taxation would inflate the labor costs of UO production least, of QV-investment creation and use second most, and of PPR execution and use most.

Obviously, the preceding results can be generalized to cases in which (1) the relevant resource users' private costs are inflated not only by the taxes the workers they directly employ must pay on the wage package the resource users pay them but also by the sales, value-added, or property taxes the resource users must pay for the nonlabor inputs their resource uses consume and the taxes their nonlabor input suppliers' employees must pay on the wage packages they earned by producing the nonlabor inputs the relevant resource uses consumed and in which (2) labor costs and other input costs constitute respectively different percentages of the private costs of the various resource uses among which choices must be made. If the differences in the effective tax rates applied to the earned income of different workers or the effective tax rates applied respectively to earned income and nonlabor-input sales cause the absolute tax inflation in the private costs of the different resource uses among which a choice must be made to differ, the tax regime will cause production-process-choice misallocation, PPR-to-PPR misallocation, UO-to-UO misallocation, QV-to-QV misallocation, and total-UO/total-QV/total-PPR misallocation whenever (the amount by which the associated tax inflation of the private cost of the most-allocatively-efficient resource use in a relevant set of possible resource uses *exceeds* the tax inflation of the private cost of a less-allocatively-efficient resource use in that set) *is larger than* (the amount by which the allocative efficiency of the most-allocatively-efficient resource use in the relevant set *exceeds* the allocative efficiency of the less-allocatively-efficient resource use in question).

BUYER SURPLUS

Buyer surplus is the difference between the price a buyer pays for something he purchases and the lower price he could pay for it and perceive himself to break even on the transaction. In an otherwise-Pareto-perfect economy, buyer surplus will cause or tend to cause resources to be misallocated because it deflates the private benefits of the business choices that generate it—that is, because it represents a private and allocative benefit the business choice in question generated that is external to the business (is realized by the buyer who secured the surplus). As I have already noted, rather than "no misallocation-causing buyer surplus," the traditional list of Pareto-optimal conditions contains the more limited condition of no public goods. I have substituted a no-misallocation-causing buyer-surplus condition for the traditional no-public-goods condition because, both in an otherwise-Pareto-perfect economy and in actual economies, public-goods situations are just one of several types of situations in which buyer surplus will generate misallocation by deflating the private benefits a business decision will generate for the business. I will now define *public goods*, explain why they will give rise to misallocation in an otherwise-Pareto-perfect economy, explain why they will be less likely to give rise to misallocation in our actual economy (in which prices are supra-competitive), and finally explain why in an otherwise-Pareto-perfect economy buyer surplus may generate QV-to-QV, PPR-to-PPR, and total-UO/total-QV/total-PPR misallocation even if no public goods exist.

Properly defined, a *public good* is a good that would be economically efficient to produce at its economically efficient output—namely, on the otherwise-Pareto-perfect assumption on which public-good analysis is conventionally based, the output at which its demand curve cuts its marginal cost curve from above—whose marginal cost curve is lower than its average total cost curve at the output in question. Standard examples of public goods are bridges and national defense (where each unit of output is the protection provided for one member of the society). From the perspective of economic efficiency, public goods are problematic in an otherwise-Pareto-perfect economy because in such an economy (1) with one minor, irrelevant qualification,[17] the demand curve (DD) for each product (which indicates the highest dollar value that successive units of the good in question will have for the possibly different buyers who value them most highly) will equal its marginal allocative value (MLV) curve (which indicates the allocative value generated by the consumption of successive units of the good in question[18]), (2) the marginal cost (MC) curve for each product will equal its marginal allocative cost (MLC) curve (which indicates the allocative value of the goods that would be produced with the resources used to produce the last unit of the product in question if they were not used to produce that last unit), and (3) the average total cost curve for each product will equal the average total allocative cost curve for that product.[19] More specifically, each public good will create economic-efficiency problems in an otherwise-Pareto-perfect economy regardless of the way in which its pricing and producers are handled:

1. if any producer of a public good will be required to price it at the single per-unit price that would result in its being produced in the economically efficient quantity (once the investment necessary to produce it has been made)—that is, to price it at its MC at the output at which DD = MLV cuts MC = MLC from above—and is given no subsidy for producing the good in question, no potential producer of a public good will build the plant to produce the good in question because the price he will be required to charge for the good is lower than the average total cost of producing the quantity of the good he will be required to produce despite the fact that the production of that quantity of the good would have been economically efficient (because the buyer surplus that the good's purchasers would have realized by purchasing the units that would be economically efficient to sell would exceed the loss the relevant producer would sustain from supplying it on the terms in question), and economic inefficiency equal to the amount by which the supply of the economically efficient output of the public good would have increased economic efficiency will result;
2. if any producer of a public good will be allowed to set the lowest, uniform per-unit price that would enable him to earn a normal rate of return by supplying the public good—the price that equals the height of DD at the output at which DD cuts the average total cost curve (ATC) from above or is tangent to ATC—or if such a good's producer is allowed to charge a higher price than the one just specified (for example, his conventional profit-maximizing price, the price at which the conventional MR curve cuts MC from above), the public good will be supplied, but its output will be lower than the allocatively efficient output: the resulting allocative inefficiency will equal the area between DD = MLV and MC = MLC between the actual output and the allocatively efficient output (the output at which DD = MLV cuts MC = MLC from above);
3. if any producer of a public good will be required to set a single, uniform price equal to the MC he will incur to produce the last unit of the public good whose supply would be allocatively efficient (the price equal to his MC at the

output at which the public good's DD = MLV curve cuts its MC = MLC curve from above) but will be given a subsidy equal to the difference between the total cost he will incur to supply the economically efficient quantity of the public good and the revenue he would obtain by supplying that quantity of the good at the uniform price in question, the public good will be supplied in the economically efficient quantity, but the financing of the subsidy in question will generate economic inefficiency both by generating allocative transaction costs and by distorting the profitability of various other choices (regardless of whether the government finances the subsidy by levying taxes on the margin of income, by printing money and causing inflation, or by charging supra-competitive prices for goods and services it supplies); and

4. if any producer of a public good will be required to produce the allocatively efficient output of the public good but will be allowed to cover the loss he would incur by doing so if he charged a uniform per-unit price for the public good by charging higher prices for one or more intramarginal units—an option that might not be available, given the private cost of practicing such price discrimination—the public good will be produced in the economically efficient quantity but economic inefficiency will result to the extent that the public-good producer generates allocative market research costs when identifying the dollar value that particular potential buyers place on the public good, administrative allocative charging costs when implementing the more complicated pricing system, and various kinds of allocative costs to prevent the arbitrage that would otherwise reduce the profits he can earn by engaging in price discrimination while causing economic inefficiency in its own right (such as by increasing the allocative cost of the arbitraged good's being delivered to its consumer and eliminating the allocative-efficiency gain that the initial buyer's purchase and consumption of the relevant unit would otherwise have generated).

Although public goods (and the buyer surplus that causes goods to be public goods) will cause economic inefficiency in an otherwise-Pareto-perfect economy, the public-good problem is likely to be less important in our actual, otherwise-Pareto-imperfect economy than in an otherwise-Pareto-perfect economy. In particular, because in the real world a public-good producer may well be withdrawing the resources he uses to produce marginal units of the public good from unit output production by nondiscriminating imperfect competitors, the public good's MLC will probably tend to exceed its MC in the real world. If it does, allowing its producer to cover his supra-MC ATC by setting his price above the marginal cost he would have to incur to produce the unit that would bring the output of the good to the level at which the DD curve for the good cuts its ATC curve from above or is tangent to its ATC curve may cause no misallocation (and will certainly cause less misallocation than would otherwise be the case) since the price that equals ATC and exceeds MC may not exceed MLC (which will also exceed MC in the circumstances described) and will certainly exceed MLC in such circumstances by less than it would otherwise have done.

However, the fact that public goods may cause less economic inefficiency in our actual economy than economists seem to suppose does not suggest that buyer surplus causes less misallocation in our actual economy (indeed, would cause less misallocation in an otherwise-Pareto-perfect economy) than traditional analysts—who implicitly assume that buyer surplus causes problems only by giving rise to public goods—appear to believe. This conclusion reflects the fact that in both an otherwise-Pareto-perfect economy and our actual economy buyer surplus can cause at least three types of economic inefficiency by deflating the private benefits a resource user can derive from a resource use even when the buyer surplus does not give rise to a public good.

I have already noted the first of these possibilities. In an otherwise-Pareto-perfect economy, buyer surplus will sometimes cause QV-to-QV misallocation by critically distorting the relative profitability of two rival QV investments, each of which would be profitable if, but only if, the other were not made. More specifically, since the otherwise-Pareto-perfect assumption guarantees that the economic efficiency of each of these two investments equals the sum of the profits and buyer surplus it will generate, buyer surplus will cause the less-economically-efficient QV investment to be made instead of the more-economically-efficient QV investment whenever the following condition is satisfied: (the amount by which the buyer surplus that would be generated by the use of the more-economically-efficient QV investment—the sale of the product it will create or the operation of the distributive outlet it will create—*exceeds* the amount of buyer surplus that would be generated by the less-economically-efficient QV investment) *is larger than* (the amount by which the economic efficiency of the more-economically-efficient investment *exceeds* the economic efficiency of the less-economically-efficient investment), where I am defining the economic efficiency of each investment on the assumption that neither investment would be made if the one in question were not made.

Buyer surplus can also deflate the private benefits a PPR project confers on its owner. In fact, the buyer surplus generated by two sorts of transactions can have this effect. The first is the buyer surplus generated by the sale of the intramarginal units of the product whose production process the PPR project is designed to alter. If the PPR discovery causes any user to increase his unit output by reducing his marginal costs over the relevant range, the discovery's value to its user(s) and hence the private benefits the PPR project confers on its owner will be deflated by any buyer surplus the additional sales generate. (Of course, if the PPR discovery causes its users to reduce their unit outputs by increasing their marginal costs over the relevant range [which it could do if it reduced their fixed costs sufficiently], any associated reduction in buyer surplus could inflate the discovery's value to its users and hence the private benefits the PPR project yielded its owner.) Second, if the owner of the PPR project does not use the discovery exclusively himself, the private benefits it yields him will be deflated by any buyer surplus the buyers or licensees of his discovery realize on their purchase of it or the right to use it.

In any event, in both an otherwise-Pareto-perfect economy and our actual, highly-Pareto-imperfect economy, the buyer surplus that the sale of PPR discoveries can generate can cause PPR-to-PPR misallocation for the same reasons and in the same circumstances as the buyer surplus that QV investments generate can cause QV-to-QV misallocation. More specifically, the buyer surplus that PPR projects generate will cause a less-economically-efficient PPR project to be substituted for a more-economically-efficient PPR project whenever (the amount by which the buyer surplus that would be generated by the sale and use of the discovery the more-economically-efficient project makes *exceeds* the buyer surplus that would be generated by the sale and use of the discovery some less-allocatively-efficient substitute PPR project would make) *is larger than* (the amount by which the former project's economic efficiency *exceeds* the latter project's economic efficiency) where, once more, the economic efficiency of each project is measured on the assumption that no such project will be executed if it is not executed.

Finally, buyer surplus can also cause total-UO/total-QV/total-PPR misallocation in both an otherwise-Pareto-perfect economy and our actual, highly-Pareto-imperfect economy—in particular, will cause such misallocation whenever the fact that the last actual resource use or resource uses in one of the above categories was more profitable than the next resource use or resource uses in another category was critically affected by the fact that the less profitable alternative resource use of a different type would have generated more buyer surplus than the more profitable actual resource use actually generated.

HUMAN ERRORS (INDIVIDUAL NONSOVEREIGNTY AND NONMAXIMIZATION)

I will combine my treatment of the final two Pareto-optimal conditions—individual sovereignty (all choosers have all the information they need to discover the choice that would maximize their interests, broadly defined[20]) and individual maximization (each chooser makes the choice that the information at his disposal should lead him to believe will maximize his interests, broadly defined—*inter alia,* no chooser makes any mathematical error that results in his failing to make the choice the information he possesses implies would be optimal for him). In particular, the text that follows will use the expression "human errors" to refer to these two types of imperfections (since human errors in the form of choices that are not in the best interest of the chooser are the likely consequence of each of these two types of imperfections). In so doing, I will ignore the possibility that, in individual instances in which both types of imperfections are present, the imperfections in question can perfectly offset each other (and for that reason not generate any economic inefficiency in an otherwise-Pareto-perfect economy).[21]

Although a chooser's nonsovereignty will not distort the actual private benefits, private cost, or profits yielded by the choice he is assessing, they will distort his perception of these benefits, costs, and profits and will tend on that account to cause him to make choices that are not in his interest and that, in an otherwise-Pareto-perfect economy, are economically inefficient. Thus, a consumer who overestimates the value of a unit of some product will overestimate the private benefits it will confer on him and hence the profitability of his purchasing it; similarly, a consumer who underestimates the private cost of purchasing some product (who underestimates the interest he will have to pay on an installment purchase or the price of some product per ounce) will overestimate the profitability of his purchasing it. In both cases, if the consumer can change the quantity of the relevant product he purchases by infinitesimally small amounts (so that he perceives himself just to be breaking even on his final purchase), the distortions in the perceived profitability of his last purchase will cause him to purchase the wrong amount of the relevant good (on the above assumptions, too many units) from his own perspective and, in an otherwise-Pareto-perfect economy, from the perspective of economic efficiency as well. If the good in question can be purchased only in lumpy increments, such nonsovereignty or nonmaximization may not critically affect the profitability of the buyer's choice: since the buyer may have perceived that his decision to buy or not to buy an extra, lumpy unit of a product would yield him significant profits, his misperception of the actual profitability of this choice may not have critically affected his perception of its profitability or, therefore, the choice he made—that is, may not cause misallocation in an otherwise-Pareto-perfect economy by causing him to perceive as profitable (unprofitable) a purchase that was unprofitable (profitable) for him.

Precisely the same analysis applies to producer errors. A producer who overestimates the marginal physical product of a particular input (MPP)—the amount by which the last unit of this input would increase his unit output (or, by extension, the contribution it would make to his completion of a QV-investment or PPR project)—or who makes a mathematical error that causes him to underestimate the amount a marginal unit of that input would cost him will on these accounts tend to find it profitable to

1. make unprofitable substitutions of production processes that use more of the input in question for production processes that use less of it;
2. produce additional units of his output whose production is in fact unprofitable;
3. make an unprofitable decision to
   - A. substitute a QV investment whose execution and use consumes more of the input in question for one whose execution and use consumes less of it or
   - B. make a QV investment whose execution and use consumes some of the input in question as opposed to making no QV investment at all; and
4. make an unprofitable decision to
   - A. substitute a PPR project whose execution and use consumes more of the input in question or will yield a discovery whose use will save less of the input in question for a PPR project whose execution consumes more of the input in question or will yield a discovery whose use will save more of the input in question or
   - B. execute an additional PPR project when he would otherwise not have done so.

Once more, errors of this kind will always critically affect the error-maker's perception of the profitability of last choices that are infinitesimally small but may or may not critically affect the error-maker's perception of the profitability of last choices that are lumpy (since the perceived profitability of those last choices may diverge significantly from zero): unit output choices come closest to being infinitesimally small though a few producers who use more than one production process to produce their product may be able to make tiny variations in the proportions of the output they produce with the different production processes they employ; choices to use one rather than another production process exclusively, choices between rival QV-investment or PPR projects, and choices to execute or not to execute any QV-investment or PPR project are always lumpy (given the economies of scale in making such investments and, usually, in using particular production processes). Once more as well, errors of this kind that lead the error-maker to make choices that are privately unprofitable will also always lead him to make choices that are economically inefficient in an otherwise-Pareto-perfect economy.

One final point. Although the nonsovereignty and nonmaximization of a chooser will not distort the actual private benefits, private cost, or profits any choice will confer or impose on him, they will distort the private cost to others of using the resources whose private value or cost the error-maker misestimates and hence the profits that would be yielded by the alternative uses to which these latter actors would put the resources in question: since these alternative users of the resources in question will have (in effect) to bid them away from the error-maker, in an otherwise-Pareto-perfect economy, any mistake the error-maker makes that leads him to offer too high (too low) a price for such resources from the perspective of his own actual interests will increase (decrease) the price that others must pay to withdraw these resources from his use above (below) the allocative cost of their using these resources.

I have now explained how an individual departure from each of the seven Pareto-optimal conditions (how an individual Pareto imperfection of each type) will tend to distort the private cost, private benefits, and profits yielded by various choices and delineated many of the kinds of resource misallocation that Pareto imperfections of each type will either cause or tend to cause in an otherwise-Pareto-perfect economy. The next section builds on this analysis by illustrating the way in which the various Pareto imperfections interact to cause a particular type of economic inefficiency—the kind that can be generated by choices between supplying a marginal unit of unit-output-producing market labor and consuming a marginal unit of leisure.

The Way in Which the Various Pareto Imperfections Interact to Cause Economic Inefficiency: The Allocation of Time between Unit-Output-Producing Market Labor and Leisure

After delineating the assumptions on which it proceeds, this subsection (1) elaborates on the meaning of the statement that, from the perspective of economic efficiency, an individual worker has devoted too much or too little time to unit output production relative to the amount of time he devoted to leisure production, (2) explains why no misallocation between unit-output-producing market labor and leisure will be generated if all the Pareto-optimal conditions are fulfilled (because neither the private benefits to the worker of performing a marginal unit of unit-output-producing market labor nor the private cost to the worker of performing such labor will be distorted and the worker in question will make the labor/leisure choice that is most profitable for him), (3) explains why and how each type of Pareto imperfection would individually cause such labor/leisure misallocation in an otherwise-Pareto-perfect world, (4) explores how the various types of Pareto imperfections interact to create the aggregate distortion in the profits a potential unit-output-producing worker can cause by performing a marginal unit of such labor, and (5) illustrates how various sets of Pareto imperfections could perfectly counteract each other in relation to this type of misallocation—*inter alia,* how, in a world in which two or more such imperfections are present, the aggregate distortion in the profits a potential unit-output-producing worker could make by performing a marginal unit of unit-output-producing market labor could be zero (why the profits the relevant worker would secure by performing such labor could equal the allocative efficiency of the relevant labor's being performed).

This subsection's analysis of the relationship between the fulfillment of the various Pareto-optimal conditions and the extent of the misallocation that will be generated by an individual worker's choice between supplying an additional unit of unit-output-producing market labor and consuming an additional unit of leisure is based on the following six assumptions or definitions:

1. most obviously, the relevant worker's labor would be unit-output-producing as opposed to QV-investment-creating or PPR-executing;
2. if the relevant worker decides not to supply an additional unit of market labor, he will consume leisure instead (as opposed to performing do-it-yourself labor);
3. the dollar value of a marginal unit of leisure to the worker reflects the dollar value to him of substituting that unit of leisure for the unit of labor he would otherwise devote the relevant unit of time to performing (that is, reflects both the intrinsic attractiveness to him of the leisure in question and the intrinsic attractiveness or unattractiveness to him of the labor in question);
4. the worker in question can vary the quantity of unit-output-producing market labor he performs by infinitesimally small amounts;
5. the marginal allocative product of labor curve—the curve that indicates the marginal allocative value that successive units of the relevant worker's

unit-output-producing market labor will generate—is downward sloping and continuous; and

6. the worker's marginal allocative value of leisure curve—the curve that indicates the allocative value generated by the worker's consumption of successive units of leisure—is also downward sloping and continuous (the dollar value to him of successive units of leisure diminishes continuously).

On the above assumptions, a worker who is choosing between performing unit-output-producing market labor and consuming leisure will have allocated his time economically efficiently if—at the labor/leisure time division he chose—the marginal allocative product of his labor (which equals both the allocative benefits the marginal unit of labor generated and the allocative cost of the marginal unit of leisure the worker forwent to perform the last unit of labor) equals the marginal allocative cost of labor (the allocative value that would have been generated by his consumption of the unit of leisure he forwent to perform his marginal unit of labor). Let the subscript L stand for labor, the subscript Le stand for leisure, MLP_L stand for the marginal allocative product of labor, and MLV_{Le} stand for the allocative value that would be generated by the consumption of the marginal unit of leisure.

If, on the above assumptions, $MLV_{Le} < MLP_L$ in equilibrium, too little labor will have been performed from the perspective of allocative efficiency because the allocative value of the leisure that the performance of an additional unit of labor would sacrifice would be lower than the allocative value that the relevant labor would generate. Thus, if $MLV_{Le} = \$8.50 < MLP_L = \$9$, the performance of an additional unit of labor would increase allocative efficiency by $.50. (The total amount of labor/leisure misallocation might be more than $.50—would equal the sum of the increases in allocative efficiency that would have been generated by all the additional units of labor [not just the first additional unit of labor] whose performance would have been allocatively efficient [if the quantity of labor performed were more than one unit below the quantity of the relevant type of labor whose performance would have been allocatively efficient].)

Similarly, if, on the above assumptions, $MLV_{Le} > MLP_L$ in equilibrium, too much labor will have been performed from the perspective of allocative efficiency because the allocative value that would be generated if an additional unit of leisure were consumed would be greater than the allocative product that would be sacrificed if one fewer unit of labor were performed. Thus, if $MLV_{Le} = \$9.25 > MLP_L = \$9$, the performance of the last unit of labor that was performed would have misallocated resources by \$.25. Finally, if $MLV_{Le} = MLP_L$, one will not be able to increase allocative efficiency by altering the quantity of labor performed. Thus, if $MLV_{Le} = MLP_L = \$9$, a decision to increase the quantity of labor performed would be allocatively inefficient since the MLP of that additional unit of labor will be lower than \$9—given assumption (5)—while the allocative value of the unit of leisure that would be forgone was \$9. Similarly, if $MLV_{Le} = MLP_L = \$9$, a decision to decrease the quantity of labor performed by one unit would be allocatively inefficient since the allocative value of the additional unit of leisure that that choice would create would be less than \$9—given assumption (6)—while the allocative product of the unit of labor that was forgone was \$9.

The series of identities (definitions) and equalities on the following page demonstrate that, if all the Pareto-optimal conditions are fulfilled, unit-output-producing workers will allocate their time economically efficiently between performing unit-output-producing market labor and producing leisure. The conditions indicated above or below the arrows leading from any equality sign indicate the subset of Pareto-optimal conditions whose fulfillment is a sufficient condition for the equality in question to obtain. Three horizontal lines between any two symbols indicate that the relevant relationship is an identity (that the equality in question is definitional).

I will start by pointing out that (1) if all the conditions indicated above and below the arrows are fulfilled, MLC_L (the marginal allocative cost of labor) will equal MLP_L (the marginal allocative product of labor), and no misallocation between unit-output-producing market labor and leisure (henceforth, no labor/leisure misallocation) will be generated and (2) taken together, the relevant conditions amount to the condition that all the various Pareto-optimal conditions (no monopoly, no monopsony, no externalities, no taxes on the margin of income, all actors are sovereign maximizers, and no problems caused by buyer surplus) are fulfilled.

I will now begin in the middle of the series of identities and equalities with $MRP_L \equiv MPP_L(MR_G)$ where G stands for the good the relevant labor would produce and explain what each symbol in the above series denotes and why each equality in the above chain will be achieved if the conditions listed above or below the relevant equal sign are fulfilled. MRP_L is the marginal revenue product of labor—the private value to the worker's employer (the producer [prod.] of G) of the last unit of labor of the type the worker performed with the skill and assiduity with which he performed his work. MRP_L is defined to

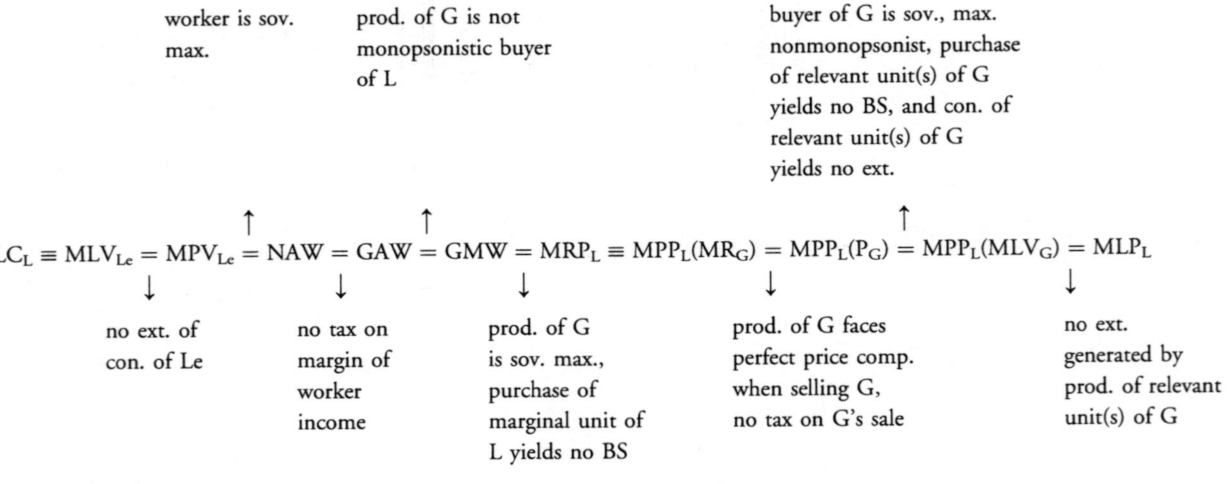
worker is sov. max.
prod. of G is not monopsonistic buyer of L
buyer of G is sov., max. nonmonopsonist, purchase of relevant unit(s) of G yields no BS, and con. of relevant unit(s) of G yields no ext.
↑
↑
↑
MLC_L ≡ MLV_Le = MPV_Le = NAW = GAW = GMW = MRP_L ≡ MPP_L(MR_G) = MPP_L(P_G) = MPP_L(MLV_G) = MLP_L
↓
↓
↓
↓
↓
no ext. of con. of Le
no tax on margin of worker income
prod. of G is sov. max., purchase of marginal unit of L yields no BS
prod. of G faces perfect price comp. when selling G, no tax on G's sale
no ext. generated by prod. of relevant unit(s) of G

Equations and Identities

equal the marginal physical product of that marginal unit of labor (MPP_L) in terms of the good G it is producing *times* the average amount of marginal revenue the marginal worker's employer obtains by selling the units of good G the marginal unit of labor produced for him.

Two points should be made about this identity. First, the MR symbol conventionally stands for the additional revenue the relevant seller obtained by selling his last unit of G, not the *average* amount of marginal revenue he obtained by selling the units of output the marginal unit of labor produced. Because those two figures will differ when $MPP_L > 1$, I should make clear that I am using MR_G to stand for the relevant average MR_G figure. (I will also use P_G to stand for the average price for which the units of output produced by the marginal unit of labor could have been sold by a perfectly discriminating seller and MLV_G to stand for the average allocative value of the units of output the marginal unit of labor produced.) I could avoid this awkwardness by assuming that the physical product of the marginal unit of each type of labor was one—that is, by defining the magnitude of that unit of labor to produce this conclusion. Second, in assuming that $MRP_L = MPP_L(MR_G)$, I am assuming that the relevant seller has to incur no additional distributive costs to sell the additional units of output the marginal unit of labor he hires produces for him. Obviously, this assumption also affects my definition of the marginal allocative product of the relevant type of labor. Since on our Pareto-perfect assumptions any such private distributive costs will equal their allocative counterparts, this assumption that there are no relevant distributive costs is not critical to any significant conclusion this analysis generates. In any event, on these symbol definitions and this assumption, $MRP_L \equiv MPP_L(MR_G)$ is an identity.

Moving to the right from this identity, the chain of equalities indicates that under the indicated conditions $MPP_L(MR_G) = MPP_L(P_G)$. This will be the case if (1) good G is produced under perfectly competitive conditions (since under those conditions $P = MR = MC$) and (2) no taxes (no sales taxes, no excise taxes, no value-added taxes, no consumption taxes) are levied on the sale of the relevant marginal units of G (since, if such taxes were levied, the before-tax price of G to its seller—which is the price for which the symbol P_G stands in the equality in question, which we are assuming equals MR_G—would be lower than the after-tax unit price its buyer paid for it—which is the price that equals MLV_G if the conditions listed in the next paragraph are fulfilled).

The next equality to the right substitutes MLV_G for P_G. This substitution will be permissible if the following conditions are fulfilled:

1. the sale of the units of G that the marginal unit of labor produced generated no buyer surplus (no BS)—if it did generate buyer surplus, $MLV_G > P_G$;
2. the relevant buyer was sovereign and maximizing—if the relevant buyer paid more for the unit of G than it was worth to him (because he overvalued it or did his math wrong), MLV_G would be less than P_G, and if the relevant buyer paid less for the good than it was actually worth to him (because he undervalued it or did his math wrong), MLV_G would be higher than P_G;
3. the relevant buyer was a nonmonopsonist—if he were a nondiscriminating monopsonist, (A) he would face an upward-sloping supply curve and would always raise the price he paid for his intramarginal units to the higher price he had to pay to elicit the supply of any additional (marginal) unit he purchased, (B) the marginal cost (MK) to him of buying the marginal unit would therefore exceed its price (since MK would include the higher payments he would choose to pay for intramarginal units when he bought the marginal unit in question), and hence (C) *ceteris paribus,* MLV_G would exceed P_G; and
4. the consumption of the units of the good the marginal unit of labor would produce generated no externalities—if it generated external costs, MLV_G would tend to be lower than P_G on that account, and if it generated external benefits, MLV_G would tend to be higher than P_G on that account.

The last equality to the right asserts that $MPP_L(MLV_G)$ equals the marginal allocative product of labor (MLP_L). MLP_L will equal the allocative value of the output the marginal unit of labor produced if the labor in question generated no externalities (or if any externalities generated by the labor in question netted out to zero). If the relevant labor generated net external costs, MLP_L would be less than $MPP_L(MLV_G)$. If the relevant labor acts generated net external benefits, MLP_L would exceed the allocative value of the output the marginal unit of labor produced.

The forgoing identities and equalities imply that in an economy in which the relevant unit-output-producing worker's employer faces perfect price competition, neither this employer nor the buyer of the output of the worker's marginal labor is a monopsonist, neither the performance of the marginal unit of labor nor the consumption of the output it produces generates any externality, no taxes are levied on the sale of the output in question, the buyer of the output in question is a sovereign maximizer, and the sale of the relevant output generates no buyer surplus, $MRP_L = MLP_L$.

We can now move to the left of MRP_L. GMW stands for the gross ("gross" because the figure is not net of the taxes the relevant employees would have to pay on the relevant wages) marginal-wage cost to the relevant employer of hiring the last unit of labor. The first equality to the left of MRP_L indicates that MRP_L equals GMW: this equality will hold if the relevant employer is a sovereign maximizer and his purchase of the relevant worker's marginal unit of labor generates no buyer surplus for him (no BS) since then he will just break even on his purchase of the relevant worker's marginal unit of labor.

GAW is the gross average wage the relevant employer pays his workers. $GMW = GAW$ (as the second equality to the left of MRP_L asserts) if the relevant employer is not a monopsonist of labor—that is, if he faces a horizontal supply curve of labor. If the relevant employer is a monopsonist of the relevant type of labor who does not engage in costless perfect price discrimination when hiring labor, $GAW < GMW$.

The third equality to the left of MRP_L asserts that the net average wage (NAW) equals GAW. This equality will obtain when there are no taxes on the margin of the income of the marginal worker. If there are such taxes, $NAW < GAW$.

The next equality to the left asserts that MPV_{Le}—the marginal private value of leisure (to its consumer—that is, to the potential worker)—equals NAW. This equality will obtain if the potential worker in question is a sovereign maximizer since such an individual will continue to labor until the net wage he receives for the last unit of labor he supplies just equals the private value to him of the unit of leisure he has to forgo to work. If the relevant worker places too high (too low) a value on his marginal unit of leisure, the (actual) MPV_{Le} (private value to the worker of the marginal unit of leisure) will be lower than (higher than) NAW.

The next equality to the left asserts that the allocative value generated by the relevant worker's consumption of his marginal unit of leisure (MLV_{Le}) equals its private value to him. This equality will obtain if the relevant worker's consumption of his marginal unit of leisure generates no (net) externalities. If his consumption of that unit generates net external costs (because he uses his leisure time to yell counterproductively at his spouse or kids or to drive around and thereby generate pollution and congestion externalities),

$MLV_{Le} < MPV_{Le}$. If, in the other direction, his consumption of the marginal unit of leisure generates net external benefits (because he spends the time being a supportive Little League coach), $MLV_{Le} > MPV_{Le}$.

Finally, we come to another definition. The marginal allocative cost of labor (MLC_L) is defined to equal the marginal allocative value of the leisure that will be forgone to create the marginal unit of labor.

In short, the equalities and identities to the left of MRP_L in our chain of relationships reveal that $MRP_L = MLC_L$ if both the relevant worker's prospective employer and the worker himself are sovereign maximizers, if the employer in question is not a monopsonistic buyer of labor, if there are no taxes on the margin of the relevant worker's income, and if the relevant worker's consumption of leisure generates no externalities. Combining the assumptions that will secure the equalities to the left of MRP_L with those that will secure the equalities to the right of MRP_L reveals that MLC_L will equal MLP_L (there will be no labor/leisure misallocation) if the following conditions are fulfilled:

1. the employer of the relevant unit-output-producing worker faces perfect price competition when selling the output the worker produces for him;
2. the relevant employer is not a monopsonistic buyer of labor, and the actors who purchase his output are not monopsonistic buyers of the goods he produces;
3. neither the marginal unit of labor in question, nor the consumption of the goods it would produce, nor the consumption of the leisure the relevant worker would have to forgo to perform the marginal unit of labor would generate any (net) externalities;
4. no taxes are levied on either the sale of the output the relevant marginal unit of labor would produce or the wages the relevant laborer would be paid for supplying the relevant marginal unit of labor;
5. the employer of the relevant worker, the customers of that employer, and the worker himself are all sovereign maximizers; and
6. neither the sale of the marginal unit of labor nor the sale of the output that the marginal unit of labor would produce generates any buyer surplus.

This list demonstrates that if all the various Pareto-optimal conditions are fulfilled there will be no misallocation between unit-output-producing market labor and leisure.

The preceding conclusion can be explained in distortion-analysis terms. I will start by focusing on the private benefits, allocative benefits, private cost, and allocative cost of the marginal unit of labor—that is, on $PB_{\Delta L}$, $LB_{\Delta L}$, $PC_{\Delta L}$, and $LC_{\Delta L}$. $PB_{\Delta L} = NAW$, and $LB_{\Delta L} = MLP_L$. The preceding analysis explained why if (1) the worker's potential employer faces perfect competition both as a seller of the product G the worker will produce and as a buyer of labor, (2) the worker's employer is a sovereign maximizer, (3) the worker's potential employer realizes no surplus when buying the worker's labor, (4) no externalities are generated by either the worker's labor or the consumption of the output it produced, (5) the buyer of the output is a sovereign maximizer, (6) the buyer of the output has no monopsonistic power as a buyer of the product the worker's labor would produce, (7) the buyer of the output secures no surplus when purchasing the product of the worker's marginal labor, and (8) no taxes are levied either on the sale of the worker's marginal product or on the worker's marginal income, $NAW = PB_{\Delta L}$ will equal $MLP_L = LB_{\Delta L}$—that is, $PB_{\Delta L}$ will not be distorted. The preceding analysis also explained why, if the relevant worker was a sovereign maximizer and his consumption of leisure generated no externalities, $MPV_{Le} = PC_{\Delta L}$ will equal $MLV_{Le} = LC_{\Delta L}$—that is, $PC_{\Delta L}$ will not be distorted. Obviously, since if all the above (Pareto-optimal) conditions are fulfilled neither $PB_{\Delta L}$ nor $PC_{\Delta L}$ will be distorted, $P\pi_{\Delta L}$ will also not be distorted. Therefore, if the worker in question is a sovereign maximizer, no misallocation will be generated by his allocation of time between unit-output-producing market labor and leisure.

Now that we have seen how the fulfillment of all the Pareto-optimal conditions will guarantee that no misallocation will be generated between unit-output-producing market labor and leisure, it should be possible to explain how an individual Pareto imperfection of each type will generate this kind of resource misallocation in an otherwise-Pareto-perfect economy. If the worker's prospective employer faces a downward-sloping demand curve and cannot costlessly engage in relevant price discrimination, the imperfection in the price competition he faces will cause misallocation between market labor and leisure by deflating (1) the private benefits the worker's employer can secure by hiring him—by reducing MRP_L below MLP_L—and derivatively (2) the private benefits the worker's marginal labor would confer on the worker (the private cost to the worker of consuming leisure) by reducing $MW = GAW = NAW = PB_{\Delta L} = LC_{\Delta Le}$ below $MLP_L = MLC_{Le}$. In an otherwise-Pareto-perfect economy, any such imperfection in the price competition the relevant worker's employer faces will therefore cause the worker to consume more leisure than is allocatively efficient by critically deflating the private benefits he can obtain by performing a marginal unit of labor and thereby critically deflating the profits he can secure by doing so (by critically deflating the private cost to him of consuming a marginal unit of leisure and thereby critically inflating the profits he can secure by consuming that leisure).

If the buyer of the output the worker's marginal unit of labor produces is a monopsonist who cannot costlessly engage in relevant price discrimination, the monopsony power of this buyer—by raising the private cost to him of purchasing the output the worker's marginal unit of labor produced above its price—will deflate the private benefits the worker's employer can secure by purchasing the worker's marginal unit of labor (by causing the price and marginal revenue he can obtain for the output that labor will produce to fall below the allocative value of that output—its value to its consumer) and, derivatively, the gross and net wage cost to the worker of consuming a marginal unit of leisure. Accordingly, at least in the circumstances described, any imperfection in the buyer competition faced by his employer's customers will also cause the worker to consume too much leisure from the perspective of economic efficiency by critically inflating the profitability of his consuming one or more marginal units of leisure (by critically deflating the profitability of his performing a marginal unit of labor).

In an otherwise-Pareto-perfect economy, any monopsony power the worker's employer possesses when purchasing labor will yield the same result in the same way if the employer cannot costlessly engage in relevant price discrimination. In particular, by inflating the private cost to the employer of hiring a marginal unit of labor, the employer's monopsony power will cause him to offer the worker a gross wage rate for his marginal unit of labor that is lower than MLP_L, thereby deflating the private cost to the worker of consuming a marginal unit of leisure and critically inflating the profitability to him of consuming one or more marginal units of leisure.

Any externality generated by the consumption of marginal units of G, the performance of marginal units of labor, or the consumption of marginal units of leisure will cause misallocation between unit-output-producing market labor and leisure in an otherwise-Pareto-perfect economy. First, in an otherwise-Pareto-perfect economy, the non-internalization of any external costs generated by the consumption of the good the relevant worker's marginal labor produces will cause such misallocation by reducing his labor's marginal allocative product below that product's value to both its consumer and the worker's employer—that is, by inflating the value of his services to his employer and hence his wage and the private cost of a marginal unit of leisure to him, thereby inducing him to consume too little leisure from the perspective of economic efficiency. Second, the non-internalization of any external benefits generated by the consumption of the good the relevant worker's marginal labor produces will have precisely the opposite effect—that is, will deflate the value of his services to his employer and hence his wage and the private cost of leisure to him and thereby induce him to consume too much leisure from the perspective of economic efficiency. Third, any external costs and benefits that are generated directly by the relevant worker's marginal labor will have the same distorting effect on the value of his services to his employer, his wage, and the private cost of leisure to him and hence the same tendency to cause him to make an economically inefficient labor/leisure choice as did respectively any external costs or benefits generated by the consumption (as opposed to the production) of the units of output his marginal labor produced. Fourth, in an otherwise-Pareto-perfect economy, the non-internalization of any external costs generated by the relevant workers' consumption of marginal units of leisure will induce him to consume too much leisure from the perspective of economic efficiency by causing the private benefits that his consumption of marginal units of leisure confers on him to exceed the net allocative benefits his consumption of these units of leisure generates, and in such an economy, the non-internalization of any external benefits generated by the relevant worker's consumption of marginal units of leisure will induce him to consume too little leisure from the perspective of economic efficiency by deflating the private benefits that his consumption of the relevant units of leisure confers on him and hence the profitability of his consuming them.

In an otherwise-Pareto-perfect economy, both a tax on the sale of the units of the good the relevant worker's marginal labor produces and a tax on the marginal income the worker earns by performing that labor will cause the worker to consume too many units of leisure from the perspective of economic efficiency by deflating his net wage and hence the private cost of the leisure to him. Sales taxes will generate this outcome by reducing the before-tax price (the marginal revenue) his employer obtains on the units of output the worker's marginal unit of labor produces below the allocative value of that output (its dollar value to its consumer, which equals its after-tax price on the applicable no-monopsony, no-human-error, and no-buyer-surplus assumptions)—that is, by deflating the worker's gross and net wage and hence the private cost of marginal units of leisure to him. A tax on the relevant worker's marginal income will generate this outcome by reducing his net wage (which equals the private cost of marginal units of leisure to him) below his gross wage (which on our otherwise-Pareto-perfect assumption equals both the private benefits his marginal services confer on his employer and the allocative benefits these services generate [the marginal allocative product of his labor]).

Buyer surplus can be generated by two transactions that are relevant to the allocative efficiency of a worker's marginal choice between performing market labor and consuming leisure: the sale of the output his marginal labor will produce and the purchase of his labor by his employer. In an otherwise-Pareto-perfect economy, any buyer surplus generated by either of these transactions will cause the worker to consume too much leisure from the perspective of allocative efficiency by deflating the private cost to him (the net wage he must forgo) to consume marginal units of leisure. Any buyer surplus generated by the sale of the output the worker's marginal units of labor produces will have this effect because it will deflate the private benefits the worker's marginal labor confers on his employer and hence the gross wage the employer pays him. Any buyer surplus generated by the employer's purchase of the marginal unit of labor of the relevant worker will deflate the private benefits the labor confers on the worker directly by reducing these benefits below the private benefits his marginal unit of labor confers on his employer, which on our otherwise-Pareto-perfect assumption equal the marginal allocative product of the worker's labor.

Human error (caused by nonsovereignty or nonmaximization) can affect all three choices with which this analysis is concerned and, in an otherwise-Pareto-perfect economy, will cause misallocation between the performance of market labor and the consumption of leisure regardless of the choice it affects. Thus, if the buyer of the output that the relevant worker's marginal labor produces pays more for it than it is really worth to him, this error will inflate the private benefits that the worker's marginal labor confers on his employer. Concomitantly, this error will inflate the gross and net wage the worker is paid and the private cost to him of consuming leisure, thereby causing him to consume too little leisure from the perspective of allocative efficiency. If the potential buyer of the output in question offers to pay less for it than it would really be worth to him without believing that he would realize buyer surplus on his purchase at the price he was offering,[22] this error will deflate the private benefits the worker's marginal labor confers on his employer and concomitantly the private cost to the worker of consuming leisure, thereby causing him to consume too much leisure from the perspective of allocative efficiency. If the worker's employer pays the worker more for his marginal labor than that labor is really worth to his employer, this error will cause the worker to consume too little leisure by inflating the gross and net wage the worker can earn by supplying his marginal unit of labor and hence the private cost to the worker of consuming one or more marginal units of leisure. If the worker's employer offers to pay the worker less than the worker's services are worth to the employer without realizing that he would profit from the transaction in which he was proposing to engage, this error will cause the worker to consume too much leisure from the perspective of economic efficiency in an otherwise-Pareto-perfect economy by deflating the private benefits the worker can obtain (the net wage) by supplying a marginal unit of his labor and concomitantly the private cost to him of one or more marginal units of leisure. Finally, in an otherwise-Pareto-perfect economy (in which the actual profits the worker would obtain by consuming a marginal unit of leisure would be undistorted), if the worker consumes more (less) leisure than is actually in his interest, this error will lead him to generate labor/leisure misallocation by consuming more (less) leisure than was allocatively efficient for him to consume.

I will now delineate a worst-case example that illustrates the way in which the various possible individual Pareto imperfections that would cause misallocation between unit-output-producing market labor and leisure on their own could interact to cause such misallocation. The case is a worst case in that all the Pareto imperfections it includes cut in the same direction—in particular, would tend on their own to cause the worker in question to consume too much leisure from the perspective of allocative efficiency. I will begin at the equality farthest to the right in the series of equalities and identities that appears at the beginning of this subsection and move progressively to the left.

To ease the exposition, I will assume that MPP_L is 1. Assume in addition that $MLP_L = \$9$. The first Pareto imperfection to be considered is the one that can cause $MPP_L(MLV_G)$ to diverge from MLP_L. Assume that the last unit of labor the relevant worker supplies generates \$.50 in external benefits, thereby deflating the private benefits that the last unit of labor confers on the worker's employer and hence on the worker. On this assumption, $MPP_L(MLV_G) = MLV_G$ (given our assumption that $MPP_L = 1$) is $\$8.50 < \$9 - MLP_L$—that is, the dollar value that the marginal physical product of labor generates for its consumer is \$8.50.

Consider next the various Pareto imperfections that can cause P_G to be lower than MLV_G and therefore $MPP_L(P_G)$ to be lower than $MPP_L(MLV_G)$. Assume that the consumption of the output the marginal unit of labor would produce will generate \$.25 in external benefits. This externality (which will also deflate the private benefits the worker's marginal unit of labor confers on his employer and derivatively on him) implies that the consumer of the output the relevant marginal unit of labor would produce would just break even by purchasing it if it cost him \$8.25—that \$8.25 is the highest price the relevant buyer could pay for this unit without incurring a loss if the purchase would not alter the cost to him of other units of the good consumed that he would purchase in any event. Assume further that the consumer undervalues the unit of output in question by \$.15 (believes that it is worth \$8.10 to him). This assumption implies that the highest price he will pay for this unit is \$8.10. Assume, in addition, that the consumer overestimates the cost to him of purchasing the unit by \$.20: this implies that the highest price he will be willing to pay for this unit is \$7.90. On top of this, assume that the relevant buyer is a monopsonist and correctly perceives that, if he pays a price that he believes to be \$7.50 for the unit in question, his decision to do so will raise the cost to him of the intramarginal units of the relevant product he would purchase in any event by \$.40. On these assumptions, the relevant buyer will believe that if he pays what he thinks is a price of \$7.50 for that unit he will just break even on the transaction in question (when in fact he would be making a \$.35 profit on the deal). Finally, assume that the buyer correctly believes that he can obtain \$.12 in buyer surplus by purchasing the unit. On this last assumption, the buyer will offer a price of \$7.38 for the unit of output that the relevant worker's marginal unit of labor would produce—a price that is \$.87 below the value of that unit of output to the buyer, a price that would further deflate the private benefits the worker's marginal unit of labor would confer on his employer and derivatively on him. On these assumptions, then, although $MLP_L = \$9$, $MPP_L(MLV_G) = \$8.25$, and $MPP_L(P_G) = \$7.38$.

I turn now to the Pareto imperfections that can cause MR_G to be lower than P_G and concomitantly MRP_L to be lower than $MPP_L(P_G)$. Assume initially that a sales tax, excise tax, value-added tax, or consumption tax is levied on the sale of the workers' marginal physical product. The price of \$7.38 is the after-tax price the relevant buyer will offer. The worker's employer will receive not that price but the pre-tax price of the unit in question—say, \$7.10 if the tax on its sale or consumption is \$.28. Assume next that the worker's employer faces a downward-sloping demand curve for G and does not find it profitable to maintain his prices on his intramarginal units of G while reducing his price for the marginal unit of G that the worker's last unit of labor produces. In this case, $MR_G <$ (before-tax) P_G—say, $MR_G = \$6$ while (before-tax) $P_G = \$7.10$. On these assumptions, then, $MPP_L(MR_G) = \$6 < MPP_L(P_G) = \$7.38$.

The next set of imperfections that need to be examined are those that can cause GMW to be lower than $MRP_L \equiv MPP_L(MR_G) = \$6$ on our assumptions. If the worker's employer underestimates the private benefits the worker's marginal unit of labor will confer on him by \$.13 and overestimates by \$.08 the cost to him of paying the worker \$5.79, the greatest amount of additional wage costs the employer will believe he can incur to secure the worker's marginal unit of labor and break even on the transaction will be \$5.79. If, in addition, the employer believes he can secure \$.20 in surplus when purchasing the relevant worker's marginal unit of labor, he will be willing to incur only \$5.59 in wage costs to secure the worker's marginal unit of labor. On these assumptions, then, $GMW = \$5.59 < MRP_L = \$6$.

Moreover, if the worker's employer is a nondiscriminating monopsonistic buyer of labor, he may have to incur \$.39 in extra labor costs on the intramarginal units of labor he buys to pay the worker \$5.20 for his marginal unit of labor. If so, the gross (before-tax) average wage the worker will be offered for his marginal unit of labor will be \$5.20—that is, $GAW = \$5.20 < GMW = \$5.59$.

The next Pareto imperfection that can cause misallocation between the performance of unit-output-producing market labor and the consumption of leisure is a tax on the worker's marginal income. If the worker must pay taxes on the margin of income (say, must pay 20 percent of his marginal income to the government), his net wage for his marginal unit of labor will be only 80 percent of \$5.20—that is, $NAW = \$4.16 < GAW = \$5.20$.

The penultimate set of Pareto imperfections that should be considered in the current context are those that may cause MPV_{Le} to be lower than NAW. Basically, MPV_{Le} will be lower than NAW either if the worker overestimates NAW or if he acts as if MPV_{Le} is higher than it actually is. Thus, if the worker overestimates by \$.16 the taxes he will have to pay on the income he can earn by performing a marginal unit of labor (believes that those taxes will be \$1.20 rather than \$1.04 and that his NAW will be \$4 rather than \$4.16), the fact that he supplied his marginal unit of labor will imply that he believed that MPV_{Le} was \$4 if his supply decision was not erroneous. If, in addition, the worker overvalued the last unit of leisure he forwent by \$.25, the private value of that unit to him will have been \$3.75 rather than \$4. Hence, on the assumptions just delineated, $MPV_{Le} = \$3.75 < NAW = \$4.16$.

Finally, we must take account of the Pareto imperfection that can cause MLV_{Le} to diverge from MPV_{Le}. Assume that the relevant worker's consumption of the unit of leisure he forwent to perform his last unit of labor would have generated \$.17 in external costs. On this and all the preceding Pareto-imperfection assumptions the current example makes, $MLV_{Le} \equiv MLC_L = \$3.58 < MPV_{Le} = \$3.75$.

Hence, if the economy contained all the Pareto imperfections I just assumed were extant, $MLC_L = \$3.58$ would be substantially below $MLP_L = \$9$ (concomitantly, $MLV_{Le} = \$3.58$ would be substantially below $MLC_{Le} = MLP_L = \$9$) in equilibrium, and too little labor would be performed (too much leisure would be consumed) from the perspective of economic efficiency if the worker in question made the labor/leisure choice he perceived to be in his interest. The combination of this example's specific assumptions and our initial general assumptions that the quantity of labor supplied can be varied by infinitesimally small amounts and that the relevant MPP_L, MLV_G, and MLV_{Le} curves are downward sloping and continuous implies that in this case allocative efficiency would be increased by infinitesimally less than ($\$5.42 = \$9 - \$3.58 = MLP_L - MLC_L = MLC_{Le} - MLV_{Le}$) if an additional unit of labor were performed. Of course, the total amount of misallocation the relevant worker's choices between performing market labor and consuming leisure will have generated in this situation will be higher than \$5.42 if (as is usually the case) the allocatively efficient number of units of labor for the relevant worker to supply exceeds the number he did supply by more than one unit.

As already indicated, the preceding example describes a worst-case scenario in which each of the extant Pareto imperfections would individually cause too little unit-output-producing labor to be performed in an otherwise-Pareto-perfect economy. I will now present a best-case scenario in which the extant Pareto imperfections not only cut in different directions but, taken as a group, perfectly counteract each other. Although the allocatively efficient amount of unit-output-producing market labor could be performed in a relevantly-Pareto-imperfect economy either because, taken together, the Pareto imperfections did not distort the profits the relevant worker could obtain by supplying the marginal unit of labor that would bring the total amount of labor he supplied to the allocatively efficient level or because any distortion they did generate in the profits he could obtain by supplying the relevant unit of labor was perfectly offset by errors the relevant worker made in calculating those profits, the following example focuses on the former, zero-aggregate-distortion possibility.

Fortunately, the broad structure of the example I am seeking to provide is clear. It is created by the following two sets of facts:

1. the profits a unit-output-producing worker can realize by supplying a marginal unit of labor will always be deflated by any external benefits that the performance of his marginal unit of labor generates, any external benefits generated by the consumption of the output that his marginal unit of labor will produce, any external costs that are generated by his consumption of a marginal unit of leisure, any monopsony power enjoyed either by the consumers of the output his marginal unit of labor produces or by his employer as a buyer of the kind of labor the relevant worker supplies, any taxes levied on the sale of the output the relevant worker's marginal unit of labor produces, any taxes levied on the marginal income of the worker in question, any tendency of the potential consumers of the output the relevant worker's marginal unit of labor produces to undervalue these units or to make some kind of mathematical error that results in their offering a lower price than they could profitably offer to secure the product, any tendency of the relevant worker's potential employer to undervalue his marginal unit of labor or for some other reason to mistakenly offer less for his marginal services than would be in the employer's interest to offer, and any imperfection in the price competition that the relevant worker's potential employer would face when selling the units of output the relevant worker's marginal unit of labor would produce;[23] and
2. the profits a unit-output-producing worker can realize by supplying a marginal unit of labor will always be inflated by the non-internalization of any external costs generated by his marginal production efforts or the consumption of the units of output his marginal labor produces, by the non-internalization of any external benefits generated by his consumption of the marginal unit of leisure, and by any nonsovereignty or nonmaximization of the consumers of the output his marginal labor produces that results in their incurring more costs to secure these units (for example, paying higher prices for these units) than is in their interest.

I will now illustrate the possibility that a series of Pareto imperfections, each of which would individually distort the profits a worker can realize by consuming a marginal unit of leisure rather than supplying a marginal unit of unit-output-producing labor, can perfectly counteract each other in the sense of yielding a zero aggregate distortion in the profits that such a choice will yield. I start with an overview of the example.

The example in question has four defining features. First, some Pareto-optimal conditions are fulfilled (there are no monopsony, no buyer surplus, and no human errors). Second, the example assumes that the economy contains two types of Pareto imperfections—taxes on the margin of income and imperfections in the price competition faced by the worker's employer when selling the output that the worker's marginal labor produces—that would individually deflate the profits the worker can realize by performing a marginal unit of labor in an otherwise-Pareto-perfect economy. Third, the example assumes that the economy contains three types of externalities—external costs generated directly by the performance of the marginal unit of labor, external costs generated by the consumption of the goods the marginal unit of labor produces, and external benefits generated by the worker's consumption of marginal units of leisure—that would individually inflate the profits the worker can realize by performing a marginal unit of labor. And fourth, the example assumes that, taken together, the deflating and inflating imperfections just listed perfectly counteract each other.

I now will delineate the example itself. It assumes that

1. $MLP_L = \$9$;
2. $MPP_L(MLV_G) = \$10$ (because the last unit of labor generates \$1 in external costs of production: given those externalities, MLP_L will equal \$9 only if the consumption of the output that the last unit of labor produced generated \$10 in net allocative benefits);
3. $MPP_L(P_G) = \$9.20$ (because the consumption of the output produced by the last unit of labor generates \$.80 in external benefits: if $MPP_L(MLV_G)$ is \$10 and \$.80 of the allocative value of the output the marginal unit of labor produced reflected benefits its consumption conferred on nonconsumers, the output's consumers must have obtained \$9.20 from consuming it, and if those consumers were sovereign, maximizing nonmonopsonists who secured no buyer surplus on their purchases of the units of the good in question, \$9.20 will equal the number of units *times* the price of the good);
4. $MPP_L(MR_G) = \$8$ (because the consumers of the output produced by the last unit of labor supplied must pay \$.20 in taxes to purchase the output in question and the worker's imperfectly competitive employer accepts \$1 less on his intramarginal units when he reduces his price to sell the extra output produced by the last unit of labor);

5. $GAW = GMW = MPP_L(MR_G) = \$8$ (because the Pareto-optimal conditions whose fulfillment is a sufficient condition for these equalities are satisfied);
6. $NAW = \$7$ (because the worker must pay \$1 in taxes on the gross income he is paid for his marginal unit of labor);
7. $MPV_{Le} = NAW = \$7$ (because the worker is a sovereign maximizer); and
8. $MLV_{Le} \equiv MLC_L = \$9 = MLP_L$ (because the consumption of the unit of leisure the worker would have to forgo to supply a marginal unit of labor would generate \$2 in external benefits).

On these assumptions, then, taken together the three types of externalities that would individually tend to induce a unit-output-producing worker to perform too much labor from the perspective of allocative efficiency would perfectly counteract the two types of Pareto imperfections—imperfections in price competition and (sales and earned-income) taxes on the margin of income—that would individually tend to induce a unit-output-producing worker to perform too little labor from the perspective of allocative efficiency: on the facts assumed, no misallocation between the performance of unit-output-producing market labor and the consumption of leisure would be generated—$MLC_L = \$9 = MLP_L$.

Four closing comments. First, the last example can be used to illustrate the critical point made by The General Theory of Second Best. On its assumptions, a policy of removing all taxes on the margin of income and all imperfections in price competition would create rather than eliminate misallocation between the performance of unit-output-producing market labor and the consumption of leisure because, in relation to this type of allocative choice, the original imperfections of these types perfectly counteracted the distorting impact of the externalities that (I am assuming) would remain in the system after the taxes on the margin of income and price-competition imperfections were removed. Similarly, on its assumptions, a policy that would internalize all externalities would create rather than eliminate misallocation between the performance of unit-output-producing market labor and the consumption of leisure because, in relation to this type of allocative choice, the original externalities perfectly counteracted the taxes on the margin of income and the imperfections in price competition that would remain in the system if the externalities were eliminated.

Second, a dose of reality. At least in my judgment, in our current economy, too much time is devoted to leisure consumption and not enough to unit-output-producing market labor from the perspective of economic efficiency. This conclusion reflects my reasonably-well-informed view that the other imperfections that are present in the system do not fully offset and may well exacerbate the tendency of taxes on the margin of monetary income and imperfections in price competition to inflate the profitability to workers of substituting leisure for unit-output-producing market labor.

Third, those economists who claim that taxes on the margin of income will not cause misallocation between the performance of unit-output-producing market labor and the consumption of leisure if the supply curve of the relevant type of labor is vertical over the relevant range are incorrect (at least if the relevant verticality does not reflect a discontinuity in the relevant marginal private and allocative value of leisure curves or the relevant marginal revenue product and marginal allocative product of labor curves). In the absence of relevant discontinuities, the fact that the relevant supply curve of labor is vertical (perfectly inelastic) will reflect the fact that the income effect of a decrease in the net wage generated by a tax on the margin of income—the effect such a decrease would have by reducing the worker's income even if it did not affect his choice by altering the relative prices of leisure and the goods that wages could be used to purchase—is not only positive but perfectly offsets the negative substitution effect of a decrease in the net wage of labor on the quantity of labor supplied—the effect that the decrease in the net wage would have on the quantity of labor supplied even if it did not affect the relevant worker's income by reducing the price of leisure relative to the prices of the goods that wages could be used to purchase. This reality supports my critique because, unlike the substitution effect of the tax (which is relevant to the economic efficiency of the tax's impact on labor/leisure misallocation), the income effect is not relevant to the tax's impact on labor/leisure misallocation. In an otherwise-Pareto-perfect economy, a tax on the margin of income will always cause labor/leisure misallocation (on the continuity and labor-quantity-variability assumptions I am making): if the tax does not alter the quantity of labor supplied, it will still cause labor/leisure misallocation by increasing the quantity of labor whose supply is allocatively efficient (since the fact that the income effect of the tax on the quantity of labor supplied is positive means that, holding constant the relative prices of leisure and the goods or services that can be purchased with wages, the workers in question will find it profitable to supply more labor when their real income is reduced by a tax on their marginal income).

Fourth, a possible response to the existing Pareto imperfections that may reduce the misallocation generated by choices between performing unit-output-producing market labor and consuming leisure: if income taxes, sales taxes, and imperfections in price competition cannot be or will not be eliminated, one might be able to reduce such misallocation by making the sales-tax rate applied to the sale of a good increase with the extent to which the good is a complement of leisure. Of course, even if such a policy would reduce labor/leisure misallocation and could be devised and implemented without generating any allocative transaction costs, it might be misallocative: the amount of misallocation it would generate by inducing buyers to consume leisure and its complements in economically inefficient proportions and by inducing consumers to purchase goods that are sometimes complements of leisure in economically inefficient quantities when they are not functioning as complements of leisure may exceed the amount by which it would reduce the relevant labor/leisure misallocation.

SECTION 2. THE VOCABULARY, SYMBOLS, THEORETICAL BASIS FOR, AND BASIC OUTLINE OF THE DISTORTION-ANALYSIS APPROACH TO ECONOMIC-EFFICIENCY ASSESSMENT

This subsection of Chapter 3 is divided into three parts. The first elaborates on the vocabulary of distortion analysis and delineates the symbols that stand for its conceptual components. The second discusses the key relationships on which the distortion-analysis approach is based. And the third outlines the distortion-analysis approach to economic-efficiency assessment.

The Vocabulary and Symbols of Distortion Analysis

In the distortion-analysis terminology that I have developed, the private benefits that a choice confers on the chooser (PB), the private cost that a choice imposes on a chooser (PC), and the profits a choice yields a chooser ($P\pi$) are said to be distorted when they differ from their allocative counterparts—the allocative benefits they generate (LB), the allocative costs they generate (LC), and their allocative efficiency (LE). More specifically, a PB, PC, or $P\pi$ figure is said to be inflated when it exceeds its allocative counterpart and deflated when it is lower than its allocative counterpart.

The distortion analyses that I execute distinguish two basic types of distortions: (1) the aggregate distortion in some figure (ΣD)—the net distortion in the indicated private figure generated by all the relevant Pareto imperfections in the economy acting in concert—and (2) seven individual-Pareto-imperfection-generated distortions (one for each type of Pareto imperfection)—the distortion that would be created by each particular type of Pareto imperfection if no other type of Pareto imperfection were present in the system (the monopoly distortion [MD], the monopsony distortion [ND], the externality distortion [XD], the tax on the margin of income distortion [TD], the distortion caused by various choosers' nonsovereignty [NSD], the distortion caused by various choosers' nonmaximization [NMD], and the buyer-surplus distortion [BSD]). All distortions in the text that follows will be symbolized as $_{\ldots}D(P_{\ldots})_{\Delta\ldots}$. In this notation, (1) the one or two letters that appear instead of the first ellipsis before the D that precedes the parenthesis in any distortion symbol indicate whether the distortion in question is an aggregate distortion or, if it is not, the particular individual-Pareto-imperfection-generated type of distortion being referred to, (2) the nonsubscript letter that appears instead of the second ellipsis, which follows the P (for private) in the parentheses that follow the first two or three letters, indicates whether the private figure whose distortion the symbol references is a private-benefit, private-cost, or private-profit figure, and (3) the letters that appear instead of the third ellipsis, which is in a subscript to the letters inside the parentheses, indicate the type of resource use that has generated the benefits, cost, or profits to whose possible distortion the symbol in question refers—for example, ΔUO stands for a decision to produce a marginal unit of output, ΔQV for one to create a marginal QV investment, and ΔPPR for one to execute a marginal PPR project. The presence of the symbol Δ before UO, QV, or PPR in a subscript indicates that the choice in question was to produce a marginal in the sense of last (least profitable but not unprofitable) unit of output of some good, to create and use a last QV investment in some area of product-space, or to execute and use a last PPR project in some area of product-space. When it is relevant to indicate the area of product-space in which the last resource use in question took place, that area is indicated by an uppercase letter at the end of the subscript in question.

Some examples may be helpful. In my system, $\Sigma D(PB_{\Delta UOX})$ stands for the aggregate distortion (the distortion generated by the interaction of all relevant Pareto imperfections in the system) in the private benefits the producer of a last unit of product X obtained by producing that unit; $MD(PC_{\Delta QVX})$ stands for the distortion that imperfections in seller competition would generate in an otherwise-Pareto-perfect economy (the monopoly distortion) in the private cost the investor who created the last QV investment to be introduced into area of product-space X incurred to do so; and $XD(P\pi_{\Delta PPRX})$ stands for the distortion that the extant externalities would generate in an otherwise-Pareto-perfect economy (the externality distortion) in the profits that the investor who executed the last PPR project to be executed that was designed to reduce the cost of producing product X earned by doing so.

Distortion analysis uses two other sets of terms worth noting at this juncture. First, distortion analysis distinguishes additive cases from nonadditive cases. The former are cases in which the relevant ΣD can be expressed as a sum of the individual-Pareto-imperfection-generated distortions—that is, cases in which ΣD = MD + XD + ... The latter are cases in which ΣD does not equal the sum of the individual-Pareto-imperfection-generated distortions—indeed, in which, in general, the individual-Pareto-imperfection-generated distortions do not even appear as arguments in the relevant aggregate-distortion formula.

Second, in additive cases, distortion analysis distinguishes between offsetting and compounding Pareto imperfections or distortions. In particular, in additive cases, imperfections or distortions are said to be compounding when they have the same sign and offsetting when they have the opposite sign.

It will usually be far easier to predict the effect of a given policy on a particular type of misallocation in additive than in nonadditive cases because in additive cases one can make the relevant predictions without measuring any relevant $\Sigma D(P\pi_{\Delta\ldots})$—namely, by focusing exclusively on the relative size and correlation between the eliminable distortions and the remaining distortions. For this reason, it is unfortunate that no or virtually no resource-use choices present additive as opposed to nonadditive cases.

The Relationships from Which the Distortion-Analysis Approach to Economic-Efficiency Assessment Derives

SOME DEFINITIONS AND BACKGROUND ISSUES

This subsection delineates the relationships on which distortion analysis builds and explains why, at a minimum, they create the possibility that it may be third-best allocatively efficient to base economic-efficiency assessments on data on particular types of distortions. However, before proceeding with these tasks, it will be helpful to (1) define three concepts the relevant analyses employ, (2) delineate an ambiguity in a component of one of these concepts—the notion of marginality—that reflects a reality that militates against the third-best allocative efficiency of the distortion-analysis approach, (3) explain why this reality probably does not significantly reduce the TBLE of the distortion-analysis approach even if it does reduce the accuracy or cost-effectiveness of the assessments that approach makes of the impact of any private choice or public policy on the total misallocation generated by all economically inefficient decisions to use resources in any particular way, and (4) call attention to an obvious but often ignored fact about the total amount of economic inefficiency in any economy that affects the focus of distortion analysis.

I start with the three definitions. In the text that follows, the *marginal* resource use of any type is defined to be the least profitable but not unprofitable resource use of that type that occurred or would occur under specified conditions. Second, the aggregate distortion in the profits yielded by any such marginal resource use (or indeed by any nonmarginal resource use) is defined to equal the difference between the (supernormal) profits yielded by that resource use and its impact on economic efficiency—a difference generated by the interaction of all the Pareto imperfections in the system that would individually distort the profits the resource use in question yielded. Third, the aggregate *percentage* distortion in the profits yielded by any marginal resource use is defined to equal the ratio of the aggregate distortion in the profits yielded by that resource use to its allocative cost (that is, the allocative value that the resources it consumed would have generated in their alternative use—in conventional terms, to the social opportunity cost of the resources being devoted to the marginal use in question). This aggregate percentage distortion will be symbolized as $\Sigma D(P\pi_{\Delta\ldots})/LC_{\Delta\ldots}$ where the deltas in the subscripts indicate that the resource use to which the relevant information relates is a marginal resource use in the above sense and the ellipses in the subscripts indicate that the marginal resource use in question could be of any type (that for the relevant purpose one need not specify whether it is UO-producing, QV-investment-creating, PPR-executing, or some other sort of resource use such as adopting an accident-loss-rendering and/or pollution-loss-reducing production process).

The ambiguity to which I earlier referred relates to the way in which economists use the word *marginal.* Sometimes, economists use this word in the way I have just defined it: as a reference to the least profitable but not unprofitable (in this sense, last) resource use of a particular type. But sometimes, they use the word *marginal* in the mathematical sense of being infinitesimally small. The ambiguity arises because in the real world the least profitable but not unprofitable resource use of any type may not be infinitesimally small. Thus, although the last decision to increase the unit output of some product might involve the allocation of a very small (if not infinitesimally small) amount of resources to the production of that product (enough additional resources to increase its output by one unit), the last decision to increase the amount of resources devoted to QV-investment creation or PPR execution in any area of product-space might be quantitatively lumpy as opposed to infinitesimally small (because of economies of scale in the use of resources for these purposes over the relevant range). As I have already indicated, in the text that follows, I will be using the word *marginal* in the sense of last or least profitable but not unprofitable and not in the mathematical sense of infinitesimally small. Resource uses that are marginal in my sense may or may not be marginal in the mathematical sense.

I now need to point out the significance of this definition for the accuracy of distortion-analysis assessments of the economic efficiency of (1) the marginal (in the sense of last) resource use of any type and (2) the total amount of economic inefficiency generated by all economically inefficient resource uses of the type in question. If all last resource uses of any type were infinitesimally small and all those who realize the profits or losses generated by last resource uses were sovereign maximizers, the last resource use of any type would just break even ($P\pi_{\Delta\ldots} = 0$), and the identity $\Sigma D(P\pi_{\ldots}) \equiv P\pi_{\ldots} - LE_{\ldots}$ would imply that $LE_{\Delta\ldots} = -\Sigma D(P\pi_{\Delta\ldots})$—that is, one could infer the amount by which the last resource use of any type increased or decreased economic efficiency from the aggregate distortion in the profits it yielded. Indeed, as I will argue (admittedly more contestably), if the above conditions were fulfilled, it would also be TBLE to infer the total amount of economic inefficiency generated by the economically inefficient resource uses of any particular type from the aggregate percentage distortion in the profits yielded by the marginal use of that type. However, even if the owners of all last resource uses were sovereign maximizers and made the decision to execute the last resource use in question, $LE_{\Delta\ldots}$ would usually not equal $(-\Sigma D[P\pi_{\Delta\ldots}])$ if the last resource use was lumpy as opposed to being infinitesimally small. Since the profits yielded by the $(n+1)$th lumpy resource use of a given kind will normally be significantly lower than the profits yielded by the nth resource use of that kind, the last resource use of any lumpy kind will usually yield positive (supernormal) profits (whose existence will be compatible with the next resource use of the kind in question's generating a loss [that is, subnormal profits]). Obviously, if $P\pi_{\Delta\ldots} > 0$, the identity $\Sigma D(P\pi_{\Delta\ldots}) \equiv P\pi_{\Delta\ldots} - LE_{\Delta\ldots}$ will not imply that $LE_{\Delta\ldots} = -\Sigma D(P\pi_{\Delta\ldots})$ but instead will imply that $LE_{\Delta\ldots} = P\pi_{\Delta\ldots} - \Sigma D(P\pi_{\Delta\ldots}) > -\Sigma D(P\pi_{\Delta\ldots})$. Thus, if $P\pi_{\Delta\ldots} > \Sigma D(P\pi_{\Delta\ldots}) > 0$, the last resource use of the type in question will be economically efficient even though its profit yield was inflated, and if the lumpiness of resource uses of the type in question would cause the private profitability and economic efficiency of the first extramarginal resource use of the type in question to be significantly lower than its counterpart for the marginal use of the relevant kind, the fact that the profit yield of that marginal use was deflated will not guarantee that additional resource uses of the relevant kind would be economically efficient even though it would imply that the marginal use did increase economic efficiency by a significant amount. Obviously, this reality implies that, when marginal resource uses are lumpy, one needs to know both $P\pi_{\Delta\ldots}$ and $\Sigma D(P\pi_{\Delta\ldots})$ to assess accurately the economic efficiency of the relevant last resource use and (as we shall see) the total amount of economic inefficiency caused by all economically inefficient resource uses of the relevant type.

However, although it will not be possible to generate as accurate estimates of the economic efficiency of last resource uses of any type or the total amount of economic inefficiency generated by the economically inefficient resource uses of any type from percentage-profit-distortion data when the last resource uses in question are lumpy as when they are infinitesimally small, this fact does not significantly undermine the case for the third-best allocative efficiency of an appropriately adjusted distortion-analysis approach to assessing the allocative efficiency of any private choice or public policy. Unfortunately, you will not be in a position to evaluate my argument for this conclusion until I describe the relationships on which the distortion-analysis approach I am recommending builds and explain why I think those relationships favor the third-best allocative efficiency of that approach.

At this juncture, I will confine myself to two observations. First, in addition to relevant distortion data, the distortion-analysis approach I am recommending can take account of the profits yielded by the marginal (last) resource uses on which it focuses and the amounts by which the profits yielded by successive, extramarginal (intramarginal) resource uses of each relevant type would be lower (higher) than the profits yielded by the marginal resource use of that type. Second, the fact that the profits some such marginal uses generate are not zero is compatible with the existence of a strong, positive correlation between (1) the magnitude of the positive distortion in the profits yielded by any marginal resource use and both (2) the probability that the marginal resource use in question was allocatively inefficient and (3) the probable amount by which it reduced economic efficiency. I will return to this issue at the end of this subsection.

The final preliminary point was presaged by the preceding sentence's focus on marginal resource uses whose profit yield was inflated rather than on all marginal resource uses: the total amount of economic inefficiency in an economy equals either the amount of misallocation caused because, from the perspective of economic efficiency, too many resources are allocated to some types and/or subtypes of uses or the amount of misallocation caused because, from the perspective of economic efficiency, too few resources are allocated to certain types and/or subtypes of uses. The total amount of economic inefficiency in an economy does *not* equal the sum of these two amounts—that is, does *not* equal the amount of misallocation caused because too many resources are allocated to some uses *plus* the amount caused because too few resources are allocated to some uses. To equate total misallocation with this sum would be to engage in double-counting. If too many resources are allocated to some uses, too few must be allocated to other uses: the total misallocation equals either the misallocation caused by the underallocation of resources to those uses to which too few resources were devoted or the misallocation caused by the overallocation of resources to those uses to which too many resources were devoted. Those two amounts of misallocation not only are equal but are the other sides of the same coin. Hence, if we ignore the possibility that the marginal resource uses in question may not have been in the interest of their respective owners, distortion analysis must focus on either those resource uses whose marginal exemplars' profit yields were inflated or those resource uses whose marginal exemplars' profit yields were deflated. I should say that, although the preceding point should be obvious, it appears not to be: some estimates of the so-called welfare costs of monopoly assume that the misallocation monopoly causes equals the sum of the economic inefficiency monopoly generates by causing too many resources to be devoted to certain uses *plus* the economic inefficiency it generates by causing too few resources to be devoted to other uses.

THE RELATIONSHIPS ON WHICH DISTORTION ANALYSIS BUILDS

In any developed economy, a huge number of resource uses of different kinds will be marginal or last in the sense of being the least profitable but not unprofitable use of the relevant kind. Thus, there will be last allocations of resources to the production of units of each product the economy produces, last allocations of resources to the creation of QV investments in each (arbitrarily designated) area of product-space it is convenient to specify, and last allocations of resources to the execution of PPR projects that relate to the production processes used to produce the products in each of the various areas of product-space in question. If the relevant data could be obtained, one could generate a distribution of the aggregate percentage distortions in the profits yielded by all of the last resource uses in the economy or two separate distribution of the aggregate percentage distortions in the profits yielded by the economy's last resource uses whose profit yields were respectively (1) not inflated and (2) not deflated. Each of these latter two distributions would have an absolute weighted-average value and an absolute weighted-average deviation from that weighted average where the weights assigned to each data point are proportional to the allocative cost of the resource use to which it refers.

The distortion-analysis approach to allocative-efficiency assessment builds on the following four relationships:

1. *ceteris paribus,* the total amount of misallocation in an economy will increase with the absolute weighted-average value of the items in the distribution of non-negative percentage distortions in the profits yielded by those of the economy's marginal resource uses whose profit yields were not deflated where the weights are assigned as previously stated to the various marginal-resource-use percentage-profit-distortion figures;
2. *ceteris paribus,* the amount by which a given reduction (increase) in the weighted-average value of the above distribution will decrease (increase) the total amount of economic inefficiency in the economy will increase with the pre-choice or pre-policy weighted-average magnitude in question;
3. *ceteris paribus,* the total amount of misallocation in an economy will increase with the weighted-average absolute deviation of the distribution of percentage distortions in the profits yielded by those of the economy's marginal resource uses whose profits were inflated (deflated), where the weights are assigned as previously stated; and
4. controlling for the above weighted-average deviation, the total amount of misallocation in an economy will increase with the weighted-average squared deviation of the indicated percentage-profit-distortion distribution.

Obviously, these four relationships support the distortion-analysis approach to allocative-efficiency assessment because they imply that, *ceteris paribus,* one will be able to predict the impact of a private choice or public policy on economic efficiency from its impact on the weighted-average magnitude of the above marginal-resource-use non-negative-percentage-profit-distortion distribution, the pre-choice or pre-policy absolute magnitude of that weighted average, and the relevant private choice's or public policy's impact on the weighted-average absolute and weighted-average squared deviation of that distribution.

As the preceding paragraph suggests, one could analyze the allocative efficiency of a particular public policy or private choice by focusing on (1) the relevant pre-policy or pre-choice attributes of the distribution of non-negative aggregate percentage profit distortions of the marginal resource uses of *all types* whose profitability was inflated (or deflated) and (2) the impact of the policy or choice in question on those attributes. However, I suspect that it will be more practicable to proceed by focusing initially on the counterpart information for the non-negative segments of the aggregate-percentage-profit-distortion distributions for *each individual type* of resource use in the economy and then deriving a conclusion about the overall economic efficiency of the policy or choice from the separate conclusions the initial analysis generated about its impact on the amount of misallocation generated by the allocatively inefficient resource uses of these output types.

Diagram I illustrates the relationships from which the distortion-analysis approach to allocative-efficiency assessment derives. Diagram I's vertical axis measures dollars, and its horizontal axis measures in dollars the total allocative cost of devoting the resources allocated to the type of resource use in question to that use ($TLC_{R/\ldots}$). Ostensibly (see below), Diagram I contains two curves—a marginal allocative value curve ($MLV_{\Delta R/\ldots}$), which indicates the allocative value that would be generated by the allocation of successive units of resources (R) measured by the allocative cost of their allocation to the use in question (...) and a marginal allocative cost curve ($MLC_{\Delta R/\ldots}$), which indicates the marginal allocative cost of allocating successive resources to the use in question (the allocative value that the successive resources in question would have generated in their alternative uses). In Diagram I, $MLV_{\Delta R/\ldots}$ is constructed to be downward sloping because, for two reasons, the allocative value generated by the allocation to any use of each successive batch of resources whose allocative cost is $1 will be lower than that of its predecessor: (1) even if the successive batches of resources whose devotion to the use in question would entail $1 in allocative costs were physically equally large and had the same physical product, the allocative value of (A) the successive, equally large increases in unit output that those resources would yield, (B) the successive QV investments they would create, or (C) the successive PPR

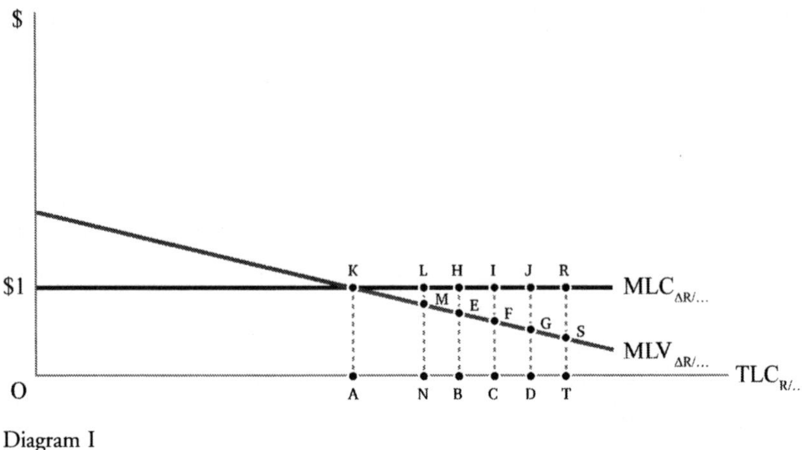

Diagram I

projects they would execute would decline, and (2) the successive batches of resources of an allocative cost of $1 that would be allocated to any given purpose would be progressively physically smaller because the alternative uses from which the resource components of each such batch would be withdrawn would be progressively more allocatively valuable. In Diagram I, $\text{MLV}_{\Delta R/\ldots}$ is constructed to be not only downward sloping but also linear. This latter, unrealistic assumption was adopted solely for expositional reasons: its substantive cost will be discussed later in this section. Finally, in Diagram I, $\text{MLC}_{\Delta R/\ldots}$ is constructed to be horizontal at the height $1. This construction reflects the obvious fact that the marginal allocative cost of each successive $1 in resources (measured by the allocative cost of their allocation to the resource use in question) is $1. In Diagram I, the allocatively efficient amount of resources (measured in terms of the allocative cost of devoting them to the resource use in question) to devote to the use to which any pair of $\text{MLV}_{\Delta R/\ldots}$ and $\text{MLC}_{\Delta R/\ldots}$ curves relates is OA—the amount at which the $\text{MLV}_{\Delta R/\ldots}$ curve cuts the $\text{MLC}_{\Delta R/\ldots}$ curve from above at point K, and the total misallocation generated by all allocatively inefficient allocations of resources to the relevant use is the area between the $\text{MLV}_{\Delta R/\ldots}$ and $\text{MLC}_{\Delta R/\ldots}$ curves between the actual amount of resources allocated to the use in question and the amount of resources whose allocation to that use would have been allocatively efficient.

Diagram I is designed to illustrate the basis of a distortion analysis that focuses on resource uses to which too many resources have been devoted from the perspective of economic efficiency—that is, all the points indicated in

Diagram I other than points A and K refer to allocations in which more than OA in resources has been devoted to the indicated type (or types) of resource use. One further fact should be noted at the outset: in Diagram I, NB = BC = CD = DT, and (given that the $MLV_{\Delta R/\ldots}$ and $MLC_{\Delta R/\ldots}$ curves are linear) HE − LM = IF − HE = JG − IF = RS − JG. The point of this construction is connected to the fact that—if the last resource use of the indicated type yields zero (supernormal) profits—the distance between the MLC and MLV curves at the resource quantity in question will indicate not only the amount by which the allocation of the indicated last unit of resources (measured in allocative [social opportunity] cost terms) to the use in question will have increased (or decreased) economic inefficiency but also the negative of the aggregate distortion in the profits yielded by that last resource use: if $P\pi_{\Delta\ldots} = 0$, the definition $\Sigma D(P\pi_{\Delta\ldots}) \equiv P\pi_{\Delta\ldots} - LE_{\Delta\ldots}$ will imply that $\Sigma D(P\pi_{\Delta\ldots}) = -LE_{\Delta\ldots}$.

Diagram I has been constructed on the basis of two other assumptions. First, Diagram I (that is, the analysis I will base on Diagram I) assumes that the $MLV_{\Delta R/\ldots}$ curve it contains is not only linear but also applies to all types of resource uses. This assumption was adopted purely for expositional reasons. However, it does conceal an issue that a third-best allocatively efficient distortion analysis would have to consider. That issue has nothing to do with Diagram I's related unrealistic assumption that it would be allocatively efficient to devote the same quantity of resources (OA)—measured in terms of the allocative cost of their being devoted to the use in question—to each type of resource use to which the economy devotes resources (the quantity at which the $MLV_{\Delta R/\ldots}$ curve for each such type of resource use cuts the $MLC_{\Delta R/\ldots}$ curve for that use from above). Instead, it has to do with Diagram I's assumption that each $MLV_{\Delta R/\ldots}$ curve will have the same shape between the actual quantity of resources devoted to the use to which it refers and the quantity whose devotion to that type of resource use would be allocatively efficient. More specifically, Diagram I's assumption that each such curve is linear over the relevant range will lead it (1) to underrepresent the amount of misallocation that will be associated with any given $\Sigma D(P\pi_{R/\Delta\ldots})$ figure if the $MLV_{\Delta R/\ldots}$ curve for the relevant resource use is convex to the origin over the relevant range and (2) to overrepresent the amount of misallocation that will be associated with any given $\Sigma D(P\pi_{R/\Delta\ldots})$ figure if the $MLV_{\Delta R/\ldots}$ curve is concave to the origin over the relevant range. Of course, if an appropriate initial analysis revealed that *ex ante* it would be TBLE to investigate and take account of the shape of the actual $MLV_{\Delta R/\ldots}$ curve for each relevant type of resource use between the actual and allocatively efficient amounts of resources devoted to it, the version of distortion analysis that would be TBLE would include at least some analysis of the shape of the relevant curves over the resource-devotion ranges in question.

Second, Diagram I's construction of the $MLV_{\Delta R/\ldots}$ and $MLC_{\Delta R/\ldots}$ curves it contains as continuous implicitly assumes that over the relevant ranges the quantity of resources devoted to any type of resource use can be varied by infinitesimally small amounts without sacrificing economies of scale. This assumption is important for two reasons. First, it is important because, in combination with the assumption that the relevant marginal-resource-use owners are sovereign maximizers and did control the relevant marginal-resource-use decision, it yields the conclusion that $P\pi_{\Delta\ldots} = 0$ for all types of resource uses and hence (as we have already noted) that $(-LE_{\Delta\ldots})$ for all resource-use types equals $\Sigma D(P\pi_{\Delta\ldots})$ for that resource-use type. Second, the assumption is important because, by implying that all last resource uses will entail the same allocative cost (say, \$1), it implies that the weighted-average value of the items in the non-negative segment of the percentage-profit-distortion distribution on which distortion analysis focuses will equal the mean of that distribution and that the weighted-average absolute deviation from the mean of the items in that distribution-segment will equal the mean deviation from that distribution's mean. Relatedly, the fact that the allocative cost of all the relevant-marginal resource uses is the same permits me to illustrate my points by focusing on the absolute means, mean absolute deviations, and mean squared deviations of the aggregate-profit-distortion distributions in question rather than on their more complicated aggregate-*percentage*-profit-distortion-distribution counterparts.

Diagram I can be used to illustrate the four relationships that create the possibility that the distortion-analysis approach to allocative-efficiency assessment may be TBLE and to explain the connection between those relationships and the possible TBLE of distortion analysis. The first relationship is that the total amount of misallocation generated by all the economically inefficient resource-use decisions of any specified type whose marginal exemplars' profit yields are inflated will increase with the weighted-average mean of the distribution of non-negative distortions in the profits yielded by marginal resource uses of the type in question. Assume that the profit yield of *n* marginal resource uses in the economy are inflated and that the $\Sigma D(P\pi_{\Delta R/\ldots})$s for each of these marginal resource uses are not only positive but also the same so that the mean of the relevant

$\Sigma D(P\pi_{\Delta R/\ldots})$ distribution equals the $\Sigma D(P\pi_{\Delta R/\ldots})$ for each marginal resource use in the economy. Now assume that $MLV_{\Delta R/\ldots}$ is the MLV curve for the allocation of successive batches of resources whose allocative cost was \$1 to the resource uses in question—for example, to the production of additional units of each of the economy's products, the creation of additional QV investments in the economy's various areas of product-space, and the execution of additional PPR projects related to the production process that would be used to produce the products produced in the economy's various areas of product-space. As Diagram I illustrates, the total amount of misallocation in the economy will increase with the $\Sigma D(P\pi_{\Delta R/\ldots})$ figure for each marginal resource use—that is, with the mean of the $\Sigma D(P\pi_{\Delta R/\ldots})$ or $\Sigma D(P\pi_{\Delta R/\ldots})$ distribution. As we have seen, on our assumptions that the relevant resource-use owners are sovereign maximizers and that the amount of resources devoted to each resource use can be varied by infinitesimally small amounts without sacrificing any economies of scale, $P\pi_{\Delta R/\ldots} = 0$, and $\Sigma D(P\pi_{\Delta R/\ldots})$ for each type of resource use will equal $-(MLV_{\Delta R/\ldots} - MLC_{\Delta R/\ldots}) = (MLC_{\Delta R/\ldots} - MLV_{\Delta R/\ldots})$ for the marginal resource use in question. Thus, in Diagram I, (1) if $(MLC_{\Delta R/\ldots} - MLV_{\Delta R/\ldots}) = \Sigma D(P\pi_{\Delta R/\ldots})$ for each of the n marginal resource uses whose profit yield is inflated (if the mean of the relevant aggregate-profit-distortion distribution) is RS, total misallocation will be n(area KRS); (2) if the distortion for each marginal resource use in question (the mean of the associated distortion distribution) is the smaller amount JG, total misallocation will be the smaller amount n(area KJG); (3) if the distortion in question is the still smaller amount IF, total misallocation will be the still smaller amount n(area KIF); and so on. Relatedly, Diagram I illustrates the fact that, controlling for the mean of the pre-policy or pre-choice aggregate-profit-distortion distribution, the amount by which the policy increases (decreases) economic efficiency will increase with the amount by which it decreases (increases) the weighted-average mean of the distribution in question. Thus, if one assumes that the pre-policy $\Sigma D(P\pi_{\Delta R/\ldots})$ for each marginal resource use in the economy and hence the mean of the relevant distribution were both RS, a policy that reduces that distortion and mean by the smaller amount (RS – JG)—that is, from RS to JG—will increase economic efficiency by n(area JRSG), while a policy that reduces that distortion and mean by the larger amount (RS – IF)—that is, from RS to IF—will increase economic efficiency by the larger amount n(area IRSF). And, in the other direction, if one assumes that the pre-policy $\Sigma D(P\pi_{\Delta R/\ldots})$ for each marginal resource use in the economy and hence the mean of the relevant distribution were both IF, a policy that increases those distortions and hence that mean by the smaller amount (JG – IF) would increase economic inefficiency by less than would a policy that would increase them by the larger amount (RS – IF)—that is, would increase total economic inefficiency by *n*(area IJGF) rather than by *n*(area IRSF).

Diagram I can also be used to illustrate the second relationship that favors the TBLE of the distortion-analysis approach—namely, the fact that, controlling for the magnitude of the impact of any policy on $\Sigma D(P\pi_{\Delta R/...})$ for each of the economy's marginal resource uses for which that distortion is positive and hence for its impact on the mean of the distribution of such distortions, the amount by which the policy in question would increase or decrease economic efficiency will increase with the magnitude of the mean of the pre-policy distribution in question. Recall that, in Diagram I, RS – JG = JG – IF = IF – HE = HE – LM. Then note that, in Diagram I, the amount by which a policy that reduces each $\Sigma D(P\pi_{\Delta R/...})$ by RS – JG from the larger pre-policy magnitude RS to the lower amount JG will reduce total resource misallocation on that account—*n*(area JRSG)—is larger than the amount by which a policy that reduces $\Sigma D(P\pi_{\Delta R/...})$ for each marginal resource use in the economy by the same amount (by JG – IF = RS – JG) from the smaller pre-policy magnitude JG to the still lower IF will reduce total resource misallocation—*n*(area IJGF)—and so on and so forth.

Diagram I can be used in addition to illustrate the third relationship that I previously claimed favors the TBLE of the distortion-analysis approach to allocative-efficiency assessment: the fact that, controlling for the weighted-average mean of the $\Sigma D(P\pi_{\Delta R/...})$ distribution for marginal resource uses whose profit yields were inflated, the total amount of misallocation generated by economically inefficient resource uses will increase with the mean deviation of the distribution in question. To see why this relationship obtains, compare the following two situations that Diagram I can be used to illustrate. In the first, half of the positive $\Sigma D(P\pi_{\Delta R/...})$s are JG, and half are HE. In the second, all of the $\Sigma D(P\pi_{\Delta R/...})$s are IF. Since JG – IF = IF – HE, the mean of the segment of the first non-negative $\Sigma D(P\pi_{\Delta R/...})$ distribution is the same as that of the second. However, the average absolute deviation of the distribution associated with the first situation (JG – IF = IF – HE) is larger than the zero average absolute deviation associated with the second situation. For our purposes, the critical fact is that the total misallocation generated by the economically inefficient resource uses present in the first (higher-absolute-average-deviation situation)—(*n*/2)(area KHE) + (*n*/2)(area KJG)—is larger than the total misallocation generated by the economically inefficient resource uses present in the second situation—*n*(area KIF). This result reflects the fact that the increase in misallocation associated with each increase in $\Sigma D(P\pi_{\Delta R/\ldots})$ from IF to JG is larger than the decrease in misallocation associated with each decrease in $\Sigma D(P\pi_{\Delta R/\ldots})$ from IF to HE (so that area IJGF is larger than area HIFE) despite the fact that the difference between JG and IF equals the difference between IF and HE. I should point out that this outcome reflects the same reality that underlies the second relationship just discussed—namely, the fact that the amount by which economic efficiency will be increased by any given reduction in the mean of the distribution of non-negative aggregate profit distortions will rise with the magnitude of the pre-change mean of the distribution in question (the reality that the amount of misallocation generated by the allocation of each successive resource-value unit to some use that was economically inefficient will rise [that the distance between $MLC_{\Delta R/\ldots}$ and $MLV_{\Delta R/\ldots}$ increases] as one moves to the right beyond the allocatively efficient resource allocation OA). Finally, Diagram I can be used to illustrate the fourth relationship that favors the TBLE of distortion analysis. To see why, controlling for the absolute mean deviation discussed in the preceding paragraph, the amount of misallocation in an economy will increase with the average squared deviation of the positive (or negative) segment of the distribution of distortions of the profit yields of its marginal resource uses, compare (1) a situation in which the aggregate profit distortion is LM in one industry, RS in one industry, and IF in two industries with (2) a situation in which the aggregate profit distortion is HE in two industries and JG in two industries. The two distortion distributions in question have the same mean (IF) and the same mean deviation (HE – IF) = (JG – IF). However, the first distribution differs from the second in two respects that bear on this fourth relationship: (1) more misallocation results from the first distribution than from the second—2 (area KHE) + 2 (area KJG) > area KLM + area KRS + 2 (area KIF) and (2) the average squared deviation of the second distribution exceeds its counterpart for the first—$(2[HE - IF]^2 + 2[JG - IF]^2)/4 > ([LM - IF]^2 + 0^2 + 0^2 + [RS - IP]^2)/4$.

One issue remains to be discussed: the extent to which the preceding analysis is compromised by its admittedly unrealistic assumption that the last resource use of any subtype will be infinitesimally small (because there are no economies of scale in devoting resources to any use over the relevant range). As already indicated, in conjunction with the assumption that the relevant resource uses maximized their owners' interests or profits, this assumption contributed to the relevance of data on the aggregate-profit distortion in the profits yielded by marginal resource uses by guaranteeing that all such resource uses would yield zero profits so that the identity $\Sigma D(P\pi_{\Delta R/\ldots}) \equiv P\pi_{\Delta R/\ldots} - LE_{\Delta R/\ldots}$ implies that $LE_{\Delta R/\ldots} = -\Sigma D(P\pi_{\Delta R/\ldots})$.

I now want to explain why the fact that there are economies of scale in many types of marginal resource uses does not significantly undermine the case for the third-best allocative efficiency of the distortion-analysis approach to economic-efficiency assessment. The existence of such economies of scale is troublesome because (1) in the vast majority of instances in which economies of scale cause marginal resource uses to be lumpy, $P\pi_{\Delta R/\ldots}$ will be positive so that $LE_{\Delta R/\ldots}$ will exceed $-\Sigma D(P\pi_{\Delta R/\ldots})$ and (2) since, in virtually all cases in which the relevant marginal resource use is lumpy, the first and many successive intramarginal (extramarginal) resource uses will also be lumpy.

The facts listed after (1) cause difficulties because when $P\pi_{\Delta R/\ldots} > 0$ and therefore $LE_{\Delta R/\ldots} > -\Sigma D(P\pi_{\Delta R/\ldots})$

1. one cannot assume that the marginal resource use will be allocatively inefficient whenever $\Sigma D(P\pi_{\Delta R/\ldots}) > 0$ even if the relevant resource user is a sovereign maximizer;
2. the misallocation the marginal resource use will have caused when $\Sigma D(P\pi_{\Delta R/\ldots}) > 0$ and $LE_{\Delta R/\ldots} < 0$ will not equal $-\Sigma D(P\pi_{\Delta R/\ldots})$ even if the relevant resource user is a sovereign maximizer—in particular, will equal $P\pi_{\Delta R/\ldots} - \Sigma D(P\pi_{\Delta R/\ldots})$ in such cases; and
3. even if the first extramarginal resource use was infinitesimally small and the relevant resource user was a sovereign maximizer, the misallocation the relevant aggregate distortion—$\Sigma D(P\pi_{\Delta R/\ldots}) < 0$—generated by deterring the first extramarginal resource use will not equal or be infinitesimally less than $|\Sigma D(P\pi_{\Delta R/\ldots}|$—in particular, will equal or be infinitesimally smaller than $P\pi_{\Delta R/\ldots} + |\Sigma D(P\pi_{\Delta R/\ldots})|$.

The fact listed after (2) in the preceding paragraph causes difficulties because it complicates the analysis of (1) the magnitude of the allocative inefficiency generated by the allocatively inefficient resource uses of the relevant type caused by the Pareto imperfections that caused $\Sigma D(P\pi_{\Delta R/\ldots})$ to be positive and (2) the magnitude of the allocative-efficiency gains that would have been generated by the allocatively efficient resource uses of the relevant type deterred by the Pareto imperfections that caused $\Sigma D(P\pi_{\Delta R/\ldots})$ to be negative.

However, for two reasons, these realities do not seriously undermine the allocative-efficiency case for the distortion-analysis approach to economic-efficiency assessment. First, to the extent that it would be *ex ante* economically efficient to analyze the impact of such lumpiness on the connection between the effect of a policy on the weighted-average absolute value of the items in the relevant aggregate-percentage-profit distribution-segment and the weighted-average deviation and weighted-average squared deviation from that weighted-average figure, the distortion-analysis approach could include such an analysis. Second, because there is no reason to believe that there is any correlation between the $(P\pi_{\Delta R/\ldots}/LC_{\Delta R/\ldots})$ and the $(\Sigma D[P\pi_{\Delta R/\ldots}]/LC_{\Delta R/\ldots})$ ratios for the economy's various marginal resource uses, across all cases the $(\Sigma D[P\pi_{\Delta R/\ldots}]/LC_{\Delta R/\ldots})$ ratios for different marginal resource uses whose profit yields were inflated seem likely to be highly positively correlated (1) with the probability that the marginal resource use in question was economically inefficient, (2) with the ratio of the economic inefficiency it generated to its allocative cost, and (3) with the ratio of the total misallocation generated by the relevant subtype of resource use to the marginal resource use's allocative cost, it may not be TBLE to expand the distortion-analysis approach to take account of the reality that many if not most marginal resource uses are lumpy.

Distortion Analysis: A General Outline

The distortion-analysis approach to economic-efficiency assessment builds on the relationships that the preceding subsection established. This subsection outlines the twelve-step variant of distortion analysis that I think would be third-best allocatively efficient in the medium to long run. This time frame is relevant because the account that follows assumes that it will be TBLE to do as much theoretical work as is possible. I admit that in the short run it may be TBLE to not do theoretical work that would be warranted if time were of no concern.

In my judgment, the following protocol describes the approach to allocative-efficiency analysis that is third-best allocatively efficient in situations in which the analyst has enough time to complete his work for it to be TBLE for him to strive to perfect any relevant theoretical analysis and it is not TBLE to consider the possibility that the allocative efficiency of marginal-resource-use decisions will be affected by economic-actor errors:

1. identify the various types and subtypes of resource uses in the economy in question;
2. develop formulas for the aggregate percentage distortion in the profits yielded by the marginal resource use of each such type and subtype—formulas that relate this distortion primarily to the various Pareto imperfections the economy contains;
3. combine this theoretical work with existing information on and guesstimates of the pre-choice or pre-policy magnitude of the parameters

whose relevance stage 2's theoretical work establishes to identify those marginal resource uses whose profit yields seem likely to be inflated;

4. take a minimally-adequately-large random sample of these marginal resource uses and combine the formulas in question and the data that are already available to estimate the aggregate percentage distortion in the profit yields of the marginal resource uses in question;
5. estimate the weighted-average value, weighted-average absolute deviation, and weighted-average squared deviation of the distribution of the non-negative aggregate percentage profit distortions just estimated;
6. analyze the way in which the private choice or public policy whose allocative efficiency is to be scrutinized would affect (or did affect) the economy's various Pareto imperfections;
7. calculate the post-choice or post-policy aggregate percentage distortions in the profits yielded by the marginal resource uses previously investigated, the weighted-average mean of the distribution of those post-choice or post-policy percentage-profit-distortion figures, and the weighted-average absolute deviation and weighted-average squared deviation of that distribution;
8. generate an initial estimate of the allocative efficiency of the private choice or public policy under scrutiny from the forgoing estimates of the pre-choice or pre-policy weighted-average absolute value of the items in of the above percentage-profit-distortion distribution, the impact of the choice or policy on that weighted-average figure, and the impact of the choice or policy on the weighted-average absolute deviation and weighted-average squared deviation of that distribution;
9. analyze
   A. the probability that enlarging the size of the random sample of marginal resource uses and/or collecting additional data on particular Pareto imperfections or other parameters whose relevance stage 2's theoretical work established would change one's conclusion about the allocative efficiency of the private choice or public policy in question (in comparison with either a do-nothing alternative or some available positive alternative) to various extents,
   B. the weighted-average allocative value of any such increase in the accuracy of one's assessment of the economic efficiency of the option under consideration (for example, no direct benefit would be yielded by an upward revision of the estimate of the allocative efficiency of a policy that would be enacted anyway at least in part because the less complete analysis deemed it to be economically efficient), and

C. the allocative cost of collecting the additional data in question (taking into consideration both the fact that those costs almost certainly would not equal the private cost of the relevant data collection even if no allocative inefficiencies had to be generated to finance the data collection in question and the fact that—regardless of how the associated expenditures were financed—their financing would generate allocative inefficiencies);

10. if the results of the stage 9 analysis implied that it would be *ex ante* third-best allocatively efficient to collect additional data on one or more parameters, collect those data and use them to reanalyze the allocative efficiency of the private choice or public policy under consideration;
11. repeat stage 9 to determine whether additional data should be collected and, if the conclusion is that such data should be collected, collect them and use them to reanalyze the allocative efficiency of the choice or policy under consideration; and
12. continue this process until the stage 9 protocol implies that it would not be TBLE to collect additional data and then announce the conclusion that the preceding analysis generated in a publication that articulates its theoretical and empirical bases and the protocols that were used to develop the information in question.

Two admissions. First, I realize that the preceding outline is far from complete and that, at least to some extent, in this context as in many others, the omitted details are important. Second, the preceding outline ignores a serious infinite-regress problem. As the outline indicates, an analyst who wants to adopt a TBLE version of the distortion-analysis approach would have to continuously assess the third-best allocative efficiency of collecting additional data on the parameters that the theory demonstrates would be relevant to the allocative efficiency of the policy or policies under consideration. In fact, such an analyst would also have to continuously assess the third-best allocative efficiency of doing additional theoretical work that would bear on the allocative efficiency of those policies. The infinite-regress problem derives from the following fact: before thinking about the TBLE of collecting particular additional data or doing particular additional theoretical work, the analyst who wanted to behave third-best allocative efficiently would have to give third-best allocatively efficient attention to whether he should think about the third-best allocative efficiency of doing the empirical or theoretical work in question. And before doing that, he should give third-best allocatively efficient attention to whether it would be third-best allocatively efficient to think about whether he should think about whether it would be third-best allocatively efficient to do the work in question. And so on and so forth. My outline of the third-best allocatively efficient variant of distortion analysis simply cuts this Gordian knot.

SECTION 3. SOME ANALYSES OF VARIOUS TYPES OF PROFIT DISTORTIONS

This section develops concrete examples of the kind of profit-distortion formulas and analyses that distortion analysis employs. In recognition of the fact that the marginal allocation of resources to virtually all types of uses are not infinitesimally small, the formulas this section develops focus on the distortion in the profits yielded by the marginal exemplar of the various types of resource uses in the economy (such as unit-output-producing uses, QV-investment-creating uses, PPR-execution uses, and accident-or-pollution-loss-reducing [AP-loss-reducing] uses) rather than on the marginal resource allocated to each of these uses. Some of the formulas indicate the monopoly distortion in the profits yielded by the marginal exemplar of some indicated type of use; some, the externality distortion in the profits yielded by the marginal exemplar of an indicated type of use; some, the aggregate distortion in the profits yielded by the marginal exemplar of an indicated type of use. For expositional reasons, some of the formulas this section develops will be based on unrealistic assumptions about the types of uses from which the resources consumed by an analyzed marginal resource use will be withdrawn. For example, the formulas for various distortions in the profits yielded by the production of a marginal unit of any product will assume that all the resources that the production of that unit consumes are withdrawn from the production of units of other products already in production. However, this section also analyzes some of the various aggregate distortions on which it focuses on realistic assumptions about the types of uses from which the resources allocated to the marginal use in question will be withdrawn. Finally, although for the most part this section makes no attempt to generate conclusions about the magnitude or even the sign of the distortions it analyzes, it does contain some speculations about the sign of some distortions that are generated by combining the formula for or theoretical analysis of that distortion with some guesstimates of at least the relative magnitudes of some of the parameters whose relevance its theoretical analysis establishes and some analyses of the policy implications of these guesstimates.

I want to admit at the outset that, although my experience as an antitrust scholar and lawyer may give readers some reason to defer to my judgments about such matters as the incidence of imperfections in price and QV-investment competition (at least in the United States), I have no expertise that merits any deference being given to my speculations about the magnitudes of the various kinds of conventional externalities generated in the economy or the extent to which the potential external benefits yielded by knowledge creation are prevented and internalized by the combination of intellectual-property (IP) law (patent, copyright, and trade-secret law) and the ability of innovators to keep at least some kinds of discoveries secret. I persist with these speculations nonetheless partly to make the book's economic-efficiency analyses more concrete and interesting, partly to give readers a better feel for the kind of analysis that may be third-best allocatively efficient when speed has a positive value, but partly (relatedly) because I share the lawyer's sympathy for basing policy conclusions on empirical guesses when time is of the essence (that is, for third-best analysis) as opposed to the typical mathematical economist's sympathy for getting things exactly right (that is, for second-best analysis).

Various Types of Distortions in the Profits Yielded by Different Kinds of Allocations of Resources to the Production of Marginal Units of Output

MD($P\pi_{\Delta UOX}$) WHEN THE RELEVANT RESOURCES ARE WITHDRAWN EXCLUSIVELY FROM THE PRODUCTION OF OTHER PRODUCTS (Y)

In my terminology, the monopoly distortion in any private benefit, cost, or profit figure is the distortion that the extant imperfections in seller competition would generate in that figure in an otherwise-Pareto-perfect economy. The particular monopoly distortion that this subsection analyzes is the monopoly distortion that imperfections in price competition would generate in an otherwise-Pareto-perfect economy in the profits yielded by the type of resource reallocation that can give rise to UO-to-UO misallocation—the type that involves resources being withdrawn from the production of product Y and reallocated to the production of product X. As the first subsection of Section 1 of Chapter 4 discusses, the traditional analysis of the allegedly misallocative effects of imperfections in seller competition (the so-called deadweight loss or social cost of monopoly) focuses exclusively on this type of allocation and misallocation.

The chain of equalities that follows yields a formula for the monopoly distortion in question. One symbol not previously explained appears in this chain—$MRT_{Y/X}$, the marginal rate at which the economy can transform Y into X. If at the margin it would be possible to produce four units of Y with the resources required to produce a marginal unit of X, the marginal rate of transformation of Y into X would be 4/1. In a Pareto-perfect economy, $MRT_{Y/X}$ would equal MC_X/MC_Y: in such a world, if the cost to X's producer of producing a marginal unit of X was four times as high as the cost to Y's producer of producing a marginal unit of Y, the fact that, at the margin, X would be *privately* four times as expensive to produce as Y would imply that at the margin it would also be *allocatively* four times as expensive to produce as Y (that the economy could produce four additional units of Y with the resources that the production of the last unit of X consumed). I must emphasize, however, that $MRT_{Y/X}$ may not equal MC_X/MC_Y when the economy is not Pareto perfect since in that eventuality the producers of X and/or Y may not have to pay for all the resources their production of marginal units of these products consumes, may pay different prices for some input they both use, and (more generally) may not pay the marginal allocative cost of using each input they do use.

I will first derive the formula for the distortion on which we are now focusing and then explain the six lines of the derivation in order. The relevant derivation is:

1. $MD(P\pi_{\Delta UOX}) = MD(PB_{\Delta UOX}) - MD(PC_{\Delta UOX}) =$
2. $(PB_{\Delta UOX} - LB_{\Delta UOX}) - (PC_{\Delta UOX} - LC_{\Delta UOX}) =$
3. $(MR_{\Delta UOX} - P_{\Delta UOX}) - (MC_{\Delta UOX} - MRT_{Y/X}[MLV_Y]) =$
4. $(MR_X - P_X) - (MC_X - [MC_X/MC_Y]P_Y) =$
5. $-P_X + (MC_X/MC_Y)P_Y =$
6. $MC_X([P_Y/MC_Y] - [P_X/MC_X])$.

The equality in line (1) manifests the fact that any distortion in the profits yielded by any choice equals the distortion in the private benefits the choice yields the chooser *minus* the distortion in the private costs it imposes on him. If, for example, the relevant Pareto imperfection or imperfections inflate the private benefits and costs of the choice in question by the same amount, the profits the choice yields the chooser will not be distorted.

The substitutions that convert the right side of the equation in line (1) into line (2) reflect nothing more than the facts that, by definition, the distortion in the private benefits a choice yields the chooser equals the difference between those private benefits and the allocative benefits the choice yields and the distortion in the private costs a choice confers on the chooser equal the difference between those private costs and the allocative costs the choice generates. The substitutions that convert line (2) into line (3) reflect the following realities:

1. the private benefits X's producer secures by producing a marginal unit of X will equal $MR_{\Delta UOX}$ in an otherwise-Pareto-perfect economy in which the sale of this unit does not affect the profits its producer makes by selling other products or the same product at future times;[24]
2. in an otherwise-Pareto-perfect economy, the allocative benefits generated by the production of a marginal unit of any product equal the price for which it is sold;
3. by definition, the private cost to a producer of producing a marginal unit of his product is the marginal cost of his producing this unit; and
4. by definition in a UO-to-UO allocation situation, the allocative cost of producing a marginal unit of one product (X) is equal to the allocative value of the units of the other product (Y) that will be sacrificed when the unit of the first product (X) is produced, which equal the number of units of that other product Y that will be sacrificed to secure the resources used to produce a marginal unit of X ($MRT_{Y/X}$) *times* the (average) marginal allocative value of those sacrificed units ($AMLV_Y$, which I signify here as MLV_Y).

The substitutions that convert line (3) of the formula into line (4) reflect the following realities:

1. MR_X, P_X, and MC_X are simply other symbols for, respectively, $MR_{\Delta UOX}$, $P_{\Delta UOX}$, and $MC_{\Delta UOX}$;
2. in an otherwise-Pareto-perfect economy, $MRT_{Y/X} = MC_X/MC_Y$; and
3. in an otherwise-Pareto-perfect economy $P_Y = MLV_Y$ (at least if we assume that the assumption that no problems are caused by buyer surplus eliminates any problems that might arise if more than one unit of Y must be sacrificed to produce a marginal unit of X).

The substitution of line (5) for line (4) reflects (1) the fact that in an otherwise-Pareto-perfect economy $MR = MC$ so that the elimination of MR_X and $-MC_X$ from line (4) does not affect its value and (2) the fact that $-(-[MC_X/MC_Y]P_Y) = (MC_X/MC_Y)P_Y$. To convert line (5) into line (6), one need only divide each term in line (5) by MC_X and then multiply the resulting sum by MC_X—a procedure that does not affect the value of the relevant expression since $(MC_X/MC_X) = 1$.

In any event, the preceding chain of equalities demonstrates that the monopoly distortion in the profits that will be yielded by the production of a last unit of product X that is created with resources that would otherwise have been used to produce more of product Y is $MC_X([P_Y/MC_Y] - [P_X/MC_X])$. Note that this result implies that, in an otherwise-Pareto-perfect economy, imperfections in the price competition faced by the producer of X will not distort the profits he can realize by producing a marginal unit of X with resources that would otherwise produce more units of Y if $(P_Y/MC_Y) = (P_X/MC_X)$.[25]

XD($P\pi_{\Delta UOX}$) WHEN THE RELEVANT RESOURCES ARE WITHDRAWN FROM THE PRODUCTION OF OTHER PRODUCTS (Y)

This subsection examines a chain of identities and equalities that yield the expression that equals the above distortion on the assumption that all the relevant externalities are externalities of production. The chain contains two symbols that have not been previously defined—MC^*_X and MC^*_Y. The asterisks in these symbols indicate that the relevant MC figures have been adjusted to reflect the net external costs (or benefits) generated by the production of the marginal unit of the indicated product. The adjustments in question cause (MC^*_X/MC^*_Y) to equal $MRT_{Y/X}$ regardless of whether (MC_X/MC_Y) equaled $MRT_{Y/X}$ (that is, regardless of whether the externalities generated by the production of a marginal unit of each product constituted the same percentage of the [internal] marginal cost of producing the relevant unit of that product).

The relevant chain is

1. $XD(P\pi_{\Delta UOX}) = XD(PB_{\Delta UOX} - XD(PC_{\Delta UOX}) =$
2. $(PB_{\Delta UOX} - LB_{\Delta UOX}) - (MC_{\Delta UOX} - MLC_{\Delta UOX}) =$
3. $-MC_X + MRT_{Y/X}(MLV_Y) =$
4. $-MC_X + (MC^*_X/MC^*_Y)P_Y =$
5. $-MC_X + (MX^*_X/MC^*_Y)MC_Y =$
6. $MC^*_X([MC_Y/MC^*_Y] - [MC_X/MC^*_X])$.

I will comment on only those substitutions in the above chain that are different from those made in the preceding subsection. In line (3), zero is substituted for $PB_{\Delta UOX} - LB_{\Delta UOX}$ because that substitution is warranted by the assumption that the economy is otherwise-Pareto-perfect—namely, that there are no externalities of consumption and that the relevant buyers are sovereign, maximizing nonmonopsonists whose purchase of the marginal unit in question confers no buyer surplus on them. In line (4), (MC^*_X/MC^*_Y) is substituted for $MRT_{Y/X}$ because, in an otherwise-Pareto-perfect economy in which there are externalities of production, $MRT_{Y/X}$ will equal (MC^*_X/MC^*_Y)

but may not equal (MC_X/MC_Y). In line (5), P_Y is substituted for MC_Y because the assumption that there are no imperfections in seller competition implies that $P_Y = MC_Y$. And line (6) can be derived from line (5) by dividing both terms in line (5) by MC^*_X and multiplying the resulting sum by MC^*_X.

The preceding chain demonstrates that the distortion that externalities of production will generate in the profits yielded by the production of a marginal unit of product X that is produced with resources withdrawn exclusively from the production of Y equals $MC^*_X([MC_Y/MC^*_Y] - [MC_X/MC^*_X])$. Note that this conclusion implies that, in an otherwise-Pareto-perfect economy, externalities generated by the production of a marginal unit of X with resources withdrawn exclusively from the production of Y will not distort the profits that the production of a marginal unit of X yields its producer if the production of the sacrificed units of Y would have generated externalities and $(MC_Y/MC^*_Y) = (MC_X/MC^*_X)$.

MD/XD($P\pi_{\Delta UOX}$) WHEN THE RELEVANT RESOURCES ARE WITHDRAWN EXCLUSIVELY FROM THE PRODUCTION OF OTHER PRODUCTS (Y)

I will let the symbol MD/XD($P\pi_{\Delta UOX}$) stand for the distortion with which this subsection is concerned. The following chain of identities and equalities yields the formula for this distortion:

1. $MD/XD(P\pi_{\Delta UOX}) = MD/XD(PB_{\Delta UOX}) - MD/XD(PC_{\Delta UOX}) =$
2. $(PB_{\Delta UOX} - LB_{\Delta UOX}) - (PC_{\Delta UOX} - LC_{\Delta UOX}) =$
3. $(MR_{\Delta UOX} - MLV_{\Delta UOX}) - (MC_{\Delta UOX} - MRT_{Y/X}[MLV_{\Delta UOY}]) =$
4. $(MR_X - P_X) - (MC_X - [MC^*_X/MC^*_Y]P_Y) =$
5. $-P_X + (MC^*_X/MC^*_Y)P_Y =$
6. $MC^*_X([P_Y/MC^*_Y] - [P_X/MC^*_X]) =$
7. $MC^*_X([P_Y/MC_Y][MC_Y/MC^*_Y] - [P_X/MC_X][MC_X/MC^*_X])$.

Two points should be noted about this conclusion. First, UO-to-UO misallocation is not an additive case—that is, $MD/XD(P\pi_{\Delta UOX}) \neq MD(P\pi_{\Delta UOX}) + XD(P\pi_{\Delta UOX})$. To confirm this fact, compare the sum of the distortion formulas generated in the preceding two subsections with the formula generated in this subsection. Indeed, not only does MD/XD ($P\pi_{\Delta UOX}$) not equal the sum of MD($P\pi_{\Delta UOX}$) and XD($P\pi_{\Delta UOX}$), the formulas for the latter two distortions are not even arguments in the formula for the former distortion. Second, the preceding conclusion confirms the basic point of second-best theory. In particular, line (6) above confirms the following two related realities: (1) neither the fact that a producer of X faces imperfect price competition (that $P_X > MC_X$) nor the fact that his marginal acts of production generate externalities (that $MC_X^* > MC_X$) guarantees that the profits X's producer will realize by producing a marginal unit of X will be distorted (that the production of X relative to Y will be allocatively inefficient in an otherwise-Pareto-perfect economy) and, relatedly, (2) policies that reduce or eliminate the imperfections in the price competition that the producers of X and/or Y face and/or that reduce or eliminate the externalities that the production of marginal units of X and/or Y generates may increase UO-to-UO misallocation between the production of X and Y by increasing the distortion in the profits yielded by the production of a marginal unit of either product—for example, by increasing the absolute value of the expression in line (6) above.

$\Sigma D(P\pi_{\Delta UOX})$ WHEN THE RELEVANT RESOURCES ARE WITHDRAWN EXCLUSIVELY FROM THE PRODUCTION OF OTHER PRODUCTS (Y)

The preceding subsection analyzed the distortion in the profits that would be yielded by the production of the marginal unit of one product (X) with resources withdrawn exclusively from the production of other products (Y) by the imperfections in seller competition and externalities of production in the economy if it were otherwise-Pareto-perfect. In fact, of course, all economies contain all the other kinds of Pareto imperfections previously listed (monopsony, externalities of consumption, taxes on the margin of income, human errors, and buyer surplus), and unless the distorting effects of the various incarnations of these other individual types of Pareto imperfections perfectly offset each other, they will collectively change the distortion in the profits yielded by the production of a marginal unit of X. This subsection explains how, even if one continues to assume that all resources used to produce the marginal unit of X were withdrawn from the production of products Y, the presence of those other types of Pareto imperfections will cause the formula for $\Sigma D(P\pi_{\Delta UOX})$ to differ from the formula for $MD/XD(P\pi_{\Delta UOX})$.

Monopsony, externalities of consumption, taxes on the margin of income, human errors, and buyer surplus will not cause the first three lines of the analysis of $\Sigma D(P\pi_{\Delta UOX})$ to differ from their counterparts in the analysis of $MD/XD(P\pi_{\Delta UOX})$. However, they will cause line (4) of the analysis of $\Sigma D(P\pi_{\Delta UOX})$ to differ in three ways from line (4) of the analysis of $MD/XD(P\pi_{\Delta UOX})$. First, as we have seen, to the extent that the consumption of the marginal unit of X generates externalities, that the consumer of that unit is a monopsonist, that the consumer of that unit miscalculates the additional cost he can incur to purchase that unit and remain equally well off or miscalculates the cost of purchasing a marginal unit of that product, that the consumer of the unit gains buyer surplus on the relevant purchase, or that a sales, excise, or value-added tax is levied on the sale of the marginal unit of X, MLV_X will differ from P_X (unless the relevant effects of these various imperfections happen to perfectly offset each other). More specifically, *ceteris paribus,*

1. $MLV_X > P_X$ if the consumption of the marginal unit of X generates external benefits;
2. $MLV_X < P_X$ if the consumption of the marginal unit of X generates external costs;
3. $MLV_X > P_X$ if the buyer of the marginal unit of X is a nondiscriminating monopsonist of this product (who faces an upward-sloping supply curve for X);
4. $MLV_X > P_X$ if the buyer of the marginal unit of X underestimated the cost he could incur to purchase the marginal unit of X and break even on the transaction or overestimated the cost to him of purchasing the marginal unit of X;
5. $MLV_X < P_X$ if the buyer of the marginal unit of X overestimated the cost he could incur to purchase the marginal unit of X and break even on the transaction or underestimated the cost of purchasing the marginal unit of X;
6. since the price of any good in all the preceding analyses is always the pre-tax price, $MLV_X > P_X$ if a sales tax, value-added tax, or excise tax is levied on the sale of the marginal unit of X; and
7. $MLV_X > P_X$ if the purchaser of the marginal unit of X obtains buyer surplus on his purchase.

If, for simplicity, we let P^*_X stand for an adjusted price that equals MLV_X, P^*_X will have to be substituted for the P_X term in line (4) of the analysis of MD/XD($P\pi_{\Delta UOX}$) to produce an expression that equals $\Sigma D(P\pi_{\Delta UOX})$.

The second way in which line (4) of the analysis of $\Sigma D(P\pi_{\Delta UOX})$ differs from line (4) of the analysis of MD/XD($P\pi_{\Delta UOX}$) parallels the first. For the same reasons that P^*_X had to be substituted for P_X in the relevant line, an adjusted-price term $P^*_Y = MLV_Y$ will have to be substituted for the P_Y in line (4) of the analysis of MD/XD($P\pi_{\Delta UOX}$) whenever one or more of these additional imperfections is present in the system and they do not collectively perfectly offset each other insofar as the possible divergence between MLV_X and P_X is concerned.

The third way in which line (4) of the MD/XD($P\pi_{\Delta UOX}$) analysis must be altered to take account of the other Pareto imperfections that are relevant to the analysis of $\Sigma D(P\pi_{\Delta UOX})$ relates to the way in which MC_X and MC_Y must be adjusted to create an MC^*_X/MC^*_Y figure that equals $MRT_{Y/X}$. When XD($P\pi_{\Delta UOX}$) and MD/XD($P\pi_{\Delta UOX}$) were being analyzed, the MC figure had to be adjusted to take account of the externalities generated by the production of the marginal unit of X and the sacrificed units of Y. In an economy in which other Pareto imperfections are present, MC_X and MC_Y may have to be adjusted on other counts as well. Most importantly, to the extent that the percentage of MC_X that consists of tax payments that X's producer must pay directly or indirectly in the form of the higher gross wages he must pay to workers whose marginal income is taxed was higher (lower) than the percentage of the relevant (MC_Y)s that consists of tax payments the relevant Ys' producers would have to pay to secure the resources they would use to produce the sacrificed Y, $MRT_{Y/X}$ will be higher (lower) than MC_X/MC_Y. If precisely the same labor would be used to produce the relevant X and the relevant Y, such tax differences would arise if the percentage of the overall benefits the workers in question would earn if they produced X that was taxable differed from the percentage of those benefits the workers in question would earn if they produced Y that was taxable—for example, if the X labor were more or less attractive than the Y labor, money wages aside. If the labor resource flow was not directly from the production of Y to the production of X but (for example) from the production of Y to the production of Z, from the production of Z to the production of W, and from the production of W to the production of X, a relevant tax difference would arise in an economy in which tax rates were progressive (increased with taxable income) if the production of the marginal unit of X consumed more-skilled and hence better-paid labor than did the production of the sacrificed Y. In any event, when the issue is $\Sigma D(P\pi_{\Delta UOX})$, not only externality-related adjustments but also tax-related adjustments will have to be made to MC_X and/or MC_Y to produce a MC^*_X/MC^*_Y ratio that equals $MRT_{Y/X}$. Obviously, if line (4) of the $\Sigma D(P\pi_{\Delta UOX})$ analysis substitutes P^*_X for the P_X in line (4) of the MD/XD($P\pi_{\Delta UOX}$) analysis, P^*_Y for the P_Y in line (4) of the MD/XD($P\pi_{\Delta UOX}$) analysis, and a different MC^*_X and a different MC^*_Y for the (MC^*_X) and (MC^*_Y) that appeared in line (4) of the MD/XD($P\pi_{\Delta UOX}$) analysis, $\Sigma D(P\pi_{\Delta UOX})$ will turn out to equal $MC^*_X([P^*_Y/MC^*_Y] - [P^*_X/MC^*_X]) = MC^*_X([P^*_Y/P_Y][P_Y/MC_Y][MC_Y/MC^*_Y] - [P^*_X/P_X][P_X/MC_X][MC_X/MC^*_X])$ in lines (6) and (7) of the $\Sigma D(P\pi_{\Delta UOX})$ analysis where MC^*_X and MC^*_Y in this analysis differ from MC_X and MC_Y for more reasons than did their counterparts in the MD/XD($P\pi_{\Delta UOX}$) analysis.

$\Sigma D(P\pi_{\Delta UOX})$ ON REALISTIC ASSUMPTIONS ABOUT THE USES FROM WHICH THE RESOURCES CONSUMED BY THE PRODUCTION OF THE MARGINAL UNIT OF X ARE WITHDRAWN

All the preceding analyses of various distortions in the profits yielded by the production of the marginal unit of an existing product have assumed that the resources used for this purpose were withdrawn from the production of other existing products. That assumption is unrealistic. Even if leisure is classified as an existing product so that the preceding analyses can be said to encompass any flow of resources from leisure production to the production of other existing goods, the analyses that have so far been executed have ignored the fact that some of the resources that the production of marginal units of existing products consume are withdrawn from QV-investment creation and PPR execution. This subsection outlines the way in which the formula for $\Sigma D(P\pi_{\Delta UOX})$ will be affected by this reality.

$\Sigma D(P\pi_{\Delta UOX}) = \Sigma D(PB_{\Delta UOX}) - \Sigma D(PC_{\Delta UOX})$. If, as we previously assumed, all the resources the production of the marginal unit of X consumes were withdrawn from the production of other products Y, $\Sigma D(PC_{\Delta UOX})$ would equal the difference between the allocative value of the sacrificed units of Y and their private value to their producers—that is, the difference between the sum of the marginal allocative products (the allocative value) the resources used to produce the marginal unit of X would have generated in their alternative uses and the total of the marginal revenue products (the relevant private value) they would have generated in their alternative uses (where the relevant private value is the value of the resources to their alternative purchasers since the producer of X had to bid them away from those other unit output producers, not [at least directly] their value to the buyers of the goods those alternative purchasers would have used them to produce). In a situation in which some of the resources the production of a marginal unit of X consumes are withdrawn from unit-output-producing uses, some from QV-investment-creating uses, and some from PPR-executing uses, the preceding difference will be only one component of $\Sigma D(PC_{\Delta UOX})$. The other components of that aggregate distortion will be (1) the difference between the total allocative product that those resources the production of the marginal unit of X withdrew from QV-investment-creating uses would have generated in those alternative uses and the total private benefits they would have conferred on the QV investors who would otherwise have used them to create QV investments and (2) the difference between the total allocative product that those resources the production of the marginal unit of X withdrew from PPR-executing uses would have generated in those alternative uses and the total private benefits they would have conferred on the PPR owners who would otherwise have used them to execute PPR projects—that is, will be the sum of the aggregate distortions in the private benefits the resources in question would have conferred on those of their alternative buyers who would otherwise have used them to create QV investments or execute PPR projects.

Obviously, the formula for $\Sigma D(P\pi_{\Delta UOX})/LC_{\Delta UOX}$ will have to be altered to reflect the fact that some QV-to-UO and PPR-to-UO resource flows will actually take the place of some of the UO-to-UO resource flows I originally assumed the production of marginal units of X involved. Unfortunately, I cannot explain how this alteration will affect $\Sigma D(PB_{\Delta UO})/LC_{\Delta UO}$ until I develop formulas for $\Sigma D(PB_{\Delta QV})/PB_{\Delta QV}$ and $\Sigma D(PB_{\Delta PPR})/PB_{\Delta PPR}$, which I will do respectively later in this chapter.

However, at this juncture, I do want to outline why I think that the net effect of the ΔQV-to-ΔUO and ΔPPR-to-ΔUO resource-flows will be to decrease the deflation of $PC_{\Delta UO}$ and hence to increase the deflation of $P\pi_{\Delta UO}$ for all existing products. This conclusion reflects two empirical premises. The first (whose theoretical basis I will explain later in this chapter) is that the private benefits of creating a marginal QV investment—that is, the operating profits that will be generated by the use of the marginal QV investment (such as the sale of the new product it creates)—are inflated: this premise implies that, to the extent that the production of the relevant marginal unit of output withdraws resources from the creation of a marginal QV investment, $PC_{\Delta UO}$ will be inflated and $P\pi_{\Delta UO}$ will therefore be deflated. The second (whose theoretical basis I will also explain later in this chapter) is that the private benefits of executing a PPR project—the profits its owner can realize by using the discovery himself, licensing others to use it, or selling it outright to someone else—are deflated but by a smaller percentage than the percentage by which the private benefits of producing a marginal unit of output are deflated: this premise implies that the substitution of PPR-to-UO resource flows for some of the UO-to-UO resource flows the original analysis posited will also reduce the amount by which $PC_{\Delta UO}$ is deflated and hence increase the deflation of $P\pi_{\Delta UO}$.

THE RATIO OF TOTAL UO-TO-UO MISALLOCATION IN THE ECONOMY TO THE AMOUNT OF RESOURCES DEVOTED TO UNIT OUTPUT PRODUCTION

The preceding analyses demonstrate that the ratio of the amount of UO-to-UO misallocation generated in an economy to "the amount of resources" (see below) it allocates to unit output production will increase with the difference between the P*/MC* ratios of goods between whose production resources flow (where P*/MC* can also be expressed as [P*/P][P/MC][MC/MC*]). This subsection explains why I think that this ratio difference and, concomitantly, UO-to-UO resource misallocation are far smaller in virtually all economies than most observers seem to believe.[26] Since both the traditional economic-efficiency rationale for antitrust and the conventional analysis of the so-called welfare cost of monopoly focus almost exclusively on this type of misallocation, this conclusion is of considerable significance.

My conclusion that UO-to-UO misallocation is far less extensive than many appear to believe is based on five sets of empirical assumptions. The first is the assumption that the QV-to-UO and PPR-to-UO resource flows that take place in any economy do not significantly affect the magnitude of its UO-to-UO misallocation. Basically, this assumption is that the $\Sigma D(PB_{\Delta QV}/PB_{\Delta QV}$ and $\Sigma D(PB_{\Delta PPR})/PB_{\Delta PPR}$ ratios for the QV investments and PPR projects sacrificed to produce marginal units of different products are the same and that the production of marginal units of different products withdraw resources in the same proportions from alternative QV-investment-creating and PPR-executing uses. This first assumption is important in the current context because it implies that UO-to-UO misallocation can be inferred from the difference between each product's P*/MC* ratio and the weighted-average P*/MC* ratio of the products from whose production the former product's production withdraws resources.

The second empirical assumption is that the production of marginal units of any product does not withdraw resources from the production of a random sample of the other goods in the economy, a random sample whose weighted-average P*/MC* ratio would equal its weighted-average economy-wide counterpart, but from a subset of the economy's other products that are atypically competitive with the product in question. Thus, a government policy that breaks up a price-fixing agreement between two firms in industry X will—by reducing their products' prices—increase the outputs of those products and reduce the outputs of other products not randomly but to an extent that increases with the degree to which they are competitive with the products whose prices were reduced (roughly speaking, the frequency with which they and the price-fixed products were well placed to obtain the patronage of the same buyers).

The third through fifth sets of empirical assumptions are that the differences between the (P*/P), (P/MC), and (MC/MC*) ratios of different products are respectively highly negatively correlated with the extent to which they are competitive with each other. I will now investigate each of these last three claims in turn.

In brief, I believe that two products that are highly competitive with each other tend to have P*/P ratios that are closer to each other than either is to the economy's weighted-average P*/P ratio because the consumption of highly rivalrous goods is likely to generate atypically similar amounts of externalities relative to their cost and because the buyers of rivalrous goods are likely to make atypically similar mistakes when valuing them and/or determining the price they can profitably pay for them (given their assessment of their value).

Three arguments underlie my belief that there is a strong, negative correlation between the difference between the P/MC ratios of the economy's various pairs of products and the extent to which the products in question are competitive with each other. First, goods that are highly competitive with each other tend to have similar marginal costs. Second, because goods that are highly competitive with each other tend to be similarly differentiated, their suppliers tend to have similar distributions of competitive advantages and hence similar highest non-oligopolistic price *minus* marginal cost (HNOP – MC) differences. And third, because producers of goods that are highly competitive with each other tend to have similar numbers of close rivals for the patronage of the buyers they are respectively privately best placed to supply and to be similarly placed in other respects that affect their ability to obtain oligopolistic margins either naturally or through contrivance,[27] they tend to secure similar oligopolistic margins on their sales.

Finally, three considerations favor my belief that there is a strong negative correlation between the difference between the ratios of external to internal marginal costs of production of the economy's various pairs of products and the extent to which the products in question are competitive with each other. First, once again, goods that are highly competitive with each other tend to have similar marginal costs. Second, the production of goods that are highly competitive with each other tends to generate atypically similar amounts of external marginal costs because the goods tend to be produced with similar technologies and similar inputs. Third, the production of goods that are highly competitive with each other tends to generate atypically similar amounts of external marginal costs because their producers tend to belong to the same lobbying groups and hence to be equally successful at preventing the promulgation of externality-internalizing legislation, administrative regulations, and judicial rulings.

Of course, I recognize that the last two correlations in particular are far from perfect. The P/MC ratios of coal and oil are quite different from each other, and I would not be surprised to discover that the ratios of internal to external marginal costs for tin cans and bottles differ to a greater extent than do their average economy-wide counterparts. Still, I do think that the second and third empirical premises of my speculative conclusion are substantially accurate. To the extent that they and their three predecessors are correct, my speculative conclusion will be justified: UO-to-UO resource flows will not take place between the production of a product X with whatever P*/MC* ratio it has and a set of sacrificed products Y whose weighted-average P*/MC* ratio equals its weighted-average counterpart for the economy but between the production of additional units of product X whose P*/MC* ratio deviates in some way from its weighted-average economy-wide counterpart and the production of units of the members of product set Y whose weighted-average P*/MC* ratio deviates from its economy-wide counterpart in the same direction as and (I suspect) to only a slightly smaller extent than does P_X^*/MC_X^* (slightly smaller because X's production will reduce the sales of some distant competitors). If this is the case, the $\Sigma D(P\pi_{\Delta UO})/LC_{\Delta UO}$ ratios for all products in the economy will be quite similar and the amount of UO-to-UO resource misallocation will be far smaller than would otherwise be the case.

One final related matter requires consideration. The first sentence in this subsection enquoted the expression "the amount of resources" devoted to unit output production in the economy. In previous subsections, the counterpart amounts were usually measured by their allocative costs and occasionally measured by their private costs. In the current context, the amount in question should really refer to something like the allocative cost of the resources the economy devoted to unit output production. My problem is that, since additional production-process research would have no allocative value if no units of output were produced and since the allocative benefits generated by the use of any additional QV investments that were created would be drastically affected by the economy's failure to use its existing QV investments, I do not know what "the allocative cost of all the resources devoted to unit output production in a given economy" means. Hence, the "amount of resources" devoted to unit output production in the economy cop-out.

IMPLICATIONS FOR THE ALLOCATIVE EFFICIENCY OF THE PERCENTAGE OF THE ECONOMY'S RESOURCES DEVOTED TO UNIT-OUTPUT-PRODUCING USES

I have already indicated why I believe that too few resources are allocated to the production of goods other than leisure relative to the amount allocated to the production of leisure. I now want to outline the arguments that have led me to reach the following three conclusions:

1. from the perspective of economic efficiency, too few resources are allocated to unit-output-producing uses as opposed to QV-investment creation and use;
2. probably, from the perspective of economic efficiency, too few resources are allocated to the production of existing products through existing production processes as opposed to PPR execution and use; and
3. almost certainly, from this perspective, too few resources are devoted to the production of existing products with existing technologies as opposed to the combination of QV-investment creation and use and PPR execution and use—that is, almost certainly, economic efficiency would be increased if, without generating any allocative transaction costs, one reallocated some percentage of the resources currently devoted to QV-investment creation and use and the same percentage of the resources currently devoted to PPR execution and use from a random sample of the marginal uses of each of these types to a random sample of unit-output-producing uses that are currently just extramarginal.

The reason that the following discussion does no more than *outline* the basis of these speculations is that my argument for these conclusions depends on various empirical assumptions I make about the determinants of the magnitudes of $\Sigma D(P\pi_{\Delta QV})/LC_{\Delta QV}$ and $\Sigma D(P\pi_{\Delta PPR})/LC_{\Delta PPR}$ whose relevance I cannot establish before I develop formulas for these distortions later in this chapter.

In brief, I am confident that an allocative-transaction-costless shift of a significant amount of resources from a random sample of marginal QV-investment-creating-and-using uses to a random sample of marginal unit-output-producing uses would increase economic efficiency because I am confident not only that $\Sigma D(P\pi_{\Delta UO})$ is negative for the production of marginal units of virtually all existing products but also that $\Sigma D(P\pi_{\Delta QV})$ is positive for the creation and use of the vast majority of marginal QV investments. In particular, for reasons I will explain later in this section, I am confident that $\Sigma D(P\pi_{\Delta QV})$ is positive for all marginal QV investments that are not truly innovative (in my judgment, the vast majority of all marginal [indeed, of all] QV investments) and for virtually all marginal QV investments that are innovative. The claim that $\Sigma D(P\pi_{\Delta QV})$ is positive for the creation and use of the vast majority of innovative marginal QV investments reflects my admittedly contestable belief that, across all cases, the combination of our intellectual-property (IP) laws (patent, copyright, and trade-secret laws) and the ability of product innovators to keep secret the content of their new product and the production process used to produce it prevents other firms from obtaining many benefits from the innovator's discovery and at least internalizes and may even overinternalize the knowledge-creation-related benefits the discovery does confer on other businesses.

My belief that economic efficiency would be increased by an allocative-transaction-costless reallocation of a significant amount of resources from a random sample of marginal PPR-executing uses to a random sample of marginal unit-output-producing uses reflects my judgment that, although the economy-wide weighted-average $\Sigma D(P\pi_{\Delta PPR})/LC_{\Delta PPR}$ ratio is negative, its absolute value is lower than its $\Sigma D(P\pi_{\Delta UO})/LC_{\Delta UO}$ counterpart. This judgment reflects my guesstimates of the magnitudes of many of the parameters in the formula for $\Sigma D(P\pi_{\Delta UO})$ that this subsection developed and of many of the parameters in the formula for $\Sigma D(P\pi_{\Delta PPR})$ that I will develop later in this section. *Inter alia,* it reflects my judgment that the combination of our existing IP laws and the ability of production-process discoverers who use their discovery exclusively in their own operations to keep their innovation secret substantially reduces the knowledge-creation-related benefits the discovery confers on other businesses and substantially compensates the discoverer for any such benefits his efforts did generate.

My confidence that an allocative-transaction-costless reallocation of a significant amount of resources from a random sample of marginal QV-investment-creating-and-using uses and PPR-executing-and-using uses to a random sample of marginal unit-output-producing uses would increase economic efficiency is based on four empirical premises that I have already delineated and in some instances at least partially justified:

1. the weighted-average $\Sigma D(P\pi_{\Delta UO})/LC_{\Delta UO}$ ratio in the economy is negative;

2. the weighted-average $\Sigma D(P\pi_{\Delta QV})/LC_{\Delta QV}$ in the economy is positive;
3. the weighted-average $\Sigma D(P\pi_{\Delta PPR})/LC_{\Delta PPR}$ ratio in the economy, though negative, is less negative than the weighted-average $\Sigma D(P\pi_{\Delta UO})/LC_{\Delta UO}$ ratio in the economy; and
4. more of the economy's resources are devoted to QV-investment creation and use than to PPR execution and use so that even if the weighted-average $\Sigma D(P\pi_{\Delta PPR})/LC_{\Delta PPR}$ ratio is more negative than the weighted-average $\Sigma D(P\pi_{\Delta UO})/LC_{\Delta UO}$ ratio, a random reallocation of resources from marginal QV-investment-related uses and marginal PPR-related uses to unit-output-producing uses would increase economic efficiency.

Of course, I am aware that the persuasiveness of this conclusion depends on the persuasiveness of the arguments I will make below about the signs and absolute values of the economy's weighted-average $\Sigma D(P\pi_{\Delta QV})/LC_{\Delta QV}$ and $\Sigma D(P\pi_{\Delta PPR})/LC_{\Delta PPR}$ ratios. However, despite this fact, I thought that even at this juncture, it was worthwhile to outline why I think that total-UO/total-QV/total-PPR misallocation is present in the economy—in particular, *inter alia,* that from the perspective of economic efficiency too few resources are allocated to unit-output-producing uses.

$\Sigma D(P\pi_{\Delta QV})$ on Varying Assumptions about the Types of Resource Uses the Creation and Use of Marginal QV Investments Sacrifice

SOME ANALYSES

This subsection's analyses of various distortions in the profits yielded by marginal QV investments follows the preceding subsection's practice of generating its conclusions from separate analyses of the relevant distortions in the private cost and private benefits of the marginal resource uses in question. It is important to note at the outset that in the QV-investment context I distinguish two categories of costs and two categories of benefits. The two categories of costs—each of which has two subtypes—are completely independent of each other. The first category of costs contains the private and allocative cost of *creating* the QV investment (symbolized respectively as $PC_{\Delta QV}$ and $LC_{\Delta QV}$). The second category of costs contains the private and allocative cost of *using* the marginal QV investment (symbolized respectively as $PC_{U\Delta QV}$ and $LC_{U\Delta QV}$). In the text that follows, I will be defining the private and allocative costs of creating a marginal QV investment in what I take to be a conventional way—namely, to refer respectively to the private and allocative cost of the resources consumed by the creation of the marginal QV investment in question. Equally conventionally, I will be defining the private and allocative cost of using a marginal QV investment to equal respectively the private and allocative (variable) cost of producing units of the product the investment created, of operating the outlet the investment created, of using the capacity the investment created, or of selling and distributing the inventory the investment created. This conventional definition is not inevitable: one could also define the relevant costs to include any costs or losses the use of the marginal QV investment generated by taking sales from the investor's preexisting projects, by inducing rivals to respond in nonretaliatory ways that still reduced those projects' profit yields, or by inducing rivals to retaliate against the maker of the marginal QV investment. In the text that follows, I will classify the latter types of costs or losses as negative private and allocative benefits. I have made this choice purely for expositional reasons (partly because each of the costs in question has a possible positive benefit counterpart). As defined, the private cost of using the QV investment is a negative component of what I will term the private (total) benefits the marginal QV investment generates—that is, the contribution the use of the marginal QV investment makes to the total supernormal profits the QV investor's organization generates. Relatedly, the allocative cost of using the QV investment affects the allocative efficiency of using the QV investment once it has been created—that is, the allocative efficiency of using the QV investment rather than costlessly destroying it. In any event, in the text that follows, the private cost of using the marginal QV investment will be symbolized as $PC_{U\Delta QV}$ or PC_{UOn}, and the allocative cost of using the marginal QV investment will be symbolized as $LC_{U\Delta QV}$ or LC_{UOn} where *n* stands for the new product, distributive outlet, capacity, or inventory the relevant marginal QV investment created.

Before proceeding, I should clarify my distinction between the cost of creating and the cost of using a QV investment by listing the kinds of costs I place in each category. Not surprisingly, the specific kinds of costs that belong in each category vary with the type of QV investment in question.

When the relevant QV investment creates a new product variant, the private and allocative costs of *creating* it consist of the private and allocative costs of (1) the market research in which the investor engaged to discover the attributes that any new product he might develop should contain prior to creating the new product he introduced, (2) the technical work he did to design the product variant he introduced (as well as various alternatives he eventually rejected), (3) the technical work he did to discover how best to produce his new product variant, (4) the cost he incurred to build and operate any pilot plant or less comprehensive production facility he constructed to produce initial exemplars of the new product, (5) the market research he did to test consumer reactions to his new product and various alternatives he eventually rejected (reactions both to hypothetical products that contained specified attributes and to actual exemplars of the product he actually introduced) to help him to decide whether to introduce the product and how to promote it, (6) the basic promotional campaign he ran to launch the new product, and (7) the plant and equipment he constructed or bought to produce his new product. By way of contrast, when a QV investment creates a new product variant, the cost of *using* the QV investment in question consists of the variable costs the investor incurs to produce and distribute his new product and any promotional costs he incurs to advertise it after it has been launched.

When a new QV investment creates a new distributive outlet, the private and allocative costs of creating the QV investment consist respectively of (1) the private and allocative costs of the background market research in which the investor engaged before reaching his initial conclusions about the location and other attributes that any new distributive outlet he created should contain, (2) the private and allocative costs of the initial designs of his new distributive outlet and its rejected alternatives, (3) the private and allocative costs of any market research he did to test those initial designs, (4) the private and allocative costs he incurred to finalize his outlet design and build the new distributive outlet, and (5) the private and allocative promotional costs he incurred to launch his new distributive outlet. By way of contrast, when a QV investment creates a new distributive outlet, the private and allocative costs of *using* the QV investment consist respectively of the private and allocative variable cost of buying and distributing the goods sold and the private and allocative variable cost of promoting both their sale and the outlet itself (the operating costs of running the new distributive outlet).

When a QV investment creates additional capacity or inventory (which increase the average speed with which the investor can supply his customers throughout a fluctuating-demand cycle), the private and allocative costs of *creating* the QV investment consist respectively of the private and allocative costs of building the capacity (including any related design costs) or the private and allocative costs of producing and storing the inventory in question. By way of contrast, (1) when the QV investment creates capacity, the private and allocative costs of *using* the QV investment consist respectively of the private and allocative variable costs of producing and distributing the units of product the capacity is used to produce and the private and allocative costs of advertising their availability, and (2) when the QV investment creates inventory, the private and allocative costs of *using* the QV investment consist respectively of the private and allocative costs of selling and delivering the inventory in question and any additional private and allocative advertising costs the investor generated to promote the product and its availability because he had more units available for sale.

As already indicated, I will also distinguish two categories of benefits that a marginal QV investment may generate. Each of these two categories of benefits has the same two subtypes as does its cost counterparts—a private subtype and an allocative subtype. However, the two categories of benefits are not independent: in particular, for each subtype, one is a component of the other. I will begin by describing the vocabulary I will use to refer to each category of private benefits and then specify the vocabulary I will use to refer to each category of the allocative benefits generated by a marginal QV investment.

The first category of private benefits (the use of) a marginal QV investment generates is the total revenue that use generates directly (symbolized as TR_{UOn})—the dollar sales of the new good (*n*) the marginal QV investment creates, the dollar sales of the (new) distributive outlet it creates, the amount of dollars for which the new inventory it creates is sold, or the dollar sales that are generated by the sale of the extra units of his product that the new capacity the marginal QV investment creates enables the investor to produce. The private benefits of the marginal QV investment are just one component of the second category of relevant private benefits I wish to distinguish—the (total) private benefits the (use of the) marginal QV investment confers on the marginal QV investor.

In my vocabulary, the (total) private benefits a marginal QV investment yields the QV investor who made it (symbolized as $PB_{\Delta QV}$) equal the amount by which the *use* of the marginal QV investment increases its maker's overall supernormal profits (once the marginal QV investment has been made). More specifically, $PB_{\Delta QV}$ *equals* (1) TR_{UOn} *minus* (2) $PC_{U\Delta QV}$ (the variable cost the marginal QV investor had to incur to produce the product his marginal QV investment created, to operate the outlet it created, to make use of the capacity it created, or to sell and distribute the inventory it created) *plus* (3) any amount by which the marginal QV investment increased the operating profits yielded by the marginal QV investor's preexisting QV investments—for example, (A) by increasing the demand for his old products by enabling him to offer a full line or by improving his reputation for quality or (B) by doing less damage to his preexisting projects' profit yields by taking sales away from his old products directly and inducing his rivals to alter their conduct in ways that reduce his old products' profit yields than would otherwise have been done by any rival QV investment the marginal QV investment deterred, *minus* (4) any positive difference between (A) the amount by which the marginal QV investment decreased the operating profits of the marginal QV investor's preexisting projects by taking sales from them or inducing rivals to respond in nonretaliatory ways that reduce those projects' profit yields and (B) the amount by which those profit yields would otherwise have been reduced for analogous reasons by any rival QV investments the marginal QV investment deterred, *minus* (5) any positive difference between (A) the amount by which the marginal QV investment reduced the profit yields of the marginal QV investor's preexisting projects by inducing rivals to retaliate and (B) the amount by which those projects' profit yields would otherwise have been reduced by rival retaliation against any rival QV investment the marginal QV investment deterred, *plus* (6) any supernormal profits the marginal QV investment yielded the investor by making it profitable for him to make a future QV investment he would not otherwise have found profitable or by increasing the profitability of a future QV investment he would have found profitable in any event by increasing the completeness of his product line or improving his reputation for quality.

Before proceeding to the allocative counterparts of these two categories of private benefits that marginal QV investments can generate, I should point out that the (total) private benefits in question—$PB_{\Delta QV}$—are different from the private (supernormal) profits the marginal QV investment yields—$P\pi_{\Delta QV}$. In particular, $P\pi_{\Delta QV} = PB_{\Delta QV} - PC_{\Delta QV}$.

The allocative counterpart to TR_{UOn} is the (net) allocative benefits generated directly by the consumption of the units of the product the marginal QV investment created, the units of the goods distributed by the outlet the marginal QV investment created, the units of the investor's old product produced by the capacity created by the marginal QV investment, or the units of the investor's old product that were supplied out of the inventory the marginal QV investment created. I will use the symbol LB_{UOn} to stand for this concept. As we have seen, LB_{UOn} may differ from TR_{UOn} because the consumers of the units in question misvalued them, realized buyer surplus on them, or were monopsonists when buying the relevant good or service and did not engage in perfect price discrimination when purchasing it, because the consumption of the units in question generated external benefits or costs, or because the availability of the new product increased the value of the producer's other products by enabling him to provide buyers with a full line or changing the image of his other products or their consumers' feelings of security in buying and using them. (Any externalities generated by the production or distribution of the relevant goods or services are taken into account when analyzing the relationship between $PC_{U\Delta QV}$ and $LC_{U\Delta QV}$.)

The allocative counterpart to $PB_{\Delta QV}$—$LB_{\Delta QV}$—equals the allocative-efficiency gain that is generated by the use of the marginal QV investment once it has been created—that is, the allocative-efficiency gain that would be generated by a decision to use that investment in the way in which it was used rather than to costlessly destroy it. This allocative-efficiency gain equals (1) LB_{UOn} *minus* (2) $LC_{U\Delta QV}$, which could also be symbolized as LC_{UOn} and which equals the allocative cost that the investor's use of the marginal QV investment generates by withdrawing from other uses the resources he buys to use his marginal QV investment *plus* the external allocative costs the investor's use of the QV investment generates because (A) the investor does not have to pay anything for some of the resources his use of the marginal QV investment (his production and distribution of the relevant goods and services) consumes and (B) the buyers of the product or services in question do not have to pay anything for some of the resources their shopping for the relevant goods or services consumes, *minus* (4) the allocative-efficiency loss the marginal QV investment generates because of the factors that resulted in the investor's having a monopolistic QV-investment incentive to make it *minus* (5) any allocative-efficiency loss the marginal QV investment generates by increasing the amount of retaliation in which firms engage.

One final reminder. $LB_{\Delta QV}$ is not the same as $LE_{\Delta QV}$. In particular, $LE_{\Delta QV} = LB_{\Delta QV} - LC_{\Delta QV}$.

$\Sigma D(PB_{\Delta QV})$ WHEN THE USE OF THE MARGINAL QV INVESTMENT WITHDRAWS RESOURCES EXCLUSIVELY FROM THE PRODUCTION OF EXISTING PRODUCTS

Both imperfections in price competition and imperfections in QV-investment competition can distort $PB_{\Delta QV}$ for a marginal QV investment whose use withdraws resources exclusively from alternative unit-output-producing uses. I will first analyze the distorting impact of imperfections in price competition on $PB_{\Delta QV}$ on the above assumption about the source of the resources the use of marginal QV investments consumes and then analyze the distorting impact of imperfections in QV-investment competition on $PB_{\Delta QV}$ on that assumption.

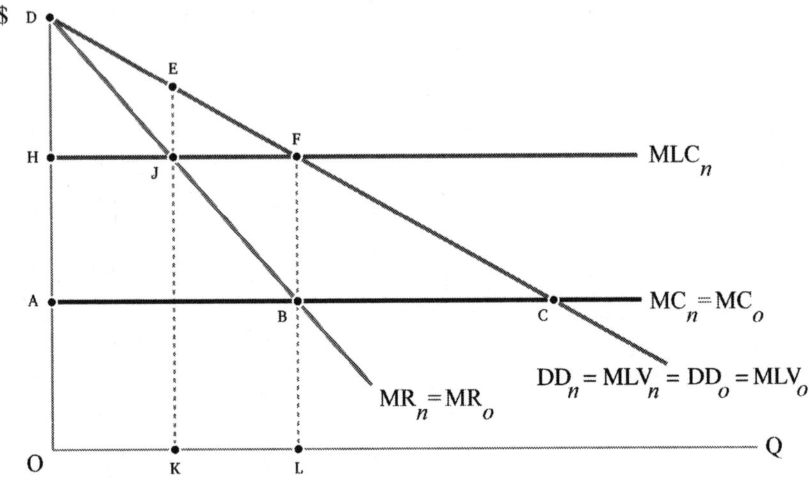

Diagram II

Diagram II illustrates the distorting effect that imperfections in price competition will have on $PB_{\Delta QV}$ by distorting both its TR_{UO_n} component and its $LC_{U\Delta QV}$ (that is, LC_{UO_n}) component. In Diagram II, (1) DD_n and MR_n indicate the demand and marginal revenue curves that the marginal QV investor in question will face when selling his new product *n*; (2) MC_n indicates the marginal cost curve the relevant QV investor will face on *n*; (3) DD_n is assumed to be identical to DD_o—the demand curves for each of the old products *o* that will lose sales to the new product *n* when it is produced; (4) MC_n is assumed to be identical to MC_o—the marginal cost curve for each of the old products from whose production resources will be withdrawn when *n* is produced; (5) DD_n is assumed to coincide with MLV_n (and DD_o is assumed to coincide with MLV_o) because the monopoly-distortion analysis assumes away the human errors, monopsony, and externalities of consumption that can cause MLV to diverge from DD; and (6) MLC_n is assumed to exceed MC_n—indeed, to exceed MC_n by just the amount that causes the output of *n* (the output OL, the output at point B at which MR_n cuts MC_n from above) to be allocatively efficient (to be the output at point F at which MLV_n cuts MLC_n from above). I take this assumption that the output of *n* will be allocatively efficient to be a neutral assumption. In any event, it is a corollary of the combination of (1) my assumption that the new product's demand and marginal cost curves will be identical to their counterparts for the old products from whose production the new product's production withdraws resources and (2) the monopoly-distortion analysis's assumption that the imperfections in seller competition on which we are focusing are the only type of Pareto imperfection in the economy. The first of these two assumptions implies that P_n/MC_n will equal P_o/MC_o for each of the relevant *o*s, and, as we have seen, in an otherwise-Pareto-perfect economy, resources will not be misallocated between the production of two products or between the production of one product and the production of a set of other products if each of the products in question has the same P/MC ratio (and none has any complements). I hasten to add that the assumptions that $DD_n = DD_o$ and that $MC_n = MC_o$ are plausible, given that the new product will primarily take sales away from products that are highly competitive with it. One final point: Diagram II's assumption that DD_n and DD_o are linear and that MC_n and MC_o are horizontal are made purely to facilitate the exposition. No significant conclusion I reach is critically affected by these last assumptions.

Now that I have described Diagram II, I can use it to analyze $MD(PB_{\Delta QV})$ on the assumption that all the resources that the use of the relevant marginal QV investment consumes are withdrawn from unit-output-producing uses. As Diagram II reveals, on this assumption, two imperfections or sets of imperfections in price competition will distort $PB_{\Delta QV}$. First, the imperfections in the price competition faced by the producers of the old products whose outputs will be reduced when the new product created by the marginal QV investment in question is produced will inflate $PB_{\Delta QV}$ by deflating $PC_{U\Delta QV}$ (by causing $PC_{U\Delta QV}$ to be lower than $LC_{U\Delta QV} \equiv LC_{UO_n}$). More specifically, the imperfections in the price competition faced by the producers of *o* will generate this outcome by reducing the private value these resources will have for the producers of *o* from whom the owner of the marginal QV investor will bid them away when he uses his marginal QV investment ($MRP_{R/o}$—the marginal revenue product the resources R would generate for the producers of *o*, which is infinitesimally less than the sum the marginal QV investor will have to pay for them) below the marginal allocative product they would generate in the employ of these producers of *o* ($MLP_{R/o}$). In terms of Diagram II, this effect is manifest by MC_n's being lower than MLC_n.

Second, at least if I attribute the buyer surplus that the sale of *n* will generate to the imperfections in price competition the relevant QV investor will face when selling *n*, the imperfections in price competition the owner of the marginal QV investment faces when selling *n* or operating the new distributive outlet the marginal QV investment creates will deflate $PB_{\Delta QV}$ by the buyer surplus in question. In other terms, the imperfections in price competition the owner of the marginal QV investment faces when selling *n* will deflate $PB_{\Delta QV}$ by causing TR_{UOn} to be lower than LB_{UOn}.

In Diagram II, the inflation of $PB_{\Delta QV}$ associated with the tendency of the imperfections in price competition the producers of products *o* face to deflate the private cost to the QV investor of using his QV investment by producing units of *n* (area HFBA) is bigger than the deflation of $PB_{\Delta QV}$ generated by the buyer surplus the sale of *n* generates (area DFH). This difference is not attributable to the fact that the DD curves in Diagram II are constructed to be linear and/or to the fact that the MC curves in Diagram II are constructed to be horizontal. More positively, the difference in question reflects the fact that, if $MC_n = MC_o$ for each old product and the production of *n* reduces by one unit the output of each old product whose output it reduces, the per-unit deflation in the variable cost of producing the new product *n* will equal the difference between the heights of the DD_o and MR_o curves (between P_o and MR_o) for each old product *o* at its actual output—that is, the additional buyer surplus the producers of the old products generated before the QV investment was made by reducing their old products' prices sufficiently to enable them to sell their marginal units of the old products—while the per-unit (buyer-surplus) deflation in the revenue the QV investor obtained by selling *n* equals the lower, average difference in the heights of DD_n and MR_n between the *y*-axis (output zero) and *n*'s actual output. In Diagram II, the output both of each of the old products *o* and of the new product *n* is OL = AB (the outputs at which MR_o cuts MC_o from above for each product *o* and MR_n cuts MC_n from above); the per-unit deflation of the private variable cost of producing *n* is FB; and the per-unit deflation in the revenue the QV investor secured by selling units of his new product is EJ. The fact that in Diagram II the per-unit deflation in the revenue the QV investor secured by selling units of *n* equals the difference between DD_n and MR_n at half the output of *n* (OK $= [\frac{1}{2}]$OL) and the related fact that the per-unit revenue deflation in question (EJ) is one-half the per-unit deflation in the private variable cost of producing *n* (HA) are artifacts of Diagram II's arbitrary assumption that DD_n and DD_o are not only identical but linear and the preceding analysis's assumption that the production of *n* reduces the output of each *o* whose output it reduces by exactly one unit. However, as previously indicated, the conclusion that the inflation in $PB_{\Delta QV}$ that is caused by the imperfections in price competition faced by the producers of *o* exceeds the deflation in $PB_{\Delta QV}$ caused by the imperfection in price competition that the marginal QV investor will face when selling *n* does not depend on these assumptions: indeed, although, *ceteris paribus*, the ratio of the above inflation to the above deflation will fall below two if the individual old products' outputs drop by more than one unit, the ratio may be higher than two if DD_n is not linear—for example, if DD_n is concave to the origin.

Although Diagram II does not illustrate this possibility, imperfections in QV-investment competition can also distort $PB_{\Delta QV}$. More particularly, to the extent that a marginal QV investment reduced the profit yields of the investor's other QV investments more by taking sales away from the products or outlets they created and by inducing his rivals to respond in a nonstrategic way than those preexisting projects' profit yields would otherwise have been reduced in these ways by any rival QV investment the marginal QV investment in question deterred, $PB_{\Delta QV}$ will have been deflated by the associated monopolistic QV-investment disincentives that confronted the investor in question. *A fortiori,* to the extent that the marginal QV investment reduced the profit yields of the investor's preexisting projects not only in the above ways but also by inducing a rival to make a QV investment that neither he nor anyone else would otherwise have made, $PB_{\Delta QV}$ will have been deflated by the associated natural oligopolistic QV-investment disincentives that confronted the investor in question. Finally, if the marginal QV investor faced retaliation barriers to expansion or entry, $PB_{\Delta QV}$ will have been deflated on their account as well to the extent that the private cost the retaliation imposed on the investor exceeded the allocative inefficiency the retaliation generated. On the other hand, to the extent that the marginal QV investment increased the profit yields of the investor's other projects because the damage it did to those projects' profit yields by taking sales from them and inducing rivals to respond in damaging though nonstrategic ways was smaller than the damage that would otherwise have been done to them both directly and indirectly by the rival QV investment(s) the marginal QV investment deterred, $PB_{\Delta QV}$ will have been inflated by the monopolistic QV-investment incentives the investor had to make the marginal QV investment.

If I were forced to make an informed guesstimate (informed by my experience as an antitrust scholar and lawyer), I would suggest that, in a substantial majority of cases, the relevant imperfections in QV-investment competition inflated $PB_{\Delta QV}$. This conclusion is based on the following empirical assumptions: (1) antitrust enforcement has largely eliminated retaliation barriers to expansion and entry, and (2) most marginal QV investors are established firms that had monopolistic QV-investment incentives to make their marginal QV investment because they found themselves in a situation in which (A) someone else would make a QV investment in their area of product-space if they did not, (B) their QV investment would deter the established or potential competitor in question from making a QV investment in their area of product-space, and (C) the deterred rival QV investment would have reduced the profit yields or the marginal QV investor's preexisting projects by more than his own QV investment reduced those profits relative to the *status quo ante.* Assumption (2C) in turn reflects my belief that the deterred rival QV investment (1) would have been located closer in product-space to the marginal QV investor's preexisting projects than its own new project would be, (2) would have been operated in a more competitive way that would be more damaging to the marginal QV investor's other projects' profit yields than was the marginal QV investor's marginal QV investment (proximity considerations aside), and (3) would have been more likely than the marginal QV investor's marginal QV investment to induce the marginal QV investor's other rivals to increase the competitiveness of their decisions (at least when the rival project in question would have been introduced by a new entrant).

In my judgment, then, both the extant imperfections in price competition and the extant imperfections in QV-investment competition will tend to inflate $PB_{\Delta QV}$ for marginal QV investments whose use withdraws resources exclusively from alternative unit-output-producing uses. My conclusion, then, is that in virtually all cases $MD(PB_{\Delta QV})$ will be positive for all such marginal QV investments.

$MD(PC_{\Delta QV})$ WHEN THE RESOURCES USED TO CREATE THE MARGINAL QV INVESTMENT ARE WITHDRAWN EXCLUSIVELY FROM THE PRODUCTION OF MARGINAL UNITS OF EXISTING PRODUCTS

To the extent that the marginal QV investor withdrew the resources he used to create his marginal QV investment from unit-output-producing uses by producers who faced downward-sloping demand curves and would not have engaged in perfect price discrimination when selling the sacrificed units of output, the imperfections in price competition faced by these alternative users of the resources in question will have deflated the private cost of creating the QV investment by reducing the private value of the resources to these alternative users (the total of the marginal revenue products they would have generated for the relevant producers) below the allocative value these resources would have generated in these alternative users' employ (the total of the marginal allocative products they would have generated if used to produce marginal units of their alternative users' products). The imperfections in the price competition faced by the alternative employers of the resources the marginal QV investment consumed will also have deflated their value to their alternative users to the extent that the sale of the additional units of output that these alternative users would have employed them to produce would have reduced the profits these alternative users made on other products by inducing their competitors to make a response that had this effect. Since $PC_{\Delta QV}$ for any marginal QV investment whose creation withdrew resources exclusively from the production of marginal units of existing products will not be affected by (1) any imperfections in price competition that the marginal QV investor faced when selling the new product or operating the new distributive outlet the marginal QV investment created, (2) any imperfections in QV-investment competition he confronted when making the QV investment in question, or (3) any other imperfection in seller competition, $MD(PC_{\Delta QV})$ for any marginal QV investment that withdrew the resources its use consumed exclusively from alternative unit-output-producing uses will be negative—that is, the relevant imperfections in seller competition will deflate $PC_{\Delta QV}$ for such marginal QV investments in an otherwise-Pareto-perfect economy.

MD($P\pi_{\Delta QV}$) FOR A MARGINAL QV INVESTMENT WHOSE CREATION AND USE WITHDREW RESOURCES EXCLUSIVELY FROM THE PRODUCTION OF EXISTING PRODUCTS

We have now concluded that the relevant imperfections in competition will inflate $PB_{\Delta QV}$ and deflate $PC_{\Delta QV}$ for any marginal QV investment whose creation and use withdrew resources exclusively from unit-output-producing uses. Obviously, these conclusions imply that the relevant imperfections in competition will inflate $P\pi_{\Delta QV}$ for such QV investments.

$\Sigma D(PB_{\Delta QV})/LC_{\Delta QV}$ FOR THE USE OF A MARGINAL QV INVESTMENT THAT WITHDREW RESOURCES EXCLUSIVELY FROM THE PRODUCTION OF EXISTING PRODUCTS

The private benefits yielded by the use of marginal QV investments are distorted not only—as we have just seen—by imperfections in seller competition and the buyer surplus generated by the use of the QV investments in question but also by all the other types of Pareto imperfections in the economy. This subsection analyzes $\Sigma D(PB_{\Delta QV})/LC_{\Delta QV}$ on the unrealistic assumption that all the resources the use of the relevant marginal QV investment consumes were withdrawn from the production of marginal units of existing products. The analysis has three components. The first focuses on the ways in which the economy's various Pareto imperfections would distort the private cost of using a marginal QV investment if its use withdrew resources exclusively from the production of existing products—in particular, on $\Sigma D(PC_{U\Delta QV})/LC_{U\Delta QV}$ for such a marginal QV investment. The second focuses on the ways in which the economy's various Pareto imperfections would distort the after-tax benefits such a marginal QV investor would obtain by using his marginal QV investment if he did not have to pay anything for the resources his use of his marginal QV investment directly consumed. And the third combines the results of its two predecessors to generate a conclusion about $\Sigma D(PB_{\Delta QV})/LC_{U\Delta QV}$.

(i) $\Sigma D(PC_{U\Delta QV})/LC_{U\Delta QV}$ for a Marginal QV Investment Whose Use Withdrew Resources Exclusively from the Production of Units of Existing Products

When all the resources consumed by the use of a marginal QV investment were withdrawn from unit output production, $\Sigma D(PC_{U\Delta QV})$ will equal (1) the (negative) difference between the (private) value of those resources to their alternative employers and the total of the marginal allocative products (TMLP) the resources in question would have generated in these alternative employers' employ *minus* (2) the TMLP in their alternative employ of the resources the use of the marginal QV investment consumed for which the marginal QV investor paid nothing *plus* (3) the difference between the factor taxes the marginal QV investor paid directly or indirectly to buy or use the resources in question and the factor taxes their alternative employers would have had to pay to buy and use them. In the preceding formulation, the (private) value of the resources in question to these alternative employers equals the total of the conventional marginal revenue products (TMRP) they would have yielded for them by increasing these sellers' outputs and sales of the goods they would have produced for them *minus* any amount by which this use of the resources in question would have reduced the profits their alternative employers made when selling other goods by altering the competitive decisions of rivals: the assumption that the relevant resources were withdrawn from the sellers of the old products rules out the possibility that their value to these alternative employers would also be reduced because their use by them would have cannibalized the sales of these alternative users' other products (since if they would have done so the QV investor's purchase of the resources would not have reduced the total amount of resources the putative alternative user actually employed in all his operations, would not have actually withdrawn resources from these putative alternative resource users because the putative alternative users would have continued to use them to produce units of their other products). In the preceding formulation, the TMLP of the resources in their alternative uses equals the private value to their consumers of the goods these resources would have produced in their alternative uses *plus* any external benefits *minus* any external costs that the goods' consumption would have generated. In the preceding formulation, the item that appears after (2) is simply the external allocative cost generated by the use of the marginal QV investment.

The first term in the preceding list of three was *resource*-oriented—that is, was the difference between the private value that the alternative employers of the *resources* the use of the marginal QV investment consumed placed on them and the allocative product these *resources* would have generated in these alternative employers' hands. For expositional reasons, I will now substitute for this resource-oriented term an equivalent *output*-oriented term. The equivalent *output*-oriented term is "the difference between the private value to the alternative users of the resources in question of the output these actors would have used them to produce and the allocative value of the sacrificed output."

Assume that the use of the marginal QV investment (say, the production and sale of actual units of the new product *n* it created) reduced the output of k old products and that the symbol $\sum_{o=1}^{k}$ stands for the sum of the figure for which the ellipses stand across all the old products o_1 to o_k whose outputs were reduced by the production of the new product *n*. Then, in a Pareto-perfect economy, the following relationships will obtain:

1. the prospective private value of the sacrificed units of old products to their prospective producers will be $\sum_{o=1}^{k} AP_{SU_o}(SU_o)$ where the subscript SU_o stands for sacrificed units of the *o* in question[28] and where AP_{SU_o} stands for the average before-tax price of the sacrificed units of each indicated old product (since $P_o = MR_o$ for each unit and the sale of the sacrificed units would not have affected the profits the seller earned on his other products);
2. the allocative value of the sacrificed units of old products will also be $\sum_{o=1}^{k} AP_{SU_o}(SU_o)$ (since the consumption of the sacrificed units would not have generated any external costs or benefits, no taxes would have been levied on the sale of the sacrificed units, and the buyers of the sacrificed units would have been nonmonopsonistic, sovereign maximizers whose purchase of the units in question would have yielded them no buyer surplus);
3. the allocative product in their alternative use of the resources the use of the marginal QV investment consumed would have equaled the allocative value of the sacrificed units of output they would have produced (since the

production of those units of output would have generated no external costs or benefits);

4. the marginal QV investor would have paid for all the resources his use of his marginal QV investment consumed (since his use of his marginal QV investment would have generated no external costs); and
5. neither the marginal QV investor nor the alternative employer of the resources in question would have paid any factor taxes to buy or use the resources the marginal QV investor's use of his QV investment consumed.

Hence, in a Pareto-perfect economy,

6. $\sum D(PC_{U\Delta QV}) = (\sum_{o=1}^{k} AP_{SU_o}[SU_o] - \sum_{o=1}^{k} AP_{SU_o}[SU_o]) - 0 + 0 = 0.$

However, the various Pareto imperfections that exist in real economies will change each of the first five preceding conclusions and presumptively the sixth as well. Thus, *ceteris paribus,* the net revenue the relevant resources' alternative users would have obtained by using them to produce additional units of *o* if they did not have to pay for the resources in question will be less than $\sum_{o=1}^{k} AP_{SU_o}(SU_o)$ when the producers of the sacrificed old products face downward-sloping demand curves and do not engage in perfect price discrimination and/or when the sacrificed sales of *o* would have elicited responses from their rivals that would have reduced the profits the sale of their other products yielded. Similarly, *ceteris paribus,* $\sum_{o=1}^{k} AP_{SU_o}(SU_o)$ will exceed the allocative value of the sacrificed units of *o* to the extent that the sacrificed units' buyers would have overestimated their value to them or the sacrificed units' buyers would have underestimated the actual cost to them of buying the units in question on the terms on which the relevant transaction would have been consummated, while, *ceteris paribus,* $\sum_{o=1}^{k} AP_{SU_o}(SU_o)$ will be lower than the allocative value of the sacrificed units of *o* to the extent that the consumption of the sacrificed units of *o* would have generated net external benefits, the sacrificed units' buyers would have secured buyer surplus as a result of their sale or would have had to pay monopsony rents to suppliers of intramarginal units to purchase the sacrificed units (because the buyers faced upward-sloping supply curves on the sacrificed products and would not engage in perfect price discrimination when purchasing the units in question), to the extent that the sacrificed units' buyers would have underestimated their value to them or overestimated the cost that the terms on which they would have purchased them would have imposed on them, to the extent that the consumption of the units in question would have generated external benefits, or to the extent that the buyers of the units in question would have had to pay taxes to purchase them. Of course, even if $\sum_{o=1}^{k} AP_{SU_o}(SU_o)$ does equal the allocative value of the sacrificed units of *o,* it will not equal the allocative product that the resources the use of the marginal QV investment withdrew from the production of *o* would have generated in this alternative use if the production of *o* generated external costs or benefits: to the extent that the production of the sacrificed units of *o* would have generated external costs (benefits), the private value to the producers of *o* of the resources the use of the marginal QV investment withdrew from them would have been inflated (deflated) on this account, and, *ceteris paribus,* the cost of these resources to the marginal QV investor would concomitantly have been inflated (deflated). Finally, and obviously, *ceteris paribus,* (1) to the extent that the production of the sacrificed units of *o* would have generated net external costs (benefits), $\Sigma D(PC_{U\Delta QV})$ will be positive (negative) on their account (since the value of the resources in question to their alternative employers and hence their cost to the marginal QV investor would be inflated [deflated] by the non-internalization of the external costs [benefits] in question), (2) to the extent that the use of the marginal QV investment (say, the production of the new product *n* it creates) generated external costs, $\Sigma D(PC_{U\Delta QV})$ will be negative on this account,[29] and (3) to the extent that the marginal QV investor paid factor taxes (indirectly or directly) to buy and/or use the resources the use of this marginal QV investment consumes that exceeded the taxes that their alternative employers would have had to pay to buy and/or use them, $\Sigma D(PC_{U\Delta QV})$ will be positive on that account as well.

This last point requires some elucidation. The relevant factor taxes include the property taxes that the marginal QV investor paid on the land and buildings he used to produce the new product *n* and the additional taxes of this sort the producers of *o* would have had to pay to purchase or use the land or buildings they would have used to produce the sacrificed units of *o.* The factor taxes also include any income taxes that the workers the marginal QV investor hired to produce *n* paid on the taxable income they received from him and the income taxes those workers would have paid on the taxable income they would have received from the producers of *o* who would otherwise have hired them. Finally, the relevant factor taxes include any sales or excise taxes the marginal QV investor paid on the inputs he used to produce *n* and the sales or excise taxes the producers of the sacrificed units of *o* would have paid to buy or use the factors they would have used for this purpose.

Obviously, any of the above sorts of factor taxes the marginal QV investor paid to use his QV investment will have inflated $PC_{U\Delta QV}$ (at least if, as I am assuming, the taxes in question are not externality-internalizing taxes). Equally obviously, the factor taxes that the producers of *o* would have had to pay to produce the sacrificed units of *o* will have deflated $PC_{U\Delta QV}$ by deflating the private value of the relevant resources to the producers of *o*.

The preceding two sentences imply that factor taxes will on balance have inflated $PC_{U\Delta QV}$ if the factor taxes the marginal QV investor paid to use his marginal QV investment exceeded the factor taxes the producers of *o* would have paid to use those factors to produce the sacrificed units of *o* and will on balance have deflated $PC_{U\Delta QV}$ if the factor taxes the marginal QV investor paid to use his marginal QV investment exceeded the factor taxes the producers of *o* would have paid to use those factors to produce the sacrificed units of *o*. Therefore, the relevant factor taxes will be consequential if, but only if, the marginal QV investor and the producers of *o* respectively paid and would have paid different amounts of factor taxes to buy and use the resources the former withdrew from the latter. There are several reasons why this condition may be fulfilled: (1) the applicable formal property-tax rate or the property valuation to which this rate is applied may vary with the use to which the property in question is put or the location of the relevant building sites, (2) the percentage of the wage package that the marginal QV investor paid the relevant workers that constitutes taxable income may differ from its counterpart for the wage package the producers of the sacrificed units of *o* would have paid them (for example, the marginal QV investor may offer more [less] attractive work or working conditions and lower [higher] monetary [taxable] recompense)—a difference that may affect the taxes levied on the relevant labor not only by affecting the taxable income that that labor was paid but also the tax rate applied to that income if the applicable tax regime did not apply a flat tax to earned income, and (3) sales taxes on other sorts of inputs may also vary with the use to which the factor in question is put or the location of the factor user—for example, factor buyers who will use the factors in certain ways or are located in certain areas may pay lower sales taxes on the inputs they purchase or be exempt from paying any sales taxes at all on the purchase of certain or any factors of production.

It should now be possible to produce a formula for $\Sigma D(PC_{U\Delta QV})/LC_{U\Delta QV}$. For simplicity and because I suspect it will prove to be TBLE to ignore these possibilities, the formula I delineate will assume that $PC_{U\Delta QV}$ will not be distorted by human errors, the monopsony power of the sacrificed units of *o*'s buyers, or (at least) by the combination of such Pareto imperfections.

On these assumptions, $\sum_{D}(PC_{U\Delta QV}) = \sum_{o=1}^{k}(AMR_{SU_o} - AP_{SU_o})SU_o - \sum_{o=1}^{k}(AXLBC_{SU_o})SU_o + \sum_{o=1}^{k}AXLCP_{SU_o}(SU_o) - AXLCP_n(Q_n) - \sum_{o=1}^{k}ASTR_{SU_o}(AP_{SU_o})SU_o - \sum_{o=1}^{k}AFTR_{SU_o}(AVC_{SU_o})SU_o + AFTR_n(AVC_n)Q_n$ where AMR_{SU_o} stands for the average marginal revenue that the sale of the sacrificed units of the *o* in question would have generated, AP_{SU_o} stands for the average price for which the sacrificed units of the *o* in question would have been sold, SU_o stands for the number of units of the *o* in question that would have been sacrificed, $AXLBC_{SU_o}$ stands for the average external allocative benefits that would have been generated by the consumption of the sacrificed units of the *o* in question, $AXLCP_{SU_o}$ stands for the average external allocative costs that would have been generated by the production of the sacrificed units of the *o* in question, $AXLCP_n$ stands for the average external allocative costs that were generated by the production of *n* (once the QV investment that created *n* was completed), Q_n stands for the quantity of *n* that was produced, $ASTR_{SU_o}$ stands for the average sales-tax rate that would have been applied to the sales of the sacrificed units of the *o* in question, $AFTR_{SU_o}$ stands for the average factor-tax rate that would have been applied to the factors that would have produced the sacrificed units of the *o* in question, AVC_{SU_o} stands for the average variable cost of producing the sacrificed units of the *o* in question, $AFTR_n$ stands for the average factor-tax rate that was applied to the factors used to produce the units of *n* that were produced, and AVC_n stands for the average variable cost of producing the units of *n* that were produced. Obviously, on the assumption that no relevant distortions are generated by human errors or monopsony, the formula for $\Sigma D(PC_{U\Delta QV})/LC_{U\Delta QV}$ will equal the above formula divided by $LC_{U\Delta QV}$.

Before proceeding to the aggregate distortion in the additional (after-tax) revenue the use of the marginal QV investment will generate for its owner, I want to emphasize that I have no doubt whatsoever that on the weighted average $\Sigma D(PC_{U\Delta QV})$ would be negative if the use of marginal QV investments withdrew resources exclusively from the production of existing products. Indeed, I would be very surprised if, on this assumption, $\Sigma D(PC_{U\Delta QV})$ were positive for any marginal QV investment in any existing economy. The only conceivable exception would be a marginal QV investment whose use generated substantial external benefits that withdrew resources from the production of old products produced under unusually competitive conditions whose production and consumption generated substantial external costs. I doubt that these conditions are ever fulfilled to the extent necessary to render $\Sigma D(PC_{U\Delta QV})$ positive.

(ii) The Aggregate Distortion in the Amount by Which the Use of a Marginal QV Investment Would Increase the After-Tax Supernormal Profits of the Investor's Organization If He Did Not Have to Pay for the Resources the Use of This Investment Consumed

This subsection focuses on the aggregate distortion in the after-tax gain or net revenue that the use of a marginal QV investment would yield the investor in question if, counterfactually, the investor had to pay nothing for the resources the use of his marginal QV investment consumed and the resources his use of his marginal QV investment consumed would have had a zero allocative product in their alternative uses. If the marginal QV investment created a new product, the aggregate distortion in question would be the aggregate distortion in the net revenue the QV investor would secure by selling the units of *n* he produced rather than costlessly reneging on a sale he had arranged and costlessly destroying his output of *n*.

The analysis that follows will attribute to the use of the marginal QV investment some effects that might more accurately be attributed to its creation—the benefits that the marginal QV investment confers on the QV investor by deterring someone else from making a QV investment in the relevant area of product-space, the losses that the marginal QV investment imposes on the marginal QV investor by inducing someone else to make a nonstrategic QV investment that neither the induced investor nor anyone else would otherwise have made, the losses that the marginal QV investment imposes on the marginal QV investor by inducing a rival to retaliate, the benefits the marginal QV investment in question confers on other businesses and/or their customers by creating knowledge that those businesses use, the losses that the creation and use of the marginal QV investment in question impose on others who value having the latest thing by lowering the value to them of other goods in their possession, and the losses that the creation and use of the marginal QV investment imposes on others by inducing them to develop a preference for having the latest thing.

For the same reasons that in the last subsection I ignored the human-error distortions and monopsony distortions in $PC_{\Delta QV}$, I will ignore them in the current context as well—that is, I will assume that the relevant human-error and monopsony distortions are zero. On that assumption, the relevant after-tax private gain will still be distorted by the buyer surplus the use of the marginal QV investment (the sale of *n*) generates, by any monopolistic QV-investment incentives the marginal QV investor had to make his marginal QV investment, by any monopolistic or natural oligopolistic QV-investment disincentives he confronted in relation to his marginal QV investment, by any retaliation barriers he faced in relation to the marginal QV investment in question, by any external costs or benefits the consumption of *n* generates, by any external benefits the production of *n* generates, and by any additional income taxes the marginal QV investor had to pay because he executed the marginal QV investment in question. I will now address each of these possibilities in turn.

The imperfections in price competition that the marginal QV investor faced when selling his new product *n* will deflate the relevant private gains by the amount of buyer surplus *n*'s sales generate—$BS_n = (AP_n - AMR_n)Q_n$. As we saw earlier, if (1) DD_n is linear, (2) DD_n coincides with DD_o for each old product whose output the use of the marginal QV investment reduces, and (3) the production of *n* reduced the output of each such *o* by one unit, the absolute value of this $(AMR_n - AP_n)Q_n$ distortion in the relevant private gain will be twice the absolute value of the $\sum_{o=1}^{k} (AMR_{SU_o} - AP_{SU_o})(SU_o)$ distortion in $PC_{U\Delta QV}$. Indeed, even if the above assumptions are replaced with more realistic counterparts, the absolute value of the former distortion will exceed the absolute value of the latter distortion (indeed, may even be more than twice the absolute value of the latter distortion).

The imperfections in the QV-investment competition that the marginal QV investor faced in the area of product-space in which the marginal QV investment was located can either inflate or deflate the private gains on which we are now focusing. Such imperfections will inflate these private gains to the extent that the marginal QV investor had a monopolistic QV-investment incentive to make the marginal QV investment. They will deflate these private gains to the extent that he had a monopolistic or natural oligopolistic QV-investment disincentive to make it or faced a retaliation barrier to making the marginal QV investment in question. For reasons that I have previously explained, the absolute value of the distortions in question will, if anything, be larger than the private incentives, disincentives, or barriers that lay behind them. Thus, the distortion created by monopolistic QV-investment incentives will be larger than those incentives because, to the extent that the investor's marginal QV investment would induce his rivals to charge higher prices than they would have charged had the rival investment it deterred been made instead, it would misallocate resources on that account. The negative distortion associated with any non-critical monopolistic QV-investment disincentives will be absolutely larger or smaller than those disincentives to the extent that they reflect the investment's inducing the investor's rivals to charge lower prices since those price reductions would increase economic efficiency at the same time that they imposed losses on the investor. The distortion associated with any non-critical natural oligopolistic QV-investment disincentives an investor faces will equal those disincentives *minus* the amount by which the investment decreases allocative efficiency by inducing a rival to make a QV investment that would not otherwise have been made. Finally, the distortion associated with the retaliation barriers the marginal QV investor faced on the marginal QV investment will be larger than the private loss the relevant retaliation inflicted on him because, regardless of the type of retaliation the investment induces, the immediate impact of the retaliation in question will be misallocative. Thus, retaliatory price cuts tend to misallocate resources to the extent that they lead to the retaliator's making sales that he is privately and presumptively allocatively worse placed to make (though, admittedly, their impact on allocative efficiency will be uncertain if the target ends up retaining the sale in question at a lower price than he would otherwise have secured). And retaliatory advertising campaigns and product or outlet relocations probably misallocate resources across all cases since the inherent unprofitability of such moves creates a presumption that they are allocatively inefficient.

The formula I will delineate at the end of this subsection for the aggregate distortion in the private gains on which it focuses will ignore this complication. In that formula, $M_{\Delta QV}$, $O_{\Delta QV}$, and $L_{\Delta QV}$ will stand for the monopolistic disincentives, natural oligopolistic disincentives, and retaliation-barrier-related disincentives the marginal QV investor had to make his marginal QV investment, all three terms will be preceded by a minus sign, and $M_{\Delta QV}$ will itself be negative (while $-[M_{\Delta QV}]$—which will stand for any monopolistic QV-investment incentive a marginal QV investor had to make the marginal QV investment in question—is positive).

The private gains on which this subsection is focusing will also be distorted by various types of externalities other than the conventional externalities of production that (as we saw) distort $PC_{U\Delta QV}$. I will start with the two types of externalities whose distorting impact on the relevant private gains is easiest to analyze and then proceed to other types of externalities whose relevant impact is more difficult to assess.

The first type of externality whose distorting impact on the private gains on which this subsection focuses is easy to assess is any external allocative benefits that are generated either by the production of the new product the relevant marginal QV investment created or by the operation of the new distributive outlet it created. The non-internalization of these external benefits will obviously deflate the private gains in question. In the formula for the aggregate distortion in these private gains, these external benefits will be preceded by a minus sign and be symbolized as $TXLBP_n$, which stands for the total external allocative benefits generated by the production of *n*.

The second type of externality in this category is the conventional net external benefits or costs generated by the consumption of the new product the marginal QV investment created or by the operation of the distributive outlet it created. The consumption of a new product created by a marginal QV investment will generate conventional external benefits (costs) if non-buyers secure net equivalent-dollar gains (losses) from seeing, smelling, or hearing these products being consumed by others or simply by knowing that others are consuming these goods in circumstances in which these gains (losses) are not internalized to the buyers. In the formula for the aggregate distortion in the private gains on which this subsection focuses, the distortion generated by such conventional consumption externalities will be symbolized as $-NXLBC_n$, which stands for *minus* the net external allocative benefits of consumption generated by the consumption of the new product *n* that the relevant marginal QV investment created where $NXLBC_n$ will be negative (so that the term in question will be positive) when the consumption of *n* generates net external costs.

The third type of externality that is relevant in this context is somewhat more difficult to handle because the magnitude, indeed, the very existence of the externalities in question is certainly controversial and may be legitimately contestable. Those externalities are the external costs that the sale and possibly the mere availability of any new product a marginal QV investment creates impose on those buyers who desire to have "the latest thing" by lowering the value to them of rival products they already own or would otherwise have purchased and conceivably by encouraging members of the society in question to develop an allocatively inefficient generic taste for having the latest thing. I suspect that new products and the publicity that attends their launching tend to create substantial external costs of both these kinds. However, I acknowledge my inability to substantiate this suspicion with anything like scientifically acceptable evidence. In any event, to the extent that the availability and sale of the new product a marginal QV investment creates generates external costs of these kinds, the private gains on which this subsection focuses will be inflated by their non-internalization. In the formula for the aggregate distortion in these private gains, the distortion the non-internalization of such externalities generated will be preceded by a plus sign and symbolized by

$TXLC(LT)_{(A/C)n}$, which stands for the total external allocative costs that the availability and consumption (A/C) of the new product *n* generates by appealing to or promoting preferences for having the latest thing (LT).

Although I am certain that no one will doubt the existence of the fourth type of externality that is relevant in this context, its magnitude will be extremely difficult to determine. This fourth category contains the congestion-related and pollution-related external benefits that would be yielded by the use of marginal QV investments that created additional or more-locationally-convenient distributive outlets. Two subsets of such external benefits are worth distinguishing. First, to the extent that the new distributive outlet reduces the number of buyers who patronize preexisting distributive outlets, it will confer actual-shopping-decongestion external benefits on those buyers who patronize these other distributive outlets. Second, at least if the operation of the new, additional, or locationally superior distributive outlet does not change any relevant buyer's residential-location decision or any buyer-employing business's location decision, it will tend to generate external benefits by reducing the amount of traffic-congestion externalities and transportation-pollution externalities that its customers generate when traveling to shop by reducing the distance that they must travel to buy the sort of goods it supplies (though, admittedly, this effect will be offset to the extent that the locational convenience the new distributive outlet supplies induces the relevant buyers to make additional shopping trips).

The magnitude of the external benefits the operation of an additional or more-locationally-convenient distributive outlet will generate on all the preceding accounts will be difficult to measure. The net external effects of the operation of such a distributive outlet (located, say, in the suburbs) will be even more difficult to determine if it induces its customers to change their residential locations (for example, to move from the central city to the suburbs by making suburban shopping more convenient) and perhaps additionally and relatedly by inducing the employers of the relevant buyers to relocate as well (by improving the suburban labor pool). When the creation and use of a distributive outlet causes such location shifts, it will generate not only shopping externalities and traveling-to-shop externalities but also commuting-to-work externalities and the externalities individuals generate when engaged in activities other than shopping or commuting. These issues are far too complex to be addressed here.[30] The formula for the aggregate distortion in the private gains with which this subsection is concerned will not make specific reference to them. In that formula, the term that refers to the distortion in the relevant private benefits generated by the non-internalization of the shopping-congestion-related and traveling-to-shop congestion-and-pollution-related external benefits the operation of the additional or more-locationally-convenient distributive outlet a marginal QV investment created will be preceded by a minus sign and symbolized by $TXL(GP)B_{\Delta QV}$ where (GP) stands for congestion-and-pollution-related.

The fifth and final category of externalities that can distort the private gains on which this subsection focuses are the knowledge-creation-related external benefits a marginal QV investment can generate. Although, like the overwhelming majority of all QV investments, the overwhelming majority of marginal QV investments generate no new technological or commercial information (for example, create a soap with a green stripe rather than a blue stripe, create a 28 inch TV set whereas previously the closest available product variants were 26 inch or 30 inch TVs, add a distributive outlet on 50th Street to the outlets already in operation on 40th and 60th Streets), a minority of QV investments are technologically or commercially innovative (create a flat-screen TV or build a store that contains washers and dryers as well as exercise equipment that people can use when waiting for their laundry to be washed and dried). Sometimes, a QV investor who has made a truly innovative product discovery can prevent other producers and their customers from profiting from the knowledge he created by using patent and copyright law to bar them from doing so or by keeping secret the production process he uses to produce his newly discovered product or the nature of the intermediate product he discovered (by using it exclusively in his own operations and/or licensing others to use it only on condition that they not reveal information about the product to third parties). However, to the extent that the discoverer cannot prevent other producers and their customers from profiting from the information he created, the private gain on which we are focusing will be deflated *unless the State compensates him for the benefit his QV investment conferred on other producers and their customers.* The preceding sentence implies that no (non-internalized) external benefits would be generated by a truly innovative marginal QV investment that created information from which other producers and their customers profited if the State awarded the marginal QV investor in question a sum of money equal to the benefits his efforts conferred on other producers and their customers. The system of intellectual-property (IP) law (patent, copyright, and trade-secret law) currently in force does not provide for such direct monetary awards. Instead, it rewards patent holders and copyright holders by giving them the exclusive right to control the use of their discovery for a specified period of time. Actually, this description is somewhat inaccurate: in practice, patent and copyright protection is not infinitely broad, does not prevent other businesses and their customers from profiting from the patent holder's or copyright holder's discovery or, more broadly, from the information their successful research effort generated. The important point in the present context is that this system will sometimes inflate and sometimes deflate the net-revenue expectations of a prospective investor in an innovative product R&D QV-investment project.

Some elaboration is required. In virtually all cases, a prospective, innovative, product-R&D investor should not and will not believe that—if his project succeeds—it will yield a discovery that would not otherwise ever be made. Instead, this prospective investor should and will recognize that his investment will advance the weighted-average date on which the discovery should be expected to be made. This reality creates the possibility that IP law can either inflate or deflate the net-revenue expectations that a marginal, innovative, product-R&D (QV) investor should and will have. For example, assume (counterfactually) that the applicable IP law will prevent any other business or its customers from profiting from any discovery the relevant innovative product-R&D project yields during the period in which his patent rights are operative. In this case, the law will inflate (deflate) the net revenue a perfectly-informed, prospective QV investor will expect his QV investment to yield him if the number of days during which the law accords him the exclusive right to control the use of any discovery he made is higher than (is lower than) the number of days by which *ex ante* his project advanced the weighted-average date on which the discovery should have been expected to be made. Assume next that the protection the IP law provides is less broad—that, even during the period in which the patent is operative, other businesses and their customers can profit by using the discovery or some of the information the research that led to it generated in various ways, including perhaps ways that reduce the net revenue the discoverer can obtain by using it. In this situation, IP law will deflate the net revenue the QV investor expects to obtain from his project on the weighted average unless its protection lasts sufficiently longer than the number of days by which his investment should have been expected *ex ante* to advance the discovery's date to compensate him both for the benefits other businesses and their customers obtained as a result of using the discovery or the information the marginal QV investor created during the period whose length coincides with the number of days by which his efforts advanced the expected date of the discovery and for the loss the other businesses' use of his discovery imposed on him during the period in question. Obviously, this conclusion implies that in some cases—namely, when the length of the patent protection exceeds the number of days by which the successful researcher's efforts should have been expected *ex ante* to advance the date on which the discovery would be made by more than the number of days it would have to exceed the latter number to offset the fact that the protection the law provided him was partial in that, even during the period in which his patent was operative, it did not prevent other businesses and their customers from profiting from the information he discovered—existing IP law would raise the revenue a well-informed prospective researcher would expect his project to yield him on the weighted average above the weighted-average-expected allocative value of his project.

Although it is far from clear whether, across all marginal, innovative, product-R&D QV investments, the combination of the applicable IP law and the relevant discoverers' ability to keep their discoveries secret inflates or deflates the relevant investors' net-revenue expectations and net-revenue outcomes, I suspect that, at least in the United States, the potential external benefits generated by marginal, technologically or commercially innovative QV investments are at least as likely to have been overinternalized as underinternalized by IP law. I hasten to repeat, however, that my experience in this area is far too limited for this judgment to deserve much deference.

The preceding analysis implicitly assumed that the discovery in question had a technological component that made it patentable. Many commercial innovations have no such component. The QV investments that create and make use of such discoveries will confer considerable benefits on copycat businesses and their customers. The formula for the aggregate distortion in the private gains on which this subsection is focusing contains an $XL(K\text{-}R)B_{\Delta QV}$ term preceded by a minus sign that reflects this reality where $XL(K\text{-}R)B_{\Delta QV}$ stands for the external, allocative, knowledge-related (K-R) benefits generated by the marginal QV investment in question.

The final category of Pareto imperfections that require consideration are taxes on the margin of income. Two types of such taxes will distort the private gains on which this subsection is focusing. The first taxes that are relevant in this context are the sales taxes that buyers of the new product *n* pay on their purchases of this product. Such sales taxes deflate the relevant private gains by reducing the average (net) price the marginal QV investor obtains for the units of *n* he sells below the average (gross) price their consumer paid for them (which would equal their average allocative value in an otherwise-Pareto-perfect economy). The formula for the aggregate distortion in the private gain with which we are now concerned contains an $ASTR_n(P_n)Q_n$ term that is preceded by a minus sign to reflect this reality where $ASTR_n$ stands for the average sales-tax rate applied to the sale of the *n* (or the sales made by the distributive outlet the marginal QV investment created).

The second tax and final imperfection that needs to be considered in the current context is the tax levied on the profits the tax laws deem the marginal QV investment to have generated. Clearly, in an otherwise-Pareto-perfect world, such taxes will deflate the private gains in question. The formula for the aggregate distortion on which this subsection is focusing reflects this fact by including a $T\pi T_{\Delta QV}$ (total profit tax) term preceded by a minus sign.

In any event, the formula for the aggregate distortion in the after-tax gain (private benefits) a marginal QV investor would secure by using his marginal QV investment—for $\Sigma D(PB_{\Delta QV})$—if no private or allocative costs were generated by that use (if $PC_{U\Delta QV} - LC_{U\Delta QV} = 0$) is $-(AP_n - AMR_n)Q_n - (M_{\Delta QV}$ or $O_{\Delta QV}) - L_{\Delta QV} - TXLBP_n - NXLBC_n + TXLC(LT)_{(A/C)n} - TXL(GP)B_{\Delta QV} - XL(K\text{-}R)B_{\Delta QV} - ASTR_n(Q_n) - T\pi T_{\Delta QV}$. Relatedly, the formula for the percentage distortion in the relevant after-tax gain will be the above formula divided by the allocative cost of creating and using the marginal QV investment in question—$LC_{\Delta QV}$.

(iii) $\Sigma D(PB_{\Delta QV})/LC_{\Delta QV}$ for a Marginal QV Investment Whose Use Withdrew Resources Exclusively from the Production of Existing Products

The aggregate percentage distortion in the private benefits of using a marginal QV investment equals the aggregate percentage distortion in the after-tax private gains the marginal QV investor would obtain by using the marginal QV investment if the private and allocative cost of his doing so was zero *minus* the aggregate percentage distortion in the private cost he would have to incur to use his QV investment. Therefore, the formula for $\Sigma D(PB_{\Delta QV})/LC_{\Delta QV}$ for a marginal QV investment whose use withdrew all the resources it consumed from the production of existing products would be equal to the formula the preceding subsection developed for the percentage distortion in the relevant private gains *minus* the formula its predecessor developed for the percentage distortion in the relevant private costs if neither human errors nor monopsony distorted either the figures in question or the difference between them and the behaviors that generate monopolistic and natural oligopolistic QV-investment disincentives, monopolistic

QV-investment incentives, and retaliation barriers to QV investing do not affect economic efficiency. If I rearrange the terms in these formulas to place those that relate to the same type of Pareto imperfection next to each other, $\Sigma D(PB_{U\Delta QV})/LC_{\Delta QV}$ will equal $(1/LC_{\Delta QV})$ *times* the following expression:

$$
\begin{aligned}
&-(AP_n - AMR_n)Q_n + \sum_{o=1}^{k}(AP_{SU_o} - AMR_{SU_o})SU_o - (M_{\Delta QV} \text{ or } O_{\Delta QV}) \\
&-LB_{\Delta QV} + \sum_{o=1}^{k}(AXLBC_{SU_o})SU_o - NXLBC_n - \sum_{o=1}^{k}(AXLCP_{SU_o})SU_o \\
&+AXLCP_n(Q_n) + TXLC(LT)_{(A/C)_n} - TXL(GP)B_{\Delta QV} - XL(K-R)B_{\Delta QV} \\
&+\sum_{o=1}^{k} ASTR_{SU_o}(AP_o)SU_o - ASTR_n(P_n)Q_n + \sum_{o=1}^{k} AFTR_{SU_o}(AVC_{SU_o})SU_o \\
&-AFTR_n(AVC_n)Q_n - T\pi T_{\Delta QV}.
\end{aligned}
$$

Before proceeding, I want to explain why I believe that $\Sigma D(PB_{\Delta QV})$ would be positive for all or virtually all marginal QV investments if all the resources their use consumed were withdrawn from the production of existing products. In my judgment,

1. the second term in the above expression—$\sum_{o=1}^{k}(AP_{SU_o} - AMR_{SU_o})SU_o$—will exceed the first—$(AP_n - AMR_n)Q_n$—by a substantial amount: both terms will usually be large; the absolute value of the second would be twice that of the first if DD_n and all the DD_o curves were linear, if DD_n coincided with each DD_o curve, and if the use of the marginal QV investment reduced the output of each *o* product whose output it reduced by only one unit; and the substitution of more realistic assumptions for the three assumptions just delineated will not critically affect the above conclusion;
2. $-(M_{\Delta QV}$ or $O_{\Delta QV})$ will usually be positive because most marginal QV investors have monopolistic QV-investment incentives to make their marginal QV investments;
3. $L_{\Delta QV}$ will normally be zero because, at least in the United States, the antitrust laws usually deter firms from retaliating against their rivals' QV investments;
4. across all cases and in the most individual cases, the consumption of the new product the marginal QV investment creates will generate the same conventional externalities as did the consumption of the units of the old products sacrificed when the new product was produced;
5. across all cases and in most individual cases, the production of the new product will generate the same conventional externalities as did the

production of the units of the old products sacrificed when the new product was produced;

6. across all cases and in most individual cases, the marginal QV investor will pay the same amount of factor taxes on the resources he employs to use his marginal QV investment as their alternative employers would have paid to use them;
7. across all cases and in most individual cases, the sales taxes that are levied on the sales of the new product or distributive outlet will equal the sales taxes that would have been levied on the sales of the old products that were sacrificed when the new product was produced;
8. although the external benefits generated by the use of marginal QV investments that created an additional or more-locationally-convenient distributive outlet may be significant, I doubt that their non-internalization fully offsets the net inflation in $PB_{\Delta QV}$ generated by all the other Pareto imperfections in the system;
9. the overwhelming majority of marginal QV investments are neither technologically nor commercially innovative, and capitalist economies' IP laws probably fully internalize—indeed, may overinternalize—the benefits that technologically innovative product-research projects confer on other businesses and their customers by yielding knowledge that the discoverer is unable to keep secret; and
10. although the business-income taxes levied on the taxable income the tax laws deem to have been generated by marginal QV-investment projects deflate the private benefits they yield their owners, I do not think that they fully counteract the distortion in those benefits that the economy's other Pareto imperfections generate (despite the fact that they are levied on the undistorted as well as the distorted profits the marginal QV investment yields).

In any event, for the above reasons, I am confident that the mean of the $\Sigma D(PB_{\Delta QV})/LC_{\Delta QV}$ distribution would be positive if the use of all marginal QV investments withdrew resources exclusively from the production of existing products. I also believe that on this assumption $\Sigma D(PB_{\Delta QV})$ would be negative either never or for only a very few marginal QV investments. In my judgment, $\Sigma D(PB_{\Delta QV})$ will be most likely to be negative for marginal QV investments (1) that are located in areas of product-space whose pricing is unusually competitive (whose use withdrew resources from the production of old products whose prices are close to their marginal costs and revenue) and (2) create either commercial innovations that have no technological basis (whose pirating the IP laws do not prevent) or distributive outlets whose operation generates a substantial reduction in congestion and pollution externalities.

$\Sigma D(PB_{\Delta QV})/LC_{\Delta QV}$ FOR A QV INVESTMENT WHOSE CREATION WITHDREW RESOURCES EXCLUSIVELY FROM THE PRODUCTION OF EXISTING PRODUCTS

Good news. We have already done all the real work necessary to develop a formula for this distortion. In particular, I must make only four obvious changes to convert the formula previously developed for $\Sigma D(PC_{U\Delta QV})/LC_{U\Delta QV}$ into the formula for $\Sigma D(PC_{C\Delta QV})/LC_{C\Delta QV}$. First, the denominator must be changed from $LC_{U\Delta QV}$ to $LC_{C\Delta QV}$. Second, although no change in the relevant symbols need be made on this account, it must be recognized that in the formula for $\Sigma D(PC_{C\Delta QV})$ all the figures that refer to something related to the sacrificed units of *o* refer to the units of the *o* in question that would be sacrificed to free the resources that the creation (rather than the use) of the marginal QV investment consumed and that the relevant (SU_o)s refer to the units of the *o* in question that would be sacrificed to free the resources the *creation* of the relevant marginal QV investment consumed. Third, in the formula for $\Sigma D(PC_{C\Delta QV})$, the term $AXLCP_n(Q_n)$ will be replaced by the term $TXLC_{C\Delta QV}$ (which stands for the total external allocative costs generated by the creation of the marginal QV investment in question). Fourth and finally, in the formula for $\Sigma D(PC_{C\Delta QV})$, the term $AFTR_n(AVC_n)Q_n$ will be replaced by the term $AFTR_{C\Delta QV}(BTPC_{C\Delta QV})$ where $BTPC_{C\Delta QV}$ stands for the before-tax private cost of creating the marginal QV investment in question. Thus, on the assumption that there are no human errors and no monopsony, $\Sigma D(PC_{C\Delta QV}) = \sum_{o=1}^{k} (AMR_{SU_o} - AP_{SU_o})SU_o - \sum_{o=1}^{k} (AXLBC_{SU_o})SU_o + \sum_{o=1}^{k} AXLCP_{SU_o}(SU_o) - TXLC_{C\Delta QV} - \sum_{o=1}^{k} ASTR_{SU_o}(AP_o)SU_o - \sum_{o=1}^{k} AFTR_{SU_o}(AVC_{SU_o})SU_o + AFTR_{C\Delta QV}(BTPC_{C\Delta QV})$. Because (1) the first (monopoly) term is negative, (2) the fifth (sales-tax) term is preceded by a minus sign, (3) there is no reason to believe that across all cases the sum of the second through fourth (externality) terms will deviate significantly from zero, and (4) there is no reason to believe that across all cases the sum of the sixth and seventh (factor-tax) terms will deviate significantly from zero, I am confident that the mean of the distribution of $\Sigma D(PC_{C\Delta QV})$ figures would be negative if the creation of marginal QV investments withdrew all the resources they consumed from the production of existing products. Indeed, I cannot imagine a realistic scenario in which $\Sigma D(PC_{C\Delta QV})$ would be positive for any individual marginal QV investment on the above assumption.

$\Sigma D(P\pi_{[C+U]\Delta QV})/LC_{[C+U]\Delta QV} \equiv \Sigma D(P\pi_{\Delta QV})/LC_{\Delta QV}$ ON THE UNREALISTIC ASSUMPTION THAT THE CREATION AND USE OF ALL MARGINAL QV INVESTMENTS WITHDREW RESOURCES EXCLUSIVELY FROM THE PRODUCTION OF EXISTING PRODUCTS

I have just argued that $\Sigma D(PB_{U\Delta QV})$ would be positive for all or virtually all marginal QV investments if the use of all such investments withdrew resources exclusively from the production of existing products and that $\Sigma D(PC_{C\Delta QV})$ will be negative for all marginal QV investments on the preceding assumption. Obviously, taken together, these two conclusions imply that the mean of the distribution of $\Sigma D(P\pi_{\Delta QV})$s would be positive for all or virtually all marginal QV investments if the creation and use of all marginal QV investments withdrew resources exclusively from the production of existing products.

$\Sigma D(P\pi_{\Delta QV})/LC_{\Delta QV}$ ON REALISTIC ASSUMPTIONS ABOUT THE TYPES OF USES FROM WHICH THE RESOURCES THE CREATION AND USE OF MARGINAL QV INVESTMENTS WITHDREW RESOURCES

Although some of the resources consumed by the creation and use of marginal QV investments will be withdrawn from the production of existing products, other such resources will be withdrawn from the execution of production-process research or from non-innovative attempts to reduce the cost of producing relevant quantities of existing products (for example, by engaging in plant modernization, constructing entirely new plants, or shifting to known production processes that are otherwise-more-expensive but less-AP-loss-prone). In order to generate any conclusions about the impact of these resource flows on $\Sigma D(PC_{C\Delta QV})/LC_{C\Delta QV}$ and $\Sigma D(PC_{U\Delta QV})/LC_{U\Delta QV}$, I would have to analyze $\Sigma D(PB_{\Delta PPR})/PB_{\Delta PPR}$ for the sacrificed PPR projects and $\Sigma D(PB_{\ldots})/PB_{\ldots}$ for the sacrificed plant modernization, new-plant construction, and production-process shifts and then compare these figures with the $\Sigma D(PB_{R/UO})/PB_{R/UO}$ ratio for the unit-output-producing resource uses for which these other types of sacrificed resource uses would be substituted. To understand why, note the following two facts. First, since the private benefits that the resources the creation and use of a marginal QV investment consume would have generated in their alternative uses equal their private cost to the QV investor while these resources' allocative product in their alternative uses equals the allocative cost of the marginal QV investor's using them (the sum of the private benefits they would have generated for their alternative users and the distortion in those private benefits), the $\Sigma D(PB_{\Delta\ldots})/PB_{\Delta\ldots}$ ratios for the alternative uses of the resources the creation and use of a marginal QV investment consume will indicate whether the resource flows in question inflate or deflate $PC_{C\Delta QV}$ and $PC_{U\Delta QV}$ and the percentage by which they inflate or deflate them. Second, since these flows of resources from non-UO uses to QV-investment-creation-and-use uses will replace some of the flows of resources from UO uses to QV-investment-creation-and-use uses we originally assumed the creation and use of all marginal QV investments exclusively entailed, even if the $\Sigma D(PB_{\Delta\ldots})/PB_{\Delta\ldots}$ ratio for each of the non-unit-output-producing types of resource uses from which the creation and use of a marginal QV investment withdrew resources were negative, the existence of these alternative resource-use-type flows will reduce the absolute value of the negative $\Sigma D(PC_{C\Delta QV})$ and $\Sigma D(PC_{U\Delta QV})$ figures if the weighted-average $\Sigma D(PB_{\Delta\ldots})/PB_{\Delta\ldots}$ ratio for the sacrificed resource uses of the non-unit-output-producing resource-use types from which the creation and use of a marginal QV investment withdrew resources was lower than the weighted-average $\Sigma D(PB_{\Delta\ldots})/PB_{\Delta\ldots}$ ratio for the unit-output-producing resource uses for which these non-unit-output-producing (sacrificed) resource-use-type flows are in fact substituted.

I did not pick the example the preceding sentence analyzed by chance. In my judgment, the weighted-average $\Sigma D(PB_{\Delta\ldots})/PB_{\Delta\ldots}$ ratio for the non-unit-output-producing resource uses that will be sacrificed when marginal QV investments are created and used will be negative but absolutely lower than the weighted-average $\Sigma D(PB_{\Delta\ldots})/PB_{\Delta\ldots}$ ratio for the unit-output-producing resource uses that would have been sacrificed by the creation and use of marginal QV investments if the relevant non-unit-output-producing resource uses were not sacrificed in their stead. Later in this section, I will explain why $\Sigma D(PB_{\Delta\ldots})/PB_{\Delta\ldots}$ for the sacrificed PPR-executing resource uses is likely to be negative but absolutely smaller than its counterpart for the unit-output-producing resource uses whose sacrifice they (in one sense) replace. The same basic argument will yield the same conclusion for the $\Sigma D(PB_{\Delta\ldots})/PB_{\Delta\ldots}$ ratio for the plant modernization and cost-reducing new-plant-construction resource uses that are sacrificed when marginal QV investments are created and used. Although, for reasons I will delineate later in this section, the $\Sigma D(PB_{\Delta\ldots})/PB_{\Delta\ldots}$ ratio for the various AP-loss-reducing resource uses from which the creation and use of marginal QV investments withdraw resources may be positive rather than negative, the percentage of the resources that the creation and use of marginal QV investments consume that they withdraw from AP-loss-reducing uses is too small to call into question my conclusion that, although the fact that some of the resources the creation and use of marginal QV investments consume are withdrawn from non-unit-output-producing uses does reduce the absolute value of $\Sigma D(PC_{C\Delta QV})/LC_{C\Delta QV}$ and $\Sigma D(PC_{U\Delta QV})/LC_{U\Delta QV}$, the existence of these flows will not cause the percentage distortion in question to be zero or positive—that is, does not alter the fact that the aggregate distortions in the private cost of creating and using QV investments will compound the tendency of the inflation in $PB_{\Delta QV}$ to cause $\Sigma D(P\pi_{\Delta QV})$ to be positive not just for the economy's weighted-average marginal QV investments but for all or virtually all marginal QV investments in the economy.

SOME IMPLICATIONS OF THE PRECEDING ANALYSES

This subsection analyzes the implications of the preceding analyses for three issues that affect the allocative efficiency of many policies.

(i) Implications for the Determinants of Whether an Area of Product-Space Receives an Allocatively-Inefficiently-High Percentage of the Economy's Total QV Investment

Inter-industry QV-to-QV misallocation is present to the extent that the marginal QV investments in different areas of product-space generate different ratios of allocative benefits to allocative costs. If the marginal QV investments in all areas of product-space yielded just normal rates of return, those areas of product-space whose marginal QV investments had $\Sigma D(P\pi_{\Delta QV})/LC_{\Delta QV}$ ratios that were lower than their weighted-average economy-wide counterpart would, from this perspective, have too low a proportion of the resources the economy devoted to QV-investment creation.

I want to comment on six of the concrete implications of this abstract conclusion for the areas of product-space that will tend to have a proportion of the QV investments the economy creates that is economically inefficiently high. First, *ceteris paribus,* an area of product-space will tend to have a proportion of the economy's QV investments that is allocatively inefficiently high if its $([P_n - MC_n]/P_n)([P_nQ_n]/PC_{\Delta QVn})$ ratio is higher than its weighted-average economy-wide counterpart. To see why, note the following facts:

1. the absolute value of $-(AP_n - AMR_n)Q_n$ in the formula for $\Sigma D(PB_{\Delta QV})$ will be far lower than the value of $\sum_{o=1}^{k}(AP_{SU_o} - AMR_{SU_o})SU_o$ in that formula;

2. the difference in the value of the two terms will increase with the value of $P_n - MR_n = P_n - MC_n$, which will approximately equal $(\sum_{o=1}^{k} (P_o - MR_o)SU_o$;
3. $(P_n - MC_n)Q_n = ([P_n - MC_n]/P_n)(P_nQ_n)$; and
4. there is a high and strong correlation between $PC_{\Delta QV}$ and $LC_{\Delta QV}$ for the different marginal QV investments in the economy.

Second, if I am right that virtually all marginal QV investors have monopolistic QV-investment incentives to make their marginal QV investment and face no significant retaliation barriers on that investment, the preceding analysis implies that the likelihood that an area of product-space will have a proportion of the relevant economy's QV investment that is allocatively inefficiently high will increase (roughly speaking) both with the extent to which the established firms that operate within it individually own atypically high shares of its QV investment and with the extent to which insider information on favorable QV-investment opportunities increase the probability that its marginal QV investments will be made by one of its established firms as opposed to a potential entrant.

Third, since I suspect that in all economies less than 100 percent of the accident and pollution losses businesses generate are internalized to them, the preceding analysis also implies that the probability that an area of product-space will have a proportion of the QV investment created in the economy in which it is located that is allocatively inefficiently high will also increase with the ratio of the allocative accident and pollution costs the creation and use of its marginal QV investments generate to the other allocative costs they generate. This conclusion reflects an assumption that the creation and use of the marginal QV investment in any area of product-space will withdraw resources from the creation and use of other QV investments whose weighted-average ratio of accident-and-pollution allocative costs to other allocative costs equals its economy-wide counterpart.

Fourth, the probability that an area of product-space will have a proportion of the relevant economy's QV investment that is allocatively inefficiently high will be inversely related to the likelihood that its marginal QV investments will be commercially but not technologically innovative if the following three conditions are fulfilled:

1. technological product-innovators can substantially prevent other businesses and their customers from profiting from the innovators' discoveries by keeping them secret and securing IP-law protection;

2. the IP laws internalize or overinternalize to technological product-innovators any benefits other businesses and their customers secure from these innovators' discoveries; but
3. commercial innovators whose discoveries have no technological basis are unable to prevent other businesses and their customers from profiting from their discoveries and cannot secure rewards from the legal system that internalize the benefits their discoveries confer on such other parties.

I should add that I believe that, at least in developed economies, all three of the above conditions are fulfilled.

Fifth, *ceteris paribus,* an area of product-space will tend to have a proportion of the relevant economy's QV investment that is allocatively inefficiently high if the effective tax rate applied to its actual profits is lower than its weighted-average economy-wide counterpart.

Sixth, finally, and somewhat overlappingly, since lobbying, campaign contributions, and bribery yield external benefits for nonpayers who gain from the favorable legislation, executive-branch decisions, and judicial rulings they secure (for example, on various tort-law, environmental-law, IP-law, tax-law, and antitrust-law issues), I expect on this account as well that the probability that an area of product-space will have a proportion of the resources the economy devotes to QV-investment creation that is allocatively inefficiently high will increase with the concentration of its sales since the extent to which a group of sellers can spend the amount of money on lobbying, political-campaign contributions, and bribery that is in their collective parochial interest will increase with the concentration of the group.

(ii) Implications for the Magnitude of the Ratio of QV-to-QV Misallocation to the Allocative Cost of the Resources Devoted to QV-Investment Creation Relative to the Magnitude of the Ratio of UO-to-UO Misallocation to the Allocative Cost of the Resources Devoted to Unit Output Production

This subsection argues that QV-to-QV misallocation constitutes a higher percentage of the allocative cost of the resources devoted to QV-investment creation than UO-to-UO misallocation constitutes of the allocative cost of the resources devoted to unit output production. However, before proceeding, I want to explore the referents of the two allocative-cost concepts in question.

To see why the concept of the allocative cost of all QV investments is problematic, note that, if no QV investments were created, the only products that could be produced would be products that nature produced whose value did not have to be discovered (since the effort that led to the discovery of the value of a product of nature either in its raw state or if processed in some way would be a QV investment), and the only PPR that could be done would relate to the harvesting or possibly the processing of these obviously valuable products of nature. I do not think it would be useful to define the allocative cost of all the resources devoted to QV-investment creation to equal the allocative value they would have generated had they been used instead to harvest such products of nature or execute production-process research into the cheapest way of harvesting or processing them. I therefore am defining the concept the allocative cost of all the QV investments in an economy to equal the sum of the allocative values that the resources consumed by the creation of each QV investment in the economy would have generated in the most profitable non-QV-investment-creating use to which they could have been put had the QV investment in question been the only QV investment actually created that was sacrificed to unit-output-producing or PPR-executing uses.

The concept the allocative cost of the resources devoted to the production of all the unit output produced in the economy is equally problematic. Thus, if no resources were to be devoted to unit output production, the allocative value these resources would generate in their alternative QV-investment-creating and PPR-executing uses would be zero (since no units of any newly created product would ever be produced and no discovered cheaper production process would ever be used). I therefore am defining the concept the allocative cost of all the resources an economy devotes to unit-output production to equal the sum of the allocative values that the resources that were used to produce each unit of the economy's actual output would have generated in their most profitable QV-investment-creating or PPR-executing uses if that unit of output were the only unit of output to be sacrificed to QV-investment-creating or PPR-executing uses.

Now to the substantive point. When discussing the extent of UO-to-UO resource misallocation, I pointed out that both the amount of such misallocation and the percentage that that amount constitutes of the private cost of the resources devoted to unit output production are reduced by the fact that UO-to-UO resource flows tend to take place between the production of goods that

1. are highly competitive with each other (and hence tend to have similar P/MC ratios);
2. are produced with similar technologies (and hence tend to have similar MC/XMC [that is, MC/MC*] ratios on that account);
3. are subjected to laws and regulations that are equally effective at internalizing the accident and pollution losses the production of the goods in question generate (and hence tend to have similar MC/XMC [that is, MC/MC*] ratios on this account as well); and
4. whose sales are subjected to the same tax rates (and hence whose P*/P ratios tend to be similar).

Therefore, the (P*/MC*) = (P*/P)(P/MC)(MC/MC*) ratio for any product is likely to be similar to the weighted-average P*/MC* ratio of the products whose unit outputs are sacrificed when an additional unit of the product in question is produced (say, a product whose price has dropped because a horizontal merger in which its producer had engaged was dissolved). This fact in turn implies that the percentage of the resources that the economy devotes to unit output production that is allocated to producing units of output of a particular product whose P*/MC* ratio is higher than (lower than) its weighted-average economy-wide counterpart will not differ from the percentage of those resources that would be allocatively efficient to devote to the production of this product (given the total amount of resources the economy devotes to unit output production) to the extent that it would if the weighted-average P*/MC* ratio of the goods whose outputs are reduced when the good in question is produced equaled the economy-wide weighted-average P*/MC* ratio. I do expect that goods whose P*/MC* ratios are higher than their economy-wide weighted-average counterparts will be underproduced from the perspective of economic efficiency, given the total amount of resources devoted to unit output production in the economy, because some of the resources their production would consume would be withdrawn from the production of distant substitutes whose weighted-average P*/MC* ratio will be much closer to its economy-wide counterpart. However, the extent of the underproduction in question and hence of the resulting UO-to-UO misallocation will be much smaller than it would be if the production of each product withdrew the same percentage of the resources devoted to the production of each other individual product.

The same point could be put in percentage-profit-distortion terms. Since the P*/MC* ratio for any product is similar to the weighted-average P*/MC* ratio for the products from whose production the former product's production withdraws resources, the absolute value of its negative $\Sigma D(PB_{\Delta UO}/LC_{\Delta UO}$ ratio (which, roughly speaking, reflects it own P*/MC* ratio) will be much more similar than it would otherwise be to the absolute value of its negative $\Sigma D(PC_{\Delta UO})/LC_{\Delta UO}$ ratio (which, roughly speaking, reflects the weighted-average P*/MC* ratio of the products from whose production its production withdraws resources). Therefore, the weighted-average value and weighted-average absolute and squared deviations of the relevant $\Sigma D(P\pi_{\Delta UO})/LC_{\Delta UO}$ distribution will be much smaller than they would otherwise be, and UO-to-UO misallocation will be much smaller than it would otherwise be.

Nothing similar causes the items in the $\Sigma D(PB_{\Delta QV})/LC_{\Delta QV}$ distribution to be small. If an additional QV investment is created in one area of product-space because the producers who are operating within it succeed at fixing their prices, the resources that would be used to create that QV investment if they all were withdrawn from alternative QV-investment-creating uses would not be withdrawn from the creation of QV investments in neighboring areas of product-space that contain products that are atypically competitive with the products produced by the price fixers. To the contrary, the price-fixing that increases equilibrium QV investment in one area of product-space will tend to increase equilibrium QV investment in neighboring areas of product-space: a rise in the prices charged by one set of rivalrous firms whose products are less competitive with the products of a second set of rivalrous firms than they are with each other's products though they are more competitive with the products of this second set of firms than they would be with a random sample of the products produced by the economy will tend to increase QV investment not only in the first set of firms' area of product-space but also in the second set of firms' area of product-space by raising the rate of return both sets of firms realize on the QV investments they owned in the original position. Hence, if anything, events or policies that cause an additional QV investment to be created in one area of product-space will tend to withdraw resources from QV-investment-creating uses in areas of product-space whose products are less-than-typically competitive with the products of the area of product-space in which the additional QV investment is created—products whose weighted-average $\Sigma D(PB_{\Delta QV})/LC_{\Delta QV}$ ratio would if anything diverge from its economy-wide counterpart in the opposite direction from the direction in which the weighted-average $\Sigma D(PB_{\Delta QV})/LC_{\Delta QV}$ ratio in the area(s) of product-space in which additional QV investments would be made would diverge from its economy-wide counterpart. Since, then, the absolute values of the negative $\Sigma D(PB_{\Delta QV})/LC_{\Delta QV}$ and $\Sigma D(PC_{\Delta QV})/LC_{\Delta QV}$ ratios for the marginal QV investment in any area of product-space are likely to diverge in opposite directions from their weighted-average economy-wide counterparts, the weighted-average deviation of the distribution of $\Sigma D(P\pi_{\Delta QV})/LC_{\Delta QV}$ ratios is likely to be higher on this account than it otherwise would be, and on this account QV-to-QV resource misallocation is likely to constitute a higher percentage of the total allocative cost of the resources QV-investment creation consumes than would otherwise be the case.

Obviously, both the fact that UO-to-UO resource flows take place between the production of products whose producers face atypically similar imperfections and the fact that QV-to-QV resource flows take place between the creation of QV investments whose creators face atypically different imperfections favor the conclusion that QV-to-QV resources misallocation constitutes a higher percentage of the allocative cost of the resources the economy devotes to QV-investment creation than UO-to-UO resource misallocation constitutes of the allocative cost of the resources the economy devotes to unit output production.

(iii) Implications for QV-to-QV Resource Misallocation and the Analysis of the Economic Efficiency of Various Public Policies

Three points. The first is that policies will tend to reduce QV-to-QV misallocation to the extent that they reduce the weighted-average deviation of the distribution of $\Sigma D(P\pi_{\Delta QV})/LC_{\Delta QV}$ ratios in the economy.

The second is that, in determining the impact of any policy whose direct impact on the $\Sigma D(P\pi_{\Delta QV})$ figures it affects derives from its impact on one or two terms in the formula for $\Sigma D(P\pi_{\Delta QV})$, one must take account of the fact that changes in those terms will affect the value of other terms in the formula. Take, for example, a policy that reduces the prices charged in the short run for the products supplied at the pre-policy QV-investment equilibrium in the relevant area of product-space. Such a policy will clearly directly affect $\Sigma D(P\pi_{\Delta QV})/LC_{\Delta QV}$ for the (changing) marginal QV investment in that area of product-space in two ways: by lowering (1) the absolute value of (A) $AMR_n - P_n$ in the $(AMR_n - AP_n)Q_n$ term in the formula for $\Sigma D(P\pi_{\Delta QV})/LC_{\Delta QV}$ (where n is now the product produced by the changing marginal QV investment in the relevant area of product-space, which will not be new in its post-policy incarnation) and (B) the $\sum_{o=1}^{k}(AMR_{SU_o} - AP_{SU_o})$ element of the $\sum_{o=1}^{k}(AMR_{SU_o} - AP_{SU_o})SU_o$ term in that formula (though the price of both the product created by the different QV investment that will be marginal at the new, lower, equilibrium-QV-investment level that will prevail after QV investment adjusts to the policy-induced price reduction at the original equilibrium-QV-investment level and the prices of the products created by the QV investments in that area of product-space that will be intramarginal at the new equilibrium from whose production the production of the marginal product withdrew resources will be higher than they were in the immediate post-policy nonequilibrium situation) and (2) by causing both Q_n and $\sum_{o=1}^{k} SU_o$ in the above terms to be higher than they were in the pre-policy equilibrium. However, the policy will also affect the value of $\Sigma D(P\pi_{\Delta QV})/LC_{\Delta QV}$ in a number of other indirect ways. First, by changing the equilibrium-QV-investment level, it may affect the ($M_{\Delta QV}$ or $O_{\Delta QV}$) term in the formula for $\Sigma D(P\pi_{\Delta QV})/LC_{\Delta QV}$ both by affecting (1) whether the potential investor that was in a position to make the least unprofitable QV investment that could have been made in the new equilibrium was an established firm or a potential competitor, (2) whether the investor in question faced monopolistic QV-investment incentives rather than monopolistic or natural oligopolistic QV-investment disincentives if it was an established firm, and (3) the size of any such incentives or disincentives it faced (by affecting the quantity of QV investments it owned in the relevant area of product-space in equilibrium). Second, by changing both Q_n and $\sum_{o=1}^{k} SU_o$, the policy in question will affect all the externalities of consumption and production terms, all the sales-tax terms, and all the factor-tax terms in the formula for $\Sigma D(P\pi_{\Delta QV})/LC_{\Delta QV}$. Third, by affecting the profits the businesses in the relevant area earned, the policy will affect the profit-tax term in the $\Sigma D(P\pi_{\Delta QV})/LC_{\Delta QV}$ formula. Fourth, by affecting the concentration of QV-investment ownership in the relevant area of product-space (by causing some QV investments to be withdrawn), the policy may affect the monopoly terms, the AP-loss externality terms, the knowledge-creation externality terms, and the tax terms in the formula for $\Sigma D(P\pi_{\Delta QV})/LC_{\Delta QV}$ by affecting the ability of the firms in that area of product-space to secure favorable antitrust, tort, environmental, IP, and tax legislation, executive-branch regulations and enforcement decisions, and judicial rulings by engaging in lobbying, making campaign contributions, and paying the amount of bribes that were in their collective parochial interests.

The fifth and final point is more concrete and relies on a number of empirical speculations. In my judgment, policies that bring the weighted-average

([P – MC]/P)(sales/QV investment) ratio of the products to which they directly apply closer to its weighted-average economy-wide counterpart will tend to reduce QV-to-QV misallocation, and policies that cause this ratio in the areas of product-space to which they are applied to diverge more from its weighted-average economy-wide counterpart will tend to increase QV-to-QV misallocation. This conclusion implies, for example, that the effect of anti-price-fixing policies or prohibitions of horizontal mergers that would decrease price competition on QV-to-QV misallocation will depend on the magnitude of the above ratio in the industries to which they are applied—that, at least in relation to their impact on QV-to-QV misallocation, appropriately selective versions of such policies will be more economically efficient than universally or randomly applied versions of such policies.

The preceding abstract conclusion also implies that the effect that policies that increase QV-investment competition in the areas of product-space to which they are applied will have on QV-to-QV misallocation will also depend on whether, pre-policy, the above ratio is higher or lower than its weighted-average economy-wide counterpart. Thus, policies that are designed to prevent retaliation against QV investments or prohibitions of conglomerate mergers or acquisitions that would reduce QV-investment competition by eliminating an effective potential entrant to the area of product-space in which they will occur will increase QV-to-QV misallocation if they are applied in areas of product-space that contain products whose weighted-average pre-policy ([P – MC]/P)($PQ/PC_{\Delta QV}$) ratio is lower than its economy-wide counterpart. Once more, therefore, at least in relation to QV-to-QV misallocation, selective application will be superior to universal or random application.

Various Types of Distortions in the (Supernormal) Profits Yielded by Various Kinds of Reallocations of Resources to the Execution of Marginal PPR Projects

MD($PB_{\Delta PPR}$) WHEN THE EXECUTION OF THE PROJECT WITHDREW RESOURCES EXCLUSIVELY FROM UNIT-OUTPUT-PRODUCING USES

This analysis assumes that the owner of each marginal PPR project both does PPR and produces the good G_I to whose production process his marginal PPR project relates. Indeed, the analysis assumes that the owners of all marginal PPR projects will use the discoveries they yield exclusively themselves—will not sell them to anyone else or even license others to use the discovered production processes. This assumption will be relaxed in the next subsection when it analyzes the distortion in $PB_{\Delta PPR}$ that may be generated if the discoverer sells his discovery or the right to use his discovery to others who have monopsony power in their roles as discovery-buyers.

Initially, the analysis that follows also assumes plausibly, though not universally correctly,[31] that the discovered production process reduces the marginal cost of producing G1. This assumption will be relaxed at the end of this subsection.

Finally, the analysis that follows assumes at the outset that all the resources that the owner of the marginal PPR project used post-discovery to produce both his pre-discovery output of G1 and any extra units of G1 the discovery made it profitable for him to produce were withdrawn from the production of units of output of other goods G2 . . . N.

Before one can analyze the way in which imperfections in seller competition can distort $PB_{\Delta PPR}$ on the above assumptions, one must first explain the various ways in which a production-process researcher can profit by using his production-process discovery himself. The use of a production-process discovery can benefit such a discoverer in three ways: (1) by reducing the cost the researcher/producer has to incur to produce his pre-discovery output of G1, (2) by enabling the researcher/producer to earn additional profits by increasing his unit output of G1 (to the extent that the discovery reduces his marginal costs at and beyond his pre-discovery output), and (3) by inducing the exit of a rival product that will not be immediately replaced by another rival product that is as competitive with the PPR investor's products as the exited product was (by reducing the researcher's marginal costs and thereby making it inherently profitable [that is, profitable for nonstrategic reasons] for him to reduce the price he charges for the good G1 whose cost of production the production-process research was designed to reduce). At least on our current assumptions (and almost certainly on realistic assumption as well), imperfections in price competition will deflate the private benefits that production-process research confers on its owner in the first two ways described above. However, the imperfections in competition that underlie the third way in which PPR can benefit a researcher will inflate $PB_{\Delta PPR}$.

I will first explain these conclusions and then illustrate the first two diagrammatically. The imperfections in competition that distort the private benefits a marginal PPR project confers on its owner by reducing the cost he has to incur to produce his pre-discovery output of the good G1 whose cost of production the PPR discovery reduced are imperfections in the price competition faced by the producers of those products G2 . . . N from whose production resources were withdrawn to produce the pre-discovery output of G1. These imperfections in price competition deflate the private benefits in question by deflating the private benefits the resources the discovery enables the PPR investor to save when producing his pre-discovery output of G1 would have conferred on the producers of G2 . . . N pre-discovery had they not originally been used to produce G1 and hence the private cost of those resources pre-discovery to the owner of the marginal PPR project. Obviously, this deflation in the pre-discovery cost of the resources the discovery will enable its owner to save will deflate the private benefits his use of the discovery will confer on him.

Two imperfections in price competition distort the profits that a marginal-cost-reducing PPR project confers on its owner by making it profitable for him to expand his output of the good whose cost of production the PPR discovery reduces. First, the imperfections in the price competition faced by the producers of G2 . . . N whose unit outputs will be reduced when additional units of the PPR investor's product are produced inflate the profits the investor realizes by expanding his output by deflating the cost he has to incur to bid the resources he will use for this purpose away from their alternative employers. Second, the imperfections in the price competition the investor in the marginal PPR project faces when selling the good G1 deflate the profits the project enables him to earn by expanding his output by putting him in a position in which his output expansion will increase the amount of buyer surplus consumers of his product G1 secure.

For our purposes, the crucial fact is that the former inflation of this component of $PB_{\Delta PPR}$ will clearly exceed the latter deflation. To see why, make the neutral assumption that DD_{G1} is downward sloping and coincides with the demand curve for each product whose output is reduced when G1's output is increased ($DD_{G2 \ldots N}$) and that the pre-discovery MC_{G1} curve coincides with the marginal cost curve of each of these latter products (so that pre-discovery the outputs of all these goods were the same). Then note the following three facts: (1) the amount of buyer surplus generated by the sale of additional units of any product whose supplier is a nondiscriminator who faces a downward-sloping demand curve (the difference between the heights of DD and MR for such a nondiscriminator) will increase with the original output of the product in question; (2) a marginal-cost-decreasing PPR project will increase the output of the good G1 to whose production process it relates while decreasing the output of the goods G2 . . . N from whose production resources are withdrawn when G1 is produced; and (3) the increase in the output of G1 will be higher than the decrease in the output of each product in the set G2 . . . N whose output is reduced when G1's output is increased. Taken together, these neutral assumptions and realities imply that (1) the buyer surplus that would have been generated by the sale of each of the last units of the other products G2 . . . N that will be sacrificed when G1's output is increased (which causes the allocative value of each such unit to exceed its private value to its producers, thereby deflating the private cost to the production-process researcher of the resources he used to produce each additional unit of G1 the production-process discovery made it profitable for him to produce—that is, the deflation in the average marginal cost of producing the additional units in question) *will be smaller than* (2) the average buyer surplus generated by the sale of the additional units of G1 whose production the PPR project in question would induce—that is, the deflation in the average private benefit the PPR investor secured by producing the additional units of output the PPR discovery made it profitable for him to produce.

The imperfections in competition that can distort $PB_{\Delta PPR}$ by creating a situation in which the producer/discoverer's use of the discovery the relevant project yields leads to the exit of a product rival are the imperfections in price and QV-investment competition that the discovery generates and the imperfections in QV-investment competition that account for the fact that the product (QV investment) that the PPR project's use causes to exit will not be immediately replaced by a QV investment (product) of another rival that is equally competitive with the PPR owner's final goods as the exited good was. It should be obvious that the benefits a PPR project confers on its owner by driving out a rival final product that will not be immediately replaced by an equally competitive rival final product are purely private gains. Indeed, to the extent that any increase in prices the exit causes misallocates resources, the associated inflation of $PB_{\Delta PPR}$ will be larger than the profits the induced exit confers on the PPR investor—that is, will equal the sum of those profits and the engendered misallocation.

Diagram III illustrates the first two ways in which a PPR project benefits a PPR owner who uses the discovery it yields exclusively himself and the ways in which imperfections in price competition distort those benefits. Diagram III contains a demand curve, a marginal allocative value curve, a marginal revenue curve, two marginal cost curves, and two marginal allocative cost curves.

The demand curve in Diagram III—DD_{G1}—coincides with the marginal allocative value curve in the diagram—MLV_{G1}. The coincidence of these two

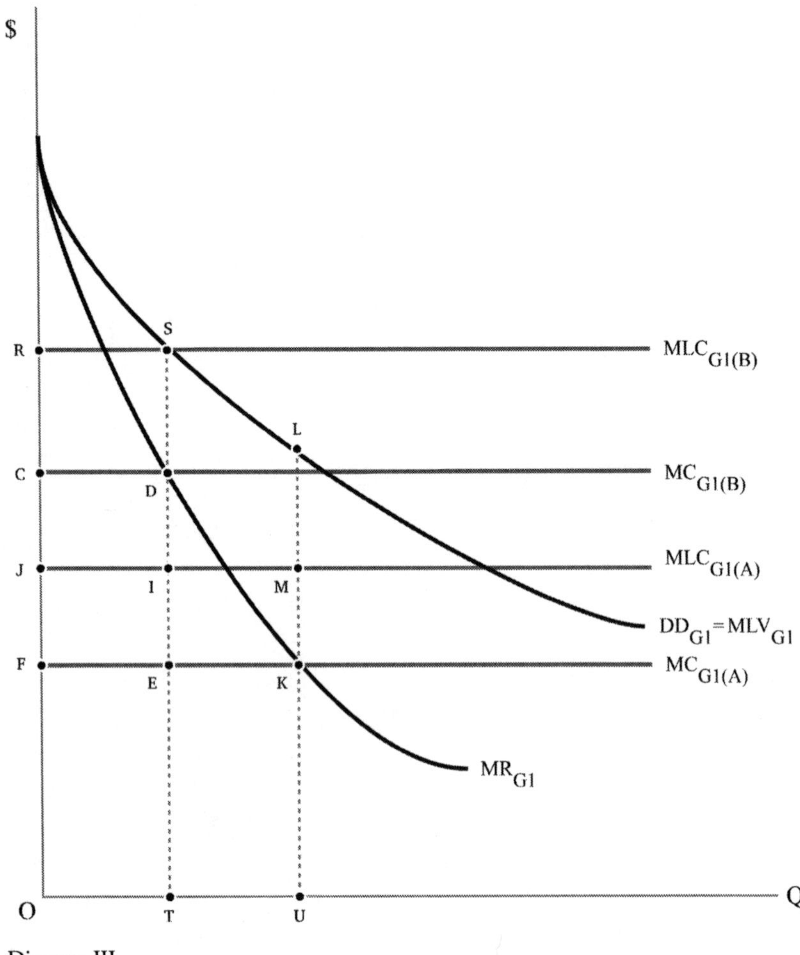

Diagram III

curves reflects the fact that the current monopoly-distortion analysis's otherwise-Pareto-perfect assumption rules out the human errors, monopsony, and externalities of consumption that can cause DD_{GI} to diverge from MLV_{GI}. The marginal revenue curve in Diagram III—MR_{GI}—coincides with the curve that indicates the private benefits that the sale of successive units of GI confers on their producer because the analysis's otherwise-Pareto-perfect assumption rules out the consumer ignorance and externalities of consumption that can cause sales to yield producers promotional benefits and the producer ignorance that can cause the production of additional units of output to generate learning-by-doing benefits.

In Diagram III, $MC_{G1(B)}$ indicates the marginal costs the researcher had to incur to produce successive units of G1 before he discovered his new production process (the subscript B stands for before), and $MC_{G1(A)}$ indicates the (lower) marginal costs the researcher must incur to produce successive units of G1 with the new production process that the marginal PPR project in question discovered (the subscript A stands for after). $MLC_{G1(B)}$ indicates the marginal allocative cost of producing successive units of G1 with the pre-discovery production process, and $MLC_{G1(A)}$ indicates the marginal allocative cost of producing successive units of G1 with the new production process the marginal PPR project discovered (after the discovery was made). In Diagram III, $MLC_{G1(B)} > MC_{G1(B)}$ and $MLC_{G1(A)} > MC_{G1(A)}$. This construction reflects two assumptions: (1) the assumption already articulated that units of G1 are produced with resources that are withdrawn exclusively from other unit-output-producing uses and (2) an assumption that the products G2 . . . N from whose unit output production the resources used to produce G1 are withdrawn are produced by nondiscriminating imperfect competitors who face downward-sloping demand curves. Although this second assumption is realistic, Diagram III's construction of $MLC_{G1(B)}$ to be 50 percent higher than $MC_{G1(B)}$ and $MLC_{G1(A)}$ to be 50 percent higher than $MC_{G1(A)}$ reflects an implicit assumption that is not realistic—namely, that the P/MR and P/MC ratios of the other products G2 . . . N from whose production resources are withdrawn when G1 is produced equal 3/2. I hasten to add, however, that this assumption has been made solely to make the diagram more readable: no conclusion on which I rely depends on its accuracy. Diagram III's assumption that all four cost curves it contains are horizontal is also made solely for expositional reasons. Finally, Diagram III adopts what I take to be the neutral assumption that the pre-discovery output of G1 (the output at which MR_{G1} cuts MC_B from above at point D—CD = OT = RS) is the output that is allocatively efficient to produce with the original production process—the output at which MLV_{G1} cuts $MLC_{G1(B)}$ from above at point S. Implicitly, this construction is based on the assumption I have articulated that, pre-discovery, the P/MR = P/MC ratio for G1 equals the P/MC ratio for each of the products G2 . . . N whose unit outputs are reduced by G1's production.

We can now use Diagram III to illustrate my claim that on the assumptions now being made the relevant imperfections in competition will deflate the private benefits a marginal-cost-reducing PPR project confers on the PPR investor/producer who owns it both (1) by reducing the cost he must incur to produce his pre-discovery unit output and (2) by enabling him to profit by expanding his output. I shall begin with the former deflation. In Diagram III, the allocative benefits the PPR project generates by discovering a production process whose use reduces the marginal cost of producing the pre-discovery output of G1 (OT) equals area RSIJ, while the private benefits the project confers on the PPR investor by reducing the variable cost he incurred to produce his pre-discovery output is the smaller area CDEF. As Diagram III manifests, the relevant allocative benefits exceed their private counterparts—that is, the private benefits in question are deflated. Thus, in Diagram III, area RSIJ is bigger than area CDEF: since $MLC_{G1(B)}$ is (3/2)$MC_{G1(B)}$ and $MLC_{G1(A)}$ is (3/2) $MC_{G1(A)}$, (1) $MLC_{G1(B)} - MLC_{G1(A)}$ must be (3/2)($MC_{G1(B)} - MC_{G1(A)}$), and (2) the allocative benefits the discovery generates by reducing the allocative cost of producing G1's pre-discovery output—($MLC_{G1(B)} - MLC_{G1(A)}$)JI = area RSIJ—must be (3/2)(the private benefits the discovery generates by reducing the private costs the PPR investor must incur to produce his pre-discovery output—[$MC_{G1(B)} - MC_{G1(A)}$]FE = area CDEF).

Diagram III also manifests the fact that the relevant imperfections in competition deflate the private benefits the PPR project confers on its owner by making it profitable for him to increase his output. In Diagram III, the production of the additional TU units of G1 that the relevant production-process discovery induces the PPR investor to produce—by reducing MC_{G1} from $MC_{G1(B)}$ to $MC_{G1(A)}$ and hence changing the point at which MR_{G1} cuts the changing MC_{G1} curve from above from point D to point K—increases allocative efficiency by the area SLMI—the area between MLV_{G1} and $MLC_{G1(A)}$ between outputs OT and OU—while increasing the investor's profits by the smaller amount area DKE—the area between MR_{G1} and $MC_{G1(A)}$ between outputs OT and OU. The difference between areas SLMI and DKE is the monopoly deflation in this component of $PB_{\Delta PPR}$.

What would the preceding analyses imply about the sign of MD($PB_{\Delta PPR}$) for a marginal-cost-reducing PPR project if all the resources consumed by the production of the good G1 whose cost of production the relevant PPR discovery reduced were withdrawn from the production of other goods G2 . . . N produced by nondiscriminating imperfect competitors who faced downward-sloping demand curves? First, since the relevant imperfections in competition deflate both the private benefits such a project generates by reducing the cost its owner must incur to produce his pre-discovery output and the private benefits it generates by making it profitable for him to expand his unit output, MD($PB_{\Delta PPR}$) will clearly be negative for such PPR projects in those cases in which the investor's use of the project does not induce the exit of a product (a QV investment) that is competitive with GI—that is, in the vast majority of cases. In fact, although this conclusion obviously reflects some empirical judgments that I will not even try to justify, I suspect that $MC(PB_{\Delta PPR})$ will be negative for this type of PPR project even when the discovery it creates does induce one or more product rivals of the final good GI to exit.

Before concluding this subsection, I want to investigate how my analysis and conclusions would be altered if the discovered production process (1) would have no effect on its users' marginal cost curves (would reduce the average total cost its users had to incur to produce their pre-discovery outputs solely by reducing their fixed costs) and (2) would increase its users' marginal cost curves (but would reduce the average total cost they had to incur to produce their pre-discovery outputs by reducing the average fixed cost they had to incur to do so by more than it increased the average variable cost they had to incur to produce that output). I will begin by analyzing the way in which such changes in assumptions will affect both the private benefits the use of the discovery would enable the discovery-owner to obtain by reducing the cost he had to incur to produce his pre-discovery output and the associated monopoly distortion in $PB_{\Delta PPR}$. No significant change will have to be made in the analysis of either those benefits or the related monopoly distortion if the discovery's use would have no impact on the marginal cost curve its user faced or would raise the average variable cost he would have to incur to produce his pre-discovery output without changing his marginal cost at that pre-discovery output. So long as the discovery did not make it profitable for its user to reduce his output by increasing his marginal cost at his pre-discovery profit-maximizing output and the discovery's user's production of his pre-discovery output withdrew resources exclusively from the production of products produced by nondiscriminating imperfect competitors who faced downward-sloping demand curves, the change in assumption we are now considering would affect neither $PB_{\Delta PPR}$ nor $MD(PB_{\Delta PPR})$: both the private cost-saving in question and the monopoly distortion in that private benefit will not be affected in any way by whether the cost-saving was a saving in variable or fixed costs.

However, if the use of the discovered production process raised the user's marginal cost at his pre-discovery output, both the private benefit in question and the monopoly distortion in that benefit would be affected: in this case, the relevant private benefit would be the (smaller) reduction in the total cost the discovery's user had to incur to produce his (lower) post-discovery output, and the distortion in that private benefit would be reduced approximately proportionately to the private benefit in question. In these sorts of cases, it will also be necessary to reanalyze the magnitude of and monopoly distortion in the second type of private benefit that marginal-cost-reducing production-process discoveries generate for their users—the profit they enable their users to obtain by increasing the unit output of the product the discovered production process can be used to produce. Obviously, if the production process the marginal PPR project discovers would have no impact on its user's marginal costs at his pre-discovery profit-maximizing output, no private benefits of this kind will be generated, and concomitantly there will be no monopoly distortion in those private benefits. If the use of the discovered production process would raise its user's marginal costs at his pre-discovery profit-maximizing output, its use will make it profitable for him to reduce his unit output; the profits he earned pre-discovery by producing the eliminated output with the old production process will have to be subtracted from the other benefits the use of the discovered production process will generate to determine ($PB_{\Delta PPR}$); and the relevant imperfections in price competition will cause this private loss to exceed its allocative-efficiency counterpart—that is, will deflate $PB_{\Delta PPR}$ on this account.

Diagram IV illustrates this possibility. $DD_{GI} = MLV_{GI}$, MR_{GI}, $MLC_{GI(B)}$, and $MC_{GI(B)}$ are the same in Diagram IV as in Diagram III. The difference is that, in Diagram IV, $MLC_{GI(A^*)} > MLC_{GI(B)}$ and $MC_{GI(A^*)} > MC_{GI(B)}$ are substituted for Diagram III's $MLC_{GI(A)} < MLC_{GI(B)}$ and $MC_{GI(A)} < MC_{GI(B)}$. In Diagram IV, the use of the discovered production process will raise the user's marginal costs by EC from CO to EO and reduce his profit-maximizing output by GT from CD = OT to EF = OG. Since the profits the discovery user made pre-discovery by producing those GT units of output (area FDJ in Diagram IV) are higher than the amount by which the pre-discovery production of those units increased economic efficiency (area WSV in Diagram IV) (given that MR_{GI} will drop faster than $DD_{GI} = MLV_{GI}$ over the relevant range and that concomitantly FJ will be larger than WV in Diagram IV), the relevant imperfections in price competition will inflate this loss the discovery imposes on its user and hence deflate the associate (negative) private benefit in this case as well.

Finally, when the use of the discovered production process will have no impact on its user's marginal cost at his pre-discovery output or will increase that marginal cost, it will also be necessary to reanalyze whether the discovery may benefit its user by driving a rival out (as it might when the use of the discovery reduced the user's marginal costs at his pre-discovery output). In fact, it is clear that the discovery will not benefit the discoverer/producer who

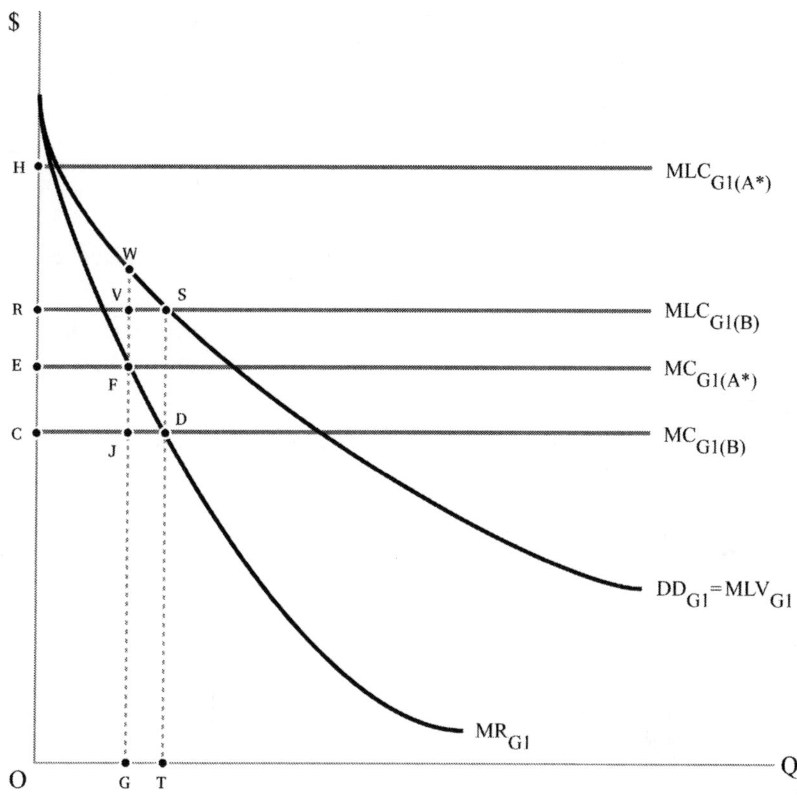

Diagram IV

made it when its use will not affect his marginal costs at his pre-discovery output by driving a rival out since in that case its use will not make it non-strategically profitable for him to lower the price he charges for G1. Indeed, if the discovery's use increases the discoverer's marginal costs at his pre-discovery output, it may actually impose a loss on him by rendering it inherently profitable for him to increase his price of G1 in circumstances in which either of two conditions is fulfilled:

1. (A) his original price but not his increased price would have led a product that competes with G1 to be withdrawn, and (B) the withdrawn product would not have been replaced immediately by another product that was as competitive with the discoverer's products as the withdrawn product had been; or

2. the higher price induces a rival to make a QV investment in the relevant area of product-space or makes it necessary for the discoverer to make an additional QV investment to deter a rival from doing so.

If I am correct that in a world that contains imperfections in seller competition but no other type of Pareto imperfection, the survival of the rival product in question would increase economic efficiency by causing prices to be lower than they otherwise would be, the private loss in question would deflate $PB_{\Delta PPR}$ in such a case not just by the amount of the loss but by that amount *plus* the amount by which the survival of the rival product would increase allocative efficiency. In such a case, then, the relevant imperfections in competition would tend to deflate $PB_{\Delta PPR}$ by causing the discovery's use to impose a loss on the user by producing an effect that would increase allocative efficiency. On the other hand, if the discovery's use caused an additional QV investment to be made in the relevant area of product-space, the distorting impact of the relevant imperfections in competition will depend on whether the associated misallocation is larger or smaller than the loss the discoverer/producer sustains on this account.

$\Sigma D(PB_{\Delta PPR})$ WHEN THE EXECUTION OF THE MARGINAL PPR PROJECT WITHDREW RESOURCES EXCLUSIVELY FROM UNIT-OUTPUT-PRODUCING USES

All types of Pareto imperfections can individually distort $PB_{\Delta PPR}$. Thus, $\Sigma D(PB_{\Delta PPR})$ is affected not just by imperfections in seller competition and related buyer surplus but also by monopsony, various kinds of externalities, various kinds of taxes on the margin of income, and human errors caused by nonsovereignty and nonmaximization. Because the same kinds of taxes and human errors that distorted $PB_{\Delta QV}$, $PC_{\Delta QV}$, and hence $P\pi_{\Delta QV}$ in various ways will affect $PB_{\Delta PPR}$, $PC_{\Delta PPR}$, and hence $P\pi_{\Delta PPR}$ in precisely the same ways, I will ignore them here and in the rest of this chapter. However, because I suspect that monopsony is more likely to distort $PB_{\Delta PPR}$ and hence $P\pi_{\Delta PPR}$ than it is to distort $PB_{\Delta QV}$ and $P\pi_{\Delta QV}$ and that certain types of externalities are also more likely to distort $PB_{\Delta PPR}$ and $P\pi_{\Delta PPR}$ than to distort $PB_{\Delta QV}$ and $P\pi_{\Delta QV}$, I will consider these imperfections and their distorting impacts in the PPR context.

When analyzing the aggregate distortions in $PB_{\Delta QV}$ and $P\pi_{\Delta QV}$, I ignored monopsony on the empirical ground that the marginal QV investor almost certainly did not possess or exercise any monopsony power when buying the resources he used to create his marginal QV investment or to produce units of the product it created, the alternative users of those resources also almost certainly did not possess or would not have exercised any monopsony power as buyers of the resources in question, and the potential customers of neither the marginal QV investor in question nor the unit-output producers from whom the relevant QV investor withdrew resources would have had monopsony power when buying the goods these parties did sell or might have sold them. To the extent that it proves TBLE to investigate these possibilities, my failure to address them when analyzing $\Sigma D(PB_{\Delta QV})$ and $\Sigma D(P\pi_{\Delta QV})$ is unjustified.

This analysis of $\Sigma D(PB_{\Delta PPR})$ will still be based on the following assumptions:

1. marginal production-process researchers do not have monopsony power when purchasing the resources the execution or use of the PPR projects consumes;
2. the unit output producers from whom the execution of marginal PPR projects withdraws resources would not have any monopsony power when buying those resources; and
3. neither the buyers of the product whose production process the marginal PPR project will alter nor the buyers of the products whose outputs that project's execution would reduce have any monopsony power when buying the products in question.

However, this analysis will take into consideration the possibility that the marginal production-process researcher may not use his discovery exclusively himself and that one or more purchasers of his discovery or the right to use his discovery may have monopsony power (the fact that some of the discovery's purchasers will be able to secure buyer surplus because transaction costs make it unprofitable for the production-process discoverer to practice perfect price discrimination when licensing the right to use his discovery is analogous to the fact that, for the same reason, the sale of the new product created by the marginal QV investment will create buyer surplus). I consider this possibility in the PPR context because I suspect that PPR innovators are far more likely than product innovators to sell their patents and ideas or to license the right to use their discoveries to parties with monopsony power. In part, I base this judgment on a perception that, despite the fact that some of the relevant information is somewhat impacted (is more available to producers of the product whose cost of production the PPR project is seeking to reduce), independent research labs (which do not produce and are not well placed to produce the good to whose production process the research relate and are therefore more likely to sell their discoveries than are product discoverers) account for a far higher percentage of production-process innovations than of technological product innovations. And in part, I base this judgment on an assumption that the number of possible buyers of production-process discoveries is likely to be relevantly smaller than the number of possible buyers of product discoveries. In any event, to the extent that the marginal production-process researcher sells his discovery or the right to use it to others and their monopsony power enables these buyers or licensees to secure surplus on the transactions in question, that surplus (and the monopsony power that accounts for at least some of it) will deflate $PB_{\Delta PPR}$.

The second nonmonopoly type of Pareto imperfection I want to discuss in conjunction with $\Sigma D(PB_{\Delta PPR})$ are externalities. Because their magnitude and distorting effects will not be different in the PPR context from what they were in the QV-investment context, I will not revisit here the externalities (1) that might have been generated by the production and consumption of the units of output sacrificed when the marginal PPR project is executed, (2) that were generated by the production and consumption of the pre-discovery output of G1, and (3) that would be generated by the production of any additional output of G1 the discovery causes to be produced. However, I will discuss (1) the possible differences between the knowledge-creation-related externalities generated respectively by production-process and product discoveries and (2) externalities that might be generated by PPR that was designed to discover less-AP-loss-prone ways of producing products.

I can think of five reasons why the ratio of the (uninternalized) externalities generated by the weighted-average marginal PPR project to its allocative cost may differ from its counterpart for marginal QV investments:

1. the weighted-average number of days by which successful marginal PPR projects should have been predicted *ex ante* to advance the date on which the discovery they made would be made may be different from its counterpart for successful marginal product-research projects;

2. the breadth of the protection that our patent laws give production-process patent holders may be different from its counterpart for product patent holders;
3. production-process discoverers may be more able to keep their discoveries secret than product discoverers: although rivals may be able to infer some features of a discovered production process through aerial reconnaissance of the buildings in which the process is used (yes, it does happen) or by bribing the managers and staffs of the discoverer, reverse engineering will clearly be more practicable when the discovery is a product in the public domain than when it is a production process that potential copycats are not in a position to observe directly;
4. the ability of production-process discoverers to internalize what would otherwise be the external benefits their research efforts generate by buying up producers of the product to whose production their discovery relates and producers of complements of that product may be greater than the ability of product discoverers to achieve this result by buying up potential producers of the product they discovered or producers of complements of that product; and
5. although a considerable percentage of product discoveries involve no technological advance and therefore receive no protection from patent laws, virtually all production-process discoveries do involve a technological advance and therefore do qualify for patent-law protection.

Although the last three of these points favor the conclusion that knowledge-creation-related externalities are less likely to deflate (more likely to inflate) $PB_{\Delta PPR}$ than $PB_{\Delta QV}$ and are likely to deflate $PB_{\Delta PPR}$ (inflate $PB_{\Delta PPR}$) by less (by more) if they do deflate (inflate) it, my ignorance about (1) the number of days by which successful marginal PPR projects and successful marginal product R&D projects should have been expected *ex ante* to advance the date on which the discovery they made was made and (2) the relative breadths of the protection that patent law gives production-process discoverers and product discoverers deters me from even speculating on this issue. I included this analysis despite this fact because I suspect that it will prove to be TBLE to investigate it more thoroughly in various policy-analysis contexts.

The only type of externality distortion in $PB_{\Delta PPR}$ I want to discuss at this juncture relates to a small subset of PPR projects—namely, those that are designed to discover a less-AP-loss-prone way to produce an existing product.

In fact, for reasons that will become apparent in a moment, it may actually be more accurate to characterize this distortion as a monopoly/externality distortion in $PB_{\Delta PPR}$. I will assume at the outset that the following five conditions are fulfilled:

1. the relevant potential production-process researcher is a monopolist of the good to whose production process the relevant marginal PPR project relates;
2. no independent research firm could possibly find it profitable to discover the less-AP-loss-prone production process the monopolist could discover (because some of the information needed to make the discovery is available only to producers of the product in question—that is, is impacted);
3. the monopolist in question would be held liable for the accident and pollution losses his operation imposed on others only if his generation of those losses was found negligent (only if the private cost to him of reducing these losses by $X by making a type of avoidance move whose rejection is assessed for negligence[32] was lower than the amount by which that move would have reduced the AP losses he should have expected to impose on others whose losses the law deems relevant);[33]
4. prior to the discovery, the monopolist/production-process researcher in question would not have been found negligent for the AP losses the discovery would enable him to prevent (because the additional private cost of shifting to any known, safer production process was higher than the amount by which he should have concluded the use of that safer process would reduce the AP losses he would generate and his rejection of the PPR project in question would not be assessed for negligence); and
5. after the discovery, the monopolist/production-process researcher in question would be liable for any AP losses he could have prevented by shifting to the discovered production process (because the private cost of the shift to the discovered process would be lower than the amount by which he should have concluded the shift would reduce the AP losses he generated).

Clearly, in this situation, the private benefits of the relevant PPR project will be deflated: although the use of the discovered process will reduce the private and presumptively the allocative AP losses that are generated, the project will not benefit the discovery's user on that account since, had the project not been executed, he would not have been liable for these losses. On these facts, in the typical situation in which the safer production process is privately more expensive (AP-loss consequences aside), the PPR project that discovered the safer production process would be unprofitable even if it were allocatively efficient—would reduce its owner's profits by the sum of the private cost of its execution, the additional other costs he had to incur to produce the output he used the discovered process to produce, and the profits he made pre-discovery on the units of output he no longer produced post-discovery (if at the monopolist's pre-discovery output the private marginal costs of the safer production process were higher than those of the more dangerous process for which it was substituted).

Admittedly, the deflation in question will disappear if the monopolist is strictly liable (and no other doctrine or information imperfection will enable him to escape liability) or if the monopolist knows that, if he does not make the relevant discovery, an independent research firm will make it on the same day he would. The deflation in question will also be smaller if the relevant producer/production-process researcher is not a monopolist of the good to whose production process the discovery relates both because, to the extent that others produce the good in question, (1) it is more likely that they would discover the safer production process if he did not and (2) he will be able to profit by licensing these others to use his discovery (rather than incurring the higher cost of using it himself). Nevertheless, I am certain that, in a significant number of cases, the combination of the monopoly power of the potential researcher both as a producer of the good in question and as the executer of the relevant PPR project and the failure of tort and environmental law to internalize to such potential researchers the costs their failure to do the research in question would impose on others will deflate $PB_{\Delta PPR}$.

I should say that an analogous benefit deflation can arise in the product-R&D QV-investment context. In this case, the marginal projects whose private benefits are deflated will be designed to discover new product variants whose production and consumption combined will be less-AP-loss-prone (or less-AP-loss-prone distributive outlets, whose location is *inter alia* a product attribute). In one sense, this deflation is even less susceptible to remedy: to the extent that our current tort and environmental laws not only do not make producers strictly liable for the AP-loss consequences of their failing to substitute the production of product variants whose production and consump-tion combined are less-AP-loss-prone for the production of product variants whose production and consumption combined are more-AP-loss-prone, they do not hold them liable for the AP losses their rejections of such avoidance moves generate when those rejections would be deemed negligent if they were assessed for negligence (because they do not assess such rejections for negligence). Hence, neither pro-competition policies nor policies that make independent research firms more profitable will be able to eliminate or reduce the deflation in the private benefits that would be yielded by product R&D into safer product variants. I ignored this possibility earlier in this chapter when analyzing particular QV-investment-related issues partly for expositional reasons but primarily because I suspect that it is far less important empirically in the QV-investment context than in the PPR context. In any event, if it would be TBLE to analyze this possibility in the QV-investment context, the QV-investment analysis should be expanded to do so.

A final assertion: although this subsection has not considered many of the Pareto imperfections that can distort $PB_{\Delta PPR}$, I am confident that a more complete analysis would not alter the conclusion suggested by the analyses that have been executed that $\Sigma D(PB_{\Delta PPR})$ is negative for the vast majority of marginal PPR projects in the economy.

$\Sigma D(PB_{\Delta PPR})$ ON REALISTIC ASSUMPTIONS ABOUT THE USES FROM WHICH THE EXECUTION AND USE OF MARGINAL PPR PROJECTS WITHDREW RESOURCES

The preceding analyses of $MD(PB_{\Delta PPR})$ and $\Sigma D(PB_{\Delta PPR})$ assumed that all the resources consumed by the use of the production process the marginal PPR project discovered would be withdrawn from unit-output-producing uses. In a world in which virtually all producers face downward-sloping demand curves and do not engage in perfect price discrimination, this assumption made it likely that $MLC_{GI(B)}$ would exceed $MC_{GI(B)}$, that $ALFC_{GI(B)}$ (the average allocative fixed cost of producing GI with the pre-discovery production process) would exceed $AFC_{GI(B)}$, and that $MLC_{GI(A)}$ would exceed $MC_{GI(A)}$. As we saw, the facts that $MLC_{GI(B)}$ exceeded $MC_{GI(B)}$ and that $ALFC_{GI(B)}$ exceeded $AFC_{GI(B)}$ implied that, *ceteris paribus*, the private cost-savings that the production-process discovery would enable its user to achieve on his pre-discovery output would be lower than their allocative counterparts—that is, that the relevant imperfections in seller competition would deflate this component of $PB_{\Delta PPR}$. On the other hand, as we also saw, the fact that $MLC_{GI(B)}$ exceeded $MC_{GI(B)}$ implied that, *ceteris paribus*, the profits a marginal-cost-reducing production-process discovery would enable its user to secure by increasing his unit output would be inflated (by the difference between the allocative and private cost of the output expansion). Roughly speaking, the former deflating effect will exceed the latter inflating effect if the discovery user's pre-discovery output was more than half his post-discovery output. Since few production-process discoveries will make it profitable for their users to double or more than double their output, I believe that—by increasing the ratio of MLC_{GI} to MC_{GI} (see below)—the assumption that all the resources the production of GI consumes would be withdrawn from other unit-output-producing uses favors the conclusions that $MD(PB_{\Delta PPR})$ and $\Sigma D(PB_{\Delta PPR})$ will be negative—that is, that on balance the relevant private benefits are deflated.

The fact that, in reality, some QV-to-PPR-use resource flows will (so to speak) be substituted for some of the UO-to-PPR-use resource flows that the preceding subsections assumed would be exclusively involved in PPR execution and use is relevant because, as we have seen, $\Sigma D(PB_{\Delta QV})$ will be positive whereas $\Sigma D(PB_{\Delta UO})$ was negative. Just as the negative value of $\Sigma D(PB_{\Delta UO})$ implied that the UO-to-PPR-use resource flows would deflate $PB_{\Delta PPR}$, the positive value of $\Sigma D(PB_{\Delta QV})$ implies that the QV-to-PPR-use resource flows inflate $PB_{\Delta PPR}$. One question that might be asked, then, is: will the deflation of $PB_{\Delta PPR}$ caused by the UO-to-PPR-use resource flows be only partially offset, fully offset, or outweighed by the inflation in $PB_{\Delta PPR}$ caused by the QV-to-PPR-use resource flows? The answer to this question depends on (1) the proportions of $PC_{U\Delta PPR}$ that the cost of resources withdrawn respectively from unit-output-producing and QV-investment-creating uses respectively constitute, (2) the absolute value of the economy's weighted-average (negative) $\Sigma D(PB_{\Delta UO})/PB_{\Delta UO}$ ratio, and (3) the absolute value of the economy's weighted-average (positive) $\Sigma D(PB_{\Delta QV})/PB_{\Delta QV}$ ratio. Because the use of the PPR discovery does not consume resources that are particularly technologically gifted or skilled, I suspect that the ratio of the resources the use of marginal PPR projects consumes that are withdrawn respectively from unit-output-producing and QV-investment-creating uses somewhat exceeds the ratio of the private cost of the resources the economy devotes to unit-output-producing uses to the private cost of the resources the economy devotes to QV-investment-creating uses—a ratio that I suspect is at least 5/1. Hence, although I believe that the economy's weighted-average $\Sigma D(PB_{\Delta QV})/PB_{\Delta QV}$ ratio is considerably higher than the absolute value of the economy's weighted-average $\Sigma D(PB_{\Delta UO})/PB_{\Delta UO}$ ratio, I do not think that the former ratio is a sufficient multiple of the absolute value of the latter ratio to make the inflation in $PB_{\Delta PPR}$ caused by the relevant QV-to-PPR-use resource flows as large as the deflation in $PB_{\Delta PPR}$ caused by the relevant UO-to-PPR-use resource flows. I therefore think that, although both $MD(PB_{\Delta PPR})$ and $\Sigma D(PB_{\Delta PPR})$ will be absolutely lower because some of the resources consumed by the use of PPR discoverers will be withdrawn from QV-investment-creating uses, $PB_{\Delta PPR}$ will still be deflated by the interaction of the various Pareto imperfections in the economy even though some of the resources consumed by the use of PPR discoveries are withdrawn from QV-investment-creating uses.

$\Sigma D(PC_{C\Delta PPR})$ ON REALISTIC ASSUMPTIONS ABOUT THE USES FROM WHICH THE EXECUTION OF MARGINAL PPR PROJECTS WITHDRAWS RESOURCES

The preceding subsection explained why I think that $\Sigma D(PC_{U\Delta PPR})$ will be negative even though the marginal production-process researcher will have to pay inflated prices for some of the resources the creation of his production-process discovery consumes—namely, for those resources the use of his discovery withdraws from QV-investment-creating uses. With one significant alteration, that analysis will also apply *mutatis mutandis* to $\Sigma D(PC_{C\Delta PPR})$. The alteration reflects the fact that productive resources are not equally productive in the various types of uses to which they might be put. More specifically, the alteration reflects the fact that the technologically gifted and trained labor that PPR consumes is likely to be withdrawn almost exclusively from product R&D—that is, from technologically innovative QV-investment-creating uses. To the extent that this is the case, the ratio of the private costs that marginal PPR-project owners incur to withdraw resources from QV-investment-creating uses to execute their projects to the private costs they incur to withdraw resources from unit-output-producing uses to execute their projects will exceed the ratio of the private cost of creating all the QV investments the economy created to the private cost of all unit output production in the economy. At a minimum, this reality implies that the absolute value of the aggregate (negative) percentage deflation in $PC_{C\Delta PPR}$—$\Sigma D(PC_{C\Delta PPR})/PC_{C\Delta PPR}$—will be lower than its counterpart for $PC_{U\Delta PPR}$. In fact, it could cause $PC_{C\Delta PPR}$ not to be distorted at all or even to be inflated. The analysis that follows will assume that although the QV-to-PPR-creation resource flows will reduce the absolute value of the (negative) $\Sigma D(PC_{C\Delta PPR})/PC_{C\Delta PPR}$ ratio, it will not cause that distortion to be zero or positive. For present purposes, I am simply asserting this conclusion, which obviously depends on a large number of empirical assumptions I have not even attempted to justify and could not justify in any scientifically acceptable manner. Those who are unhappy with this assertion should recall that the point of this analysis is not to justify any particular policy conclusion but to delineate and justify the approach I am arguing one should take to economic-efficiency assessment.

$\Sigma D(P\pi_{\Delta PPR})/LC_{\Delta PPR}$ ON REALISTIC ASSUMPTIONS ABOUT THE USES FROM WHICH THE CREATION AND USE OF MARGINAL PPR PROJECTS WITHDRAW RESOURCES

The preceding two subsections explained why I believe that for virtually all marginal PPR projects in the economy (1) $\Sigma D(PB_{\Delta PPR})$ and hence $\Sigma D(PB_{\Delta PPR})/LC_{U\Delta PPR}$ and (2) $\Sigma D(PC_{C\Delta PPR})$ and hence $\Sigma D(PC_{C\Delta PPR})/LC_{C\Delta PPR}$ are negative. Although these conclusions do not themselves imply anything about the sign of the weighted-average economy-wide $\Sigma D(P\pi_{\Delta PPR})/LC_{\Delta PPR}$ ratio or the absolute value of this weighted-average percentage profit distortion relative to that of its $\Sigma D(P\pi_{\Delta UO})/LC_{\Delta UO}$ counterpart, the analyses of these two subsections do provide some basis for concluding (1) that the weighted-average economy-wide $\Sigma D(P\pi_{\Delta PPR})/LC_{\Delta PPR}$ ratio will be negative and (2) that the absolute value of this weighted-average ratio will be lower than the absolute value of its weighted-average unit output counterpart—$\Sigma D(P\pi_{\Delta UO})/LC_{\Delta UO}$. *Inter alia*, the first of these conclusions reflects two facts: (1) the fact that the percentage of the resources that the creation of marginal PPR projects consumes that is withdrawn from QV-investment creation is higher than the percentage of the resources that the use of marginal PPR-project discoveries consumes that is withdrawn from QV-investment creation and (2) the fact that the monopoly deflation in the private cost of producing the goods to whose production marginal PPR discoveries relate inflates one component of $PB_{\Delta PPR}$. The second of these two conclusions reflects the fact that the percentage of the resources that the execution and use of marginal PPR projects consume that is withdrawn from QV-investment creation is higher than the percentage of the resources that the production of marginal units of existing products consumes that is withdrawn from QV-investment-creating uses and too many other considerations to be listed here.

In any event, the concrete economic-efficiency assessments that follow will (when relevant) proceed on the far-from-satisfactorily-explained assumption that the above two conclusions are correct. Once more, those who disapprove can console themselves with the fact that the point of Part II is to delineate and justify the approach to economic-efficiency assessment I claim is TBLE, not to generate any particular policy conclusion or set of policy conclusions.

PPR-TO-PPR MISALLOCATION: ITS CAUSE AND SOME POLICY-ANALYSIS IMPLICATIONS

At the most abstract level, it is easy to explain the cause of PPR-to-PPR misallocation and the type of policy that would reduce such misallocation.

The extant Pareto imperfections will cause PPR misallocation if and to the extent that they cause $\Sigma D(P\pi_{\Delta PPR})/LC_{\Delta PPR}$ to differ among the marginal PPR projects in the economy. Concomitantly, government policy will reduce PPR-to-PPR misallocation if it reduces the weighted-average deviation of the distribution of $\Sigma D(P\pi_{\Delta PPR})/LC_{\Delta PPR}$ ratios in the economy—that is, if it causes resources to be reallocated from PPR uses in which $\Sigma D(P\pi_{\Delta PPR})/LC_{\Delta PPR}$ is less negative to PPR uses in which $\Sigma D(P\pi_{\Delta PPR})$ is more negative, assuming that my conclusion that $\Sigma D(P\pi_{\Delta PPR})$ is negative for (virtually) all marginal PPR projects in the economy is correct. The tricky bit is to be more specific about the causes of PPR-to-PPR misallocation and to generate related policy conclusions that are more concrete and therefore more useful.

Unfortunately, to perform these tasks even with a modicum of success, I have to make some assumptions that are clearly contestable. I will assume first (and I think quite reasonably) that the production-process discoveries that marginal PPR projects yield will reduce the marginal costs of their users and be used not only by their discoverer (say, the producer of G1) but also (under license) by his product rivals (the producers of G2 . . . N). In part, this latter assumption reflects my conclusion that a refusal by the discoverer to license his rivals to use his discovery would be predatory and violative of the Sherman Act's[34] prohibition of monopolizing or attempting to monopolize. I will assume second (and much more contestably) that the weighted-average P/MC and P*/MC* ratios of the products from whose production the production of G1 . . . N withdrew resources will deviate from their economy-wide counterparts in the same direction but to a slightly smaller extent than the weighted-average P/MC and P*/MC* ratios of G1 . . . N. As I explained earlier, this assumption reflects my contestable belief that there is some tendency for products that are moderately but not closely competitive with each other to be similarly differentiated and to be produced and distributed with similar technologies (to be produced and distributed under conditions of similar economies of scale relative to the extent of their sales and to have similar XMC/MC ratios). In any event, to the extent that this is the case, there will be some tendency for $\Sigma D(P\pi_{\Delta PPR})/LC_{\Delta PPR}$ to be more negative in areas of product-space whose weighted-average P/MC or P*/MC* ratio is higher than its economy-wide counterpart.

To facilitate my explanation, I will designate the goods from whose production the production of G1 . . . N withdraws resources "goods H1 . . . K" and ignore the externalities and other Pareto imperfections that can cause P* to diverge from P and MC* to diverge from MC. Let us focus first on the tendency of the use of the discovered process to benefit the user by reducing the private cost he had to incur to produce his pre-discovery output. Since this component of $PB_{\Delta PPR}$ will be deflated by $\sum_{H=1}^{K} (P_{H(B)}/MC_{H(B)})SU_{H(B)}$ $(\sum_{G=1}^{N} AVC_{G(B)}[Q_{G(B)}])$ where $SU_{H(B)}$ refers to the number of units of the H in question that were sacrificed when the pre-discovery output of G1 . . . N was produced, the deflation in question will increase with $\sum_{H=1}^{K} (P_H/MC_H)$ and hence on my assumption with $\sum_{G=1}^{N} (P_{G(B)}/MC_{G(B))}Q_{G(B)}$. Consider next the tendency of the use of the discovered process to benefit its user by making it profitable for him to increase his output. Since the amount by which the associated allocative-efficiency gain will exceed the profit gain in question—that is, the deflation in this component of $PB_{\Delta PPR}$—will increase with the extent to which G1 . . . N were underproduced pre-discovery, my assumption—which implies that the amount by which $\sum_{G=1}^{N} (P_{G(B)}/MC_{G(B)})\ Q_{G(B)}$ exceeds $\sum_{H=1}^{K} (P_{H(B)}/MC_{H(B)})Q_{H(B)}$ will increase with the former ratio and that therefore the extent to which G1 . . . N are underproduced from the perspective of economic efficiency will increase with the former ratio—will also imply that the deflation in this second component of $PB_{\Delta PPR}$ will increase with the pre-discovery weighted-average P/MC ratio of the products in the area of product-space on which G is located.

Unfortunately, although it would be helpful if one could conclude that PPR-to-PPR misallocation would be reduced by policies that increased PPR in areas of product-space whose products' weighted-average P/MC (actually, P*/MC*) ratio was higher and decreased PPR in areas of product-space whose products' weighted-average P/MC ratio was lower, another consideration cuts against this conclusion. There is almost certainly some positive correlation between what might crudely be called seller concentration in various areas of product-space and the weighted-average P/MC ratio of the products that the relevant areas of product-space contain, and (as I have already argued) there is also good reason to believe that there is a positive correlation between the concentration of the seller side of an industry and the favorability of the (1) antitrust, IP, tort and environmental, and tax legislation, (2) executive-branch regulations, regulatory rulings, and enforcement policies, and (3) judicial decisions than do industries that are less concentrated. Since this political-economy reality favors the conclusion that, *ceteris paribus,* $\Sigma D(P\pi_{\Delta PPR})/LC_{\Delta PPR}$ will tend to be less negative in more concentrated areas of product-space (with higher-than-average weighted-average P/MC ratios) than in less concentrated areas of product-space (with lower-than-average weighted-average P/MC ratios), I cannot even guess whether on balance policies that increase PPR in areas of product-space with higher P/MC ratios while decreasing it in areas of product-space with lower P/MC ratios will tend to reduce PPR-to-PPR misallocation. However, if such policies would reduce this type of misallocation, that reality would favor the allocative efficiency of reducing the effective tax rate applied to the profits yielded by PPR projects in areas of product-space whose weighted-average P/MC ratios were higher than their economy-wide counterpart while increasing the effective tax rate applied to the profits yielded by PPR projects in areas of product-space whose weighted-average P/MC ratios were lower than their economy-wide counterpart. Moreover, if such policies would reduce PPR-to-PPR misallocation, this reality would also favor enforcing pro-price-competition policies (especially nonstructural pro-price-competition policies such as prohibitions of price-fixing) more aggressively in areas of product-space in which the weighted-average P/MC ratio was higher than its economy-wide counterpart.

The preceding discussion did not address the tendency of our current negligence system to deter the execution of allocatively efficient PPR projects designed to discover less-AP-loss-prone production processes. Although it is somewhat misleading, though accurate, to describe the nonexecution of such projects as an example of PPR-to-PPR misallocation (since such projects would be allocatively efficient even if their execution did not withdraw resources exclusively from the execution of other PPR projects), I do want to describe some policies that might reduce the amount of misallocation of this type in the economy.

The most obvious response to this problem is to make producers strictly liable for the accident and pollution losses they impose on others. If this response is not politically available or (contrary to my conclusion) would be allocatively inefficient or undesirable overall, one might reduce this type of misallocation by a small amount by changing our negligence practice by assessing for possible negligence the failure of injurers to avoid by doing PPR into less-AP-loss-prone production processes: my pessimism about the contribution such a change would make primarily reflects the difficulty triers-of-fact would have in identifying the relevant PPR opportunities available to the injurers in question and assessing the negligence of their rejecting them (even with the help of expert witnesses or court masters). Third, deconcentrating antitrust policies might reduce such misallocation by making it less likely that the firm or firms in a position to increase allocative efficiency by doing such research would be in a position in which each would know that, if it did not make the discovery in question, no one else would and by increasing the profits a producer/discoverer could earn from his discovery by licensing others to use it. Fourth, the State might also be able to reduce such misallocation by paying monetary awards to producers who did relevant research or who made such discoveries when it would not otherwise be profitable for them to do so or by subsidizing the operation of independent (nonproducer) research firms that engage in the relevant type of research.

TOTAL-UO/TOTAL-QV/TOTAL-PPR MISALLOCATION: SOME SPECIFICS AND THEIR POLICY-ANALYSIS IMPLICATIONS

Total-UO/total-QV/total-PPR misallocation is present in the economy to the extent that economic efficiency would be increased if the proportions in which the economy's resources were allocated among unit-output-producing, QV-investment-creating, and PPR-executing uses were appropriately altered—for example, if resources were withdrawn from a random sample of marginal QV-investment projects and reallocated to a random sample of originally just-extramarginal unit-output-producing and PPR-executing uses. The preceding subsections have argued that $\Sigma D(P\pi_{\Delta QV})/LC_{\Delta QV}$ is positive, that $\Sigma D(P\pi_{\Delta PPR})/LC_{\Delta PPR}$ is negative, and that $\Sigma D(P\pi_{\Delta UO})/LC_{\Delta UO}$ is even more negative than $\Sigma D(P\pi_{\Delta PPR})/LC_{\Delta PPR}$. These conclusions imply that economic efficiency would be increased if resources were withdrawn from a random sample of marginal QV-investment-creating uses and reallocated to random samples of just-extramarginal PPR-executing and/or unit-output-producing uses or if resources were withdrawn from a random sample of marginal PPR-executing uses and reallocated to a random sample of just-extramarginal unit-output-producing uses.

If it were not for the difficulty of identifying the unit-output-producing and PPR-executing resource uses that are just-extramarginal and/or the direct and indirect allocative cost of financing the subsidization of all unit output production and all PPR, one might be able to increase allocative efficiency overall by reducing total-UO/total-QV/total-PPR misallocation by subsidizing marginal (or all) unit-output-producing resource uses and marginal (or all) PPR-executing resource uses but not marginal (or all) QV-investment-creating resource uses. In practice, however, I suspect that other types of policies will be able to make more of a contribution to economic efficiency by reducing total-QV/total-UO/total-PPR misallocation.

I would first recommend pro-*price*-competition policies, whose execution will tend to reduce the total amount of resources devoted to QV investment (by reducing the weighted-average rate of return that will be generated by any given set of QV-investment projects in the relevant area of product-space) while increasing unit output production and PPR. Of course, certain policies that reduce total-UO/total-QV/total-PPR misallocation by increasing price competition (such as prohibitions of horizontal mergers that would reduce production-optimum misallocation by enabling the merging firms to produce their original outputs more cheaply) may reduce economic efficiency overall, but the fact that price reductions will reduce total-UO/total-QV/total-PPR misallocation will favor the overall allocative efficiency of any policy that reduces prices. I hasten to add, however, that the same cannot be said for pro-QV-investment-competition policies such as policies against conglomerate mergers that eliminate effective potential entrants into the relevant area of product-space. Although such policies may have other effects that make them economically efficient or desirable overall, they will tend to increase total-UO/total-QV/total-PPR misallocation by increasing the total amount of resources the economy devotes to QV-investment creation.

Obviously, the impact of policies that would externalize pollution, accident, and congestion externalities on total-UO/total-QV/total-PPR misallocation depends on the quantity and character (costs or benefits) of the externalities that would have been or were generated pre-policy by the production of extramarginal units of output, the execution of extramarginal PPR projects, and the creation and use of marginal QV investments. I would guess that (1) the relevant unit output production generates external pollution and accident costs, (2) the execution of the relevant marginal PPR projects would generate neither external costs nor external benefits of the relevant kinds, (3) the use of the relevant marginal PPR projects would generate external pollution and accident costs (to the extent that it caused its users to increase their unit outputs by decreasing their marginal costs[35]), though the relevant externalities would constitute a lower percentage of the allocative cost of the relevant PPR projects' creation and use than the external costs of the extramarginal unit output production would constitute of its allocative cost, (4) the creation of both product-creating and distributive-outlet-creating QV investments would generate external pollution and accident costs, (5) the use of most product-creating QV investments would not generate any external accident or pollution costs, and (6) the use of most distributive-outlet-creating QV investments would generate accident, pollution, and congestion-related external benefits by reducing the amount of such external costs that are generated. For these reasons, I would also guess that policies that effectively internalized all external accident, pollution, and congestion external costs would increase total-UO/total-QV/total-PPR misallocation more by reallocating resources from unit-output-producing to PPR-executing uses and from unit-output-producing to distributive-outlet-creating (QV-investment-creating-subtype) uses than they would decrease total-UO/total-QV/total-PPR misallocation by reallocating resources from product-creating (QV-investment-creating-subtype) uses to PPR-executing uses. I hasten to add that such externality-internalizing policies might still be allocatively efficient and desirable overall. However, their impact on total-UO/total-QV/total-PPR misallocation seems likely to me to count against their allocative efficiency and overall desirability.

The third and final type of policy that might be commended by its impact on total-UO/total-QV/total-PPR misallocation is an IP policy. From the perspective of total-UO/total-QV/total-PPR misallocation, it might be desirable to give production-process discoverers longer and broader patent protection than product discoverers.

Although all these suggestions are tentative and contestable, I hope they give some sense of the way in which the approach to economic-efficiency assessment I am advocating would work as well as of the relevance of total-UO/total-QV/total-PPR misallocation to economic-efficiency analysis.

The Aggregate Distortion in the Profits Yielded by a Marginal Decision by a Producer to Shift to a Known, Less-AP-Loss-Prone Production Process

So far, Chapter 3 has focused on unit-output-producing, QV-investment-creating, and PPR-executing uses. However, economic actors sometimes make other sorts of resource-consuming choices. This subsection focuses on a choice to shift to a known, otherwise-more-expensive production process that is less-AP-loss-prone that a tort-law doctrine induced a producer to make by imposing liability on him for any losses his rejection of this avoidance move imposed on those victims whom tort law entitles to recovery. More particularly, this subsection analyzes the aggregate distortion in the profits yielded by a marginal choice of this kind—that is, a choice that yielded its maker private benefits that just exceeded the private costs it imposed on him.

The traditional law and economics analysis assumes that (allocative-transaction-cost considerations aside) anytime a tort-law regime induces a producer to engage in such avoidance it will increase allocative efficiency on this account. This assumption reflects the FBLE-analysis premise that the profits such a choice would yield the producer who made it would not be distorted. I will now provide a skeletal example that illustrates the fact that even if (1) the tort-law regime's liability rules are first-best allocatively efficient (for example, combine strict liability with a comprehensively-and-accurately-applied contributory-negligence doctrine), (2) the tort-law regime entitles all direct victims and their empathizers and sympathizers to legal recovery, (3) no potential injurer, potential victim , judge, or jury ever makes an error, and (4) private transactions costs do not make it profitable for nonentitled victims to sue, entitled victims not to sue, nonliable injurers to pay victims, or parties to settle for more or less than the expected trial outcome, imperfections in the economy unrelated to tort-law doctrines, tort-law-participant errors, and tort-dispute-processing transaction costs will be likely to distort the profits such a production-process shift yields the producer who makes it and may very well cause a shift that is profitable to be allocatively inefficient (may have inflated the profits of such a shift by more than the shift increased the relevant producer's profits). The example is skeletal because I will not even attempt to justify its assumptions about such things as the percentage distortion in the private benefits generated by resource uses of different types, the percentages of the economy's resources that are devoted to different types of uses, the extent to which the economy's resources are specialized, or the percentage of the loss that the avoidance move in question could prevent that would have consisted of lost wages, medical expenses, and any reduction in the victims' abilities to enjoy their lives, given the resources they can purchase.

In any event, the example that follows makes the following assumptions:

1. the production-process shift in question does not induce the producer who makes it to change his unit output: he produces one unit of his product with the safer production process and would have produced one unit with his original, more dangerous production process;
2. accident-and-pollution-loss consequences aside, the safer production process is \$100 privately more expensive to use;
3. the use of the safer production process reduces the losses the producer imposes on others and hence the damages he has to pay by infinitesimally more than \$100 (hereinafter by \$100);
4. the $\Sigma D(PB_{\Delta UO})/PB_{\Delta UO}$ ratio for the resources the use of the safer production process withdraws from unit-output-producing uses is -25%; the weighed-average $\Sigma D(PB_{\Delta QV})/PB_{\Delta QV}$ ratio for the resources

the use of the safer production process withdraws from QV-investment creation is +75%; and the weighed-average $\Sigma D(PB_{\Delta PPR})/PB_{\Delta PPR}$ ratio for the resources the use of the safer production process withdraws from PPR execution is −6%;

5. 1% of the resources that the shift to the safer production process consumes are withdrawn from the production of leisure;
6. the PB of leisure production are not distorted;
7. 80% of the economy's resources are devoted to unit output production, 15% to QV-investment creation, and 5% to PPR execution;
8. because (A) the percentage of the resources devoted to PPR execution that consists of scientifically gifted and trained labor is much higher than the percentage of the resources devoted to QV-investment creation that consists of such labor, which in turn is much higher than the percentage of the resources devoted to unit output production that consists of such labor and (B) such resources are specialized in the sense that they are much more productive when used in ways that take advantage of their special attributes, 83% of the resources the shift to the safer production process consumes are withdrawn from unit output production, 13% from QV-investment creation, and 4% from PPR execution;
9. the losses that the shift to the safer production process (for example, one that involves the use of a higher smoke stack or a catalytic converter) would prevent consist of illnesses that would have been caused by the pollution the safer production process would prevent;
10. the victims of the pollution the shift would prevent would be workers picked (so to speak) randomly from the working population of the economy: 80% of these workers would have performed unit-output-producing labor; 15%, QV-investment-creating labor; and 5%, PPR-executing labor;
11. the percentage distortions in the wages paid those workers equal the percentage distortions in the private benefits their efforts conferred on their employers—that is, the wages paid the unit-output-producing workers were 25% below their allocative product, the wages paid the QV-investment creators were 75% above their allocative products, and the wages paid the PPR-executing workers were 6% below their allocative products; and
12. of the \$100 loss the shift to the safer production process would prevent, \$70 consist of lost wages, \$20 consist of medical expenses (which will not be distorted), and \$10 consist of the monetary value of the pain,

Table 1A $\Sigma D(PC_{\Delta PPS})$

	The PC to the Avoiding Producer of the Resources He Withdrew From the Indicated Type of Use to Execute the Relevant PPS	Σ%D(PC) for PC in Indicated Category	ΣD(PC) for PC in Indicated Category
Resources Withdrawn from Leisure Production	(1%)$100 = $1	0%	$0
Resources Withdrawn from UO-Increasing Uses	(83%)$99 = $82.17	−25%	−$20.5425
Resources Withdrawn from QV-Creating Uses	(13%)$99 = $12.87	+75%	+$9.6525
Resources Withdrawn from PPR-Executing Uses	(4%)$99 = $3.96	−6%	−$.2376
TOTAL	$100		−$11.1276

suffering, and reduced ability to enjoy (↓ATE) the victim would have experienced (which will also not be distorted).

Tables IA and IB analyze respectively the $\Sigma D(PC_{\Delta PPS})$ and $\Sigma D(PB_{\Delta PPS})$ to the avoiding producer for the marginal production-process shift (hence the subscript of ΔPPS) on which the above example focuses. As the tables respectively reveal, on the assumptions of the example they explore, the private cost of the marginal production-process shift in question will have been deflated by $11.1276 (so that the allocative cost of the shift was $111.1276), and the private benefits of the shift in question will have been deflated by $6.335 (so that the allocative benefits of the shift were $106.335). Obviously, these conclusions imply that, in the situation described, the marginal production-process shift that the first-best allocatively efficient tort law induced the relevant producer to make (made it infinitesimally profitable for him to make) will have misallocated resources by $4.7926 = $111.1276 − $106.335.

Table 1B $\Sigma D(PB_{\Delta PPS})$

	The PB to the Avoiding Producer of Preventing the Loss in the Indicated Category	Σ%D(PB) for the Prevented Loss in the Indicated Category	ΣD(PB) for the Prevented Loss in the Indicated Category
Prevented Lost Wages of Unit-Output-Producing Victims	80% ($70) = $56	−25%	−$14
Prevented Lost Wages of QV-Investment-Creating Victims	15%($70) = $10.50	+75%	+$7.875
Prevented Lost Wages of PPR-Executing Victims	5%($70) = $3.50	−6%	−$.21
Prevented Medical Expenses	$20	0%	$0
Prevented Pain, Suffering, and Reduced Ability to Enjoy	$10	0%	$0
TOTAL	$100		−$6.335

SECTION 4. THREE DISTORTION ANALYSES OF IMPORTANT POLICY OPTIONS THAT ARE LESS COMPLETE THAN WOULD BE TBLE

This section exemplifies distortion analysis by delineating significant elements of the theoretical component of the distortion analysis of (1) the allocative efficiency of prohibiting contrived oligopolistic pricing,[36] (2) the antitrust, tax, and intellectual-property policies that would reduce the amount of resource misallocation we cause by devoting allocatively inefficient quantities of resources to product R&D and PPR, (3) the impact of a shift from a negligence/contributory-negligence to a strict-liability/contributory-negligence tort-liability system on the amount of misallocation that potential injurers and potential victims cause by making allocatively inefficient AP-loss-avoidance (henceforth, APLA) decisions. I include this material both to convey a better sense of the content and usefulness of the distortion-analysis approach to allocative-efficiency assessment and to provide reference points for Chapter 4's critiques of the conventional analysis of the allocative efficiency of various government policies.

The Allocative Efficiency of a Universal Prohibition of Contrived Oligopolistic Pricing

The TBLE version of the distortion-analysis approach to this issue would proceed by listing the various types of resource misallocation a universal prohibition of contrived oligopolistic pricing would affect, developing formulas for the aggregate distortion in the profits yielded by each relevant type of resource use, collecting data on the parameters whose relevance these formulas reveal, generating estimates of the pre-policy absolute weighted-average values and weighted-average absolute and squared deviations from those weighted-average values of the positive segments of the distributions of the aggregate percentage distortions in the profits yielded by marginal resource uses of each type, generating estimates of the impact of the anti-contrived-oligopolistic-pricing policy in question on the weighted-average values and weighted-average absolute and squared deviations from those weighted-average values of the distribution-segments in question, and finally generating estimates of the allocative efficiency of the policy under investigation from these estimates of the policy's impacts on these weighted-average values and deviations. This subsection will not execute such an analysis. Instead, after (1) discussing the effect of a universal prohibition of contrived oligopolistic pricing on allocative transaction costs, it will (2) use distortion analysis to explain why such a policy seems likely always to reduce certain types of resource misallocation directly by deterring the practice of contrived oligopolistic pricing, (3) use distortion analysis to explain why such a policy seems likely to increase allocative efficiency indirectly by deterring companies from making choices whose profitability was critically affected by their increasing the ability of the choosers to contrive oligopolistic prices, and (4) use distortion analysis to explain why such a policy can and the circumstances in which it will increase or decrease other types of resource misallocation directly by deterring the practice of contrived oligopolistic pricing.

Before proceeding, a preliminary point: I will be assuming *ad arguendo* that the anti-contrived-oligopolistic-pricing policy under review will succeed in eliminating all such pricing (and all related variable-cost quality-fixing as well).[37] It should be noted that my assumption that the policy under investigation is neither selectively applied to some but not other areas of product-space nor selectively effective in the sense of deterring a higher percentage of contrivance in some areas of product-space in which it is applied than in other areas in which it is applied does not imply that it will have the same effect on P, P − MC, or P/MC in all areas of product-space. This conclusion reflects the obvious fact that the extent of contrived oligopolistic pricing (as well as the ratios of the most profitable noncontrived prices sellers in different areas of product-space could charge to their marginal costs) will vary substantially among the economy's various areas of product-space.

I will now explain why I cannot generate any useful generalizations about the relevant relationships through pure *a priori* analysis. In the analysis that follows, COM stands for the oligopolistic margin a seller is able to contrive; HNOP stands for a seller's highest non-oligopolistic price—the price he would find most profitable to charge in a perfectly informed world if he had to assume that his rivals' responses would not be influenced by any perception they might have that he might react to those responses; and NOM stands for the natural oligopolistic margin a seller can secure—the margin he can secure because his rivals correctly perceived that it would be possible and inherently profitable for him to react to responses to his initial price (1) that they would find profitable if he would not react to them and (2) that would render his initial price unprofitable. It would clearly be helpful if the pre-policy average COM/(HNOP + NOM) ratio or the pre-policy COM/MC ratio in the economy's various areas of product-space were highly correlated with its sellers' average pre-policy P/MC ratio or if the average COM in any area of product-space was highly correlated with its seller' average pre-policy P − MC gap. Unfortunately, however, theoretical analysis does not support the existence of any of these relationships, and the empirical data one would need to test for them has never been collected. Admittedly, increases in the average pre-policy (HNOP + NOM) − MC difference for the products in any area of product-space will tend to cause the average COMs in that area to rise by increasing the ratio of the harm that a retaliator can inflict on anyone who has stolen a customer to whom the retaliator charged an oligopolistic price by stealing the undercutter's customer in return at any given cost to himself. However, increases in the average pre-policy (HNOP + NOM) − MC figure in any area of product-space will also tend to cause the average COMs in that area of product-space to fall by raising the amount of safe profits the sellers that operate in it must put at risk to attempt to secure a contrived oligopolistic margin rather than a price equal to the sum of the HNOP and NOM. The complete analysis is far more complicated. However, even if one takes everything into account, one will not be able to establish through *a priori* analysis any correlation either (1) between the average pre-policy COM/MC ratio in any area of product-space and the average pre-policy P/MC ratio in that area of product-space or (2) between the average pre-policy COM in any area of product-space and the average pre-policy ([P – MC]/P) ratio in that area of product-space. Hence, even if one could ignore the facts that (1) the average XMC/MC or MC*/MC ratio in the economy's different areas of product-space differ significantly and are not highly correlated with the average P/MC ratio in those areas of product-space and (2) the average sales-to-QV-investment ratio in the economy's different areas of product-space differ significantly and are not highly correlated with each other, one could not infer much about whether an area of product-space has too high a proportion of the resources the economy devotes to unit output production or QV-investment creation from data on its average pre-policy or post-policy COM or COM/P ratio. This reality will obviously reduce my ability to assess the impact of a universally applied and universally effective prohibition of contrived oligopolistic pricing on inter-industry UO-to-UO misallocation and inter-industry QV-to-QV misallocation.

THE EFFECT OF A UNIVERSAL PROHIBITION OF CONTRIVED OLIGOPOLISTIC PRICING ON ALLOCATIVE TRANSACTION COSTS

Two points. Distortion analysis sheds no light on the first. At least if I relax my assumption that the relevant prohibition of contrived oligopolistic pricing would be universally effective, the policy in question would increase transaction costs not only by (1) the transaction cost of devising it, enacting it, and hiring and training people to enforce it but also by (2) the variable transaction cost of discovering violations, (3) the variable transaction cost of prosecuting, defending, and adjudicating the cases brought against alleged violators, and (4) the transaction costs that contrivers generate to conceal their contrived oligopolistic communications and any retaliation that their contrivance entails (say, by substituting less detectable and provable but more-transaction-costly retaliatory advertising campaigns and outlet-location decisions for more detectable and provable but less-transaction-costly retaliatory price cuts). In the other direction, a policy of prohibiting contrived oligopolistic pricing will tend to reduce related transaction costs by reducing the amount of contrived oligopolistic pricing in which sellers engage and hence the total amount of transaction costs they generate when engaged in such contrivance and by eliminating the transaction costs that aspiring contrivers would have generated by practicing predation, executing mergers, and making QV investments whose profitability would otherwise have been critically increased by their tendency to increase the profitability of contrived oligopolistic pricing to their perpetrators. I suspect that, on balance, prohibitions of contrived oligopolistic pricing will increase private transaction costs.

Distortion analysis does shed light on the second point to be made about the allocative transaction cost of the policy in question. Because the resources that are consumed when transaction costs are generated are withdrawn from alternative uses in which the private value they would have generated for their employers would have been distorted by the interaction of the various Pareto imperfections in the economy, the net effect of a prohibition of contrived oligopolistic pricing on allocative transaction costs is almost certainly different from its net impact on the private transaction costs just listed.

THE VARIOUS TYPES OF RESOURCE MISALLOCATION THAT A PROHIBITION OF CONTRIVED OLIGOPOLISTIC PRICING WOULD ALMOST CERTAINLY REDUCE DIRECTLY

The conclusions this subsection articulates all reflect conclusions about the percentage distortions in the profits yielded by various types of resource uses that Sections 2 and 3 of this chapter generated. These conclusions imply that a universally effective (or even a realistically effective) nonselective prohibition of contrived oligopolistic pricing will reduce the following eight types of resource misallocation:

1. by reducing prices, it will reduce the amount of misallocation caused by individuals' substituting leisure and do-it-yourself labor for market labor;
2. to the extent that the policy reduces the salaries and hence the tax rate applied to the marginal incomes of the deterred contrivers' workers by reducing the profits of the deterred contrivers, it will reduce the amount of X-inefficiency-related misallocation these workers generate by substituting untaxed conventional fringe benefits, attractive physical working conditions, preferred coworkers, and less arduous work-regimes for taxable monetary income (that is, for the goods they could purchase with such income);
3. to the extent that the policy would be enforced progressively over time and hence would cause prices to decline over time, it will reduce the misallocation caused by individuals' making economically inefficient substitutions of present consumption for future consumption;
4. to the extent that the policy will prevent undercutting competitive inferiors from stealing customers from privately-better-placed rivals—in particular, to the extent that it deters (A) price cuts by noncontrivers designed to beat

contrived oligopolistic offers and (B) price cuts by contrivers designed to punish those who have undercut their contrived oligopolistic offers, it will reduce intra-industry UO-to-UO misallocation;

5. to the extent that the policy will redistribute income from the richer to the poorer (because on the weighted average the shareholders and employees whom contrivance benefits are richer than the consumers whom it harms), it will reduce resource misallocation by (I hope) appealing on balance to the external distributive preferences of the members of the society in question, by reducing the amount of misallocation people generate because the consumption-option that is in their individual interest is less allocatively efficient than some less-externality-prone alternative, by reducing the amount of misallocation caused by crime, and by reducing the amount of misallocation that is generated by underinvestment in the human capital of the poor (particularly of poor children);
6. by reducing prices and thereby increasing the proportion of the economy's resources devoted to unit output production and PPR while decreasing the proportion of the economy's resources devoted to QV-investment creation, the policy will reduce total-UO/total-QV/total-PPR misallocation;
7. to the extent that the policy will prevent producers of identical inputs from stealing customers from a position of competitive inferiority by deterring the charging of contrived oligopolistic prices that are undercut and retaliation by contrivers who have been undercut, it will reduce production-optimum misallocation on this account; and
8. to the extent that the policy will prevent producers of identical final products from charging discriminatory prices to steal the customers of better-placed contrivers or to retaliate against undercutters who have beaten their contrived oligopolistic offers, it will reduce consumption-optimum misallocation on this account.

THE CONTRIBUTION THAT A UNIVERSALLY EFFECTIVE PROHIBITION OF CONTRIVED OLIGOPOLISTIC PRICING WOULD PROBABLY MAKE TO ECONOMIC EFFICIENCY INDIRECTLY BY DETERRING SELLERS FROM MAKING CHOICES WHOSE PROFITABILITY WOULD OTHERWISE HAVE BEEN CRITICALLY AFFECTED BY THEIR TENDENCY TO INCREASE THE SELLERS' ABILITY TO CONTRIVE OLIGOPOLISTIC MARGINS

Although limitations of space prevent me from providing a full account of the factors that influence the profitability of contrived oligopolistic pricing,[38] I hope it is obvious that businesses may be able to increase the profitability of such pricing by driving rivals out through predation, by eliminating rivals by consummating horizontal mergers, and sometimes by making QV investments that deter rival established firms from executing QV-investment expansions or potential competitors from executing new entries. All such moves can increase the profitability of contrivance by reducing the number of rivals who would find it profitable to undermine the potential contriver's contrived oligopolistic price if they did not anticipate the contriver's reacting strategically to such a move and by improving the perpetrator's array of competitive positions vis-à-vis the remaining potential underminers of his contrived oligopolistic prices. In some (I suspect, many) cases, the contribution that the relevant predation, mergers, and QV investments would make to the profits the perpetrator could make by practicing contrived oligopolistic pricing if such pricing were not prohibited would critically affect the profitability of the conduct in question—that is, a universally effective prohibition of contrived oligopolistic pricing would deter at least some acts of predation, some horizontal mergers, and some QV investments by preventing them from increasing their perpetrators' profits by increasing the profits these actors can make by practicing contrived oligopolistic pricing (and a less-than-fully-effective prohibition of contrived oligopolistic pricing would deter a smaller number of choices of these kinds by critically reducing their certainty-equivalent profitability).

Two facts support my conclusion that these indirect effects of contrived-oligopolistic-pricing prohibitions will increase allocative efficiency—that the contrived-oligopolistic-pricing-profitability-enhancing behaviors such prohibitions would deter would have been allocatively inefficient. First, any tendency of the behaviors in question to increase the profits their perpetrators would be able to obtain by practicing contrived oligopolistic pricing would *inflate* their profitability—indeed, would inflate their profitability not just by the profits they yielded on this account but by the sum of those profits and the misallocation any additional contrived oligopolistic pricing it caused to be practiced would generate by increasing prices in the relevant areas of product-space. Second, the profit yields of the conduct in question would be inflated even if it did not enable its perpetrators to obtain higher COMs. Thus, the profits yielded by predation would be inflated even if it did not increase the predator's COMs because the profits it yielded the predator by increasing his competitive advantages and natural oligopolistic margins are a private gain that, if anything, will be associated with a total-UO/total-QV/total-PPR misallocation-related allocative-efficiency loss. And again, the profits that would have been yielded by the deterred horizontal mergers would have been inflated even if they would not have increased their participants' COMs (1) because the profits they would have yielded the merger partners by increasing their competitive advantages by freeing them from each other's competition and the profits they would have yielded the merger partners by increasing their NOMs by increasing their competitive advantages increase total-UO/total-QV/total-PPR misallocation and (2) because the merger partners are intrinsically indifferent to the allocative-efficiency losses their merger would generate even if it would affect no one's COMs by increasing the prices their rivals charge their rivals' customers by making the price the merged firm would have to charge a rival's customer to steal him more discriminatory than the same price would have been pre-merger for the relevant independent merger partner (whose prices to its own customers were lower than the price the merged firm would have charged these buyers to the extent that the merger partners were each other's closest competitors for the patronage of some buyers). Finally, for reasons that this chapter has already explored, any tendency of prohibitions of contrived oligopolistic pricing to reduce equilibrium QV investment in the areas of product-space in which the deterred contrivance would have been practiced will increase the policy's economic efficiency.

THE VARIOUS TYPES OF RESOURCE MISALLOCATION WHOSE MAGNITUDES SUCH AN ANTI-CONTRIVANCE POLICY WOULD BE LIKELY TO AFFECT DIRECTLY BUT COULD EITHER INCREASE OR DECREASE

Universally applied and effective prohibitions of contrived oligopolistic pricing seem likely to affect the magnitude of inter-industry UO-to-UO and QV-to-QV misallocation but could either increase or decrease each of these types of misallocation. I will now analyze each of these possibilities in turn.

For simplicity, I will assume that the only Pareto imperfections in the system are imperfections in price competition and externalities of production. On this assumption, the total elimination of contrived oligopolistic pricing will reduce (increase) inter-industry UO-to-UO misallocation if it reduces (increases) the weighted-average deviation of the distribution of P/MC* ratios in the economy. Unfortunately, because I do not know the relationships between the average COM/MC ratio in an area of product-space and either its average ([HNOP + NOM] – MC)/MC ratio or its XMC/MC ratio, I do not know whether a policy that would eliminate all COMs would increase or decrease inter-industry UO-to-UO misallocation. All I can say is that a selective policy that targeted contrived oligopolistic pricing in areas of product-space whose pre-policy P/MC* ratios were higher than average would reduce this type of resource misallocation. However, I suspect that, even if one considered the transaction-cost savings that would be generated by an enforcement decision not to prosecute contrivance in some areas of product-space, a decision to enforce the anticontrivance policy in this selective way would be misallocative on balance, given its impact on the kinds of economic inefficiency the omitted prosecutions would have decreased.

The analysis of the impact of a universally effective prohibition of contrived oligopolistic pricing on inter-industry QV-to-QV misallocation parallels the analysis of such a prohibition's impact on inter-industry UO-to-UO misallocation. Once more, four points are relevant. First, such a policy will decrease (increase) such misallocation if the amount by which they reduce the average rate of return yielded by the QV investments in any area of product-space is positively correlated with the aggregate distortion in the rate of return yielded by the marginal QV investment in the area of product-space in question. Second, on balance, the relevant *a priori* arguments leave one uncertain about the existence and/or sign of any such correlation. Third, a selective enforcement policy that targeted contrivance in areas of product-space in which the above aggregate distortion was higher than average would probably reduce inter-industry QV-to-QV misallocation. However, fourth, even if one considers the allocative-transaction-cost savings one could secure by not enforcing a prohibition against contrived oligopolistic pricing in areas of product-space that contain too low a proportion of the resources the economy devotes to QV-investment creation from the perspective of allocative efficiency and assumes that such a policy would also (as it might not) decrease inter-industry UO-to-UO misallocation, it would probably decrease economic efficiency overall.

I have just executed a distortion analysis of the allocative efficiency of prohibiting contrived oligopolistic pricing that was quite thorough theoretically (if one deems it to have incorporated the earlier analyses of Chapter 3) but made use of virtually no empirical data. If one could ignore the allocative-transaction-costliness of such a prohibition, this analysis would justify the conclusion that a prohibition of contrivance that was applied universally would almost certainly increase allocative efficiency and that a more-selectively-applied prohibition of contrived oligopolistic pricing that would be more likely to reduce inter-industry UO-to-UO and/or inter-industry QV-to-QV misallocation would probably be less allocatively efficient than a more universally applied policy. Although I suspect that these conclusions would not change if the allocative-transaction-cost consequences of the various anticontrived-oligopolistic-pricing policies were taken into account, it would almost certainly be *ex ante* TBLE to collect data on the allocative-transaction-cost consequences of such policies and on the other parameters that will affect the magnitude and, in some instances, the sign of its impact on the various types of allocative efficiency it would affect before reaching even an initial conclusion about the most-allocatively-efficient contrived-oligopolistic-pricing policy to adopt.

INCREASING THE ALLOCATIVE EFFICIENCY OF THE QUANTITY OF RESOURCES DEVOTED RESPECTIVELY TO PRODUCT R&D AND PPR THROUGH ANTITRUST, TAX, AND INTELLECTUAL-PROPERTY (IP) POLICY

Earlier in this chapter, I argued for the admittedly contestable conclusions that the economies of developed countries currently devote too many resources to product R&D and too few to PPR from the perspective of allocative efficiency. Primarily, these conclusions are contestable because we do not have sufficient data on (1) the benefits that knowledge-creating research confers on businesses that use the information that discoverers generate without compensating them for it (given our current patent, copyright, and trade-secret laws and limitations in the ability of discoverers to keep their unpatented discoveries secret) and (2) the relationship between the length of the protection that our IP law gives discoverers and the number of days by which their research efforts should have been predicted *ex ante* to advance the date of the discovery they made. This subsection ignores any doubts that could be raised about the preceding conclusions—that is, delineates the antitrust, tax, and IP policies that would reduce the amount of misallocation that developed economies generate by devoting allocatively inefficient quantities of resources to product R&D and PPR on the assumption that such economies currently devote too many resources to product R&D and too few to PPR.

I start with antitrust policy because the underlying theoretical points have already been made. As we have seen, antitrust policy will reduce the amount of allocative inefficiency we generate by devoting too many resources to product R&D insofar as it increases price competition (to the extent it does so) but will increase the amount of allocative inefficiency we generate by devoting too many resources to product R&D insofar as it increases QV-investment competition. The price-competition conclusion improves the allocative-efficiency case not only for prohibitions of contrived oligopolistic pricing but also for prohibitions of predation, of mergers that would decrease price competition, and of QV-investment expansions by established firms in areas in which they are already operating (though I suspect that the latter prohibition would still be allocatively inefficient on balance). The QV-investment-competition conclusion weakens the allocative-efficiency case for prohibiting (1) retaliation against QV investments by established firms or new entrants and (2) conglomerate mergers that would reduce QV-investment competition in the area of product-space in which they occur by eliminating an effective potential entrant (though, once more, I suspect that on balance such prohibitions are still likely to be allocatively efficient and *a fortiori* desirable overall). As we have also seen, antitrust policies will reduce the amount of allocative inefficiency we generate by devoting too few resources to PPR insofar as it increases price competition. This conclusion favors the allocative efficiency of the same range of antitrust policies as did its product-R&D counterpart.

I turn next to tax policy. In order to render unprofitable the marginal and intramarginal product-R&D projects I am assuming are allocatively inefficient, one would have to put a tax surcharge on the economic profits yielded by all marginal and some intramarginal product-R&D projects (or perhaps more practicably and allocatively efficiently on all product-R&D projects) that is high enough to render the allocatively inefficient product-R&D projects unprofitable (but, particularly if the surcharge is applied universally, not so high as to render unprofitable allocatively efficient product-R&D projects). Obviously and unfortunately, to determine the size of the most-allocatively-efficient surcharge (expressed, say, as a percentage of the private cost of the projects to which it applies), one would have to calculate the ratio of the pre-policy inflation of the profits that such projects yield to the private cost of the projects in question. For this purpose, one would have to collect data on all the Pareto imperfections and other parameters that determine the inflation in question. In order to render profitable all otherwise unprofitable PPR projects that would be allocatively efficient, one would have to subsidize such projects (perhaps through investment-credit or accelerated-depreciation provisions that cause the effective tax rate that is applied to them to be negative) sufficiently to make them profitable post-tax. Once more, in order to calculate the most-allocatively-efficient subsidy (expressed as a percentage of the private cost of the PPR projects in question), one would have to collect data on all the parameters that determine the ratio of the aggregate distortion in such projects' profit yields to the private cost of such projects and use those data to calculate the distortion in the profits of the projects in question. Of course, the allocative efficiency of such tax and subsidy policies will depend on more than the allocative inefficiency of the product-R&D projects they deter and the allocative efficiency of the PPR projects they cause to be executed. It will also depend on (1) the allocative transaction costs that the drafting, passage, and implementation of the policies in question will generate, (2) the allocative-efficiency gains the tax surcharges in question would yield by generating revenue (to the extent that the surcharges apply to projects they do not deter) that obviates the government's financing its operations in other, misallocative ways or foregoing allocatively efficient expenditures, and (3) the allocative-efficiency losses the de facto subsidy yields by inducing the government to increase the other (misallocative) taxes it levies and/or the prices it charges for goods and services it supplies, to cause more inflation, or to forego other allocatively efficient expenditures.

The analysis of the IP-policy implications of the conclusions that we devote too many resources to product R&D and not enough to PPR from the perspective of allocative efficiency parallels the analysis of the tax-policy implications of these conclusions. First, these conclusions favor shortening the length and narrowing the breadth of the IP-law protection we give to product discoverers and extending the length and widening the breadth of the IP-law protection we give to production-process discoverers. Second, to determine the IP-law changes that would most reduce the amount of misallocation we cause by devoting the wrong quantity of resources to product R&D and PPR respectively, one would have to calculate the current aggregate distortion in the profits such projects yield and the amount by which various changes in IP law would affect their profit yields. Third, the overall allocative efficiency of the proposed IP-law changes would reflect not only their impact on the misallocation we cause by devoting the wrong quantity of resources to different types of R&D but also their impact on allocative transaction costs and the amount of misallocation that is generated by the underutilization of discovered information. The changes in IP law under consideration would affect allocative transaction costs not only because they would be allocative-transaction-costly to devise, enact, and apply but also because they would affect the number of patent and copyright applications that are made (by affecting both the number of discoveries that are made and the proportion of discoverers who seek patent and copyright protection), the allocative transaction costs generated by the creation and enforcement of licensing agreements, the allocative transaction costs discoverers who choose not to obtain patent protection generate to keep critical aspects of their discoveries secret, the allocative transaction costs aspiring copycats generate when attempting to uncover secret features of unpatented discoveries, and the allocative transaction costs generated by the making, defending, and processing of patent, copyright, trade-secret, and licensing-agreement legal claims.

Although these distortion analyses of the antitrust, tax, and IP policy-implications of the conclusion that we currently devote too many resources to product R&D and too few to PPR from the perspective of allocative efficiency are far from TBLE, I hope they do provide some sense of both the distortion-analysis approach and its usefulness. They should also establish a basis for Section 3 of Chapter 4's critique of the consensus view of economists, law and economics scholars, and politicians about the policies that should be adopted to increase the allocative efficiency of the quantity of resources we devote to R&D.

THE IMPACT OF A SHIFT FROM A NEGLIGENCE/CONTRIBUTORY-NEGLIGENCE TO A STRICT-LIABILITY/CONTRIBUTORY-NEGLIGENCE TORT-LIABILITY SYSTEM ON THE AMOUNT OF MISALLOCATION GENERATED BY THE ACCIDENT-AND-POLLUTION-LOSS-AVOIDANCE (APLA) DECISIONS OF POTENTIAL INJURERS, OF POTENTIAL VICTIMS, AND OF THE TWO COMBINED

Shifts from a negligence/contributory-negligence[39] to a strict-liability/contributory-negligence[40] tort-liability regime will affect allocative efficiency not only by changing the amount of misallocation generated by the economically inefficient avoidance decisions of the potential injurers and potential victims but also by affecting the total allocative transaction costs that AP-loss contingencies and realities cause to be generated and the impact of AP-loss insurance on allocative efficiency. However, to save space, this subsection will focus exclusively on the impact of the relevant shift on the amount by misallocation generated by the economically inefficient avoidance decisions of potential injurers and potential victims. Indeed, its analysis of even these two issues will address only the major imperfections that are relevant to their resolution.[41]

The following protocol outlines the variant of the distortion-analysis approach to these issues that would be TBLE if there were no need to continuously consider whether to collect additional data on relevant parameters:

1. identify all the imperfections (see below) that would individually distort the profits yielded by any APLA decision a potential injurer or potential victim could make;

2. develop a formula that would reveal the way in which these imperfections interact to distort the profit-yields of the marginal APLA decisions of potential injurers and potential victims;
3. collect data on the pre-shift magnitudes of the parameters whose relevance this formula reveals;
4. calculate the aggregate distortion in the profits yielded by the marginal APLA decisions of all types made by potential injurers and potential victims;
5. determine the weighted-average value and the weighted-average absolute and squared deviations of the positive or negative segment of the aggregate-percentage-profit-distortion distributions in question;
6. determine the impact of the shift on the magnitudes of these imperfections identified in stage one and hence on the weighted-average value and weighted-average absolute and squared deviations of the relevant segments of the distributions in question;
7. estimate the impact that the shift would have on the amount of misallocation that the economically inefficient APLA decisions of potential injurers and potential victims would generate if these tort cogenerators never made avoidance-decision mistakes from its effect on the weighted-average value and weighted-average absolute deviation of the distribution-segments in question; and
8. adjust this estimate to take account of the errors potential injurers or potential victims would commit when making APLA decisions.

However, to save space, this subsection will confine itself to (1) listing the major imperfections that would individually distort the profits a potential injurer or potential victim could earn by making APLA moves of various types in a negligence/contributory-negligence regime, (2) commenting on the probable sign of the aggregate distortion in the profits potential injurers and potential victims could earn by making marginal APLA moves of different types in such a regime, and (3) examining the ways in which a shift from negligence/contributory negligence to strict liability/contributory negligence would affect the relevant imperfections, the impact of such a shift on the absolute weighted-average value and weighted-average absolute and squared deviations of the distortion distributions in question, the impact of such a shift on the APLA-decision errors potential injurers and potential victims commit, and (derivatively) the impact of the shift on the amount of misallocation generated by the economically inefficient APLA decisions of potential injurers and potential victims.

The analysis that follows is based on three assumptions about the way in which negligence and contributory negligence are defined and applied. First, it assumes that, in practice, avoidance-move rejections by potential injurers (potential victims) that are assessed for negligence (contributory negligence) are deemed negligent (contributorily negligent) if the private cost that the rejected move would have imposed on the potential injurer (potential victim) was lower than the amount by which he should have been predicted *ex ante* it would reduce the weighted-average amount of private accident and pollution losses he would impose on those of his victims who are eligible to obtain legal redress (on the victim himself) on (1) the legally accurate assumption that, in practice, negligence and contributory-negligence calculations focus on the private (equivalent-dollar) cost that the rejected avoidance move would have imposed on the potential injurer or potential victim who might have made it rather than on the allocative cost the actor in question would have generated by making it and on the (weighted-average-expected) private (equivalent-dollar) benefits that the rejected avoidance move would have conferred on its traditional beneficiaries (that is, on those possible victims who are eligible to obtain legal redress) rather than on the (weighted-average-expected) allocative benefits it would have generated, (2) the legally accurate assumption that the courts' definitions of negligence and contributory negligence ignore any impact a rejected avoidance move would have had on the tort-contingency-related risk costs that possible accident-and-pollution (AP) victims bear, and (3) the legally inaccurate assumption that the relevant private costs and private benefits that a particular potential tort co-generator's execution of a given avoidance move would generate are calculated on an individualized basis—that the courts do not assume that all potential injurers or victims other than those who have obviously relevant disabilities such as blindness are equally-cost-effective potential avoiders.

Second, the analysis makes the legally inaccurate assumption that no potential victim will be found contributorily negligent for rejecting an avoidance move that would not be part of the most-allocatively-efficient set of avoidance decisions in an otherwise-Pareto-perfect economy because, in such an economy, it would be less allocatively efficient than an avoidance move that at one time was available to the potential injurer. An alternative, coincident formulation of this assumption is that no victim will be found contributorily negligent for rejecting an avoidance move whose private cost to him would have been lower than the private benefits it should have been expected to generate by reducing the weighted-average amount of accident or pollution losses he should have expected to suffer if no one would have avoided if he did not when, at least at some point in time, the potential injurer could have made an avoidance move whose weighted-average-expected private benefits exceeded its private costs by an amount that was larger than the amount by which the private benefits of the potential victim's privately best avoidance move exceeded its private cost.[42] More formally, if we let B_V stand for the cost to the potential victim of the privately best avoidance move available to him, $(\downarrow PL)_V$ stand for the amount by which that move would reduce weighted-average-expected AP losses, B_I stand for the cost to the potential injurer of the privately best avoidance move available to the potential injurer, and $(\downarrow PL)_I$ stand for the amount by which the potential injurer's privately best avoidance move would reduce weighted-average-expected AP losses, the preceding assumption is that no *V* will be found contributorily negligent despite the fact that $B_V < (\downarrow PL)_V$ if $(\downarrow PL)_V - B_V < (\downarrow PL)_I - B_I$.

Third, the analysis makes the legally accurate assumption that, in practice, the rejection of only a small subset of the various types of avoidance moves available to potential injurers and potential victims will actually be assessed for negligence or contributory negligence. It may be useful to illustrate this third point. Take, for example, a potential injurer who is a manufacturer. This type of actor may be able to reduce the AP losses he generates in at least the following five ways: (1) by shifting to a known, less-AP-loss-prone production process, (2) by shifting to a known, less-AP-loss-prone location (to whose substitution relevant buyers would be indifferent, AP-loss consequences aside), (3) by shifting to the production of a known, alternative product variant whose production and consumption combined would be less-AP-loss-prone, (4) by reducing his unit output, and (5) by doing research directed at discovering less-AP-loss-prone production processes, locations, and product variants and shifting to the less-AP-loss-prone option the research discovered. In practice, a manufacturer's rejection of only one of these types of avoidance moves is assessed for negligence—namely, his rejection of a known, less-AP-loss-prone production process. Although a manufacturer's location-choice might make him liable as a nuisance, nuisance analysis is not negligence analysis; similarly, although a manufacturer's design of the product variant he produces (his product-variant choice) may make him liable under products-liability law, the relevant design-defect analysis is also not a negligence analysis (under a different name); moreover, manufacturers whose liability is governed by a negligence standard are also never found liable for producing too many units of their product or failing to do an adequate amount of research into less-AP-loss-prone production processes, locations, or product variants.

This drastic limitation in the set of avoidance options whose rejection by injurers is assessed for negligence is not limited to cases in which the injurer is a manufacturer. Thus, although decisions by car-driver injurers to drive too fast, to drive when intoxicated or tired, to operate cars knowing that the brakes are faulty, or perhaps to operate cars that have not undergone the safety inspections required by statute are assessed for negligence, decisions by car-driver injurers to drive more rather than less, to take more-accident-prone rather than less-accident-prone routes, or to operate heavier vehicles with higher bumpers that are likely to impose more accident losses on others when involved in an accident of a given type than would lighter vehicles with lower bumpers are never in practice assessed for negligence.

I should add that the set of avoidance-move types whose rejection by potential victims is assessed for contributory negligence constitutes a similarly restricted subset of the full set of avoidance-move types available to such actors. Thus, although the choice of a pedestrian who was a potential victim of an automobile-pedestrian accident to run out into the street in front of oncoming traffic or to become intoxicated in a situation in which he might go for a walk in a drunken state will be assessed for negligence, decisions by pedestrians to walk more rather than less, to take more-accident-prone rather than less-accident-prone lawful routes, to walk at night or in inclement weather, or to wear dark, nonreflective clothing is not in practice assessed for contributory negligence. Similarly, decisions by car buyers to purchase more expensive cars that will be more expensive to replace or repair if damaged in an accident are never assessed for contributory negligence. In any event, the analysis of the effect of a shift from negligence to strict liability on the aggregate distortion in the profits potential injurers and potential victims can obtain by making different types of APLA moves will reflect these doctrine-application realities.

One final introductory point. Throughout this subsection, the term *imperfection* refers not just to one of the seven types of Pareto imperfections previously defined but also to tort doctrines, tort-related transaction costs, tort insurance, errors made by judges and juries in tort cases, and errors made by tort injurers and tort victims that might cause potential injurers or potential victims to make allocatively inefficient APLA decisions in an otherwise-Pareto-perfect economy.

THE IMPACT OF A SHIFT FROM A NEGLIGENCE/CONTRIBUTORY-NEGLIGENCE TO A STRICT-LIABILITY/CONTRIBUTORY-NEGLIGENCE TORT-LIABILITY REGIME ON THE AMOUNT OF MISALLOCATION GENERATED BY ECONOMICALLY INEFFICIENT APLA DECISIONS BY POTENTIAL INJURERS

I will address this issue by listing the various imperfections that can distort the avoidance incentives of potential injurers, analyzing the sign of the distortion each of these imperfections will generate in the profitability of avoidance to potential injurers and the direction of the errors these parties are likely to make in this context, and then assessing the likely impact of the shift in question on the relevant aggregate distortion and errors and derivatively on the amount of misallocation that potential injurers are likely to generate by making economically inefficient avoidance decisions.

(i) The Major Imperfections That Can Cause Potential Injurers Who Are Operating under a Negligence/Contributory-Negligence Regime to Make Allocatively Inefficient APLA Decisions

I have already discussed the most important such imperfection—namely, the fact that in practice the rejection by potential injurers of many of the types of APLA moves that are available to them is not assessed for negligence, henceforth "imperfection (1)." Restrictions in the application of the negligence doctrine will cause $PB_{\Delta APLA}$ for all potential injurers operating under a negligence/contributory-negligence regime to be zero for all APLA moves whose rejection will not be assessed for negligence, regardless of the other imperfections that are present in the economy—that is, will cause $\Sigma D(PB_{\Delta APLA})$ to equal $(-LB_{\Delta APLA})$ for such avoidance moves regardless of the other imperfections that are in the system. The other imperfections that can cause a potential injurer operating under a negligence/contributory-negligence regime to make an allocatively inefficient APLA decision in an otherwise-Pareto-perfect economy (by critically distorting the profits he can earn by making an allocatively efficient avoidance decision and/or by causing him to make an APLA decision that is not in his interest) can all be critical when the rejection of the avoidance move in question would be assessed for negligence.

I will now list seventeen additional significant imperfections—"imperfections (2)–(18)"—that belong in this category:

2. some victims who are entitled to recover may not sue (for example, because they do not know that their loss was caused by someone's wrongdoing, because they cannot identify the wrongdoer who injured them, because they do not know that the law entitles them to recover their loss from the wrongdoer who injured them, because they do not believe that the legal system will treat them justly, or because the private transaction costs of pursuing a legal claim [including the psychological cost of dealing with lawyers] are prohibitive);
3. some victims may not be entitled to recover because the tort law restricts recovery (A) to parties on whom the accidents or pollution in question had a physical impact or (B) to parties who had reasonable grounds to believe that they might experience such a physical impact (because the tort law denies recovery to witnesses of an accident who were never at physical risk, to all relatives and friends of traditional AP victims except [to some extent] for their spouses [who can recover for the loss of consanguinity], and to potential victims who bore preventable AP-loss-related risk costs—indeed, the common law does not allow even those parties who are considered to be entitled to recoveries to obtain compensation for the risk costs they sustained);
4. some victims may be barred from recovery by a fellow-servant rule or by the contributory-negligence, "last clear chance," or "assumption of risk" doctrines (or may have their recoveries reduced by the comparative-negligence doctrine);[43]
5. although this outcome is inconsistent with the common law's normal attitude toward mitigation, traditional tort doctrine precludes those victims whom the injurer's failure to avoid has induced to incur costs before the accident has occurred or pollution has been generated to prevent the occurrence of the accident or pollution in question or to reduce the loss any accident or pollution that occurs would generate from recovering any such avoidance costs they incurred for these purposes;
6. judges and juries may misestimate (across all cases, I believe they tend to underestimate) those portions of victims' losses that victims are entitled to recover;
7. victims who do sue may tend to settle for less than the verdict they would obtain at trial (A) because their expected mechanical trial-costs are higher than those of defendants (who tend to be repeat players), (B) because they are more risk averse than defendants, (C) because the dispute imposes more risk on them than defendants who are larger, face less risk in relation to the

individual case because they hold a portfolio of similar risks, or can take advantage of economies of scale in securing tort insurance, (D) because they have a greater financial need than do defendants to resolve a dispute quickly, (E) because defendants are more likely to be repeat players who have a stake in developing a reputation for hanging tough, and (F) because plaintiffs are more likely to be influenced by lawyers on contingency fees who find settlements that are against their clients' interests to be in their own interests because the lawyers incur a higher percentage of the joint lawyer-client opportunity costs of going to trial than of the weighted-average-expected increase in recovery that a decision to go to trial is predicted to generate;

8. in independent, simultaneous causation cases[44] and in some step-function-loss cases,[45] the law's "but-for cause" definition of "cause-in-fact" will prevent it from securing allocatively efficient care by eliminating the private monetary benefits avoidance will confer on any care-providing injurer;
9. judges and juries may make false-negative[46] findings of cause-in-fact;
10. the "scope of liability" ("proximate cause") doctrine may not deem the injurer to be a legally accountable cause of the loss even though his act was unambiguously a probabilistic cause of the loss and did increase weighted-average-expected AP losses on balance;
11. judges or juries may make false-negative findings on scope of liability (proximate cause);
12. judges or juries may make false-negative findings on negligence even when they do analyze the negligence of the rejected APLA move;
13. the injurer may be partially or totally judgment-proof because he can declare bankruptcy and (in the case of corporate injurers) his shareholders enjoy the benefits of limited liability;
14. the injurer may be partially insured in a situation in which his future insurance premiums will not rise by the amount of the payments his insurance company must make on his behalf;[47]
15. imperfections in seller competition may distort the profits yielded by shifts to known, otherwise-more-expensive, AP-loss-reducing production processes—more specifically, will probably tend to inflate those profits by deflating the private cost of such moves by more than they deflate the private benefits they would confer on the potential injurer's potential victims;
16. incentive distortions that arise because there is a conflict of interest between the potential injurer who will have to pay (say, a corporation) and the actor who makes the relevant avoidance decision (say, an employee)—

a conflict that is likely to be most important in cases in which the loss may be detected only after the passage of a considerable period of time, given that (A) the employee who is responsible for the avoidance decision in question is likely to be working for a different company, retired, deceased, or in any event insufficiently penalizable by the relevant employer at the time at which the loss is detected and the employer is sued and (B) the relevant employee's current rewards are a function of the company's current profits or his estimated contribution to its current profits;

17. imperfections in the information possessed by potential injurers about the tort-liability regime under which they were operating, the range of avoidance moves available to them, the private cost of each of the avoidance moves in question, the amounts by which those moves would reduce the probability of the various types of accidents and losses they might generate, the probability that their potential victims would be eligible to recover and would sue, the probability that their victims would be barred from recovery or have their recoveries reduced by their contributory negligence, assumption of risk, or failure to take advantage of a last clear chance to prevent the accident, the likelihood that their victims would settle, the weighted-average-expected amount by which the settlement settling victims would accept would fall below the award they would receive at trial; and
18. imperfections in the attentiveness of potential injurers or in their mathematical calculations of $(\downarrow PL)_I$, P_I, and/or the profitability of avoidance, given the information they possessed.[48]

(ii) The Sign of the Distortions the Imperfections in Question Will Generate in $P\pi_{\Delta APLA}$ and the Direction of the Errors Potential Injurers Commit When Making APLA Decisions

Fourteen of the first sixteen imperfections in the preceding list clearly deflate the profits a potentially liable injurer can earn by engaging in AP-loss avoidance. The only exceptions are imperfections (6) and (15). I have no doubt that the sign of the distortion generated by imperfection (6) is also negative—that, at least across all cases, the damages that victims are awarded for those losses that are recoverable fall below the losses in question. I also think that the information deficiencies and the miscalculations and inattentiveness that constitute (respectively) imperfections (17) and (18) would also cause potential injurers to underavoid from the perspective of allocative efficiency in an otherwise-Pareto-perfect economy. The only countervailing consideration is the distortion generated by imperfection (15)—imperfections in the price competition faced by (1) alternative users of the resources that safer production processes would consume and (2) the employers of the potential victims whose losses the relevant avoidance would prevent: for reasons that were examined earlier in this chapter, I believe that these imperfections in price competition will inflate $P\pi_{\Delta APLA}$ for the shifts to safer but otherwise-more-expensive production processes whose rejection is in practice assessed for negligence that tort law would be needed to secure. I have no doubt that this monopoly inflation in $P\pi_{\Delta APLA}$ does not alter the conclusion the $\Sigma D(P\pi_{\Delta APLA})$ will be negative for all or virtually all avoidance moves whose rejection is assessed for negligence and that the errors that potential injurers commit when making APLA decisions will exacerbate the tendency of the above aggregate distortion to make them reject even those allocatively efficient avoidance moves whose rejection will be assessed for negligence.

The preceding conclusions imply that, *ceteris paribus,* potential injurers who are operating in a negligence/contributory-negligence tort-liability regime will generate economic inefficiency by failing to make allocatively efficient APLA moves not only when the moves in question are moves whose rejection is not in practice assessed for negligence but also when the rejected moves are types whose rejection will be assessed for negligence. Although, obviously, the following statement reflects a large number of empirical assumptions for which I have provided no evidence whatsoever, I believe that the absolute value of the mean of the distribution of the aggregate (negative) distortion in the profits that would be yielded by APLA moves whose rejection would be assessed for negligence that is generated by the combination of imperfections (2)–(16) in the preceding list is high and, relatedly, that in negligence/contributory-negligence jurisdictions imperfections (2)–(16) will cause a great deal of misallocation by rendering it unprofitable for potential injurers to make allocatively efficient avoidance moves whose rejection will be assessed for negligence. This conclusion is regrettable in itself and implies as well that any tendency of potential injurers to underestimate the profitability of avoidance—because of imperfections (17) and (18)—will be more misallocative than it would otherwise be. In any event, both (1) the fact that in practice the rejection of many types of avoidance moves is not assessed for negligence and (2) the other 17 imperfections listed above will cause potential injurers who are operating under a negligence/contributory-negligence tort-liability regime to misallocate resources by rejecting allocatively efficient APLA moves.

(iii) The Impact of a Shift from a Negligence/Contributory-Negligence to a Strict-Liability/Contributory-Negligence Tort-Liability Regime on the Relevant Distortions in $P\pi_{APLA}$ for Potential Injurers, the APLA-Decision Errors Potential Injurers Make, and, Derivatively, the Amount of Misallocation That Economically Inefficient APLA Decisions by Potential Injurers Generate

The shift from a negligence/contributory-negligence to a strict liability/contributory-negligence tort-liability regime will affect six of the imperfections that would tend to deter potential injurers from making avoidance moves whose (B_I)s were less than their $(\downarrow[PL]_I)$s. First, most obviously, and most importantly, the shift will eliminate the deflation in PB_{APLA} and $P\pi_{APLA}$ for potential-injurer avoidance moves whose rejection would not in practice be assessed for negligence. Second, the shift will eliminate the deflation in PB_{APLA} and $P\pi_{APLA}$ for potential-injurer avoidance moves whose rejection will be assessed for negligence generated by the possibility that the trier-of-fact will make a false-negative error on the negligence issue. Third, the shift will tend to increase the deflation in PB_{APLA} and $P\pi_{APLA}$ for potential-injurer avoidance moves generated by what I take to be the tendency of triers-of-fact to award damages to victorious victims that are lower than the sum of the legally recoverable losses they sustained. This conclusion reflects (1) the fact that plaintiff-lawyers will find it much more difficult to put on evidence of injurer-wrongdoing in strict-liability cases than in negligence cases and (2) the fact that jury-awarded damage awards tend to increase with the jury's conclusions about the seriousness of the defendant's wrongdoing. Fourth, to the extent that victims do not sue because their distrust of the legal system leads them to believe that debatable issues such as negligence will be resolved against them and the private transaction cost of litigating deters victims with uncertain prospects of recovery from suing, the shift from negligence to strict liability will tend to reduce the deflation in the private benefits that potential-injurer avoidance will yield potential injurers that is generated by the failure of victims who are entitled to recoveries to sue by eliminating an issue that victims may think will be incorrectly resolved against them and by reducing the transaction cost of litigating. Fifth, the shift will tend to reduce the deflation in PB_{APLA} and $P\pi_{APLA}$ for potential-injurer avoidance moves by reducing the amount by which settlements fall below weighted-average-expected trial-outcomes. This conclusion reflects the fact that the shift from negligence to strict liability will reduce both the mechanical transaction cost and the risk cost of litigating for both parties. It also reflects the fact that the absolute reductions in both types of costs are likely to be bigger for plaintiffs than for defendants because plaintiffs are likely to face higher costs of both kinds than defendants (in the case of mechanical transaction costs because plaintiffs are not so likely to be repeat players as defendants and in the case of risk costs because plaintiffs will tend to be smaller and more risk averse than defendants as well as because the fact that plaintiffs are less likely to be repeat players implies that they will face lower risk costs in relation to individual cases because they have a portfolio of similar risks). Sixth, the shift will tend to reduce the amount of misallocation potential injurers generate by rejecting allocatively efficient avoidance moves because they critically underestimate the profits they can earn by avoiding. In part, the shift will yield this effect by rendering irrelevant the tendency of potential injurers to underestimate the probability that their conduct will be negligent or will be found negligent. In part, it will do so because, to the extent that it encourages potential injurers to take out or even consider taking out tort-liability insurance, it will tend to increase the probability that insurance companies will directly inform them of the risk they are running, condition their coverage on their making what in fact are allocatively efficient avoidance moves, require them to set up safety committees that will lead them to discover relevant facts or avoidance options, and/or confront them with premiums that correct their misperception of the accident and pollution losses they should expect to generate for which they will be held liable.

Two conclusions are warranted. First, the shift from negligence/contributory negligence to strict liability/contributory negligence will clearly reduce the deflation in $P\pi_{APLA}$ for potential injurers in relation to avoidance moves whose rejection would not be assessed for negligence. Second, although this conclusion reflects various empirical assumptions for which I have submitted no evidence whatsoever, outside of one category of cases that I will note,[49] I also think that a shift from negligence/contributory negligence to strict liability/contributory negligence will clearly reduce the amount of misallocation that potential injurers generate by making economically inefficient avoidance choices about executing moves whose rejection will be assessed for negligence. Put crudely, I base this latter conclusion on a belief that (1) the reduction in the aggregate deflation of the profitability of avoidance to injurers that the shift will generate by eliminating false-negative errors on the negligence issue, reducing the percentage of legally entitled victims who fail to sue or pursue their claims, and reducing the percentage by which settlements fall below expected trial-outcomes will be larger than the increase in the relevant aggregate deflation it will generate by increasing the percentage by which damage awards fall below recoverable losses and (2) the shift will also reduce the amount of misallocation potential injurers generate by rejecting avoidance moves whose rejection will be assessed for negligence by preventing them from making errors.

THE IMPACT OF A SHIFT FROM A NEGLIGENCE/CONTRIBUTORY-NEGLIGENCE TO A STRICT-LIABILITY/CONTRIBUTORY-NEGLIGENCE TORT-LIABILITY REGIME ON THE AMOUNT OF MISALLOCATION GENERATED BY ECONOMICALLY INEFFICIENT APLA DECISIONS BY POTENTIAL VICTIMS

This analysis is structured in precisely the same way as was the analysis of the impact of the relevant shift on the amount of misallocation generated by economically inefficient APLA decisions by potential injurers.

(i) The Major Imperfections That Can Cause Potential Victims Who Are Operating under a Negligence/Contributory-Negligence Regime to Make Allocatively Inefficient APLA Decisions

Three sets of imperfections can cause potential tort victims to make allocatively inefficient avoidance decisions: (1) tort-law doctrines and practices, first-party tort-loss insurance contracts and worker's-compensation programs, and government-transfer programs (unemployment insurance, disability insurance, welfare payments, subsidized or free medical services) that would in any event externalize from the victim to injurers, insurance companies, or the government some or all of the losses the victims could prevent themselves from initially sustaining by engaging in avoidance, (2) imperfections in seller competition and/or other Pareto imperfections not directly caused by tort-doctrine or tort-process imperfections that would distort the profits a potential injurer could make by avoiding in an otherwise-Pareto-perfect economy, and (3) the errors that potential victims commit when making APLA decisions. The first of these sets of imperfections clearly tend to induce potential victims to misallocate resources by rejecting allocatively efficient APLA moves; I believe that the third (potential-victim errors) does so as well; and although I acknowledge that the second set of imperfections just listed will inflate the profitability of most relevant types of avoidance moves to potential victims who would otherwise ultimately bear some portion of any loss they initially suffered (for the same reasons that it will inflate the profitability of the relevant types of avoidance moves to potential injurers), I am confident that this inflation will rarely cause potential victims to make allocatively inefficient avoidance moves and will certainly not alter the conclusion that across all cases potential victims will cause more misallocation by rejecting allocatively efficient APLA moves than by making allocatively inefficient APLA moves.

The rest of this subsection focuses on the factors that will influence the extent to which the avoidance incentives of potential victims are deflated by the prospect of their receiving compensation from their injurers if the relevant tort-law regime is a negligence/contributory-negligence system. In such a regime, this tort-law deflation in the profits that potential-victim avoidance will yield the potential victim will be larger

1. the greater the probability that the loss will have been caused by a human injurer (as opposed to nature alone) who is legally responsible for his choices and not judgment-proof;
2. the smaller the probability that the victim in question would be held not to be entitled to recover because he was not the type of victim whom tort law entitles to recover;
3. the smaller the probability that the injurer will be incorrectly held not to be the cause-in-fact of the victim's loss;
4. the smaller the probability that all of the victim's possible injurers will be held not to be the cause-in-fact of the victim's loss because the only relevant evidence on this issue was evidence on the contribution that each possible injurer's activity made to the *ex ante* probability of the loss's occurring and each possible injurer's activity contributed 50 percent or less of the *ex ante* probability of the relevant loss's occurring;
5. the smaller the probability that the injurer will be found not to be the proximate cause of the victim's loss either because that finding is correct under the prevailing proximate-cause (scope-of-liability) doctrine or because a false-negative finding on proximate cause is made;
6. the smaller the probability that the injurer would not be held negligent because he was not in a position to make an APLA move whose rejection would violate the Hand test for negligence;
7. the smaller the probability that his injurer would not be held negligent because all avoidance moves that were available to him whose rejection would violate the Hand test for negligence were types of moves whose rejection would not in practice be assessed for negligence;
8. the smaller the probability that the trier-of-fact would make a false-negative finding on the negligence issue even if he did assess for negligence the injurer's negligent rejection of an avoidance move;
9. the smaller the probability that the victim would be barred from recovery by a fellow-servant, assumption-of-risk, or last-clear-chance doctrine, even if he was not contributorily negligent;

10. the greater the probability that the avoidance move for which $B_v < \downarrow (PL)_v$ was a type of move whose rejection would not in practice be assessed for contributory negligence;
11. the smaller the probability that the potential victim would erroneously be found to be contributorily negligent;
12. the smaller the amount by which the weighted-average-expected damages that the victim would be awarded would fall below his actual loss;
13. the smaller the amount by which the sum for which the victim should expect on the weighted average to settle will fall below the weighted-average-expected damages he should anticipate being awarded if he goes to trial; and
14. the smaller the transaction cost to the victim (including the private value of his time, the aggravation he will experience, his lawyers' fees, and his court fees) of seeking compensation for his losses.

(ii) The Impact of a Shift from a Negligence/Contributory-Negligence to a Strict-Liability/Contributory-Negligent Tort-Liability Regime on the Tort-Law-Generated Distortion in $P\pi_{APLA}$ for Potential-Victim Avoidance Moves, the First-Party Tort-Loss-Insurance Distortion in $P\pi_{APLA}$ for Such Moves, the APLA-Decision Errors Potential Victims Commit, and, Derivatively, the Amount of Misallocation Potential Victims Generate by Making Economically Inefficient APLA Decisions

Before proceeding, I want to explain why I am focusing on a shift to a strict-liability/contributory-negligence regime rather than on a shift to a strict-liability regime that, like the current common-law alternative, does not incorporate a contributory-negligence doctrine. The reason is that I am certain that the inclusion of even our current, restrictively applied contributory-negligence doctrine in a strict-liability regime would increase allocative efficiency. It should be obvious that, transaction-cost considerations aside, the inclusion of such a contributory-negligence doctrine in a strict-liability regime will reduce the amount of misallocation potential victims generate by rejecting allocatively efficient avoidance moves whose rejection would be assessed for contributory negligence by reducing the deflation in the profits potential victims can earn by making such moves by the mathematical product of the damages the potential victims in question would otherwise have been able to collect from their injurer and the probability that the trier-of-fact will correctly find contributorily negligent the victim's contributorily negligent rejection of the avoidance move in question. Admittedly, the inclusion of a contributory-negligence doctrine in a strict-liability regime will increase the amount of misallocation potential injurers generate by rejecting allocatively efficient avoidance moves by deflating the profits they can earn by making such moves by creating the possibility that their victims will be barred from recovery by a correct or incorrect finding that they were contributorily negligent—particularly if contributory negligence is defined in the current way to encompass cases in which $0 < \downarrow(PL)_V - B_V < \downarrow(PL)_I - B_I$. However, even if any resulting allocative inefficiency is combined with any additional allocative transaction costs that the inclusion of a contributory-negligence doctrine causes to be generated, I am convinced that these allocative costs of the contributory-negligence doctrine's inclusion will be lower than the allocative benefits it generates by inducing potential victims to make allocatively efficient avoidance moves whose rejection would be assessed for contributory negligence.

I will now address the issues listed in the heading of this subsection. To begin, a shift from a negligence/contributory-negligence to a strict-liability/contributory-negligence tort-liability regime will affect the tort-law-related distortion in $P\pi_{APLA}$ for all potential-victim avoidance moves (including all potential-victim marginal avoidance moves) in four major ways: in particular, will

1. increase the deflation in $P\pi_{APLA}$ for all potential-victim avoidance moves by eliminating the possibility that their injurers will be found not liable because they had not in fact been negligent or had been negligent in rejecting an avoidance move whose rejection would not in practice have been assessed for negligence or because the trier-of-fact will have mistakenly found non-negligent their rejection of an avoidance move whose rejection the trier-of-fact did assess for negligence;
2. decrease the deflation in $P\pi_{APLA}$ for all potential-victim avoidance moves by increasing the amount by which damage awards fall below recoverable losses by precluding tort victims from putting on evidence about the injurer's fault whose introduction would tend to increase the damages the juries award;
3. decrease the deflation in $P\pi_{APLA}$ for all potential-victim avoidance moves by reducing the difference between the weighted-average settlement tort victims accept and the weighted-average damage award they would receive at trial by reducing the private transaction cost and riskiness of litigating by removing the negligence issue from the litigation (given the tendency of tort victims [A] to face higher litigation costs than [repeat player] tort injurers, [B] to be smaller and hence more risk adverse than tort injurers, [C] to have smaller

risk portfolios and to have their risk costs per risky event reduced to a smaller extent by their involvement in multiple risky situations); and

4. increase the deflation in $P\pi_{APLA}$ for all potential-victim avoidance moves by decreasing the transaction cost and risk cost of both litigating the associated tort claim and negotiating its settlement by removing the negligence issue from the controversy.

In addition, by reducing the likelihood that potential victims will take out first-party tort insurance by reducing the amount of tort losses they would end up bearing if not insured (a factor that is made relevant by the fact that the private transaction cost of taking out such insurance will not rise proportionately with the weighted-average losses the insurance buyer would suffer if not insured), the shift from negligence to strict liability will reduce the frequency with which $P\pi_{APLA}$ for potential-tort-victim avoidance moves is deflated by first-party tort insurance.

Relatedly, by reducing the percentage of potential tort victims who investigate the possibility of taking out first-party tort insurance as well as the percentage of such actors who actually take out such insurance, the relevant shift will (I believe) increase the extent to which potential tort victims misallocate resources by rejecting allocatively efficient avoidance moves that would have been profitable for them to make by depriving them of the information about their risk exposure that tort premiums would provide as well as of the advice and sometimes the useful commands (conditions for coverage) of the insurance companies to whom they make inquiries and/or from whom they buy insurance.

What do the preceding conclusions imply for the effect of a shift from a negligence/contributory-negligence to a strict-liability/contributory-negligence tort-liability regime on the amount of misallocation potential victims generate by making economically inefficient APLA decisions? It would clearly be TBLE to obtain a lot more information before attempting to answer this question. For example, it would be useful to obtain information on the relative size of (1) the misallocation the shift's tendency to reduce the percentage of potential tort victims that takes out first-party tort insurance prevents by reducing the frequency with which potential tort victims reject allocatively efficient avoidance moves because they are insured and their insurer has been unable to overcome the associated moral-hazard problem and (2) the misallocation this tendency of the shift causes by depriving potential victims of the information that would deter them from mistakenly rejecting allocatively efficient avoidance moves or eliminating insurance-company-imposed contractual duties that would deter them from rejecting the moves in question. It would also be useful to obtain information on the relative sizes of the second through fourth weighted-average deflation changes I initially indicated the shift would generate in a world without tort insurance. Finally, it would be useful to obtain information on the frequency with which the shift would increase the deflation in $P\pi_{APLA}$ for potential-victim avoidance moves because in practice actual victims' actual injurers would not be found negligent. However, although the magnitude and even the sign of the net impact that the shift will have on $\Sigma D(P\pi_{APLA})$ for all potential-victim avoidance moves including potential-victim marginal avoidance moves in the first four ways just described will clearly depend on whether the potential injurer was in a position to make an avoidance move whose rejection would be assessed for negligence and would in fact be negligent, I suspect that across all cases potential injurers will not be in such positions sufficiently often for the shift to increase substantially the absolute value of the weighted-average value of the distribution of $\Sigma D(P\pi_{\Delta APLA})$s for potential-victim marginal avoidance moves and thereby to increase the amount of misallocation potential victims generate by rejecting allocatively efficient avoidance moves.

(iii) The Impact of a Shift from a Negligence/Contributory-Negligence to a Strict-Liability/Contributory-Negligence Tort-Liability Regime on the Total Amount of Misallocation Generated by Allocatively Inefficient APLA Decisions Made by Potential Injurers and Potential Victims

The preceding two subsections explained why the relevant shift seems likely to reduce the misallocation generated by economically inefficient APLA decisions by potential injurers and to increase the misallocation generated by economically inefficient APLA decisions by potential victims. In my judgment, the shift will reduce potential-injurer APLA-decision misallocation by more than it will increase potential-victim APLA-decision misallocation. I will not list all the empirical assumptions that underlie this conclusion. However, I will say that, to a considerable extent, it reflects my belief that the number of allocatively efficient avoidance moves that the shift will make profitable for potential injurers to make because their rejection would not in practice be assessed for negligence is far greater than the number of allocatively efficient avoidance moves this shift will deter potential victims from making by increasing the probability that they will be able to recover any loss they critically suffer from their injurers.

Chapter 4 Some Second-Best-Theory Critiques of Canonical Allocative-Efficiency Analyses and of the Standard Justifications for Ignoring Second Best

Chapter 3 explained The General Theory of Second Best and delineated and exemplified an approach to allocative-efficiency assessment that I believe responds appropriately to second-best theory. More specifically, Chapter 3 argued that this distortion-analysis approach is third-best allocatively efficient in that it takes appropriate account of the multiplicity of resource-use types, the Pareto-imperfectness of all economies, the fact that the allocative efficiency of reducing or eliminating a target imperfection depends on the other imperfections that will remain in the system, and the inevitable cost and imperfectness of both theoretical and empirical work. Chapter 3 also made two important critical assertions about the scholarly literature on the allocative efficiency of proposed or actual legislation, judge-announced legal doctrines, and legal-case resolutions. First, the vast majority of welfare economics and law and economics analyses of the allocative efficiency of particular pieces of legislation or judicial rulings have ignored The General Theory of Second Best—that is, have proceeded on the first-best premise that one can accurately assess the allocative efficiency of any public policy that is designed to reduce or eliminate a particular Pareto imperfection on the assumption that the target imperfection is the only relevant Pareto imperfection in the economy. Second, the small minority of studies that do attempt to analyze the way in which the existence of a specified nontarget imperfection affects the allocative efficiency of eliminating or reducing a target imperfection, though making real contributions, fail to consider many types of imperfections and many types of resource misallocation they should take into account and, derivatively, articulate conclusions that second-best theory demonstrates they have not justified.

Chapter 4 has two sections. Section 1 illustrates and justifies Chapter 3's negative assertions about the economic-efficiency-analysis canon by describing the standard analysis of nine allocative-efficiency issues and demonstrating that all fail to take appropriate account of The General Theory of Second Best. Section 2 then describes the reaction of economists to The General Theory of Second Best and criticizes the variety of arguments that economists and legal academics who have some knowledge of second-best theory use to justify ignoring it.

SECTION 1. NINE ALLOCATIVE-EFFICIENCY ISSUES WHOSE CANONICAL ANALYSES FAIL TO RESPOND APPROPRIATELY TO SECOND-BEST THEORY: DESCRIPTIONS AND CRITIQUES

The Deadweight Loss Caused by an Individual Monopoly (That Is, Imperfections in Price Competition)

The traditional allocative-efficiency rationale for pro-competition policies focuses exclusively on the supposed tendency of individual imperfections in price competition to generate a deadweight loss by reducing the output that the non-perfect competitor finds most profitable below the output that would be most allocatively efficient for him to produce (by reducing marginal revenue below price).[1] More particularly, the traditional economic-efficiency rationale for antitrust is that pro-price-competition policies will eliminate or reduce this deadweight loss by eliminating or reducing the individual imperfections in price competition that first-best analysis claims cause it.

Economists and law and economics scholars have traditionally illustrated this analysis through diagrams that resemble Diagram V. The facts that DD, MR, and MC are all linear in Diagram V and that MC is horizontal play no critical role in either the traditional analysis or in the critique that follows.

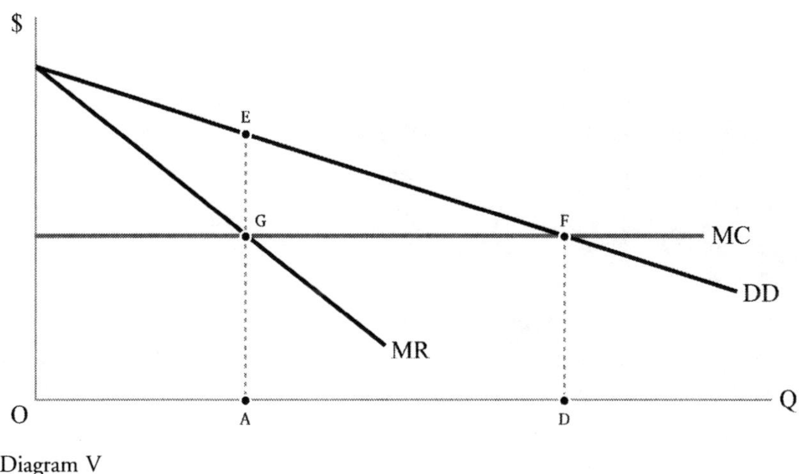

Diagram V

The traditional proof and diagrammatic illustration of the supposed tendency of an individual monopoly to generate a deadweight loss of the kind just described assumes that DD = MLV and MC = MLC (in essence, that the target imperfection in price competition is the only [relevant] Pareto imperfection in the economy). In Diagram V, in which the actual output is OA (the output at which MR cuts MC from above at point G), these assumptions are manifest by the claim that the allocatively efficient output is OD (that the output at which DD cuts MC from above at point F is the output at which MLV [not shown] cuts MLC [not shown] from above) and that the resulting deadweight loss is area EFG (that the area between the DD and MC curves [that are shown] between the actual and allegedly allocatively efficient outputs equals the area between the MLV and MLC curves [that are not shown] between the outputs in question). As Chapter 3 indicated, in our actual, highly-Pareto-imperfect world, DD will equal MLV and MC will equal MLC only rarely and fortuitously. Thus, unless the relevant imperfections perfectly counteract each other, DD will not equal MLV if the relevant consumers are not sovereign, do not maximize, or are monopsonists or if the relevant consumption generates externalities (even if one could ignore the divergence between DD and MLV generated by the income elasticity of demand). Similarly, in our actual, highly-Pareto-imperfect world, unless the relevant imperfections perfectly counteract each other, MC will not equal MLC when the production of the good in question generates externalities (since, for example, if the production generates external costs, producers will not pay anything for some of the resources the production of the good in question consumes) or various other Pareto imperfections individually distort the private value to their alternative users of the resources the production of the units in question would consume (since in this eventuality the private cost to a producer of the resources he purchases to produce his unit output [which equals their private value to their alternative users] will not equal the allocative cost of his using these resources [which equals the allocative product they would have generated in their alternative users' employ]).

Diagram VI illustrates the analysis of the deadweight loss that an individual monopoly will generate in a world that contains Pareto imperfections other than the individual imperfection in price competition in question. At least, Diagram VI illustrates that analysis on the simplifying assumption that the various Pareto imperfections that can individually cause DD to diverge from MLV perfectly counteract each other—that DD = MLV. Both to ease the exposition and because the canonical analysis I am criticizing makes this assumption as well, the analysis of Diagram VI also assumes that all the resources that the production of the monopolized good (say, X) consumed were withdrawn from the production of units of other products ($Y_{1...N}$, henceforth Y) already in production.

Diagram VI carries over the same DD, MR, and MC curves that Diagram V contained. However, in Diagram VI, DD_X is explicitly indicated to coincide with MLV_X. Diagram VI also differs from Diagram V in that it contains three MLC_X curves that diverge from MC_X. Although, as Chapter 3 explained, all

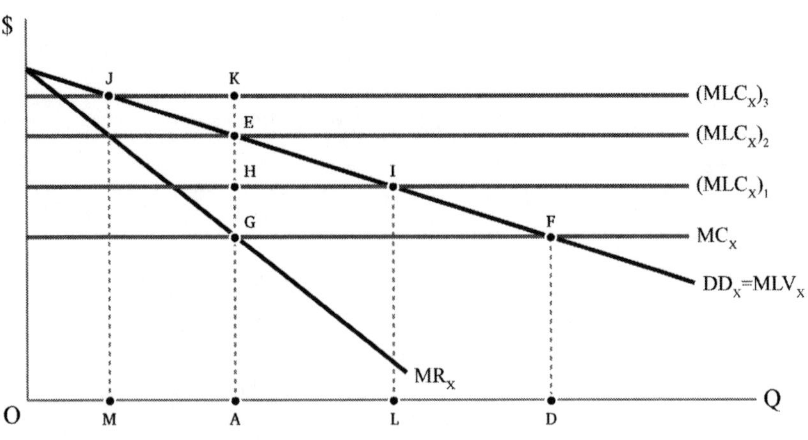

Diagram VI

the various types of Pareto imperfections could cause MLC_X to diverge from MC_X, I will assume here that the relevant divergences are caused by three Pareto imperfections:

1. imperfections in the price competition faced by the producers of Y1 . . . N (the alternative users of the resources the production of X will consume)—imperfections that deflate MC_X (cause it to be lower than MLC_X) by deflating the private value of the resources in question to Y1 . . . N by reducing the marginal revenue they can obtain by using those resources to produce marginal units of their products below the allocative value of those units;
2. external costs that would be generated by the production of the units of Y1 . . . N; that would be sacrificed if additional units of X were produced—external costs whose non-internalization will inflate MC_X by inflating the private value of the resources in question to the producers of Y1 . . . N; and
3. external costs that would be generated by the production of the relevant additional units of X—external costs whose non-internalization will obviously deflate MC_X.

Diagram VI makes the assumption that, taken together, these imperfections will always deflate MC_X—that is, cause MC_X to be lower than MLC_X. Although this assumption may be inaccurate in a few cases, I believe it will be correct in virtually all situations, at least if (as the canonical analysis assumes) all the resources that would be consumed by the production of additional units of X would be withdrawn from the production of units of other existing products.

In any event, Diagram VI distinguishes three situations. In all three, the actual output stays the same at OA—the output at which MR_X cuts MC_X from above at point G. However, in all three, the allocatively efficient output (determined by the intersection of the relevant MLC_X curve with the unchanging DD_X curve, which is assumed to coincide with MLV_X) is lower than OD—the output at which DD_X cuts MC_X from above at point F. In the first situation, in which MLC_X is assumed to equal $(MLC_X)_1 > MC_X$, the other imperfections that are present in the system reduce the extent of the deadweight loss the imperfection in price competition in X generates from area EFG to area EIH while reducing the allocatively efficient output from OD to OL—the output at which $DD_X = MLV_X$ cuts $(MLC_X)_1$ from above at point I—but do not change the conclusion that the monopolized good is still underproduced from the perspective of allocative efficiency. In the second, in which $MLC_X = (MLC_X)_2$, the imperfections that cause MLC_X to exceed MC_X do change the conclusion that the monopolized good is underproduced from the perspective of allocative efficiency: by reducing the allocatively efficient output from OD to OA—the output at which $DD_X = MLV_X$ cuts $(MLC_X)_2$ from above at point E—the other Pareto imperfections in question perfectly counteract the tendency of the monopoly in X to cause too few units of X to be produced (create a situation in which the actual output is the allocatively efficient output). Finally, in the third situation, in which $MLC_X = (MLC_X)_3$, the imperfections that cause MLC_X to exceed MC_X yield an outcome in which—despite the fact that X's producers face imperfect price competition—X's output is too high from the perspective of allocative efficiency: by reducing the allocatively efficient output from OD to OM—the output at which $DD_X = MLV_X$ cuts $(MLC_X)_3$ from above at point J—the imperfections in question more than offset the tendency of the monopoly in X to cause too few units of X to be produced (cause too many units of X to be produced from the perspective of allocative efficiency—in particular, cause a deadweight loss equal to area JKE to be generated on this account).

Chapter 3 explained the circumstances in which these three outcomes will respectively be generated on the assumptions on which this critique is proceeding. If we continue to define MC^*_X and MC^*_Y in some way that guarantees that MC^*_X/MC^*_Y equals the marginal rate at which the economy can transform Y into X, (1) X will be underproduced (as it was when MLC_X equaled $[MLC_X]_1$) if $P_X/MC^*_X > P_Y/MC^*_Y$, (2) X will be produced in the allocatively efficient quantity (as it was when $MLC_X = [MLC_X]_2$) when $P_X/MC^*_X = P_Y/MC^*_Y$, and (3) X will be overproduced from the perspective of economic efficiency (as it was when $MLC_X = [MLC_X]_3$) if $P_X/MC^*_X < P_Y/MC^*_Y$. As Chapter 3 explained, these conclusions reflect the fact that in an otherwise-Pareto-perfect economy X and Y will be produced in allocatively efficient proportions to each other if and only if the rate at which individual consumers can exchange Y for X (P_X/P_Y)[2] equals the rate at which the economy can transform Y into X (MC^*_X/MC^*_Y).[3] Thus, X will be underproduced relative to Y if $P_X/MC^*_X > P_Y/MC^*_Y$ because in these circumstances P_X/P_Y, which equals the rate at which individual consumers can exchange Y for X, will be greater than MC^*_X/MC^*_Y,[4] the rate at which the economy can transform Y into X, and all buyers would have been better-off (in a preferred position) had they been allocated less Y and the additional units of X that could have been produced had the units of Y withdrawn from them not been produced.[5]

Obviously, these conclusions imply not only that individual monopolies will not always produce deadweight losses in the form of UO-to-UO misallocation in our actual, highly-Pareto-imperfect world but that pro-price-competition policies will increase economic efficiency by reducing such UO-to-UO misallocation if and only if (roughly speaking) they reduce the difference between the P/MC* ratios of pairs of products between whose production resources flow (which, as we also saw in Chapter 3, many policies of this sort will not do).

In short, the canonical analysis of the deadweight loss of monopoly is undermined by its first-best character. An analysis of the impact of individual imperfections in price competition on UO-to-UO misallocation that takes appropriate account of second-best theory and the relevant facts reveals that the traditional analysis's conclusions are wrong and that the correct analysis of this issue does not support the policy conclusions that have traditionally been drawn from the canonical analysis.

The Economic Efficiency of a Marginal-Cost-Reducing Horizontal Merger That Also Reduces Output: Oliver Williamson's "Welfare Trade-Off" Analysis

In two canonical articles,[6] Oliver Williamson analyzed what he called "the *welfare* trade-off" and I would call "the *allocative-efficiency* trade-off"[7] involved in assessing the allocative efficiency of a horizontal merger between or among producers of identical products or services (say X) that simultaneously reduces both the (private) marginal cost of producing each unit of the good in question by generating efficiencies and the unit output of the good by reducing the price competition the relevant producers face (paradigmatically, by converting the industry in question from a perfectly competitive industry into a pure monopoly). Williamson's analysis is based on the same two broad assumptions that we just saw underlie the traditional analysis and diagrammatic representation of the deadweight loss of monopoly—namely, that $DD_X = MLV_X$ and $MC_X = MLC_X$. His first-best analysis and conclusions must therefore be rejected for the same reasons that the traditional analysis of and conclusions about the deadweight loss of monopoly must be rejected.

Diagram VII has been devised to illustrate both the Williamson analysis of the relevant allocative-efficiency trade-off and the second-best critique of that analysis on the assumption that the relevant merger would convert a perfectly competitive industry into a pure monopoly. In this diagram, the $(MC_{IND})_B$ curve is the pre-merger industry supply curve—the curve that indicates the marginal cost the industry would have to incur to produce successive units of

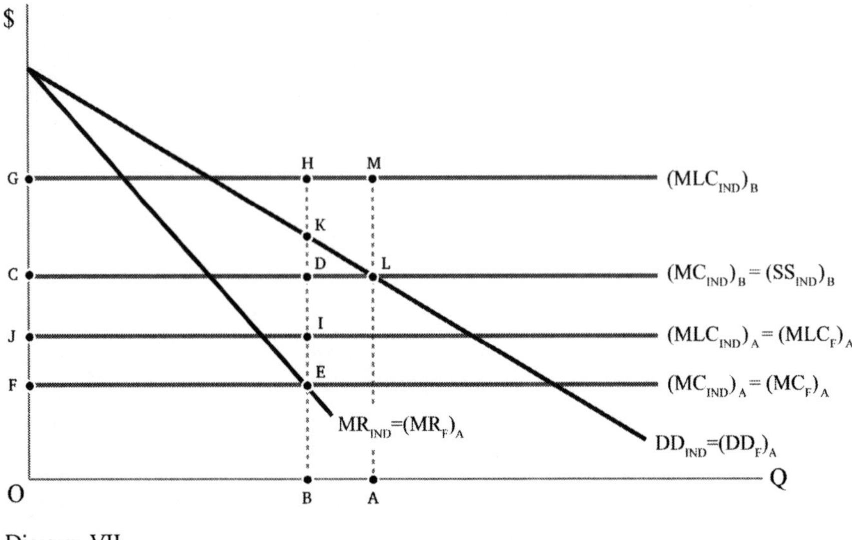

Diagram VII

product X *before* (hence sub-B) the merger was executed. The height of $(MC_{IND})_B$ also indicates the marginal cost that each firm in the industry would face pre-merger until it reached its capacity, which presumably is a small percentage of the pre-merger output of the industry (since pre-merger the industry is assumed to be perfectly competitive). In addition, the segment of $(MC_{IND})_B$ between C and L equals the demand curve each firm F in the industry faced before the merger—$(DD_F)_B$. This representation reflects the fact that each firm in a perfectly competitive industry will face a horizontal demand curve whose height equals MC at the output at which DD_{IND} cuts MC_{IND} from above. The segment of $(MC_{IND})_B$ between C and L will also equal the marginal revenue curve each firm in the industry faced before the merger—$(MR_F)_B$.

The $(MC_{IND})_A$ curve in the diagram represents the marginal cost that the monopolistic merged firm would face post-merger (sub-A for after the merger). In particular, in this diagram, $(MC_{IND})_A$ is assumed to be 40 percent of $(MC_{IND})_B$. Although this figure (that is, the assumption that the merger will reduce MC_X by 60 percent) will almost always be unrealistically high (was adopted solely to promote diagrammatic clarity), the assumption that $(MC_{IND})_B$ exceeds $(MC_{IND})_A$ was made because Williamson assumes that the merger to be evaluated will reduce the marginal cost of producing the good in question.

DD_{IND} in Diagram VII is the industry demand curve for the product the merger partners produce. DD_{IND} also is the demand curve that the merged firm F faces post-merger—$(DD_F)_A$—since post-merger the industry is a pure monopoly. For the same reason, $(MR_F)_A$ coincides with MR_{IND}. The construction of the $(MR_F)_A$ curve assumes that the merged firm will not practice price discrimination.

The diagram also contains two MLC curves. In particular, it assumes that $(MLC_{IND})_A = (MLC_F)_A > (MC_{IND})_A = (MC_F)_A$, that $(MLC_{IND})_B > (MC_{IND})_B$, and that $(MLC_F)_B > (MC_F)_B$. Each of these assumptions reflects a more basic assumption that units of the product produced by the merged company will be produced with resources that would otherwise have been used to increase the unit output of one or more other goods that would be sold under imperfectly competitive conditions by nondiscriminators—that is, the assumption that the private value that the resources in question would generate for their alternative users (the private cost of those resources to the producer or producers of X) would be lower than the allocative value they would generate in the alternative users' employ (the allocative cost of X's producer's or producers' using those resources). In the diagram, $(MLC_{IND})_B = 1.5(MC_{IND})_B$ and $(MLC_{IND})_A = 1.5(MC_{IND})_A$. These assumptions are undoubtedly unrealistic: the relevant MLC/MC ratios will be far closer to one. They have also been made solely to increase the clarity of the diagram and are not critical to the conclusion I want to establish—namely, that Williamson's analysis of both the allocative-efficiency gains the merger in question will generate by lowering the marginal cost of producing the post-merger output of X and the allocative-efficiency loss that he assumes it will generate by preventing some units of X from being produced at their pre-merger MC are inaccurate (would be accurate if and only if $DD = MLV$ and $MC = MLC$ or the divergences between DD and MLV on the one hand and MC and MLC on the other perfectly [and fortuitously] counteracted each other).[8]

I will now use Diagram VII to illustrate and criticize Williamson's analysis of the trade-off that must be made to calculate the allocative efficiency of a horizontal merger that simultaneously reduces both (1) the unit output of the merger partners' product X from OA—the output at which DD_{IND} cuts $(MC_{IND})_B = (SS_{IND})_B$ from above at point L—to OB—the output at which $(MR_F)_A$ cuts $(MC_F)_A$ from above at point E—and (2) MC_X from $(MC_{IND})_B = CO$ to $(MC_{IND})_A = FO$. As I have already indicated, Williamson analyzed the allocative efficiency of such a horizontal merger on the implicit first-best assumptions that $DD_{IND} = MLV_X$, that $(MC_{IND})_B = (MLC_{IND})_B$, and that $(MC_{IND})_A = (MC_F)_A = (MLC_F)_A$. On these assumptions, Williamson concluded that the merger would increase allocative efficiency by reducing the private and allocative cost of producing X's post-merger output (OB) by area CDEF and would decrease allocative efficiency by preventing the production of BA units of X whose pre-merger production at $(MC_{IND})_B = CO$ increased allocative efficiency by area KLD (the area between the DD_{IND} curve [which Williamson assumed coincided with MLV_X] and the pre-merger MC_{IND} curve [which Williamson assumed coincided with $(MLC_{IND})_B$] between the pre-merger and post-merger outputs of X). According to Williamson, then, the net allocative efficiency of the merger whose effects are portrayed in Diagram VII equaled area CDEF *minus* area KLD.

However, if one relaxes Williamson's first-best, otherwise-Pareto-perfect assumption and assumes that the imperfections that are present in the system other than the post-merger imperfection in the price competition faced by the merged producer of X caused $(MLC_{IND})_B$ to equal $1.5(MC_{IND})_B$ and $(MLC_{IND})_A$ to equal $1.5(MC_{IND})_A$ as the construction of Diagram VII assumes, both the allocative-efficiency gain that the merger will generate by reducing the allocative cost of producing the post-merger output of X and the allocative-efficiency effect of the merger's reducing X's output by BA units will be different from the value Williamson assigned to them. Thus, on the assumptions on which Diagram VII's construction is based,

1. the allocative-efficiency gain the merger will generate by reducing the allocative cost of producing the post-merger output of X—OB—will be area GHIJ, not area CDEF, where area GHIJ is (1.5)area CDEF, and
2. the merger will have increased economic efficiency by area HMLK, not decreased it by area KLD, by preventing the production of BA units of X at their pre-merger allocative cost.

Admittedly, this diagram's unrealistically high estimate of the percentage by which MLC_X exceeds MC_X causes it to exaggerate the percentage by which Williamson's otherwise-Pareto-perfect assumption led him to underestimate the production-optimum-related allocative-efficiency gains the mergers he was analyzing would generate: the percentage by which Williamson's estimate underestimates this gain equals the percentage by which MC_X is deflated (if, pre-merger, the private cost of the resources the mergers enabled the merged firm to save was deflated by Z percent, the private savings the merger effectuates will also be deflated by Z percent, and Williamson's estimate of the allocative gains in question will therefore be Z percent too low). However, as long as MLC_X exceeds MC_X to some extent, Williamson's estimate of this gain will be too low. Moreover, Diagram VII's implication that the mergers Williamson is analyzing will increase allocative efficiency by preventing the production of some units of the product in question at their pre-merger cost (instead of decreasing allocative efficiency in this way, as Williamson claimed) is consistent with the assumption that premerger the industry in question was perfectly competitive since in that case its pre-merger P/MC ratio would almost certainly have been lower than its weighted-average counterpart for the products whose unit outputs its production reduced and there is no general reason to believe that the MC/MC* ratio for X will tend to be sufficiently lower than its weighted-average counterpart for these other products to call into question Diagram VII's assumption that, pre-merger, X was overproduced from the perspective of allocative efficiency. Of course, the merger in question could reduce allocative efficiency by preventing the production of units of X at their premerger marginal cost by raising P_X/MC_X sufficiently to produce this result. However, even then, Williamson's estimate of the amount by which the merger would reduce allocative efficiency in this way would overestimate the allocative-efficiency loss by measuring it on the assumption that $(MLC_{IND})_B$ was lower than it actually was.

In short, if one substitutes more realistic assumptions for Williamson's first-best, otherwise-Pareto-perfect assumptions, the analysis of the allocative efficiency of the type of merger he considered might not involve the kind of trade-off he thought it involved—that is, allocative efficiency might be increased by the unit output reductions the mergers he analyzed generated as well as by the marginal-cost reductions they yielded. Moreover, even if the relevant unit output reductions were misallocative (so that a trade-off would have to be made), Williamson's assumptions would lead him to underestimate the relevant allocative-efficiency gain and overestimate the relevant allocative-efficiency loss. Thus, Williamson's failure to respond appropriately to second-best theory not only undermines his analysis but also leads him to reach conclusions that are both inaccurate and biased against the allocative efficiency of the subset of horizontal mergers he was investigating.[9] This critique of Williamson's trade-off analysis is therefore far from academic in the pejorative sense of that word.

The Allocative Efficiency Both of the Quantity of Resources Economies Devote to R&D and of Various Policy Proposals for Reducing the Misallocation Caused by Underinvesting in R&D

Not only the vast majority of politicians but also virtually all economists[10] and legal scholars believe that we devote too few resources to R&D (indeed, to investment in general) from the perspective of economic efficiency.[11] This allocative-efficiency conclusion has led these observers to recommend tax policies, IP-law changes, and antitrust-law modifications that are designed to increase allocative efficiency by increasing the amount of resources that the economies to which they would apply devote to R&D. More specifically, these experts have recommended increasing the quantity of resources we devote to R&D by giving investors in R&D various tax breaks, by lengthening and broadening patent-law protection, by strengthening trade-secret protection, and by granting antitrust exemptions to mergers, acquisitions, and joint ventures that would increase the quantity of R&D in which their participants engage but would still decrease competition on balance (or violate the Sherman Act [roughly speaking] because their participants' *ex ante* perception that the acts in question would be profitable was critically affected by the participants' belief that they might reduce the absolute attractiveness of the offers against which they would have to compete in the future in some way that would critically inflate its profitability in an otherwise-Pareto-perfect economy).[12]

I have four general objections to the preceding economic-efficiency conclusions and the policy proposals they have spawned and one specific objection to the antitrust-exemption proposal just delineated. The first general objection is that the relevant conclusions and proposals do not distinguish between product R&D and PPR. The second general objection is that the relevant economic-efficiency analyses do not pay appropriate attention to the possibility that—by providing discoverers with protection that at least in some respects is broader and longer than the protection they could secure for themselves if they could keep their discovery absolutely secret—the relevant countries' patent and copyright laws partially or fully internalize or overinternalize to discoverers the benefits their discovery confers on others by providing them with information for which they did not have to pay or by enabling them to secure buyer surplus by purchasing the information in question. The third general objection is that most of the relevant economic-efficiency analyses are first-best in character—that is, ignore the fact that the profitability of product R&D and PPR projects is distorted by imperfections other than the externalities of knowledge creation on which they focus. In particular, the standard analyses ignore the fact that imperfections in price competition almost certainly inflate the profits yielded by product R&D and deflate the profits yielded by PPR.[13] The fourth general objection is really a pair of objections that are corollaries of the first three: (1) the consensus economic-efficiency conclusion seems to me to be overbroad—although there are good reasons for believing that $\Sigma D(P\pi_{\triangle PPR})$ is negative, there are also good reasons for believing that $\Sigma D(P\pi)$ for marginal product R&D is positive—and, relatedly, (2) policies that are designed to reduce the misallocation that is generated by our devoting the wrong quantity of resources to R&D must distinguish between product R&D and PPR—namely, must encourage PPR but discourage product R&D. None of the tax, IP, or antitrust proposals that have been made to reduce the misallocation we generate by investing the wrong quantity of resources in R&D distinguishes between product R&D and PPR.

My last objection is an additional objection to the proposal that mergers, acquisitions, and joint ventures that increase the quantity of resources devoted to R&D[14] receive antitrust exemptions. As Chapter 3 demonstrated, any tendency of such an antitrust exemption to decrease price competition will on that account tend to increase the extent to which we overinvest in product R&D and the extent to which we underinvest in PPR from the perspective of allocative efficiency—that is, will on these accounts disserve the proposed exemption's goal of reducing the amount of misallocation we generate because, from the perspective of allocative efficiency, we devote the wrong amounts of resources to product R&D and PPR.

In short, although the standard analyses of (1) the economic efficiency of the quantity of resources we devote to R&D and (2) the policy implications of this type of resource misallocation have other deficiencies as well, both are undermined by their failure to take appropriate account of The General Theory of Second Best. Once more, this omission has led economists and law and economics scholars to reach inaccurate economic-efficiency conclusions and propose policies that are less economically efficient and desirable overall than various alternatives would be.

The "Social Costs" of Monopoly[15]

In 1953, Arnold Harberger published an article that attempted to measure the amount of economic inefficiency that imperfections in competition ("monopoly," in his terms) generated in the United States.[16] Harberger's approach to this issue contains three flaws that Chapter 3 points out. First, Harberger assumes that the only type of resource misallocation monopoly causes is the type I denominate UO-to-UO misallocation. Second, and relatedly, Harberger focuses exclusively on imperfections in price competition—that is, he ignores the effect of imperfections in QV-investment competition on economic efficiency. And third, Harberger's method of estimating the amount of UO-to-UO misallocation in the United States is implicitly based on the first-best, otherwise-Pareto-perfect assumptions that DD = MLV and MC = MLV.[17] This section ignores the second of these errors and explores the third and first—that is, both the way in which they affect Harberger's estimate and the extent to which Harberger's errors were corrected in the vast body of literature his canonical article spawned.

I start with Harberger's failure to deal with the realities on which second-best theory (subsequently) focused. If, as I believe, MLC exceeds MC (or at least would exceed MC if, as Harberger implicitly assumes, all the resources used to produce additional units of any product X are withdrawn from the production of other existing products Y1 . . . N), Harberger's approach will lead him to overestimate UO-to-UO misallocation in two ways. First, it will lead him to overestimate the misallocation caused by the underproduction of those goods to whose production too low a proportion of the resources the economy devotes to unit output production are allocated. Second, it will lead him to conclude that many goods to whose production too high a proportion of the resources the economy devotes to unit output production are allocated[18] are underproduced. This second mistake is particularly damning, given that the total amount of UO-to-UO misallocation in any economy does not equal the sum of the amount of misallocation caused by the relative underproduction of some goods and the amount of misallocation caused by the relative overproduction of other goods—in particular, equals either of these (equal) amounts of misallocation, which are each other's flip sides.

Admittedly, the vast quantity of literature Harberger's article spawned[19] does make a number of different criticisms of his approach to UO-to-UO misallocation measurement.[20] However, none of these articles notes, much less criticizes, the otherwise-Pareto-perfect assumption his method implicitly adopts: not only Harberger but also his progeny ignore The General Theory of Second Best.

Although Harberger's failure to respond appropriately to the interdependencies whose importance second-best theory subsequently emphasized biases his estimate of the allocative-efficiency cost of monopoly upwards by leading him to overestimate the amount of UO-to-UO misallocation monopoly causes, his failure to recognize that imperfections in competition cause many more types of misallocation than UO-to-UO misallocation obviously biases his estimate of the allocative-efficiency cost of monopoly downwards. A number of the articles written in response to Harberger recognize this fact. Thus, Cowling and Mueller include in their estimate of the economic inefficiency that monopoly causes the advertising costs that firms incur to develop competitive advantages that enable them to secure supra-marginal-cost prices,[21] and Posner argues that the economic inefficiency that monopoly causes includes the economic inefficiency generated by the full range of conduct in which firms engage to put themselves in a position to charge such prices[22] (which should include not just advertising existing products but also QV investments, predation, mergers, acquisitions and joint ventures, lobbying for protectionist legislation and administrative regulations, and the various other kinds of conduct that enables them to secure contrived oligopolistic margins). However, although these scholars deserve praise for pointing out this second deficiency of Harberger's estimate, their own approach to these additional types of monopoly-caused misallocation is far from satisfactory (for example, assumes that $X in advertising expenditures generate $X in misallocation[23]) or fail to indicate how one should determine (1) whether the various kinds of conduct in which firms engage to enhance their ability to charge supra-competitive prices are economically efficient or inefficient, (2) when some conduct of a particular relevant type (such as making QV investments) could be either allocatively efficient or allocatively inefficient, whether and the amount by which all the induced behavior of the relevant type combined increased or decreased economic efficiency, or (3) when a particular type of relevant conduct is economically inefficient, how economically inefficient it is.

In short, the substantial literature on "the social costs" of monopoly manifests the errors that Chapter 3 explains and tries to correct. Some of the errors lead the scholars who make them to overestimate the economic-efficiency cost of imperfections in competition; other errors that Chapter 3 discusses cause them to overestimate these costs; and the scholars in question make additional errors that also would render their estimates inaccurate if they were individually the only errors the analyses in question contained. I believe that, even in our otherwise-highly-Pareto-imperfect economy, imperfections in competition cause far more misallocation than existing estimates suggest. However, I have not tried to justify this conclusion here. The point of this subsection is simply that the current approaches to this issue are invalidated by their failure to use an appropriate checklist of the various types of misallocation imperfections in competition can cause, to take account of imperfections in QV-investment competition as well as of imperfections in price competition, and to respond appropriately to The General Theory of Second Best.

The Economic Efficiency of Internalizing External Accident and Pollution Costs in General and of Shifting from a Negligence/Contributory-Negligence to a Strict-Liability Tort-Liability Regime in Particular

THE FIRST-BEST CHARACTER OF THE ARGUMENTS MADE FOR THE ALLOCATIVE EFFICIENCY OF INTERNALIZING EXTERNAL ACCIDENT AND POLLUTION COSTS IN GENERAL

The standard law and economics argument for the allocative efficiency of internalizing external accident and pollution costs is a first-best-allocative-efficiency argument in that it assumes that, if the external costs generated by any choice are internalized by the prospect of paying an appropriate tax or damage award, the private cost of any avoidance move will equal its allocative cost, the private benefits of any avoidance move will equal the allocative benefits it would generate, and the profits any avoidance move would yield will equal its impact on allocative efficiency.[24] *Inter alia,* this series of first-best assumptions derives from the assumptions that (1) DD = MLV, (2) the private cost to a producer of reducing the externalities of production he generates by reducing his unit output is not distorted by any other Pareto imperfections such as the imperfections in price competition that he and his input rivals face, and (3) the private cost to a prospective QV investor of preventing the generation of externalities by declining to make a QV investment whose creation would have generated externalities is not distorted by any other Pareto imperfections such as the imperfections in price competition he and his input rivals face or any buyer surplus the sales of the product his QV investment would have created would generate.

The vast majority of the pure economics analyses of this issue with which I am familiar are also first best.[25] Admittedly, a few economists who have analyzed the allocative efficiency of internalizing external costs have recognized that any imperfections in price competition faced by a producer who is an external-cost generator will counteract the tendency of the non-internalization of any externalities he generates to cause him to produce too many units of his product from the perspective of allocative efficiency—that is, to deter him from engaging in allocatively efficient avoidance by reducing his unit output. However, even those scholars who make this point ignore the other Pareto imperfections that distort the profits that an externality-reducing unit output reduction will generate and ignore second-best theory more generally when analyzing the allocative efficiency of internalizing external accident and pollution costs.[26]

Chapter 3 explains why a second-best-allocative-efficiency analysis of the allocative efficiency of internalizing external accident and pollution costs would have to take into account all the other types of Pareto imperfections that can individually distort the private cost of avoidance to a potential injurer or potential victim or the private benefits that a potential injurer's or potential victim's avoidance move will confer on the avoider in question. The conclusions that Chapter 3 establishes imply *inter alia* that any analysis that ignores these other imperfections will fail to reveal that a policy that internalizes to an actor the allocative external costs he generates will sometimes render profitable allocatively inefficient avoidance moves (because their private costs are critically deflated) and will sometimes fail to render profitable allocatively efficient avoidance moves (because their private costs are critically inflated). Those conclusions imply as well that any such analysis will also fail to reveal that, because a policy that internalizes to potential avoiders the private losses their avoidance would have prevented them from imposing on the conventional victims of the accidents or pollution they would otherwise have caused may not internalize the allocative costs their avoidance would have prevented, even if the relevant avoidance moves' private costs are not distorted, such a policy may not render profitable allocatively efficient avoidance moves (because the external private losses the relevant actors could have prevented their conventional victims from experiencing are lower than the allocative external losses they could have prevented) or may render profitable allocatively inefficient avoidance moves (because the private external losses the relevant actors could have prevented their conventional victims from experiencing are higher than the allocative external costs they could have prevented). In other words, Chapter 3 establishes conclusions that imply that, regardless of whether the policies they recommend are designed to internalize the allocative or the private external costs that potential injurers and victims could prevent, the internalization policies that first-best-allocative-efficiency analyses recommend will fail to eliminate all externality-related allocative inefficiency—that is, will be less than maximally allocatively efficient in an allocative-transaction-costless world.[27] In fact, I am confident that, even when allocative transaction costs are taken into account, the third-best allocatively efficient approach to analyzing the allocative efficiency of externality-internalizing policies will take account of a large number of Pareto imperfections other than the externalities at which the policies are targeted.

Chapter 3 establishes the following propositions:

1. the allocative efficiency of the impact of a universal internalization policy on the relative outputs of various goods in production—that is, on UO-to-UO misallocation—depends *inter alia* on whether such a policy will cause the P/MC* ratios of the products between whose production resources flow to converge or diverge (roughly speaking, on the correlation between the MC/MC* and the P/MC ratios of the different products between whose production resources flow—that is, on whether, in any relevant product set, those products with lower-than-average MC/MC* ratios [those products whose production is atypically externality-prone] tend to have higher-than-average P/MC ratios);
2. the allocative efficiency of such a policy's impact on the allocation of resources between unit-output-producing, QV-investment-creating, and PPR-executing uses—that is, on total-UO/total-QV/total-PPR misallocation—depends (roughly speaking) on whether QV-investment creation and use is more prone to generate external costs than are unit output production and consumption and PPR creation and use (since imperfections in price competition [and, I suspect, tax policy] will cause too many resources to be devoted to QV-investment creation and too few to unit output production and PPR execution in an otherwise-Pareto-perfect world); and
3. the allocative efficiency of such a policy's tendency to induce AP-loss generators to avoid by shifting to otherwise-more-expensive production processes depends (roughly speaking) on the relative magnitudes of the original externality deflation in the profits such a shift would yield and the monopoly inflation in the profits in question.

Although, obviously, I do not have enough factual information to determine the amount of empirical research that would be TBLE to execute when devising externality-internalizing policies, to identify the extent to which a more selective internalization policy would be more allocatively efficient than a universal internalization policy (practicability and allocative transaction costs aside), or to identify the more selective internalization policy that would be most allocatively efficient, all things considered, I am confident that the first-best allocatively efficient approach to externality-internalization policy is not third-best allocatively efficient and that, even when allocative transaction costs are taken into account, an analysis that pays attention to various relevant nontarget Pareto imperfections will yield different conclusions about the internalization policy that is most allocatively efficient than would an analysis that considers transaction costs but is otherwise first-best allocatively efficient.

THE STANDARD LAW AND ECONOMICS ANALYSIS OF THE ALLOCATIVE EFFICIENCY OF SHIFTING FROM A NEGLIGENCE/CONTRIBUTORY-NEGLIGENCE TO A STRICT-LIABILITY TORT-LIABILITY REGIME

Chapter 3 outlines a distortion-analysis approach to analyzing the allocative efficiency of shifting from a negligence/contributory-negligence to a strict-liability/contributory-negligence tort-liability regime—the approach to this issue that I believe is TBLE. For two reasons, this subsection focuses on a shift from a negligence/contributory-negligence system to a strict-liability regime that does not contain a contributory-negligence doctrine: strict liability without contributory negligence is the current doctrinal alternative, and, relatedly, a shift to strict liability without contributory negligence is the choice whose allocative efficiency law and economics scholars have studied.

When the shift from negligence/contributory-negligence to strict liability involves dropping the contributory-negligence doctrine, it will clearly generate a larger increase in the amount of misallocation potential victims cause by rejecting avoidance moves whose rejection is really contributorily negligent and therefore presumptively allocatively inefficient. When the relevant shift is to a strict-liability regime that contains a contributory-negligence doctrine, it will tend to[28] misallocate resources by inducing potential victims to reject those avoidance moves whose rejection is contributorily negligent (and is therefore presumptively allocatively efficient) but will not be assessed for contributory negligence (or will not be found contributorily negligent) by deflating the private benefits of those moves to a victim by enabling him to secure compensation for the losses he could have prevented from an injurer who was not negligent, whose negligent rejection of an avoidance move would not be assessed for negligence, or whose negligent rejection of an avoidance move would be incorrectly found not to have been negligent. When the relevant shift is to strict liability without contributory negligence, the shift will, for the same reason, misallocate resources by deterring potential victims from making *all* avoidance moves whose rejection would be contributorily negligent (and is therefore presumptively allocatively inefficient)—that is, from making presumptively-allocatively-efficient avoidance moves regardless of whether the rejection of the moves in question would be assessed for contributory negligence, would be misassessed as being not contributorily negligent, or would not be contributorily negligent.

In any event, the traditional law and economics analysis of the shift from a negligence/contributory-negligence system to a strict-liability regime that does not include a contributory-negligence doctrine has two components: (1) an analysis of the effects of the shift in question on (allocative) transaction costs and (2) an analysis of its impact on the amount of misallocation that the economically inefficient avoidance decisions of potential injurers and potential victims generate. I will now argue that both components of the conventional analysis are undermined by their first-best character.

(i) The Traditional and More Modern Law and Economics Analysis of the Effect of the Shift on (Allocative) Transaction Costs

The first-best assumptions of the original law and economics analysis of the transaction-cost consequences of shifting from a negligence/contributory-negligence regime to a strict-liability system led the relevant scholars to conclude that such a shift would increase the (allocative) transaction costs generated by the assertion, defense, and processing of tort-law claims (henceforth, "legal-claim transaction costs") and would not affect total AP-loss-related (allocative) transaction costs in any other way. It also renders valid (that is, consistent with its [other] assumptions) the original law and economics analysis's implicit assumption that any relevant private transaction costs that might be generated would equal their allocative counterparts. I will now explain each of these claims in turn.

To see why the original analysis's legal-claim transaction-cost conclusion follows from its otherwise-Pareto-perfect assumption, note that

1. if injurers, victims, judges, and juries are sovereign maximizers and the legal system makes it privately profitable for judges and juries to make legally correct decisions, no transaction costs will ever be generated by the making and processing of AP-loss-related tort-law claims in a negligence regime because, on these assumptions, no potential injurer will ever be negligent and no actual victims will ever bring an AP-loss-related tort-law claim; and
2. under strict liability, private transaction costs will be generated by AP-loss-related tort-law claiming because AP-loss claims will be valid.

To see why the original analysis's otherwise-Pareto-perfect assumption rules out the possibility that AP-loss contingencies might generate any transaction costs other than legal-claim transaction costs, note that this assumption rules out private tort-loss insurance and any tort-loss-related government-transfer programs. Obviously, the relevant analysis's otherwise-Pareto-perfect assumption also guarantees that private transaction costs will equal their allocative counterparts (for the same reason that it guarantees that all other private costs equal their allocative counterparts).

Of course, in reality, the economy is not otherwise-Pareto-perfect and, consequently, none of the above three conclusions is correct. Thus, for at least five reasons, AP-loss-related tort-law claims will be made, and legal-claim transaction costs will be generated in a negligence/contributory-negligence regime. First, some claims are made because potential injurers are sometimes negligent because they are not sovereign maximizers. Second, some claims are made because one or more of the tort-law-doctrine, claiming-process, and decision-making imperfections that Chapter 3 lists make it *ex ante* profitable for potential injurers to be negligent (a separate possibility if one defines a potential injurer's sovereignty to be compatible with his being uncertain about whether the various imperfections in tort-law doctrine, claiming processes, and decision making will actually eliminate or critically reduce his liability). Third, some claims are made because the private transaction costs that potential injurers must incur to defend a suit make it profitable for the potential injurer to pay off someone who is in fact making a nuisance claim. Fourth, some claims are made because potential injurers may be found negligent despite the fact that their behavior would not qualify as negligent under the Hand test: this result could obtain because the trier-of-fact made a simple mistake, because the trier-of-fact did not appreciate the stochastic character of due care, or because tort-law doctrine instructs the trier-of-fact to assume (often counterfactually) that the defendant was as able as the average member of the community to avoid the AP loss in question in an allocatively efficient way. Fifth, some claims are made because victims (or potential plaintiffs) are not sovereign maximizers.

Once one admits that legal claims will be made in a negligence/contributory-negligence regime, the traditional *a priori* argument for the conclusion that the shift from a negligence/contributory-negligence system to a strict-liability regime will increase the private transaction costs generated by legal claims will no longer be applicable. Instead, the analysis of the effect of such a shift on the private transactions costs generated by legal claims will have to include empirical investigations of the four ways in which it will affect such transaction costs.

First, one will have to analyze the way in which such a shift will increase legal transaction costs by changing the number and amount of valid claims. Unfortunately, the sign of this effect cannot be predicted on an *a priori* basis. On the one hand, the shift will increase the number and amount of valid claims by increasing the percentage of losses for which injurers are liable. On the other hand, the shift will also affect the number and amount of valid claims by changing the number and amount of losses that take place by increasing potential injurers' avoidance and decreasing potential victims' avoidance. Admittedly, although the preceding two conclusions imply that one cannot predict the effect of the shift in question on the number and amount of valid claims on an *a priori* basis, I am confident that the shift from negligence to strict liability will tend to increase legal transaction costs by increasing the number and amount of valid legal claims.

Second, one will have to examine the extent to which such a shift will tend to increase legal transaction costs by increasing the percentage of valid legal claims that are actually asserted both by reducing the transaction cost to victims of pursuing their claims and by making some more optimistic that justice will be done by eliminating a factual issue (negligence) that they may fear juries will resolve incorrectly against them.

Third, one will have to investigate the extent to which such a shift will tend to decrease legal transaction costs directly by decreasing the transaction cost of litigating or settling any relevant claim by making it unnecessary to try or discuss the negligence issue.

Fourth, one will have to study the uncertain effect that such a shift will have on legal transaction costs by influencing the percentage of claims that are settled. *Ceteris paribus,* legal transaction costs will tend to be lower if claims are settled as opposed to litigated. Unfortunately, one cannot predict the impact of a shift from a negligence/contributory-negligence system to a strict-liability regime on settlement rates on an *a priori* basis because such a shift will have offsetting effects on two of the major factors that economic theory predicts will determine whether a given dispute is settled as opposed to litigated. Assuming for simplicity that neither party expects to obtain any strategic gains or suffer any strategic losses from the litigation of the dispute in question (for example, that no favorable or unfavorable legal precedent will be set at trial, that no effective method of proof or argument will be revealed, and that the relevant parties' negotiating reputations will be unaffected), maximizing sovereigns will settle whenever the joint savings that settlement will generate for them by obviating litigation (which is more transaction costly than are settlement negotiations) exceed any positive difference between the weighted-average-expected amount the plaintiff expects to obtain at trial and the weighted-averaged-expected sum the defendant believes the plaintiff will be awarded. A shift from a negligence/contributory-negligence system to a strict-liability regime will have an uncertain effect on the probability that this condition will be satisfied because it will simultaneously decrease the joint transaction-cost savings that settlement will generate (because the negligence issue will be more expensive to litigate than to discuss during settlement negotiations in both mechanical and risk-cost terms) and decrease the likely extent to which defendants and plaintiffs disagree about trial-outcomes (because defendants and plaintiffs will probably both tend to be unduly optimistic about the resolution of both the negligence issue and all other relevant issues).

The preceding analyses imply that the effect of a shift from negligence to strict liability on legal transaction costs cannot be predicted on an *a priori* basis. Although my intuition is that shifts to strict liability will increase legal transaction costs, the more I speculate about this issue, the less certain I become. Certainly, it would be TBLE to do far more research on the various empirical issues this question implicates. Nevertheless, the following analysis will assume that a shift from a negligence/contributory-negligence regime to a strict-liability system will increase legal-claim private transaction costs.

More recent law and economics analyses of the allocative efficiency of a shift from a negligence/contributory regime to a strict-liability system (and of various other tort-law-doctrine issues) do acknowledge the obvious reality that under a negligence/contributory-negligence regime some tort cases will be brought and some legal-claim private transaction costs will be generated.[29] Unfortunately, these analyses do not properly appreciate all the various ways in which the doctrinal shift on which this subsection focuses (and various other doctrines as well) would affect the amount of legal-claim private transaction costs that will be generated. Still, as I have just indicated, I agree with their conclusion that a shift to strict liability will increase legal-claim private transaction costs.

However, the more modern literature still does not acknowledge that a shift to strict liability will affect total private transaction costs in ways other than by affecting legal-claim private transaction costs or that private transaction costs and therefore private-transaction-cost effects may diverge from their allocative counterparts. I will now discuss each of these issues in turn.

First, a shift from a negligence/contributory-negligence to a strict-liability tort-liability regime will clearly affect the private transaction costs generated by AP-loss insurance and government transfers. To the extent that the shift in question would reduce the number of first-party insurance policies that potential AP-loss victims take out by more than they increase the number of tort-liability insurance policies that potential AP-loss injurers take out, it may reduce the amount of transaction costs that insurance contracting generates (though, of course, ultimately, the more relevant effect is the allocative efficiency of any associated change in insurance contracting). Similarly, to the extent that the relevant shift reduces the number and amount of medical-care, disability, unemployment, and welfare claims the government must process and pay by enabling the relevant victims to collect from their injurers and perhaps to finance their timely participation in rehabilitation programs that reduce the probability of their being dependent on state help, the shift may reduce the transaction costs generated by the relevant government-transfer programs.

Although I suspect that a shift from a negligence/contributory-negligence to a strict-liability regime will reduce both insurance-related transaction costs and government-transfer-related transaction costs, I have no sense of the magnitude of these two impacts. Still, these possibilities almost certainly reduce the amount by which the shift in question increases all types of transaction costs combined.

Finally, three points about the relationship between the private and allocative transaction costs that are generated in connection with AP-loss contingencies. First, just as monopoly distorts (I suspect, deflates) the private cost of all other types of resource uses, it distorts the private-transaction-cost consequences of a shift to strict liability. Thus, if monopoly deflates private transaction costs, a shift that increases (decreases) the private transaction costs in question by $X will increase (decrease) the allocative transaction costs in question by more than $X.

The second and third points assume that the relevant allocative transaction costs include the misallocation that governments will cause to finance any related transfer payments. The second point turns on the fact (assumption) that a shift to strict liability will have a non-zero net impact on the amount of transaction costs the government incurs for which it does not receive full compensation. On the one hand, a shift to strict liability will increase the net transaction cost to the government of supplying judicial and court services by increasing the amount of such services it must supply (assuming that, as is presently the case in the United States, the parties to a litigation are not required to pay the full, conventionally calculated dollar cost to the government of supplying the court services they receive). On the other hand, a shift from negligence to strict liability will probably reduce the transaction cost to the government of its various transfer-programs by reducing the number of AP-loss-related transfer-claims made to the government and concomitantly the transaction cost of handling all AP-loss-related transfer-claims.

The second point is that the allocative cost associated with these uncompensated transaction costs exceeds its private counterpart not only for the reasons previously discussed but also because the government will tend *ceteris paribus* to misallocate resources when it finances the net fiscal loss in question. Certainly, this conclusion will be warranted if the government finances this fiscal loss by raising taxes on the margin of income or by taking steps that increase inflation. It will also be warranted if the government finances this fiscal loss by cutting or eliminating other expenditures that would have been allocatively efficient.

The third point relates to the tendency of a shift to strict liability to reduce the amount of AP-loss-related transfer-payments that the government must make. This reduction in transfer-payments should not be considered to be a transaction-cost saving: in itself, the substitution of tort damage-awards for government transfer-payments has no impact on allocative efficiency.

In short, the first-best character of the original law and economics analyses of the transaction-cost consequences of shifting from a negligence/contributory-negligence to a strict-liability tort-liability regime rendered their treatment of the effect of the shift on legal-claim private transaction costs irrelevant and prevented the analysts from appreciating (1) that the shift in question would also affect the transaction costs generated by AP-loss-related private insurance and government transfers and (2) that all relevant private transaction costs and private-transaction-cost effects are likely to differ from their allocative counterparts. Although more recent work has done a somewhat better job of analyzing the relevant shift's likely impact on legal-claim private transaction costs, the relevant scholars' continuing inclination to make otherwise-Pareto-perfect assumptions has prevented them from recognizing that the shift in question will affect other sorts of transaction costs than legal-claim transaction costs or from appreciating the fact that the shift's impact on allocative transaction costs is likely to be different from its impact on private transaction costs.

(ii) The Traditional Law and Economics Analysis of the Impact of Such a Shift to Strict Liability on the Amount of Misallocation Generated by the Economically Inefficient Avoidance Decisions of Potential Injurers and Potential Victims

The traditional law and economics analysis of the impact of a shift from a negligence/contributory-negligence to a strict-liability tort-liability regime on avoidance-decision misallocation has three major deficiencies. One is its first-best character. However, before explaining the basis of this criticism and the way in which this deficiency affects the traditional analysis's conclusions, I want to discuss the other two shortcomings of the traditional law and economics approach to this issue.

The first of these additional deficiencies relates to the assumptions the traditional analysis makes about the set of avoidance moves whose rejection is in practice assessed for negligence (or implicitly [see below] contributory negligence). The earliest law and economics scholarship on the allocative efficiency of a shift from a negligence/contributory-negligence regime to a strict-liability system implicitly assumed that, under a negligence/contributory-negligence regime, the rejection of all types of avoidance moves would be assessed for negligence or contributory negligence. In 1980, Steven Shavell wrote an important article[30] that pointed out that this assumption is incorrect in that refusals by tort-loss cogenerators to avoid by reducing their activity levels (in particular, by producers to reduce their unit outputs and, by extension, by drivers to reduce the amount they drove and by pedestrians to reduce the amount they walked) are not in practice ever assessed for negligence. Although economists and law and economics scholars now take this doctrinal or doctrine-application reality into account when assessing the effect of a shift from a negligence/contributory-negligence regime to a strict-liability system on the amount of misallocation generated by the economically inefficient avoidance decisions of potential injurers and potential victims (or assessing the allocative efficiency of any other doctrine or policy to whose allocative efficiency it is relevant), they continue to ignore the fact that activity-level reductions are not the only type of avoidance move whose rejection is never assessed for negligence. Thus, as Chapter 3 points out, decisions by manufacturers not to reduce the AP losses they generate by shifting their locations, by changing the product variants they produce, or by doing research into less-AP-loss-prone production processes, locations, or product variants are never in practice assessed for negligence; decisions by car drivers not to reduce the accident losses they cause by driving cars that are more brightly colored, cheaper, lighter in weight, or equipped with bumpers of standard height or by taking routes or driving at times or in weather in which they are less likely to be victims of other drivers' negligence or their own and other drivers' bad luck are never assessed for negligence or contributory negligence; and decisions by pedestrians not to reduce the accident losses they generate by wearing brighter clothing or taking (lawful) routes or walking at times or in weather in which they are less likely to be victims of driver negligence or bad luck are never in practice assessed for contributory negligence.

The second deficiency of the standard law and economics analysis of the shift on which we are now focusing that has nothing to do with second-best theory is that, in practice, virtually all analysts of the impact of the relevant shift to strict liability on the misallocation generated by the economically inefficient avoidance decisions of potential injurers and potential victims have focused exclusively on its impact on the misallocation that potential injurers' economically inefficient avoidance decisions generate—that is, have ignored the fact that at the same time that the shift in question reduces the misallocation that potential injurers' avoidance decisions generate by making potential injurers liable for any losses they generate by rejecting avoidance moves whose rejection was negligent and therefore presumptively allocatively inefficient but whose rejection would not in practice be assessed for negligence (or would in practice be misassessed to be not negligent), it will increase the amount of misallocation that potential victims generate by rejecting allocatively efficient avoidance moves both (1) by relieving the victims of the loss they would otherwise suffer by rejecting avoidance moves whose rejection would be contributorily negligent and would be found to be contributory negligence in circumstances in which the injurer would otherwise be liable because he would be found negligent and (2) by deflating their incentives to make allocatively efficient avoidance moves of any type (inflating the profitability of rejecting avoidance moves of all types) by enabling them to recover any loss they initially suffer because they have rejected an avoidance move made relevant by an injurer's conduct from an injurer who would not have been found liable in a negligence regime because he was not negligent, because his rejection of the avoidance moves he negligently rejected would not in practice be assessed for negligence, or because his negligent rejection of some avoidance move would be misassessed as being not negligent.

I have already mentioned the third deficiency of the standard law and economics analysis of the impact of a shift from a negligence/contributory-negligence regime to a strict-liability system on the amount of misallocation generated by economically inefficient avoidance decisions—its first-best character (that is, its assumption that the legal system and broader economy contain no Pareto imperfection other than the standard of liability that would individually distort the profit yield of any potential injurer's or potential victim's avoidance decision). Chapter 3 lists a huge number of (1) tort-claim-process-related realities, (2) tort-doctrine imperfections, and (3) Pareto imperfections that are not generated by either of the preceding two realities that would individually distort the profit yield of avoidance of any type to potential injurers and/or potential victims in an otherwise-Pareto-perfect economy and that will cancel each other out only rarely and fortuitously.

Chapter 3 also makes strong arguments for three conclusions that imply that the standard analysis's otherwise-Pareto-perfect assumption (that is, first-best character) will cause it to underestimate the amount by which the relevant shift to strict liability will reduce the amount of misallocation generated by economically inefficient avoidance moves—an error that may critically affect the analysis's assessment of the overall allocative-efficiency of such a shift, given its (contestable) conclusion that the shift in question will increase (allocative) transaction costs. First, Chapter 3 explains why the other imperfections in the system almost certainly would deflate the profit yield of both injurer-avoidance and victim-avoidance if the liability of co-generators of tort losses were governed by a negligence/contributory-negligence regime.[31] Second, by explaining why a shift from a negligence/contributory-negligence to a strict-liability/contributory-negligence regime would almost certainly decrease the negative distortion in the profits injurers would obtain by avoiding and would increase the negative distortion in the profits victims would obtain by avoiding, Chapter 3 provides sound reasons for concluding that a shift from a negligence/contributory-negligence tort-regime to a tort regime of strict liability without contributory negligence would affect the distortion in these profit yields in the same direction as the shift it investigated: indeed, if anything, the shift to a strict-liability regime that does not include a contributory-negligence doctrine will tend to generate an even larger decrease in the negative distortion in the profits injurers would obtain by avoiding (because it eliminates the negative distortion in those profits generated by the possibility that the injurer's victim will be barred from recovery by his contributory negligence) and will tend to generate an even larger increase in the negative distortion in the profits victims would obtain by avoiding (at least when the avoidance move in question is a type whose rejection would have been assessed for contributory negligence). Third, Chapter 3 points out that if one makes what seem to me to be plausible assumptions about the frequency with which potential injurers and potential victims can make allocatively efficient avoidance moves and about the frequency with which allocatively efficient avoidance moves would increase allocative efficiency by different amounts (roughly speaking, that potential injurers are more likely to be able to engage in allocatively efficient avoidance than are potential victims and that the distributions of allocatively efficient potential-injurer and potential-victim avoidance moves in a diagram in which the allocative efficiency of the moves in question is measured along the horizontal axis and the number of moves of given allocative efficiency is measured along the vertical axis are relatively flat over the relevant ranges) and recognizes that the allocative-efficiency gain that is generated by a given decrease in the negative distortion in the profitability of a choice when that decrease critically affects the profitability of the choice will increase with the absolute value of the original distortion in the choice's profitability (and, admittedly, that the allocative-efficiency loss that is generated by a given increase in the negative distortion in the profitability of a choice when that increase critically affects the profitability of the choice will increase with the absolute value of the original distortion in the choice's profitability), it becomes clear that the negative distortions in the profit yields of potential-injurer and potential-victim avoidance moves that are caused by the interaction of the various imperfections the standard analysis ignores increase the amount by which a shift from a negligence/contributory-negligence regime to a conventional strict-liability system will reduce avoidance-decision misallocation (increase the amount by which the shift decreases potential-injurer avoidance-decision misallocation by more than it increases the amount by which the shift increases potential-victim avoidance-decision misallocation).

In short, in my judgment, the failure of the conventional analysis to take account of the other imperfections the economy and legal system contain causes it to underestimate the amount by which a shift from a negligence/contributory-negligence to a conventional strict-liability tort-liability regime will reduce avoidance-decision misallocation. If the conventional analysis's contestable conclusion that this shift will increase (allocative) transaction costs were correct, its first-best character would critically affect its assessment of the overall allocatively inefficiency of the shift in question—that is, would cause the relevant analysts to conclude that such a shift would be allocatively inefficient when it would actually be allocatively efficient.

The Allocative Efficiency of Making Scope-of-Liability (Proximate-Cause) Determinations Depend on Whether the Injurer Is Strictly Liable or Liable Solely for the Consequences of His Found Negligence: A Critique of Shavell's Second-Best-Type "Crushing Liability" Argument

Injurers who would otherwise be liable for an accident or pollution loss they caused are sometimes relieved of liability on scope-of-liability (proximate-cause) grounds—that is, on the ground that in some sense their choice was not sufficiently connected to the loss to make them legally responsible for it. In practice, the probability that a court will relieve an injurer of liability on this ground is inversely related to the size of the loss, the *ex ante* probability of its occurrence, and the foreseeability of the loss.

In 1980, Steven Shavell wrote a canonical article on the economic efficiency of the scope-of-liability doctrine.[32] In addition to describing the way in which the courts have applied the doctrine, Shavell lists the types of misallocation whose magnitude the doctrine affects, analyzes the doctrine's likely effect on transaction costs, investigates whether the courts' treatment of the factors they consider to be relevant to a loss's falling within an injurer's scope of liability is allocatively efficient, and argues (in effect) that the common law's failure to adopt a proportionate-liability approach to cases in which cause-in-fact must be inferred (if it is to be inferred at all) from the contribution that each possible injurer's activity made to the *ex ante* probability of the loss's occurring justifies the conclusion that, everything considered, the fact that an injurer is strictly liable (as opposed to being liable solely for the consequences of his found negligence) favors the allocative efficiency of dismissing cases against the injurer in question on scope-of-liability grounds.

The text of this subsection delineates and criticizes Shavell's analysis of and conclusion about the first, third, and fourth of these issues. Because my criticisms of Shavell's analysis of the allocative efficiency of the courts' conclusions about the relevance of the size, probability, and foreseeability of a loss to whether it falls within the injurer's scope of liability are unrelated to second-best theory or the tendency of economists to underestimate the number of ways that resources are used, they are presented in note 36.

SHAVELL'S CLAIMS ABOUT THE TYPES OF MISALLOCATION WHOSE MAGNITUDES SCOPE-OF-LIABILITY DISMISSALS WILL AFFECT

Shavell claims that scope-of-liability dismissals will affect three types of misallocation: (1) allocative transaction costs (which, for this purpose, in common with the traditional analysis, I am considering to be a type of misallocation), (2) the misallocation caused by potential injurers' economically inefficient avoidance decisions, and (3) the misallocation caused by potential victims' economically inefficient avoidance decisions. More specifically, Shavell believes that proximate-cause dismissals will reduce (allocative) transaction costs, increase the amount of misallocation that potential injurers' economically inefficient avoidance decisions generate, and decrease the amount of misallocation that potential victims' economically inefficient avoidance decisions generate. The next two subsections focus on Shavell's analysis of the impact of scope-of-liability dismissals on the first two types of misallocation just listed.[33]

SHAVELL'S ANALYSIS OF AND CONCLUSIONS ABOUT THE IMPACT OF THE SCOPE-OF-LIABILITY DOCTRINE ON (ALLOCATIVE) TRANSACTION COSTS

Although Shavell does recognize that in individual cases a scope-of-liability doctrine could increase the transaction cost[34] of litigating a case, he regards this as "an unlikely possibility"[35] and is confident that across all cases the doctrine will reduce legal-claim transaction costs (and, he seems to assume, overall transaction costs). I have four objections to Shavell's analysis of this transaction-cost-impact issue. First, Shavell's conclusion that scope-of-liability dismissals are highly likely to reduce legal-claim transaction costs seems to be based on a misunderstanding of the way in which tort trials are structured. Shavell seems to be assuming that the proximate-cause issue will be tried and resolved first—before any evidence is introduced on cause-in-fact, negligence, contributory negligence, or damages—and concomitantly that if the case is decided on proximate-cause grounds those other issues will not have to be litigated. At present, except in what I assume is the rare instance in which the trial judge grants the defendant a summary judgment on the ground that no reasonable trier-of-fact could conclude that the defendant's choice was a proximate cause of the victim's loss, the scope-of-liability issue is decided after all the other issues are tried. Rather than reducing transaction costs by obviating the litigation of the causation, negligence, contributory negligence, and damages issues, the doctrine increases transaction costs when the actual doctrine makes relevant facts that would not otherwise have to be established (as it often will in strict-liability cases) and/or when the proximate-cause issue is raised but resolved in the plaintiff's favor (though, admittedly, the doctrine may reduce transaction costs by obviating the trier-of-fact's resolving the causation, negligence, contributory-negligence, and/or damages issues if the relevant trier-of-fact concludes that the case can be decided on proximate-cause grounds before fully addressing the other issues that would otherwise have to be considered).

Second, although my judgment on this issue is certainly contestable, I think that, even if the scope-of-liability issue were tried and resolved before any other issue, the probability that the doctrine would increase the transaction cost of litigating given cases is far higher than Shavell suggests. Even on the above counterfactual assumption, the scope-of-liability doctrine will increase the transaction cost of litigating a particular case in two sets of circumstances: (1) when the scope-of-liability issue is resolved in the plaintiff's favor and factual determinations must be made to resolve this issue that would not otherwise have to be made and/or (2) when the scope-of-liability issue is resolved in the defendant's favor but its resolution is more transaction costly than the resolution of all the other issues (cause-in-fact, negligence, contributory negligence, damages, and so on) whose litigation and resolution (we are assuming counterfactually) the scope-of-liability dismissal obviates. The first of these sets of conditions is often fulfilled in both negligence and strict-liability cases, and the second is frequently fulfilled in strict-liability cases (though, admittedly, these conclusions reflect various unarticulated assumptions I am making about the facts the courts deem relevant to the resolution of the scope-of-liability issue).[36]

Third, Shavell ignores the fact that the scope-of-liability doctrine affects legal-claim transaction costs by changing the percentage of claims that are settled in a direction that cannot be predicted through *a priori* argument. Two effects are relevant in this connection:

1. the doctrine tends to decrease the settlement rate by adding another issue to the litigation on whose resolution both parties tend to be too optimistic—that is, by increasing the amount by which the tort injurer's and tort victim's estimates of the weighted-average-expected trial-outcome differ; and
2. the doctrine also affects the settlement rate by changing the positive difference between the transaction cost of litigating and the transaction cost of settling—namely, will decrease the settlement rate if (as Shavell supposes) it decreases this difference but will increase the settlement rate if (as I believe) it increases this difference.

Fourth, just as the traditional analysis of the impact of a shift from negligence to strict liability on total transaction costs ignores its impact on the transaction costs generated when people enquire about tort insurance, take out tort-loss-related insurance policies, make and resolve tort-loss-related insurance claims, and make and process tort-loss-related government-transfer claims (as well as on the misallocation the government causes when financing its consideration and payment of tort-loss-related transfer-claims), Shavell also assumes that the only type of transaction costs the proximate-cause doctrine will affect are legal-claim transaction costs.

I would want to obtain a considerable amount of information about a variety of different factual issues before reaching any final conclusion about the impact of the scope-of-liability doctrine on allocative transaction costs. Given the way in which trials are currently structured, I suspect that the doctrine will increase, not decrease, total allocative transaction costs. But even if this judgment is premature, I am certain that Shavell's conclusion that the doctrine is "highly unlikely" to increase (allocative) transaction costs is unjustified and inaccurate.

Shavell's Implicitly-Second-Best-Type Argument for the Allocative Efficiency of Counting the Fact That an Injurer Is Strictly Liable as Opposed to Being Liable (If at All and at Most) for the Consequences of His Found Negligence in Favor of Deciding a Tort Suit for the Injurer on Scope-of-Liability Grounds

Shavell did not use second-best terminology to describe his argument for the allocative efficiency of making the standard of injurer liability a determinant of whether a loss the relevant legal system concluded the injurer caused should be placed within the scope of his liability. However, his argument for doing so is one of the few second-best-type arguments in the law and economics literature. Shavell's argument can be outlined in the following second-best-theory-oriented way. First, the common law of torts holds a possible injurer liable only if the victim can demonstrate that, more probably than not, the defendant was the cause-in-fact of his loss.[37] Second, in some cases, this causation issue must be resolved by determining whether the defendant's (henceforth, the putative injurer's) activity contributed more than 50 percent of the *ex ante* probability of the occurrence of the loss that actually did eventuate.[38] Third, in such cases, the common law's binary approach to cause-in-fact will inflate the profits that a putative injurer who would be held liable for a loss if found to be its cause-in-fact can obtain by reducing his activity's contribution to the *ex ante* probability of the loss's occurring from above 50 percent to 50 percent or less than 50 percent.[39] Fourth, in some cases in which the common law's cause-in-fact requirement—its commitment to a binary approach to cause-in-fact—inflates the profits a potential injurer can earn by avoiding, it will cause misallocation by rendering profitable an allocatively inefficient avoidance move. Fifth, this outcome is far more likely when the putative injurer is strictly liable than when he is liable only for the consequences of his found negligence: when the potential injurer is strictly liable, absent a scope-of-liability doctrine, he will be liable for all losses he is found to have caused, including all losses he could have prevented only by making avoidance moves that would be allocatively inefficient on otherwise-Pareto-perfect assumptions; when the potential injurer's liability is governed by a negligence/contributory-negligence system, he will be liable for failing to prevent losses he is found to have caused by rejecting avoidance moves whose execution would have been allocatively inefficient in an otherwise-Pareto-perfect economy only if his rejection of the move in question is incorrectly found to have been negligent and his victim is not found to have been contributorily negligent. Sixth, one way to reduce the amount of avoidance-decision misallocation caused by a doctrine that is not first-best allocatively efficient and that inflates the profitability of avoidance is to introduce a second doctrine that is not first-best allocatively efficient that would deflate the profitability of avoidance in an otherwise-Pareto-perfect economy and that will reduce the aggregate distortion in the profits avoidance will yield the avoider in a world in which the first "imperfect" doctrine is still present. Seventh, the scope-of-liability doctrine is a Pareto-imperfect doctrine that deflates the profits a potential injurer can secure by avoiding. Eighth, the impact of the scope-of-liability doctrine on the amount of misallocation potential injurers' economically inefficient avoidance decisions generate will be favorable (or less unfavorable) when the potential injurer is strictly liable than when he is liable (if at all and at most) only for the consequences of his found negligence because the law's approach to cause-in-fact is more likely to inflate the profitability of avoiding to strictly liable injurers than to injurers who are liable (if at all and at most) only for the consequences of their found negligence. Therefore, ninth, everything considered, allocative efficiency will be promoted by counting in favor of a scope-of-liability dismissal the fact that the putative injurer in question is strictly liable as opposed to being liable (if at all and at most) for the found consequences of his found negligence.

I do not like criticizing this argument. Although I would have preferred Shavell to have articulated his position in the explicitly-second-best-theory-oriented way I have just done, he deserves credit for having made this type of argument even in the terms he used to express it. Still, although Shavell's recognition that (1) the shift from negligence to strict liability affects the aggregate distortion in the profits that potential injurers can obtain by avoiding and (2) this impact of the shift in liability standard will affect the impact that the scope-of-liability doctrine has on the amount of misallocation potential injurers generate by making economically inefficient avoidance decisions are both steps in the right direction, the "everything considered" part of the ninth step of the argument I articulated and Shavell makes (though not in these words) is not only unwarranted by the rest of his argument but also totally unjustified in fact.

Shavell writes as if the only difference between strict-liability and negligence/contributory-negligence regimes that is relevant to the impact of the scope-of-liability doctrine on the amount of misallocation generated by potential injurers' economically inefficient avoidance decisions is the fact that the relevant injurers' avoidance incentives will be more likely to be inflated by the law's binary approach to cause-in-fact if the injurer is strictly liable than if he is liable (if at all and at most) for the consequences of his found negligence. In fact, empirically, the impact that the liability rule has on $\Sigma D(P\pi_{APLA})$ for potential injurers through its effect on the distortion in the profits they can earn by avoiding that is caused by the common law's binary conception of causation is almost certainly far less significant than the impact that a shift from negligence to strict liability has on $\Sigma D(P\pi_{APLA})$ for potential injurers for other reasons that are relevant far more often—*inter alia,* by eliminating the deflation in $\Sigma D(P\pi_{APLA})$ that is generated by the fact that the rejection of some types of avoidance moves is never assessed for negligence, by eliminating the deflation in $\Sigma D(P\pi_{APLA})$ for potential injurers that is generated by the possibility of false-negative findings on negligence, by reducing the deflation in $\Sigma D(P\pi_{APLA})$ for potential injurers caused by the failure of legally entitled victims to sue by decreasing the percentage of cases in which potential injurers who rejected avoidance moves whose Bs were less than their $\downarrow$(PL)s and whose rejection is assessed for negligence are not sued because of the transaction cost of suing or the victim's belief that he would not be treated fairly (by reducing the transaction cost of litigating and eliminating two issues [negligence and contributory negligence] on which a mistake could be made), by decreasing the deflation in $\Sigma D(P\pi_{APLA})$ for potential injurers caused by the prospect that entitled victims would settle for less than they would get at trial (by reducing the transaction cost of litigating and reducing the riskiness of litigation), by eliminating the deflation in $\Sigma D(P\pi_{APLA})$ for potential injurers caused by the possibility that the victim's recovery will be eliminated or reduced by his actual or found contributory negligence, and by increasing the deflation in $\Sigma D(P\pi_{APLA})$ generated by the tendency of triers-of-fact to award damages that do not fully compensate legally entitled victims (by militating against or preventing plaintiffs' lawyers from introducing evidence of injurer-wrongdoing).

Two conclusions, therefore, seem justified. First, a TBLE analysis of the way in which the standard of injurer liability affects the impact of scope-of-liability dismissals on the amount of misallocation that the economically inefficient avoidance decisions of potential injurers generate is far more complicated than Shavell's analysis acknowledges—would involve the consideration of a large number of ways that the standard of liability will affect $\Sigma D(P\pi_{APLA})$ for potential injurers that Shavell fails to take into account. Second, Shavell's failure to consider the other imperfections that distort the profits that potential injurers can realize by avoiding in a strict-liability and/or negligence regime seems likely to have led him to reach a false conclusion about whether strict liability favors or disfavors the allocative efficiency of scope-of-liability dismissals. At this juncture, the first point should be self-evident. The second point can be derived from various conclusions Chapter 3 establishes. Thus, the argument that Chapter 3 makes for the conclusion that the shift from a negligence/contributory-negligence to a strict-liability/contributory-negligence regime will increase the amount of misallocation that potential injurers generate by making economically inefficient avoidance decisions by more than it decreases the amount of a misallocation that potential victims generate by making economically inefficient avoidance decisions implies *a fortiori* that the scope-of-liability doctrine will increase the sum of the amounts of misallocation that potential injurers and potential victims generate by making economically inefficient avoidance decisions by more when the injurer is strictly liable and does not have the option of escaping liability by establishing the victim's contributory negligence than when the injurer's liability would be determined under a negligence/contributory-negligence regime if he were found to be the legal cause of the victim's loss. Moreover, since if anything scope-of-liability dismissals will reduce legal-claim allocative transaction costs by less and increase government-transfer allocative transaction costs and government-transfer-finance-related misallocation by more when the injurer is strictly liable than when his liability is governed by a negligence/contributory-negligence system, the arguments of Chapter 3 also imply that, all things considered, the scope-of-liability doctrine will be more allocatively inefficient when the injurer is strictly liable than when it is combined with a negligence/contributory-negligence tort-liability regime.

To repeat: this subsection has two central points: (1) although Shavell should be praised for making a second-best-type argument for his conclusion that strict liability counts in favor of the allocative efficiency of scope-of-liability dismissals, the second-best-style analysis he executed is far from third-best allocatively efficient in that it ignores a wide range of additional imperfections that are relevant to his conclusion, and (2) Shavell's failure to consider these additional imperfections not only prevents his analysis from justifying the conclusion he claims to have established but also leads him to reach a conclusion that seems likely to be wrong. Even if partial moves toward TBLE analysis are steps in the right direction, analyses that ignore many but not all nontarget imperfections cannot justify conclusions that do not make reference to these omissions and may well generate conclusions that are seriously wrong.

The Allocative Efficiency of the Alleged Common-Law Practice of Making Members of an Industry Strictly Liable in Tort When the Industry Is in Its Infancy and Liable Only If Negligent When It Is Mature

In 1981, William Landes and Richard Posner contributed an article, "The Positive Economic Theory of Tort Law," to a symposium titled *Modern Tort Theory.*[40] In this article, Landes and Posner argue, *inter alia,* that their hypothesis that the common law is allocatively efficient is supported by the purported fact that the common law holds members of a given industry strictly liable when the industry is in its infancy and liable only if found negligent when it is mature.[41] This subsection states and criticizes the argument Landes and Posner made to support their conclusion that the legal practice they describe is allocatively efficient as well as the conclusion itself.

Landes and Posner make the following survival-related argument for their claim that it is allocatively efficient to make members of an industry strictly liable when the industry is in its infancy and liable only if negligent when it is mature:

> During the early stages of development of a new product or activity, we lack sufficient experience to determine whether the benefits of the product exceed its full costs including costs to third parties (*e.g.,* property owners who suffer ground damage from airplane crashes). One way to gather such information is to hold the producer or user strictly liable for accidents to third parties resulting from the activity. Strict liability forces the innovator to internalize all the costs of his activity. If the activity still flourishes in spite of a strict liability standard, we can be confident that its benefits exceed its full costs or, equivalently, that eliminating or greatly reducing the new activity would not be optimal. At this point the argument in favor of strict liability weakens. Experience already has demonstrated that the activity's

benefits exceed its full costs, and society is now being burdened with the greater administrative costs associated with an increasing number of claims brought about by the growth of the activity. We would predict, therefore, a shift toward negligence and away from strict liability as a new industry or activity matures.[42]

This survival argument suffers from five deficiencies. I will start with the two that are the standard deficiencies of economics and law and economics allocative-efficiency analyses on which this chapter has focused. First, Landes and Posner's argument is a first-best argument—that is, it assumes that the profitability and allocative efficiency of new activities (indeed, of all activities) will be equal to each other if the AP losses they impose on others are fully internalized by tort law (or, at least, that other Pareto imperfections will never critically distort the profitability of an enterprise). In so doing, Landes and Posner's argument ignores the wide variety of other imperfections that distort the profitability of activities—most importantly, monopoly imperfections, tax imperfections, the externalities that would otherwise have been generated by the resource uses from which the new activity withdraws the resources it consumes, and the external benefits associated with any knowledge created by the new activity (which may be negative if innovation law overinternalizes what would otherwise be the relevant external benefits). One simply cannot assume that the fact that an infant industry has survived despite the fact that its members had to pay all the AP losses they generated (*inter alia,* because they were strictly liable for these costs) demonstrates the allocative efficiency of the industry's survival or creation. Nor can one assume that the death of an infant industry in these circumstances demonstrates the allocative inefficiency of its survival or creation.

Second, Landes and Posner's argument focuses on only one of the types of avoidance moves that may be allocatively efficient for potential injurers to make—namely, the decision of a potential injurer to exit (to reduce its output to zero). Landes and Posner completely ignore the possibilities that both in an industry's infancy and in its maturity a shift from negligence to strict liability may reduce the amount of misallocation an industry's members' economically inefficient avoidance decisions generate by inducing them to reduce their unit outputs without going out of business altogether, to change their locations, to change the product variants they produce, and to do research into less-AP-loss-prone production processes, locations, and product variants and put their discoveries to use. This omission is a variant of the failure of standard allocative-efficiency analyses to take account of the impact of the policies under scrutiny on most of the types of resource misallocation whose magnitudes they affect. I do not know whether a shift from negligence to strict liability will be more likely to increase allocative efficiency by inducing an industry's members to avoid by reducing without eliminating their unit outputs, by changing their locations, by changing the product variant they produce, or by doing and adopting the results of additional AP-loss-reducing research when the industry is in its infancy than when it is mature. My point is not that these possibilities disfavor Landes and Posner's conclusion or even that I know how they will cut[43] but that they are sufficiently likely to affect Landes and Posner's conclusion for their consideration to be third-best allocatively efficient.

The next three deficiencies of Landes and Posner's argument do not relate to this chapter's central themes, though the obviousness of the errors in question do raise questions about why these highly intelligent scholars made them. The third objection is that even if an investment's lifetime profits always equaled its lifetime allocative efficiency, one could not assume that the fact that an infant industry survived strict liability demonstrates the allocative efficiency of its survival because the members of the infant industry may have been willing to accept losses during their industry's infancy in order to obtain the gains that they would secure in their industry's maturity when the shift from strict liability to negligence enabled them to avoid compensating the victims of some of the AP losses they generated (when there is an advantage to entering sooner rather than later).

The fourth objection to Landes and Posner's argument is that, even if Landes and Posner were correct in arguing that the fact that an infant industry survived the imposition of strict liability demonstrated the allocative efficiency of its survival, this would prove that strict liability would not be able to increase allocative efficiency by eliminating allocatively inefficient mature industries only if the relevant conditions were the same in the industry in its mature and infant stages. Once one recognizes that the relevant *ceteris* may not be *paribus*—for example, that an industry's products may become less attractive to consumers over time, that its non-AP-loss allocative costs may rise over time, or that the pollution or accidents it causes may become more costly over time (because of population growth, population shifts, or changes in the polluting activities of others), it becomes clear that strict liability may not only increase allocative efficiency by eliminating a mature industry whose survival through its infancy was allocatively efficient but may be as likely to do so as it was originally likely to increase allocative efficiency by preventing the industry's foundation or eliminating it in its infancy. In particular, strict liability will be as likely to lead to the allocatively efficient destruction of a mature industry as it will be to cause the allocatively efficient prevention of the creation of a new industry or destruction of that industry in its infancy if the percentage of mature industries that experience changes that make their operation allocatively inefficient despite the fact that they were allocatively efficient in their infancy is as high as the percentage of infant industries whose infancy is allocatively inefficient.

The fifth and final objection to Landes and Posner's survival-related argument is that, even if it established the allocative inefficiency of making members of mature industries strictly liable, this fact would not establish the allocative efficiency of the alleged common-law pattern of making members of an industry strictly liable when it is in its infancy and liable only if found negligent when it is mature (and hence confirm their hypothesis that the common law is economically efficient) because it would not establish the allocative efficiency either of making members of mature industries liable only if negligent as opposed to not liable at all or members of infant industries strictly liable rather than liable only if found negligent, liable under other conditions, or not liable at all. This objection reflects the tendency of injurer liability to increase both allocative transaction costs and the amount of misallocation that potential victims generate by making economically inefficient avoidance decisions.

In fact, even if Landes and Posner's actual argument were replaced with a correct argument of the type they were trying to make, it would not establish the allocative efficiency of the way in which Landes and Posner claim the common law changes the standard of liability it imposes on the members of a given industry through time or, concomitantly, confirm their general hypothesis that the common law is economically efficient. At best, the type of argument Landes and Posner were trying to make could establish that the overall allocative efficiency of strict liability relative to that of negligence is greater in an industry in its infancy than in its mature stage of development. That fact would not establish the allocative efficiency of the common law's alleged tendency to make members of an industry strictly liable when the industry is in its infancy and liable only if found negligent when the industry is mature because it is fully consistent with

1. negligence being more allocatively efficient than strict liability both when an industry is in its infancy and when it is mature;
2. strict liability being more allocative efficient than negligence both when an industry is in its infancy and when it is mature; and
3. some standard of liability other than either strict liability or negligence (for example, strict liability *plus* contributory negligence) being more allocatively efficient than either of those standards when an industry is in its infancy and/or when an industry is mature.

As I have already suggested, Landes and Posner's claims that (1) common-law courts hold the members of a given industry strictly liable when the industry is in its infancy but liable only if found negligent when it is mature and (2) this (alleged) judicial practice is economically efficient are important because (if correct) they would support Landes and Posner's more general claim that (in some sense) the common law is economically efficient. I want to close this discussion by pointing out that even if (1) Landes and Posner's description of the relevant judicial practice were correct and (2) a legal system that was required to apply the same standard of liability to all infant industries and the same standard of liability to all mature industries (which may or may not be identical to the standard applied to infant industries) would find it most allocatively efficient to apply a strict-liability tort-liability regime to all infant industries and a negligence/contributory-negligence tort-liability regime to all mature industries, for two reasons the relevant legal practice would not support Landes and Posner's hypothesis that all judicially announced law is allocatively efficient: (1) because nothing requires the legal system to apply the same standard of tort liability to all infant industries and the same (possibly different) standard to all mature industries and (2) because it is extraordinarily unlikely that it will prove to be third-best allocatively efficient to apply the same standard of tort liability to all infant industries and/or the same (possibly different) standard of tort liability to all mature industries.

In short, neither the argument that Landes and Posner did make nor the sort of argument they tried to make can establish the allocative efficiency of the common law's response to the maturation of an industry and, therefore, neither can confirm the hypothesis that the common law is allocatively efficient. Moreover, if Landes and Posner's account of American tort law is correct, it is extraordinarily unlikely that its use of liability standards is third-best allocatively efficient.

The Allocative Efficiency of "Ideal" Housing Codes—of Housing Codes That Are Designed to Increase Allocative Efficiency

Housing codes are usually municipal ordinances that specify various attributes that each dwelling unit within the relevant jurisdiction must possess. Typically, housing codes establish such things as the maximum distance between electrical outlets, the quality of electric wiring, the ventilation above cooking facilities, the minimum distance between lavatories and sinks, the quantity and quality (nonflammability) of the insulation that must be placed in a dwelling unit, and the fire alarms that all dwelling units must possess. Housing codes can also require dwellings to have various aesthetic attributes or to contain such components as garages or carports. In practice, housing codes are often controlled by and serve the parochial interests of the builders, electricians, plumbers, and others who supply the attributes the codes require. For this reason, most actual housing codes are allocatively inefficient or, at least, are less allocatively efficient than such regulations could be.

This subsection is not concerned with the political economy or allocative efficiency of actual housing codes. Instead, it addresses the standard law and economics analysis of the allocative efficiency of housing codes that are ideal in the sense that they were designed to increase allocative efficiency. More particularly, this subsection presents and criticizes the traditional law and economics argument for the conclusion that, no matter how well-motivated from the perspective of allocative efficiency, housing codes will inevitably misallocate resources both (1) by inducing some dwelling owners to make economically inefficient decisions to incorporate housing attributes into them that they would not otherwise have individually chosen to include and (2) by inducing some owners of subcode units whose supply would have been allocatively efficient to abandon those units or convert them into nonresidential uses that are less economically efficient.[44]

The traditional law and economics analysis of the allocative efficiency of ideal housing codes is a first-best-allocative-efficiency analysis. It assumes that, were it not for the housing code (which creates a Pareto imperfection by prohibiting the individual, actual, and prospective owners of dwellings from making the housing-attribute choices that would otherwise maximize their individual interests), the economy would contain no Pareto imperfections. If this otherwise-Pareto-perfect assumption were correct, the traditional analysis's conclusions would clearly be warranted. Since the private cost to the property owner of any improvement to code would equal the allocative cost, the private benefits to the property owner of any improvement to code would equal the allocative benefits, and all dwelling owners and occupiers would be sovereign maximizers, the fact that, absent the code, the dwelling owner would not choose to supply some attribute the code would require him to supply would demonstrate that its allocative cost was higher than the allocative benefits its supply would generate. Similarly, since the revenue that the supply of any housing unit the code causes to be withdrawn would have generated for its supplier would equal the allocative benefits its supply would have generated, the private cost the prospective supplier would have had to incur to supply the unit in question would equal the allocative cost of its supply, and the relevant prospective supplier would have been a sovereign maximizer, the fact that the subcode unit that the code causes to be withdrawn or not to be supplied in the first place would otherwise have been supplied implies not only that its supplier would have perceived its supply to have been profitable but that its supply would have increased both its supplier's profits and allocative efficiency.

Of course, in a world in which the economy is not otherwise-Pareto-perfect, the preceding argument does not apply: the private cost of improving a unit to code may not equal the allocative cost of doing so, the perceived private value of the improvement to code to the occupier of the dwelling unit who determines how much will be paid for it or who makes the improvement in a unit he both owns and occupies may not equal the allocative benefits the improvement to code generates, the private cost of supplying the subcode units the code causes to be withdrawn or not built (as opposed to being upgraded or replaced) may not equal the allocative cost of their supply, the private benefits those withdrawn units would have conferred on their occupiers (and owners when the two are different) may not equal the allocative benefits they would have generated, and (least importantly in this context) the housing-attribute choices that would have been made absent the code may not have been profitable for the individual occupiers and owners of housing units who made them because those individuals may not be sovereign maximizers. As we shall see, in such circumstances, housing codes that are designed to increase allocative efficiency may well succeed in doing so.

Diagrams VIII and IX illustrate respectively the traditional law and economics analysis of the possibility of increasing allocative efficiency through housing codes and an analysis of this possibility that rejects the traditional analysis's otherwise-Pareto-perfect assumption. Both diagrams contain static representations of curves that change over time: since housing units last for more than one time period and both the demand for housing and the marginal cost of supplying subcode housing of any specified quality or code-quality housing will change over time (as properties deteriorate and require repair), the curves in Diagrams VIII and IX should be interpreted to indicate the present value of the market value, allocative value, private supply cost, and allocative supply cost of the units over their lifetimes.

Diagram VIII illustrates the traditional law and economics analysis. It contains two industry demand curves and two industry marginal cost (MC) or supply (SS) curves. In Diagram VIII (and in Diagram IX), the subscript S stands for subcode and the subscript C stands for code. Diagram VIII assumes

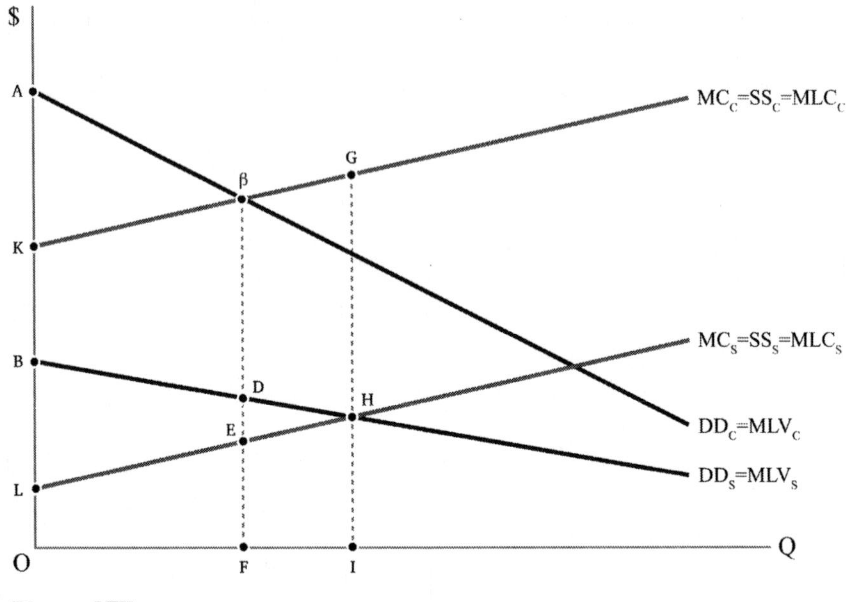

Diagram VIII

that the housing market is perfectly competitive, that all subcode units are identical, and that all code units are identical. In Diagram VIII, DD_C converges on DD_S as one moves to the right. This construction, which is not essential to any important conclusion I will use the diagram to illustrate, seems to me to be realistic: if one assumes (admittedly contestably) that the upgrades of the units to code will not change the identity of the units' occupiers (will not lead to gentrification), DD_C would converge on DD_S if the individual occupiers' evaluations of both the subcode units (in comparison with such alternatives as doubling up, moving away, or living rough on the streets) and the improvements to code were positively income-elastic (if, for example, the people who placed the highest dollar value on the subcode unit [because they were wealthier than other occupiers of the relevant units] also placed the highest dollar value on the improvement to code [for the same reason]).[45] Because Diagram VIII is constructed on the traditional analysis's otherwise-Pareto-perfect assumption, $DD_S = MLV_S$ and $DD_C = MLV_C$.

Diagram VIII also contains two industry marginal cost (MC) or supply (SS) curves. $MC_S = SS_S$ indicates the marginal cost of supplying successive subcode units (of the quality we assume all subcode units have), and $MC_C = SS_C$ indicates the marginal cost of supplying successive code units.

MC_S slopes up to the right because (1) more resources have to be used to maintain successive units at the subcode quality-level in question, (2) because the individual units of resources that would have to be purchased to maintain successive housing units at the relevant subcode quality-level would be increasingly expensive to purchase, and/or (3) because the private value that the successive land and building units that could be withdrawn from housing uses would have for buyers who would put them to alternative uses would decline. Diagram VIII's construction of $MC_C = SS_C$ to be parallel to $MC_S = SS_S$ manifests an assumption that it would be equally privately costly to bring each original subcode unit up to code[46]—in particular that the private cost of bringing each subcode up to code was equal to the length of the line segment $KL = \beta E = GH$ (by construction). Because Diagram VIII is constructed on the traditional analysis's otherwise-Pareto-perfect assumption, $MC_C = SS_C$ equals MLC_C and $MC_S = SS_S$ equals MLC_S in the diagram so that the allocative cost of bringing each unit up to code also equals $KL = \beta E = GH$.

I can now use Diagram VIII to illustrate the traditional argument that, even with the best of will, one could not devise a housing code that is allocatively efficient on the diagram's otherwise-Pareto-perfect assumption. In Diagram VIII, the implementation of the housing code converts a situation in which originally OI subcode units were supplied (the number of units at which DD_S cuts SS_S from above at point H) to a situation in which OF code units are supplied (the number of units at which DD_C cuts SS_C from above at point β).[47] The code therefore has two effects. First, it causes FI subcode units to be withdrawn (abandoned or converted to other uses). Second, it causes OF subcode units to be improved to code.

Since the analysis's otherwise-Pareto-perfect assumption guarantees that $DD_S = MLV_S$, that $SS_S = MLC_S$, and that the individuals who supplied and occupied the FI units pre-code that the code caused to be withdrawn were sovereign maximizers, it should be no surprise that the original supply of those units was allocatively efficient and, concomitantly, that their code-induced withdrawal was allocatively inefficient. In Diagram VIII, the resulting inefficiency equals area DHE—the area between the $DD_S = MLV_S$ and $SS_S = MLC_S$ curves between the outputs OI and OF.

On Diagram VIII's otherwise-Pareto-perfect assumption, the housing code's second effect—its causing OF subcode units to be upgraded to code—is also allocatively inefficient. In terms of the diagram, the misallocation in question is the difference between the amount by which the improvements to code increase the market value of the units (the dollar value of the units to the payers who occupy them)—area AβDB—and the allocative cost of the improvements—area KβEL. To see why the latter area exceeds the former, note that the relevant analysis's otherwise-Pareto-perfect assumption guarantees that (1) the largest amount by which any code-induced improvement of a housing unit to code increases its market value will be lower than the private cost the unit's owner had to incur to improve it to code (since otherwise the improvement to code would have been profitable and would have been made in the absence of the code) and (2) the allocative benefits that are generated by any code-induced improvement to code will fall below the allocative costs it generates by the same amount as its private benefits to the owner of the improved unit would have fallen below the private cost he would have had to incur to bring his unit up to code had the code not penalized noncompliance. In Diagram VIII, this assumption is manifest by the fact that AB (the highest market value increase [and allocative benefit] generated by any improvement to code) is lower than KL, the private (and allocative) cost of improving each unit to code.

Diagram IX contains all the curves and points that Diagram VIII contains. However, in Diagram IX, (1) the DD_C and DD_S curves contain oPp superscripts that indicate that they are constructed on the assumption that the economy is otherwise-Pareto-perfect, (2) a distinction is drawn between the DD_C^{oPp} and DD_S^{oPp} curves on the one hand and the DD_C^R and DD_S^R curves on the other, where the superscript R indicates that the curve in question is being calculated on realistic assumptions about the Pareto perfectness of the economy, and (3) the two DD_S curves, the two DD_C curves, the MC_C curve, and the MC_S curve are not assumed to coincide respectively with the (realistic) MLV_C^R, MLV_S^R, MLC_C^R, and MLC_S^R curves. Indeed, Diagram IX contains MLV_C^R, MLV_S^R, MLC_C^R, and MLC_S^R curves that diverge respectively from their private counterparts.

I will now

1. explain why and how the two DD^{oPp} curves are likely to diverge from their DD^R counterparts;
2. examine why and how MLV_S^R and MLV_C^R are likely to diverge from DD_S^R and DD_C^R respectively;
3. explore why and how MLC_S^R and MLC_S^R are likely to diverge from their private counterparts; and
4. examine the implications of these conclusions for the possible allocative efficiency of ideal housing codes.

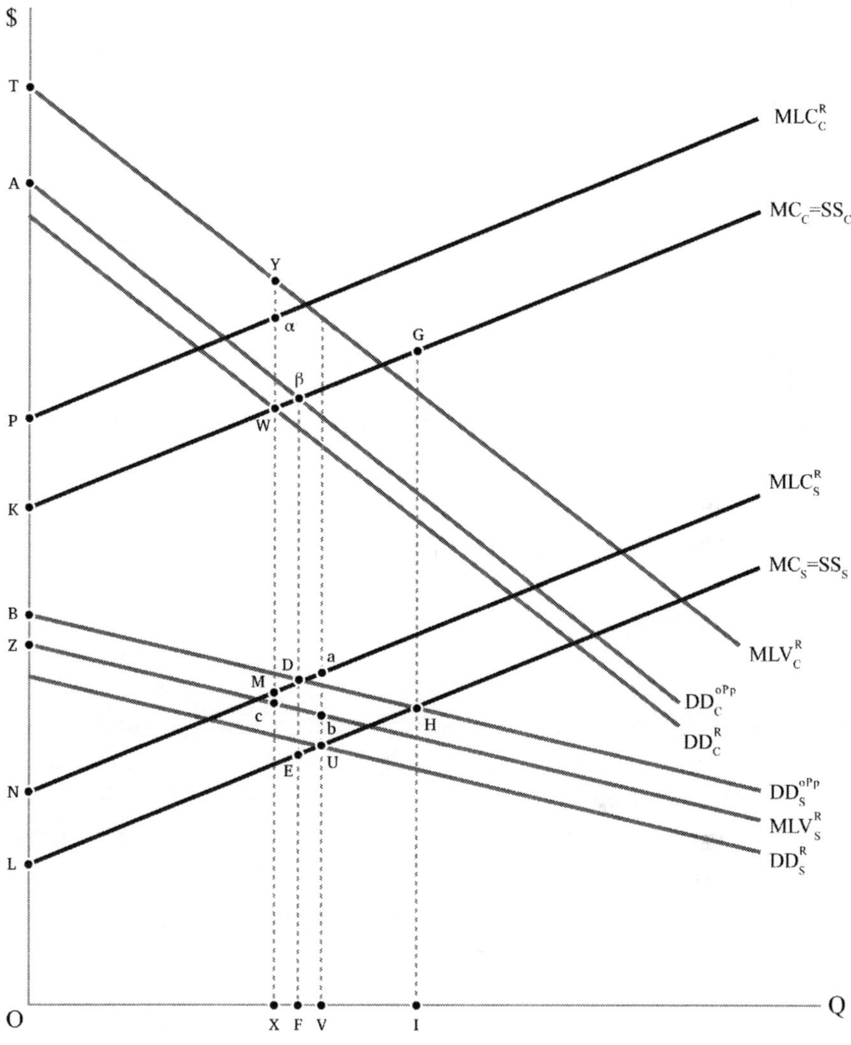

Diagram IX

However, before proceeding to these tasks, I need to address a relevant "compared to what" issue. When determining the demand for any good, one assumes that the alternative to the good's supply is its nonsupply. Diagram VIII therefore implicitly defined DD_S on the assumption that the alternative to the supply of the subcode units in question was their abandonment. It also implicitly defined DD_C on the assumption that the alternative to the supply of the code-quality units in question was the abandonment of the subcode units that could be upgraded to code. All this is painfully obvious. In practice, however, it appears not to have been so obvious that the relevant MLV curves should be based on the same comparisons—that is, that both the MLV_C^R and the MLC_S^R curves should be calculated on the assumption that the alternative to occupying the relevant units is occupying other units (often, moving away), doubling up, or living rough. The same issue has to be resolved in relation to the relevant MC and MLC^R curves. If, as I will be assuming for expositional reasons, the relevant subcode units are already in existence, the various marginal cost and marginal allocative cost curves should be calculated on the assumption that the alternative to continuing to supply the subcode unit of given quality or to upgrading the unit to code is converting the unit into some other type of use or abandoning it altogether.[48] On this assumption, MC_S for any unit is the private cost of maintaining the original subcode quality of the unit in question *plus* either (1) the opportunity cost of not devoting the property to some profitable nonresidential use (if that were the relevant alternative) or (2) the insurance premiums and property taxes the property owner could avoid by abandoning the property (if abandonment were the most profitable alternative to maintaining the property at its original quality-level); MLC_S^R for any unit is the allocative cost of maintaining the original subcode quality of the unit in question either *plus* the allocative gain that the relevant property would have generated in its alternative use if the option that was the most profitable alternative to maintaining the property as a residential unit was converting it into some other type of use or *minus* the allocative loss that the relevant property would have generated had it been abandoned if that was its owner's most profitable option;[49] MC_C for any unit is the private cost of upgrading the unit to code and maintaining it as the code requires *plus* either the private opportunity cost of forgoing the opportunity to devote the property to some profitable nonresidential use (if that were the most-privately-attractive alternative to using the property as a code-quality residential unit) or the insurance premiums and property taxes one could avoid by abandoning the property if that were the owner's most profitable alternative; and MLC_C^R for any unit is the allocative cost of upgrading the property to code and maintaining its code quality *plus* the allocative gain that would have been generated by the alternative positive use to which the property would have been put had it been withdrawn from the housing market or *minus* the allocative loss that would have been generated by the abandonment of the property (if that were the most-privately-attractive alternative to improving it to code and if, as I am contestably assuming, the property would generate net allocative costs if it were abandoned).

I begin by explaining why and how DD_S^R diverges from DD_S^{oPp} and why DD_C^R diverges from DD_C^{oPp}. Diagram IX is constructed on the assumption that the DD_S^R curve will be considerably below the DD_S^{oPp} curve. This relationship reflects the fact that, in the real world, the dollar value of a subcode unit to the individual who pays for it will be reduced by the external costs that other subcode units in its neighborhood impose on the owners and occupiers of the (neighboring) subcode unit in question. These external costs include the costs associated with (1) the risk that neighboring subcode units may generate fire and disease that may spread to their neighbors, (2) the possibility that neighboring subcode units may be inhabited by occupiers who commit crimes against their neighbors or interact unpleasantly with them, (3) the possibility that the occupants of neighboring dwelling units may impose congestion costs on their neighbors, and (4) the possibility that the neighboring subcode units may be unpleasant to look at. Somewhat more contestably, Diagram IX also constructs DD_C^R to be lower than DD_C^{oPp}, though the difference between the heights of these two curves is considerably smaller than the difference between the heights of their DD_S counterparts. My assumption that DD_C^R is lower than DD_C^{oPp} reflects my belief that (1) even a housing code that is as allocatively efficient as such a regulation can be will not prevent the occupants of a code-quality unit from imposing fire-and-disease-related external costs on their neighbors (since it will not be allocatively efficient or even possible to eliminate the possibility of such externalities being generated), (2) even the occupants of code-quality housing will probably impose congestion costs on their neighbors, and (3) any external benefits code-quality units confer on their neighbors because they are attractive to look at or because their inhabitants interact pleasantly with their neighbors are unlikely to offset fully the external costs that the first two items in this list identify. My assumption that the distance between DD_C^{oPp} and DD_C^R is smaller than the distance between DD_S^{oPp} and DD_S^R reflects an assumption that the upgrading of neighboring units to code will reduce the amount of fire-and-disease-related externalities they generate, make it more likely that they will be attractive rather than unattractive to look at, and make it more likely that their occupants will interact with their neighbors in ways that confer external benefits on them rather than impose external costs on them.

Diagram IX is also based on the assumptions that MLV_S^R exceeds DD_S^R and that MLV_C^R exceeds DD_C^R. Those assumptions relate to the possibility that occupying a subcode unit rather than doubling up or living rough[50] or occupying a code unit in a neighborhood in which all units meet code requirements as opposed to a subcode unit in a neighborhood in which many units are subcode will increase the lifetime allocative product of the children in the relevant households by placing them in warmer, quieter, more healthful dwellings in better neighborhoods. To the extent that this is the case,[51] there are three related reasons why DD^R may fall below MLV^R: (1) the relevant heads of households may systematically underestimate the contribution that living in a code unit in a code-quality neighborhood as opposed to living in a subcode unit in a worse neighborhood or the contribution that living in a subcode unit as opposed to doubling up or living rough will make to their children's allocative product; (2) the relevant heads of household may place less than a $1 value on a $1 increase in their children's equivalent-dollar welfare; and (3) the children in question may obtain less than a $1 gain for each dollar increase in their allocative products (because part of the increase in their productivity is secured by their employers or buyers of the products they produce and/or part is offset by an increase in the taxes they pay or a decrease in the transfer payments they receive). I should add that, although I do believe that Diagram IX's assumption that MLV_S is lower than DD_S^{oPp} is realistic, I have no confidence in its construction of MLV_C as being higher than DD_C^{oPp}. I did not want to construct MLV_C to coincide with DD_C^{oPp} (since that outcome would be purely fortuitous) and, having no reason to believe that it would be more likely to be higher than DD_C^{oPp} than lower than DD_C^{oPp}, constructed it to be higher than DD_C^{oPp} for purely visual reasons.

Diagram IX also manifests the fact that, in the real world, MC_S is unlikely to coincide with MLC_S^R and MC_C is unlikely to coincide with MLC_C^R. Four sets of Pareto imperfections are likely to be salient in this context. The first are imperfections in seller competition. As we have seen, these imperfections will tend to make MC_S and MC_C fall below MLC_S^R and MLC_C^R respectively to the extent that the maintenance of the subcode unit at its original subcode quality (and the construction of the subcode unit if we are assuming that the policy might affect the number of such units that are built) and the improvement of subcode units to code withdraw resources from unit-output-producing uses by imperfectly discriminating imperfect competitors or from PPR-executing uses and will tend to make MC_S and MC_C exceed MLC_S^R and MLC_C^R respectively to the extent that the above activities withdraw resources from QV-investment-creating uses. On balance, I suspect that the relevant imperfections in price competition will deflate MC_S and MC_C—that MLC_S^R and MLC_C^R will tend to exceed their private counterparts on this account. The second set of salient Pareto imperfections are the external costs (noise and congestion externalities) that the maintenance and upgrading of subcode units will generate:[52] obviously, these externalities will also tend to cause MLC_S^R and MLC_C^R to exceed their private counterparts. The third set of salient Pareto imperfections are (part of) the taxes that the workers who maintain or upgrade subcode units must pay on the income they derive from performing the labor in question: to the extent that the workers in question would otherwise have devoted the time they allocated to maintaining or improving the relevant dwelling units to the production of leisure, the taxes they had to pay on the marginal income they derived from working on the relevant units would inflate their cost to the units' owners—that is, would cause MC_S to exceed MLC_S^R and MC_C to exceed MLC_C^R. The fourth set of salient imperfections are the property taxes that dwelling owners must pay on their property. These taxes will inflate MC_S for property owners who, if they did not devote their property to subcode residential housing, would either abandon it or convert it into something with a lower assessed value (for example, would tear down the building and use the land as a parking lot), will deflate MC_S for property owners who would turn the property into a nonresidential entity (say, a liquor store) that would have a higher assessed value, and will inflate the private cost of improving the unit to code to the extent that doing so increases the assessed value of the property. Indeed, the code will also inflate the private cost of improving a subcode unit to code as opposed to abandoning it by increasing the property's assessed value by increasing the quality of the neighborhood in which it is located.

Obviously, since two of the most relevant types of Pareto imperfections deflate MC_S and MC_C and two inflate them, one cannot determine whether the relevant allocative costs exceed or are lower than their private counterparts through *a priori* argument. To be honest, I have little confidence in my suspicion that MLC_S^R exceeds MC_S and that MLC_C^R exceeds MC_C. Diagram IX does construct the two allocative cost curves higher than their private counterparts, but this construction primarily reflects my desire to combat the traditional assumption that the allocative and private cost curves in question coincide. Nevertheless, because I see little reason to assume that—if MLC_S^R exceeds MC_S and MLC_C^R exceeds MC_C—the allocative figures will exceed the private figures by different percentages, the percentage by which Diagram IX constructs MLC_S^R to be above MC_S equals the percentage by which it constructs MLC_S^R to be above MC_S.

I should now be able to use Diagram IX to illustrate the impact that the housing code whose effects it illustrates will have first on the number of housing units supplied and second on allocative efficiency. I should say at the outset that the allocative-efficiency conclusion I derive from the diagram will have to be revised to take account of some allocative costs and benefits that the curves in the diagram cannot or, as I have defined them, do not reflect.

The housing code whose effects are depicted in Diagram IX will reduce the number of units supplied from OV (subcode) units to OX (code) units—that is, will cause XV housing units to be withdrawn. OV is the number of housing units at which DD_S^R cuts $MC_S = SS_S$ from above at point U, and OX is the number of housing units at which DD_C^R cuts $MC_C = SS_C$ from above at point W. I hasten to point out that, in the real world, housing codes may not reduce the number of housing units supplied. If the neighborhood effects I described are sufficiently strong, the codes may make it profitable for all owners of the original subcode units to continue to devote their properties to residential uses even if each would prefer not to improve his unit to code—that is, each property owner may profit at least as much from his neighbors' improving their units to code as he loses by improving his unit to code. (Indeed, in many cases, individual improvements to code that would not have been profitable absent the housing code may be profitable when the code is in force—that is, the improvement of the neighborhood may increase the additional rent an individual improvement to code will enable the property owner to obtain by improving his unit to code sufficiently to render profitable improvements that would not have been profitable absent the code-induced neighborhood upgrade, even if one ignores the penalties the code imposes on nonconforming property owners.) In fact, in many cases, I suspect, the implementation of an ideal housing code may actually increase the number of housing units supplied. Diagram IX's construction to the contrary is a construction against interest in that—by disfavoring the allocative efficiency of housing codes—it cuts against my conclusion that the conclusions of the traditional first-best-allocative-efficiency analysis are seriously wrong.

In any event, on the assumptions that Diagram IX manifests, the housing code whose effects it illustrates will (1) *increase* allocative efficiency by area Mabc by causing XV subcode units to be withdrawn (by the area between MLC_S^R and MLV_S^R between housing "output" OX and OV) and (2) *increase* allocative efficiency as well by the difference between area TYcZ and area PαMN (where the former area equals the amount by which the improvement to code increased the allocative benefits generated by the units in question—

the area between MLV^R_C and MLV^R_S between quantities zero and OX—and the latter area equals the allocative cost of the improvements in question—the area between MLC^R_C and MLC^R_S between quantities zero and OX). Obviously, both these conclusions contradict their traditional counterparts: at a minimum, then, the substitution of more-or-less-realistic assumptions about the Pareto imperfectness of the economy for the traditional analysis's otherwise-Pareto-perfect assumption creates the possibility that an appropriately designed housing code could increase allocative efficiency.

As I have already indicated, the preceding analysis ignores a number of the ways in which housing codes can affect allocative efficiency. I will address three such impacts here. First, ideal housing codes will generate allocative costs to the extent that their drafting, passage, and implementation consume allocatively valuable resources.

Second, ideal housing codes will generate allocative costs to the extent that the government's efforts to finance its housing-code expenditures by raising the taxes it levies, by increasing the prices it charges for goods and services it sells, by generating inflation, or by forgoing various other expenditures would have decreased allocative efficiency.

Third, ideal housing codes may generate either net allocative benefits or net allocative costs by satisfying or dissatisfying on balance the external distributive preferences of members of the society in question. Obviously, this allocative-efficiency-relevant impact of ideal housing codes will depend on both the external distributive preferences of the relevant society's members and the actual distributive impact of the code in question. The actual distributive impact will depend *inter alia* on three factors: first, the ratio of the percentage of subcode units the code causes to be improved to the percentage it causes to be abandoned or converted to nonresidential uses; second, the percentage of any improved units that are rented or sold to middle-class or wealthy tenants; and third, the relative magnitudes of the equivalent-dollar gains the code confers on the units' individual original owners by inducing their neighbors to alter (or abandon) their properties to the equivalent-dollar losses it imposes on the relevant properties' individual owners (given the decisions made by their neighbors) by requiring them to alter their units.[53] These factors will substantially affect the impact of the relevant code *inter alia* on

1. the workers who would improve the units to code or would have maintained the relevant units at their original subcode quality-level;
2. the adult poor tenants of the original subcode units taken as a group;

3. the children of those heads of household (housing codes that increase the quality of the housing units that poor families inhabit probably redistribute income from the adult members of those families to their children); and
4. the non-poor potential owners and renters of the improved units.

To the extent that the relevant population's external distributive preferences are utilitarian, equal-utility egalitarian, or equal-resource egalitarian, an ideal housing code's external-distributive-preference-related impact on allocative efficiency will also be affected by such facts as

1. the extent to which the subcode units were owned by lower-middle-class families as opposed to wealthier individuals—for example, were the original family homes of lower-middle-class families who continued to own them after moving from the central city to the suburbs;
2. the difference between the income/wealth positions of the renters of the subcode units whom the code would harm even if it did not lead to gentrification and the income/wealth positions of the probably-better-off renters of the subcode units whom the code would benefit (whose superior income/wealth positions would lead them to place a higher value both on the original subcode unit [as opposed to doubling up, moving away, squatting, or living rough on the streets] and on the improvement to code), and
3. the income/wealth positions of the building-trade personnel whom an ideal housing code would presumably benefit.

Obviously, then, even if one could be certain that all the relevant external distributive preferences were utilitarian, equal-utility egalitarian, or equal-resource egalitarian, one would need a great deal of data to determine whether housing codes would yield allocative gains or losses on their account.

Although I suspect that the three impacts that housing codes will have on allocative efficiency that do not show up in Diagram IX count against their allocative efficiency on balance, their presence does not critically affect my conclusion that housing codes that focus on external-cost-generating housing attributes may well be able to increase allocative efficiency. This subsection has therefore shown not only that the traditional law and economics analysis of the allocative efficiency of ideal housing codes is based on otherwise-Pareto-perfect assumptions that are unrealistic but also that an alternative analysis that takes the relevant Pareto imperfections into account implies that the traditional conclusion that housing codes must be allocatively inefficient is seriously misguided.

The Approach Admiralty Courts Have Taken to Setting Marine-Salvage Awards: A Critique of the Allocative Efficiency of the Practice and of a Canonical Landes and Posner Argument for Its Allocative Efficiency

When a successful marine salvor has not been able to enter into a binding compensation agreement, an admiralty court is often called on to determine the percentage of the value of the lives and objects he saved that he can keep. In a classic article, William Landes and Richard Posner argue that the relevant "judge-made" law "is consistent with" and displays "impressive congruence with" their hypothesis that "the rules of judge-made law are best explained as efforts—however unwitting—to bring about [economically-]efficient results."[54] This subsection summarizes and criticizes the argument that Landes and Posner make for the allocative efficiency of judicially announced marine-salvage law. Their marine-salvage argument is important not only because marine salvage is an important social phenomenon and the article in which the argument is made is canonical but also because many law and economics scholars make analogous arguments to establish the allocative efficiency of various other bodies of judge-announced law.

If space were costless and reader patience infinite, I would preface my critique of this Landes and Posner argument with a thorough account of the approach to determining such marine-salvage awards that would be third-best allocatively efficient and a related critique of the third-best allocative efficiency of the approach to such awards that the courts are reported to have taken.[55] Rather than providing such an account and critique, however, I will restrict myself to outlining the approach to marine-salvage awards that would be third-best allocatively efficient for courts to take, pointing out various complications with which this approach would have to cope, explaining why the most-allocatively-efficient awards courts could make would not constitute the most-allocatively-efficient response the State could make to marine-peril contingencies (that is, explaining the trade-offs the courts will have to make when determining the least-allocatively-inefficient award they could make in a given case), and criticizing some features of the actual judicial practice from the perspective of allocative efficiency.

To simplify the exposition, I assume that a judicial system's approach to determining the awards it will make to successful marine salvors will not affect allocative efficiency by changing the allocative transaction cost of resolving marine-salvage-award cases, the misallocation the government generates to finance the associated judicial activity, or the net external-distributive-preference-related allocative gains or losses the relevant cases' disposition generates. On this assumption, a judicial system's approach to calculating marine-salvage awards will affect allocative efficiency by influencing

1. the amount of misallocation caused by the fixed-cost (background) choices of potential marine rescuers (choices about constructing salvage ships, adapting nonsalvage ships to increase their ability to perform rescues, hiring and training officers and crew to perform marine rescues, and deploying ships that could effectuate marine rescues);
2. the amount of misallocation caused by the variable-cost (foreground) choices of potential rescuers (choices about whether to attempt given rescues and the characteristics of any rescue attempt that is made);
3. the amount of misallocation caused by the various background avoidance choices made by potential marine rescuees—decisions about whether to purchase passenger or cargo ships; to buy ships with thicker hulls; to keep spare parts (such as propellers and engine components) on board; to hire more and better trained mechanics; to give officers and crew more safety training; to pack cargo in water-resistant or flame-resistant containers; to stow cargo in safer positions; to reduce the physical volume, value, vulnerability, or dangerousness of the cargo carried; to reduce the number, vulnerability, and wealth (life value) of the passengers transported; to reduce the number of trips each ship makes in any given time period; to travel by more circuitous but safer routes; to travel at safer times of the year; to travel under safer weather conditions; and so on; and
4. the misallocation generated by the foreground decisions of owners of imperiled ships to reject or accept offers of rescue assistance.

Obviously, on the above assumption, the most-allocatively-efficient approach a judicial system could take to determining marine-salvage awards is the approach that will lead it to make the awards that minimize the sum of these four types of misallocation.

I will now discuss three features of the marine-salvage situation that complicate the approach that would be third-best allocatively efficient for a judicial system to take to the calculation of marine-salvage awards. The first such complication is that the four types of choices just listed—decisions involving the fixed cost of marine-salvage operations, decisions involving the variable cost of rescue attempts, decisions by potential rescuees to avoid or not avoid marine perils, and decisions by potential rescuees to accept or reject rescue-attempt offers—are all interdependent. This interdependence is important in the current context because it implies that the compensation that courts require marine rescuees to pay rescuers who have not been able to negotiate binding prices for their services affect each of these types of decisions as well as the misallocation they generate not only directly but also indirectly by affecting the other types of marine-peril-related decisions with which each of these types of decisions is interdependent.

The second reality that complicates the third-best allocatively efficient approach to marine-salvage-award calculation is the fact that the economy contains many Pareto imperfections that would individually distort the profits yielded by the four types of choices just described in an otherwise-Pareto-perfect economy. The set of imperfections that would be second-best allocatively efficient to take into account include (1) the external costs that each rescue attempt that is made on a given body of salvage that multiple parties attempt to rescue generate because each such rescue attempt reduces the weighted-average amount of salvage the other rescue attempts should be expected to rescue, (2) the external environmental costs generated by some rescue attempts (such as those that entail dumping the fuel of the imperiled ship to facilitate refloating it), (3) the external benefits that each seaman's rescue efforts confer on the owners of the salvage ship for which he works, the ship's officers, and the other members of the crew, (4) the various Pareto imperfections (perhaps most importantly imperfections in price competition) that distort the private fixed cost of building and adapting salvage ships, some of the variable costs of rescue attempts, the costs potential rescuees incur to make their physical ships safer, the cost to potential rescuees of taking longer but safer routes, the cost to potential rescuees of reducing the number of voyages they make, and so on, and (5) any externalities that are generated by any insurance coverage that owners of imperiled ships have on their ships, cargo, and officers' and crews' lives. Admittedly, at least in the short run, it may prove to be third-best allocatively efficient for a judicial system to ignore some of these imperfections when calculating the salvage awards that would be most allocatively efficient for them to make. However, it will be TBLE for the courts to take some of these imperfections into account, and even if it is not, their existence will complicate the analysis that is *ex ante* TBLE for courts to execute by requiring them to consider whether it would be TBLE to alter their awards to reflect the distortions these imperfections jointly generate.

The third reality that complicates the approach that would be TBLE for a judicial system to take to the calculation of marine-salvage awards is the fact that, only rarely and fortuitously, would some award-formula (or set of awards) cause all four types of marine-peril-related decisions I previously delineated to always be made economically efficiently. To determine the award-formula that will be TBLE, a judicial system will have to calculate the impact of various awards on each type of misallocation they will affect and trade off against each other the allocative-efficiency gains and losses that various award-changes will generate.

My next observation follows directly from the preceding point. At least some law and economics scholars seem to assume that—if the courts make the marine-salvage awards that are the most-allocatively-efficient awards they could make—marine-peril-related misallocation will be eliminated. As the preceding discussion implies, this optimistic conclusion is unwarranted. The courts simply do not have the policy instruments they would need to induce all the relevant types of decisions to be made allocatively efficiently. To secure such an outcome, they would have to be empowered *inter alia* to subsidize fixed-cost marine-rescue expenditures as well as to grant awards to successful marine salvors. My previous assertion that the TBLE approach for courts to take to the calculation of marine-salvage awards involves their discovering the award-formula that makes the most-allocatively-efficient trade-off they can strike among the various types of allocative-efficiency gains and losses that different awards can generate is compatible with the most-allocatively-efficient award-formula they can adopt's being the least-allocatively-inefficient award-formula they can adopt—that is, with the possibility that the most-allocatively-efficient award a court can make will not eliminate all marine-peril-related avoidance-choice misallocation. In other words, even if courts use the marine-salvor-award formula that is TBLE taken by itself, a system of TBLE judicial marine-salvage awards is unlikely to constitute the most-allocatively-efficient response the State could make to marine-peril contingencies. Of course, this reality does not disprove the claim that—given the options available to them—the approach the courts have taken to calculating marine-salvage awards is TBLE or surprisingly close to TBLE.

I will now analyze the second-best and third-best allocative efficiency of the approach the courts have taken to calculating the total award to make in any marine-salvage case.[56] I will start by describing the approach the courts are reported to have taken to calculating the award a successful marine rescuer who has not been able to negotiate a binding price for his services must be paid by the rescuee. I should state at the outset that the account that follows ignores the very real possibility that, despite the courts' and many legal scholars' claims to the contrary, court-ordered marine-salvage awards are not controlled by any formula—indeed, are not even guided in any coherent way by the factors the courts claim determine the awards they make. In other words, this section assumes that Gilmore and Black are wrong when they conclude that trial judges set marine-salvage awards by "pull[ing] an arbitrary figure out of the air."[57] More specifically, the analysis's assumptions about the content of the positive law of marine salvage are based on the account of the 1958 Kennedy treatise on *The Law of Civil Salvage*.[58] According to this treatise, courts determine the compensation they award in marine-salvage cases by considering the following factors:

A. As regards the salved property:
  1. the degree of danger, if any, to human life;
  2. the degree of danger to the property; and
  3. the value of the property salved.

B. As regards the salvors:
  1. the degree of danger to human life;
  2. the salvors' (a) classification [in my terms—professional, semi-professional, casual], (b) skill and (c) conduct;
  3. the degree of danger, if any, to property employed in the salvage service and its value;
  4. the (a) time occupied and (b) work done in the performance of the salvage service;
  5. responsibilities incurred in the performance of the salvage service—e.g., such as the risk that one might incur liability to passengers or shippers through deviation or delay; and
  6. losses or expense incurred in the performance of the salvage services—e.g., losses of profitable trade, expenses to repair damage to the ship or its gear, the cost of fuel consumed.[59]

This basic account needs to be supplemented in at least eight ways. First, at least in the United States, awards are not given to so-called pure-life salvors—that is, to salvors who have rescued lives but no property. Second, the value attributed to lives saved and injuries sustained is far lower than their allocative value. Third, although item B(2)(c)—salvor conduct—does cover individual-salvor decisions to execute a rescue-attempt variant that unjustifiably (allocatively inefficiently?) interferes more with the success of other rescue attempts than an alternative rescue-attempt variant he could have executed would have done, item B(2)(c) appears not to cover the possibility that, from the perspective of allocative efficiency, too many rescue attempts were made in the case in question—though, as the next comment indicates, the courts may take account of this possibility when adjusting the award they make in response to their calculation of items A(1) and A(2) in the above list. Fourth, there is some reason to believe that courts define factors A(1) and A(2)—the degree of danger to life and property—to take into consideration not only the probability that the salvage in question would be "saved" by nature or by the self-rescue efforts of the imperiled ship if no one else made a rescue attempt but also the probability that the salvage would have been rescued by another salvor had the successful salvor in question not made a rescue attempt. Although, as we shall see, such a practice would have problematic effects on decisions to invest in marine-salvage operations, it would make the award a successful salvor received depend on whether the full set of rescue attempts to which his effort belonged was allocatively efficient. Fifth, although item B(2)(a)—the type of salvor involved in a particular case—does suggest that the courts take account of differences in the amount of fixed costs of salving that different types of salvors have incurred and other items in the list—all items in set B other than item B(2)(a)—suggest that the courts take account of the variable cost of successful rescue attempts, nothing in the list suggests that the courts consider the other facts that influence the ratio of the successful salvor's investment in his salvage business to his total variable cost of salving or the percentage by which the awards he receives when his rescue attempts are successful must exceed the variable cost he incurred to execute his successful rescue attempts for him to cover his salvage business' fixed costs—namely, if the calculation is made on a ship-by-ship basis, the number of rescue attempts he will use the ship in question to make and the percentage of those rescue attempts that will be successful. Sixth, nothing in the list suggests that the courts consider whether the current level of salvage-operation investment is allocatively efficient. Seventh, except to the extent that the salvor owns the cargo he is carrying, will personally have to compensate the cargo's owner for any cargo that is lost or damaged, or will have to pay higher insurance premiums or incur other costs if he goes bankrupt because of his inability to compensate owners of lost or damaged cargo to whom he was liable, the list of salvor-attributes the courts consider does not contain the value of any cargo the salvor ship was carrying and the probability that the rescue attempt would cause it to be lost or damaged to any given extent—factors that will influence both the allocative and the private variable cost of the rescue attempt.[60]

Eighth, as another leading treatise on marine salvage recognized, in practice, the factors listed under heading A are by far the most important determinants of the awards that are made, and "the time and labor expended by the salvors in rendering the salvage service"—factor B(4)—and "the value of the property employed in rendering the service and the danger to which such property was exposed"—factor B(3)—are the least important.[61]

I will now analyze in order the second-best and third-best allocative efficiency of the approach the courts have taken to determining the protocol they should use to calculate the total award to make to individual successful marine salvors and the protocol they are reported to have followed when making such decisions in individual cases. As we have seen, any analysis of the second-best allocative efficiency of the courts' approach will assume that the courts could execute or commission all relevant theoretical and empirical analyses perfectly and costlessly.

On this assumption, there are twelve categories of reasons why the approach courts have taken to calculating marine-salvage awards is not or seems unlikely to be second-best allocatively inefficient. The first two relate to more general features of the courts' treatment of this issue. The last ten relate to specific features of the protocol the Kennedy treatise claims the courts follow. The first reason—though certainly not dispositive—clearly has some relevance. To my knowledge, no admiralty court has ever said that its decision was designed to minimize allocative inefficiency. Admittedly, such courts have sometimes explained their decisions in terms of consequences whose effectuation might be associated with increases in allocative efficiency. However, the correlation in question is far from clear, and the judges seem to value the consequences to which they refer for reasons other than their connection to allocative efficiency. Thus, when courts justify their salvage awards by citing their tendency to encourage maritime commerce by reducing its hazards,[62] it is not clear that they have increasing allocative efficiency by encouraging maritime commerce in mind. When courts justify their marine-salvage awards on the ground that they reward Good Samaritans,[63] it is not clear that the judges want to encourage Good Samaritanism if and only if it is allocatively efficient: to the contrary, they seem to be motivated by a distributive preference for rewarding Good Samaritans regardless of whether the Good Samaritans' conduct in the case was allocatively efficient. In fact, even when the courts in question make reference to goals whose attainment seems likely to be allocatively efficient, other things being equal—such as preventing unjust enrichment,[64] deterring the theft of unguarded property,[65] and preventing the waste that bilateral monopoly may cause in rescue situations in which time is of the essence[66]—the judges' interest seems to be in the distributive desirability of securing these results (for example, of preventing exploitation in bilateral-monopoly situations) rather than in the allocative efficiency of doing so. Admittedly, for some purposes, including those of Landes and Posner, the important question is not *why* judges resolve issues allocatively efficiently (if they do) but *whether* they resolve cases allocatively efficiently. For these purposes, the critical issue is whether the marine-salvage-award protocol the courts use is third-best allocatively efficient. However, the fact that the courts have never indicated that they were trying to make the awards that would minimize allocative inefficiency and have made some statements that suggest that they were not trying to achieve this goal clearly bears on whether their approach was third-best, much less second-best, allocatively efficient.

Second, and relatedly, nothing suggests that the courts are attempting to calculate the marine-salvage awards they are making by following either of the most abstract protocols that could be SBLE (or TBLE):

1. by listing the various types of allocative costs marine peril can generate, delineating the various ways in which marine-salvage awards can affect each of these types of allocative costs, determining the magnitude of each such type of cost that would result if any given marine-salvage-award protocol were followed, and identifying the protocol (formula) whose use would minimize the sum of such costs or (probably more allocatively efficiently)
2. by listing the various types of marine-peril-related misallocation that can be generated, delineating the various ways in which marine-salvage awards can affect the amount of each such type of misallocation that is generated, determining the magnitude of each such type of misallocation that would be generated if any given such protocol were followed, and identifying the protocol (formula) that would minimize the sum of the relevant types of misallocation.

Thus, no court has ever tried to determine the award-formula that would eliminate each particular type of marine-peril-related misallocation that might be generated, noticed that the formula that would eliminate one such type of misallocation would not eliminate all the other types of marine-peril-related misallocation that could be generated, tried to determine the factors that would influence the amount of marine-peril-related misallocation of each relevant type that would be generated if the awards made deviated in either direction by various amounts from the awards that would eliminate that type of misallocation, attempted to determine the amount of misallocation of each relevant type that would be generated if a given set of awards were made (if a given award-calculation protocol were followed), or attempted to identify the set of awards (the award-calculation protocol) that would minimize the sum of the marine-peril-related misallocation that was generated.

The next ten reasons focus on specific features of the courts' reported protocol. Third, the reported protocol is not a formula. No court has ever articulated the formula by which it calculates the award it makes in individual cases. Even if the courts had supplied the list of factors that the Kennedy treatise and other scholarly works claim influence judicial decisions and that list covered all the factors courts take into account when calculating marine-salvage awards, such a list would not constitute a formula—that is, would not allow potential marine salvors and potential marine rescuees to predict accurately the awards that will be made. I can imagine conditions under which it would be second-best allocatively efficient for courts to provide less rather than more guidance about their future decisions to these parties—for example, when the awards that are second-best allocatively efficient are higher than the awards that would minimize the misallocation that potential rescuees generate but lower than the awards that would minimize the misallocation that potential rescuers generate and the courts' concealment of their intentions leads potential rescuees to underestimate the awards that the court will make and potential rescuers to overestimate those awards. However, I suspect that the conditions for this result will rarely obtain. In general, even if (counterfactually) the courts were basing their marine-salvage awards on a formula that was second-best allocatively efficient, their failure to delineate the formula they were using would be allocatively inefficient.

Fourth, although the list of factors that allegedly influence the marine-salvage awards courts make contains many items that do relate to considerations that affect the award that would minimize particular types of marine-peril-related misallocation (such as the amount of marine-salvage-operation investment the salvor has made), the items in the list that do relate to such parameters do so only crudely. For example, although the salvor's classification (professional, semi-professional, casual) does relate to the fixed costs of salvage-operation investment the salvor's salving operating profits must cover, it is a far-from-accurate surrogate for such fixed-cost data.

Fifth, even when the list of factors contains some components of a figure that is relevant to the calculation of the second-best allocatively efficient award, it omits other components of the figure in question. Thus, although the list contains most components of the private variable cost of rescue attempts, it omits the weighted-average-expected amount of variable costs a rescue attempt will impose on the attempter by increasing the probability that the cargo he is carrying will be lost or damaged. Similarly, although the list contains many components of the private and allocative benefits that a rescue attempt should be expected to generate *ex ante,* it omits the weighted-average-expected value of the lives that may be saved in pure-life-salvage situations.

Sixth, even when the list includes some relevant factor, in practice the courts may mismeasure the factor in question. Thus, the general view is that courts undervalue lives saved and at risk and injuries prevented or sustained.

Seventh, the list omits a number of determinants of the positive economic consequences of the awards given that an allocatively efficient protocol would take into account. For example, the list does not include the number of rescue attempts the successful salvor will make with the salvage ship in question or the percentage of those attempts that will be successful (which one would have to know in addition to his fixed costs and the private variable cost of his successful rescue attempts to determine the percentage by which the average award he receives when successful must exceed the average private variable cost of his successful rescue attempts for him to earn a normal rate of return on his current salvage-operation investments).

Eighth, the list does not make reference to many determinants of the allocative efficiency of the positive economic consequences of the use of a particular award-protocol. For example, it ignores the allocative efficiency of the current level of salvage-operation investment (which will depend on the allocative cost of successive salvor investments and their impact on the allocative-efficiency gains that actual rescue attempts generate once the relevant investments are made, the allocative efficiency of the avoidance moves they induce potential rescuees to reject, and the allocative efficiency of the rescue-attempt offers they induce potential rescuees to reject [by increasing the salvage awards courts will make]).

Ninth, as I have already indicated, the list seems not to reflect the possibility that the awards made may cause misallocation by inducing an allocatively inefficient number of rescue attempts to be made or inducing potential rescuees to reject offers to execute allocatively efficient rescue attempts.

Tenth, the list clearly does not cover the allocative efficiency of the pre-incident avoidance-decisions of the rescuee.

Eleventh, although the list does cover the externalities a rescue attempt would otherwise generate by interfering unnecessarily with other rescue attempts made on the same body of salvage and although various international conventions and privately developed governance-structures have internalized to salvors much of the environmental consequences of their actions that admiralty law failed to internalize,[67] the list clearly does not make reference to most of the various Pareto imperfections that will individually and collectively distort the private value of the property and lives saved, the private fixed salvage-operation costs of the salvor, the private variable cost of rescue attempts, and the private cost of potential rescuees' avoidance moves.

Twelfth, although I assume that, unlike the list, the judges have indicated the direction in which their awards will be affected by variations in the parameters the list contains, the judges have not indicated the amounts by which the awards they announce will be affected by given variations in each such parameter, and (even if there is reason to believe that the courts have varied their awards in the right direction with changes in the parameters in question) there is no reason to believe that they have varied their awards to the right extent in response to changes in these parameters.

Of course, the preceding demonstration that the approach the courts have taken to calculating marine-salvage awards is not second-best allocatively efficient does not establish the third-best allocative inefficiency of their handling of this issue. However, I see absolutely no reason to believe that all or even most of the features of the courts' approach that grounded the third through twelfth reasons for concluding that it was not second-best allocatively efficient were third-best allocatively efficient.

It should now be possible to criticize Landes and Posner's canonical argument for their conclusion that what they refer to as "judge-made" marine-salvage law "is consistent with" and displays "impressive congruence with" their hypothesis that "the rules of judge-made law are best explained as efforts—however unwitting—to bring about [economically-]efficient results."[68]

Basically, Landes and Posner proceed by (1) listing the factors that the courts have taken into consideration when making marine-salvage awards,[69] (2) explaining that the factors in the list do affect the award that would be allocatively efficient in a given case or would play a role in the most-allocatively-efficient formula that courts could use to calculate marine-salvage awards and that the courts vary the awards they make in the allocatively efficient direction in response to variations in the magnitude of the factors they consider,[70] and (3) offering arguments for the allocative efficiency of courts' ignoring certain factors that would otherwise have been allocatively efficient for them to take into account.[71]

The implausibility of many of these latter arguments aside, this type of argument has the following deficiencies:

1. the argument's analysis of the allocative efficiency of the courts' response to the factors they do take into account is undercut by its failure to take account of the full range of choices (for example, decisions related to the fixed cost of rescue attempting) whose selection and allocative efficiency both the factors in question and marine-salvage awards affect;
2. the argument's analysis of the impact of the courts' responses to the factors they consider on the substance and allocative efficiency of the choices it recognizes those responses affect is undercut by its failure to recognize the interdependence of many of the choices in question and the fact that the allocative efficiency of many individual choices depends in part on the effect they will have on other marine-peril-related choices;
3. its analysis of the impact of marine-salvage awards on the allocative efficiency of the choices it recognizes those awards will affect (and hence its analysis of the allocative efficiency of particular marine-salvage awards or of particular formulas for calculating such awards) is undermined by its failure to take account of the fact that the courts have ignored many of the determinants of the awards that would be most allocatively efficient for them to make—*inter alia,* the full range of Pareto imperfections that individually and in combination distort the profitability of the choices the awards affect and/or cause individual choosers to make choices that are not in their individual interest; and
4. its analysis of the allocative efficiency of judicially prescribed salvage-awards is limited by its failure to consider whether the courts have made the awards they issue vary to the allocatively efficient extent in response to given changes in the value of the factors they consider (by its focusing exclusively on whether the courts vary the awards they make in response to changes in the value of relevant parameters in the allocatively efficient direction).

As I have already indicated, part of my interest in Landes and Posner's argument for the allocative efficiency of admiralty law's approach to marine-salvage awards derives from the fact that this argument is a prototype for the argument they and others use to establish the allocative efficiency of common-law doctrines in general. I therefore want to comment on the extent to which the preceding critique of their marine-salvage argument applies to its analogues.

Admittedly, some of the deficiencies of the argument I just criticized will not appear when the judicial decisions under scrutiny are binary rather than continuous—for example, when the issue is whether (1) a particular defendant is strictly liable or liable only for the consequences of his negligence or (2) a particular defendant's conduct was negligent. However, other deficiencies of Landes and Posner's marine-salvage-award argument are equally salient when the judicial decisions whose supposed allocative efficiency is being established are binary. For example, as an earlier subsection of this chapter demonstrated, Landes and Posner's argument for the allocative efficiency of the (alleged) common-law practice of holding members of an industry strictly liable during the industry's infancy but liable only if found negligent when the industry has matured was flawed *inter alia* by its failure to consider the full range of allocatively inefficient decisions that businesses could make that would not in practice be assessed for negligence and the large number of Pareto imperfections other than AP-loss externalities not internalized by liability rules that could distort the profitability of the choices in question (and whose magnitude would, in different cases, increase and decrease as the industry in question matured). Landes and Posner's tendency to ignore some of the avoidance moves whose rejection may be affected by a judicial choice also undermines their analysis of the allocative efficiency of the way in which courts have applied particular doctrines. Thus, as Bob Rabin pointed out,[72] Posner's conclusion that a trolley company had not behaved negligently in a case in which a plaintiff was electrocuted when a long wire he was carrying came into contact with uninsulated overhead trolley wires beneath an overpass was critically affected by Posner's failure to consider the possible negligence of the trolley company's failure to post warnings on both sides of all such overpasses—that is, the failure to consider the possibility that even if the trolley company's decision to place the necessarily uninsulated wires overhead rather than in the ground was not negligent, its failure to post warnings may have been negligent.

In my judgment, the common law is not in general allocatively efficient, and the resolutions of common-law issues that are correct as a matter of law will not always be allocatively efficient. I have chosen to conclude this section of Chapter 4 with a critique of the canonical law and economics assessment of the way in which courts have calculated marine-salvage awards because of the importance I place on refuting the claim that so-called judge-made (that is, judge-announced) law is allocatively efficient.

Chapter 3 asserted that (1) the vast majority of economics and law and economics analyses of the allocative efficiency of particular legislation or judicially announced law are first-best-allocative-efficiency analyses, (2) the few articles that take some account of second-best theory do not take full account of the implications of that theory, and (3) this failure of the relevant scholars to respond appropriately to The General Theory of Second Best not only undermines their analyses but leads them to reach allocative-efficiency conclusions that are generally seriously inaccurate. Section 1 of Chapter 4 has discussed nine canonical articles or bodies of literature that support these claims.

SECTION 2. THE ARGUMENTS THAT ECONOMISTS AND LAW AND ECONOMICS SCHOLARS USE TO JUSTIFY IGNORING SECOND-BEST THEORY: A CRITIQUE

Not only welfare economists but also economists in general reacted in one voice to Lancaster and Lipsey's publication of "The General Theory of Second Best" in 1956: "Woe is we!" they all cried. In terms of substantive response, the next six years contained little else than stunned silence, accompanied by business as usual. Then, in 1962, E. J. Mishan published an article[73] that economists concluded took them off the second-best-theory hook. Mishan established the following result: if one is trying to analyze the allocative efficiency of reducing or eliminating a Pareto imperfection in one sector of the economy (the target sector) and no resources flow either from that sector to other sectors or from other sectors to that sector, one need not take account of the Pareto imperfections that are located in the other sectors of the economy when analyzing the allocative efficiency of reducing a Pareto imperfection in the target sector. This argument is correct. However, Mishan's argument does not significantly undermine the practical importance of second-best theory because, in practice, resources always flow between or among different sectors of the economy.

Contemporary economists' reaction to second-best theory is equally problematic. In part because I once organized a symposium entitled "Second-Best Theory and Law and Economics,"[74] I have had literally dozens of conversations with economists about their knowledge and use of The General Theory of Second Best. The vast majority of these academics responded simply by stating either that they know nothing about second-best theory or that all they know about it is that the profession has decided to ignore it. All the scholars who responded in one of these ways went on to say that they had no interest in learning anything about second-best theory. Some explained that their lack of interest in second-best theory reflects their more general lack of interest in methodological issues.

A few scholars responded to my inquiry by stating The General Theory of Second Best accurately and then saying: "The profession has decided to ignore it. I don't see why I should be any different." The most surprising fact about this second set of conversations is that many of the economists in this group actually have executed very useful, though partial, second-best-allocative-efficiency analyses of particular problems—for example, analyses that consider the relevance for the allocative efficiency of internalizing externalities of the facts that (1) tortfeasors and victims may not be sovereign or maximizers and (2) even those judges or juries who attempt to maximize allocative efficiency may be thwarted by imperfections in the information available to them or by their own conceptual errors. Apparently, these scholars do not realize that allocative-efficiency analyses that attempt to take human errors into account are preliminary second-best or third-best analyses.[75] A small number of the economists with whom I have tried to discuss second-best theory indicated that they knew what it is about and claimed that they do take second-best theory into account, citing and describing articles they wrote or (more often) lectures they gave to prove their point. Unfortunately, further discussion quickly revealed that the analyses they had executed were either non-second-best, micro-economic, general-equilibrium analyses of the effect of some choice on price, unit output, or profits or extremely superficial and partial second-best analyses of a trivial problem that failed to take account of the factors that would clearly play a dominant role in any third-best-allocative-efficiency analysis of the relevant issue or policy.

A significant minority of the scholars with whom I have discussed second-best theory made arguments that they thought justified their individual and our profession's collective decision to ignore it. Seven of these arguments have been made sufficiently often to merit some attention.[76] I will now discuss each of these arguments in turn.

First, several economists have tried to justify ignoring second-best theory by arguing that it does not offer a clear or useful alternative to FBLE analysis and that it therefore leaves economists with nothing to say. I reject this justification for two reasons. First, I deny its premise: in my judgment, one can derive from second-best theory the basic structure of the TBLE approach one ought to take to allocative-efficiency analysis if one's (proximate) goal is to maximize allocative efficiency. Second, even if no positive use could be made of second-best theory, that fact would not justify ignoring its negative corollary that, unless a sound argument to the contrary can be devised, there is no reason to believe that the policies recommended by FBLE analyses will even tend to increase allocative efficiency. If second-best theory really did imply that economists have nothing to say, economists should shut up rather than continuing to say things that second-best theory has shown they have failed to justify.

A second argument with which several economists have tried to justify their failure to take account of second-best theory is that it ignores the point of making simplifying assumptions. In one sense, the premise of this argument is correct: in itself, The General Theory of Second Best does ignore the point of simplifying assumptions. However, this fact does not reduce its value or justify the profession's ignoring it. More particularly, the fact that second-best theory ignores the point of simplifying assumptions

1. does not undercut its negative corollary that, unless one can make an appropriate argument to the contrary (an argument that takes account of the point of simplifying assumptions), there is no reason to assume that a policy that reduces the number and/or magnitude of the Pareto imperfections in the economy will tend on that account to increase allocative efficiency and
2. does not prevent it from making a positive contribution by enabling economists to develop a third-best allocatively efficient approach to identifying the simplifying assumptions that are *ex ante* allocatively efficient and *ex ante* allocatively inefficient to make.

In short, although second-best theory does ignore the point of simplifying assumptions, the more telling observation is that it reveals the importance of the economics profession's ignoring the allocative-efficiency cost of the simplifying assumptions the profession makes and provides a structure for identifying *ex ante* allocatively efficient simplifications.

A third supposed justification for dismissing second-best theory that I have heard economists repeatedly offer is that TBLE approaches may be misused by the bad guys to produce bad results since, unlike FBLE decision rules, TBLE analysis allows decision makers to be influenced by guesstimates of facts and thereby authorizes exercises of judgment that can lead to abuse. I have four responses to this contention: (1) in my judgment, it will usually be possible to prevent this kind of abuse of process; (2) a full TBLE analysis should take the possibility of this kind of decision-making malfeasance into account; (3) economists do not have a great deal of expertise in relation to this possibility; and (4) if economists are really ignoring second-best theory for this kind of reason, they should indicate that fact so that their audience realizes that their objection to second-best theory is political-administrative rather than (as they usually suggest) technically economic.

A fourth reason that some economists have given for ignoring second-best theory is that even sophisticated analyses can sometimes yield wrong conclusions. I have two responses to this contention. First, even if this contention did justify the conclusion that no allocative-efficiency analysis could be third-best allocatively efficient—that no allocative-efficiency analysis could generate higher allocative benefits than costs, it would not justify basing predictions on FBLE analysis: if this argument is correct, economists should simply admit that they cannot predict the allocative efficiency of any choice sufficiently accurately for it to be allocatively efficient for them to attempt to do so. Second, I do not think that the reality that TBLE analyses will sometimes generate incorrect conclusions justifies the conclusion that it will never be *ex ante* allocatively efficient or desirable overall to execute TBLE analyses—that no analysis that attempts to take account of the positive insights of second-best theory will ever be worth its cost (will ever be better than simply admitting that one cannot say anything valuable about the allocative efficiency of the choices under consideration).

A fifth purported justification for ignoring second-best theory is that the best way to analyze the allocative efficiency of policies is to analyze the actual effects (equivalent-dollar gains and losses?) generated by similar policies in the past. I have three responses: (1) the empirical analyses that those who make this argument cite in support of this claim are actually not allocative-efficiency analyses but micro-economic analyses of the effects of policies on prices, unit outputs, and profits; (2) it rarely will be allocatively efficient to assess the allocative efficiency of even a past policy by analyzing directly the equivalent-dollar gains it conferred on its beneficiaries and the equivalent-dollar losses it imposed on its victims; and (3) the kind of empirical analyses that can reveal the allocative efficiency of past policies must be grounded on the type of theoretical understanding that second-best theory provides.

A sixth common argument for ignoring second-best theory is that the policies that FBLE analysis has recommended have turned out to be desirable. I have four responses: (1) some of these policies did increase allocative efficiency, and some did not; (2) one cannot argue for the allocative efficiency of FBLE analysis by giving a few examples of reductions in Pareto imperfections that increased allocative efficiency; (3) the facts that these scholars often cite to demonstrate the allocative efficiency of the policy recommendations generated by FBLE analysis often do not establish their allocative efficiency—relate to micro-economic effects (such as effects on prices, unit outputs, and profits) whose allocative-efficiency implications are unclear; and (4) even if FBLE analysis would produce more allocatively efficient results than my investigations suggest, FBLE analysis would rarely be third-best allocatively efficient.

A seventh and final argument that some economists use to justify ignoring second-best theory is that the theory devalues allocative-efficiency analysis and thereby reduces the quality of public decision making by increasing the effect of other kinds of analysis on the decisions that are made. I have four responses: (1) second-best theory does not devalue allocative-efficiency analysis and should not reduce the impact of such analyses on public decision making—to the contrary, if economists responded appropriately to second-best theory, the theory could very well increase the impact that economists' allocative-efficiency conclusions have on public decision making both by enabling them to take messy reality into account and by increasing the accuracy of the advice they give; (2) the economists who have made this argument have not specified the criteria by which they think public decisions should be judged; (3) these economists have provided no theoretical or empirical reason to conclude that any increase in the impact of non-allocative-efficiency considerations on public decisions would make them worse; and (4) academic economists are obligated to speak the truth, not to lie to improve social outcomes.

Section 1 of Chapter 4 provides evidence of the continuing failure of economists and law and economics scholars to respond appropriately to The General Theory of Second Best when executing allocative-efficiency analyses and demonstrates that this error has led the economists who made it to reach allocative-efficiency conclusions that seem likely to be highly inaccurate. Section 2 of Chapter 4 argues that the intelligent scholars who persist in ignoring second-best theory have tried to justify this choice with arguments that cannot bear the slightest scrutiny. I do not know which section's conclusions are more disturbing.

Part Three **The Relevance of Allocative-Efficiency Conclusions**

Part III focuses on (1) the relevance of the allocative efficiency of a choice or course of conduct to its justness or moral desirability, moral-rights considerations aside, in the societies at which the economists this book discusses are directing their policy recommendations and (2) the relevance of the allocative efficiency of an interpretation or application of the law to its correctness as a matter of law in the societies in question. Chapter 5 presents my own analysis of and conclusions about these issues, and Chapter 6 delineates and criticizes various arguments and contrary conclusions that have respectively been made and reached about them by respected economists and law and economics scholars.

Since both chapters focus on the relevance of allocative-efficiency conclusions to prescriptive-moral evaluation and the assessment of the internal-to-law correctness of conclusions about various types of legal rights, I will devote the rest of this lengthy introduction to Part III to the following tasks:

1. explaining the assumptions I will be making about the various moral types of societies that can be distinguished;

2. elaborating on and illustrating the two types of prescriptive-moral discourse (moral-rights discourse and moral-ought discourse) engaged in by the members and governments of the moral type of society at which the economists on whom this book focuses usually direct their policy recommendations—namely, rights-based societies of moral integrity;
3. delineating the different types of approaches that various scholars take to the analysis of justice, including the philosophically informed empirical approaches that I think should be used respectively to determine whether a given society has a conception of justice and, if it does, the moral norm it is committed to instantiating through its moral-rights discourse and conduct;
4. asserting that the societies for which the scholars on whose work this book focuses are making policy recommendations are liberal, rights-based societies and delineating some of the concrete corollaries of the liberal norm to whose instantiation these societies are committed;
5. delineating the ultimate values to which significant percentages of those societies' members are personally committed;
6. outlining the moral-rights and moral-ought arguments that can legitimately be made in the societies in question;
7. distinguishing the different types of legal rights that exist in such societies (in particular, distinguishing them by their "point");
8. defining and distinguishing the concepts of "legitimate" and "valid" legal argument;
9. describing my own conclusions (A) about the valid and legitimate way in any rights-based society to determine the answer that is correct as a matter of law to questions about the existence of particular legal rights that are purportedly moral-rights-based and (B) about the different valid and legitimate way in any rights-based society to determine the answer that is correct as a matter of law to questions about the existence of legal rights that are not moral-rights-based; and
10. describing and commenting on the two other jurisprudential schools that probably have most adherents in the contemporary American legal academy—legal realism and legal positivism.

SECTION 1. THE DIFFERENT MORAL TYPES OF SOCIETIES

In my judgment, it is useful to distinguish four moral types of societies. Immoral societies are societies that base a requisitely important set of their choices on decision criteria that are immoral—that violate an ineliminable feature of the moral. For example, a society will be immoral if, out of prejudice, its members and governments regularly choose to punish or disadvantage particular society members because of their possession of an attribute (such as their gender or race) whose possession has no moral relevance.

Amoral societies are societies whose members and governments (1) base a requisitely important set of decisions that are morally significant on one or more decision criteria that are morally irrelevant, though their use does not manifest any prejudice or other evil intent, or (2) vary the defensible, moral criteria they use to resolve moral issues in an *ad hoc* way. For example, a society will be amoral if it chooses to determine the amount of resources that different individuals receive (measured, say, by their allocative value) by the number of pins they carry around in their pockets when no consequentialist argument can be made for doing so.

Goal-based societies of moral integrity are societies whose governments and members do not draw a strong distinction between the just and the good (or, relatedly, between moral-rights discourse and discourse about what morally ought to be done) but whose governments can be said to make their moral-ought decisions sufficiently consistently from the perspective of a defensible moral norm to deserve to be denominated societies of moral integrity. Although the governments and members of goal-based societies may sometimes use moral-rights and moral-obligations language, that language is typically used in such societies to express moral-ought, goal-oriented conclusions about which the speaker feels strongly and/or of whose correctness the speaker is sure. In any event, in goal-based societies, even when prescriptive-moral analyses that are couched in moral-rights terms are substantively different from moral-ought (goal-oriented) analyses, moral-ought conclusions trump moral-rights conclusions when the two favor conflicting choices or courses of action.

Finally, rights-based societies of moral integrity are societies that draw a strong distinction between the just and the good and are committed to instantiating the just over the good (to securing moral rights even when some defensible conception of the good must be sacrificed to some extent to do so) when the just commends a choice or course of conduct that the relevant conception of the good disfavors. Thus, in rights-based societies, individuals cannot morally justify an act that violates someone's moral rights by demonstrating that they believe for non-parochial reasons that one morally ought to engage in the conduct that violates the moral right in question, and the State cannot morally justify violating someone's moral rights by citing the fact that the rights-violating choice it wants to make would enable it to secure some morally defensible goal it was authorized to pursue. Indeed, in rights-based societies, individuals whose sincere moral convictions lead them to violate the moral rights of others and governments that violate moral rights to secure perfectly legitimate goals are subjected to a weighty type of moral criticism on that account.[1]

SECTION 2. THE TWO TYPES OF MORAL DISCOURSE IN WHICH THE MEMBERS AND GOVERNMENTS OF RIGHTS-BASED SOCIETIES ENGAGE

As I have already indicated, one of the defining characteristics of a rights-based society is the fact that its members and governments engage in two, strongly distinguished types of prescriptive-moral discourse—moral-rights discourse and moral-ought discourse. These two types of discourse differ in four respects. First, they differ in that they are grounded on different moral norms. For convenience, I call the moral norm from which moral-rights conclusions are derived the society's "basic moral principle" and any of the moral norms from which moral-ought conclusions can be derived in a rights-based society "personal ultimate values." Second, the source of the binding force of the norms that the two types of discourse employ is different. The individual members of, participants in, and governments of a rights-based society are bound by its basic moral principle even if they never personally advocated or explicitly agreed to be bound by it: they are bound by it solely by their membership or participation in the society in question. By way of contrast, the members of and participants in the society are (in a somewhat different sense) bound by the personal ultimate value to which they have committed themselves by their voluntary commitment to that norm (though individuals of integrity can change their minds about the moral norm they are personally committed to instantiating if they do so for proper reasons—for example, not because doing so serves their parochial self-interest). Third, moral-rights discourse and moral-ought discourse differ in that they have different domains: although the moral-ought question is always pertinent (since an individual can always ask whether he morally ought to fulfill a particular moral obligation), many private and State choices do not implicate anyone's moral rights (though, of course, one can always investigate whether a particular choice does implicate such rights). Fourth and relatedly, as the previous sentence implies, moral-rights discourse and moral-ought discourse also can differ in that the conclusions they generate can favor different and conflicting acts or courses of conduct.

It may be useful to illustrate the difference between moral-rights and moral-ought discourse. For this purpose, I need to specify the moral norm to whose instantiation the rights-based society in question is committed (its basic moral principle). Because I think that the United States and virtually all of the other countries at which the policy recommendations made by the economists I am criticizing are directed are *liberal,* rights-based societies, I will assume that the society in my example is a liberal, rights-based society—that is, a society whose concrete moral-rights commitments derive from a basic commitment to treating all moral-rights bearers for whom it is morally responsible with appropriate, equal respect and to showing appropriate (in the case of its members) or appropriate, equal (in the case of its governments) concern[2] for these individuals as well—in part for their "utility" as economists understand this concept but preeminently for their having and seizing the opportunity to lead lives of moral integrity by taking seriously both their moral obligations and the dialectical task of choosing and conforming their lives to a morally defensible, personally chosen conception of the good. Assume that I am a member of a liberal, rights-based society. Assume in addition that I have asked someone (call her Jill) to give me advice on a paper I have written before I present it at an academic conference. We can ask two different prescriptive-moral questions about Jill's position: whether Jill has a moral obligation to help me in this way and whether she morally ought to do so. My point is that different issues and moral norms are germane to answering these two questions and conflicting answers may be given to them. In particular, since, in liberal, rights-based cultures, Jill would not have a moral obligation to provide me with such assistance unless she (1) had promised to do so, (2) had a special status relationship to me (perhaps was a relative, friend, or member of my academic department), and/or (3) was a culpable cause-in-fact of my requiring assistance (had carelessly or willfully misinformed me of the date on which I was supposed to give the paper or had delayed and handicapped my preparation by failing to fulfill her obligation to return overdue books I had requested at the library), the internally correct answer to the above moral-obligation question would turn on the resolution of these promissory, status, and culpable-cause-in-fact issues.[3]

However, these issues may not be decisive—indeed, may not be relevant at all—to the determination of what Jill morally ought to do from one or more defensible personal-ultimate-value perspectives. Thus, the fact that Jill clearly does not have a moral obligation to help me with my work—had made no relevant promise, had no prior relationship with or connection to me, and was not a cause-in-fact of my need for help—leaves open the question of what she morally ought to do in the situation in question. For example, an unconventional utilitarian who accepts the coherence of the distinction between moral-rights claims and moral-ought claims and who recognizes that the society in question engages in a bifurcated prescriptive-moral discourse that pays heed to this distinction will still conclude that Jill morally ought to help me if he concludes that the all-things-considered utility cost to Jill of supplying the relevant help is lower than the all-things-considered net utility benefits to me and others of her doing so. Similarly, an unconventional utilitarian who recognizes that Jill has a moral obligation to help me because she had promised to do so, had a relevant status relationship to me, or was a culpable cause-in-fact of my needing help may still conclude that she morally ought not do so if her helping me will reduce total utility.

SECTION 3. THE DIFFERENT APPROACHES THAT PHILOSOPHERS AND OTHERS TAKE TO THE ANALYSIS OF JUSTICE (MORAL RIGHTS)

A significant number of philosophers (so-called Foundationalists) believe that one can derive an objectively true and hence universally applicable conception of justice (in my terms, basic moral principle) through purely conceptual analysis—in particular, from the concept of the moral, human freedom, human flourishing, or human nature. Although I do not deny the possibility that some such Foundationalist analysis may succeed, I have never been convinced by any such argument. I acknowledge that certain features of the moral are ineliminable—that is, that morality is not completely socially negotiable. However, I do not think that the ineliminable features of morality are sufficiently rich and varied to yield a unique, objectively true conception of justice. As the preceding discussions manifest, I believe that, rather than trying to discover such a universally applicable conception of justice through pure conceptual analysis, one should try to identify the moral type and more specific moral commitments of individual societies by executing philosophically informed empirical analyses of their members' and governments' prescriptive-moral discourse, perceptions, and conduct.[4]

The definitions of the four moral types of societies I find worth distinguishing implicitly reveal the empirical protocols I think one should use to identify them. Thus, to determine whether a society is moral-rights-based, one must observe (1) whether its members and governments distinguish moral-rights claims from moral-ought claims linguistically and use different arguments when asserting, defending, and evaluating these two types of prescriptive-moral claims and (2) whether they believe that moral-rights conclusions trump moral-ought conclusions when the two conflict (conform their conduct to the moral-rights conclusion when the two conflict and subject those who violate moral rights to instantiate some personal ultimate value to severe moral criticism and possibly material sanctions as well).

At this juncture, however, the more relevant empirical protocol is the approach one should take to identifying the basic moral principle of a rights-based society. In my judgment, conclusions about the abstract moral norm (the basic moral principle) on which a particular rights-based society is committed to grounding its moral-rights discourse and conduct should be based on the application of two criteria. The first, "best fit" criterion focuses on how closely the following facts fit the claim that each of the various candidates for the relevant rights-based society's "basic moral principle" title is in fact its basic moral principle: (1) the moral-rights claims that were made and not made, (2) the arguments that were made and not made in support of and against these claims by the disputants and those who evaluated the claims in question (by observers and any official decision makers who address the issue), (3) the conclusions that were reached about the claims in question both by those who resolved them and by others, (4) how close the "cases" in question were perceived to be (where "cases" is enquoted because the overwhelming majority will not be legal cases), (5) how certain not only decision makers but also observers were about the correct resolution of the claims in question, and (6) the extent to which the conduct of the members and governments of the society in question was consistent with the moral obligations they would have if the respective candidates for the society's basic-moral-principle title were its basic moral principle.

The second criterion one should use to evaluate candidates for a rights-based society's "basic moral principle" title is an "explicability of non-fit" criterion. This criterion is relevant because the damage that a non-fit does to the candidacy of a defensible moral norm for a rights-based society's basic-moral-principle title is reduced (the non-fit should be discounted) to the extent that the non-fit is explicable in certain ways—that is, because the basic moral principle of such a society is the moral norm that best discounted-fits the facts it should fit. In any event, this explicability-of-non-fit criterion focuses on the extent to which non-fits can be explained by (1) the greater power of the non-fit's beneficiaries (though explanations of this kind call into question the society's moral integrity), (2) the presence of conventional transaction costs or other types of costs that make it unattractive for parties to pursue justified moral-rights claims, attractive for parties to pursue unjustified moral-rights claims, attractive for parties to oppose justified moral-rights claims, or unattractive for parties to oppose unjustified moral-rights claims, (3) the fact that the claimants, defendants, decision makers, or observers whose conduct or perceptions did not fit the relevant candidate did not adequately consider the choices they made, the moral conclusions they reached, or the perceptions they expressed (for example, the fact that the choices and evaluations in question were made in haste under emergency conditions), (4) conceptual errors that the relevant actors may very well have made (for example, confusions among the psychological, welfare, and entitlement senses of interest or concern), or (5) empirical or other sorts of errors that may have been made in good faith by relevant actors, deciders, or observers.

SECTION 4. THE COMMITMENTS OF A LIBERAL, RIGHTS-BASED SOCIETY

As I have already asserted, I believe that an acceptably thorough and philosophically informed empirical analysis of the facts the preceding paragraph claimed are relevant to the identification of a rights-based society's basic moral principle would yield the conclusion that the United States and most of the other countries for which the economists on whom this book focuses are making policy recommendations are *liberal,* rights-based societies of requisite though certainly imperfect moral integrity in the sense in which I previously defined the term *liberal.*[5]

It would be helpful to begin this account by describing three incommensurabilities that liberalism recognizes that significantly affect the obligations and rights of the members of and participants in a liberal, rights-based society. First, liberalism draws a strong distinction between (1) the satisfaction a choice confers on the individual who made it or someone else by satisfying his prejudices or indulging his preference to inflict pain or other sorts of losses on others, to degrade them, or to control them when doing so cannot be justicized (shown to be just) and (2) the satisfaction a choice confers on the chooser or someone else for other, non-illiberal reasons. Thus, although liberalism recognizes that individuals have a right to allow certain choices (say, an individual's choice of a spouse) to be influenced by prejudice, in general, liberalism does not place a positive weight on the utility people obtain by disadvantaging or harming the targets of their prejudices: indeed, in general, from a liberal perspective, the fact that a choice's attractiveness to the chooser was critically affected by the satisfaction it gave him by disadvantaging someone against whom he was prejudiced renders it morally impermissible (rights-violative). Liberalism also does not place a positive value on the satisfaction a choice gives the chooser or someone else because it satisfies the relevant individual's desire to inflict pain on or impose some other type of loss on its target, to degrade its target, or to control its target when these effects cannot be justicized: indeed, once more, the fact that the relevant choice's attractiveness to the chooser was critically affected by its indulging such an illiberal preference will render it morally impermissible from the perspective of liberalism.

Second, liberalism places a lexically higher value on any effect a choice has on the opportunity that a relevant creature has to lead a life of moral integrity than on any impact it has on what I will refer to as "mere utility." In other words, from a liberal perspective, the fact that a choice will reduce on balance the opportunity that relevant individuals have to lead lives of moral integrity to the smallest possible extent will render it morally impermissible (rights-violative), regardless of the extent to which it increases total utility, and the fact that a choice will increase on balance the opportunity that relevant individuals have to lead lives of moral integrity will render it morally permissible (and in some instances morally obligatory), regardless of the extent to which it would decrease total utility.

Third, liberalism draws a strong distinction between the duties that the members of and participants in a liberal, rights-based society have to avoid imposing losses on each other and the duties they have to assist (say, to rescue) each other. The liberal position on the duty to rescue accommodates two conflicting implications of liberalism's placement of a preeminently high value on individuals' having and seizing the opportunity to lead lives of moral integrity. In the one direction and most obviously, liberalism's valuation of individuals' having and seizing the opportunity to lead lives of moral integrity favors the existence of a duty to rescue imperiled moral-rights-holders who would or might otherwise die, suffer neurological injuries that would prevent them from leading lives of moral integrity, or suffer other sorts of injuries that would strongly militate against their leading lives of moral integrity by subjecting them to life-dominating pain or depression. In the other direction, less obviously and admittedly more contestably, at least to the extent that (1) individuals are more likely to seize the opportunity to lead lives of moral integrity if they perceive themselves to be the authors of their own lives and (2) the imposition of positive duties on them works against their feeling that they control their choices, liberalism's prioritization of individuals' having and seizing the opportunity to lead lives of moral integrity disfavors the imposition of positive duties on individuals in general and duties to rescue in particular. The liberal accommodation of these two conflicting implications of the preeminently high value it places on individuals' having and seizing the opportunity to lead lives of moral integrity is that (assuming that they have made no relevant promise, have no relevant status relationship with the potential rescuee, and were not the culpable cause of the potential rescuee's imperilment) the individual members of and participants in a liberal, rights-based society have a moral duty to rescue or provide assistance to each other if and only if (1) the relevant rescue attempt would reduce the probability that the potential rescuee would suffer a (nonmonetary) loss that would preclude him from or strongly militate against his having and seizing the opportunity to lead a life of moral integrity and (2) the relevant rescue attempt would not (A) impose a significant risk that the rescue attempter would suffer a substantial bodily injury or death and (B) consume an exorbitant amount of the potential rescuer's time.

I should add that the expression *nonmonetary* in the preceding sentence reflects the principle that I call "liberal dualism"—a principle that specifies most broadly that the moral obligations that the members of and participants in a liberal, rights-based society have when acting in nonpolitical capacities are different from the moral obligations that the governments of such a society have and that its members have when voting for State policies or their political representatives. Thus, because (1) the individual members of and participants in a liberal, rights-based society are not the cause-in-fact of the poverty of others that would deprive them of or strongly undermine their opportunity to lead lives of moral integrity and (2) would not be culpable for their poverty even if for some reason they caused it (for example, because their superior skill caused a competitor to become impoverished by forcing him into bankruptcy), in their private capacities, better-off individuals do not have a moral obligation to rescue impoverished society members from poverty that precludes them and their families from leading lives of moral integrity (though they may be morally obligated to support State policies that prevent poverty from depriving moral-rights bearers for whom the State is responsible from having a meaningful opportunity to lead lives of moral integrity).[6]

Before proceeding to list the most important concrete moral obligations of the members of, participants in, and governments of a liberal, rights-based society, I should point out one additional implication of the principle of liberal dualism that bears on the content of some tort-related and contract-related moral obligations in such societies: because the individual members of and participants in such societies are not culpable causes-in-fact of each other's income/wealth positions (which affect the marginal utility of money to them) or dispositions to obtain utility from material resources (which affect the marginal utility of money to them, given their income/wealth positions), (1) any duty an individual potential injurer has not to discount the losses his choices may impose on others by causing them to suffer injuries or illnesses and/or other material losses that would deprive them of mere utility (as opposed to depriving them of the opportunity to lead lives of moral integrity for nonmaterial reasons) should focus on the equivalent-dollar effects the choice may generate rather than on its impact on mere utility, and (2) any duty a contract participant has not to discount his contract partner's interests when making choices that relate to his performance obligations is a duty not to make a relevant choice against his contract partner's interest that the chooser would not have found attractive had he not placed a lower weight on the average dollar of any equivalent-dollar loss he should have expected it to impose on his contract partner than on the average equivalent-dollar gain it would confer on him.

I will now delineate four sets of moral obligations that the members of and participants in a liberal, rights-based society share. The first set is made up of moral obligations that are created by intimate relationships and certain status relationships that liberalism values *inter alia* but especially for the contribution they make to their participants' taking their lives morally seriously. Although these conclusions are clearly contestable, I believe that, in a liberal, rights-based society, a participant in such a relationship who is in a position to do so has a moral obligation to take positive steps to secure and preserve his relationship partner's opportunity to lead a life of moral integrity and to place far more similar weights on the other's and his mere utility than he is obligated to do to the utility of others with whom he has no such relationship. Thus, parents have moral obligations to their children and vice versa, and spouses have moral obligations to each other that they do not have to strangers. These obligations clearly include obligations to provide financial support and (in the case of parents to children) certain kinds of emotional and education inputs and may extend to a duty to provide transplant-material even when doing so creates some risk of death or substantial bodily harm (for example, in the case of future illness or injury).

The second set of liberal moral obligations that individuals have relates to contract formation and performance. The individual members of a liberal, rights-based society have an obligation not to induce others to enter into contracts through fraud, deceit, misrepresentation, or coercion and (as I have already indicated) an obligation within a contractual relationship to reject performance choices that would impose losses on their contract partners that would be unattractive for the chooser if he placed the same weight on the average equivalent-dollar gain or loss it generated for his contract partners as on the average equivalent-dollar gain or loss it generated for him.

The third set of moral obligations that liberalism imposes on individuals is covered by tort law and sometimes criminal law. Liberalism places a moral obligation on individuals not to invade each other's privacy unjustifiably. It also declares morally impermissible all choices whose attractiveness to the chooser was critically affected by his desire to inflict pain on, impose other sorts of losses on, degrade, or control others (when the actor's behaving in these ways cannot be justicized). The liberal duty of appropriate, equal respect and appropriate concern also renders it morally impermissible for any member of or participant in a liberal, rights-based society (1) to commit an assault or battery, (2) to engage in libel, slander, defamation, or intentional misrepresentation, (3) to intentionally subject someone to emotional distress, (4) to obtain benefits from another through fraud or deceit, (5) to harm someone by abusing a legal process or engaging in malicious prosecution, or (6) to falsely imprison someone, regardless of whether the injurer committed the relevant acts because he valued harming, degrading, or controlling his victims. In addition, in some circumstances, liberalism imposes duties on choosers to avoid imposing accident and pollution losses on others whom they do not wish to harm. In particular, when the loss in question is a mere-utility loss, liberalism requires the relevant chooser to make all avoidance moves he believed or should have believed *ex ante* would have generated higher certainty-equivalent allocative benefits than costs (even if the individual did not think in such terms). When the loss might deprive a victim of the opportunity to lead a life of moral integrity, liberalism obligates the potential avoider to make all avoidance moves that he believed or should have believed *ex ante* would reduce the extent to which on balance he deprived others of the opportunity to lead lives of moral integrity by imposing (nonmonetary) accident and pollution losses on them (assuming that the move would not endanger his opportunity to lead a life of moral integrity). As I have already indicated, each member of and participant in a liberal, rights-based society also has a duty to attempt to rescue others whose opportunities to lead lives of moral integrity are imperiled when (1) the attempt would reduce the probability that the potential rescuee would suffer such a loss, (2) the attempt would not subject the rescuer to a significant risk of substantial bodily harm, (3) the attempt would not consume an exorbitant amount of the potential rescuer's time, and (4) the potential rescuer was uniquely well placed to effectuate the rescue (or to contribute to the probability of rescue by adding his attempt to that of others who were better placed to execute the rescue than he was or were as well placed as he was to effectuate the relevant rescue).

The fourth set of moral obligations that the members of and participants in a liberal, rights-based State share relates to their property rights. Liberalism is not hostile to private property. To the contrary, within limits, liberalism may be favorably disposed to private property for three reasons. First, a properly regulated system of private property may—by increasing allocative efficiency—increase a society's ability to provide its members with the material wherewithal that will contribute to their having and seizing the opportunity to lead lives of moral integrity. Second, at least if it is combined with appropriate redistributive policies, a system of private property—by increasing allocative efficiency—can also contribute to the mere utility of the society's members and participants. Third, liberals also value private property to the extent that private property protects it owners' privacy by establishing a physical space in which an owner is relatively protected against private or State intrusion and/or financial security that protects the individual against private and State interference more generally. Of course, liberalism would impose some limits on private property—not only those suggested by the possibility that such property may be used in an externality-generating, allocatively inefficient way but also (more fundamentally) by the moral right of all members of and participants in a liberal, rights-based society to the resources that will significantly contribute to their being in a position to lead lives of moral integrity. In any event, the members of and participants in a liberal, rights-based society have a moral duty not to commit theft or unlawful conversion, not to trespass on other people's land, and not to violate rights to real and other types of property in any other way.

Now that I have given this admittedly partial account of the moral obligations of the members of and participants in a liberal, rights-based society, I can proceed to the moral obligations of such a society's government. *Inter alia,* the government of a liberal, rights-based society is obligated

1. not itself to violate the contract, tort, and property rights of those for whom it is responsible or to discriminate against them;

2. to take all steps consistent with its overarching obligation to maximize the rights-related interests of the members of and participants in its society to deter individual rights-violations (*inter alia* by educating those for whom it is responsible to respect each other's rights and by providing appropriate legal disincentives to rights-violations);
3. to provide victims of moral-rights violations with a meaningful opportunity to obtain redress from those individuals who have violated their rights (that is, to secure its subjects' secondary, corrective-justice rights);
4. to provide each victim of a moral-rights violation who, through no fault of his own, is unable to identify the particular wrongdoer who injured him among a set of wrongdoers who have caused the kind of loss he suffered with a legal right to obtain compensation from the wrongdoers in question;[7]
5. to secure for each moral-rights-bearer for whom it is responsible whatever he needs (nutrition, health care, housing, psychological nurturing, general education, exposure to alternative conceptions of the good and lifestyles, privacy, the opportunity to enter into and maintain intimate relationships, relative real income, and so on) to have a meaningful opportunity to lead a life of moral integrity;
6. not to violate the liberty interests of those for whom it is responsible (to inhibit or prevent them from living lives that their conception of the good commends) unless doing so promotes the rights-related interests of the society's members and participants on balance, to take all steps consistent with its overarching duty to promote its subjects' rights-related interests to prevent private actors from violating each other's liberty interests, and to provide those whose liberty interests have been violated with effective legal redress against the violators;
7. to provide all competent members of the society in question with an appropriate, equal opportunity to influence the content of the laws that will subsequently govern them;
8. to give each moral-rights holder for whom it is responsible appropriate opportunities to participate in any judicial or administrative proceeding that affects his welfare or the protection of his moral rights;
9. to subject its decisions to appropriate quality-control;
10. not to impose a loss on someone for whom the society in question is responsible for no good reason at all (even if the relevant choice was subjected to appropriate quality-control); and
11. not to promote a particular conception of the good (as opposed to the desirability of leading a life of moral integrity, which entails *inter alia*

developing a defensible personal conception of the good and making choices that are consonant with it).

SECTION 5. SOME PERSONAL ULTIMATE VALUES TO WHICH SIGNIFICANT PERCENTAGES OF THE MEMBERS OF CONTEMPORARY LIBERAL, RIGHTS-BASED SOCIETIES SUBSCRIBE

As I have already indicated, the numerous moral choices in a rights-based society that do not implicate someone's moral rights are not supposed to be controlled by the moral norm the society is committed to instantiating. Instead, the prescriptive-moral evaluation of these choices must be based on some (defensible) personal ultimate value. I will now list and define the five categories of personal ultimate values that, I suspect, have the most support in contemporary liberal, rights-based societies. The first such category is utilitarian values. Many members of contemporary liberal, rights-based societies believe that, rights-considerations aside, utility considerations determine what morally ought to be done.[8] In fact, contemporary utilitarians fall into two camps: the classical utilitarian believes that any claim (choice) should be evaluated solely by whether its recognition (selection) increases or decreases the total utility of all creatures whose utility counts, while the "modern" utilitarian believes that any claim (choice) should be evaluated solely by whether its recognition (selection) increases or decreases the average utility of all creatures whose utility counts. This difference may be salient when the number of creatures whose utility counts will be affected by the option that is selected.

A second personal ultimate value to which some members of contemporary liberal, rights-based societies subscribe is equal-utility egalitarianism. According to this norm, moral-rights considerations aside, private choices, government choices, or claim resolutions should be evaluated exclusively by their impact on the equality of the utility experienced by the relevant society's moral-rights holders.

A third personal ultimate value to which some members of liberal, rights-based societies are committed is equal resource egalitarianism. According to this norm, moral-rights-considerations aside, the choice that morally ought to be made in any situation is the choice that would reduce to the greatest extent possible the inequality of the amount of resources (measured, presumably, by their allocative cost) allocated to the society's various moral-rights holders.

A fourth personal ultimate value to which some members of contemporary liberal, rights-based society subscribe is equality-of-opportunity egalitarianism. According to this value (cluster of values), moral-rights-considerations aside, one morally ought always to make the choice that minimizes the inequality of the opportunities that the society's various moral-rights holders have to do the things that the supporters of the relevant variant of this value believe all people should have the same opportunity to do. (The variants of this value differ by the nature of the opportunities that they posit should be distributed equally.) I should add that, presumably, variants of each of the last three values just described can also be distinguished by the metric their respective supporters believe should be used to measure the inequalities with which they are concerned ("presumably" because I am unaware of any attempt by the proponents of these values to articulate the inequality-metric they think is appropriate).

The final "personal ultimate value" to which many members of contemporary liberal, rights-based societies are committed is libertarianism. In practice, libertarianism has two components. The first is a distributive component. Libertarians believe that each moral-rights holder has a moral right to (and certainly morally ought to be allowed to keep) all wealth and income he secured without directly violating a moral right of anyone else—all wealth and income he secured by earning it by performing labor[9] or investing, by finding it, by securing it through luck in general, or by obtaining it as a gift or bequest. The second component of libertarianism is a liberty component. In practice, those self-styled libertarians who focus on concrete legal problems tend to base their analysis of liberty issues on the assumption that people can make themselves anew at any time; that they are always able to choose their values, preferences, dispositions, and so on; that they are uninfluenced or at least unencumbered by experience. At least, that is the inference I draw from the fact that libertarians assume that there are no prerequisites for individuals' having the capacity to exercise autonomy in a meaningful way or, more concretely, that one cannot justify (for example) restricting the opportunity that adults have to access pornography on the Internet by citing the possible damage that children might suffer if the scheme that facilitated adult access to such material enabled kids to access it as well.[10] I should add that these two components of libertarianism may be connected. Just as the liberty component of libertarianism assumes that individuals will their values, preferences, and dispositions, its distributive component may reflect an assumption that individuals will (are morally responsible for) their own productivity (though it clearly also reflects an unargued-for and to my mind dubious premise that individuals are entitled to keep the proceeds of their luck).

I began this discussion of libertarianism by enquoting its characterization as a "personal ultimate value" system. I did so because of my doubts about the moral status of libertarianism—about whether libertarian "values" are defensible in the sense of deserving to be called moral values at all. Basically, my concern is empirical. People do not will—are not morally responsible for—their productivity. In my judgment, regardless of whether an individual's labor product is measured in marginal or average terms or in terms of value to employer or allocative product, the vast majority of interpersonal differences in labor productivity reflect things over which individuals have no control—their genetic endowments, the nutrition they received *in utero,* the material and psychological resources they were given in their infancy, the family and neighborhood environments in which they grew up, the educational resources with which they were supplied, the utility preferences that members of their society (or people more generally) have for the goods and services they were capable of supplying, the distribution of income in their society or in the world (which will affect the market value of their labor, given the preferences of their output's potential consumers), the number of people in their society (or in the world) who can provide the types of labor they can supply, the availability of complements to the products they can produce, and so on. Even if one assumes that individuals are partly responsible for their labor product (as any moral analysis almost certainly must do since it must reject strict determinism), the assumption that people are sufficiently morally responsible for their labor productivity for it to be just to allow them to keep the fruits of their labor strikes me as being disqualifyingly unrealistic. I also do not think that one can defend the luck component of the libertarian distributive norm—that one can demonstrate that people are entitled to keep the proceeds of their own luck. Libertarianism's implicit assumption that individuals create their own preferences, values, and dispositions also strikes me as disqualifyingly unrealistic. In any event, that is why I enquoted the expression "personal ultimate value" when using it to classify or characterize libertarianism.

SECTION 6. THE STRUCTURE OF MORAL-RIGHTS ARGUMENT AND DIFFERENT TYPES OF MORAL-OUGHT ARGUMENT

Now that I have delineated and elaborated on the liberal norm that grounds the moral-rights commitments of the societies at which most of the policy recommendations of the economists this book is criticizing are directed and the various personal ultimate values to which significant percentages of those societies' individual members subscribe, I can block out the structure of moral-rights argument and different types of moral-ought argument. Moral-rights arguments have five steps:

1. determine whether the society in question is a moral-rights-based society (by using the protocol previously described);
2. if the society in question is moral-rights-based, identify its basic moral principle (by using the protocol previously described);
3. determine the set of creatures that are moral-rights holders in the society in question by (1) evaluating the candidates for the society's moral-status-determining-attribute title by (A) assessing the fit between each and the substantive moral rights that the society's moral-rights holders have and the fit between each and the conclusions the society's members and governments have reached about the moral-rights-bearing status of different creatures and (B) discounting the non-fits associated with each candidate by their discount-justifying explicability and (2) examining the implications of one's moral-status-defining-attribute conclusion for the rights-bearing status of different actual creatures;
4. analyze the society's basic moral principle and the relevant facts to determine whether the choice to be assessed either violates a *prima facie* negative right of a moral-rights holder for whom the chooser is responsible or is *ceteris paribus* required by someone's *prima facie* positive right against the chooser in question; and
5. analyze the society's basic moral principle and the relevant facts to determine whether the rejection of a choice that would otherwise be required by the *prima facie* moral right of a relevant moral-rights holder is rendered just by its increasing the extent to which the total rights-related interests of all relevant moral-rights holders are secured or (where relevant) whether the execution of a choice that would otherwise be forbidden by the *prima facie* right of a relevant moral-rights holder is rendered just by its decreasing the extent to which the total rights-related interests of all relevant moral-rights holders are secured.

I will now outline the basic structure of moral-ought arguments. Like all moral-rights arguments, all moral-ought arguments have to resolve the boundary-condition issue: in the case of moral-ought arguments, have to determine the creatures whose positions the evaluator believes morally ought to be considered. After that, however, moral-ought arguments diverge into two families.

The first family of moral-ought arguments proceeds from a value perspective that gives utilitarian considerations some weight. In a rights-based society, not only pure utilitarian moral-ought evaluations but also moral-ought evaluations that proceed from a mixture of utilitarian and other values (such as equal-utility, equal-resource, or equal-opportunity egalitarianism) can best be executed through the following eight-step procedure (assuming that the evaluator can make any morally permissible change from the status quo or no change at all and believes that we morally ought to fulfill our obligations):

1. determine the set of moral-rights holders;
2. determine whether a particular choice is required or prohibited by the rights of any moral-rights holder—if a particular choice is required by our moral-rights-commitments, that choice morally ought to be made; if a particular choice is prohibited by our moral-rights-commitments, follow the rest of the protocol to determine which nonproscribed choice morally ought to be made; if a particular choice is neither required by nor prohibited by our moral-rights commitments, follow the rest of the protocol to determine which choice morally ought to be made;
3. use economic-efficiency analysis to predict the equivalent-dollar gains that each morally permissible change from the status quo will confer on its beneficiaries and the equivalent-dollar losses it will impose on its victims;
4. specify the personal ultimate value or personal-ultimate-value combination on which the relevant moral-ought conclusion will be based—*inter alia,* specify the facts that the value in question makes germane to the consideration of the distributive desirability of the choice in question;[11]
5. collect the facts that the above value or value-combination deems relevant to the distributive desirability of the choice in question;
6. use the value-specification in (4) and the facts in (5) to generate weights to be attached to the average equivalent-dollar gain and average equivalent-dollar loss yielded by each morally permissible change from the status quo;
7. for each relevant change from the status quo, calculate the weighted equivalent-dollar gains the change would generate, the weighted equivalent-dollar losses the change would generate, and the difference between them; and
8. evaluate all changes or no change according to the net weighted equivalent-dollar effect of each; recommend the change with the highest positive net weighted equivalent-dollar gain or recommend no change if all changes would yield lower net weighted equivalent-dollar gains than losses (the

evaluator should be indifferent to making a change that yields equal net weighted equivalent-dollar gains and losses).

The second set of moral-ought arguments proceeds from purely nonutilitarian values. Although some of these values focus on the intent of the actors to bring about certain consequences that are perceived to be bad in themselves, I will focus on values in this set that give no weight to total utility for other sorts of reasons. For example, someone who is committed exclusively to an equality-of-utility or equality-of-opportunity value will not be willing to trade any inequality of these sorts for any increase in utility. And again, a pure libertarian will not be willing to trade even the smallest increase in the divergence between the incomes individuals receive and what they deserve according to libertarian notions for any increase in utility or economic efficiency. Moral-ought evaluations that proceed from this second set of values will start with the same two steps with which their utilitarian counterpart began and then proceed as follows:

3. specify the personal ultimate value or personal-ultimate-value combination on which the relevant moral-ought conclusion will be based;
4. collect the facts that the above value or value-combination deems relevant;
5. use the relevant value or value-combination to assess the moral desirability of each morally permissible choice; and
6. recommend the choice that is most desirable.

If the actor does not believe he always morally ought to fulfill his societally imposed commitments, step 2 drops out, and the fact that an option fulfills or violates those commitments is relevant only insofar as it has consequences he values.

SECTION 7. THE TYPES OF LEGAL RIGHTS THAT EXIST IN MORAL-RIGHTS-BASED SOCIETIES

For current purposes, three or perhaps four categories of legal rights are worth distinguishing. The first contains the legal counterparts of the moral rights the society in question is committed to securing. Since I believe that rights-based societies are morally obligated to make moral rights legal rights unless doing so would sacrifice, on balance, the rights-related interests of those for whom they are responsible, I believe that this category of legal rights is quite extensive—includes not only fundamental-fairness-type constitutional rights but also all private-law (contract-law, tort-law, and property-law) rights that are the legal counterparts to contract-related, tort-related, and property-related moral rights, many of which I previously listed. I might add that, in my judgment, to be legitimate, the common law of all rights-based societies that have such a body of law must be exclusively concerned with giving legal force to contract-related, tort-related, and property-related moral rights.[12] The second category of legal rights contains legal rights that were created by legislation (including administrative rule-making or judicial decision making that was in fact legislative) that was successfully designed to effectuate a legitimate personal ultimate value (to achieve a legitimate goal). The third category of legal rights contains legal rights that were created by legislation that was designed to secure the parochial interests of its supporters.[13] A fourth category of legal rights that may be worth distinguishing in some contexts contains legal rights that were created by legislation that was promulgated mistakenly with the intention of securing moral rights, achieving defensible goals, or promoting the parochial interests of its supporters or beneficiaries.[14]

SECTION 8. LEGITIMATE AND VALID LEGAL ARGUMENT

In my terminology, a legal argument or the use of an argument to determine the answer to a legal-rights question that is correct as a matter of law is "legitimate" in a given society if it is consistent with (in some instances, is required by) that society's moral commitments. By way of possible contrast, in my terminology, a legal argument is "valid" in a given society if in that society it plays a role in the determination of the answers to individual legal-rights questions that are correct as a matter of law.

Legal arguments can be legitimate only in societies of moral integrity because only such societies have moral commitments. As I have already indicated, both goal-based societies and rights-based societies can have moral integrity. In goal-based societies, legal arguments are legitimate if and only if their use is consistent with the relevant society's moral-ought commitment. In rights-based societies, legal arguments are legitimate if and only if their use is consistent with the relevant society's moral-rights (justice) commitments.

If all societies of moral integrity were societies of perfect moral integrity, there would be no difference between the set of legal arguments that are legitimate and the set that are valid in any society of moral integrity. In reality, however, societies that fulfill their moral commitments sufficiently to warrant the conclusion that they are societies of moral integrity will almost always be societies of imperfect moral integrity. For example, the constitutions of some such societies have provisions whose concrete implications were understood by their ratifiers that are inconsistent with the society's moral commitments.[15] In any such society, legal arguments that are based on the text and history of those morally illegitimate constitutional provisions will be valid even though they are illegitimate, and the answers to legal-rights questions that they favor may be correct as a matter of law even though they are immoral (illegitimate) by the society's own standards. Because the following discussion of legal argument applies to legal argument in the United States and will be read by people who, by and large, are most interested in American legal practice, I should point out that—with two probable exceptions[16]—since the Reconstruction amendments, the United States Constitution contains no provisions that are inconsistent with the country's moral commitments. I therefore believe that, in the contemporary United States, legitimate and valid legal argument coincides in all cases that do not involve the exceptions in question.

SECTION 9. MY OWN POSITION ON LEGITIMATE AND VALID LEGAL ARGUMENT IN A LIBERAL, RIGHTS-BASED SOCIETY

I start with an admission. My own (liberal-legalist) account of legitimate and valid legal argument in liberal, rights-based societies is highly contested. In fact, the majority of American law professors would almost certainly reject it in favor of some variant of legal realism or legal positivism. For this reason, after this section presents my position, the next discusses the positions that legal realists and legal positivists take on valid legal argument in the societies on which they focus.[17]

My conclusions about the structure and content of legitimate and valid legal argument in a liberal, rights-based society are substantially grounded on the following moral axiom: for a rights-based (or goal-based) society to have moral integrity, its legal-argument practice and the conclusions it reaches about the answers to legal-rights questions that are correct as a matter of law must be consistent with its moral commitments. This axiom implies not just that the basic moral principle to which a rights-based society of moral integrity is committed is part of its law (*inter alia,* that all moral rights are *prima facie* legal rights) but also that the principle in question operates more widely to determine the moral legitimacy and presumptive validity of using the other types of argument that members of our culture have used to determine the answer to legal-rights questions that are correct as a matter of law—more specifically, (1) to identify the variants of the general modes of legal argument that have been used in the relevant legal culture whose use is respectively (A) morally legitimate and valid and (B) morally illegitimate and invalid and (2) to establish the legal force in particular situations of those types of argument whose use is valid.

Some elaboration may be useful. I will therefore explain the way in which arguments of moral principle inform the use of the other general modes of legal argument that are employed in the United States. The first general mode I will consider is textual argument. Textual argument focuses on such things as the ordinary or technical meaning at the time of its relevant use of the language of a legally relevant utterance or text (constitution, statute, ordinance, administrative regulation, contract, corporate charter, trust agreement, and so on); whether a particular interpretation of a component of that text or utterance would render one or more of its other components irrelevant or would contradict one or more of its other components; whether a particular interpretation of a component of a text or utterance would balance the values, interests, or goals at stake in the way in which they were balanced by the other components of the relevant document or utterance; the nature of the document or utterance being considered (whether it is a constitution, statute, ordinance, or private contract); and the placement of the relevant language in the document or utterance as a whole (whether a disputed provision of a constitution is in a power-creating or power-limiting section of the document, whether a disputed provision in a contract is in a duty-creating or remedial section of the document). A rights-based society's basic moral principle can make the greatest positive contribution to textual analysis when the language in question refers to some justice-related moral norm, as do constitutional references to "unenumerated rights," "privileges or immunities," and "equal protection" and private-law references to "good faith," "fair notice," or "unconscionable" conduct. The fact that the society in which such language is being used is a (liberal) rights-based society implies that the relevant expressions should be interpreted by reference to its basic (liberal) moral principle—that the interpreter need not rely on his own or someone else's personal ultimate values to concretize them. A rights-based society's basic moral principle can also inform textual analysis when the relevant text is ambiguous but may well be communicating an instruction or announcing an arrangement that contradicts the society's moral commitments. In such circumstances, the rights-based society's basic moral principle may favor giving the relevant text a saving construction or declaring the law it promulgates void as unconstitutional (the private arrangement it articulates void as *contra bones mores*).

A second general mode of argument that is sometimes used to interpret written communications or utterances is structural argument. Structural argument interprets vague or ambiguous language in light of the point of the arrangement to which the language relates (the *raison d'être* of the government a constitution organizes and controls, the goal a statute was designed to secure, or the goal a contract was formed to achieve). The basic moral principle of a rights-based society informs its structural constitutional arguments because the point of such a society's government is to secure the moral rights that are corollaries of that principle. A rights-based society's basic moral principle will also sometimes inform structural arguments that are used to interpret statutes, ordinances, and administrative rules—will disfavor conclusions that particular pieces of legislation are designed to achieve goals whose pursuit would violate the society's moral commitments and (in a few instances) will suggest that a statute was passed to secure moral rights that could not otherwise be secured (for example, that the common law's adoption of a binary approach to cause-in-fact precludes it from securing).[18]

A third general mode of argument that is sometimes used in (liberal) rights-based societies to determine the answer to a legal-rights question that is correct as a matter of law is historical argument. As I have already indicated, some historical arguments focus on the meaning of a text or utterance's individual words or expressions in the relevant context at the time they were written or spoken. Other historical arguments focus on such things as the alternative textual formulations that were rejected; the causes (historical antecedents) of the enactment's passage or contract's formation; the content of other decisions made contemporaneously by an enactment's supporters or a contract's participants; and statements made contemporaneously by an enactment's supporters or a contract's participants about the values they were hoping to further or more concrete goals they were trying to secure. Some American lawyers and legal scholars have argued that one should use narrow-gauged historical analysis to determine the extensions of constitutional or statutory language even when the language in question refers to moral concepts. For example, some such experts have argued that the answer to whether criminal statutes prohibiting homosexual acts (but not analogous heterosexual acts) violate the privileges or immunities or equal protection clause of the Fourteenth Amendment turns on whether the conduct in question was criminalized by any or some percentage of the states at the time of the amendment's ratification. Arguments of moral principle (more accurately, the argument that justifies the philosophically informed empirical procedure I think one must use to identify the specific moral commitments of a given rights-based society) imply that the appropriate historical analysis is far more broad-gauged: that the society's relevant commitments can be identified only by examining the way in which, throughout its history, its members and governments have valued and treated (1) the various kinds of interests that homosexuals have in engaging in homosexual acts and (2) the various kinds of interests that people who disapprove of such conduct have in its criminalization. Although the criminal status of homosexual acts in different states at the time of the Fourteenth Amendment's ratification is certainly relevant to this broad enquiry, "philosophical analysis" indicates that such facts represent only a tiny percentage of the data that are relevant to the resolution of the moral and constitutional issue in question.

A fourth general mode of argument that is used in at least some rights-based societies is argument that focuses on the holdings of prior cases, canons of statutory construction, and various other kinds of legal practice. Not all rights-based societies rely on legal precedent to give their society's members and participants fair notice of the laws that apply to them: the practice of precedent is but one of a number of ways in which such societies can fulfill this moral duty. However, arguments of moral principle (or perhaps I should say an understanding of the ways in which precedent practices can affect rights-related interests) can reveal the details of the practice of precedent that can fulfill a (liberal) rights-based society's overarching moral duty. The crucial issue is: What weight should be given to a precedent that was wrong as a matter of law when first announced or that has been rendered inapplicable to a subsequent case that is in some ways similar to the case in which the precedent was announced by changes in the facts that affect the various interests that the initial decision had to accommodate? Arguments of moral principle imply (moral analysis implies) that an initially wrong decision should not be followed unless the net rights-related interests it sacrificed (its repetition would sacrifice, fair-notice considerations aside) were less weighty than the fair-notice rights-related interests that would be sacrificed by not following the precedent (where the latter interests are interests of individuals [not the State] who relied on the precedent reasonably [could not be expected to have realized that the precedent was or might well have been wrong or is no longer applicable to their situation]).[19]

The fifth and final general mode of legal argument that is used in the United States (in addition to arguments of moral principle) is called "prudential argument." In fact, this expression is used to refer to a wide range of arguments: arguments that focus on (1) the utility consequences of the legal-decisions that might be made, (2) the likelihood that the addressees of a particular legal ruling will obey them, (3) the likelihood that lower courts will follow or executive-branch officials will enforce particular judicial rulings, (4) the extent to which the members of American society will be willing to accept particular judicial rulings, (5) the losses that will result if the members of and participants in American society react to particular rulings by violating other laws, and (6) the likelihood that particular rulings will reduce the judicial system's ability to perform its functions in the future (for example, that public officials will react to particular rulings by packing the courts or reducing their jurisdiction and that the public will react to such rulings by disobeying the courts' future rulings more generally). Although I admit that the following conclusion is contestable, in my judgment, the use of the last five variants of prudential argument just listed is morally impermissible: rights-based societies cannot justicize rejecting legal conclusions that would otherwise be correct as a matter of law because their members and participants would not obey them, their officials would not enforce them, their members and participants would respond to them by acting lawlessly more generally, and/or their officials would react to them by undermining the judicial branch of the government. Societies of moral integrity are morally obligated to react to the prospect of such moral-rights violations by acting to deter them and prosecuting or rejecting the actual violators, not by giving in to the potential wrongdoers.

Before proceeding to outline the structure of what I take to be the legitimate and valid way to assess claimed legal rights of the various types that individuals can have in rights-based societies, I want to point out one consequence of (1) the distinction between a society's basic moral principle and the personal ultimate values to which its members subscribe and (2) the fact that arguments of moral principle are the dominant form of legitimate and valid legal argument in rights-based societies: both this distinction and this fact favor the existence of answers to all legal-rights questions that are uniquely correct as a matter of law. Thus, the distinction in question favors the existence of such answers because it implies that the substance of (at least the *prima facie*) legal rights of a rights-based society's members and participants can be objectively determined by using the protocol I have outlined to identify the society's basic moral principle and analyzing that principle's concrete corollaries—that is, because it implies that the underlying moral rights of such a society's members and participants can be objectively identified, that moral-rights claims are critically different from strongly supported or confidently asserted personal-ultimate-value-based moral-ought claims. And the dominance hypothesis favors the existence of answers to legal-rights questions that are uniquely correct as a matter of law because it (1) implies that certain arguments (such as narrow-gauged historical arguments, arguments based on morally illegitimate precedent-practices, and various types of morally illegitimate prudential arguments) that may disfavor the conclusions that arguments of moral principle commend do not count at all (precisely because their use would be morally illegitimate) and, relatedly, (2) informs the content of (co-opts) the arguments that it indicates should be used to determine the answers to legal-rights questions (requires textual argument to take account of the distinction between moral principles and personal ultimate values, structural argument to recognize the point of rights-based societies, historical argument about the meaning or concrete extensions of justice-related concepts to be broad-gauged rather than narrow-gauged, and arguments from precedent to reflect the various ways in which the use of precedent affects relevant individuals' rights-related interests).

I should now be able to outline the structure of legitimate and valid legal argument in a liberal, rights-based society. Not surprisingly, in my view, that structure depends on whether the disputed legal right is or would be moral-rights-based. If the asserted legal right is moral-rights-based, after noting that fact, the legal argument should articulate the liberal moral norm and analyze whether the right in controversy is a concrete corollary of the basic right of all members of and participants in a liberal, rights-based society to appropriate, equal respect and appropriate or appropriate, equal concern. I should add that although, ideally, the relevant basic-moral-principle conclusions should be generated by the philosophically informed empirical analysis I have described and its concretization should be achieved through an appropriately-fact-sensitive conceptual analysis of that principle's corollaries, it would not be surprising (and may even be third-best desirable, given the fact that lawyers, judges, judicial clerks, and adjudicative processes are not ideal for these purposes) for courts to rely more heavily on constitutional texts, statutory texts, and related judicial opinions than would be warranted if they could costlessly collect perfect data of the more general sorts I have described and costlessly execute perfect analyses of the required types. If the preceding analysis yields the conclusion that the plaintiff's moral right has been violated, the court would then have to consider whether the plaintiff had no legal right (1) because the choice that violated his moral right was authorized by or required by a morally illegitimate constitutional provision whose relevant extensions were understood by the provision's ratifiers at the time of ratification, (2) because the State could not enforce the moral right in question without disserving on balance the rights-related interests of the moral-rights holders for whom it was responsible, or (3) because the private actor who had violated the relevant moral right had reasonably relied on an incorrect judicial decision declaring his conduct lawful or an unconstitutional (because moral-rights-violative) statute that authorized him to make the choice that had violated the moral right at issue in the case in question. I should add that, in my judgment, in all cases in the third category and in all cases in the second category in which the making of the relevant determinations and the payment of the relevant compensation would not disserve rights-related interest on balance,[20] plaintiffs who have not been able to secure legal vindication of their moral rights for the above reasons have a moral right to be compensated for their loss by the State.

Obviously, arguments of moral principle are supposed to play a far less significant role in the resolution of legal cases in which the asserted legal right is not moral-rights-based but was created by a piece of legislation or constitutional provision that was designed either perfectly or imperfectly to achieve a morally defensible goal or to serve the parochial interests of its beneficiaries. In such cases, arguments of moral principle do play some background role—determine some of the attributes of the decision-making process that can be legitimately used to resolve them, have some effect on the doctrine of precedent the courts are morally obligated to employ if they employ such a doctrine at all, prohibit judges from being influenced by prejudice or making decisions in an ad hoc way, and so on. Primarily, however, such cases are to be resolved through textual, structural, historical, precedent-related, canon-of construction-practice-related, and consequentalist-prudential argument. I do not think that liberal, moral principles determine the precise way in which such cases must be resolved. Thus, although liberalism does require the State to put the addressees of the law in a position in which they can learn their legal rights and obligations, it does not require the courts to follow judicial precedents: the required fair notice could be given by telling the population that the courts were bound by the consensus views of academic commentators on the answers to legal-rights questions that are correct as a matter of law as expressed in leading commentaries and instructing the courts to follow those views as well. Liberalism also does not dictate the morally legitimate way for the courts of liberal, rights-based States to resolve cases in which legislative-drafting errors have been made—that is, cases in which the text of a statute does not express the specific intention of the legislature (as it can be inferred from independent evidence—explanatory statements by key legislative actors, the language of rejected drafts, other statutes passed contemporaneously, and so on) or creates a regime that will not serve the defensible or parochial goal extrinsic evidence reveals motivated the legislature (more precisely, the subset of legislators who voted for the legislation in question). I suspect that it may be desirable for courts in countries that have parliamentary systems of government, in which corrective legislation can be more easily enacted, to follow the text of statutes and for courts in countries that have congressional systems of government, in which it is more difficult for corrective legislation to be passed, to be guided by the intentions of the legislature.[21] But, for present purposes, the wisdom of this proposal is neither here nor there. Liberalism requires no more than that the approach the courts take to this issue is neither illicitly motivated nor ad hoc.

SECTION 10. TWO PROMINENT ALTERNATIVE JURISPRUDENTIAL POSITIONS: LEGAL REALISM AND LEGAL POSITIVISM

As I indicated earlier, my position on legitimate and valid legal argument in the countries to whose governments the economists this book is criticizing are making policy recommendations is not shared by most contemporary American legal academics.[22] To prepare the way for Part III's analyses of the relevance of the economic efficiency of an interpretation or application of the law for its correctness as a matter of law, I will therefore give an account of the two alternatives (or sets of alternatives) to my position in the contemporary American legal academy: the legal-realist position and the legal-positivist position.

From a jurisprudential perspective, the legal realists are not a uniform group. Some legal realists believe that there is no internally right answer to some legal-rights questions because the relevant legal rights turn on the proper interpretation of open-textured language in a constitution, statute, administrative regulation, or judicial opinion whose meaning is critically indeterminate. Some legal realists believe that there is no internally right answer to some legal-rights questions because the relevant legal rights turn on legal practices (for example, canons of statutory construction or practices of determining the substance and assessing the weight of precedents) that are irresolvably critically internally inconsistent. And some legal realists are uninterested in whether there are internally rights answers to all legal-rights questions: they are interested in what determines the answers that judges give to *intellectually contestable* or *socially contested* legal-rights questions regardless of whether these questions are *essentially contestable* (and, relatedly, in the most effective way for lawyers to argue cases whose internally correct resolution is contestable or socially contested).[23]

Legal realists do not explicitly address how judges are morally obligated to or morally ought to decide cases to which there are internally right answers.

However, quite clearly, some legal realists would reject the preceding distinction between moral-rights argument and moral-ought argument as being either incoherent or ignored in our social practice and would reject as well the claim that there are unique, internally correct answers to legal-rights questions whose answers are intellectually contestable. However, I do think that some legal realists do believe in the coherence and relevance of the distinction between the just and the good, believe as well in the existence of answers to contestable legal-rights questions that are uniquely correct as a matter of law, and think that judges not only are morally obligated to but morally ought to do their best to resolve disputes about contestable legal-rights issues in the way that is internal-to-law correct. At least, this conclusion is supported not only by direct comments by some leading legal realists[24] but also by the fact that legal realists such as Karl Llewellyn have concluded that when dealing with contract or commercial disputes that cannot be resolved by reference to language alone (whatever that might mean) judges morally ought to make the decision that conforms with the relevant subcommunity's practice and expectations.[25] In cases in which legal realists believe there is no internally right answer, they seem to think that judges morally ought to make good policy choices by combining sound social science with personal ultimate values that they do not specify and whose contestability they ignore. I am certain that most legal realists recognize that the approach that would be most desirable for a court to take to the resolution of a question for which no answer is uniquely correct as a matter of law and the conclusion that would be most desirable for a court to reach about that issue might be different from their legislative or administrative-agency counterparts—that the differences among the training of those institutions' personnel (decision makers and staffs), the decision-making procedures they are required to or have the funds to employ, the policy instruments they are authorized to use, their capacities to fund and monitor various solutions, and so on might affect what they morally ought to do. But the legal realists have not, to my knowledge, developed anything like a comprehensive protocol or set of protocols for judges to use when deciding cases for which there is no answer that is uniquely correct as a matter of law.

The second alternative to my position on legitimate and valid legal argument in the societies with which this book is concerned that I will discuss is legal positivism, the jurisprudential school that I suspect has plurality if not majority support in contemporary American legal academia. All legal positivists believe that any type of society's narrowly defined valid-legal-argument practice is self-validating. In other words, legal positivists believe that the fact that a general mode of argument (or, indeed, some variant of that mode of argument) has been used and accepted as valid requisitely often by a society's lawyers and judges to establish the answer to a legal-rights question that is correct as a matter of law in that society renders that type of argument or argument-variant legally valid (that is, relevant to the determination of the answer to a legal-rights question in the society that is correct as a matter of law). Relatedly, legal positivists believe that, in the societies whose respective valid-legal-argument practices they are describing (all of which are rights-based, though many legal positivists would not acknowledge this fact even if they did grant the coherence of the concept in question), arguments that derive from the basic moral principle the relevant societies are committed to instantiating are not generically valid legal arguments. More specifically, legal positivists claim that such arguments of moral principle are irrelevant to the determination of the answer to a legal-rights question that is correct as a matter of law in any society unless the moral principle in question has been cited by an authoritative court in that society (or, more restrictively, was said by such a court to have critically affected its resolution of a legal-rights issue) or has been cited by the legislative body that passed the legislation whose interpretation is at issue in the case at hand as a justification for the legislation in question (or, more restrictively, has been said by the legislature that passed the legislation in question to have been the principle that the relevant legislation was designed to instantiate). Legal positivists base this claim about the legal relevance of moral norms on two purported empirical observations: (1) lawyers in the societies whose valid-legal-argument practices they are trying to describe have not used the type of moral argument I call arguments of moral principle when arguing for their clients' positions in legal-rights disputes or when assessing their clients' legal rights in the course of providing them with legal advice in situations in which such arguments would be relevant to the resolution of the legal-rights issue under consideration if they were valid legal arguments (because the legal right at issue, if it existed, would derive from a moral right) sufficiently often for such arguments to be valid legal arguments, and (2) judges in these societies have not relied on arguments of moral principle requisitely often when resolving disputes over legal rights that, if they existed, would derive from moral rights sufficiently often for such arguments to be valid legal arguments.

A few legal positivists (the tiny minority who believe that arguments from legal precedent dominate any conceivable combination of the other sorts of arguments that are legally valid in the societies whose valid legal arguments they are attempting to catalog) believe not only that a society's narrowly defined legal-argument practice is self-validating but also that any narrow legal-rights conclusion that the society's courts have persistently reached when addressing the narrow issue in question is self-validating. However, the vast majority of legal positivists seem to agree with my colleague Philip Bobbitt's position that no individual type of legal argument that is validated by use dominates the other types of valid legal argument. Since Bobbitt's overall position is prototypical,[26] I will summarize it here. First, Bobbitt ignores or rejects my notion of legitimate legal argument—that is, legal argument that is consistent with the moral commitments of the society in which it is used. Second, and relatedly, Bobbitt implicitly rejects the possibility that a general mode of legal argument or a particular variant of some general mode of legal argument can be invalidated by its use's moral illegitimacy in my sense (if it would otherwise be validated by the frequency of its use). Third, and again relatedly, Bobbitt contends that all general modes of legal argument and all specific variants of those general modes (including variants that are inconsistent with each other) are validated by use—are valid if they have been used requisitely often by lawyers when arguing before courts (and presumably when preparing and giving legal advice to clients) and by judges when questioning lawyers at oral argument or writing opinions to justify their resolution of the cases in question. Fourth, Bobbitt lists and gives accounts of the general modes and more specific variants of legal argument that are used in the Untied States: textual, structural, historical, precedent-related or other-legal-practice related, prudential, and (his own notion) "ethical."[27] Fifth, Bobbitt contends that, if a particular answer to a legal-rights question is favored by all variants of legal argument that have been validated by use, that answer is correct as a matter of law. However, if more than one answer that could be given to a particular legal-rights question is favored by some and disfavored by other validated variants of legal argument, no answer to the legal-rights question at issue is correct as a matter of law, and the judge must choose among the answers that are favored by at least one mode of valid legal argument by exercising his conscience (by which I assume Bobbitt means by using a personal ultimate value to determine what he morally ought to do).

On Bobbitt's account, then, which I think would be accepted by the vast majority of legal positivists, the appropriate way for a judge to address a legal-rights question would be (1) to identify all variants of legal argument that have been validated through use in his legal culture, (2) to determine the answer to the question at issue that is favored by each of those validated variants, (3) if all validated variants of legal argument favor the same answer, to give that answer to the relevant legal-rights question, but (4) if more than one possible answer to the relevant legal-rights question is favored by some validated legal-argument variant, to choose the individual answer that is favored by at least one valid legal-argument variant that he thinks in the circumstances morally ought to be given.[28]

Now that I have explained the relevant moral and jurisprudential concepts and positions, Chapter 5 can proceed to analyze (1) the relevance of the allocative efficiency of a choice to its (A) justness or (B) moral desirability, moral-rights considerations aside, and (2) the relevance of the allocative efficiency of a conclusion about the answer to a legal-rights question to its correctness as a matter of law, and Chapter 6 can proceed to analyze the correctness of the arguments that various economists and law and economics scholars have made and the conclusions they have reached about the relevance of a prescriptive-moral conclusion's allocative efficiency to its prescriptive-moral correctness and the relevance of a legal interpretation's or application's allocative efficiency to its correctness as a matter of law.

Chapter 5 The Prescriptive-Moral and Legal Relevance of Allocative-Efficiency Conclusions

This chapter analyzes the relevance of the allocative efficiency of a choice to its justness in a liberal, rights-based society and to its moral desirability, moral-rights considerations aside, and the relevance of the allocative efficiency of an interpretation or application of the law to its correctness as a matter of law or its moral desirability in a liberal, rights-based society. The chapter has four sections. Section 1 analyzes the connection between a choice's allocative efficiency and its justness in a liberal, rights-based society; Section 2, the connection between a choice's allocative efficiency and its moral desirability, moral-rights considerations aside, in such a society; Section 3, the connection between the allocative efficiency of a legal interpretation or application and its correctness as a matter of law on the assumptions that the society in question is a liberal, rights-based society and that my conclusions about valid legal argument in such a society are correct; and Section 4, the connection between the allocative efficiency of a legal interpretation or application and either its correctness as a matter of law or its moral desirability if no unique, internally right answer can be given to the legal question on two different sets of assumptions: respectively, that the legal realists and the legal positivists are correct about valid legal argument and the existence of unique, internally correct answers to legal-rights question in the societies whose legal practices they study.

SECTION 1. THE RELEVANCE OF A CHOICE'S ALLOCATIVE EFFICIENCY TO ITS JUSTNESS IN A LIBERAL, RIGHTS-BASED SOCIETY

This section argues that the allocative efficiency of a choice is neither a necessary nor a sufficient condition for its justness in a liberal, rights-based society. It has two subsections. The first supports this conclusion by delineating one issue that plays an important role in moral-rights analyses to whose resolution allocative-efficiency analysis can make no contribution and four morally salient distinctions to which allocative-efficiency analysis is inherently insensitive. The second justifies and illustrates this conclusion by demonstrating the possible allocative inefficiency of six of the concrete moral rights of a liberal, rights-based society's members and participants.

Five Deficiencies of Allocative-Efficiency Analysis from the Perspective of Moral-Rights Analysis

The first feature of allocative-efficiency analysis that precludes it from being an algorithm for moral-rights analysis in a liberal, rights-based society is its inability to contribute to the identification of those creatures (and, derivatively, entities) that are moral-rights holders in such societies. As I have indicated, the various candidates for the title of "attribute that makes a creature a moral-rights holder" in a liberal, rights-based society should be judged by two criteria. The first is a closeness-of-fit criterion: how well does the candidate fit (1) the substance of the moral rights of moral-rights holders in the society in question and (2) the conclusions that the society's members and governments have reached about the moral-rights-bearing status of different creatures? The second is an explicability-of-non-fits criterion: to what extent is the damage done to the relevant candidates' candidacies by the non-fits with which each is associated reduced by their non-fits' exonerating explicability? The attribute that makes a creature a moral-rights holder in a particular rights-based society is the attribute that best discounted fits the facts it should fit (where individual non-fits are discounted by their exonerating explicability). There is no reason to believe that allocative-efficiency analysis is an algorithm for this protocol. Indeed, that is an understatement. Among other reasons, allocative-efficiency analysis cannot be an algorithm for determining the creatures that are moral-rights-bearing because it cannot even determine the creatures who count in allocative-efficiency analysis[1]—the creatures whose equivalent-dollar gains and losses are part of allocative-efficiency calculations.[2] I should add that an analogous inability of allocative-efficiency analysis—its inability to identify the creatures whose utility or treatment is valued by the applicable personal ultimate value—also precludes it from being an algorithm for any type of moral-ought analysis.

Four other features of the concept of allocative efficiency preclude allocative-efficiency analysis from functioning as an algorithm for the resolution of moral-rights questions in a liberal, rights-based society. The first three are its insensitivity to the three incommensurabilities that Section 4 of the introduction to Part III indicated often play a critical role in liberal, moral-rights analyses. First, because the allocative efficiency of a choice or policy does not depend on whether the equivalent-dollar gains and losses it generates derive from licit or illicit preferences, allocative-efficiency analysis cannot accurately capture the importance for the analysis of liberal moral rights of the distinction between illicit and licit preferences—that is, is insensitive to the impact on liberal, moral-rights conclusions of the fact that an act was critically motivated by prejudice or by the desire to inflict pain or other sorts of losses on, to degrade, or to control its victim unjustifiably. Second, because the allocative efficiency of a choice or policy does not depend on whether the equivalent-dollar gains and losses it generates derive from its effects on mere utility or on the opportunity rights-bearers have to lead lives of moral integrity, allocative-efficiency analysis cannot accurately capture the importance to the analysis of liberal, moral rights of the distinction between causing people to experience mere-utility losses and preventing them from leading lives of moral integrity or subjecting them to life-dominating pain or depression that strongly militates against their leading such lives. Third, because the allocative efficiency of a choice or policy does not directly depend on whether the choice is to avoid harming someone or to provide assistance to someone, allocative-efficiency analysis cannot accurately capture the significance for liberal, moral-rights analysis of the distinction between actively harming someone and failing to provide someone with assistance. In addition, and somewhat overlappingly, allocative-efficiency analysis cannot accurately capture the significance for liberal, moral-rights analysis of the distinction between an individual's psychological or material-welfare interest or concern in an event, choice, or piece of information and his entitlement interest or concern in it.

Some Illustrations of the Fact That Allocative-Efficiency Analysis Cannot Function as an Algorithm for the Resolution of Specific Liberal, Moral-Rights Claims

This subsection analyzes seven liberal moral rights to illustrate my conclusion that—even if one could ignore the inability of allocative-efficiency analysis to identify the creatures that are moral-rights-bearing in any rights-based society—the other insensitivities just delineated would prevent it from functioning as an algorithm for the resolution of liberal-moral-rights claims. I hasten to add that the analyses that follow will be far from complete—they are designed solely to show that the allocative efficiency of a resolution of each of the types of rights-claims I will discuss is not a necessary or sufficient condition for its correctness.

THE RIGHT TO THE RESOURCES AND EXPERIENCES THAT MAY CRITICALLY AND WILL SIGNIFICANTLY AFFECT AN INDIVIDUAL'S OPPORTUNITY TO LEAD A LIFE OF MORAL INTEGRITY

I have defined liberalism as a moral position that places a lexically higher value on moral-rights holders' having and seizing the opportunity to lead lives of moral integrity than on anything else (such as increasing mere utility). In my view, this fundamental commitment morally obligates the government of a liberal, rights-based society to secure for the moral-rights holders for whom it is responsible the prenatal care and postnatal nutrition, housing, psychological support (parenting services), medical care, general education, exposure to alternative conceptions of the good and alternative lifestyles, privacy, opportunities to form and maintain intimate relationships, and liberties that may critically affect and will certainly significantly affect their opportunities to lead lives of moral integrity. Admittedly, in many instances, decisions to make such resources and options available to particular individuals will increase the allocative product of these persons by more than such decisions' allocative cost (even if one ignores any net external-preference-derived equivalent-dollar gain the decisions generate). However, I have no doubt that, in some identifiable cases involving infants or adults with severe disabilities, the supply of the necessary resources will not be allocatively efficient. Take, for example, children born deaf and blind who have the neurological potential to lead lives of moral integrity but must receive an enormous amount of educational resources to be able to develop the cognitive abilities that will enable them to function as moral agents. A liberal, rights-based society that could do so without sacrificing rights-related interests on balance would be obligated to devote the educational resources to these individuals that would enable them to function as moral agents even when (external-preference-derived net equivalent-dollar gains aside) the allocative cost of doing so would exceed the associated increase in their conventional allocative product—indeed, the society would be obligated to supply them with such education even if doing so would be allocatively inefficient after any external-preference-derived equivalent-dollar effects were taken into account. Nor do I think that this last class of cases constitutes an empty economic box: one would have to be Pollyannish to assume that—even in a liberal, rights-based society whose members live up to their liberal commitments sufficiently for their society to deserve to be called a society of moral integrity—the net external-preference-derived equivalent-dollar gains the supply of the resources in question would generate would always be sufficiently great to render the supply of these resources allocatively efficient.

THE RIGHT TO PRIVACY

Liberalism values personal privacy highly in part because many people obtain pleasure (what economists might call utility) from their privacy but preeminently because the secrecy, solitude, and anonymity privacy affords them contribute significantly to their opportunity to lead lives of moral integrity by enabling them to form intimate relationships by putting them in a position to reveal things about themselves selectively and lowering the cost to them of being rejected or, indeed, of rejecting someone's offers of intimacy, by giving them the peace and quiet to consider what they value, by reducing the cost to them of experimenting with different values or lifestyles, and in numerous other ways.[3] For at least one and probably two reasons other than its inability to resolve the boundary condition issue, allocative-efficiency analysis cannot serve as an algorithm for the resolution of personal-privacy-right claims.

I start with the contestable reasons. External-preference-derived equivalent-dollar gains and losses aside, allocative-efficiency analysis measures the value of a particular privacy interest by the equivalent-dollar value the person who has it would place on it if he were a sovereign maximizer. This valuation would equal the value that liberalism places on the relevant privacy interest only if "being perfectly informed" entails subscribing to liberal values and appreciating the contribution that the privacy interest at issue would make to the individual's having an opportunity to lead a life of moral integrity and being able to achieve his personally chosen goals. It seems to me that if the concept of sovereignty that allocative-efficiency analysis employs is defined this encompassingly, allocative-efficiency analysis will not be able to make any distinctive contribution to prescriptive-moral analysis: all the real work will be done in the philosophical or psychological analysis of the real value of the relevant (privacy) interest to its holder. To the extent that this last conclusion is contestable, so too is my first, non-boundary-condition-related reason why the allocative efficiency of a resolution of a particular privacy claim is not a necessary or sufficient condition for its correctness from a liberal perspective. The second reason why allocative-efficiency analysis is not an algorithm for the liberal analysis of privacy rights is that allocative-efficiency analysis is insensitive to the different status of the various motivations of privacy-invaders—that is, will place the same weight on the equivalent-dollar gains the privacy-invasion confers on the invader, regardless of whether his underlying preferences were licit or illicit and regardless of whether the invader had a rights-related interest in the information he was trying to obtain (in cases in which the invader's motivation was not illicit).

The liberal analysis of a moral-rights holder's right to privacy will take account both of the privacy-related rights-related interests of the person whose privacy was invaded and of the relevant rights-related interests of the privacy-invader. I have already indicated the various ways in which different kinds of invasions of personal privacy can militate against the victim's taking his life morally seriously. It should be obvious that privacy-invasions of different types can also cost their victims utility as economists understand this concept. Moreover, to the extent that liberalism would sometimes deem permissible some types of invasions of privacy perpetrated by individuals who had a right to know the information the privacy-invasion would yield them, a liberal analysis of a personal-privacy claim might involve a determination of whether the invader had a right to know the information the invasion might yield, was merely curious, hoped to make money out of the information he obtained, or wanted to invade the victim's privacy to cause the victim pain, to degrade the victim, or to control the victim unjustifiably. Allocative-efficiency analysis is insensitive to these distinctions. Unlike a liberal analysis, an allocative-efficiency analysis will take no account, for example, of whether newspaper readers collectively place a $10,000 value on information about the subsequent life histories of television or radio quiz-show or adventure-show contestants because they are curious about them or because they need some such information to decide whether to support legislation that would put some morally legitimate limits on such programs (for example, on the minimum age of contestants).[4] Although I will not present any evidence to support this conclusion, I suspect that, in many identifiable situations, illicit motivations and widespread curiosity will render allocatively efficient some invasions of privacy that would be rights-violative in a liberal, rights-based society.[5]

LIBERTY RIGHTS

Unlike liberalism, allocative-efficiency analysis does not view (1) liberties that critically affect an individual's opportunity to lead a life of moral integrity, liberties to do things one is morally obligated to do, and liberties to do things that are specially connected to the actor's instantiating his personal conception of the good as being *incommensurate with* (2) liberties to violate the moral rights of others, liberties to commit acts that are valued because of the mere utility they will confer on the actor, and liberties to choose among options among which one is essentially indifferent.[6] Admittedly, to the extent that the members of a liberal, rights-based society place a higher non-external-preference-based equivalent-dollar value on the former categories of liberties than on the latter categories of liberties and to the extent that the members of a liberal, rights-based society have stronger external preferences for fellow-members' and other societal participants' having the former categories of liberties, allocative-efficiency assessments will reflect these higher equivalent-dollar valuations of the liberties to which liberalism will assign a lexically higher value. However, the same sorts of reasons that may make it allocatively inefficient to provide some individuals who have the neurological prerequisites for leading lives of moral integrity with meaningful opportunities to do so may make it allocatively inefficient to protect some liberal liberty rights of some members of a liberal, rights-based society: some moral-rights holders in liberal, rights-based societies may not assign as high an equivalent-dollar value to particular liberty rights as liberalism suggests they should (a value that will result in the liberty right's being protected); some such individuals may not have as strong external preferences for the protection of the liberty rights of others as liberalism suggests they should have; and some may have prejudices or other illicit motivations that cause them to place a negative equivalent-dollar value on the protection of some liberty rights of some of their society's other members and/or participants.

THE RIGHT THAT OTHERS NOT MAKE CHOICES AGAINST ONE'S INTERESTS THAT ARE ILLICITLY MOTIVATED

In my judgment, there clearly will be situations in which (whether for reasons of prejudice, sadism, or a desire to control unjustifiably) individual perpetrators will place a sufficiently high equivalent-dollar value on assaulting, raping, slandering, imprisoning, and so on their victim for such rights-violating behavior to be allocatively efficient, particularly if enough others share their preferences for the external-preference-derived equivalent-dollar effects of their conduct to be positive or at least not substantially negative. Admittedly, it may be that, even if this is the case in some situations, the situations in which it is the case will be sufficiently individually unidentifiable and uncommon for their existence to eliminate the possibility that an individual evaluator will ever confront a case in which he will recognize as allocatively efficient behavior of these sorts that is rights-violative. However, I see no basis for asserting that such a possibility will never arise.

THE RIGHT OF A POTENTIAL VICTIM OF AN ACCIDENT OR POLLUTION LOSS THAT WOULD DEPRIVE HIM OF MERE UTILITY NOT TO HAVE THE EQUIVALENT-DOLLAR MAGNITUDE OF THE LOSSES OF THIS KIND HE CONFRONTS *EX ANTE* INCREASED BY A POTENTIAL INJURER'S REJECTION OF AN AVOIDANCE MOVE THE LATTER SHOULD HAVE PERCEIVED (IN EFFECT) TO BE *EX ANTE* ALLOCATIVELY EFFICIENT[7]

As I have already suggested, in a liberal, rights-based society, potential polluters or accident causers who should expect to impose on others net AP losses of a mere-utility type (that would not deprive others of a meaningful opportunity to lead lives of moral integrity) in any way other than by imposing a monetary loss on them have two related moral obligations: (1) to do the research into the accident and pollution their activities might impose on others if they do not avoid, the avoidance moves available to them, the allocative cost of the avoidance moves that are available to them, and the allocative benefits those moves would generate (at least in part by reducing the accident and pollution losses the potential injurer would impose on others) that they would find profitable to do if they would bear any equivalent-dollar AP losses they initially imposed on others and (2) to make all avoidance moves they know of that they would find profitable to make *ex ante*, given the information at their disposal, if they were maximizers and believed that they would bear all equivalent-dollar AP losses they initially imposed on others. As I indicated, this conclusion favors the hypothesis that a variant of allocative-efficiency analysis that takes account of the imperfections in the information that would be available to an individual tort-loss co-generator if he fulfilled his related research obligations is an algorithm for the liberal analysis of moral tort rights in mere-utility-loss situations in that it proceeds from one of the assumptions that is a component of the principle I refer to as "the principle of liberal dualism"—namely, that the moral obligation that a liberal, rights-based society's members and participants have to avoid imposing mere-utility losses on each other relates to the equivalent-dollar as opposed to the utility effects they should expect *ex ante* their avoidance research and avoidance choices to have.

Nevertheless, for at least three and possibly for as many as six sorts of reasons, the conclusions that liberalism would warrant both about whether a wrong has been committed in the type of situation on which we are now focusing and about the amount of compensation a polluter or accident-causer who has wrongfully endangered his potential victims' mere-utility interests should pay his victims will not be allocatively efficient.[8] The first is that a liberal, rights-based society's members and participants have no moral duty to make the avoidance choices that maximize their equivalent-dollar gains when those choices are not required by the rights of others (or conceivably but doubtfully a duty to take their own lives morally seriously). This fact will render the correct resolution of a liberal, moral-duty question about the duty of a potential polluter or accident-causer to engage in mere-utility-loss-preventing avoidance when the fact that the potential avoider should have perceived an avoidance-move option to be *ex ante* allocatively efficient was critically affected by its tendency to confer equivalent-dollar gains on him by reducing the AP losses he suffered in his role as his own potential victim.

The second reason why the correct answer to the liberal, moral-rights questions that arise in this type of accident or pollution situation may not be allocatively efficient is that liberalism warrants the conclusion that a potential polluter or accident-causer who mistakenly believed *ex ante* that an avoidance move that was an option for him would be allocatively efficient would be morally obligated to make that move if it would reduce the equivalent-dollar AP losses others should be expected to sustain even though the move in question was actually *ex ante* allocatively inefficient. This situation could arise either because the actor in question misperceived the allocative costs and benefits of one or more of his avoidance options or because he did his math wrong. In any event, conclusions that polluters or accident-causers have acted wrongfully in these sorts of situations might misallocate resources by inducing victims to make additional moral claims that are allocative-transaction-costly.

Third, even if liberal, moral-rights conclusions do induce polluters and accident-causers whose avoidance-move rejections have wrongfully increased the certainty-equivalent mere-utility AP losses confronting their potential victims to compensate those victims for the losses they wrongfully imposed on them, the corrective-justice damage-calculation component of those conclusions may not be allocatively efficient if the profitability of the rejected avoidance moves would be distorted by the interaction of the various other Pareto imperfections present in the system (other than the externalities the avoidance-move rejection would generate in an otherwise-Pareto-perfect world if the rejecter did not compensate the victims of the rejection for the losses it imposed on them) or if the injurer in question and, more importantly, his future counterparts respectively did not and would not act as sovereign maximizers when making avoidance-move decisions. In all such situations, the damages conclusion that liberalism would warrant would not be allocatively efficient (given the allocative-transaction-costliness of securing damage-awards for nontraditional "victims" of the avoidance-move rejection and payments from the nontraditional beneficiaries of the rejection in question, such as competitors of the victims of the pollution or accident caused by the relevant avoidance move's rejection).

The next three reasons why liberal, moral-rights conclusions may not be allocatively efficient all relate to the causation component of the case a victim must establish to have a corrective-justice right to which we seem to be committed—that is, to the fact that we seem to believe that a victim is not entitled to recover from an injurer unless he can show that, more probably than not, the accused (1) made a wrongful choice that (2) violated his duty to the victim and (3) was a but-for cause of the victim's loss. In the introduction to this subsection, I characterized these three reasons as "possible" reasons why the correct liberal resolution of a relevant moral-rights claim may be allocatively inefficient because I am not convinced that liberalism or the general notion of moral duty entails this approach to moral responsibility.

The above conception of corrective-justice rights would cause any liberal analysis that incorporated it to be allocatively inefficient in three types of situations. First, it will do so in simultaneous-independent-causation cases—that is, in cases in which (1) the independent avoidance-move rejections of two or more potential polluters or accident-causers belonged to two or more different sets of sufficient conditions for the generation of the loss, (2) each such avoidance-move rejection would be allocatively inefficient if none of the avoidance moves were made, (3) all such avoidance-move rejections combined were allocatively inefficient, (4) the relevant sets of sufficient conditions were fulfilled at times that resulted in two or more such sets' causing the loss to occur simultaneously, and (perhaps redundantly) (5) the loss was not increased by the fulfillment of more than one set of the relevant sets of sufficient conditions. In situations of this kind, it would be allocatively efficient to prevent the rejection of the relevant avoidance moves. However, for two reasons, liberalism might not hold any of the actors who rejected the avoidance moves in this type of situation morally responsible for the loss that resulted. First, in this type of situation, no individual chooser was a but-for cause of the loss that resulted. (I will refer to choosers in this situation as "putative injurers" because no such choosers are but-for causes of the loss.) Second, in at least some of these situations, none of the putative injurers may have behaved wrongfully. At least, this conclusion is warranted when (1) the individual putative injurers' failures to avoid were independent—and each believed that the others would fail to avoid regardless of what he did, (2) each individual putative injurer knew that one or more others were sufficiently likely not to avoid for his avoidance-move rejection not to be *ex ante* allocatively inefficient, and (3) the profitability or attractiveness of not avoiding to each putative injurer was not critically affected by his desire to have the loss generated.

Textbook examples of situations that fall into this category include cases in which a building is simultaneously destroyed by two or more fires or an individual is simultaneously killed by two or more bullets. However, an empirically more important set of cases that may fall into this category contains cases in which a pollution loss has been simultaneously caused by two or more pollution-discharges, each of which would be a sufficient condition for the loss to be generated and none of which increased the loss that resulted, given that one or more other discharges would have occurred regardless of whether it occurred. (In each of these situations, I did not state that the act in question [setting the fire, shooting the gun, discharging the pollution] was wrongful because, even though it would have been wrongful had it been a but-for cause of the loss, it might not have been wrongful, given the fact that it was not a but-for cause of the loss unless it was critically illicitly motivated.)

Second, any liberal analysis that includes a but-for causation requirement for moral responsibility will also yield allocatively inefficient moral-rights conclusions in overdetermined step-function-loss cases. Assume that the function that relates the loss that will result from varying amounts of pollution's being put into some medium is a step function—that is, would be represented in a two-dimensional diagram in which the loss was measured along the vertical axis and the pollution along the horizontal axis as a series of disconnected horizontal lines that could be connected by verticals at their successive end and beginning points. This type of loss function is not uncommon. Thus, in the river-pollution context, no harm results below some level of pollution; suddenly, at a particular pollution level, one cannot swim in or fall into the river without incurring some health risk; over some range above that level, additional pollution does not change the resulting loss; and then suddenly at some higher level of pollution, the fish are no longer edible; again, over some range above this latter level, additional pollution does not change the environmental loss; and then suddenly, when pollution increases above some level, the fish die and the river smells. Assume in addition that (1) each of 30 polluters puts two units of pollution into some body of water without influencing his fellow polluters' decisions to pollute, (2) no loss would be generated by the presence of zero to 49.99 units of pollution, (3) $100 in mere-utility losses would be generated by the presence of 50 to 120 units of pollution, and (4) the cost to each polluter of eliminating part or all of his pollution was $4.

On these assumptions, it would be allocatively efficient for six polluters to eliminate their pollution in the situation in question (because reducing the total amount of pollutants in the water from 60 units to 48 units would increase allocative efficiency by $76 = $100 – $6[$4]). However, for two related reasons, a liberal, moral-rights analysis would not conclude that any of the polluters in question had violated a victim's moral right—(1) because no polluter was a but-for cause of the loss in question (because no individual polluter's pollution affected the loss either directly or by influencing other polluters' pollution-decisions since each's pollution raised total pollution from 58 to 60 units), and (2) because, on the above account, no individual polluter behaved wrongfully by polluting (since each's pollution was allocatively efficient—saved him $4 in abatement costs and caused no damage).

Third, if liberal, moral-rights analysis requires victims to establish that, more probably than not, all the elements of injurer culpability are satisfied, imperfections in four types of information that a liberal-moral-rights-claim evaluator would want to have may render allocatively inefficient the resolution of this type of liberal-moral-rights-claim that is morally correct. The first such type of information is information on whether a *possible* simultaneous-independent-causation case is an *actual* simultaneous-independent-causation case and, if not, on the identity of the first causer of the loss in question (that is, the causer whose choice generated the loss before any other choice could do so). If the liberal-moral-rights-claim evaluator cannot determine that there was a first causer and/or the identity of the first causer, he will not be able to conclude that any putative injurer has wronged the victim even if one putative injurer was a first causer and it would be allocatively efficient for all of them to avoid.

The second type of information that is relevant in this context relates to the identity of the putative injurer who was the but-for cause of the loss. Assume that in a non-simultaneous-causation case the party who has suffered a loss—the victim—(1) can demonstrate that two or more actors who had a relevant duty toward him made duty-violating, allocatively inefficient choices that more probably than not caused some individuals to suffer the kind of loss the victim in question suffered but (2) cannot prove that, more probably than not, any particular injurer had caused his loss. In some cases of this kind (such as when the loss was asbestositis that was caused by the inhalation of one unit of asbestos and asbestos was wrongfully put into the air that the victim breathed by two or more polluters, none of whom was more likely than not the source of the asbestos the victims inhaled[9]), at no point in time would it have been possible to identify the particular wrongdoer who harmed the victim. In other cases of this kind (such as cases in which the victim's illness was caused by his ingestion several years earlier of a medicine that was wrongfully produced and may ultimately have been supplied to him by one of two or more pharmaceutical companies, none of which was more likely than not his ultimate supplier[10]), it would have been possible at an earlier point in time to identify the particular manufacturer-wrongdoer who harmed the victim in question (namely, at the time at which the prescription-filling record was recoverable) but was no longer possible to do so at the time at which the victim's symptoms appeared, the cause of his illness was identified, or the suit was brought. In both these kinds of cases, there are wrongdoers whose allocatively inefficient wrongdoing has caused harm and individual victims who have been harmed by the allocatively inefficient wrongdoing of an individual wrongdoer whose wrongdoing harmed him. Nevertheless, in these types of cases as well, a liberal, moral-rights analysis that incorporated the binary approach to causation would conclude that the victims had no right to recover from any of their possible injurers despite the fact that a decision requiring the possible injurers to compensate the victims for their losses would provide the possible injurers with allocatively efficient avoidance incentives.

The third type of information that is relevant in this context is similar to the second. Assume that (1) the liberal-moral-rights-claim evaluator knows that a loss might have been caused by nature alone or by a combination of nature and the choice of a particular human being or human organization and (2) if human choice did play a role in the relevant loss's generation, the choice in question was wrongful and allocatively inefficient. Assume in addition that the evaluator has imperfect information about whether human choice did play a role in the generation of the loss in question—indeed, that the only information he has on this issue is information about the contribution that the possible injurer's activity made to the *ex ante* probability that the loss would occur. In an otherwise-Pareto-perfect world, the allocatively efficient way for the evaluator to respond to this sort of situation would be to hold the possible injurer responsible and conclude that he is morally obligated to pay the victim that percentage of the victim's loss that the possible injurer's activity contributed to the *ex ante* probability of the loss's occurring. However, that solution is inconsistent with the binary conception of corrective-justice rights to which we seem to be committed. Under this binary conception, the possible injurer will be morally responsible for the whole loss if his activity contributed more than 50 percent of the *ex ante* probability of its occurring and morally responsible for none of the loss if his activity contributed 50 percent or less than 50 percent to the *ex ante* probability of the loss's occurring. In an otherwise-Pareto-perfect world, this binary response will cause misallocation in two ways:

1. by deterring possible injurers in this position from making allocatively efficient avoidance moves that would reduce the contribution their activity made to the *ex ante* probability of the loss's occurring from some higher probability not above 50 percent to some lower probability not above 50 percent; and
2. by inducing possible injurers in this position to make allocatively inefficient avoidance moves that reduce their activity's contribution to the *ex ante* probability of the loss's occurring from some probability above 50 percent to a probability of 50 percent or below 50 percent.[11]

The fourth type of information that is relevant in this context relates to the wrongfulness of an injurer's and/or victim's conduct. I will illustrate this possibility with three increasingly complex examples.

The first assumes that the liberal-moral-rights-claim evaluator knows that (1) the situation in question is either an individual-care situation (one in which the most-allocatively-efficient response to the AP-loss contingency in question is for either the potential victim or the potential injurer to avoid) or a no-care situation (one in which the most-allocatively-efficient response to the relevant contingency is for no one to avoid) and (2) there is a 30 percent probability that the potential injurer could have increased *ex ante* allocative efficiency while conferring a net equivalent-dollar gain on others by avoiding, while there is no chance that the victim could have increased allocative efficiency by avoiding.

In such a situation, allocative-transaction-cost considerations aside, it would be *ex ante* allocatively efficient to find the potential injurer morally responsible because doing so would tend to induce his future counterparts to engage in allocatively efficient avoidance when they could do so without deterring his victim's future counterparts from engaging in allocatively efficient avoidance because *ex hypothesis* they could not do so. However, if liberalism is committed to a binary approach to cause-in-fact, it would be incorrect for a liberal-moral-rights-claim evaluator to find the injurer morally responsible since the probability that the injurer had behaved wrongfully was not over 50 percent—specifically, was only 30 percent.

The second wrongfulness-information example extends the first to a situation in which (1) the imperfectly informed evaluator knows that the situation was either a no-care or an individual-care situation, (2) the imperfectly informed evaluator knows that there is some possibility that the victim might have been the most-allocatively-efficient potential avoider, and (3) the relevant probabilities enable the evaluator to divide the loss in a way that guarantees that the most-allocatively-efficient avoidance move will be made, regardless of whether the potential injurer or the potential victim is the party in a position to make it. Assume, in particular, that the evaluator knows that (1) the loss is $100,000, (2) the avoidance moves the injurer and victim in question could have made would not have affected the sum of tort-loss-related risk costs that would be generated, (3) the economy is otherwise-Pareto-perfect, (4) if the potential injurer can prevent the $100,000 loss allocatively efficiently, he can do so for less than $80,000, and (5) if the potential victim can prevent the $100,000 loss allocative efficiently, he can do so for less than $15,000. In this instance, any division of the loss between the potential injurer and potential victim that future counterparts of these parties can anticipate between ($80,000 to the injurer and $20,000 to the victim) and ($85,000 to the injurer and $15,000 to the victim) will insure that allocatively efficient avoidance decisions will be made. By way of contrast, a loss-division of $100,000 to the injurer and $0 to the victim—the division a liberal-moral-rights-claim evaluator will be obligated to conclude that liberalism warrants if he finds that the probability that the injurer behaved wrongfully was higher than 50 percent and that the probability that the victim behaved wrongfully was not higher than 50 percent—will fail to induce the victim to avoid when he is the potential most-allocatively-efficient avoider, and a loss-division of $100,000 to the victim and $0 to the injurer—the division that the evaluator will be obligated to conclude that liberalism warrants if he finds that the probability that the injurer behaved wrongfully was not higher than 50 percent—will fail to induce the injurer to avoid when he is the potential most-allocatively-efficient avoider.

The third wrongfulness-information example generalizes the second still further to situations in which no loss-division could guarantee allocative efficiency in an otherwise-Pareto-perfect world because (if we assume for simplicity that the most-allocatively-efficient avoidance moves that might have been available respectively to the potential injurer and to the potential victims would have generated the same reduction in weighted-average-expected AP losses) the sum of (1) the highest cost that the potential injurer would have had to incur to generate that weighted-average-expected loss-reduction in the most-allocatively-efficient way it could manage and (2) the highest cost that the potential victim would have had to incur to generate that weighted-average-expected loss-reduction in the most-allocatively-efficient way it could manage was not lower than (3) the weighted-average-expected loss-reduction either's most-allocatively-efficient avoidance move would generate. If, in such a case, I assume optimistically but in no way critically that (1) the evaluator has information about the probability that each party will be able to generate a $100,000 reduction in weighted-average-expected losses by incurring avoidance costs within each $1,000 interval between $0 and $100,000 and (for convenience) (2) any actor who will be able to avoid at a cost within a given $1,000 interval will be able to do so at the $500 midpoint of that interval, the evaluator could determine the *ex ante* most-allocatively-efficient loss-division by starting with a loss-division of $100,000 to the victim and $0 to the injurer and asking whether, *ex ante,* weighted-average-expected allocative efficiency would be increased or decreased (A) by a shift from a $100,000/$0 to $99,000/$1,000 victim/injurer loss-division, (B) by a shift in the loss-division from a $99,000/$1,000 victim/injurer loss-division to a $98,000/$2,000 victim/injurer loss-division, and so on and so forth. As the text indicates, there is no reason to believe that this *ex ante* most-allocatively-efficient division could be made in the name of corrective justice—for example, would be the division required by a negligence/contributory-negligence or comparative-negligence doctrine. Although the loss-division that this approach would reveal to be *ex ante* most allocatively efficient might be the $100,000/$0 or $0/$100,000 victim/injurer loss-division that a liberal, moral-rights analysis would warrant in this kind of case, I suspect that this will be true only rarely.[12]

In short, for at least three and possibly for as many as six reasons, even if liberal, moral-rights conclusions were self-executing, the resolution of liberal, moral-rights claims by victims of avoidance-move rejections that increased the certainty-equivalent equivalent-dollar AP losses they confronted that would be internally correct in a liberal, rights-based society might be allocatively inefficient. The allocative efficiency of the resolution of such a moral-rights claim is therefore neither a necessary nor a sufficient condition of its correctness from a liberal perspective.

THE RIGHT OF A POTENTIAL VICTIM OF AN ACCIDENT AND/OR POLLUTION LOSS THAT MIGHT DEPRIVE HIM OF THE OPPORTUNITY TO LEAD A LIFE OF MORAL INTEGRITY NOT TO HAVE THE PROBABILITY THAT HE WOULD HAVE A MEANINGFUL OPPORTUNITY TO LEAD A LIFE OF MORAL INTEGRITY REDUCED BY A POTENTIAL INJURER'S REJECTION OF AN AVOIDANCE MOVE THE LATTER SHOULD HAVE PERCEIVED *EX ANTE* WOULD HAVE SERVED THE INTEREST OF THE RELEVANT POPULATION IN HAVING SUCH AN OPPORTUNITY

All the reasons that justify the conclusion that the correct resolution of the previous liberal, moral-rights claim may not be allocatively efficient have counterparts for the related claim with which this subsection is concerned. In addition, the internally correct resolution of this liberal, moral-rights claim may also be rendered allocatively inefficient by the difference between the value that liberalism assigns to preserving a moral-rights bearer's opportunity to lead a life of moral integrity and the equivalent-dollar value that an allocative-efficiency analysis would assign to the preservation of this opportunity.

THE RIGHT TO POSITIVE ASSISTANCE (FOR EXAMPLE, TO RESCUE-ATTEMPT SERVICES)

As Section 4 of the introduction to Part III argued, when acting in a private (that is, nonpolitical) capacity, an individual member of or participant in a liberal, rights-based society has a moral obligation to provide assistance to a fellow moral-rights holder in his society (1) to whom he has made no relevant promise, (2) with whom he has no relevant, more specific status relationship, and (3) whose need for assistance he has not culpably caused if and only if (4) he is in a sense I defined uniquely-well-placed to provide the relevant assistance, (5) his assistance will reduce the probability that its recipient will be deprived of the opportunity to lead a life of moral integrity (by suffering some type of loss other than a monetary loss), and (6) his assistance will not expose him to a significant risk of substantial bodily harm or death or consume an exorbitant amount of his time. Section 4 of the introduction to Part III argued that this conclusion represents an accommodation of two implications of liberalism. In the one direction, the preeminent value that liberalism places on individuals' having and seizing the opportunity to lead lives of moral integrity favors the conclusion that the members of and participants in any liberal, rights-based society have a moral duty to make rescue attempts that seem likely to preserve such opportunities on balance directly because the contribution they make to the opportunity the potential rescuee has to lead such a life exceeds the direct disservice the rescue attempt does to the potential rescuer's relevant opportunity. In the other direction, to the extent that (1) individuals will be more likely to seize an opportunity to lead lives of moral integrity if they perceive themselves to be the authors of their own lives and (2) the imposition of positive duties on individuals militates against their perceiving themselves in this way, liberalism disfavors imposing duties to rescue on individuals because doing so reduces the probability that they will seize their opportunity to lead lives of moral integrity—indirectly disserves the goal liberals value most highly by reducing the extent to which the society's members and participants perceive themselves to be the authors of their own lives. In any event, if this account of the liberal duty to rescue is correct, allocative-efficiency analysis cannot serve as an algorithm for the identification of those situations in which a potential rescuer has a positive duty to provide assistance. Thus, on my account, there will be no duty to provide assistance in many situations in which the provision of assistance would be allocatively efficient—for example, (1) when the assistance in question is allocatively efficient assistance that would not increase the probability that its recipient would have a meaningful opportunity to lead a life of moral integrity, (2) when the assistance in question is allocatively efficient assistance that would increase the probability that its recipient would have or would continue to have an opportunity to lead a life of moral integrity but would expose the assistance-provider to a significant risk of substantial bodily harm (even though the latter risk disserved the rescue attempter's interest in leading a life of moral integrity by less than the rescue attempt served the life-of-moral-integrity-related interest of the potential rescuer) or would consume a great deal of the assistance-giver's time and effort, and (3) when the uniquely-well-placed condition for the existence of a duty to provide assistance warrants the conclusion that no potential assistance-giver has a duty to rescue in circumstances in which a conclusion that one or more of the potential assistance-givers had such a duty would induce one or more of them to provide assistance.

Subsection 1 described one incapacity and four insensitivities of allocative-efficiency analysis that respectively guarantee and favor the conclusion that allocative-efficiency analysis cannot serve as an algorithm for resolving liberal, moral-rights questions. Subsection 1 also explained why the allocative efficiency of a particular resolution of any of seven types of moral-rights claims is neither a necessary nor a sufficient condition for its correctness from a liberal, moral-rights perspective. There can be no doubt that allocative-efficiency analysis is not an algorithm for liberal, moral-rights analysis.

SECTION 2. THE RELEVANCE OF A CHOICE'S ALLOCATIVE EFFICIENCY TO ITS MORAL DESIRABILITY, MORAL-RIGHTS CONSIDERATIONS ASIDE, IN A LIBERAL, RIGHTS-BASED SOCIETY

As Section 5 of the introduction to Part III indicated, moral-ought analysis in a liberal, rights-based society can be based on any one of a large variety of personal ultimate values. In contemporary liberal, rights-based societies, I suspect that the most popular personal ultimate values are utilitarianism, equal-utility egalitarianism, equal-resource egalitarianism, different variants of nonliberal equal-opportunity egalitarianism, libertarianism, and various sorts of retributivist values. This section explains why allocative-efficiency analysis is not an algorithm for the instantiation of any of these personal ultimate values.

I start with utilitarianism. The allocative efficiency of a choice is not a necessary or sufficient condition for its desirability from any type of utilitarian perspective because the utility-value of the average equivalent dollar won by a choice's beneficiaries will often differ from the utility-value of the average equivalent dollar lost by its victims. Thus, an allocatively efficient choice that confers $100 in gains on its beneficiaries will be undesirable from the perspective of classical utilitarianism if the average util-value (a "util" is a unit of utility) of the equivalent dollars gained was 2 and the average util-value of the equivalent dollars lost was 3, since then the choice will have generated total util-gains for its beneficiaries of $100(2) = 200$ utils and total util-losses for its victims of $70(3) = 210$ utils. In the other direction, an allocatively inefficient choice that generated $70 in equivalent-dollar gains and $100 in equivalent-dollar losses will be desirable from the perspective of classical utilitarianism if the average util-value of the equivalent dollars gained was 3 and the average util-value of the equivalent dollars lost was 2 since then the choice will have generated total util-gains for its beneficiaries of $70(3) = 210$ utils and total util-losses for its victims of $100(2) = 200$ utils. In fact, as we saw, it is not even clear that utilitarians would find it desirable to employ a variant of allocative-efficiency analysis that would calculate the winners' total equivalent-dollar gains and the losers' total equivalent-dollar losses (or the ratio of these two figures): although I suspect that utilitarians will usually find it desirable to incorporate such a variant of allocative-efficiency analysis into their evaluative protocol, they may find it more desirable to estimate the utility gains and losses a choice they are evaluating directly rather than indirectly by generating equivalent-dollar gain and loss estimates, estimating the average util-values of the equivalent dollars respectively gained and lost, and comparing the util-value-weighted equivalent-dollar gains and losses in question.

It is also extraordinarily unlikely that the various policies one would have to adopt to effectuate equal-utility, equal-resource, or nonliberal equal-opportunity egalitarianism would maximize allocative efficiency. Although such policies might do a better job than our current policies do at reducing the misallocation we generate by underinvesting in the human capital of the poor, they clearly would misallocate resources by creating divergences between the after-tax marginal wages different classes of workers earn and their marginal allocative products and by distorting the profitability of investing, and there is absolutely no reason to believe that the policies that would be most desirable from the perspectives of these equal-utility, equal-resource, and equal-opportunity norms would minimize the sum of (1) market-labor/do-it-yourself-labor/leisure misallocation, (2) savings/consumption/gifting/bequesting misallocation, and (3) underinvestment-in-human-capital misallocation.

There is also no reason to believe that the instantiation of libertarian values would be allocatively efficient. Admittedly, at least on one understanding of libertarianism, its instantiation would tend to increase allocative efficiency in three ways: (1) by causing each worker to obtain net total wages equal to the allocative product of the last worker to perform the type of labor he performed as skillfully and assiduously as he did—that is, would tend to increase allocative efficiency by eliminating misallocation among market labor, do-it-yourself labor, and leisure, (2) by eliminating taxation on gift-giving and bequesting and, hence, the misallocation such taxation causes by deterring allocatively efficient transfers of these kinds (allocatively efficient because the gift benefits both the donor and the donee), and (3) by eliminating taxation on unearned income and hence the misallocation between savings and consumption such taxes cause by deterring allocatively efficient saving. However, even if the empirical premises and basic values of libertarianism imply that libertarians should be committed to allocating resources to each worker whose allocative cost equals the allocative product of that worker's marginal counterpart, in my experience most self-styled libertarians believe that the relevant standard for rewarding the members of any class of identical workers should be the allocative product of the average worker in their class (where each labor class consists of workers who perform a given task or set of tasks equally skillfully and assiduously). Moreover, the effectuation of even marginal-worker-oriented libertarian distributive values would be likely to be allocatively inefficient for three reasons: it would be extremely allocative-transaction-costly; it would (I fear) cause us to massively underinvest in the children of the poor; and it would deprive the government of the finances it requires to engage in a wide variety of allocatively efficient supply and regulatory activities. Finally, although this claim partly depends on one's conclusions about the substance of libertarian primary moral rights, I suspect that it will not be allocatively efficient to secure the secondary, corrective-justice rights that libertarianism would require to be secured. In part (but only in small part), this last conclusion reflects the fact that, like retributivist values and other sorts of norms that value people's getting what they morally deserve, libertarianism would favor penalizing wrongdoers even if no conventional consequentialist goals would be furthered by doing so.

In short, not only is allocative-efficiency analysis not an algorithm for the instantiation of the most popular personal ultimate values to which the individual members of contemporary liberal, rights-based societies subscribe, but there also is good reason to believe that such values will often favor choices that are distinctly allocatively inefficient.

SECTION 3. THE RELEVANCE OF THE ALLOCATIVE EFFICIENCY OF A LEGAL INTERPRETATION OR APPLICATION TO ITS CORRECTNESS AS A MATTER OF LAW

Fortunately, our analysis of this issue can rely on the work we have already done. As Section 7 of the introduction to Part III points out, the members of and participants in liberal, rights-based societies can have three types of legal rights: legal rights that derive from moral rights, legal rights that were created by legislative acts that were designed to instantiate a legitimate personal ultimate value or to achieve a legitimate social goal, and legal rights that were created by legislative acts that were designed to serve the parochial interests of their supporters. In general, allocative-efficiency analysis cannot serve as an algorithm for the interpretation or concretization of any of these types of legal rights.

Thus, Section 1's demonstration that the allocative efficiency of the resolution of many liberal, moral-rights claims is not a necessary or sufficient condition for its internal correctness implies that the allocative efficiency of the interpretation or application of a moral-rights-based legal right is not a necessary or sufficient condition for its correctness as a matter of law. Indeed, Section 1's analysis implies that, with only one partial exception (relating to the moral right not to have the mere-utility AP losses one confronts increased by avoidance-move rejections by a potential injurer who should have perceived the move he rejected to be *ex ante* allocatively efficient), there is not much of a connection between the allocative efficiency of the resolution of a moral-rights-based legal-right claim and its internal-to-law correctness.

Similarly, Section 2's demonstration that allocative-efficiency analysis cannot serve as an algorithm for the application of any of the personal ultimate values to which the members of and participants in contemporary liberal, rights-based societies subscribe implies that it also cannot be used to determine the interpretation or application of most legal rights that were created to effectuate such values or achieve legitimate social goals—indeed, can be used in this way only when the proximate goal of the relevant legislative act was to increase allocative efficiency. Once more, Section 2's analysis actually suggests that there will usually not be much of a connection between the interpretation or application of personal-ultimate-value-oriented legislation that is most allocatively efficient and the one that is correct as a matter of law.

The same conclusion applies to legislation that was designed to serve the parochial interests of its beneficiaries. The fact that virtually no legislation that was enacted to serve the parochial interests of its beneficiaries will be allocatively efficient implies that the interpretation or application of such legislation that is most allocatively efficient is unlikely to be correct as a matter of law.

So far, this analysis of the relevance of the allocative efficiency of a legal interpretation or application to its correctness as a matter of law has implicitly assumed the correctness of (1) my account of legitimate and valid legal argument in a liberal, rights-based society and (2) my assumption that the United States and most of the other societies for which the economists on whom this book focuses are recommending policies are liberal, rights-based societies. I want to conclude this section by pointing out that its conclusions do not depend on these assumptions. Thus, there is no reason to believe that those legal realists who believe that (1) there are no internally right answers to contestable questions of law or any question of law and (2) judges are morally obligated to or morally ought to resolve such questions in the way that would be morally desirable if moral-rights and legal-rights considerations could be ignored would conclude that the most-allocatively-efficient resolution of the issues in question would be most morally desirable. Indeed, the preceding demonstration that the allocative efficiency of a resolution of any issue is not a necessary or sufficient condition for its desirability from any personal-ultimate-value perspective makes it extraordinarily unlikely that the relevant subset of legal realists would conclude that judges morally ought to make allocatively efficient decisions. Similarly, there is no reason to believe that the modes of legal argument that legal realists would admit determine the internally right answer to any legal-rights question to which they would concede such an answer can be given will all favor the most-allocatively-efficient answer that could be given to relevant questions of legal interpretation or application.

I turn now to the legal positivists. The argument that establishes that the relevant legal realists are unlikely to conclude that judges morally ought to supply the *ex ante* most-allocatively-efficient answer one could supply to any legal-rights question for which no answer is uniquely correct as a matter of law also establishes that legal positivists are unlikely to conclude that judges morally ought to supply the *ex ante* most-allocatively-efficient answer they could supply or the most-allocatively-efficient answer that would not be wrong as a matter of law in those instances in which the legal positivists believe no uniquely-internally-correct answer can be given to the relevant legal question (because the different modes of legal argument that, to their mind, have been validated by practice favor different answers to the relevant question).

My assessment of the relevance of the allocative efficiency of a legal interpretation or application to its correctness as a matter of law also does not depend on any assumption that the society in question is a liberal, rights-based society. Thus, Section 2's demonstration that none of what I have termed the various personal ultimate values to which individual members of liberal, rights-based societies are personally committed do not generically favor economically efficient decisions implies that the economic efficiency of a legal interpretation or application will not be a necessary or sufficient condition for its correctness as a matter of law when the legal right at issue is moral-rights-related and the society is a nonliberal, rights-based society or when the legal right is created by a goal-oriented law and the society in question is a nonliberal, goal-based society. The preceding discussion of the relevance of the economic efficiency of the interpretation or application of a goal-oriented or parochial-interest-serving piece of legislation in a liberal, rights-based society will apply with only one slight modification when the society in question is a nonliberal, rights-based society or a goal-based society: when the society is a nonliberal, rights-based society and the goal-oriented legislation is designed to instantiate liberal values, the critical point is that the economic efficiency of an interpretation or application of the relevant law is not in general a necessary or sufficient condition for its instantiating liberal values.

Chapter 5 has primarily analyzed the relevance of allocative-efficiency analysis (1) to the resolution of moral-rights questions in liberal, rights-based societies, (2) to the resolution of moral-ought questions in such societies, and (3) to the resolution of the interpretative and application issues that can be raised about the different kinds of legal rights that exist in such societies that is correct as a matter of law in such societies. It has demonstrated not only that allocative-efficiency analysis is not an algorithm for the resolution of any of these issues in a liberal, rights-based society but also that the contribution that allocative-efficiency analysis can make to the resolution of these issues is, I suspect, far more limited than not only economists but also most members of the policy audience believe.

However, I do not want to end this chapter so negatively. I will therefore close by rehearsing seven types of contributions that allocative-efficiency analysis or economics more generally can make to prescriptive-moral and/or legal analysis. First, in my judgment, allocative-efficiency analysis is relevant to the analysis of the moral and legal avoidance-obligations of a potential injurer (or victim) who was in a position to reduce the mere-utility losses he imposed on others in a liberal, rights-based society because that obligation turns on the conclusions he should have reached or did reach *ex ante* about the allocative efficiency of the avoidance-move options he rejected. Second, in my judgment, variants of allocative-efficiency analysis that yield estimates of either the total equivalent-dollar gains and losses that choices or policies will generate or the ratio of these totals to each other will almost always make a desirable contribution to the evaluation of the moral desirability of these choices from a pure utilitarian perspective or from any perspective in which utilitarian considerations are given some weight. Third, economic analysis more generally can inform the moral-ought evaluation of private choices or public policies from many different value-perspectives by identifying the winners and losers of the choices or policies in question and providing information about such things as their income/wealth positions and the relationship between their income/wealth positions and the allocative product generated by their labor and acts of saving. Fourth, by providing information that is relevant to the prediction of the utilitarian consequences of effectuating any nonutilitarian norm, allocative-efficiency analysis can contribute to an individual's personal-ultimate-value choice as well as to his analysis of whether he morally ought to fulfill his liberal obligations. Fifth, allocative-efficiency analysis can reveal the ambiguities in the formulation of particular norms (such as the "people ought to be paid according to what they produce" component of some variants of liberatarianism) and can inform the analysis of the variant of the norm that is most consistent with its rationale. Sixth, since from most value-perspectives many features of the world might be called distributive imperfections (in that each would cause the income/wealth distribution to be undesirable from the normative perspective in question if it were the only distributive imperfection in the system), second-best theory can put an evaluator in a better position to analyze the distributive desirability from many moral perspectives of a choice or policy that would change the magnitude of or eliminate one or more distributive imperfections in a world that contained other distributive imperfections. Seventh, and finally, allocative-efficiency analysis can contribute to the determination of whether a given statute, ordinance, or administrative rule was really intended to promote allocative efficiency by revealing whether its supporters were likely to have believed that it would yield this outcome as well as to the application that is correct as a matter of law of legislation whose application should be determined by its goal of increasing allocative efficiency.

Chapter 6 A Critique of Various Relevance Arguments Made by Economists and Law and Economics Scholars

This chapter has five sections. Section 1 states and criticizes various general positions that economists and law and economics scholars take on such matters as the coherence of the concept of moral rights, the coherence of moral norms that value anything other than total utility or the equality of the distribution of utility, and the moral attractiveness of any such norms that are coherent. Section 2 states and criticizes three arguments that economists and/or law and economics scholars have made for the justness of all allocatively efficient choices or decisions. Section 3 states and criticizes an argument that economists and law and economics scholars have made for the moral-ought desirability of all allocatively efficient policies. Section 4 states and criticizes two types of arguments that some law and economics scholars use to justify their conclusion that so-called judge-made law is in some sense allocatively efficient. Finally, Section 5 criticizes the conclusion of various leading industrial-organization economists and law and economics scholars that the American antitrust laws promulgate an allocative-efficiency test of legality to illustrate a more general claim (for which I offer no other evidence) that such scholars tend to conclude that legislation that I think was not passed to increase allocative efficiency was enacted to do so.

SECTION 1. SOME VIEWS ABOUT THE COHERENCE OF MORAL-RIGHTS ANALYSIS, THE COHERENCE OF LEGAL-RIGHTS ANALYSIS, AND THE ATTRACTIVENESS OF MORAL NORMS THAT VALUE SOMETHING OTHER THAN TOTAL UTILITY AND THE SHAPE OF THE DISTRIBUTION OF UTILITY THAT I BELIEVE ARE PREVALENT AMONG ECONOMISTS AND LAW AND ECONOMICS SCHOLARS

This section articulates and criticizes a variety of positions and arguments that I have repeatedly heard economists respectively take and make orally. However, I will cite only one piece of scholarship to support my claim about the prevalence of these norms among economists and law and economics scholars—Louis Kaplow and Steven Shavell's famous article on "Fairness versus Welfare."[1] I should add that this article has been reviewed favorably or cited approvingly hundreds of times by respected economists and law and economics scholars (though it has elicited far less positive responses from philosophers).

I start by reviewing two prescriptive-moral positions that many economists and law and economics scholars take whose erroneousness I have already explained: the position that economic efficiency is a value and that choices that move the society to a Pareto-superior position are always morally desirable. Economic efficiency is not an ultimate value: one cannot legitimately value net equivalent-dollar gains (greenback effects) in themselves. As I have explained, at most, economic efficiency is a proximate value that is valued because, *ceteris paribus*, choices that increase economic efficiency increase total utility. However, as we have seen, economic efficiency is not that proximately related to total utility: because the *ceteris* (the utility-value of the average equivalent dollar gained and the utility-value of the average equivalent dollar lost) are often not even close to *paribus*, many economically efficient choices do not increase total utility, and many economically inefficient choices do increase total utility.

Consider next the supposed moral desirability (undesirability) of all choices that bring the world to a Pareto-superior (Pareto-inferior) position. As the torturer/murderer example of Section 1 of Chapter 2 demonstrated, from the perspective of various norms that value the resources that people receive and the experiences they have matching their moral deserts, choices that make somebody better off without making anyone worse off will be negatively valued if the person whose position is improved does not deserve to be made better off, and choices that make somebody worse off without making anyone better off will be positively valued if the person whose position is worsened deserves to be made worse off.

I move now to new ground. In my experience, many if not most economists believe that moral-rights discourse and argument about the internally correct answer to a legal-rights claim are incoherent: "mumbo-jumbo" is the expression that these scholars have most often used when characterizing such analyses. The more cautious of these critics of moral-rights discourse and legal argument admit that such discourse and argument might be coherent but insist that, to their knowledge, no one has ever given a coherent account of them in part because no one has ever given a coherent account of either (1) any moral norm on which moral-rights analysis could be based other than utilitarianism or a norm that values the shape of the utility distribution (usually the equality of utility) as well as total utility or (2) the various types of argument that are alleged to be valid legal arguments and the way in which they can collectively generate unique, internal-to-law correct answers to (at least some) legal-rights questions. Obviously, these scholars' doubts about the coherence of what they somewhat misleadingly describe as "non-welfare" or "fairness" norms are equally strong in relation to proposals to use such norms to determine what morally ought to be done (what is morally desirable, moral-rights considerations aside). Many other economists and law and economics scholars who are less cautious (and deep down, I suspect, most of those who are more circumspect in articulating their views) claim unequivocably that all so-called fairness norms are incoherent.

I obviously do not think that the liberal norm that liberal, rights-based societies are committed to instantiating in their moral-rights discourse and moral-rights-related conduct is incoherent. Nor do I think that the various other types of norms on which moral-rights commitments or moral-ought evaluations respectively could be and are based—such as equal-resource egalitarianism, equal-opportunity egalitarianism of different sorts, and libertarianism (if it is a defensible moral position)—are incoherent. Indeed, I think that both I (in this text and elsewhere) and others have specified these norms in a way that should dispel all doubts about their coherence.

My conversations with the economists and law and economics scholars who have questioned the coherence of these norms or expressed the view that they are inherently incoherent have led me to attribute their views to a belief that any concept some of whose extensions (roughly speaking, concrete applications) are contestable is incoherent. Those scholars seem to think that if the extensions of a concept cannot be determined uncontroversially (ideally deductively in the way that something like a mathematical formula can be applied), it has no substantive meaning (denotation). I find this view bizarre. It certainly is rejected not only by philosophers and lawyers but also by historians, literary critics, and a wide variety of social scientists as well as by ordinary-language speakers in their everyday discourse.

In addition, in my experience, large numbers of economists and law and economics scholars who concede that nonwelfarist moral norms can be coherent or who are at least willing to proceed *ad arguendo* on the assumption that this is the case believe that all such norms are morally undesirable. I have heard such scholars make six arguments for this conclusion. Since all of these arguments appear in Kaplow and Shavell's article, I will focus here on their discussion of this issue.

Kaplow and Shavell's first argument against the attractiveness of fairness norms is that "little explicit justification for notions of fairness . . . has in fact been offered."[2] I have six comments. First, I disagree with their empirical premise. Second, as I am sure they would admit, even if supporters of particular fairness norms have not devoted enough attention to explaining their attractiveness, this failure might be remediable. Third, since I am not a Foundationalist, I will admit that, as an ultimate matter, the objective superiority of a moral norm cannot be established. Fourth, Kaplow and Shavell's normative discussions lead me to suspect that their conclusion that no proponent of any particular fairness norm has adequately explained its attractiveness may derive from their belief that the only kind of justification that can be justified is what they denominate a welfarist justification—that is, a justification that focuses exclusively on total utility and/or the shape of the distribution of utility. Obviously, this kind of intellectual bootstrapping would involve an unacceptable type of circularity. Fifth, Kaplow and Shavell fail to recognize that their "inadequate justification" complaint is decidedly double-edged: as an ultimate matter, they cannot demonstrate that creatures' experiencing utility is important, much less more important than anything else. And sixth, even if as an ultimate matter no moral norm can be demonstrated to be superior to all others, one might be able to determine the moral norm to whose effectuation a given society is committed.

Second, Kaplow and Shavell argue that some fairness norms are unattractive because their application will cause horizontal inequities. Thus, they claim that (liberal or libertarian) norms that favor making negligent injurers liable for the consequences of their negligence are unattractive because "most instances of negligence do not cause accidents."[3] I have two responses to this criticism. First, Kaplow and Shavell's welfarism also pays scant attention to horizontal inequities—disvalues them only to the extent that they cause those creatures who count to experience disutility because of their preference for horizontal equity. Second, from the perspective of many justice norms, horizontal-inequity considerations may be either irrelevant or relevant but not critical. Thus, from a liberal perspective, the attractiveness of requiring a culpable injurer to compensate his victims if the alternative were for the victims to be uncompensated would not be affected by the fact that other culpable actors were morally lucky in that their culpable act harmed no one.

Third, Kaplow and Shavell argue that fairness norms are unattractive because they are insufficiently forward-looking—that is, "reflect an *ex post* perspective"[4]—and as a result disserve their (alleged) goal of minimizing wrongdoing[5] or inducing beneficial behavior.[6] I have three responses. The first is admittedly just an assertion: Kaplow and Shavell create the impression that the implementation of the norms they denominate "fairness norms" will produce these effects far more often than such norms will. Second, the point of some fairness norms may not be to achieve the forward-looking consequences that Kaplow and Shavell value. Third, there is no objective basis for concluding that securing the consequences that Kaplow and Shavell value is more important than (say) punishing wrongdoers for its own sake. Once more, Kaplow and Shavell are simply privileging the effects that they value over other effects that would be more important from some perspectives that deserve to be called moral.

Kaplow and Shavell's fourth objection to fairness norms is that the implementation of some fairness notions sometimes produces perverse effects from the perspective of the goals that appear to underlie them. Thus, they argue,

> [I]n some basic settings, the only effect of choosing punishment in accordance with retributive justice (aside from raising the cost of the legal system and increasing the number of innocent victims of crime) is to preserve the profitability of crime to some potential criminals—who themselves are viewed as wrongdoers according to retributive theory. Or, pursuing the principle of corrective justice, under which wrongdoers must compensate victims for harm done independently of whether requiring such payments reduces individuals' well-being, has as its only other feature that in certain settings it favors some type of individuals over others solely on characteristics determined by chance elements that seem morally arbitrary from any plausible perspective.[7]

The two responses I made to Kaplow and Shavell's third objection to fairness norms also apply to this objection.

Kaplow and Shavell's fifth objection to fairness norms is the related objection that their implementation sometimes sacrifices "well-being."[8] I have three responses to this claim. First, it implicitly measures well-being by utility—an arbitrary choice since well-being could equally well be measured according to (for example) the extent to which the relevant individuals lead lives of moral integrity. Second, again an assertion, Kaplow and Shavell create the impression that the implementation of the norms they denominate "fairness norms" would sacrifice utility (however measured) far more often than it would. And third, beauty is symmetry. If securing justice requires the sacrifice of utility or some other maximand in which the shape of the distribution of utility perhaps as well as total utility are arguments, the maximization of utility or the securing of some exclusively-utility-oriented maximand will require the sacrifice of justice. From an ultimate perspective, this reality provides no basis for choosing between fairness and welfare.

Kaplow and Shavell's sixth, again related, and final objection to fairness norms is that any "fairness-based analysis . . . [will inevitably in some case lead] to the choice of legal rules that reduce the well-being of every individual."[9] Kaplow and Shavell believe that the fact that consistently adhering to any notion of fairness will sometimes entail rejecting a Pareto-superior choice demonstrates the undesirability of any such norm: "[I]f one adheres to the view that it cannot be normatively good to make everyone worse off, then logical consistency requires that one can give no weight in normative analysis to notions of fairness because doing so entails the contrary proposition."[10]

I have two objections to this argument. First, its conclusion does not follow from its premise: as Howard Chang has pointed out, even if Pareto-inferior positions were always morally inferior to their Pareto-superior alternatives, a decision protocol that instructs the decision maker to pick the Pareto-superior option if one is available but—if no such option is available—to use an evaluative protocol in which a fairness norm either determines the outcome by itself or plays a positive but less dominant role in the determination of the relevant decision might be morally attractive.[11] Second, Kaplow and Shavell's Pareto-superior-position-related argument must be rejected because its premise is wrong: from some normative perspectives that deserve to be called moral, a Pareto-superior option may be morally inferior to its Pareto-inferior alternative.

In short, I reject both the claim of many economists and law and economics scholars that fairness norms, moral-rights discourse, and legal argument are incoherent and the claim of many such academics that fairness norms would be unattractive even if they could be rendered coherent.

SECTION 2. THREE ARGUMENTS THAT ECONOMISTS AND LAW AND ECONOMICS SCHOLARS HAVE MADE FOR THE JUSTNESS OF ALL ALLOCATIVELY EFFICIENT CHOICES: A CRITIQUE

A Utilitarian Argument That Includes a Peculiar Response to the Alleged Impossibility of Making Interpersonal Comparisons of Utility

Some economists and law and economics scholars make the following utilitarian argument for the justness of all allocatively efficient choices:

1. the decision that maximizes the total utility of all moral-rights holders is the just decision (the decision that secures the relevant parties' moral rights);
2. given the impossibility of making interpersonal comparisons of utility, it is appropriate to assume that each equivalent-dollar gain and loss a choice generates will be associated with an equal utility-gain or utility-loss;
3. therefore, all decisions that are as allocatively efficient as they could be are just because they should be assumed to maximize total utility.[12]

Neither of the premises of this argument can bear scrutiny. Even if one ignores the problematic character of any mapping of the various types of affective experiences human beings have (ecstasy, happiness, satisfaction, pleasure, displeasure, pain, dissatisfaction, depression, terror, and so on) into utility, the difficulty that utilitarians have in justifying any boundary condition that limits the creatures whose utility counts to human beings (for example, that excludes nonhuman animals that can experience utility), the fact that utilitarianism implies that the moral quality of any individual's conduct is essentially irrelevant to the amount of resources he ought to receive (though it may be relevant for instrumental reasons), and the related fact that utilitarianism does not take the distinction between individuals seriously, no Foundationalist argument has established the objective correctness of utilitarianism, and no conventionalist argument can establish its internal correctness (since members of our culture do not decide moral-rights [justice] questions by applying a utilitarian standard). *Inter alia*, utilitarianism does not capture our moral practices because it does not distinguish between moral-rights discourse and moral-ought discourse and because it does not make the intentionality of actors directly relevant to the right answer to any moral-rights question one could pose about their position.

Moreover, even if the internally right answer to any relevant moral-rights question were always the answer that maximized *utility*, the answer to such questions that maximized *allocative efficiency* would not be the internally right answer to such questions. Certainly, a contrary conclusion cannot be established by citing the supposed impossibility of making interpersonal comparisons of utility. Such an argument fails for two reasons.

The first is admittedly contestable. I reject the premise that it is impossible to make interpersonal comparisons of utility. Certainly, we at least purport to make such comparisons frequently. Thus, we say that Ed is happier than Dick. We give a particular gift to Mary rather than to Jane because we think Mary will get more pleasure from it. Or, more complicatedly, we decide to invite Ted and Alice rather than Bob and Carol to a dinner party because we think that the former couple (though not necessarily each member of the former couple) will enjoy it more, that our other guests will get more pleasure out of meeting them, or (most generally) that the party will maximize the utility of its participants taken as a group (give its participants the best time on balance) if Ted and Alice are invited. Of course, we may be fooling ourselves when we make such calculations and statements. The kinds of evidence we use to make and evaluate the relevant claims (evidence that relates to facial expressions, tone of voice, demeanor in general, our own assessments of our own experience, the reports of others of their experiences, and so on) may not in fact be adequate for the purpose. However, I do not see how one can hold such a position without lapsing into solipsism—that is, if the kinds of evidence to which I have referred do not justify conclusions about the affective states of other minds, I do not understand the basis on which one can presume that other minds exist.

The second reason why the "impossibility of making interpersonal comparisons of utility" argument fails is that—contrary to its second premise—it is not appropriate or neutral to assume that the average equivalent dollar gained by a choice's beneficiaries and the average equivalent dollar lost by a choice's victims involve the same absolute change in utility for the party in question. This equal-utility assumption is arbitrary and counterintuitive, not neutral and appropriate. For both the preceding reasons, therefore, I would not think that one could establish the correctness of the most-economically-efficient resolution of a moral-rights issue from the perspective of either some objectively true and hence universally applicable conception of justice or any society's particular conception of justice by citing the supposed impossibility of making interpersonal comparisons of utility even if utilitarianism did capture the objectively true concept of justice or our society's justice-conception.

An Argument That Is Based on a Dubious "Envelope" Conception of Justice

The second argument that economists and law and economics scholars have made to justify their conclusion that allocative-efficiency analysis is an algorithm for the generation of moral-rights conclusions is the following "envelope conception of justice" argument:

1. justice is an increasing function of a variety of *desiderata* such as utility, equality, liberty, and autonomy;
2. decisions that increase allocative efficiency increase the extent to which these *desiderata* are secured (in comparison with the *status quo ante*) to a far greater extent than is generally recognized; therefore,
3. the choice that maximizes allocative efficiency is just.[13]

I have two objections to this argument. First, I do not think that the definition of justice its first premise contains—that the internally correct (just) moral-rights decision is the decision that maximizes some function whose value increases with the extent to which the *desiderata* in question are secured[14]—has been established by any Foundationalist argument or captures our moral-rights practices. Second, even if the argument's first premise correctly formulates the objectively correct and therefore universally applicable concept of justice or our society's conception of justice and even if its second premise correctly asserts that allocatively efficient decisions increase the extent to which the *desiderata* in its first premise's envelope formula for justice are secured in comparison with the *status quo ante*—indeed, do so to a far greater extent than is generally recognized—this argument would not justify the conclusion that allocatively efficient decisions always secure moral rights: even if the allocatively efficient decision would be more just than most suppose, some other, less-allocatively-efficient decision might promote justice as formulated even more.

An Autonomy Argument from Hypothetical Consent

The third argument that some economists and law and economics scholars use to justify their conclusion that allocatively efficient decisions are always just is the following argument from hypothetical consent:[15]

1. allocatively efficient choices (or a least a broad subset of such choices that includes virtually all the kinds of common-law decisions judges must make) are in the *ex ante* interest of everyone;
2. everyone would therefore consent to such choices *ex ante* if given the opportunity to do so;
3. the making of allocatively efficient choices is therefore consistent with (perhaps is required by) our commitment to autonomy;
4. our conception of justice makes autonomy paramount; therefore,
5. allocatively efficient choices are always just.[16]

Three objections can be made to this argument. The first is probably the least important in this context: even if, as I believe, one secures justice by making those choices that maximize moral-rights-related interests on balance and even if, in a liberal, rights-based society, the basic duty of respect generally implies that each (competent) moral-rights holder has a *prima facie* right to develop his own conception of the good and to act on that conception (constrained only by the moral rights of others), the liberal, rights-based State's commitment to autonomy will not imply that it is bound to allow individuals to make all choices they desire when their choice does not disserve the moral-rights-related interests of others. For example, a liberal, rights-based State is not obligated to allow the moral-rights holders for whom it is responsible to sell themselves into slavery, to take addictive drugs whose consumption will cause them to lose their autonomy, or to enter into various kinds of relationships that seem highly likely to cost them their autonomy. Nor, I suspect, is it required to allow them to ride motorcycles without wearing helmets, even if no one else will be affected by their avoidable injuries.

The second and third objections to the argument from hypothetical consent are more important in the current context. The second is that the autonomy argument from consent requires actual consent, not hypothetical consent. The fact that someone would have consented to something if given the opportunity to do so is not an adequate predicate for concluding that his autonomy interests are furthered by holding him to a deal or an arrangement to which he did not in fact consent. The fact that on Monday an individual would have accepted a deal or arrangement or policy that will harm some people *ex post* because at that time he did not know whether he would be an *ex post* beneficiary or victim of the choice in question does not in itself bind him to accept it on Wednesday, when he knows its actual results. Admittedly, the features of the policy that would have led him to accept it on Monday may provide a basis for the conclusion that the policy was just, but any argument that relies on those features is not a consent argument.

Third, even if hypothetical consent would establish the justness of any policy, the hypothetical-consent argument would not establish the justness of the overwhelming majority of allocatively efficient choices of any kind because neither allocatively efficient choices in general nor the economically efficient resolution of common-law-rights questions are likely to leave everyone better off *ex ante* and no one worse off *ex ante*. Proponents of the hypothetical-consent argument have vastly overestimated the frequency with which allocatively efficient policies will leave all those they affect better off *ex ante*. In my judgment, allocatively efficient policies will virtually always have one or more *ex ante* losers.[17]

Richard Posner, the major proponent of the hypothetical-consent argument for the justness of all allocatively efficient choices, has tried to respond to this reality (whose empirical importance he vastly underestimates) by insisting that "only a fanatic would insist that unanimity be required"[18] in this sort of context. In fact, however, for consent arguments to work, there must be unanimity: in this context, fanaticism is the order of the day.

In short, none of the arguments that economists and law and economics scholars have made for the supposed justness of allocatively efficient decisions can bear scrutiny.

SECTION 3. AN ARGUMENT THAT VARIOUS ECONOMISTS HAVE MADE FOR THE MORAL-OUGHT DESIRABILITY OF ALL ALLOCATIVELY EFFICIENT POLICIES

Economists have also developed an argument that they think establishes the moral-ought desirability of all allocatively efficient policies or decisions:

1. any decision that moves the economy to a Pareto-superior position (that makes somebody better off without making anyone worse off) morally ought to be made;
2. a policy of making all allocatively efficient decisions will over the long haul make some people better off and no one worse off than they would be if all allocatively efficient decisions were rejected; therefore,
3. a policy of making all allocatively efficient decisions will always be morally desirable.[19]

Unfortunately, this argument also cannot bear scrutiny: both its premises are wrong, and, even if they were right, they would not establish its conclusion. The first premise is wrong because, from some legitimate personal-ultimate-value perspectives (for example, from the standpoint of retributionist norms or, more generally, norms that value having each individual's rewards or material welfare match the quality of the relevant actor's moral performance in general), some moves to Pareto-superior positions (such as choices that benefit a heinous criminal and harm no one in any straightforward sense) may be thought to be morally undesirable. The second premise is empirically wrong because, given the fact that individual allocatively efficient decisions may have substantial adverse effects on some of their victims, even over the long haul a decision to make all allocatively efficient decisions might not move the society to a position that was Pareto-superior to the *status quo ante*. And even if the two premises of this argument were correct, the argument would not justify the conclusion that the allocatively efficient choice always morally ought to be made because from various personal-ultimate-value perspectives one or more moves that are not Pareto-superior in comparison with the *status quo ante* may be preferable to a move that is Pareto-superior in comparison with the *status quo ante*.

SECTION 4. A CRITIQUE OF TWO TYPES OF ARGUMENTS THAT LAW AND ECONOMICS SCHOLARS HAVE MADE FOR THE ALLOCATIVE EFFICIENCY OF SO-CALLED JUDGE-MADE LAW

Law and economics scholars who believe in the allocative efficiency of the law that judges announce in cases in which these scholars believe judges make as opposed to find the law attempt to justify their allocative-efficiency conclusion with two types of arguments. Chapter 4 described and criticized an example of the first type of argument in question: arguments that attempt to demonstrate the allocative efficiency of a given decision, doctrine, or body of law (in the case discussed there, the awards judges concluded marine rescuees were legally obligated to pay their salvors) by demonstrating that the relevant judges' decisions varied in the allocatively efficient direction with the case-parameters the judges took into account. As Chapter 4 argued, this type of argument is deficient in that it ignores the possibility (in the case there, the reality) that the most-allocatively-efficient decisions judges could make would also be affected by a number of case-parameters they ignored and fails to consider whether the judges' decision varied to the right extent with changes in the magnitudes of the relevant case-parameters that they did take into consideration.

Law and economics scholars who believe in the allocative efficiency of the law they (but not I) think judges make also try to justify this conclusion with a second kind of argument that might be called "storytelling." Scholars who engage in this type of storytelling try to prove the allocative efficiency of particular decisions by making up facts about individual cases that would render their actual judicial resolution allocatively efficient. Although these stories' factual assumptions might be realistic—indeed, might even be plausible—the stories often ignore other independent, often at least as likely empirical possibilities that would render the decision the judges made *ex ante* allocatively inefficient, and the scholars sometimes ignore the fact that the judges in question never adverted to, much less accepted, the accuracy of the factual assumptions that critically affected the scholars' stories' punch lines.

As Chapter 4 pointed out, Robert Rabin has provided a good example of such misleading storytelling—Landes and Posner's attempt to demonstrate the allocative efficiency of a judicial ruling that a trolley company had not behaved negligently in a case in which a plaintiff was electrocuted when a metal pole he was carrying came into contact with uninsulated overhead trolley wires beneath an overpass on which the plaintiff was walking.[20] Landes and Posner's story was that—given the low probability of this kind of loss, the fact that the wire had to be uninsulated to supply electricity to the trolley, and the high cost of placing the wire underground—the trolley company's decision to use overhead wires in the situation in question was not negligent (because the cost of placing the wires underground was higher than the weighted-average-expected reduction in accident losses placing them underground would generate). Rabin pointed out an additional possibility that Landes and Posner ignored—the possibility that, even if the trolley company's decision not to bury the necessarily uninsulated wires was not negligent, its failure to post warning-signs in these situations may have been negligent.[21]

In short, neither of the two types of argument with which law and economics scholars have tried to confirm their hypothesis that so-called judge-made law is allocatively efficient can bear scrutiny.

SECTION 5. THE TENDENCY OF ECONOMISTS AND LAW AND ECONOMICS SCHOLARS TO CONCLUDE THAT LEGISLATION THAT I BELIEVE WAS NOT DESIGNED TO INCREASE ALLOCATIVE EFFICIENCY WAS DESIGNED TO DO SO: AN ANTITRUST ILLUSTRATION

Economists and law and economics scholars vastly exaggerate the frequency with which legislation, ordinances, and administrative regulations are designed to increase allocative efficiency. I will not try to justify this claim here. Instead, I will restrict myself to illustrating it by evaluating the assumption of virtually all American economists who do antitrust economics[22] and all American legal academics who use economics to interpret and apply American antitrust law[23] that the American antitrust laws promulgate an economic-efficiency test of legality—that is, declare any behavior or practice they cover illegal if and only if that conduct (or perhaps its prohibition) would be economically efficient. More specifically, this section will begin by articulating the tests of legality that the American antitrust laws would be read to promulgate if properly interpreted, will then provide some examples that reveal that these tests do not make the economic efficiency of the conduct to which they apply a necessary or sufficient condition for its antitrust legality, and will finally discuss some confusions that may account for the relevant economists' and law and economics scholar's mistaken claim that the American antitrust laws do promulgate an economic-efficiency test of legality.

Two statutes articulate the federal American antitrust laws' tests of legality—the Sherman Act and the Clayton Act.[24] Section 1 of the Sherman Act prohibits "every contract, combination, or conspiracy in restraint of trade or commerce among the several states, or with foreign nations," and Section 2 makes it illegal for anyone to "monopolize, or attempt to monopolize, or combine or conspire . . . to monopolize" any part of interstate or foreign commerce. The Clayton Act's relevant individual provisions prohibit the various specific kinds of business conduct they respectively cover whenever the effect of that conduct may be to "lessen competition" or "create a monopoly" "in any line of commerce in any section of the country." I believe that the readings of these two statutes that are correct as a matter of law—the readings that take appropriate account of the ordinary meaning of their language, the way in which the words they use were previously used in the law where relevant, the social histories that preceded their enactment, their specific legislative histories, and the other components and overall structure of the industrial policy of which they constitute an important part—reveal that neither promulgates an economic-efficiency test of legality.[25]

I start with the Sherman Act. In my view, the Sherman Act promulgates a specific-anticompetitive-intent test of legality. More precisely, I believe that, correctly interpreted, the two relevant provisions of the Sherman Act would be read to prohibit virtually all[26] business acts or practices whose profitability was perceived by their perpetrators *ex ante* to be "critically increased" by (and therefore, *ceteris paribus* critically *inflated* by) its tendency to increase their profits (1) not by increasing their competitive advantages by reducing their marginal costs and/or increasing their product's or products' dollar value to their actual buyers or their perception of that dollar value, (2) not by reducing their fixed costs, and (3) not by enabling them to secure more profits from a given combination of marginal cost and demand curves, but (4) by increasing the demand curve they faced by reducing the absolute attractiveness of the offers against which they must compete. The language "perceived by its perpetrator(s) *ex ante* to be critically increased or *ceteris paribus* critically inflated" requires some elucidation. A perpetrator's *ex ante* perception of the profitability of his act will be critically increased by the fourth effect just listed if his perception that the act in question might generate it caused him to view as profitable an act he would otherwise have considered to be unprofitable. In the otherwise-Pareto-perfect world whose existence the phrase *ceteris paribus* indicates one must posit for these purposes, the profitability of an act that would not have been perceived by its perpetrator to be *ex ante* profitable but for his belief that it might increase his profits by reducing the absolute attractiveness of the offers against which he would have to compete in the future will be not only critically *increased* but critically *inflated* by the perceived effect in question (if it actually occurs)—i.e., this effect would render the act profitable despite the fact that it was allocatively inefficient. To see why, note that, in an otherwise-Pareto-perfect world, (1) the fact that the act would have been *ex ante* unprofitable had there been no chance that it might reduce the absolute attractiveness of the offers against which its perpetrator would have to compete in the future would imply that it was allocatively inefficient and (2) although any tendency the act in question may have to reduce the absolute attractiveness of offers against which the actor would have to compete in the future will increase its profitability in any world, in an otherwise-Pareto-perfect world it will decrease the act's allocative efficiency. In any event, on this reading, the Sherman Act will prohibit *inter alia* virtually all acts of price-fixing, all acts of predation, and mergers, acquisitions, and joint ventures that would not have been perceived by their participants to be *ex ante* profitable had they not believed that they might increase their profits by freeing them from each other's competition and possibly by reducing the competition remaining rivals would give them.

I turn now to the Clayton Act. In my view, properly interpreted, the Clayton Act would be read to promulgate a qualified (see below) anticompetitive-impact test of legality. More precisely, I believe that, with one qualification, the Clayton Act's various relevant provisions prohibit the specific type or types of conduct they respectively cover[27] if and only if an informed observer should have predicted *ex ante* that the conduct in question would on the weighted average impose a net equivalent-dollar loss on the American customers of its perpetrators and the American customers of the perpetrators' product rivals by reducing the absolute attractiveness of the offers these buyers received from their inferior (that is, worse-than-privately-best-placed) suppliers, regardless of whether this effect was a necessary cause of the conduct's harming them so long as the conduct would be predicted to harm them on balance.[28] The contestable qualification is an organizational-allocative-efficiency defense that has no textual basis in the statute but is favored not only by the Sherman Act and the commentary on that Act that preceded the initial passage of and various amendments to the Clayton Act but also by other features of American industrial policy—for example, by its granting discoverers monopoly control over their discoveries. This organizational-allocative-efficiency defense enables defendants who would otherwise be found to have violated the Clayton Act to exonerate themselves and escape liability by demonstrating that—more probably than not—the tendency of their behavior to impose net equivalent-dollar losses on relevant buyers because they reduced the attractiveness of the offers they received from their inferior suppliers was critically affected by its tendency to drive various rivals out by reducing their total competitive advantages by improving the defendants' competitive positions by increasing their organizational allocative efficiency (for example, by lowering not only their private but also their allocative marginal costs). On this reading, the Clayton Act would also prohibit many mergers, acquisitions, and joint ventures, a few acts of price discrimination, and a very small percentage of the other vertical practices it covers.

Before proceeding, I should indicate that, on my readings, the Sherman and Clayton Acts will sometimes not produce the same conclusion about the legality of particular conduct they both cover. For example, the Sherman Act would not condemn a horizontal merger that violated the Clayton Act test of legality if the tax advantages it yielded its participants were a sufficient condition for its perpetrators' *ex ante* perception that it would be profitable. But for current purposes, the crucial fact is that, on my readings, neither statute promulgates an economic-efficiency test of antitrust legality. Thus, on my readings, (1) neither statute will usually prohibit price discrimination or the more complicated types of pricing that tie-ins and reciprocity agreements can effectuate even when (as is typically the case) these pricing practices are economically inefficient and their prohibition would be economically efficient[29] and (2) neither statute's conclusion that particular conduct was illegal would be affected by the fact that (for second-best-type reasons) the reductions in competition (most often, in this context, in QV-investment competition but conceivably in a few instances in price competition) that the conduct in question was predicted to generate would increase allocative efficiency.

I want to close this section with three intellectual explanations for the mistake it claims that economists and antitrust lawyers who use economics to interpret and apply the American antitrust laws make when they claim that those laws should be applied in the way that would most increase economic efficiency. First, in my opinion, some of the scholars and lawyers in question have made this mistake (1) because they do not take legal argument seriously—at least, do not believe that an internal-to-law correct interpretation can be given to the American antitrust laws, (2) because, somewhat relatedly, they think that judges should interpret these laws in the way in which they morally ought to have been drafted (that is, to serve the public interest), and (3) because they think that these laws or all laws morally ought to be designed to increase economic efficiency to the maximum extent they can. Second, in my judgment, all of the scholars in question have been partly led to make this mistake by their ignorance of or refusal to take account of The General Theory of Second Best. Third, finally, and perhaps most surprisingly, many of the relevant economists and lawyers have been led to make this mistake by their tendency to conflate the impacts of an act on competition, on buyer (equivalent-dollar) welfare, and on economic efficiency—at least, by their tendency to believe that all acts that reduce competition also impose equivalent-dollar losses on buyers and reduce allocative efficiency, that all acts that impose equivalent-dollar losses on buyers also reduce competition and allocative efficiency, and that all acts that reduce allocative efficiency also impose equivalent-dollar losses on buyers. Perhaps the relevant economists and lawyers do know better, but if they do their discussions of the antitrust laws' tests of legality and, indeed, of antitrust policy often fail to manifest such knowledge.

Again, I have analyzed the claim of economists and economics-oriented antitrust lawyers that the federal American antitrust laws promulgate an economic-efficiency test of legality because I believe that it is an example of a much broader phenomenon—that the errors the preceding paragraph articulated cause economists and law and economics scholars to mistakenly assert that many laws establish an economic-efficiency test of legality.

In short, Chapter 6 has refuted all of the arguments that economists and law and economics scholars have made for the justness of all choices that are allocatively efficient, for the moral desirability of all such choices (moral-rights considerations aside), and for the correctness as a matter of law or moral-ought desirability of all allocatively efficient interpretations and applications of all laws that were not passed to increase allocative efficiency, regardless of whether they were moral-rights-based, moral-ought-based, passed to serve the parochial interests of their supporters, or mistaken. Chapter 6 concludes with an analysis of the American antitrust laws' tests of legality that explains why the standard view of economists that these laws should be interpreted in the most-economically-efficient way possible is incorrect and explores the errors that led economists to reach this mistaken conclusion, errors (I assert) that often lead economists and law and economics scholars to conclude mistakenly that legislation should be interpreted and/or applied in the most-economically-efficient way possible.

Conclusion

This Conclusion has four sections. The first summarizes the book. The second illustrates its critique of the way in which economists and law and economics scholars analyze allocative efficiency by criticizing a well-respected law and economics analysis of the allocative efficiency of protecting commercial and personal privacy. The third reviews some facts the book established that support the claim that the scholars whose work it criticizes either knew or should have known that they were making the mistakes it demonstrates they made. The fourth makes some brief comments about the implications of the book for economists and law and economics scholars, for the policy audience in general, and for university administrators.

SECTION 1. A SUMMARY

The book's three parts respectively address the following three issues: the correct way to define the concept of the impact of a choice or policy on allocative (economic) efficiency, the most-allocatively-efficient way to assess the allocative efficiency of a choice or policy, and the connection between allocative-efficiency conclusions and prescriptive-moral and legal conclusions. Part I begins by arguing that definitions of concepts such as the impact of a choice on allocative efficiency should be evaluated by two criteria: (1) their compatibility with ordinary and technical usage and (2) the usefulness of the concept they define. It then explains why these criteria imply that (1) a choice's allocative efficiency should be defined to equal the difference between the equivalent-dollar gains it confers on its beneficiaries and the equivalent-dollar losses it imposes on its victims, (2) the equivalent-dollar gains a choice confers on its beneficiaries equal the number of dollars they would have to receive "in an inherently neutral way" to leave them as well off as the choice would leave them, (3) the equivalent-dollar losses a choice imposes on its victims equal the number of dollars that would have to be taken from them in an inherently neutral way to leave them as poorly off as the choice would leave them, and (4) the ways in question are inherently neutral in that they are neither valued nor disvalued in themselves by the relevant parties and will not affect them indirectly by generating secondary-feedback effects. In essence, then, Part I argues that the definition of the impact of a choice on allocative efficiency that is correct in the sense in which it defines that modifier equates its constituent gains and losses with elaborated-on versions of the equivalent variations as opposed to the compensating variations in the affected parties' wealths.

Part I then explains why the definition it proposes is superior to the various definitions that economists and law and economics scholars currently use or purport to use—the Pareto-superior/Pareto-inferior definition (which creates a concept that is virtually useless), the Kaldor-Hicks test (that is not only wrong but is also biased in favor of the status quo), the Scitovsky-paradox-inspired variant of the Kaldor-Hicks test that is somewhat misleadingly called the Scitovsky test (which incorporates and therefore fails to correct the errors of the Kaldor-Hicks test), and the potentially-Pareto-superior definition (which makes some of the same errors that the Kaldor-Hicks test makes). Part I also discusses a number of subordinate issues that relate to the operationalization of the concept of the impact of a choice on allocative efficiency that it argues that many economists and law and economics scholars have mishandled: *inter alia,* whether equivalent-dollar gains and losses that reflect the relevant party's external preferences—preferences that relate directly to the consequences of a choice for others—should be counted in any allocative-efficiency calculation, whether the nature of a *desideratum* may be affected by its voluntary purchase and sale (for example, whether friendship can be bought or whether paid-for sex is the same as voluntary, non-paid-for sex or rape from either participant's perspective), and whether allocative-efficiency calculations should be based on consumer evaluations even when there is good reason to believe that the relevant consumers have, from their own perspective, misevaluated the good or service in question.

Part II focuses on the allocatively efficient way to assess the allocative efficiency of a choice or policy. Its analysis derives from The General Theory of Second Best—that is, from the fact that, since, without further information, one must assume that any two imperfections will be as likely to counteract as to compound each other, there is no general reason to believe that a policy that will reduce the number or magnitude of the imperfections in a system without removing all such imperfections will *even tend on that account* to bring one closer to the optimum.

Part II begins by defining the seven (or eight, if one includes allocative transaction costs) so-called Pareto imperfections that could cause allocative inefficiency in an otherwise-Pareto-perfect world, listing the various ways in which resources are used in our economy and hence the various types of resource misallocation that can be generated in our economy, examining the way in which imperfections of one type will cause various types of resource misallocation in an otherwise-Pareto-perfect economy, and explaining and illustrating the different ways in which two or more imperfections of the same or different types interact to cause several of the types of resource misallocation that can be generated. Part II then develops an approach to allocative-efficiency assessment that it argues is third-best allocatively efficient—that is, allocatively efficient given the plethora of Pareto imperfections of all types in the actual economy, the multiplicity of types of resource uses in the economy, and the allocative cost and inevitable imperfectness of both analytic and empirical work. This distortion-analysis approach derives from the fact that the amount of misallocation generated by the economically inefficient choices to allocate resources to any particular type of use increases with the absolute value of the weighted-average mean and weighted-average absolute and squared deviations of the distribution of positive or negative percentage distortions in the profits yielded by the least profitable but not unprofitable resource uses of that type to have been made where the distortion in the profits that a relevant resource use generates equals the difference between the profits it yielded and its allocative efficiency and the percentage distortion in question equals the ratio of the relevant profit distortion to the allocative cost of the resources the relevant resource use consumed. In any event, the distortion-analysis approach to assessing the allocative efficiency of any policy proceeds by (1) analyzing the different ways in which the economy's various Pareto imperfections interact to distort the profits yielded by each of the various types of resource-use choices the policy will affect, (2) collecting or assembling data on the pre-policy magnitudes of the various relevant Pareto imperfections, (3) analyzing the ways in which the policy would affect the magnitudes of those imperfections, (4) generating an initial estimate of the policy's impact on the total amount of misallocation in the economy by using the preceding work to estimate its impact on the absolute weighted-average mean and weighted-average absolute and squared deviations of the percentage-profit-distortion-distributions segments it would affect, (5) repeatedly assessing the *ex ante* allocative efficiency of collecting additional data on relevant parameters by determining the allocative cost of such data collection, the likelihood that it would change one's estimate of those parameters by different amounts, and the amount by which any related revision in the estimates of the magnitudes of the parameters in question would increase the *ex ante* allocative efficiency of the policy the analyst recommended by enabling him to identify a more *ex ante* allocatively efficient policy, and (6) making a final estimate of the allocative efficiency of the policy in question when the preceding analysis suggests that it would not be *ex ante* allocatively efficient to collect additional data.

Part II then illustrates this distortion-analysis approach by using scaled-down versions to analyze the allocative efficiency of (1) prohibiting contrived oligopolistic pricing (roughly speaking, price-fixing), (2) altering tax, intellectual-property, and antitrust policy to increase both product and production-process R&D, and (3) shifting from a negligence/contributory-negligence tort-liability regime to a strict-liability/contributory-negligence tort-liability regime.

After that, Part II illustrates or justifies its claim that economists and law and economics scholars almost entirely ignore The General Theory of Second Best by describing and criticizing eight canonical articles or bodies of literature that execute first-best-allocative-efficiency analyses—that is, that analyze the misallocation some Pareto imperfection generates on the assumption that it is the only Pareto imperfection in the system—and one article that takes some account of second-best theory by considering the way in which an independent imperfection affects the allocative efficiency of introducing a second imperfection selectively but continues to ignore a host of other imperfections that also affect the allocative efficiency of the proposed selective intervention. The eight first-best analyses are the traditional analyses of (1) the deadweight loss monopoly allegedly causes, (2) the trade-off involved in calculating the allocative efficiency of a horizontal merger that simultaneously reduces its participants' marginal (allocative) costs and increases the prices they charge, (3) the allocative efficiency of the quantity of resources currently devoted to R&D of all kinds, (4) the allocative-efficiency cost of monopoly, (5) the allocative efficiency of an effective, universal policy of internalizing externalities and of a more limited policy of shifting from a negligence/contributory-negligence tort-liability regime to a strict-liability tort-liability regime, (6) the allocative efficiency of the alleged common-law practice of holding the members of infant industries strictly liable while holding members of mature industries liable solely for the consequences of their found negligence, (7) the possibility of devising allocatively efficient housing codes, and (8) the allocative efficiency of marine-salvage law. The study that takes some account of second-best theory analyzes the allocative efficiency of making scope-of-liability decisions depend *inter alia* on the standard of liability that would be applied to the defendant if his case were not dismissed on proximate-cause (scope-of-liability) grounds—that is, on the ground that the loss the defendant was alleged to have caused was not for some reason a loss for which he would be legally responsible even if he could be shown to have caused it or to have caused it negligently (if his liability depended *inter alia* on his found negligence).

Part II concludes by delineating and criticizing the various arguments that those economists who admit knowing about The General Theory of Second Best claim justify ignoring it. It argues that these arguments cannot bear scrutiny—indeed, that they are troublingly misconceived or irrelevant.

Part III focuses on the connection between the allocative efficiency of a choice and its justness or moral desirability (moral-rights considerations aside) as well as on the connection between the allocative efficiency of an interpretation or application of the law and its correctness as a matter of law. Part III"s prescriptive-moral and legal analyses are based on the assumption that the societies for which the scholars the book is criticizing are making policy-recommendations and legal assessments are by and large liberal, rights-based societies—that is, societies whose members and governments (1) draw a strong distinction between moral-rights discourse and moral-ought discourse (between the just and the good), (2) are committed to instantiating the just even when the good as defensibly conceived must be sacrificed to do so, and (3) are committed to deriving their moral-rights (justice) conclusions from a basic duty to treat all moral-rights holders for whom they are responsible with appropriate, equal respect and, derivatively, for showing appropriate (in the case of individuals) or appropriate, equal (in the case of government) concern for them as well—in part, for their utility as economists would understand this concept but preeminently for their having and seizing the opportunity to lead a life of moral integrity by taking their moral obligations seriously and taking seriously as well the dialectical task of developing a morally defensible, personal conception of the good and leading a life that is consonant with that conception.

After delineating and elaborating on various moral and legal concepts that its analysis employs, Part III argues that the allocative efficiency of a choice is neither a necessary nor a sufficient condition for its justness in a liberal, rights-based society. It supports this conclusion in two ways: first, by explaining that (1) allocative-efficiency analysis can make no contribution to the analysis of an issue that must always be resolved as part of any moral-rights analysis—namely, what is the identifying attribute of a moral-rights holder (the so-called boundary-condition issue)—and (2) allocative-efficiency analysis is insensitive to four distinctions that often play a critical role in the analysis of the moral rights of moral-rights holders—the distinction between licit and illicit preferences (such as prejudices), the distinction between mere utility and the opportunity to lead a life of moral integrity, the distinction between not harming another and failing to provide assistance to another, and the related distinctions among psychological, material-welfare, and entitlement interests (concerns). Second, it establishes this conclusion by demonstrating that allocative-efficiency analysis is not an algorithm for determining the content of (1) the liberal right of a person to the resources and experiences that will critically affect his opportunity to lead a life of moral integrity, (2) the liberal right to privacy, (3) liberal liberty rights, (4) the liberal right that others not make choices against one's interest that are illicitly motivated, (5) the liberal right of potential accident and pollution victims not to have their *ex ante* mere-utility interests sacrificed by their potential injurers' rejection of avoidance moves that these potential injurers should have perceived *ex ante* (in effect) to be allocatively efficient, (6) the liberal right of potential accident and pollution victims not to have their *ex ante* interest in having an opportunity to lead a life of moral integrity sacrificed by their potential injurers' rejection of avoidance moves that these potential injurers should have perceived *ex ante* would sacrifice the net interest of the relevant population in having such an opportunity, and (7) the liberal right to positive assistance from other members of or participants in one's liberal, rights-based society.

Next, Part III demonstrates that the allocative efficiency of a choice is not a necessary or sufficient condition for its moral-ought desirability, moral-rights considerations aside, regardless of the personal-ultimate-value perspective from which the relevant evaluation is being made—for example, regardless of whether it is being made from a classical or modern utilitarian perspective, an equal-utility egalitarian perspective, an equal-resource egalitarian perspective, an equal-opportunity egalitarian perspective, or a libertarian perspective. Indeed, Part III shows that the allocative efficiency of a choice or policy is not at all relevant from the perspective of any of the nonutilitarian values just listed and that its relevance to the utilitarian evaluation of any choice or policy (1) is limited by its inability to determine the identity of the creatures whose utility counts, (2) is partial in any event in that the allocative efficiency of a choice is neither a necessary nor a sufficient condition for its desirability from a utilitarian perspective, and (3) is contingent on the utility of predicting the impact of a choice or policy on (total or average) utility not directly but circuitously by predicting equivalent-dollar gains and losses (as a variant of allocative-efficiency analysis would be able to do), determining the average utility-value of the equivalent dollars gained and lost respectively, weighting the equivalent-dollar gains and losses by their respective average utility-values, and comparing the weighted-equivalent-dollar gains and the weighted-equivalent-dollar losses.

After that, Part III demonstrates that, regardless of whether one subscribes to my position on legitimate and valid legal argument in liberal, rights-based societies, the allocative efficiency of an interpretation or application of the law is not a necessary or sufficient condition for its correctness as a matter of law or for its moral-ought desirability if no uniquely correct answer can be given to the relevant legal-rights question. More particularly, Part III demonstrates that this position is correct regardless of whether one subscribes (1) to my view that in liberal, rights-based societies arguments of moral principle (arguments that derive from the basic right to appropriate, equal respect and concern that such societies are committed to securing) are not only legitimate and valid legal arguments but are also the dominant mode of legal argument in that they operate not only directly but also by controlling the legitimacy, (almost always) the validity, and the argumentative force of the other modes and mode-variants of legal arguments used in such societies, (2) to the variant of legal realism that denies that legal argument can generate internally right answers to any or any contestable or contested legal-rights question, or (3) to legal positivism, which maintains that (A) all general modes and specific variants of legal argument that are used sufficiently often in the relevant society are validated by their use, (B) an internal-to-law right answer can be given to a legal-rights question in a given society if and only if that answer is favored by all variants of legal argument that have been validated through use, and (C) when no answer can be given to a legal-rights question that is uniquely correct as a matter of law, the judge morally ought (some might also say is morally obligated to) resolve the question by selecting from the set of answers that are favored by at least one valid legal argument the particular answer he thinks is morally most attractive. Indeed, Part III demonstrates that allocative-efficiency analysis is not an algorithm for the resolution of legal-rights questions regardless of whether the legal right (1) derives from a moral right (since allocative-efficiency analysis is not an algorithm for the resolution of moral-rights questions), (2) was created by legislation designed to promote some personal ultimate value (achieve some morally defensible good) except when the statute was designed to increase allocative efficiency (since allocative-efficiency analysis is not an algorithm for the resolution of moral-ought questions), or (3) was created by legislation designed to serve the parochial interests of some or all of its beneficiaries (since such legislation is almost always allocatively inefficient).

Part III then criticizes various positions taken by and arguments made by economists and law and economics scholars on (1) general philosophical and jurisprudential issues, (2) the relevance of allocative-efficiency conclusions to the justness and moral desirability (moral-rights considerations aside) of private choices or government policies, and (3) the relevance of the allocative efficiency of a legal interpretation or application to its correctness as a matter of law. More specifically, Part III criticizes the position of many such scholars that moral-rights talk and legal argument are incoherent ("mumbo-jumbo" is the expression that they often use) and that any norm that values anything but total utility or the shape of the utility distribution is probably incoherent and certainly undesirable. Part III also criticizes three arguments that economists and/or law and economics scholars have made for the ability of allocative-efficiency analysis to function as an algorithm for the analysis of justice—a utilitarian argument that responds inappropriately to the supposed impossibility of making interpersonal comparisons of utility, an argument that adopts an envelope conception of justice and draws a false inference from the fact that economically efficient policies are more likely to promote the norms that it assumes are arguments in the justice function than is generally recognized, and a hypothetical-consent argument that links justice to the protection of autonomy. In addition, Part III criticizes an argument for the ability of allocative-efficiency analysis to serve as an algorithm for the resolution of all moral-ought questions that claims falsely that in the long run making all allocatively efficient policy-decisions will bring the economy to a Pareto-superior position and assumes incorrectly that that fact renders such a decision protocol morally desirable from all defensible moral perspectives. After that, Part III states and criticizes two types of arguments that law and economics scholars use to confirm their hypothesis that judge-announced (in their contestable words, "judge-made") law is allocatively efficient—evidence that the damages that judges award vary in the allocatively efficient direction with the facts of the case they claim influence such damage-awards and stories that describe (contestable) factual premises that would make judicial rulings allocatively efficient. Part III concludes by illustrating its *assertion* that economists and law and economics scholars vastly exaggerate the frequency with which legislation is designed to increase allocative efficiency or should be interpreted in the most-economically-efficient way possible by challenging the claim of virtually all antitrust economists and legal scholars who use economics to interpret and apply the American federal antitrust laws that those laws promulgate or should be interpreted to promulgate an economic-efficiency test of legality.

SECTION 2. A CRITIQUE OF RICHARD POSNER'S HIGHLY REGARDED ANALYSIS OF THE ALLOCATIVE EFFICIENCY OF PROTECTING COMMERCIAL AND PERSONAL PRIVACY

In his well-respected article "The Right to Privacy,"[1] Richard Posner argues that (1) giving the discoverers of commercially valuable information monopoly control over the use of that information (protecting this type of commercial-privacy interest) is allocatively efficient because it provides potential researchers with allocatively efficient incentives to discover and use such information, (2) giving individuals a legal right to control the commercial exploitation of their images and endorsements is allocatively efficient because it enables individuals to manage the use of their images and endorsements so as to maximize their private value to their users and hence the allocative value they generate, but (3) giving individuals the legal right to prevent the disclosure of personal information about themselves is allocatively inefficient since it will increase the extent to which individuals defraud others by making it more difficult for people to discover information about each other. This section explains why each of these contentions is wrong.

Posner's argument for the allocative efficiency of giving discoverers monopoly control over the information they discovered is flawed not only in that

(1) it fails to specify the length and breadth of the control that would be allocatively efficient in an otherwise-Pareto-perfect world and (2) it fails to deal with the misallocation that such monopoly control generates by causing the discovered information to be underutilized from the perspective of allocative efficiency but also and most importantly in the current context in that (3) it fails to respond to the fact that various other imperfections in the system (most importantly, externalities and imperfections in seller and buyer competition) will render allocatively inefficient the intellectual-property-protecting regime that would be allocatively efficient in an otherwise-Pareto-perfect economy—*inter alia* imply that the most-allocatively-efficient system of intellectual-property protection would take into account the amount by which the discoverer's research project reduced the expected returns of its competitors and the various parameters that affect the magnitude of the monopoly distortion in the profits yielded by the discovery.

Posner's argument for the allocative efficiency of giving individuals control over the use of their likenesses and endorsements is based on a series of dubious empirical assumptions that underlie his implicit premise that any decision that increases the total private value of a person's likeness and endorsement to all the businesses that use it to sell their products will increase allocative efficiency on that account as well. The empirical assumptions in question relate to (1) the ways in which the relevant endorsements increase the value that the buyers of the endorsed product perceive it has for them (by providing them with information about its physical or performance attributes, by changing the associations the buyers have with the product, by changing the information a consumer of the product can communicate about himself to others by informing them of the fact that he does consume the particular product in question), (2) the sovereignty of the buyers in question and of those whom they are trying to influence, and (3) the allocative costs that the pervasive use of product endorsements (and the image advertising they encourage) generate by inducing people to take images more seriously than it is in their individual and certainly their collective interest to do.

Finally, Posner's assessment of the allocative efficiency of protecting personal privacy is based on an amazingly pessimistic assumption about the reasons individuals value their privacy (namely, because they want to keep information about themselves secret to put themselves in a position to defraud others) that totally ignores the reasons that lead liberals to place a high value on privacy. I am tempted to ask why—if Posner has such a pessimistic view of the reasons individuals want to keep facts about themselves secret—he does not have a similarly pessimistic view about why individuals want to persuade others that they have the same or similar attributes as the endorsers of the products they consume. I also cannot resist the temptation to say that, in my experience, economists more generally have what I take to be extraordinarily inaccurate views of human preferences, values, motivations, and experience.

I have included this critique of Posner's analysis of the allocative efficiency of protecting different types of privacy in the Conclusion because his analysis reflects all the types of errors that I am claiming beset conventional economic-efficiency analyses: (1) a failure to recognize that various Pareto imperfections (such as imperfections in price competition) other than the target imperfection (the externalities that would be generated if others could use an individual's discovery, likeness, or endorsement without buying the right to use it from him) can affect the allocative efficiency of reducing or eliminating a target imperfection, (2) a tendency to make unrealistic assumptions about the Pareto-perfectness of the economy (for example, about the extent to which buyers are consumer sovereigns or about the likelihood that individuals might be tyrannized by their small decisions into generating allocatively inefficient public bads), and (3) a proclivity to misassess the preferences, values, commitments, and motivations of the persons whose equivalent-dollar gains and losses are components of any allocative-efficiency calculation.

SECTION 3. SOME EVIDENCE THAT THE ECONOMISTS AND LAW AND ECONOMICS SCHOLARS WHOSE WORK I CRITICIZE KNEW OR SHOULD HAVE KNOWN THAT THEY WERE MAKING THE ERRORS THE BOOK DEMONSTRATES

Intermittently, this book points out facts that suggest that the economists and law and economics scholars who made the mistakes it discusses either knew or should have known that they were making the errors in question. This section reviews the most troubling of these facts.

First, in some instances, my suspicions were aroused by the obviousness of the errors that were made. For example, it seems suspiciously clear to me that (1) one cannot justify ignoring second-best theory by pointing out that some policies that first-best-economic-efficiency analysis would imply would be economically efficient reduced prices and increased quality and variety (facts that do not guarantee the policy's economic efficiency) or that some such policies actually did increase economic efficiency, (2) one cannot significantly undercut the force of second-best theory by pointing out that the economic efficiency of a policy that will be applied in only one sector of the economy will not be affected by imperfections in other sectors of the economy if resources do not flow between the target sector and these other sectors, (3) one cannot justify failing to analyze various types of quality-or-variety-increasing-investment misallocation by asserting that all choices or policies will have the same effect on such misallocation as on UO-to-UO misallocation, (4) one cannot demonstrate the objective superiority of utilitarian values or values that focus exclusively on total utility and the shape of the utility distribution by pointing out that the effectuation of values that are concerned with other things will sometimes or even always sacrifice utility or valued attributes of the utility distribution, (5) one cannot justify the conclusion that a concept is incoherent by establishing that some or many of its extensions are contestable, (6) one cannot demonstrate the economic efficiency of judge-made law by proving that judicial decisions vary in the economically efficient direction with variations in some of the factors judges state influenced their decisions or by telling stories about the facts of cases that make their actual judicial resolution appear economically efficient that ignore various obvious possibilities that call the relevant decision's economic efficiency into question, and (7) one cannot establish the economic efficiency of the law's handling of some issue (say, the rule of liability to be applied to some set of potential injurers) by showing that the law's resolution of this issue is more allocatively efficient than some but not all of the other ways in which it might have been resolved would have been.

Second, in some instances, questions are raised by the economics profession's responding to a proof that reveals that a definition economists are using is wrong by patching the definition to prevent it from producing the conclusion that the proof established was wrong rather than by trying to understand the error(s) in the original definition that led it to produce a wrong conclusion in the case in question and revising the definition accordingly. I have in mind the profession's responding to the Scitovsky Paradox by substituting the so-called Scitovsky test for economic efficiency for the Kaldor-Hicks test.

Third, in some instances, I am made suspicious by the economics profession's or individual economists' "forgetting" things it or they once knew—reverting to the Kaldor-Hicks test for economic efficiency, adopting the potentially-Pareto-superior test for economic efficiency even though it has many of the same defects as the Kaldor-Hicks test, and ignoring The General Theory of Second Best even when they understand its import.

Fourth, in some instances, I find problematic the extent to which the economics profession or, at least, individual economists and law and economics scholars have succeeded in maintaining their ignorance in not knowing anything about The General Theory of Second Best or not learning about or understanding the criticisms that philosophers and academic lawyers have made of some of their prescriptive-moral and legal claims.

Taken together, these facts seem to me to warrant the conclusion that the economists and law and economics scholars who made and continue to make the errors this book points out knew or should have known that they were making these mistakes. I can only speculate about the causes of this (alleged) pattern of conduct, which I do not think is in any way unique to the economics profession. Although it might be prudent for me to leave these suggestions to another day, I will offer them here. The grab bag of possibilities that occur to me includes (1) general human dispositions—resistance to cognitive dissonance and the reluctance to admit one has made mistakes, (2) the fact that economists have been professionally socialized to accept particular paradigms, (3) the desire of individual economists to advance in a profession whose gatekeepers (journal editors, referees, tenured faculty members, and department chairs) are committed to defending existing paradigms, (4) the fact that most economics journals impose strict page-constraints that make it difficult in an individual article to explain a conceptual innovation and justify it by showing how it enables its user to identify important new issues or to analyze known or new issues more satisfactorily, (5) the desire of individual economists to do private or public consulting (and the concern that communications that respond in a scientifically appropriate way to second-best theory and moral and legal complexities will be harder to understand and, on that account, less likely to get them hired and to induce their audience to listen to or adopt their suggestions), (6) the desire of individual economists to have their profession highly valued (coupled with the fear [which I believe to be unjustified] that their acknowledgement of the importance of second-best theory and philosophical and legal complexities will reduce the value others place on the information economists can provide), (7) the desire to promote their personal conception of the good (coupled with the fear that admissions that economic efficiency is not a value in itself, that utilitarianism or a distributive norm that values both total utility and the shape of the utility distribution cannot be shown to be objectively most morally desirable, and that second-best theory does undercut first-best arguments will decrease the probability that the polity will make decisions that promote the relevant economist's conception of the good), and (8) the desire to promote the public interest as it was defined through democratic political processes (coupled with the fear that the above admissions will reduce the influence of economics on public decisions and thereby disserve the democratically defined public interest and/or that any attempt by government to take account of the complexities that the above admissions indicate should be considered in a world in which perfect analytic work could be costlessly executed and perfect data could be costlessly collected would in practice be counterproductive—that the allegedly third-best protocols that government would use would produce results that were worse than those that would be yielded by philosophically and jurisprudentially naïve first-best-allocative-efficiency analyses [in part because a government that tried to intervene more sophisticatedly and selectively would be likely to become a moral-rights-violating Leviathan, a possibility to which a proper third-best analysis would give appropriate attention]).

In any event, if this book is correct in claiming that economists knew or should have known that they were making the mistakes it demonstrates and persisted in those errors despite that fact, that reality would obviously have important implications.

SECTION 4. SOME IMPLICATIONS OF THE BOOK'S CENTRAL FINDINGS

The book's most obvious implications are for economists and law and economics scholars: (1) substitute the correct, monetized definition of the impact of a choice on allocative efficiency for the various useless or incorrect definitions you are currently using; (2) substitute a third-best-allocative-efficiency analysis for the first-best-allocative-efficiency analyses you currently are executing (regardless of whether the particular distortion-analysis approach I have developed turns out to be third-best allocatively efficient); and (3) do not claim that the allocative-efficiency conclusions you generated have more prescriptive-moral or legal relevance than they actually have—either just present your allocative-efficiency conclusions as facts and let others assess their relevance or discuss their relevance with your audience in an informed, sophisticated way (which may help those you are advising discover additional information you can supply that would help them answer the prescriptive-moral or legal question at issue). Economists and law and economics scholars have an academic and moral duty to change in these ways, and the public interest would be served if they did so.

The book also has implications for the policy audience. Most obviously, it implies that the policy audience should guard against being influenced by the mistakes it argues economists are currently making. But perhaps equally importantly, its discussion of the tendency of economists to persist in making errors they know or should know they are committing and its unsupported allegation that this practice is more general among academics[2] implies that the policy audience should always take a critical stance toward the advice of experts, even when they are not being paid by special interests. The Germans have an expression: "*Papier ist geduldig*"—paper is patient; you can write anything on it. One should always be skeptical of things that are written down (or said), not only when the authors of the statements are people with special interests or their representatives but also when they are supposedly-public-spirited academics.

I am a great believer in the value of expertise—that is, I think that expert advice can make a substantial contribution to government decision making. However, this view is conditioned on the government's establishing decision-making institutions and adopting decision-making protocols that subject all expert advice to careful scrutiny and ensure that the people who make the decisions have enough expertise and communication skills to understand the soundness and contestability of the information they are given.

Finally, the book has implications for university administrators. It implies that universities should make decisions to combat the ignorance of the members of individual academic disciplines about relevant work done in other disciplines, the tendency of academics to stick to paradigms that should be overthrown (or, less comprehensively, to continue to make individual mistakes they know or should know they are making), and the disposition of academics to leave the impression that the positions they are taking on public-policy issues are based exclusively on their scientific expertise when that is not the case. Somewhat more specifically, universities should try to achieve these goals *inter alia* by establishing joint-degree programs in which relevant fields are truly integrated, encouraging faculty members in different disciplines to teach individual courses together and collaborate on research, allowing graduate students to have recognized minors in other disciplines or to satisfy part of their course requirements by taking courses in related fields, hiring and promoting people with training in more than one related field, securing recommendations on which interdisciplinary hiring and promotion decisions are based from a group of people who collectively have all the different expertises necessary to evaluate a candidate's work, securing recommendations on which single-discipline hiring and promotion decisions are based from individuals who subscribe to the relevant range of defensible paradigms in the discipline (when the field has more than one paradigm), and reviewing the hiring and promotion decisions of individual faculties to combat paradigm parochialism and individual defensiveness.

A high school English teacher once gave me the following advice: say you're going to say it, say it, and say you've said it. This effort to follow her instruction is now completed.

Notes

INTRODUCTION

1. The equivalent-dollar gain a choice confers on a particular beneficiary is the number of dollars he would have to receive to be left as well off as the choice would leave him if the grant of money did not affect him (1) directly for nonmaterial reasons because he valued or disvalued such transfers in themselves or their distributive impact or (2) indirectly for material reasons because the transfer would change the income/wealth position and derivatively the choices of one or more others in ways that affected his material interests. The equivalent-dollar loss a choice inflicts on a particular victim is the number of dollars he would have to lose to be left as poorly off as the choice would leave him if the loss did not affect him directly for the above nonmaterial reasons or indirectly for the above material reason. (In this note and in the rest of this book, the pronoun "he" is used to refer to both men and women.) For an explanation of the qualifications in the preceding two sentences, see Section 1 of Chapter 1. The expression "*equivalent*-dollar" is used because many of the effects of choices are not direct monetary effects. Indeed, in some cases, someone who has experienced an equivalent-dollar effect may not be able to capitalize this impact of the choice in question. Take, for example, someone who experiences an equivalent-dollar gain from an environmental policy that cleans the water in swampland he owns and

values (say, for sentimental reasons) but whose market value is still zero after the improvement in question.

2. For an example in which a prominent critic of law and economics takes this position, see Duncan Kennedy, *Cost-Benefit Analysis of Entitlement Problems: A Critique,* 33 STAN. L. REV. 387, 410 (1981).
3. For a discussion of this issue by a prominent welfare economist, see E. J. MISHAN, WELFARE ECONOMICS: FIVE INTRODUCTORY ESSAYS 68–72 (1964).
4. See J. R. Hicks, *The Rehabilitation of Consumer Surplus,* 8 REV. ECON. STUD. 108 (1940).
5. See Tibor Scitovsky, *A Note on Welfare Propositions in Economics,* 9 REV. ECON. STUD. 77 (1941). The name "Scitovsky test" is somewhat misleading: Scitovsky never endorsed this unjustified response to his demonstration that, in some circumstances, both a policy choice and its immediate reversal could pass the Kaldor-Hicks test. For a discussion of the Scitovsky test, see Section 3 of Chapter 2.
6. See R. G. Lipsey & Kelvin Lancaster, *The General Theory of Second Best,* 24 REV. ECON. STUD. 11 (1956) for the first formal statement of the theory.
7. Two elaborations are necessary. First, the conventional list of Pareto-optimal conditions substitutes a "no public goods" condition for my "no misallocation-causing buyer surplus" condition. My choice reflects the fact that buyer surplus can cause misallocation not only when public goods (goods whose demand curves cut their marginal cost curves from above at an output at which marginal cost is less than average total cost) are involved but also in other situations (for example, when the relevant choice is investing in the creation of one of two rival products that are not public goods and the investment that is more profitable is less economically efficient because the amount by which the buyer surplus that would be generated by the sale of the good that the less profitable investment would create *exceeds* the buyer surplus that would be generated by the sale of the good that the more profitable investment would create *is greater than* the amount by which the profits that would be yielded by the more profitable investment *exceed* the profits that would be yielded by the less profitable investment). Second, the list delineated in the text is conventional in that it omits an eighth condition that quite possibly should be included—the condition that the other seven conditions can be fulfilled without incurring any social (allocative) transaction costs. The conventional omission of this transaction-cost condition is unfortunate to the extent that it leads economists to undervalue research that seeks to devise substantive laws, legal institutions, and legal procedures that would increase economic efficiency by reducing the allocative transaction cost of responding to the other Pareto imperfections. As Guido Calabresi has observed, many economists have been dismissive of sophisticated efforts by legal academics to increase economic efficiency in these ways. See Guido Calabresi, *The Pointlessness of Pareto: Carrying Coase Further,* 100 YALE L.J. 1211 (1991). One further point about transaction costs needs to be made: both economists in general and law and economics scholars have universally ignored the fact that private transaction costs will rarely equal their allocative counterparts. In substantial part, this error reflects the relevant scholars' failure to take appropriate account of the Pareto imperfections whose presence makes The General Theory of Second Best salient.

8. See, e.g., PHILLIP AREEDA, LOUIS KAPLOW, & AARON EDLIN, ANTITRUST ANALYSIS 12–15 (6th ed. 2004).
9. See Oliver Williamson, *Economies as an Antitrust Defense Revisited,* 125 U. PA. L. REV. 699 (1977) and *Economies as an Antitrust Defense: The Welfare Trade-Off,* 58 AM. ECON. REV. 18 (1968).
10. See, e.g., Kenneth Dam, *The Economic Underpinnings of Patent Law,* 23 J. LEGAL STUD. 247 (1994) and Robert Merges and Richard Nelson, *On the Complex Economics of Patent Scope,* 90 COLUM. L. REV. 839 (1990).
11. See Arnold C. Harberger, *Monopoly and Resource Allocation,* 66 PAPERS AND PROC. AM. ECON. ASSOC. 77 (1953).
12. For standard environmental-economics textbooks whose economic-efficiency analyses totally ignore The General Theory of Second Best and whose bibliographies contain references to hundreds of economics articles that share this deficiency, see EBAN GOODSTEIN, ECONOMICS AND THE ENVIRONMENT (4th ed. 2005) and TOM TIETENBERG, ENVIRONMENTAL AND NATURAL RESOURCES ECONOMICS (4th ed. 1996). I hasten to add that some environmental-economics textbooks do contain some material that takes at least some account of second-best theory. Thus, CHARLES KOLSTAD, ENVIRONMENTAL ECONOMICS (2000) recognizes (1) (at 129–31) that any imperfections in the price competition that a pollution-generating producer faces will affect the impact of a Pigouvian pollution tax on the economic efficiency of his unit output decision and (2) (at 281–84) that the impact of Pigouvian pollution taxes on labor-leisure misallocation will be affected by the reality that market-labor-generated income but not leisure is taxed. WILLIAM BAUMOL & WALLACE OATES, THE THEORY OF ENVIRONMENTAL POLICY (2d ed. 1988), also recognizes—indeed, devotes (at 91–102) a chapter to exploring—the relevance of imperfect price competition for the economic efficiency of the impact of Pigouvian pollution taxes on the taxpayer's unit output decisions. However, neither the Kolstad textbook nor the Baumol and Oates textbook presents anything like a full second-best analysis of the problems whose solution they recognize second-best theory informs, and both ignore second-best theory more generally. For a more recent collection of articles that examines the relevance of independent taxes on the margin of income for the economic efficiency of internalizing externalities through Pigouvian pollution taxes, see ENVIRONMENTAL POLICYMAKING IN ECONOMIES WITH PRIOR TAX DISTORTIONS (Lawrence Goulder, ed. 2001). For a tort-policy analysis that completely ignores second-best theory, see William A. Landes & Richard M. Posner, *The Positive Economic Theory of Tort Law,* 15 GA. L. REV. 851 (1981). For a tort-policy analysis that takes account of one imperfection when analyzing the economic efficiency of eliminating a second potential imperfection, see Steven Shavell, *An Analysis of Causation and the Scope of Liability in the Law of Torts,* 9 J. LEG. STUD. 463 (1980). For a discussion of the deficiencies of Shavell's second-best-influenced economic-efficiency analysis, see the relevant subsection of Section 1 of Chapter 4 *infra.*
13. See Landes & Posner, *supra* note 12 at 910–11.
14. See Shavell, *supra* note 12 at 476.
15. See William A. Landes & Richard M. Posner, *Finders, Good Samaritans, and Other Rescuers: An Economic Study of Law and Altruism,* 7 J. LEG. STUD. 83 (1978).

16. Richard Posner, Economic Analysis of Law 529–63 (1st ed. 1973).
17. See John Donohue, *Some Thoughts on Law and Economics and the General Theory of Second Best,* 73 Chi.-Kent L. Rev. 257 (1998).
18. The clearest presentation of the utilitarian argument can be found in Posner, *supra* note 16 at 241. For the envelope-concept-of-justice argument, see Richard Posner, *The Ethical and Political Basis of the Efficiency Norm in Common Law Adjudication,* 8 Hofstra L. Rev. 487 (1980). The hypothetical-consent argument is best articulated in Richard Posner, The Economics of Justice 92–99, 101–03 (1981).
19. For the initial statements of the argument, see J. R. Hicks, *Foundations of Welfare Economics,* 49 Econ. J. 696 (1939) and Harold Hotelling, *The General Welfare in Relation to Problems of Taxation and of Railway and Utility Rates,* 6 Econometrica 242 (1938). See also Mitchell Polinsky, *Probabilistic Compensation Criteria,* 86 Q.J. Econ. 407, 407–12 (1972).
20. See Landes & Posner, *supra* notes 12 and 15.
21. See, e.g., Robert Bork, The Antitrust Paradox: A Policy at War with Itself 61–66 (1978); Paul Joskow & Alvin Klevorick, *A Framework for Analyzing Predatory Pricing Policy,* 89 Yale L.J. 213 (1979); and Jonathan B. Baker, *The Case for Antitrust Enforcement,* 17 J. Econ. Persp. 27 (2003).
22. See Richard M. Posner, *The Right to Privacy,* 12 Ga. L. Rev. 1363 (1980).

CHAPTER 1. THE CORRECT DEFINITION OF THE IMPACT OF A CHOICE ON ECONOMIC (ALLOCATIVE) EFFICIENCY

1. The expression "external preference" comes from Ronald Dworkin, Taking Rights Seriously 234–38 (1977). An external preference is a preference for someone else's being allocated additional resources or opportunities, fewer resources or opportunities, or a particular amount of resources or opportunities. As defined, an individual's external preferences can reflect his legitimate likes or dislikes, his prejudices, his personal moral values, or the distributive values he perceives his society to be committed to instantiating. Some law and economics scholars use the expression "disinterested preferences" instead of "external preferences." See Matthew Adler and Eric Posner, *Implementing Cost-Benefit Analysis When Preferences Are Distorted,* in Cost-Benefit Analysis: Economic, Legal, and Philosophical Perspectives 269, 281–82 (Matthew Adler & Eric Posner, eds. 2001).
2. As Part II's discussion of second-best theory reveals, this conclusion reflects various unarticulated assumptions not only about the accuracy of the crude calculations in question but also about the relative size of and correlation between the errors in the estimates or guesstimates of the relevant external-preference-related equivalent-dollar effects and the errors in the estimates of the net non-external-preference-related equivalent-dollar effects.
3. This position is much more limited than Dworkin's generic objection to counting any external-preference-related equivalent-dollar effect a policy generates. Dworkin's argument (*supra* note 1 at 234–38) is that counting such external preferences is morally unacceptable because it is inegalitarian in that it counts some individuals' benefits

more than once and some individuals' benefits less than once. Thus, according to Dworkin, any protocol for evaluating a policy that counts the external-preference-related benefits a policy generates when it benefits someone whose welfare others value is unacceptably inegalitarian because that protocol counts the relevant individual's benefits or utility twice—once when he experiences it and again when others who value his obtaining the benefit experience the benefit they obtain on that account. I do not think that such a protocol entails double-counting that is inconsistent with egalitarianism. I would say that the utility of such a beneficiary is counted only once in itself, though the fact that the relevant party experienced a gain is also relevant indirectly to the extent that others value his experiencing that gain. In my judgment, it is no more inegalitarian or morally improper for some other reason to count such indirect consequences of a direct beneficiary's gain than it would be to count the utility gains the initial benefit generated by inducing the direct beneficiary to make a choice that generated more external benefits than the choice he would have made had his real income or wealth not been increased. Although it is morally impermissible or undesirable to count the indulgence of certain types of external preferences in favor of a choice—such as those that reflect prejudices or sadistic tastes—I do not think that Dworkin's generic objection to counting any external preference can be justified.

4. For example, as Part III will assert, many economists subscribe to the incorrect view that the following moral distinctions or concepts are incoherent: (1) the distinction between the right and the good, (2) any alleged moral norm that is nonconsequentialist, (3) any alleged moral norm that renders salient anything other than the effect of a choice on total utility or on some combination of total utility and the shape of the distribution of utility, and (4) any concept whose extensions are contestable.
5. The impact of a choice on creatures whose equivalent-dollar gains and losses are not components of the economic-efficiency calculation may still be relevant to the choice's economic efficiency to the extent that creatures whose equivalent-dollar gains and losses are components of the economic-efficiency sum place positive or negative dollar valuations on the impact in question. Thus, even if the impact of a choice on the welfare of dogs is not a component of its economic efficiency, it will affect the economic efficiency of the choice in question to the extent that dog-lovers and dog-haters whose equivalent-dollar gains and losses are components of the economic-efficiency effects of any event, private choice, or public policy place positive or negative dollar valuations on the impact in question (have external preferences for or against the welfare of dogs).
6. I realize, of course, that a number of these specific conclusions are controversial. In my judgment, some who disagree with them do so because they are conflating their own religious convictions with the moral position to which our society is committed, and some do so because (for perfectly defensible reasons) they think that our State morally ought to or perhaps (given the possibility of error or malfeasance) is morally obligated to treat some creatures that are not moral-rights holders as if they were.
7. The relevant external effects will depend *inter alia* on the difference between the relevant individual's allocative product and gross wages, the difference between the taxes he pays and the allocative cost of the government's supplying him with the government services he receives, the conventional external costs and benefits he generates, the

external costs and benefits he generates in his personal relations, the external costs and benefits he generates because of the external preferences of others, the amount of charity he gives, etc.

8. If the relevant individuals would be aware of the policy that led to their creation or that affected the length of their lives, the policy's allocative efficiency would also be affected by the equivalent-dollar value they would assign to it for reasons unrelated to their valuation of their own lives or the relevant days of their lives—e.g., because their conception of the good, their perception of their moral obligations, or their religious convictions led them to place a positive or negative value on the policy in question.
9. See John Broome, *Cost-Benefit Analysis and Population* in ADLER & POSNER, *supra* note 1 at 117, 128.
10. In this case, I have quoted the word "value" because I doubt that libertarianism is a defensible value (or at least that some popular variants of libertarianism are defensible). More specifically, I question the moral status of libertarianism because it proceeds from the premise that human beings are morally responsible for their productive capacities, tastes, values, and proclivities when, I believe, interpersonal variations in these things can probably be substantially attributed to interpersonal variations in genetic endowments and environmental factors over which the relevant individuals have no control.
11. For an example of this practice, see the "revealed preference" articulation of the Pareto-superior definition of "an increase in economic efficiency"—i.e., the claim of many economists that a position should be said to be Pareto-superior to an alternative if the former position is chosen over the latter by one or more individuals and the latter position is not chosen over the former by any individual or if other decisions the affected parties have made would reveal that they would value the relevant positions in the above ways if they acted consistently and the latter decisions were actually warranted by their real preferences. This "revealed preference" articulation assumes that the fact that the former position would be chosen over the latter by someone implies that the relevant individual would be better off in the former position than in the latter, that the fact that the former position would not be chosen over the latter by anyone implies that no one would be worse off in the former position than in the latter, and that the relevant individuals acted as sovereign maximizers when making any decision from which the relative value of the positions in question to them was being inferred. None of these assumptions may be accurate in a world in which individuals can make errors.

CHAPTER 2. A CRITIQUE OF THE DEFINITIONS OF AND TESTS FOR ECONOMIC EFFICIENCY THAT ECONOMISTS AND LAW AND ECONOMICS SCHOLARS USE

1. For another situation in which a Pareto-superior choice would not be morally desirable from a defensible (liberal) moral perspective, see Amartya Sen, *The Impossibility of a Paretian Liberal,* 78 J. POL. ECON. 152 (1970).
2. See J. R. Hicks, *The Rehabilitation of Consumer Surplus,* 8 REV. ECON. STUD. 108 (1940).
3. See Tibor Scitovsky, *A Note on Welfare Propositions in Economics,* 9 REV. ECON. STUD. 77 (1941).

4. The tendency of taxes on the margin of income to cause these two types of misallocation is explained in Section 1 of Chapter 3.
5. The text's statement that proponents of the potentially-Pareto-superior definition of increase in economic efficiency focus on the existence of a policy package consisting of the policy under investigation and a money transfer that would be Pareto-superior if the money transfer would be neither allocative transaction costly nor misallocative in the two other ways delineated is actually generous. In fact, proponents of this definition ignore the fact that the financing of the money transfer will almost certainly cause misallocation among market labor, do-it-yourself labor, and leisure and misallocation among savings, consumption, and gifting or bequesting: (1) in an otherwise-Pareto-perfect world, the financing of the money transfer in any way that make its victims' losses depend on their income or wealth will cause both of these additional kinds of misallocation, (2) in such a world, the only kind of tax that will not generate those types of misallocation (a poll tax) will be particularly allocative-transaction-costly and may cause misallocation in addition by inducing one or more taxpayers to commit economically inefficient suicides, and (3) there is no reason to believe that the other Pareto imperfections in any actual economy will eliminate the tendency of any such financing arrangement to cause these types of misallocation.
6. Actually, even in an otherwise-Pareto-perfect economy, an allocative-transaction-costless money transfer could confer equivalent-dollar gains on its beneficiaries that exceed the equivalent-dollar losses it imposes on its victims by causing various individuals to alter their conduct.
7. And the fact that the policies would be economically inefficient after the money transfer was executed did not reflect the money transfer's impact on its economic efficiency.
8. In circumstances in which the relevant money transfer did not critically increase the economic efficiency of the policy whose economic efficiency is to be scrutinized.

CONCLUSION TO PART I

1. R. H. Coase, *The Problem of Social Costs,* 1 J. Law & Econ. 1 (1960).
2. The relevant transaction costs would include (1) the private/allocative costs the potential victim(s) would have to incur/generate to determine that he might suffer a loss that one or more potential injurers might avoid, to identify his potential injurer(s), to negotiate a deal with his potential injurer(s), and to enforce that deal as well as (2) the private/allocative costs the potential injurer(s) would have to incur/generate to determine that his choice might cause losses for which he might be liable, to identify his potential victim(s), to negotiate a deal with his potential victim(s), and to enforce that deal. In situations in which there are multiple injurers or multiple victims, the private and allocative transaction costs in question may be increased by holdout and free-rider problems: indeed, such problems may actually prevent what would otherwise be a jointly profitable deal from being struck.
3. Coase proceeded on the assumption that the only relevant Pareto imperfection in the system was the externality to which the rule of liability related. As a result, he ignored

the possibility that the rule of liability might affect the amount of allocative inefficiency in the system by changing the distribution of income and/or wealth. Several possibilities are relevant in this connection. First, the rule of liability may affect allocative efficiency by changing the net external benefits (costs) that are generated because people approve or disapprove of the way in which their society distributed the relevant type of loss or distributed income and/or wealth in general. Second, the rule of liability may also affect misallocation by changing the position of the poor in a way that affects (1) the misallocation caused by our tendency to underinvest in the children of the poor, (2) the misallocation caused by crime (to the extent that redistributions to the poor deter crime by improving the legitimate-conduct options of the poor and by reducing their alienation and hence increasing their distaste for crime), and (3) the misallocation the poor cause by consuming externality-generating cars and housing units by making it personally disadvantageous for them to purchase low-quality, more-external-cost-generating goods. Third, the rule of liability may also affect allocative efficiency by changing the wealth and externality-related choices of the non-poor—such as by inducing a middle-class or rich person to substitute a racy sports car, which he will drive in a more accident-prone way, for a staid station wagon, which he will drive more safely. Fourth, the rule of liability may also affect misallocation by changing the demand curves for various relevant products and thereby the amount of resource misallocation other imperfections (such as imperfections in seller competition) cause.

4. Admittedly, this claim should be qualified to reflect the fact that the government would have to generate some allocative costs to finance its supply of the good in question if it did not finance its supply by selling it.
5. See Edoh Amiran & Daniel Hagen, *Willingness to Pay and Willingness to Accept: How Much Can They Differ?*, 93 AM. ECON. REV. 458 (2003).
6. The most highly respected estimate of giving by U.S. donors in 2003 is $179.36 billion by living individuals, $21.60 billion by decedents, $26.30 billion by foundations, and $13.46 billion by corporate foundations—a total of $240.72 billion. GIVING USA: THE ANNUAL REPORT OF PHILANTHROPY FOR THE YEAR 2003 (THE CENTER ON PHILANTHROPY AT INDIANA UNIVERSITY) 6 (2004). I recognize that many economists suspect that a substantial amount of charitable giving does not manifest the donor's external preferences (say, altruism) but his desire to secure something valuable in exchange (perhaps prestige). See Oded Stark & Ita Falk, *Transfers, Empathy Formation, and Reverse Transfers,* 88 PAPERS AND PROC. AM. ECON. ASS. 271 (1998). I also recognize the difficulty of determining the relative importance of these two types of motivation. See, e.g., William Harbaugh, *The Prestige Motive for Making Charitable Transfers,* 88 PAPERS AND PROC. AM. ECON. ASS. 277 (1998). I should point out, however, that if the prestige a donor can obtain from giving does not exclusively reflect the respect he obtains by manifesting his wealth, the fact that the donor can secure prestige through such giving may well reflect the external preferences of others for the welfare of the beneficiaries of the gifts the donor makes.
7. For a summary of the results of such lab experiments, see COLIN CAMERER, BEHAVIORAL GAME THEORY 465–73 (2003). For a series of lab experiments whose participants manifested a surprisingly high degree of altruism, see Ray Fisman, Shachar

Kariv, & Daniel Markovits, *Individual Preferences for Giving,* YALE LAW & ECONOMICS RESEARCH PAPERS #306 (2005).

8. David A. Hyman, *Rescue without Law: An Empirical Perspective on the Duty to Rescue,* 84 TEX. L. REV. 653 (2006).
9. For a recent article arguing that, for second-best-theory-related reasons, traditional conclusions about the allocative inefficiency generated by commodity taxes (the conclusions generated by the conventional "excess burden triangle" formula) seriously underestimate ("in some cases by a factor of 10 or more") the misallocative effects in question, see Lawrence Goulder & Roberton Williams III, *The Substantial Bias from Ignoring General Equilibrium Effects in Estimating Excess Burden, and a Practical Solution,* 111 J. POL. ECON 898 (2003).

PART II. THE ASSESSMENT OF ECONOMIC EFFICIENCY

1. Although this proposition would be true if economic inefficiency were defined in a Pareto-inferior sense, it is not true when the concept is defined in the monetized sense in which I am defining it. Nevertheless, since the relevant inaccuracy is minor and it is expositionally useful to ignore it, I will ignore it in the text that follows.
2. Admittedly, if certain conditions were fulfilled, one would have to qualify the proposition articulated in the text, though the operational significance of the qualification is admittedly contestable. Unfortunately, to explain the conditions in question, I will have to define some concepts before it would otherwise be necessary to do so. In what follows, the distortion in the profitability of any resource-use choice will be defined to equal the difference between the profitability and allocative efficiency of the resource-use choice in question. More specifically, the monopoly (monopsony, externality, etc.) distortion in the profitability of a specified resource-use choice will be defined to equal the distortion in the profitability of that choice that would be generated by the extant Pareto imperfections of the specified type in an otherwise-Pareto-perfect economy, while the aggregate distortion in the profitability of a specified resource-use choice will equal the distortion in that choice's profitability that was (or will be) generated by the interaction of all the various types of Pareto imperfections that would individually distort the profitability of the resource-use choice in an otherwise-Pareto-perfect economy.

   The relevant qualification would be necessary if and only if one of the following three conditions is fulfilled: *viz.*, when the aggregate distortion in the profitability of a particular resource-use choice

   1. equals the sum of the individual-Pareto-imperfection distortions in the profitability of that resource-use choice,
   2. equals the sum of one or more individual-Pareto-imperfection-generated distortions and the distortion in the profitability of the specified resource-use choice generated by the interaction of the remaining relevant Pareto imperfections, or
   3. equals the sum of the distortions in those profit-yields that each type of Pareto imperfection that distorts them generates given the other Pareto imperfections in the economy when (over the relevant range) changes in one Pareto imperfection will not affect any term in the relevant sum other than the term to which it directly relates.

To see why there would be some reason to believe that reducing or eliminating a particular type of Pareto imperfection would tend to increase economic efficiency in either of the above two circumstance, note the following four facts. First, as we shall see, the total amount of misallocation generated by resource-use choices of any given type increases with the weighted-average value and weighted-average absolute and squared deviations of the distribution of positive (or negative) percentage distortions in the profitability of least profitable but not unprofitable (henceforth, marginal) resource-use choices of that type. (For the definition of percentage profit distortion and the specification of the weight to be assigned each observation, see the text at page 7 *supra.*) For simplicity, this note assumes that all resource uses in the distributions it discusses have the same marginal allocative cost.

Second, in the first type of situation described above, even if the profit distortion that would be caused by one type of Pareto imperfection in an otherwise-Pareto-perfect world (henceforth the eliminatable distortion [ED]) was randomly related to the value that the distortion in the profits of the relevant marginal resource-use choices would have if no imperfections of the relevant type were present (henceforth the remaining distortion [RD]), the elimination of ED (of the type of Pareto imperfection that generated it) will tend to reduce the mean of the distribution of positive (or negative) distortions in the profits yielded by marginal resource uses of the relevant type. More specifically, if ED and RD are not correlated, the elimination of ED will reduce the mean positive (or negative) value of ED + RD to the extent that |ED| is sometimes larger than |RD|. Admittedly, in the set of cases in which |ED| < |RD|, the elimination of ED will have no effect on the mean value of the positive (or negative) portion of the ED + RD distribution because the amount by which the elimination of ED will reduce ED + RD in the half of the relevant cases in which the two distortions have the same sign will equal the amount by which the elimination of ED will increase ED + RD in the half of the relevant cases in which the two distortions are oppositely signed. However, the elimination of ED will reduce the above mean value when |RD| < |ED| < 2|RD| because in this subset of cases the amount by which the elimination of ED will reduce |ED + RD| in the half of such cases in which ED and RD have the same sign is larger than the amount by which the elimination of ED will increase |ED + RD| in the half of such cases in which ED and RD are oppositely signed. (Thus, if |ED| = 7 and |RD| = 4, the elimination of ED will reduce |ED + RD| by 7 from 11 to 4 when the two distortions have the same sign and will increase |ED + RD| by only 1 from |3| to |4| when the two distortions have opposite signs.) Moreover, the elimination of ED will decrease the relevant mean by even more when ED and RD are randomly related and |ED| > 2|RD| because in this set of cases the elimination of ED will reduce |ED + RD| not only when ED and RD have the same sign but also when they are oppositely signed. (Thus, if |ED| = 9 and |RD| = 4, the elimination of ED will reduce |ED + RD| by 9 when the two distortions have the same sign and will reduce |ED + RD| by 1 from |5| to |4| when they are oppositely signed.)

Third, in the first type of situation delineated above, if ED and RD are not correlated, the elimination of ED will reduce the mean absolute and squared deviations of the positive (and negative) segment of the relevant profit-distortion distribution even if

|ED| < |RD|. Thus, if |RD| is 4, |ED| is 1, and the overall distribution contains 4 data points, the elimination of ED will change the relevant overall distribution of ED + RD from 5, 3, −5, −3 to 4, 4, −4, −4, thereby reducing both the mean absolute and mean squared deviations of the positive segment of the relevant distribution from one to zero.

Fourth, the analysis and conclusions of the preceding two paragraphs will also apply in the second situation previously described—namely, when ED is the distortion caused by a particular type of Pareto imperfection, the aggregate distortion in the profits yielded by the relevant resource-use choices equals ED *plus* the distortion caused by all other types of Pareto imperfections, but this latter distortion (RD) does not equal the sum of the distortions that would respectively be caused by the other types of Pareto imperfections if each were the only type of Pareto imperfection present in the economy.

Unfortunately, the usefulness of the preceding results is contestable. Neither of the first two conditions is often fulfilled. And, although the first part of the third condition is frequently fulfilled, the second part will often not be and may not be to an extent that is problematic: thus, the internalization of an external marginal cost of production may affect not only the externality term in a relevant sum but the imperfect-competition term in that sum as well by affecting the P/MC ratio of the product whose external marginal costs were internalized.

I should add that I have not been able to discover any similar profit-distortion-oriented argument for reducing the Pareto-imperfectness of the economy when the three conditions listed above are not fulfilled.

3. I should note, however, that the vast majority of economists ignore the difference between the private transaction costs in question and their allocative counterparts and that many if not most economists also tend to ignore the public-finance-related allocative costs generated by government policies that are costly for the government to design and implement—(1) the administrative allocative costs the government must generate to finance those activities and (2) the misallocation that will be generated by any taxes the government levies, any higher good-or-service prices it charges, or any inflation it generates to pay for the expenditures in question.
4. My daughter Stefanie suggested that the acronym FBLE is also appropriate because it resembles the word "feeble."
5. This statement may be overbroad. To the extent that some theoretical and empirical work that would be relevant to the economic efficiency of a policy but *ex ante* economically inefficient to execute nonetheless would provide insights or empirical information that would improve any related moral-rights or moral-ought analysis, it might be desirable overall to do the additional work in question despite the fact that it would be *ex ante* economically inefficient to do so.

CHAPTER 3. THE DISTORTION-ANALYSIS APPROACH TO ECONOMIC-EFFICIENCY ASSESSMENT

1. Admittedly, this nomenclature is somewhat inconsistent with the fact that markets cannot be defined non-arbitrarily. For my demonstration of the inevitable arbitrariness

of market definitions, see Richard S. Markovits, *On the Inevitable Arbitrariness of Market Definitions,* 2002 ANTITRUST BULL. 571 (2002). I have tried to reduce the inconsistency by using the expression intra-*industry* rather than the expression intra-*market.* I hasten to add that I distinguish intra-industry from inter-industry UO-to-UO or RUO misallocation purely for heuristic reasons: at no point do I rely on any analysis that requires me to define an industry. The preceding remarks also apply to my distinction between intra-industry and inter-industry QV-investment misallocation, which the text that follows delineates.

2. In cases in which the producers in question are competitors as buyers of inputs though they are not competitors as sellers of goods, resources could flow directly between the production of distantly competitive products. In cases in which two products have a common product rival even though the two products are not competitive with each other, resources can be conceptualized as flowing between the two products via that common rival. Of course, as the text indicates, in practice, the resources that are allocated to the production of additional units of one good are unlikely to be withdrawn exclusively from the production of other goods already in production—i.e., are likely to be withdrawn in part from uses in which they would create a new product or distributive variant, would execute a production-process-research project, and/or would produce leisure. However, for analytic purposes, it is useful to consider the factors that would determine the amount of misallocation that would be generated by decisions to produce additional units of some goods if the resources that were consumed by that production were all withdrawn from the production of units of other goods and services that have already been created.
3. For an analysis of why price discrimination and relevant externalities can cause production-optimum misallocation, see Richard S. Markovits, *The Causes and Policy Significance of Pareto Resource Misallocation: A Checklist for Micro-Economic Policy Analysis,* 28 STAN. L. REV. 1, 9–10 (1975).
4. For a discussion of all these possibilities, see *id.* at 5–9.
5. Perfect price competition occurs when two conditions are fulfilled. First, no seller has a competitive advantage over all its rivals when dealing for the patronage of any given buyer (e.g., no seller can supply any buyer with a product variant he prefers to the products offered by the seller's rivals at the same marginal cost the rivals would have to incur to supply the buyer in question, and no seller can supply any buyer with a product variant he values equally to the products offered by the seller's rivals at a lower marginal cost than the rivals would have to incur to supply the buyer in question). Second, the number of potential suppliers of any given buyer of the product in question that are equally-well-placed to obtain his patronage is too large to permit any relevant supplier from obtaining oligopolistic margins—i.e., to obtain higher prices because his rivals perceive that he can react to their responses to his price. Traditionally, economists have assumed that perfect price competition will result when an infinite number of suppliers produce identical products at identical costs. In fact, perfect competition can also result when (1) sellers produce heterogeneous products among which the relevant buyers are not indifferent if any buyer preference advantages an individual seller has over his closest rivals for a particular buyer's patronage

is perfectly offset by the marginal cost disadvantages he faces when competing against the rivals in question for the relevant buyer's patronage and (2) the number of privately-best-placed potential suppliers of each relevant buyer though not infinite is large enough to preclude them from obtaining oligopolistic margins.

6. A perfectly competitive seller's demand curve will slope down to the right beyond the output that equals industry demand at the perfectly competitive price.
7. At least if QV-investment competition is perfect, price must equal minimum average total cost (ATC) for there to be an equilibrium: if QV-investment competition is perfect and P is less than ATC, some firms will exit, and if QV-investment competition is perfect and P exceeds minimum ATC, new QV investments will be introduced into the relevant area of product-space by either expanding established firms or new entrants.
8. Actually, this conventional assumption will be true only if the sale of the marginal unit in question does not increase the profits the seller makes on other sales (1) by providing the buyer with information about the product in question (either about its performance attributes or about how to use it) that leads him and others with whom he communicates or who observe him consuming it to increase their valuation of it, (2) by increasing its value to the buyer because it is a part of a line of products and the buyer likes to have a matched set of products, (3) by deterring rivals from competing against the seller in the future (when the sale is retaliatory), or conceivably (4) by reducing the seller's future costs if (as the Boston Consulting Group has suggested is sometimes the case) the production of the marginal unit of output has enabled the relevant seller to learn by doing. I will now explain why I am justified in ignoring all these possibilities in the current context. The first and fourth (whose empirical importance I doubt) are ruled out by the individual sovereignty component of the current otherwise-Pareto-perfect assumption; the third (retaliation) possibility is ruled out by the perfect-competition assumption; and the second (full-line preference) possibility—though not ruled out by this analysis's other assumptions—can be ignored in the current context because any benefits the seller obtains on this account will not be distorted.
9. The two qualifications reflect the fact that in two sets of circumstances price will equal marginal revenue for sellers who face price competition that is not perfectly competitive. In the first such situation, the competitive advantages the seller enjoys and/or oligopolistic margins he can obtain result in his facing a demand curve that is horizontal at his profit-maximizing output (at which his MR curve cuts his MC curve from above) despite the fact that this demand curve is higher than his marginal cost curve at that output. Although this situation undoubtedly does sometimes arise, I assume that it occurs extremely rarely. In the second situation, P = MR for a seller who faces a downward-sloping demand curve where the P in question is the price he charges for his marginal unit of output because the seller need incur no costs to charge that price for his marginal unit while continuing to charge the higher price or prices he would have charged for his intramarginal units had he not produced and sold his marginal unit. I am confident that this situation will never arise: even when a seller finds it profitable to price in this way, he will have to incur costs (1) to identify his marginal

buyer (whose patronage he can obtain only at a lower price than he charged his other customers), (2) to offer him a lower price (instead of relying on a standardized posted price), (3) to arrange for his cashiers to collect a lower price from him, (4) to prevent the favored customer from engaging in arbitrage by reselling the unit to an intramarginal buyer from whom the seller would otherwise have collected a higher price (or because the buyer might or would succeed in making such a cross-sale), and (5) to deal with the tendency of such discrimination to induce nonfavored buyers to intensify their bargaining, rivals to retaliate, and/or (in certain legal regimes) nonfavored customers, rivals, or the government to bring price-discrimination suits.

10. I am ignoring a fifth related cause of nonperfect QV-investment competition—the possibility that a relevant investment might induce established rivals to make a predatory response (a response designed to induce the investor to withdraw his new QV investment or, conceivably, to exit altogether). This possibility is perfectly analogous to the retaliation possibility discussed in the text.

11. The analysis of the relationship between the loss that other sorts of retaliatory moves will impose on their target and the allocative inefficiency those moves generate is complex and its conclusions uncertain. I will focus first on the relationship between these two amounts when the retaliatory response is a price cut that does cause the target to lose customers to the retaliator. If the retaliator's private and allocative marginal costs equal his target's for the buyers the price cuts enable the retaliator to steal from his target, the allocative inefficiency the price cuts generate will equal the sum of the allocative transaction costs they generate and the target's buyer preference advantage, while the target's associated loss will equal the sum of his buyer preference advantage and any oligopolistic margin he otherwise would have secured.

When the retaliatory move is an advertising campaign, the private loss to the target will equal the private cost to him of any additional advertising he places to combat the retaliator's advertising *plus* any price cuts he makes to keep customers the retaliatory advertising would otherwise have caused him to lose *plus* any profits he originally earned on sales the retaliatory advertising costs him *minus* any profits he makes because the retaliatory advertising results in his making sales he would not otherwise have made or making sales to given buyers at higher prices than he would otherwise have secured. The allocative inefficiency the retaliatory advertising generates equals the allocative cost of the retaliator's advertising *plus* the allocative cost of any advertising it induced the target to place *plus* the allocative transaction cost of any price changes the advertising induced relevant sellers to make *minus* any increase in the value of the relevant goods to their consumers the advertiser generated by changing the goods' images or associations *plus* any economic inefficiency the advertising generated by providing misinformation to relevant buyers that led them to make economically inefficient consumption choices *minus* any increase in economic efficiency the advertising generated by providing information to relevant buyers that increased the economic efficiency of their product choices.

If the target does not respond to the retaliatory location shift in any way other than by reducing his prices, the private loss the shift imposes on its target equals the profits it causes the target to lose by reducing the prices he obtains from customers he retains whose patronage he would otherwise have secured at a higher price *plus* the private transaction cost to the target of making any price cuts the location shift induces him to make *plus* the profits the target would otherwise have made on sales the location shift causes him to lose *minus* any profits he makes on any additional sales the target's price cuts enable him to make if the location shift does not change the allocative variable cost of supplying a given number of units of the relevant, changing set of products. The allocative inefficiency the location shift generates equals the allocative cost of making the location shift *plus* the allocative transaction cost the target generates when he changes his prices in response to the location shift *plus* any amount by which the location shift reduces the allocative value of the original number of "units" sold *plus* (*minus*) the amount by which the shift and any induced price changes increase (decrease) UO-to-UO and other sorts of misallocation.

The analysis of the private loss that any additional QV investments the retaliator makes inflicts on its target is the same as its location-shift counterpart. The allocative inefficiency that such a retaliatory investment will directly generate equals the private loss the retaliatory investment would yield if one ignores any tendency it has to benefit the retaliator by deterring rivals from competing with him *plus* the amount by which the private cost of the investment is lower than its allocative cost *plus* the amount of misallocation that will be generated by the deterrent effect of the investment in question.

12. This point has been recognized by a small number of economists who have attempted to analyze product-set misallocation in some detail. See GENE M. GROSSMAN & ELHANAN HELPMAN, INNOVATION AND GROWTH IN THE GLOBAL ECONOMY 70 (1991), where the relevant effect is discussed under the name "the profit-destruction effect" and Phillippe Aghion and Peter Howitt, *A Model of Growth through Creative Destruction,* 60 ECONOMETRICA 323 (1992), where the relevant effect is discussed under the old Schumpeterian name "creative destruction." The type of misallocation I call QV-to-QV misallocation was first discussed in Harold Hotelling, *Stability in Competition,* 39 ECON. J. 41 (1929). For a more complicated and realistic analysis of this phenomenon, see Moshe Ben-Akira, André de Palma, & Jacques-Francois Thisse, *Spatial Competition with Differentiated Products,* 19 REG. SCI. & URBAN ECON. 5 (1989). For an excellent (though somewhat dated) survey of the relevant literature, see Kelvin Lancaster, *The Economics of Product Variety: A Survey,* 9 MARKETING SCI. 189, 195–201 (1990).

Unfortunately, antitrust-law professors and antitrust economists have ignored the existence of QV-to-QV misallocation and its possible antitrust-policy and antitrust-law implications. (I do not think that QV-to-QV misallocation has any implications for the interpretation or application of the American antitrust laws that is correct as a matter of law. However, since many of those scholars [to my mind, mistakenly] believe that the antitrust laws authorize the courts to make antitrust policy in the public interest and that antitrust decisions that are economically efficient are always in the public interest, many would reject my conclusion on this issue.) Fortunately, however, some of the economists who have focused on what I call QV-to-QV misallocation have addressed various related antitrust-policy issues (such as the impact of spatial-pricing policies on QV-to-QV misallocation). See, e.g., Simon P. Anderson, André de Palma, & Jacques-Francois Thisse, *Social Surplus and Profitability under Different*

Spatial-Pricing Policies, 59 So. Econ. J. 34 (1999) and Jacques-Francois Thisse and Xavier Vives, *On the Strategic Choice of Spatial Price Policy,* 78 Amer. Econ. Rev. 122 (1988). See *id.* at 136–37 for a useful bibliography.

13. I should add that in some situations—e.g., when the amount by which a prospective QV investor's new project would reduce the profit yields of his preexisting projects if it would not affect any rival's QV-investment decision is smaller than the amount by which his new QV investment would increase his preexisting projects' profit yields by deterring a rival from making a QV investment—the relevant investor will have a monopolistic QV-investment incentive to make the investment in question. I should perhaps note as well that any QV investment whose investor-perceived *ex ante* profitability is critically affected by the investor's belief that he has a monopolistic QV investment incentive to make it is on that account predatory and violative of §2 of the Sherman Antitrust Act. For a detailed discussion of the latter point, see Richard S. Markovits, *On the Possibly-Predatory Character of Nonsystems-Rivalry Investments and Systems Rivalry: Definitional, Functional, and Legal Analyses,* 2005 Antitrust Bull. 1, 8–15 (2005).
14. In fact, it is at least arguable that the actual tax condition that would have to be fulfilled for Pareto optimality to be achieved in an otherwise-Pareto-perfect economy is no tax at all: even a tax such as a poll tax that does not vary with the taxpayer's income may cause economic inefficiency by inducing a potential taxpayer to make an economically inefficient decision to kill himself by reducing the private benefits of his living below the allocative benefits.
15. The textual argument accounts for two phenomena that economists have recognized but not satisfactorily explained: (1) the tendency of monopolists to generate so-called X-inefficiency (to incur higher average total costs not fully attributable to their paying higher monetary wages for given labor to produce given quantities of given products) and (2) the tendency of monopolists to discriminate (indulge their employeres' prejudices) more in their hiring decisions. The textual argument implies that both these phenomena can be traced to (1) the fact that monopolists do pay higher (monetary *plus* nonmonetary) wages, (2) the related fact that their workers and management face higher marginal tax rates, and (3) the fact that these higher marginal tax rates make it more profitable for their workers and managers to take out their wages in nonmonetary, nontaxable, cost-raising forms (such as less arduous work regimes, more attractive physical working environments, and [from their perspective] more attractive and compatible work colleagues [*inter alia,* workmates who share their male gender, Caucasian race, and American birthplace]).
16. Taxes on the margin of income inflate gross wages because sovereign, maximizing workers (who can vary the amount of labor they can perform by infinitesimal amounts) will equate their net wage with the private cost to them of working (the private value to them of the leisure they have to forgo to work), which is the allocative cost of their working in an otherwise-Pareto-perfect economy—i.e., because such taxes raise the private cost to the employer of hiring a worker (the gross wage if he is not a monopsonist of labor) above the allocative cost of his employing the worker in question (which on our assumptions equals the net wage the relevant worker secures by performing the labor in question).

17. The qualification is that if the seller of the good in question engages in some amount of price discrimination and one or more buyers purchase multiple units of the good, a demand curve that is constructed on the assumption that the seller will not engage in price discrimination will misrepresent the value of the second and subsequent units individual buyers purchase if they gained less surplus on their earlier purchases than the curve's construction assumes and their valuation of the units in question is real-income elastic over the relevant range. This qualification will usually be empirically unimportant because for most goods both the buyer-surplus difference in question and its significance for the relevant buyer's dollar valuation of subsequent units of the good consumed will be small (second order).
18. Thus, as we saw, in an economy in which buyers are sovereign, maximizing non-monopsonists and their consumption generates no buyer surplus, the price they pay for a unit of any good will equal its dollar value to them, and in an economy in which consumption generates no externalities, the value of any unit of a good to its purchaser will equal its allocative value.
19. Both the second and the third propositions the text articulates reflect the following two facts: (1) in an economy in which all prices are perfectly competitive, no externalities are generated, and the price at which the marginal unit of any product is sold equals the allocative value of its being consumed as opposed to being costlessly destroyed, the price that any producer will have to pay to bid resources away from their alternative uses will equal their marginal allocative products in those uses, and (2) in an economy in which no externalities of production are generated, producers will have to buy all resources their production activities consume.
20. The modifier "broadly defined" is included to signal the fact that individuals can positively or negatively value the welfare of particular others or the shape of the distribution of income and wealth.
21. Thus, the nonsovereignty of a person who believes that an ounce of some product is worth $1 more to him than it actually is worth to him will perfectly offset his nonmaximization if he makes a mathematical error that leads him to conclude that the cost of purchasing an ounce of the product in question is $1 higher than it actually is.
22. To differentiate the difference to which the text refers from buyer surplus, buyer surplus must be defined to equal the difference between the value the buyer assigned to the good at the time of purchase and the price he paid for it.
23. Assuming that the imperfection caused his potential employer to face a downward-sloping demand curve and that his employer could not costlessly charge the demand price(s) for the units of output his marginal unit of labor produced without reducing the price(s) he charged for his intramarginal units.
24. More specifically, as note 8 *supra* indicated, the conventional marginal revenue the sale of a marginal unit of some product yields the seller will equal the private benefits its sale confers on him only if (1) the sale generates no promotional, learning-by-doing, or (strategic) retaliatory or predatory advantages, (2) does not reduce the profits the seller will realize by selling other products by taking sales from them, (3) does not reduce the profits the seller realizes by selling other products or the product in question in the future by inducing his rivals to respond in a strategic or nonstrategic

way that produces these effects, and (4) does not yield joint economies that increase the profits he makes when selling other goods. First, some vocabulary and then some comments. The production of an additional unit of a product is said to yield learning-by-doing advantages to the extent that the activity provides information or experience to the producer that enables him to reduce his future costs of production. Although some commentators (e.g., the Boston Consulting Group) think that the learning-by-doing advantages of producing additional units of products are substantial, I am skeptical. In my terminology, a business choice is said to be strategic if *ex ante* the chooser perceived its profitability to be critically affected by its tendency to reduce the competition he will face in the future (by driving a rival out or by deterring a rival from entering, making an additional QV investment, or competing against him more vigorously by cutting prices or in some other way) by communicating the actor's intention to respond to future competition by making one or more moves that would not otherwise be profitable to punish rivals who make competitive moves against him and/or to reward rivals who have chosen not to compete against him. By definition, all retaliatory and predatory actions are strategic in the above sense.

Basically, my equation of $PB_{\Delta UOX}$ with the conventional $MR_{\Delta UOX}$ assumes that the relevant producer's production of the marginal unit of output in question is not strategic (which could be said to be implied by the analysis's otherwise-Pareto-perfect assumption), that it will not yield promotional advantages (which is implied by the analysis's individual sovereignty assumption), that it will not yield learning-by-doing advantages (which is also implied by the analysis's individual-sovereignty assumption), that it will not yield joint economies by encouraging the buyer to purchase another product that is part of the same line to complete his set (an assumption that is not implied by the analysis's otherwise-Pareto-perfect assumption but is not in the end critical because such economies are not distorting), or by enabling the seller to take advantage of economies of scale in production or distribution (a possibility that the analysis's assumptions cannot be said to rule out but will almost certainly be *de minimis* when the triggering event is the production of a single unit of the product in question).

25. I should admit that the text's analysis of $MD(P\pi_{\Delta UOX})$ ignores one additional possibility—*viz.*, MC_X/MC_Y might not equal $MRT_{Y/X}$ if one or more producers of the inputs that were used to produce the unit of X or would have been used to produce the sacrificed Y was a monopolist who would have engaged in price discrimination when selling the resources in question by charging the producer of X and the producers of the sacrificed Y different prices for the resources in question. If this is the case, the relevant MC figures would have to be adjusted in the way that the next subsection indicates they will have to be adjusted when the production of X and/or Y generates externalities to produce an adjusted MC_X/MC_Y ratio (MC^*_X/MC^*_Y) that equals $MRT_{Y/X}$.

26. Later in this chapter, I will argue that this ratio is also substantially lower than the ratio of total QV-to-QV misallocation to the amount of resources devoted to QV-investment creation in the economy in question.

27. *Inter alia,* the ability of a privately-best-placed seller to obtain an oligopolistic margin naturally (i.e., because his rivals know that the relevant buyer will give him an opportunity to make a rebid that beats any better offer they have received from an inferior supplier and because he will find it inherently profitable to beat any offer a rival makes that beats his initial offer) is inversely related to (1) the value of speedy delivery and (2) the repeat-player status of the buyer in question (the benefits the buyer can secure by encouraging inferior suppliers to beat its best-placed supplier's oligopolistic price by accepting a better deal from an inferior supplier than its best-placed supplier originally offered despite the fact that the best-placed supplier would be willing to beat the initially better offer the inferior supplier made) and is directly related to (1) the ability of the best-placed supplier to verify both the claim of the buyer in question that the seller's initial offer had been beaten and similar claims of future buyers that this was the case and (2) the competitive advantage the best-placed supplier enjoyed in relation to the buyer in question (which will determine the profits he would have realized at the reduced price he would have to charge to beat his inferior rival's offer had he charged that lower price in the first instance). *Inter alia,* the oligopolistic margin a best-placed seller will find it profitable to contrive in his dealings with a particular buyer will be inversely related to (1) the size of the competitive advantage he enjoys in his relations with the buyer in question (the safe profits he must put at risk to contrive any oligopolistic margin), (2) the legal penalties for such contrivance, (3) the effectiveness of antitrust enforcement of prohibitions of such price-fixing, (4) the number of rivals to whom he must communicate his contrived oligopolistic intentions (the number of rivals who were second-placed to secure the relevant buyer's patronage or were worse-than-second-placed by a smaller margin than the oligopolistic margin the best-placed supplier was attempting to contrive), and (5) the cost he has to incur to inflict any given amount of harm on an undercutting rival by undercutting the rival's prices to the rival's customers (which, roughly speaking, will be inversely related to the size of the target's average competitive advantage in his dealings with buyers he is best-placed to supply that the potential retaliator will attempt to steal and directly related to the average amount by which the retaliator is worse-than-second-placed to supply the buyers in question) and would be directly related (1) the ability of the potential contriver to reduce the cost of the necessary communications by making them simply by announcing a contrived oligopolistic price (directly related to his reputation for contrivance and for not overestimating his competitive advantages), (2) the ability of the contriver to infer undercutting by inferiors from circumstantial evidence relating to the percentage of old customers whose patronage the contriver retained and the percentages of former customers of rivals and new buyers in the relevant area of product-space that the contriver secured (which will increase with the number of buyers in each of these categories, the constancy over time of the factors other than price-cutting that affect these percentages, and the ability of the contriver to predict the magnitude that the percentages in question would have absent price-cutting from competitive inferiors from data on the other determinants of those percentages), (3) the ability of the contriver to identify the undercutter—e.g., by discovering his closest competitors for the customers he lost or the rival who actually supplied his lost

customers, (4) the extent to which the potential contriver could secure the cooperation of potential undercutters by reciprocating to their forebearing the opportunity to make profits by stealing his customers (the frequency with which and the amount by which he was the rival's closest competitor for buyers they were best placed to supply), (5) the number of buyers his organization was best placed to supply across all their operations (the private benefits the potential contriver could secure by enhancing his reputation for contrivance by practicing it successfully in individual instances or making good on his threats of retaliation), etc.

28. I have chosen to use the pure subscript SU_o and the non-subscript SU_o rather than ΔQ_o to avoid the ambiguity of ΔQ_o, which might refer to either the marginal unit of *o* or the change in the output of *o*—i.e., the sacrificed units of *o*. More particularly, my decision to use these (SU_o)s partly reflects my concern that my use of ΔQV to stand for the marginal QV investment might lead readers to assume that ΔQ_o stands for the marginal unit of the old product *o* in question rather than to the relevant change in its unit output.

29. Any external benefits that are generated by the use of the marginal QV investment will be considered in the next subsection, which focuses on $\Sigma D(PB_{\Delta QV})/LC_{\Delta QV}$.

30. I have analyzed them and various related issues in an unpublished book manuscript entitled PUTTING US IN OUR PLACE: ON THE ALLOCATIVE EFFICIENCY AND OVERALL DESIRABILITY OF LARGE-LOT ZONING AND OTHER SORTS OF RESIDENTIAL-DENSITY CONTROLS.

31. A privately valuable production-process discovery could conceivably reduce the total cost of producing a relevant quantity of a particular good by reducing the fixed cost of doing so while leaving unchanged or even increasing the variable and marginal costs the discovery's user has to incur to produce the relevant quantity of the good in question.

32. In practice, the rejection of most types of avoidance moves is not assessed for negligence. Thus, although a producer's failure to adopt a known, less-accident-and/or-pollution-loss-prone (henceforth, less-AP-loss-prone) production process will be assessed for negligence, his failures to reduce the AP losses he generated by shifting to a less-externality-prone location, by shifting to the production of a different product whose production and consumption combined were less externality-prone, by reducing his unit output, or by doing research into less-externality-prone production processes, locations, or product variants are never assessed for negligence.

33. For example, in determining an injurer's negligence, the law does not consider the loss his avoidance could have prevented (1) the friends and family of the direct victim from suffering because they cared about his welfare or obtained more satisfaction from interacting with him when he was not injured, ill, or dead than they did after he suffered the loss in question or (2) witnesses of horrific accidents from suffering if they experienced no physical impact and were never under any risk of experiencing such an impact. (I should say that there is one exception to the first of these two points: the law does allow spouses to recover for any loss of consanguinity the traditional victim's injury or illness caused them to suffer.)

34. See §2 of the Sherman Antitrust Act, 26 Stat. 209 (1890) (codified as amended at 15 U.S.C.A. §§1–11). In brief, if any such refusal to deal occurred, it would be predatory because its profitability would be critically affected by its tendency to reduce

the absolute attractiveness of the offers against which the refusing discoverer had to compete not just by raising his rival's marginal costs but by driving one or more of them out.

35. In the current context, I am ignoring PPR projects that are designed to discover less-AP-loss-prone production processes.

36. In my terminology, a seller engages in oligopolistic conduct when he makes a move he would not have deemed profitable *ex ante* but for his belief that his rivals' responses might be influenced by their correct perception that he might react to those responses in a way that renders unprofitable responses that would otherwise have been profitable. In my terminology, a seller's oligopolistic conduct is said to be contrived when he induces his rivals to anticipate that he would react to otherwise profitable responses that would have rendered his initial move unprofitable in a way that would render those responses unprofitable despite the fact that the reaction in question would not have been profitable but for its tendency to increase the reactor's future profits by deterring these respondents and/or others from competing against him in the future. The anticipated reaction can be a reciprocal forebearance from undercutting and/or an act of retaliation. In the former case, the rivals' expectations will be created by an anticompetitive promise; in the latter, by an anticompetitive threat. I substitute the expression "contrived oligopolistic pricing" for "price-fixing" because price-fixing is understood to involve the exchange of anticompetitive promises, backed up perhaps by threats of retaliation, and thereby fails to cover the cases in which a seller makes no anticompetitive promise of reciprocation but relies solely on threats of retaliation to secure his rivals' collaboration. In my terminology, contrived oligopolistic pricing is contrasted with natural oligopolistic pricing, which does not involve the communication of any anticompetitive promises or threats. A seller is said to have practiced natural oligopolistic pricing when he has set a price that is higher than he would otherwise have found profitable because he expected his rivals' responses to that price to be influenced by their realization that the buyers in question would give him an opportunity to beat any more attractive offer they made in response to his initial offer and that he would find it inherently profitable to beat any such more attractive offer they would find profitable to make if he could not react to it.

37. However, I will not be assuming that the policy in question will prevent sellers in a given area of product-space from securing contrived oligopolistic restrictions in the amount of QV investments they make in that area of product-space by making and carrying out threats to retaliate against QV-investment expansions or new entries or by entering into QV-investment-restricting anticompetitive agreements.

38. For a partial list of these factors, see note 27 *supra*.

39. Roughly speaking, under this regime, a victim whom the law deems eligible to obtain compensation for accident or pollution losses it deems legally recoverable can obtain a judgment in his favor against an alleged injurer if (1) the victim can show that, more probably than not, the alleged injurer proximately caused his loss by negligently rejecting a type of avoidance move whose rejection the law assesses for negligence and (2) the alleged injurer cannot show that, more probably than not, the loss was also caused by the victim's contributorily negligent rejection of a type of avoidance move

whose rejection the law assesses for contributory negligence. In this formulation, a choice is said to be negligent or contributorily negligent if it is not "reasonable" or manifests a "lack of due care." Most law and economics scholars and many judges operationalize negligence by the so-called Hand formula for negligence. According to this formula, which assumes that the avoidance move in question would completely eliminate the possibility of the relevant loss's occurring and that all the facts it implicates are accurately perceived *ex ante* by the injurer, an avoidance move's rejection is negligent if B < PL where B stands for the burden or private cost of the rejected avoidance move to the potential injurer, P stands for the *ex ante* probability that the loss would occur if the avoidance move in question were not made, and L stands for the magnitude of any loss that would result if the injurer did not avoid. If the formula is adjusted to take account of the possibility that the relevant avoidance move might reduce without eliminating the probability of the loss's occurring and/or might reduce the size of the loss that resulted, it could be rewritten as $B < \sum_{i=1}^{n} P_iL_i - \sum_{j=1}^{m} P_jL_j$ where P_i stands for the *ex ante* probability that a loss of size L_i would occur if the injurer did not make the avoidance move in question, n is the number of different loss-sizes that could occur if the injurer did not make the avoidance move in question, P_j stands for the probability that a loss of size L_j would occur if the avoidance move in question were made, and m is the number of different loss sizes that could occur if the avoidance move were made so that the right side of the above inequality equals the amount by which the relevant avoidance move would reduce weighted-average-expected AP losses (which one might also symbolize as [↓PL]). The preceding description of the negligence/contributory-negligence tort-liability regime is rough because it ignores the fact that, in practice, courts seem to require victims to demonstrate not that the probability that the injurer was a negligent proximate cause of the victim's loss was over 50% but that the probabilities (1) that the injurer was negligent, (2) that his negligence caused the loss, and (3) that (if he was negligent) his negligence was the proximate cause of the loss were each over 50%. To see why this requirement is easier to satisfy, assume that the victim could show that each of these last three (independent) probabilities was 60%. In this situation, the victim would prevail despite the fact that the probability that the putative injurer's negligence was the proximate cause of the loss was 60%(60%)(60%) = 21.6%. I will assume that this feature of tort-law practice has been eliminated.

40. A strict-liability/contributory-negligence regime differs from a negligence/contributory-negligence regime in that it does not require victims to show that the injurer was negligent. Actual strict-liability regimes do not recognize contributory-negligence defenses. I am focusing on a strict-liability regime in which the contributory-negligence doctrine is also applied because I am certain that the combination of the strict-liability and contributory-negligence doctrines is more allocatively efficient than a pure strict-liability regime—*inter alia,* that the addition of a contributory-negligence doctrine will reduce the misallocation generated by economically inefficient APLA decisions by potential victims by more than it increases the misallocation generated by economically inefficient APLA decisions by potential injurers. For an explanation, see the text that follows.

41. I have analyzed the impacts this subsection ignores and the impacts it investigates in considerable detail elsewhere. See Richard S. Markovits, *The Allocative Efficiency of Shifting from a "Negligence" System to a "Strict Liability" Regime in Our Highly-Pareto-Imperfect Economy: A Partial and Preliminary Third-Best-Allocative-Efficiency Analysis,* 73 CHI.-KENT L. REV. 20, 40–112 (1998).
42. The text assumes (for expositional reasons only) that the situation in question is what I call an "individual-care avoidance-situation"—i.e., one in which the privately best and presumptively most-allocatively-efficient response to an accident or pollution contingency is for either the potential injurer or the potential victims to avoid. Such situations must be contrasted with both (1) "no-care avoidance-situations," in which the privately best and presumptively most-allocatively-efficient response to an accident or pollution contingency is for no one to avoid and (2) multiple-care avoidance-situations, in which the privately best and presumptively most-allocatively-efficient response is for both the potential injurer and the potential victim to engage in some avoidance (e.g., for the potential injurer to do some shoveling of the snow and for the potential victim to wear sensible shoes, walk carefully, reduce the amount of walking he does, and adjust his routes to take their relative dangerousness into account). I use the expression *multiple-care* rather than the standard expression *joint-care* to avoid the implication that such care involves coordination in the sense of advanced planning by the avoiders in question.
43. The fellow-servant rule bars a worker from suing his employer for injuries he sustained on the job as a result of a coworker's negligence. The assumption-of-risk doctrine bars victims who are deemed to have assumed the risk from recovering their loss from injurers who would otherwise be liable: victims are sometimes said to have assumed a risk when they would not be held to be contributorily negligent (in some but not all instances because the avoidance move they rejected is a type whose rejection is not in practice assessed for contributory negligence). The last-clear-chance doctrine bars victims from recovering a loss they would otherwise be able to recover if they forwent a last clear chance to prevent the loss by making an avoidance move whose B_V was less than its $(\downarrow PL)_V$, regardless of whether $([\downarrow PL]_V - B_V)$ was less than $([\downarrow PL]_I - B_I)$ for the avoidance move the injurer had rejected. Under the most comprehensive version of the comparative-negligence doctrine, a contributorily-negligent victim of a negligent injurer is not barred from recovery but has his recovery reduced by the percentage his fault constituted of the total fault of the victim and injurer combined, regardless of the absolute extent of the victim's fault or the relative extent of the injurer's and victim's faults. (Some American jurisdictions employ more limited versions of the comparative-negligence doctrine in which it applies only when the victim's fault was slight, was significantly less than the injurer's fault, or was not more than the injurer's fault.) The text has placed its reference to comparative negligence in parentheses because this doctrine is an alternative to the contributory-negligence doctrine the text is assuming is in force.
44. Standard examples are cases in which an individual is killed by two bullets that entered his body simultaneously, each of which would have killed him instantly, or cases in which a house is simultaneously destroyed by two fires that were independently set.

45. Step-function-loss situations are situations in which the loss is not a continuous function, for example, of the amount of pollution but jumps discontinuously when pollution reaches one or more particular levels. Thus, the relevant loss function would be a step function if no loss resulted when the quantity of a particular pollutant discharged into a river fell below a specifiable amount but any quantity above that amount would render the water no longer fit to drink, any quantity above some nonmarginally higher amount would discontinuously render the river unsuitable for swimming, any quantity above some nonmarginally higher level would render the river unsuitable for boating, any quantity above some nonmarginally higher level would render the fish the river contains inedible, and any quantity above some nonmarginally higher level would cause the river to smell. The function that relates the loss (measured on the vertical axis) to the amount of pollution discharged (measured on the horizontal axis) in such a case is said to be a step function because it is level at zero until some quantity of discharge is reached, then rises vertically to some positive level (the riser) when the first critical discharge-quantity is reached, stays level again (the step) until the next critical discharge-level is reached, and so on and so forth. Any body of law (such as the common law) that is designed to secure corrective justice may not be able to secure allocative efficiency in cases that involve step-function losses when it would be allocatively efficient for two or more injurers to avoid but no individual injurer's avoidance would be allocatively efficient. Assume that the loss is zero until 50 units of pollution are discharged, jumps to $100 when the discharge reaches 50 units, and stays at $100 until the discharge reaches 90 units. Now assume that 20 identical polluters discharge three units of pollution, that each could eliminate his pollution by spending $7, that the avoidance decisions of the polluters are completely independent, and that the allocative benefits and cost of the relevant avoidance moves equal their private counterparts. The allocatively efficient response would be for 4 of these polluters to eliminate their pollution since this conduct would generate $100 in allocative benefits and 4($7) = $28 in allocative costs. However, neither a negligence doctrine nor a strict-liability doctrine could secure this result since none of the individual polluters would be deemed to be a cause-in-fact of the pollution loss since none could affect the loss that resulted by avoiding (since none's avoidance would reduce the pollution loss since each's avoidance would reduce this total discharge from 60 units to 57 units, at which the loss would still be $100). (Indeed, even if this cause-in-fact problem could be surmounted, a negligence regime would not secure any avoidance in this case because no individual polluter's refusal to avoid would be negligent, given that for the individual polluter B = $7 and ↓PL = 0.)
46. I include in this category cases in which the trier-of-fact made the correct decisions on cause-in-fact, given the information that was presented to him.
47. I do not want to leave the impression that tort-liability insurance will clearly increase the amount of misallocation that potential injurers generate by making economically inefficient APLA decisions. Such insurance can reduce such misallocation (1) to the extent that the insurance company does research to discover avoidance moves that would reduce the AP losses the insured generates, conditions its coverage on the insured's making avoidance moves whose Bs are less than their (↓PL)s, requires the insured to establish worker-management safety committees, and inspects the opera-

tions of those it insures to enforce these contractual arrangements and (2) to the extent that such insurance induces potential injurers to engage in profitable and presumptively allocatively efficient avoidance by correcting their optimistic misperceptions of the liability they would face if they did not avoid by confronting them with insurance premiums that give them a more accurate view of the losses they would generate if they did not avoid (and perhaps of the extent to which they could reduce those losses by altering their plant, equipment, work regimes, personnel, and emergency procedures in various ways). Hence, tort-liability insurance might be allocatively efficient even if it increased allocative transaction costs by more than it reduced tort-related risk costs.

48. For some literature that relates to this and the preceding possibility, see George Loewenstein & Richard Thaler, *Anomalies: Intertemporal Choice,* 3 J. ECON. PERSPECTIVES 181 (1989); George Loewenstein & Draten Prelec, *Anomalies in Intertemporal Choice: Evidence and an Interpretation,* in CHOICE OVER TIME (George Loewenstein, ed. 1992); George Loewenstein, *The Fall and Rise of Psychological Explanations in the Economics of Intertemporal Choice,* in CHOICE OVER TIME 3–34 (George Loewenstein, ed. 1992); Fraten Prelec & George Loewenstein, *Decision Making over Time and under Uncertainty: A Common Approach,* 37 MGMT. SCI. 770 (1991).

49. The exception relates to cases in which cause-in-fact determinations must be based on the percentage that the putative injurer's activity contributed to the *ex ante* probability of the relevant loss's occurring. This situation arises (1) in pollution cases in which (A) the victim was exposed to pollutants discharged by more than one polluter, none of whom generated more than 50% of the pollution to which the victim might have been exposed, (B) the victim contracted an illness (such as asbestositis) that was caused by one unit of the pollutant in question or by a subset of the total amount of the relevant pollutant to which he was exposed that more than one polluter could have produced, and (C) there is do direct way to identify the source of the particular unit(s) of pollution that caused the victim's illness and (2) in some product liability cases in which the loss was generated by the consumption of a generic product (say, drug) produced by several companies in situations in which at the time the loss was discovered the victim could not establish the identity of the producer whose product he consumed. In this category of cases, which I believe constitutes a tiny percentage of the relevant universe, the avoidance incentives of potential injurers is far more likely to be critically inflated by the way in which the common law resolves the cause-in-fact issue if they are strictly liable than if they are liable only if deemed negligent.

Some explanation is required. The common law handles cause-in-fact in such cases by declaring a putative injurer to be the cause-in-fact of the loss if his activity contributed more than 50% to the *ex ante* probability of the loss's occurring (and then holds him liable for the full loss if the other conditions for liability are fulfilled) and declaring him not to be the cause-in-fact of the loss (and hence not liable at all, regardless of whether the other conditions for liability are fulfilled) if his activity contributed 50% or less of the *ex ante* probability of the loss's occurring. Under strict liability, this approach will inflate the private benefits to a potential putative injurer whose activity would otherwise contribute more than 50% but less than 100% of the *ex ante* probability of the loss's occurring of making an avoidance move that would reduce his activity's contribution to that *ex ante* probability to 50% or less. In so doing, it may critically inflate the profitability of his making the move in question. Assume, for example, that (1) if he does not avoid, a possible putative injurer's activity would contribute 60% of a 40% *ex ante* probability of a $1,000 loss's occurring—i.e., raises that probability from 16% to 40%, (2) the party in question could make an avoidance move that would cost him $300 and would reduce the *ex ante* probability of the loss's occurring from 40% to 32%—i.e., that would reduce his contribution to the probability of the loss's occurring from 24% of 40% (from 60%) to 16% of 32% (to 50%), and (3) the private cost of the avoidance move would equal its allocative counterpart, the relevant private loss would equal its allocative counterpart, and the avoidance move in question would have no impact on tort-related risk costs. In this example, the avoidance move in question would be allocatively inefficient—i.e., would produce allocative benefits of (8%)($1,000) = $80 and allocative costs of $300. However, if the relevant potential putative injurer were strictly liable (and nothing else would prevent the victims from recovering), he would find the move profitable since it would reduce his weighted-average-expected liability from (40%)($1,000) = $400 to $0 by reducing his activity's contribution to the *ex ante* probability of the loss's occurring from 60% > 50% to 50% (i.e., by reducing his contribution sufficiently for him not to be deemed a cause-in-fact of the loss) while costing him only $300. If the putative injurer's liability depended on his being deemed negligent, the common law's approach to cause-in-fact in such cases would not induce him to engage in allocatively inefficient avoidance (would not inflate the profitability of his doing so when it would be allocatively inefficient for him to avoid) because—at least on our otherwise-Pareto-perfect assumptions—he would not be found negligent for rejecting the avoidance move in question since its B = $300 exceeds its (↓[PL]) = $80. In such cases, then, the shift from a negligence/contributory negligence to a strict-liability/contributory-negligence regime might substantially increase the amount of misallocation potential injurers generate by making economically inefficient avoidance decisions. I should add that, in an otherwise-Pareto-perfect economy, the allocatively efficient way to deal with such cases is to hold each putative injurer liable for that percentage of any loss that resulted that his activity contributed to the *ex ante* probability of the loss's occurring. However, if as I believe the common law must be directed solely at securing corrective justice and if (more contestably) the common law's binary approach to cause-in-fact is an integral part of our corrective-justice commitments, the proportionate-liability approach I have just described would have to be promulgated legislatively.

CHAPTER 4. SOME SECOND-BEST-THEORY CRITIQUES OF CANONICAL ALLOCATIVE-EFFICIENCY ANALYSES AND OF THE STANDARD JUSTIFICATIONS FOR IGNORING SECOND BEST

1. See, e.g., PHILLIP AREEDA, LOUIS KAPLOW, & AARON EDLIN, ANTITRUST ANALYSIS 12–15 (6th ed. 2004).
2. Thus, if $P_X = \$3$ and $P_Y = \$1$, the individual (nonmonopsonistic) buyer will be able to exchange one X for three Y.

3. Thus, if $MC^*_X = 2$ and $MC^*_Y = \$1$, it will take twice the amount of resources to produce a marginal unit of X as to produce a marginal unit of Y, and the economy will be able to transform one unit of X into two units of Y at the margin.
4. To see why $P_X/MC^*_X > P_Y/MC^*_Y$ implies that $P_X/P_Y > MC^*_X/MC^*_Y$, multiply both sides of the first inequality by MC^*_X/P_Y and cancel terms.
5. If buyers face a P_X of \$3 and a P_Y of \$1, they will maximize by arranging their purchases so that they get three times the utility from the last unit of X they consume as from the last unit of Y they consume. If at the time in question $MC^*_X = \$2$ while $MC^*_Y = \$1$, X will be underproduced relative to Y because the economy would be able to transform a unit of Y into one-half a unit of X, which would be worth one and one-half units of Y to each of these goods' consumers on the margin.
6. See Oliver Williamson, *Economies as an Antitrust Defense Revisited*, 125 U. PA. L. REV. 699 (1977) and *Economies as an Antitrust Defense: The Welfare Trade-Off*, 58 AM. ECON. REV. 18 (1968).
7. For reasons that Section 6 of the introduction to Part III and Section 2 of Chapter 5 will discuss in some detail, regardless of whether welfare is defined in terms of utility (as most economists assume it must be defined) or in terms of some other conception of well-being, welfare is not monotonically related to economic efficiency. Williamson should not therefore have denominated the economic-efficiency trade-off he was investigating a *welfare* trade-off.
8. Like Diagrams V and VI, Diagram VII also assumes that the relevant DD and MR curves are linear and that the relevant MC and MLC curves are horizontal. These assumptions have also been made solely to facilitate the construction of Diagram VII; they do not critically affect any significant conclusion the diagram will be used to establish. (Admittedly, the combination of the assumption that MC_{IND} is horizontal and the assumption that pre-merger the industry was perfectly competitive implies that no producer must incur any fixed costs to produce X.)
9. Admittedly, the last conclusions do depend on the assumption that the production of X withdraws resources exclusively from the production of other existing products: when some of the resources that the production of X consumes are withdrawn from QV-investment-creating uses, the text's conclusions will be justified only if various additional empirical conditions are fulfilled.
10. The economists base their conclusions on both theoretical and empirical analyses. The theoretical analyses focus primarily on externality spillovers from knowledge creation. The empirical analyses attempt to measure the so-called social rate of return to R&D—roughly speaking, 100% *times* the ratio of (the difference between the economic efficiency gains generated by the use of any discovery a research project generates) to (the allocative cost of the project) *minus* 100%. The seminal theoretical work on the relationship between the economic efficiency and profitability of R&D is Kenneth J. Arrow, *Economic Welfare and the Allocation of Resources for Invention,* in THE RATE AND DIRECTION OF INVENTIVE ACTIVITY: ECONOMIC AND SOCIAL FACTORS 609 (Richard R. Nelson, ed. 1962). For some more recent theoretical work on R&D spillovers and other Pareto imperfections that would, acting on their own, cause the profitability of R&D to diverge from its allocative efficiency, see GENE M. GROSSMAN

& Elhanan Helpman, Innovation Growth in the Global Economy 43–111 (1991); Charles I. Jones & John C. Williams, *Measuring the Social Return of R&D,* 113 Q. J. Econ. 1119 (1998); James J. Anton & Dennis A. Yao, *Expropriation and Inventions: Appropriable Rents in the Absence of Property Rights,* 84 Amer. Econ. L. Rev. 190 (1994); M. Ishaq Nadiri, Innovations and Technological Spillovers 1 (Nat'l Bureau of Econ. Research, Working Paper No. 4423, 1993); Zvi Griliches, *The Search for R&D Spillovers,* 94 Scandinavian J. Econ. 29 (Supp. 1992); Jeffrey I. Bernstein & M. Ishaq Nadiri, *Research and Development and Intra-Industry Spillovers: An Empirical Application of Dynamic Duality,* 56 Rev. Econ. Stud. 429 (1989); Phillippe Aghion & Peter Howitt, *A Model of Growth through Creative Destruction,* 60 Econometrica 323 (1992); Nancy T. Gallini & Brian D. Wright, *Technology Transfer under Asymmetric Information,* 21 Rand. J. Econ. 147 (1990); Giovanni Dosi, *Sources, Procedures, and Microeconomic Effects of Innovation,* 25 J. Econ. Lit. 1120 (1988); Adam B. Jaffe, *Technological Opportunity and Spillovers of R&D: Evidence from Firms' Patents, Profits, and Market Value,* 76 Am. Econ. Rev. 984 (1986); Nancy T. Gallini & Ralph A. Winter, *Licensing in the Theory of Innovation,* 16 Rand. J. Econ. 237 (1985); Nancy T. Gallini, *Deterrence by Market Sharing: A Strategic Incentive for Licensing,* 74 Am. Econ. Rev. 931 (1984); Partha Dasgupta & Joseph Stiglitz, *Uncertainty, Industrial Structure, and the Speed of R&D,* 11 Bell J. Econ. 1 (1980); M. Therese Flaherty, *Industry Structure and Cost-Reducing Investment,* 48 Econometrica 1187 (1980); Ward Bowman, *The Incentive to Invent in Competitive as Contrasted to Monopolistic Industries,* 20 J. L. & Econ. 227 (1977); Morton I. Kamien & Nancy L. Schwartz, *Market Structure and Innovation: A Survey,* 13 J. Econ. Literature 1 (1975); Sheng Chen Hu, *On the Incentive to Invent: A Clarificatory Note,* 16 J. L. & Econ. 169 (1973); Jack Hirshleifer, *The Private and Social Value of Information and the Reward to Inventive Activity,* 61 Am. Econ. Rev. 561 (1971); and Harold Demsetz, *Information and Efficiency: Another Viewpoint,* 12 J. L. & Econ. 1 (1969).

The empirical literature includes F. M. Scherer, Innovation and Growth: Schumpeterian Perspectives (1984); Jones & Williams, *supra;* Avi Griliches, *Productivity: R&D, and the Data Constraint,* 84 Am. Econ. Rev. 1 (1994); Griliches, *supra*; Zvi Griliches & Fran Lichtenberg, *Interindustry Technology Flows and Productivity Growth: A Reexamination,* 66 Rev. Econ. & Stat. 324 (1984); Zvi Griliches & Frank Lichtenberg, *R&D and Productivity Growth at the Industry Level: Is There Still a Relationship?* in R&D, Patents and Productivity 465 (Zvi Griliches, ed. 1984); F. M. Scherer, *Inter-Industry Technology Flows and Productivity Growth,* 64 Rev. Econ. & Stat. 627 (1982); Leo Sveikauskas, *Technological Inputs and Multifactor Productivity Growth,* 63 Rev. Econ. & Stat. 275 (1981); Nestor E. Terleckyj, *Direct and Indirect Effects of Industrial Research and Development on the Productivity Growth of Industries,* in New Developments in Productivity Measurement and Analysis 359 (John W. Kendrick & Beatrice N. Vaccara, eds. 1980).

11. Thus, as Merges and Nelson have indicated, every effort to design an economically efficient patent system has proceeded on the assumption that, when it comes to invention and innovation, "faster is better." See Robert P. Merges & Richard R. Nelson, *On the Complex Economics of Patent Scope,* 90 Colum. L. Rev. 839, 878 (1990).

12. For some general proposals of this kind, see Thomas A. Piraino, Jr., *Reconciling Competition and Cooperation: A New Antitrust Standard for Joint Ventures,* 35 Wm. & Mary L. Rev. 871 (1994) and Thomas M. Jorde & David J. Teece, *Innovation and Cooperation: Implications for Competition and Antitrust,* 4 J. Econ. Persp. 75 (1990). For arguments in favor of relaxing antitrust laws specifically in the context of high-tech industries, see Thomas M. Jorde & David J. Teece, *Innovation, Cooperation, and Antitrust: Striking the Right Balance,* 4 High Tech. L. J. 1 (1989); Janusz A. Ordover & William Baumol, *Antitrust Policy and High Technology Industries,* 4 Oxford Rev. Econ. Pol'y 13 (1988); and Janusz A. Ordover & Robert D. Willig, *Antitrust for High-Technology Industries: Assessing Research Joint Ventures and Mergers,* 28 J. L. & Econ. 311 (1985). Even the few experts writing in this field who reject the case for special treatment of R&D-related efficiencies seem to accept the assumption that increases in R&D of all types would be economically efficient. See Joseph Brodley, *Antitrust Law and Innovation Cooperation,* 3 J. Econ. Persp. 97 (1990). See also M. I. Kamien, Eitan Muller, & Israel Zang, *Research Joint Ventures and R&D Cartels,* 82 Am. Econ. Rev. 1293 (1992); and K. Suzumura, *Cooperative and Noncooperative R&D in an Oligopoly with Spillovers,* 82 Am. Econ. Rev. 1307 (1992).
13. See Chapter 3's treatment of these issues. I should admit that some studies done by industrial organization economists who focus on product R&D in particular do recognize this point, if somewhat obliquely, by noting that the profits a discoverer can earn by utilizing his product discovery will be inflated to the extent that the new product's sales take profitable sales away from other producers. See Chapter 3, note 12 *supra.*
14. The actual proposals advocate exceptions for mergers, acquisitions, and joint ventures that will increase the proficiency of their participants' R&D, the quantity of resources they devote to R&D, or both. To the extent that any increase in the relevant research-proficiency is associated with their using fewer resources to generate the same set of discoveries, second-best theory implies that the associated private-cost savings will not equal their allocative counterparts—*viz.,* will exceed their allocative counterparts insofar as the saved resources are allocated to unit-output-producing or PPR-executing uses and will be lower than their allocative counterparts insofar as the saved resources are allocated to QV-investment-creating uses. To the extent that any increase in research-proficiency is associated with the researchers' generating more discoveries with the same resources, second-best theory implies that the associated private benefits will be lower than their allocative counterparts when the additional discovery is a production-process discovery and will be higher than their allocative counterparts when the additional discovery is a product discovery.
15. The expression "social costs of monopoly" comes from the literature. I have quoted "social costs" in the heading because the terminology is somewhat misleading. In economics, the expression "social cost" is ordinarily used as a surrogate for "allocative cost" in contrast to "private cost." Its use in this context to stand for "allocative-efficiency cost or loss" is misleading not only because this cost or loss equals the sum of the differences between various allocative-cost and allocative-benefit figures but also because the actual social loss that monopoly causes should be measured in terms of

utility, some alternative conception of well-being, and/or some conception of rights-related interests, not in equivalent-dollar allocative-efficiency terms.

16. Arnold C. Harberger, *Monopoly and Resource Allocation,* 66 PAPERS AND PROC. AM. ECON. ASSOC. 77 (1953).
17. Harberger assumed that the amount of misallocation generated by the underproduction of any product X equaled the size of the standard deadweight-loss triangle that would be created by its supra-marginal-cost price if the elasticity of its demand curve were unitary over the relevant range. Obviously, even if the unitary-elasticity assumption were accurate, this estimate would be accurate only if P = MLV, MC = MLC, or the divergences between P and MLV on the one hand and MC and MLC on the other hand perfectly counteracted each other.
18. *Viz.,* those goods whose P/MC* ratios are lower than their weighted-average counterparts for the goods from whose production resources would be withdrawn when additional units of the goods in question were produced.
19. For discussions of the relevant literature, see W. KIP VISCUSI, JOHN M. VERNON, & JOSEPH E. HARRINGTON, JR., ECONOMICS OF REGULATION AND ANTITRUST 86–88 (3rd ed. 2000) and PAUL R. FERGUSON & GLENYS J. FERGUSON, INDUSTRIAL ECONOMICS: ISSUES AND PERSPECTIVES 88–95 (2nd ed. 1994). See also F. M. SCHERER & DAVID ROSS, INDUSTRIAL MARKET STRUCTURE AND MARKET PERFORMANCE 33–38, 666–67 (1990); Robert T. Masson & Joseph Shannon, *Social Costs of Oligopoly and the Value of Competition,* 94 ECON. J. 520 (1984); Keith Cowling & Dennis C. Mueller, *The Social Costs of Monopoly,* 88 ECON. J. 724 (1978); Abram Bergson, *On Monopoly Welfare Losses: A Reply,* 65 AMER. ECON. REV. 1024 (1977); R. Carson, *On Monopoly Welfare Losses: A Comment,* 65 AMER. ECON. REV. 853 (1973); Dean A. Worcester, Jr., *New Estimates of the Welfare Loss to Monopoly,* 40 SO. ECON. J. 234 (1973); David R. Kamerschen, *An Estimate of the Welfare Loss from Monopoly in the American Economy,* 4 WESTERN ECON. J. 221 (1966); David Schwartzman, *The Burden of Monopoly,* 68 J. POL. ECON. 627 (1960); and George J. Stigler, *The Statistics of Monopoly and Merger,* 64 J. POL. ECON. 33 (1956).
20. For example, Cowling & Mueller, *supra* note 19 and Masson & Shannon, *supra* note 19 criticize Harberger's unitary-demand-elasticity assumption.
21. *Supra* note 19.
22. Richard Posner, *The Social Costs of Monopoly and Regulation,* 83 J. POL. ECON. 807 (1975).
23. This claim is wrong not only because the direct allocative (resource) cost of advertising will not generally equal its private counterpart but also because it fails to deal with the realities that advertising (1) can create allocative value by changing the nature of the advertised product and providing information that prevents consumers from making misallocative consumption-decisions that disserve their individual interests and (2) can also generate allocative costs by reducing the value of old products to their owners, disseminating misinformation that causes consumers to make misallocative consumption-decisions that disserve their individual interests, and most contestably and generally by disserving everyone's interest by making us more materialistic and other-directed.

24. See e.g., STEVEN SHAVELL, ECONOMIC ANALYSIS OF ACCIDENT LAW (1987) and William A. Landes & Richard M. Posner, *The Positive Economic Theory of Tort Law,* 15 GA. L. REV. 851 (1981).
25. See, e.g., two leading environmental economics textbooks and the hundreds of sources they cite: EBAN GOODSTEIN, ECONOMICS AND THE ENVIRONMENT (4th ed. 2005) and TOM TIETENBERG, ENVIRONMENTAL AND NATURAL RESOURCES ECONOMICS (4th ed. 1996).
26. See, e.g., the environmental economics textbooks written respectively by CHARLES KOLSTAD, ENVIRONMENTAL ECONOMICS (2000), and WILLIAM BAUMOL & WALLACE OATES, THE THEORY OF ENVIRONMENTAL POLICY (2d ed. 1988).
27. The other imperfections that are in the system also call into question the allocative efficiency of a health-and-safety authority's accepting as allocatively efficient any work regime agreed to by a worker-management safety committee. Even if one assumes that the workers' union representatives are perfectly informed and are motivated to maximize the workers' collective equivalent-dollar interests, distortions in the private cost of avoidance and in the private loss that work-related injuries and illnesses impose on their worker-victims may well render the work regime that maximizes the equivalent-dollar gains of a company's shareholders and workers combined less allocatively efficient than some alternative.
28. The shift will only *tend to* produce this outcome because the deflation in the relevant private benefits that a victim's avoidance confers on the victim will not always be critical.
29. See, e.g., Landes and Posner, *supra* note 24 and Steven Shavell, *An Analysis of Causation and the Scope of Liability in the Law of Torts,* 9 J. LEG. STUD. 463 (1980).
30. Steven Shavell, *Strict Liability versus Negligence,* 9 J. LEG. STUD. 1 (1980).
31. Obviously, this ignores the fact that the distortions that some of these other imperfections generate will vary with the type of avoidance move under consideration. To ease the exposition, the text will continue to ignore this important reality.
32. Shavell, *supra* note 29.
33. Because Shavell does not think that scope-of-liability dismissals will have a significant impact on potential-victim avoidance-decision misallocation (see *id.* at 496), he does not analyze this possibility. Although I do not share this empirical assumption, I will ignore this issue as well in the text that follows.
34. I should note that Shavell does not distinguish between private and allocative transaction costs.
35. See Shavell, *supra* note 29 at 471 n. 25.
36. This might be an appropriate place to state and comment on Shavell's analysis of the allocative efficiency of the courts' treatment of the facts on which they base their resolution of scope-of-liability issues. For this purpose, I will accept *ad arguendo* Shavell's assumption that the scope-of-liability doctrine will reduce the amount of transaction costs that tort-related contingencies cause to be generated. First, Shavell claims (*supra* note 29 at 484–85) that, from the perspective of allocative efficiency, the courts are wrong to count the fact that the *ex ante* probability of the relevant loss's occurring was low in favor of dismissing the suit against the injurer on scope-of-liability grounds. As Shavell correctly points out, as the probability of the relevant

loss's occurring declines, both the transaction-cost savings that dismissals will generate and the amount of misallocation they will cause potential injurers to generate by making economically inefficient avoidance decisions will tend to decline proportionately: (1) the lower the *ex ante* probability of the loss, the lower the number of losses and hence the lower the number of cases in which scope-of-liability dismissals will save transaction costs, and (2) the lower the *ex ante* probability of the loss, the smaller the deflation in avoidance incentives the prospect of the relevant dismissals will generate and hence the smaller the increase in the amount of misallocation potential injurers generate by making economically inefficient avoidance decisions. However, in my judgment, Shavell's conclusion that the courts have acted allocatively efficiently by making the probability of a scope-of-liability dismissal vary inversely with the size of the loss involved in the case in question is mistaken. Shavell's position on this issue reflects his assumption that the cost of trying cases that the injurer does not win on scope-of-liability grounds will not vary with the size of the loss the case involves (with the amount in controversy). On this assumption, the relevant judicial practice would be allocatively efficient: as the size of the loss declines, the transaction-cost savings that proximate-cause dismissals generate stay constant, but the deflation such dismissals cause in potential injurers' avoidance incentives and hence the amount of misallocation they cause potential injurers to generate by making economically inefficient avoidance decisions declines. See *id.* at 488–89. I reject Shavell's conclusion because I think that the transaction cost of trying a tort suit increases proportionately with the amount in controversy: as the loss increases, the parties spend more money on lawyers and expert witnesses. If this proportionality hypothesis is correct, the size of the loss will also be irrelevant to the allocative efficiency of dismissing a suit on proximate-cause grounds: as the loss declines, both the transaction-cost savings that dismissals generate and the amount of misallocation they cause potential injurers to generate by making economically inefficient avoidance decisions will drop proportionately. Finally, I have mixed reactions to Shavell's assessment of the allocative efficiency of the courts' tendency to be more likely to dismiss suits on proximate-cause grounds when the loss that resulted was unforeseeable. Shavell argues that both "casual empiricism" and various psychological studies imply that injurers tend to underestimate the probability of unforeseeable accidents and that this tendency favors the allocative efficiency of dismissing claims related to unforeseeable accidents because it implies that on this account such dismissals will cause potential injurers to cause less misallocation by making economically inefficient avoidance decisions than would otherwise be the case. See *id.* at 491. Although Shavell concedes that this argument is undercut by (1) the transaction cost of assessing foreseeability or potential injurers' underestimates of the probability of the loss and (2) the tendency of the foreseeability test to "reduce the incentive of parties to investigate or, at least, to carefully contemplate the potential consequences of their actions" (*id.* at 492), he fails to consider the possibility that in many cases the "specifically unforeseeable" may be foreseeable. Thus, because manufacturers who put a new pollutant into the air may have a pretty good idea of the magnitude of the loss this decision will cause even though they cannot foresee the specific character of the loss—e.g., the specific diseases it will cause—a decision to dismiss a claim made against them on the ground that the specific loss was unforeseeable would tend to cause them to increase the misallocation they generate by making economically inefficient avoidance decisions, *ceteris paribus,* by inflating the perceived profitability to them of polluting the atmosphere.

37. I believe that this feature of the common law reflects the fact that the countries that have a common law are rights-based societies, that the point of the common law of rights-based societies is to legally enforce the corrective-justice rights of their members and participants, and that the binary conception of cause-in-fact that the common law employs is part of the conceptual structure of corrective justice. For an explanation of these points, see Richard S. Markovits, *Liberalism and Tort Law: On the Content of the Corrective-Justice-Securing Tort Law of a Liberal, Rights-Based Society,* 2006 Ill. L. Rev. 243 (2006). I hasten to add that, in the type of case on which we are now focusing, the moral commitments of a liberal, rights-based society are not incompatible with its passing legislation that makes a putative injurer liable to an actual victim for part of the loss the victim suffered even though the putative injurer was not more than 50% likely to have inflicted it—i.e., such a result (secured, for example, through legislation that promulgated a market-share-liability rule) would not generically violate any moral right of the putative injurer in question.
38. In some cases of this kind, it never would have been possible to establish cause-in-fact in any other way. Asbestositis cases, in which the disease is caused by the inhalation of one unit of asbestos and the victim has been exposed to asbestos put into the environment by more than one polluter none of whom placed into the air more than 50 percent of the asbestos the victim might have inhaled, belong in this category. In other cases of this kind, although at one point in time it would have been possible for the victim to establish the identity of his injurer in some other way, at the time of trial, through no fault of the victim, it is no longer possible for him to do so. Cases in which the victim's loss was caused by his consumption of a medicine that could have been produced by more than one pharmaceutical company none of whom produced more than 50 percent of the medicine he might have consumed will fall into this second category if at the time the symptoms appeared the victim was no longer able to identify his ultimate supplier (he no longer had the relevant prescription, and the prescription record was no longer recoverable from the drugstore that retailed the medicine).
39. For some examples that illustrate this point, see note 49 of Chapter 3. The law's approach to cause-in-fact is said to impose "crushing liability" because it may make it profitable for a putatitve injurer to close down an allocatively efficient business—i.e., to avoid by exiting when the exit is allocatively inefficient.
40. See Landes & Posner, *supra* note 24.
41. I will assume *ad arguendo* that their description of the relevant common-law practice is accurate.
42. Landes & Posner, *supra* note 24 at 910–11. Landes and Posner admit (at 911) that their hypothesis has two weaknesses:

> There are, however, two factors that may work against the hypothesis. First, strict liability may not provide information on the full costs of a new activity because an

accident may result in a large number of small claims, each of insufficient amount to provide an incentive to bring a suit. If there is no feasible means of *aggregating* small claims, we are in effect in a world of no liability and can offer no hypothesis on the relative advantages of different liability rules. The other factor is that strict liability, even at the early stages of a new activity, reduces the incentives for the potential victim to take care or alter his activity level to minimize risk. These disadvantages of strict liability will tend to be minor, however, when the activity begins on a small scale, when the probability of being a victim is small, and when the victim would have to take care or change his activity level to avoid the accident before he had knowledge of whether he was likely to be a victim. If the victim's care is an important component of due care in the early stages of an activity, as it was for airplane collisions and injuries to pedestrians from automobiles (because the cost of pedestrian care is often trivial), strict liability would be inefficient even initially and we would predict that it would not be adopted.

I agree with Landes and Posner's discussion of their two qualifications except for the conclusion expressed in the last sentence of the quoted material: even if victim avoidance can increase allocative efficiency to an important extent in the early stages of a potential injurer's activity, strict liability may not be allocatively inefficient in that the allocative-efficiency gains it generates (in comparison with negligence) by inducing potential injurers to reduce their unit outputs (and change their locations, alter their product variants, and execute and make use of the discoveries generated by additional research into less-AP-loss-prone production processes, locations, and product variants) may exceed the allocative-efficiency losses it generates by deterring allocatively efficient avoidance by victims. And when potential-victim avoidance can make a substantial contribution to economic efficiency, the most-economically-efficient tort-liability regime may be strict liability with contributory negligence.

43. For example, if AP-loss-reducing research would be more allocatively efficient in an industry's infancy than in its maturity (because more improvements remain to be made when the industry is immature), a shift from negligence to strict liability will tend to increase allocative efficiency more by inducing an industry's members to do such research when the industry is in its infancy than when it is mature. If, on the other hand, AP-loss-reducing research will be more allocatively efficient in an industry's maturity than it its infancy because one cannot carry out such research allocatively efficiently until a scientific and technological base has been established by engaging in production and observing its consequences, a shift from negligence to strict liability will tend to increase allocative efficiency more by inducing the industry's members to engage in AP-loss-reducing research when it is mature than when it is in its infancy.
44. Like the traditional analysis, the analysis that follows assumes that any housing code will be perfectly enforced.
45. Admittedly, if I relaxed the assumption that all subcode units are identical and that all code units are identical to a relatively minor extent, one could also tell a story that would imply that DD_C would diverge from DD_S as one moved out to the right. This result might obtain, for example, if the highest valuers of the subcode units were elderly, long-term residents on fixed incomes who valued *their* subcode units higher

than other subcode-unit occupiers valued the units in which those other individuals lived (1) partly because the elderly residents placed a high value on staying put—i.e., strongly disvalued moving, (2) partly because they liked things the way they were, and (3) partly because they were poorer than other occupiers (and hence placed a lower-than-average *dollar* value on the improvement to code).

46. Admittedly, this assumption is probably inconsistent with the second explanation of the upward slope of MC_S.
47. To ease the exposition, I am assuming that, prior to the code, OI subcode units were in existence and that the code would cause these units either to be abandoned or to be improved to code. At the other extreme, one could also assume that, prior to the code, no housing units to which it would apply existed and that the code would cause OF code-quality units as opposed to OI subcode units to be built. On otherwise-Pareto-perfect assumptions, this difference is of no account. On realistic assumptions, the difference will be salient to the extent, for example, that the abandonment of existing occupied dwellings generates external costs.
48. Admittedly, pre-code, the owner of the subcode unit also would have the option of allowing his unit to deteriorate further—i.e., of supplying a unit that was even more subcode. The text that follows will ignore this possibility—in essence, will assume that this option will never be more profitable than maintaining the original quality of the subcode unit, converting it to a nonresidential use, or abandoning it.
49. The assumption that abandoned properties generate net allocative costs reflects a contestable judgment that on the weighted average the allocative costs they generate by facilitating and hence inducing allocatively inefficient criminal activities, causing fires (which consume valuable firefighting resources, emit pollution, and spread to surrounding properties), and housing unpleasant, disease-spreading vermin exceed the allocative benefits they generate by providing habitats for squatters. I should add that abandonment is a legal option in most if not all American jurisdictions.
50. I cannot generalize about the relevant productivity effect the code will have when it induces inhabitants of subcode units to move away.
51. I have already indicated that it may not be the case if the alternative to occupying a subcode unit in the area in which the housing code applies is moving away. It also may not be the case if the code causes gentrification and does not improve the housing stock on balance or if the code causes enough housing units to be withdrawn to worsen the conditions in which children live and work on balance.
52. Recall that I have counted the external benefits that the preservation as opposed to the abandonment of subcode units will generate as part of the MLV_S^R.
53. For a more detailed analysis of the relevant distributive impacts, see Richard S. Markovits, *The Distributive Impact, Allocative Efficiency, and Overall Desirability of Ideal Housing Codes: Some Theoretical Clarifications,* 89 Harv. L. Rev. 1815 (1976).
54. William A. Landes & Richard M. Posner, *Salvors, Finders, Good Samaritans, and Other Rescuers,* 7 J. Leg. Stud. 83, 102 (1978). I have quoted the expression "judge-made" because it implies that judges are authorized to or in these areas typically do legislate rather than find the law—a claim that I reject. I also object to Landes and Posner's use of the word *explained* in the quoted excerpt. Even if (contrary to my own view) economic efficiency best *predicts* the relevant decisions, that fact would not in itself

imply that it best *explains* these decisions. To justify the conclusion that economic efficiency best *explains* the relevant decisions in any sense, one would have to explain either why the economically efficient award is just or most desirable (moral-rights considerations aside) or (more cynically) why the relevant decisions are motivated by parochial self-interest and why the relevant decision makers would find it in their parochial self-interest to resolve such cases as economically efficiently as they could.

55. For thorough analyses of these issues, see Richard S. Markovits, The Economic Efficiency of Marine-Salvage Law: Foreground Choices, Background Choices, and a Related Critique of Landes and Posner's Classic Study (article under submission, 2007).

56. The text that follows ignores such issues as the allocative efficiency of (1) admiralty law's "no cure/no pay" rule, which denies awards to those who have made unsuccessful marine-rescue attempts, (2) the way in which admiralty law divides up marine-salvor awards among the owner, officers, and crew of the salvage ship, and (3) the way in which admiralty law allocates the duty to pay any award made to marine salvors among the owners of the property and lives that were imperiled (the so-called general average principle). I have analyzed the allocative efficiency of admiralty law's handling of these and various other issues not discussed in the text in *id.* See, e.g., *Mason v. The Bladirear,* 6 U.S. (2 Cranch) 240, 266 (1804); *B.V. Bureau Wijsmuller v. United States,* 702 F.2d 333, 337–38 (2d Cir. 1983); *Seven Coal Barges,* 21 F. Cas. 1096, 1097 (C.C.D. Ind. 1870, no. 12, 677); and the *Charles Henry, S.F. Cas.* 509, 410 (E.D.N.Y. 1865, no. 2617). This string cite is taken from *Note, Calculating and Allocating Salvage Liability,* 99 HARV. L. REV. 1896 at 1898 n. 13.

57. See GRANT GILMORE & CHARLES BLACK, THE LAW OF ADMIRALTY 563 (2nd ed., 1975).

58. See DAVID W. STEEL & FRANCIS D. ROSE, KENNEDY'S LAW OF CIVIL SALVAGE (5th ed., 1985).

59. *Id.* at 174.

60. See *Note, Calculating and Allocating Salvage Liability, supra* note 54 at 1915.

61. See MARTIN J. NORRIS, THE LAW OF SALVAGE 21–33 (1958).

62. See, e.g., *Mason v. The Blaireau,* 6 U.S. (2 Cranch) 240, 266 (1804); *B. V. Bureau Wijsmuller v. United States,* 702 F.2d 333, 337–38 (2d Cir. 1983); *Seven Coal Barges,* 21 F. Cas. 1096, 1097 (C.C.D. Ind. 1870, no. 12, 67); and *The Charles Henry, S.F. Cas.* 509, 510 (E.D.N.Y. 1865, no. 2617). This string cite is taken from *Note, Calculating and Allocating Salvage Liability, supra* note 60 at 1898 n. 13.

63. See, e.g., *The Henry Ewbank,* 11 F. Cas. 1166, 1170 (C.C.D. Mass. 1833, no. 6376).

64. See, e.g., *The Sabine,* 1010 U.S. 384, 384 (1880).

65. See, e.g., *The Clarita and the Clara,* 90 U.S. (23 Wall.) 1, 17 (1874) and *The Blackwall,* 77 U.S. (10 Wall.) 1, 14 (1879).

66. See, e.g., *Higgins, Inc. v. The Tri-State,* 99 F. Supp. 694, 698–99 (S.D. Fla. 1951) and *Magnolia Petroleum Co. v. National Oil Trans. Co.*, 281 F. 336, 339–41 (S.D. Tex. 1922).

67. See Wayne T. Brough, *Liability Salvage—by Private Ordering,* 19 J. LEG. STUD. 95, 111 (1990).

68. Landes & Posner, *supra* note 54 at 102.

69. Landes and Posner use the same list I am using—the list provided by the 1958 Kennedy treatise THE LAW OF CIVIL SALVAGE. See *id.* at 101–02.
70. See *id.* at 100–13.
71. Thus, Landes and Posner argue that the American courts' practice of counting the value of lives saved when property as well as lives have been rescued but not providing compensation for "pure life" salvors may be allocatively efficient because—although allocative efficiency will be furthered by giving potential rescuers appropriate incentives to save lives as well as property when both are imperiled—altruism may secure allocative efficiency when only lives are in danger. See *id.* at 104–05 and n. 48.
72. Robert L. Rabin, *The Historical Development of the Fault Principle: A Reinterpretation,* 15 GA. L. REV. 925, 955 (1981), discussing Landes and Posner's treatment of *Adams v. Bullock,* 227 N.Y. 208, 125 N.E. 93 (1919) in William A. Landes & Richard M. Posner, *The Positive Economic Theory of Tort Law,* 15 GA. L. REV. 851, 894 (1981). Landes and Posner's argument was that—given the low probability of this kind of loss and the high cost of placing underground the wire that caused it (which had to be uninsulated to supply electricity to the trolley)—the trolley company's decision to use overhead wires was not negligent (because the cost of placing the wires underground was higher than the reduction in weighted-average-expected accident losses placing them there would generate).
73. See Edward J. Mishan, *Second Thoughts on Second-Best,* 14 OX. ECON. PAPERS, N.S. 205 (1962).
74. See 73 CHI.-KENT L. REV. 2–274 (1998).
75. More generally, the refusal of economists to respond appropriately to second-best theory when the relevant Pareto imperfections are not imperfections in individual sovereignty (information) or maximization is puzzling, given their willingness to accept behavioral economics and the economics of information. The first behavioral-economics study to be highly respected was Herbert Simon, *A Behavioral Model of Rational Choice,* 69 Q.J. ECON. 99 (1955). The work of cognitive psychologists such as Amos Tversky and Daniel Kahneman gave behavioral economics a substantial boost. For a relevant collection of essays, see CHOICES, VALUES, AND FRAMES (Daniel Kahneman & Amos Tversky, eds. 2000). For a recent collection of behavioral-economics essays, see ECONOMIC INSTITUTIONS AND BEHAVIORAL ECONOMICS (Peter Diamond, ed. 2006). For a discussion of the use of behavioral economics in law and economics, see Christine Jolls, Cass R. Sunstein, & Richart Thaler, *A Behavioral Approach to Law and Economics,* 50 STAN. L. REV. 1471 (1998). See also the sources cited at Chapter 3, note 48 *supra.* For surveys of the economics of information by two of its Nobel-prize-winning practitioners, see Joseph E. Stiglitz, *Information and the Change in the Paradigm of Economics,* 92 AMER. ECON. REV. 460 (2002); Michael Spence, *Signaling in Retrospect and the Informational Structure of Markets,* 92 AMER. ECON. REV. 434 (2002). See also Joseph E. Stiglitz, *The Contributions of the Economics of Information to Twentieth Century Economics,* 115 Q.J. ECON. 1441 (2000).
76. I have heard each of these arguments made orally on a substantial number of occasions. For an article by a deservedly-highly-respected economist-lawyer in which all are

made, see John Donohue, *Some Thoughts on Law and Economics and the General Theory of Second Best,* 73 CHI.-KENT L. REV. 257 (1998).

PART III. THE RELEVANCE OF ALLOCATIVE-EFFICIENCY CONCLUSIONS

1. Admittedly, some would argue that one should also distinguish at least two other moral types of societies—ideal-based societies and religious societies. Traditionally, societies that are committed to basing their choices on the choices' impact on such things as (1) the number of people of a certain type the society produces or contains or (2) the number of works of art of a specified type that it produces are denominated "ideal-based societies." My characterization of such societies would depend on the nature of the valued human characteristic or the reason that the type of art was valued. In my scheme, some such societies—e.g., those that value certain types of individuals or certain kinds of art because they and/or their presence generate outcomes that can defensibly be viewed as morally desirable—would be classified as goal-based societies, while other ideal-based societies would be characterized as amoral or immoral societies. There is also no simple way to characterize the societies that others would denominate "religious societies" in my terms. To the extent that others assume that the defining characteristic of such societies is their commitment to assigning the task of evaluating all moral decisions to people at the top of a religious hierarchy—i.e., to their believing that ordinary members of the societies in question (laypeople) should cede all moral decision making to such a priestly class, I would consider such societies to be immoral, regardless of the moral quality of the choices the priests recommend. If, on the other hand, the concept of a religious society were defined to include societies whose members have a religious duty to base what I think should objectively be considered to be moral decisions on one or more religious texts that they interpret themselves, my classification of this subset of religious societies would depend on the moral quality of the decision criteria the relevant religious texts promulgate and the extent to which the texts cover all moral choices the individual members of the society confront. I should say that my inclination to classify as immoral religious societies that leave no room for individuals to engage in moral decision making also has implications for the moral status of goal-based societies whose goals are supposed to govern all choices made by their members.
2. It is morally permissible for the members but not the governments of liberal, rights-based societies to act in a way that manifests their greater concern for the welfare or interests of some relevant individuals than for the welfare or interests of other relevant individuals. This conclusion reflects the facts that (1) the legitimately favored individuals will usually be intimates of the actor in question or members of a group with which he identifies and (2) liberalism values such intimacy and (to a lesser extent) group affiliations because intimate relationships both lead to moral self-discovery and provide a context in which individuals learn to take seriously their moral obligations and their personally chosen values (in my terminology, the "personal ultimate values" that underlie their conception of the good).
3. Liberalism recognizes promissory obligations because, in fulfilling promises, the promisor shows respect for the promisee. Liberalism recognizes status obligations

because both voluntary and relevant nonvoluntary status relationships promote intimacy, and intimate relationships promote their participants' taking their lives morally seriously by helping them discover what they value and providing a context in which they have the opportunity both to fulfill important moral obligations and to actualize their personal conception of the good. Liberalism recognizes that any individual who was a culpable cause-in-fact of another's predicament has a special duty to render assistance to his victim because the duty of respect requires a culpable injurer to mitigate the harm he has wrongfully caused when he can reasonably do so.

4. Empirical approaches to determining the moral commitments of given societies are conventionally denominated "conventionalist" as opposed to Foundationalist moral analyses. (I object to the term *conventionalist* because the word *convention* is also used to describe practices that have no moral valence, such as driving on the right or the left side of the road.) In any event, most scholars who use a conventionalist approach are what might be termed pure conventionalists in that their reports are not in any way philosophically informed (perhaps I should say in that they proceed on the assumption that the moral has no ineliminable attributes, that the moral is completely socially negotiable). My conventionalist approach to moral analysis is far from pure—is highly qualified by the attention it gives to a wide range of moral distinctions and concepts that I consider to be ineliminable.

Some elaboration is required. The pure conventionalist analyzes a society's moral character and commitments on the assumption that such concepts as a society of moral integrity, moral norm, acting from a moral position, and prejudice are entirely socially negotiable. Hence, the pure conventionalist simply reports the conduct of the communities he studies that its members consider to have a moral dimension in some undefined sense—simply reports the self-described moral conventions of particular communities. The pure conventionalist does not comment, for example, on the possible moral significance of the fact that a society that is committed to liberalism in its moral-rights discourse makes legal decisions that violate liberal principles—i.e., does not comment on the implications of this inconsistency for the moral integrity of the community in question. He also does not comment on the possible moral significance of the fact that the society he is studying has a caste system that it does not try to justify or justicize (show to be just) in any way. Indeed, if the society consistently applies caste-based decision rules and decision standards, the pure conventionalist will say no more than that this practice is part of the morality of the community in question. Conventionalists who are pure in the sense in which I am using this terminology will also not ask whether a narrow-gauged practice that is inconsistent with the best account (see the following text) that can be given of a particular society's general or broad-gauged moral practice is immoral by the society's own standards: if the narrow-gauged practice is consistently followed, the pure conventionalist will describe it to be part of the community's moral practice.

An illustration may clarify this last point. Assume that the best account that can be given of a particular society's broad-gauged moral practice implies that it is a liberal, rights-based society. Assume in addition that this conclusion partly reflects the fact that members of the relevant society (1) give substantial positive weight to the interests individuals have in forming and participating in intimate relationships that contribute to their discovering their personal ultimate values as well as to their actualizing these values and fulfilling their moral obligations and (2) give a positive weight as well to the desire of individuals to experience and give pleasure. Now assume that this same society penalizes adults who participate in voluntary homosexual sexual activity on the ground that it disgusts the majority of its members even when such behavior contributes to the formation and maintenance of broader intimate relationships. Assume finally that this society imposes no penalties on adults who participate in voluntary heterosexual sexual activity that is in the relevant sense anatomically identical. The pure conventionalist would categorize this society's consistent treatment of homosexuals who engage in such sexual conduct as part of its morality. The pure conventionalist would not ask whether disgust can justify or justicize penalizing adult participants in voluntary homosexual sexual conduct. The pure conventionalist also would not ask whether this treatment of the relevant homosexuals might not be immoral by the community's own standards because it was inconsistent with the best account of the community's broad-gauged moral practice. The pure conventionalist would simply accept the community's own assessment of the morality of its narrow-gauged conduct.

As I have already indicated, I will be employing a highly qualified conventionalist approach to moral analysis, not a pure conventionalist approach. My conventionalist approach is qualified because it proceeds on the assumption that the notions moral norm, acting from a moral position, being an individual or society of moral integrity, and prejudice have some ineliminable attributes—for example, that an individual or a State cannot be said to have moral integrity unless he or it behaves morally consistently to some hard-to-specify extent. A highly qualified conventionalist would therefore conclude that a consistent narrow-gauged practice was immoral if its alleged justification (disgust) was morally unacceptable and was immoral by the community's own standards if it was inconsistent with the best account of the community's moral commitments—perhaps, with the way in which the society in question generally responded to conduct that implicated the same interests that the narrow-gauged practice affects to the same extent that they were affected by the narrow-gauged practice at issue.

5. For some of the relevant evidence, see RICHARD S. MARKOVITS, MATTERS OF PRINCIPLE: LEGITIMATE LEGAL ARGUMENT AND CONSTITUTIONAL INTERPRETATION at Chapters 3 and 4 (1998).

6. The text has ignored another feature of the liberal duty to rescue—*viz.,* that no potential rescuer has a duty to rescue unless he is uniquely well placed to effectuate the rescue in question. I can offer three justifications for this feature. The first is convincing when it applies but often is inapplicable: in many situations in which a potential rescuer knows that he is not uniquely well placed to effectuate the rescue, he can reasonably believe that any effort he makes to effectuate the rescue will not increase the probability that the potential rescuee will be saved. The second justification is that in many such situations the potential rescuer who is not uniquely well placed can reasonably believe that his rescue attempt will deter a better placed rescuer from attempting to rescue so that even if it does increase the probability of rescue it will worsen the overall certainty-equivalent outcome by increasing the probable cost to the (changing) rescue attempter. The third

justification is that any related authorization of the State to render legally enforceable a moral obligation of a non-uniquely-best-placed potential rescuer to make a rescue attempt he was not uniquely best placed to make creates a risk that the government will enforce this legal obligation selectively against its political opponents or targets of social prejudice. I should say, however, that in general I do not think it legitimate for a rights-based State to rely on this last type of (prudential) argument: a State of moral integrity should respond directly to the risk of politically corrupt or prejudice-based decisions, not eliminate the possibility of their being made by failing to create legal rights that would otherwise secure the rights-related interests of those for whom it is responsible. See Section 8 of this introduction to Part III.

7. The relevant problem arises in two kinds of cases. In the first, at no point in time could the victim have identified his wrongdoing injurer. In the second, the victim could have identified his wrongdoing injurer at one point in time but not at any time after he was aware that he had suffered a loss that someone might have wrongfully imposed on him. The former type of case is exemplified by asbestositis cases in which the loss is caused by the inhalation of one unit of asbestos in a situation in which asbestos was put into the air by more than one polluter none of whom was responsible for more than 50% of the asbestos that the victim might have inhaled. See, e.g., *Rutherford v. Owen-Illinois, Inc.*, 941 P.2d 1203 (Cal. 1997). The latter type of case is exemplified by pharmaceutical cases in which the plaintiff has been harmed by his consumption of a drug that was negligently produced or designed that could have ultimately been supplied to him by any one of a number of producers none of whom supplied more than 50% of the drug to buyers in his area. See, e.g., *Sindell v. Abbott Lab.*, 607 P.2d 924 (Cal. 1980). The State could deal with these situations by legislating a market-share-liability rule that would make each possible injurer of any such victim liable for a percentage of the victim's loss equal to the probability that the injurer in question caused that victim's loss (roughly speaking, equal to the seller's share of the relevant market).

8. Admittedly, the text is somewhat misleading in that many contemporary utilitarians share the traditional utilitarian's rejection of the distinction between the just and the good and believe that utility controls (in my terms) not only what morally ought to be done but also what justice requires.

9. Actually, libertarians are not clear about whether each individual is entitled to the revenue product of the last worker to perform the labor he performed with the skill and assiduity with which he worked, the average revenue product of the previously defined class of workers to which he belongs, the allocative product of the last worker in his class, or the average allocative product of that class of workers. Although it seems to me that the empirical and normative premises of libertarianism imply that libertarians should believe that workers are entitled to the allocative product of the last worker in their class to perform their type of labor, in my experience, when asked, libertarians tend to assert that they believe that workers morally ought to receive either (1) their gross market wage (which would equal the revenue product of the last worker in their labor class to be employed if the relevant employer was a sovereign, maximizing nonmonopsonist who obtained no surplus by hiring the last worker in question) or (2)

the average allocative product of the workers in their class. At least, in my experience, many self-styled libertarians tend to advocate distributing income according to the average allocative product of each class of workers until they learn that this standard would probably favor sanitation workers' being given more resources than doctors.

10. For a discussion of this issue, see Eugene Volokh, *Freedom of Speech, Shielding Children, and Transcending Balancing*, 1997 SUP. CT. REV. 141 (1997).

11. The following facts may be relevant to the distributive desirability of a choice: (1) the characteristics of the utility levels, more general welfare-positions, and/or general conduct of the beneficiaries and victims; (2) the moral characteristics of any acts against which the private or government choice in question is directed; and (3) the characteristics of any indirect consequences the relevant private or government choices may have. Thus, for utilitarians and various kinds of egalitarians, the relevant facts will include such category (1) items as the distribution of the beneficiaries' and victims' pre-choice wealths and incomes. For those libertarians who believe that people morally ought to be paid according to what they produce, the relevant facts will include such category (1) items as the relationship between the beneficiaries' and victims' pre-policy wealths and incomes and their libertarian-defined productivity. For retributionists and individuals who believe that people morally ought not profit from their own wrongs, the relevant facts will include such category (2) items as whether any acts to which a relevant private or government choice responds were inherently immoral.

12. For an explanation, see Richard S. Markovits, *Liberalism and Tort Law: On the Content of the Corrective-Justice-Securing Tort Law of a Liberal, Rights-Based Society*, 2006 ILL. L. REVIEW 243, 285–86 (2006).

13. I assume that such legislation is not rendered unconstitutional by the motivation of the legislators who promulgated it or by the fact that it cannot be justified from any defensible value-perspective.

14. The text assumes that mistaken legislation that is pointless—that is not desirable from any defensible moral perspective and does not even serve the parochial interests of those it was designed to benefit—is not unconstitutional on that account. In fact, I suspect that legislation that is pointless will be unconstitutional if its passage manifests the State's lack of appropriate concern for the people it disadvantages and that such legislation will manifest such a lack of appropriate concern unless it was generated by a process that did provide appropriate (though not foolproof) safeguards against such defective legislation's promulgation.

15. Of course, the failure of a society to amend its constitution to remove a provision that violates its moral commitments will count against its being a society of moral integrity: indeed, a society's failure to remove such a provision over a long period of time may justify the conclusion that it is not a society of moral integrity if the provision has a sufficiently negative impact on the rights-related interests of the society's members and participants.

16. Although a full analysis would be quite complicated, I believe that the provisions assigning each state two members in the Senate and establishing the electoral-college procedure for selecting the president are almost certainly inconsistent with the society's

liberal obligation to secure for each of its members an equal influence on the content of the laws that will subsequently govern him.

17. I have elsewhere delineated and criticized a wide variety of other positions that legal scholars have taken on valid legal argument in the United States. See Richard S. Markovits, *Legitimate Legal Argument and Internally-Right Answers to Legal-Rights Questions,* 74 CHI.-KENT L. REV. 415, 435–60 (1999) and MATTERS OF PRINCIPLE: LEGITIMATE LEGAL ARGUMENT AND CONSTITUTIONAL INTERPRETATION at Chapter 2 (1998).
18. See, e.g., Chapter 4, notes 37–38 *supra* and the accompanying text.
19. For an analysis of the liberal moral legitimacy of the American practice of precedent as reported by the Supreme Court, see RICHARD S. MARKOVITS, MATTERS OF PRINCIPLE: LEGITIMATE LEGAL ARGUMENT AND CONSTITUTIONAL INTERPRETATION 70–71 and 73–74 (1998).
20. An example may be helpful. Assume that, upon the dissolution of a marriage, the spouse who is more sinned against than sinning has a contract-type (or possibly even a tort-type) moral right to compensation from the partner. However, because one cannot make the relevant factual determinations without invading the privacy of the marital partners and stirring up antagonism between them, any attempt to make this moral right legally enforceable may disserve rights-related interests on balance not only by disserving the spouses' privacy interests but also by making it less likely that, post-divorce, they will provide (1) their children with the parenting services to which the children are morally entitled and (2) each other with the opportunity to have a role in their children's lives to which they have entitlement interests. If this is the case, a liberal, rights-based State would have no moral obligation to make the moral right in question legally enforceable: indeed, it would presumably be morally impermissible for such a State to do so. Moreover, since a liberal, rights-based State that set out to compensate the more-sinned-against-than-sinning spouse itself would have to ascertain the same intimate facts to determine which spouse it should pay and how much compensation that spouse should be paid, any substitution by the State of a State-paid-compensation scheme for the private-legal-right approach would probably be equally dubious from a liberal perspective, even if one ignores the incentives such a scheme would provide the spouses to alter or lie about their behavior to secure (higher) payments for one of them.
21. Roughly speaking, the actual practice of courts in the two types of countries follows this pattern.
22. I hasten to add that the position I am taking belongs to a family of liberal-legalist positions to which a significant number of contemporary American legal academics (most importantly, Ronald Dworkin, but also many others, such as Stephen Gardbaum and David A. J. Richards) do subscribe.
23. Some legal realists believe that the answers courts give to contested legal-rights questions can best be predicted from socioeconomic data that relate to the political power of the groups that different decisions would benefit or harm; some believe that such decisions can best be predicted from data on the personal psychological histories or value-preferences of the judges who must make them; and some think that such

decisions can best be predicted from data on various aspects of the professional socialization of judges and lawyers that may or may not include or give much emphasis to the instruction they received on legitimate and valid legal argument.

24. See, e.g., MacCormick and Wiseman's report of Karl Llewellyn's comments on this issue in Neil MacCormick & Zipporah Wiseman, *Llewellyn Revisited,* 70 TEX. L. REV. 771–775–76 (1992) (book review).
25. See KARL LLEWELLYN, THE BRAMBLE BUSH (1930) and THE COMMON LAW TRADITION: DECIDING APPEALS 122–24 (1960).
26. See PHILIP BOBBITT, CONSTITUTIONAL INTERPRETATION (1991) and CONSTITUTIONAL FATE: THEORY OF THE CONSTITUTION (1982).
27. Bobbitt stipulatively defines ethical legal argument to refer to legal argument that is grounded on the ethos of the people, which, in the case of the United States, he identifies to be the ethos of limited government. I regard the ethos of limited government to be one corollary of the United States' more pervasive liberal commitment to valuing individuals' having and seizing the opportunity to lead lives of moral integrity (more specifically, to that component of that value that relates to individuals' choosing their own conceptions of the good). Although, like me, virtually all legal positivists would accept that the other types of argument Bobbitt lists are often used in American law, many legal positivists would doubt that the category of argument Bobbitt calls "ethical argument" is a valid component of American legal-argumentation practice except to the extent that it is a component of structural constitutional argument.
28. Although Chapter 5 will assume *ad arguendo* that the legal-positivist (and legal-realist) positions on valid legal argument are correct, I want to explain why I disagree with each of the positions the text ascribes to legal positivism or some legal positivists. First, I disagree with the protocol that legal positivists use to determine the legal validity of any type of argument. Legal positivists appear to believe that the social practices from which one should infer the set of argument-types that are legally valid in a particular society consist solely of the arguments that (1) its lawyers articulate when giving legal advice and when arguing in dispute resolution processes about the answer to a legal-rights question that is correct as a matter of law and (2) its judges articulate when questioning lawyers at oral argument and justifying conclusions they have reached about the resolution of an individual legal-rights issue that is correct as a matter of law. I believe that this protocol focuses on too narrow a data set. To start, the relevant data set must be expanded to include the unarticulated arguments that seem best to explain the legal-rights conclusions that the relevant lawyers and judges argued for and reached. In addition and more importantly, it should be expanded to include data on the relevant society's lawyers,' judges,' and citizens' beliefs about such law-related matters as the connection between the answer to any legal-rights issue that arises in their society that is correct as a matter of law and their society's moral commitments, the legitimate role of judges, the moral and constitutional permissibility of *ex post facto* legislation, and the moral integrity of their society. Even those legal positivists who reject my conclusion that certain features of the moral are ineliminable (who believe that the moral status of any position is purely a matter of social negotiation) should agree that the above moral beliefs of a society's legal community and members are part

of the network of specifically legal practices from which one must infer the set of arguments that are relevant to the resolution of legal-rights issues that are correct as a matter of law in the society in question.

Second, I disagree with the legal-positivist account of the set of arguments that have been articulated by lawyers, judges, and perhaps their company when considering the resolution of legal-rights issues that is correct as a matter of law in the societies they have studied. I will limit this response to the United States, the country with whose legal-argument practice I am most familiar, though I am certain that the legal-positivist account is, if anything, even less accurate in relation to several other rights-based societies (such as the Federal Republic of Germany). Legal positivists claim that lawyers and judges have rarely made reference to what I call arguments of moral principle to resolve legal-rights issues in cases in which the asserted legal right, if it existed, would derive from a moral right. At least in the United States, I consider this claim to be inaccurate. Although I will offer no more empirical evidence to support my view than the legal positivists have offered to support theirs, I will assert that, both in the nineteenth century and (after a partial but significant hiatus) increasingly in the last 50 years, American lawyers and judges have made explicit use of what I call arguments of moral principle (as contrasted with arguments about what morally ought to be done) in their briefs, oral arguments, and opinions in both state and federal courts and when providing legal advice to clients not only in moral-rights-related constitutional-law cases and situations but also in moral-rights-related common-law cases and situations. I should add an explicability-of-non-fit argument: to the extent that arguments of moral principle were made less often than I would deem appropriate in the 50 years after 1905, that fact can at least partially be explained by the failure of the American legal community to draw the correct lesson from *Lochner v. New York* 198 U.S. 405 (1905). Rather than concluding that (1) the *Lochner* majority took the valid approach to the issue it addressed by examining the consistency of the legislation under review with the moral commitments of U.S. society but reached the wrong conclusion about the constitutionality of the relevant statute (but see below) because it mistakenly found that those commitments were libertarian and not (as my analysis suggests) liberal and (2) the appropriate response to this mistake was to be more sophisticated and systematic when attempting to identify the American rights-based society's basic moral principle, many American lawyers, jurists, and legal academics responded by concluding that one should not consider moral principles at all when determining the answer to any legal-rights question that is correct as a matter of law in the United States and resolved therefore not to make or be influenced by arguments of moral principle, and many more (who realized that the previous response would convert legal analysis into an arcane procedure disconnected with the moral disputes it is sometimes required to decide) concluded that, although their analyses of moral-rights-related legal rights would have to take arguments of moral principle into account, it would be prudent to conceal that fact whenever it was possible to do so. (I should perhaps note that the preceding sentence's assertion that the conclusion of the *Lochner* Court was wrong may be incorrect. In particular, the *Lochner* Court's conclusion that the wages-and-hours legislation it reviewed was unconstitutional may have been correct for a different reason from the one the Court cited: the legislation may have violated the equal-protection clause in that it may have been passed to protect longtime American residents against competition from recent immigrants, who were willing to work longer hours for lower wages.)

Third, I disagree with the legal-positivist conclusion that, in the rights-based societies whose valid-legal-argument practice they are attempting to describe, arguments of moral principle are not generically valid legal arguments. In part, I disagree with this conclusion because I reject the legal positivists' empirical conclusion that arguments of moral principle have not been articulated very often by the lawyers and judges of the societies they have studied. In part, I disagree because the conclusion fails to give appropriate weight to the fact that liberal arguments of moral principle provide the best explanation not only for various constitutional doctrines that they have not been explicitly used to justify but also for various common-law contracts and tort doctrines they have not been used to justify (at least by the lawyers and judges who participated in the cases in which those doctrines were announced, challenged, and applied). (For a discussion of the relevant constitutional law, see Markovits, *supra* note 19 at Chapter 3–4. For two articles that make this point respectively in relation to various, important contract-law doctrines and various, important tort-law doctrines, see respectively Daniel Markovits, *Contract and Collaboration,* 113 YALE L.J. 1417 [2004] and Markovits, *supra* note 12 at 243.) But primarily I disagree with this conclusion because it is inconsistent both with the moral axiom I have cited and with the related beliefs that (I am asserting without appropriate empirical evidence) the lawyers, judges, and citizens of at least the United States have about the relationship between the resolution of any legal-rights claim that is correct as a matter of law in the United States and America's moral-rights commitments, about the morally legitimate role of judges, about the moral permissibility and constitutionality of *ex post facto* legislation, and about the moral integrity of the United States.

Before closing this discussion, I want to respond to two objections that several legal positivists have made to the claim that some moral norms are generically inside the law. The first objection is that this claim is inconsistent with the fact that judges often contend that the law constrains them to reach legal conclusions that they do not like in the sense that they think that the law should respond to the transactions or behaviors in question differently from the way it does. I believe that in virtually all such instances the judges are asserting their belief that, from their own personal-ultimate-value perspectives, the law morally ought to be different, not their belief that the law violates the moral rights of some party (i.e., is inconsistent with the society's moral-rights commitments). To the extent that this assessment is correct, this legal-positivist rejoinder is irrelevant to my claim.

The second of these two objections is that the position I am taking sacrifices an important advantage of the legal-positivist position that law and morals are separate—*viz.,* that this legal-positivist position enables observers to criticize the law on moral grounds. I have two responses to this objection. First, even if it were true, it would have no relevance to the truth-value of the separation claim. Second, I see no connection between the separation claim and the ability of observers to criticize legislation or legal rulings on moral grounds. The belief that the moral commitments of a rights-based society of moral integrity are generically inside its law does not preclude or even militate against the believer's criticizing those components of his society's law that are not moral-rights-based on the ground that they instantiate a personal ultimate value that he finds less morally attractive than some alternative or on the ground that the law or judicial ruling in question was designed to achieve a goal that cannot be morally defended (because the goal was immoral or amoral, because the goal was to secure the parochial interests of its supporters when this was improper, or because the law or ruling was reprehensibly mistaken). Nor does a belief that law and morals are not separate in the sense that legal positivists claim they are preclude the believer from morally criticizing those components of his society's law that do instantiate its moral-rights commitments on the ground that he finds these commitments less morally attractive than some alternative set of moral commitments a society could have. In fact, the position I am taking creates an additional basis for criticizing a rights-based society's law on moral grounds—*viz.*, that some component of its law is inconsistent with its moral commitments. In short, not only is the claim that underlies the second legal-positivist objection to my position irrelevant to the truth-value of the legal-positivist separation-position, but the claim is itself mistaken.

CHAPTER 5. THE PRESCRIPTIVE-MORAL AND LEGAL RELEVANCE OF ALLOCATIVE-EFFICIENCY CONCLUSIONS

1. Many economists with whom I have discussed this issue initially argue that there is an obvious answer to the question "which creatures' gains and losses are to be counted in an allocative-efficiency calculation?"—*viz.*, those creatures who are capable of conceiving of and (ideally) articulating estimates of their (equivalent-)dollar gains and losses. In my judgment, this answer is inconsistent with current practice and impossible to justify. No one would doubt, for example, that the equivalent-dollar effects of a choice on infants must be included in any allocative-efficiency estimate despite the fact that the infants cannot conceptualize, much less calculate or articulate, these effects. Moreover, although, in my view, an appropriate analysis would yield the conclusion that the equivalent-dollar effect of a choice or event on nonhuman animals should not be included in any allocative-efficiency calculation, that conclusion also cannot be generated by allocative-efficiency analysis itself—it must be generated by an analysis of the attributes of a creature that make it moral-rights-bearing or a legitimate object of moral-ought concern. I should add that one cannot resolve this issue by pointing out that nonhuman animals cannot own property: the morality of that social reality can itself be questioned, since there is no technical or practical reason to bar such creatures from owing property given that their interest in such property (and their rights in general) could be protected by a state-appointed guardian.
2. As the text indicates, the inability of allocative-efficiency analysis to identify the creatures whose interests count always precludes such analysis from generating moral-rights conclusions. However, in one sense, this limitation of allocative-efficiency analysis is most glaring when the moral status of a creature who would be affected by a relevant choice is contestable—e.g., in some abortion situations, in some tort situations in which

a fetus is the victim, in some situations involving persons with diminished mental capacities, and in cases involving the interests of members of future generations.

3. Admittedly, the fact that the interests privacy protects are important does not establish the conclusion that the concept of privacy can play a useful role in prescriptive-moral analysis. Thus, Judith Jarvis Thomson has argued that the concept of privacy is otiose in that any prescriptive-moral conclusion it can be used to generate could be justified equally well without it by citing the fact that the conduct under investigation violated other rights (for example, property rights) of the relevant rights-holder. See Judith Jarvis Thomson, *The Right to Privacy,* 4 PHIL. & PUB. AFF. 295 (1975). I disagree for two reasons. First, in some circumstances the only right that a privacy-right-violating act violates is the right to privacy. Assume that the victim is trespassing in someone else's apartment and is looking at a pornographic picture he has stolen. Someone who goes out of his way to observe the victim engaging in this activity (say, by using some kind of X-ray or night-vision machine to enable him to see what the victim is doing) has violated the victim's privacy right but no other right the victim has. Second, in some circumstances in which the victim could demonstrate that his rights have been violated without making reference to the fact that his privacy rights have been violated—e.g., by showing that his property rights have been violated—the fact that the victim's privacy rights have been violated will still be significant in that it will affect the damages he suffered and the award to which he is morally (and legally) entitled.
4. I should say that American judicial opinions and decisions also sometimes ignore the difference between some information's being a matter of public interest in the psychological and entitlement senses. See *Sidis v. F-R Pub. Corporation,* 113 F.2d 806 (1940). The courts sometimes also make a parallel error when deciding whether someone is a public figure—a designation that affects the circumstances in which the individual is legally entitled to obtain damages from people who have published damaging, false information about him.
5. Section 2 of the book's Conclusion delineates and criticizes a canonical law and economics analysis of privacy. See Richard M. Posner, *The Right to Privacy,* 12 GA. L. REV. 393 (1978).
6. Relatedly, many economists—see, e.g., MILTON FRIEDMAN, CAPITALISM AND FREEDOM (1962)—adopt what I call a billiard-ball definition of liberty when engaged in political philosophy. On this definition, any law restricts liberty if it prohibits someone from making any choice whatsoever—if it limits his "opportunity set" in any way. Thus, in this usage, a law prohibiting someone from driving north on a one-way southbound street or a law prohibiting someone from making an unprovoked physical attack on another would be a restriction of liberty. In my judgment, this usage not only does not capture the way in which we use the concept of liberty but also creates a concept that cannot perform a useful role in prescriptive-moral or legal analysis. For the concept of liberty to do any work, some special justification must be offered for a restriction of liberty to be just or justifiable, and to my mind in ordinary circumstances, no special justification must be offered to restrict the direction in which one may drive down a street or to prohibit a person from attacking another physically. I should add that some philosophers also seem to think that liberty should be defined in

a way that does not require choice options to be morally assessed. For analyses of such so-called flat conceptions of liberty, see Hiller Steiner, *Freedom and Bivalence* in FREEDOM, POWER AND POLITICAL MORALITY: ESSAYS FOR FELIX OPPENHEIM 57 (Ian Carter and Mario Ricciardi, eds. 2001).

7. This articulation of the relevant right is intentional. In my view, a potential victim's moral right is violated by his potential injurer's rejection of an avoidance move he should have perceived (in effect) to be *ex ante* allocatively efficient even if the prospective loss in question does not eventuate. Of course, in such cases, the wronged potential victim would be morally entitled to recover only the risk cost the avoidance-move rejection imposed on him and the damage done by the disrespect he was shown. The latter sum would be quite small if the potential injurer's choice was not affected by the potential injurer's attitude toward the particular victim. (If it were not, the respect loss would be shared by all members of and participants in the society in question.) The parenthetical "in effect" that appears in this heading is included to reflect the reality that most injurers will not be thinking in allocative-efficiency terms—will be making a private cost and benefit trade-off whose relationship to its allocative counterpart they would not recognize.
8. The text will list and make a few comments on each of these reasons. They are discussed more thoroughly in Richard S. Markovits, *On the Economic Inefficiency of a Liberal-Corrective-Justice-Securing Law of Torts,* 2006 ILL. L. REV. 525 (2006).
9. See, e.g., *Rutherford v. Owens-Illinois, Inc.*, 941 P.2d 1203 (Cal. 1997).
10. See, e.g., *Sindell v. Abbott Lab.*, 607 P.2d 924 (Cal. 1980).
11. Assume, for example, that (1) the relevant actor is strictly liable, (2) cause-in-fact has to be inferred from the contribution the actor's activity made to the *ex ante* probability of the loss's occurring, (3) if the actor does not avoid, his activity will increase the probability of a $1,000 loss from 15% to 40%, (4) an avoidance move is available to the actor that would reduce his activity's contribution to the *ex ante* probability of the relevant loss's occurring from 25% to 15% (and concomitantly his percentage contribution to the *ex ante* probability of the loss's occurring from 25/40 = 62.5% > 50% to 15/30 = 50%), (5) the private cost of the relevant avoidance move is $300, (6) both the private cost of the relevant avoidance move and the loss that move would make less likely equal their allocative counterparts, and (7) all relevant parties are risk neutral. In this situation, the avoidance move would generate weighted-average-expected allocative benefits of 1%($1,000) = $100 and private benefits to the avoider of 40%($1,000) = $400 (since it would convert a situation in which he would be deemed to be the cause-in-fact of and liable for any loss that resulted—i.e., in which he faced the prospect of having to pay weighted average damages of 40%($1,000) = $400—to one in which he would not be deemed to be the cause-in-fact of any loss that resulted—i.e., in which he should not expect to pay any damages). In this situation, then, (1) the private benefits and profits the avoidance move would yield the potential avoider would be inflated by $400 – $100 = $300, and (2) this inflation would critically affect the profitability of the avoidance move in question—would render $400 – $300 = $100 profitable an avoidance move that was $300 – $100 = $200 allocatively inefficient. I should perhaps point out that the $300 inflation in the profits yielded by the relevant avoidance move equals

the sum of (1) the $150 by which the weighted-average damages the actor should expect to pay if he does not avoid ($400) exceed the weighted-average loss his activity should be expected to yield if he does not avoid (25%[$1,000] = $250) and (2) the $150 by which the $0 damages the actor should expect to pay if he does avoid falls below the 15%($1,000) = $150 in losses his activity should be expected to generate on the weighted average if he does avoid.

12. An illustration may be helpful. Assume that there is a one-in-a-million chance—a .0001% probability—that the potential victim will be able to increase *ex ante* allocative efficiency by $99,500 by reducing the weighted-average-expected loss by $100,000 at an avoidance cost of $500 and a one-in-a-hundred chance—a 1% probability—that the potential injurer will be able to increase *ex ante* allocative efficiency by $500 by reducing the weighted-average-expected loss by $100,000 by incurring $99,500 in avoidance costs. On these facts, shifting from a $100,000/$0 victim/injurer loss-division to a $99,000 / $1,000 victim/injurer loss-division would increase allocative efficiency by (1%[500] −.0001%[$99,500] = $5 − $.995 = $4.005). To determine the division of the loss that was *ex ante* most allocatively efficient, the analyst would have to repeat this calculation for each additional shift about which he had information and pick the loss-division that involved the total shift associated with the highest net gain.

CHAPTER 6. A CRITIQUE OF VARIOUS RELEVANCE ARGUMENTS MADE BY ECONOMISTS AND LAW AND ECONOMICS SCHOLARS

1. Louis Kaplow and Steven Shavell, *Fairness versus Welfare*, 114 HARV. L. REV. 961 (2001).
2. *Id.* at 1018.
3. *Id.* at 1007.
4. *Id.*
5. *Id.* at 1006.
6. *Id.* at 1008.
7. *Id.* at 1018–19.
8. *Id.* at 1011.
9. *Id.* at 1012.
10. See Louis Kaplow and Steven Shavell, *The Conflict between Notions of Fairness and the Pareto Principle*, 1 Am. L. & Econ. Rev. 63, 76 (1999).
11. See Howard Chang, *A Liberal Theory of Social Welfare: Fairness, Utility, and the Pareto Principle*, 110 Yale L.J. 72 (2000). As Chang demonstrates, Kaplow and Shavell's apparent belief to the contrary notwithstanding, they cannot incorporate his point into their position without abandoning their position. See Howard Chang, *The Possibility of a Fair Paretian*, 110 Yale L.J. 251 (2000).
12. Richard Posner made this standard economics argument in the first edition of his famous ECONOMIC ANALYSIS OF LAW 241 (1973). I have heard many economists make precisely the same argument.
13. Basically, this is the argument Richard Posner made in his article *The Ethical and Political Basis of the Efficiency Norm in Common Law Adjudication*, 8 HOFSTRA L. REV. 487 (1980).

14. Note the mathematical character of the first premise's definition of justice.
15. Admittedly, some proponents of this argument may not take it to be a separate argument for the justness of allocatively efficient decisions. These scholars may think that the supposed fact that allocatively efficiency decisions protect autonomy because they will always elicit hypothetical consent may find this conclusion salient because they believe that autonomy is one component of the kind of envelope concept of justice they (and the second positive argument just described) adopt. I should also admit that something like this hypothetical-consent argument may be playing a role in the argument that all allocatively efficient choices morally ought to be adopted because, if they were, the economy would end up in a position that would be Pareto-superior to the position that would be established if no such decisions were made. However, the importance of consent arguments in philosophical debate has led me to consider this argument separately here.
16. This argument is best articulated by Richard Posner in THE ECONOMICS OF JUSTICE 92–99 and 101–03 (1981).
17. For example, Richard Posner cites decisions about implied warranties of habitability as instances of allocatively inefficient common-law decisions that leave everyone worse off *ex ante*. *Id.* at 102. My own study demonstrates that such decisions will leave some groups whose members will be able to identify themselves *ex ante* better off and some such groups worse off. See Richard S. Markovits, *The Distributive Impact, Allocative Efficiency and Overall Desirability of Ideal Housing Codes,* 89 HARV. L. REV. 1815 (1976). I have no doubt that this is the case for most common-law decisions and *a fortiori* for public-policy choices in general.
18. See Posner, *supra* note 16 at 97.
19. See Harold Hotelling, *The General Welfare in Relation to Problems of Taxation and of Railway Utility Rates,* 6 ECONOMETRICA 242 (1938) and J. R, Hicks, *Foundation of Welfare Economics,* 49 ECON. J. 696 (1939). See also Mitchell Polinsky, *Probabilistic Compensation Criteria,* 86 Q.J. ECON. 407, 407–12 (1972).
20. See Robert L. Rabin, *The Historical Development of the Fault Principle: A Reinterpretation,* 15 GA. L. REV. 925, 955 (1981), discussing Landes and Posner's treatment of *Adams v. Bullock,* 227 N.Y. 208, 125 N.E. 93 (1919) in William A. Landes & Richard M. Posner, *The Positive Economic Theory of Tort Law,* 15 GA. L. REV. 851, 894 (1981).
21. I should note that Landes and Posner often fail to consider the full range of avoidance moves available to injurers and that this deficiency of their tort-law scholarship parallels the tendency of economists in general to ignore many of the types of misallocation that the policies they investigate can affect. For other contexts in which Landes and Posner have ignored some of the avoidance moves available to potential injurers, see Chapter 4's discussions of their arguments for (1) the allocatively efficiency of the way in which the common law varies the rule of liability it imposes on the members of an industry according to whether the industry is mature or in its infancy and (2) the allocatively efficiency of marine-salvage law.
22. See, e.g., Paul Joskow and Alvin Klevorick, *A Framework for Analyzing Predatory Pricing Policy,* 89 YALE L.J. 213 (1979).
23. See, e.g., Frank Easterbrook, *Predatory Strategies and Counterstrategies,* 48 U. CHI. L. REV. 263 (1981); ROBERT BORK, THE ANTITRUST PARADOX (1978); and Richard

Posner, *Oligopoly and the Antitrust Laws: A Suggested Approach,* 21 STAN. L. REV. 1562 (1969).

24. See Sherman Antitrust Act, 26 Stat. 209 (1890) (codified as amended at 15 U.S.C.A. §§1–11) and Clayton Act, 38 Stat. 730 (1914) (codified as amended at 15 U.S.C.A. §§12–27). The text ignores the third major federal major antitrust statute—the Federal Trade Commission Act, 38 Stat. 717 (1914) (codified as amended at 15 U.S.C.A. §§41–58)—because its operative unfair-competition test of legality has always been assumed to condemn the same conduct that the Sherman and Clayton Acts prohibit.
25. For a more detailed discussion of the proper interpretations of the Sherman and Clayton Acts, see Richard S. Markovits, *Some Preliminary Notes on the American Antitrust Laws' Economic Tests of Legality,* 27 STAN. L. REV. 841 (1975).
26. I believe that the Sherman Act covers all but one type of business conduct. The exception reflects a drafting error. As written, the Sherman Act does not prohibit unsuccessful attempts to enter into price-fixing agreements by offering to reciprocate to a rival's rejection of an otherwise-profitable opportunity to beat the offerer's contrived oligopolistic offer. Section 1 does not cover such conduct because it does not cover attempts. Section 2 does not cover such conduct because, given Section 1, its prohibition of monopolizing or attempting to monopolize should be read not to cover contracts in restraint of trade or attempts to enter into such contracts. I should add that American federal law does not contain a general attempt statute (i.e., a statute that declares criminal any attempt to do something whose successful completion is prohibited by any federal criminal statute) and that American federal courts do not read attempt provisions into federal statutes that do not contain them. I should also add that—although most antitrust-law professors seem to disagree with my conclusion that the Sherman Act does not prohibit unsuccessful attempts to enter into contracts or agreements in restraint of trade—all the criminal-law professors with whom I have discussed this issue have agreed with my conclusion. I should also point out that unsuccessful attempts to enter into price-fixing arrangements may well harm the buyers to whom they related. Assume, for example, that both a best-placed seller X1 and his closest rival X2 for a particular buyer Y1's patronage would have to incur overall marginal costs of $1 to supply Y1 and that X1 had a $.10 buyer preference advantage over X2 for Y1's patronage and a $.15 buyer preference advantage over Y1's third-placed supplier (whose marginal costs of supply were also $1). Now assume that X1 charges Y1 $1.14 for his product A1 and tries to induce X2 not to steal Y1 from him by beating this offer with a price of $1.03 by promising to reciprocate by allowing X2 to secure higher prices than he would otherwise be able to obtain from another buyer, Y2, whom X2 was best-placed to supply and X1 was uniquely-second-placed to supply. Finally, assume that X2 rejects this offer and steals Y1 from X1 by charging Y1 a price of $1.03 for X2's product A2 (which Y1 disprefers to X1's product A1 by $.10). In this example, X1's attempt to enter into an anticompetitive agreement with X2 will have cost Y1 the equivalent of $.03 by producing a situation in which he ended up buying A2 for $1.03 rather than A1 for $1.10 (the highest non-oligopolistic price X1 could have successfully charged Y1 for A1).

27. One additional clarification is required. Most of the provisions of the Clayton Act apply to an individual transaction or an individual actor's choice or course of conduct. For example, §7 addresses the legality of an individual merger or acquisition. However, I believe that §3 of the Clayton Act should usually be read to address the legality of all potential suppliers of a given set of buyers' using tie-ins and reciprocal-trading agreements, engaging in the resale price maintenance, and/or employing vertical territorial restraints and customer-allocation clauses—i.e., to declare illegal the use of such arrangements by all members of such a group who wish to employ them if the general availability of such arrangements to the relevant group of sellers would tend to "decrease competition" in the Clayton Act sense of that expression. The contrary conclusion would imply that §3 requires the courts to run a kind of paramutual system in which sellers whose survival does not depend on their using these vertical techniques are prohibited from employing them when this prohibition would help their less successful rivals survive while these less successful rivals are allowed to use the techniques in question because granting them permission to do so would help them survive. Such behavior by the courts would contravene the level-playing-field conditions that the antitrust laws are in part designed to secure.
28. The conduct that the Clayton Act covers may also harm the relevant buyers by making it profitable for the perpetrators to remove buyer surplus they would not otherwise have found profitable to exploit. According to the test of legality I am reading the Clayton Act to promulgate, conduct that should have been predicted *ex ante* to impose net equivalent-dollar losses on the relevant buyers for this reason (even considering any benefits it should have been predicted to confer on them by lowering the perpetrator's marginal costs and hence the prices he would charge on that account) would violate the Act if it would also be predicted *ex ante* to harm them on balance by reducing the attractiveness of the offers they received from their inferior suppliers so long as it would be predicted *ex ante* to inflict equivalent-dollar losses on them on balance.
29. For an explanation of these claims, see Richard S. Markovits, *Tie-ins and Reciprocity: A Functional, Legal, and Policy Analysis,* 58 TEX. L. REV. 1363 (1980).

CONCLUSION

1. See Richard M. Posner *The Right to Privacy,* 12 GA. L. REV. 393 (1978).
2. See THOMAS S. KUHN, THE STRUCTURE OF SCIENTIFIC REVOLUTIONS (1970).

Glossary of Frequently Used Symbols and the Concepts for Which They Stand

This glossary is divided into two sections. The first contains symbols and related concepts whose use is not restricted to distortion analysis. The second contains the symbols I use when executing distortion analyses.

Many of the symbols in the first section stand both for a curve and for a point on that curve. Thus, the symbol MC stands both for the marginal cost curve and for the private cost a producer incurred to produce the last unit of output of the product he produced. The glossary defines these symbols as if they referred exclusively to the relevant point. Thus, MC is defined to refer to the private cost a producer incurred to produce the last unit of the product he produced. However, as already indicated, the text sometimes uses the symbol to refer to the curve that indicates the marginal (i.e., private variable) cost the producer would have to incur to produce successive units of the product.

I. SYMBOLS AND TERMS WHOSE USE IS NOT RESTRICTED TO DISTORTION ANALYSIS

AFC average fixed (private) cost

Fixed (private) costs are (private) costs of production that do not vary with output. Average fixed (private) costs are the total fixed costs a producer has incurred (TFC) *divided by* the quantity of his output (Q): TFC/Q.

AFLC average fixed allocative cost
The fixed allocative cost of producing some good is the net allocative value or total allocative product that the non-variable-cost resources used to produce that good (the resources whose quantity does not vary with the good's output) would have generated in their alternative uses—i.e., the net equivalent-dollar gains those resources would have generated in their alternative uses. The average fixed allocative cost of producing some good exceeds the total fixed allocative cost of producing that good (TFLC) *divided by* the quantity of its output (Q): TFLC/Q.

AVC average variable (private) cost
The total variable (private) cost to a producer of producing a specified quantity of some good are those (private) costs that the producer of the units in question would incur to produce them that reflect his use of resources whose use does vary with his output of the good concerned. The average variable cost to a producer of producing some quantity of a particular good equals the total variable cost he incurs to produce that quantity of the good in question (TVC) *divided by* the quantity in question (Q): TVC/Q.

AVLC average variable allocative cost
The total variable allocative cost of a producer's producing a specified quantity of a particular good is the net allocative value or total allocative product that the variable-cost resources he would use to produce the relevant units (the resources that he uses in quantities that increase with his output) would have generated in their alternative uses—i.e., the net equivalent-dollar gains those resources would have generated in their alternative uses. The average variable allocative cost of a producer's producing a specified quantity of a given product equals the total variable allocative cost of his doing so (TVLC) *divided by* the quantity in question (Q): TVLC/Q.

DD the demand curve for a particular product (which may be specified by a subscript)
The demand curve for a particular product indicates the quantity of that product that would be sold at different (per unit) prices. DD_F stands for the demand curve for a particular product that would be faced by a given firm. DD_{IND} stands for the demand curve for a particular product that would be faced by an industry—i.e., by a set of firms that produce identical versions of the product in question and distribute them from locations and in ways among which relevant buyers are indifferent. DD_{IND} will equal DD_F if the industry in question is a pure monopoly.

LB the allocative benefits generated by a particular choice (usually specified by a subscript)
The operational definition of the allocative benefits of a choice depends in part on the nature of the choice in question. If the choice is a choice to use a particular resource to increase the unit output of a particular product, to create a quality-or-variety-increasing (QV) investment (see below), or to execute a production-process-research (PPR) project (see below), the allocative benefits of the choice equal, respectively, the net equivalent-dollar gain generated by the consumption

of the unit of output in question (as opposed to its allocatively costless destruction), the net equivalent-dollar gain generated by the use of the QV investment created (as opposed to its allocatively costless destruction), and the net equivalent-dollar gain generated by the use of the discovered production process (as opposed to its not being used). If the choice is a choice by an individual to consume a unit of a particular good, the allocative benefit is the net equivalent-dollar gain generated by his consumption of the unit in question (as opposed to the unit's allocatively costless destruction).

LC the allocative cost generated by a particular choice (usually specified by a subscript)
The operational definition of the allocative cost of a choice also depends in part on the nature of the relevant choice. If the relevant choice is to increase the unit output of a particular good, to create a particular quality-or-variety-increasing (QV) investment, or to execute a particular production-process-research (PPR) project, its allocative cost equals the allocative value (net equivalent-dollar gain) that the resources consumed by the choice in question would have generated in their alternative uses. If the relevant choice is the choice of an individual to consume an existing unit of some good, its allocative cost equals the net equivalent-dollar gain that would have been generated by the consumption of the unit in question by the alternative consumer who would have consumed it if the consumer whose choice is being analyzed did not do so.

LE the allocative (economic) efficiency of a particular choice (usually specified by a subscript)
The difference between the allocative benefits and the allocative cost of the choice in question—i.e., the net equivalent-dollar gain generated by the resource-use or consumption decision in question (if the alternative to it were the allocatively costless destruction of the resources or good in question).

MC marginal (private) cost of production
The marginal cost to a specified producer of producing a last unit of some good is the private variable cost the producer incurs to produce that unit (the product in question is sometimes specified by a subscript).

MC* adjusted marginal cost
The adjusted marginal cost of producing a last unit of some good is the relevant private marginal cost adjusted to reflect Pareto imperfections that cause the private marginal cost figure to diverge from its allocative counterpart—marginal allocative cost or MLC (see below). The text normally does not refer to the MC* of a particular product in isolation. Rather, it refers to the ratio of the MC*s of two products (say, X and Y), which is defined to equal the marginal rate at which the economy can transform one into the other—$MC^*_X/MC^*_Y \equiv MRT_{Y/X}$ (see below).

MK marginal (private) cost of purchase
The private cost a buyer must incur to purchase the last unit of some product he purchases. When the buyer is a monopsonist—i.e., faces an upward-sloping supply curve (see below)—and does not engage in price discrimination when

purchasing the product consumed, the MK to him of buying the last unit of the good in question that he purchases will exceed the price of that last unit.

MLC marginal allocative cost (of production)
The marginal allocative cost of producing the last unit of some product is the net allocative value the variable-cost resources used to produce that unit would have generated in their alternative uses—i.e., the allocative product of those resources in their alternative uses.

MLP marginal allocative product (of some resource—in this book usually labor [L]—in some specified use)
The marginal allocative product of a specified type of resource (say, labor) in a particular kind of use is the equivalent-dollar gain generated by the marginal unit of that type of resource when devoted to that use. If the resource is labor and the labor in question is being used to produce additional units of some product X, MLP_L equals the allocative value of the units of X the marginal unit of labor produced *plus* any external benefits the labor's production-activity generated directly *minus* any external costs the labor's production-activity generated directly.

MLV marginal allocative value
The marginal allocative value of the last unit of some product to be produced is the net equivalent-dollar gain generated by its consumption (as opposed to its allocatively costless destruction).

MPP marginal physical product of some type of resource (usually specified in a subscript—in this book, usually some type of labor [L]) that is devoted to producing units of output of a specified product (sometimes also identified with a subscript)
The marginal physical product of a specified resource (say, of some type of labor) is the number of units of a specified good that the resource in question is being used to produce that is produced by the last unit of that type of resource used to produce that good.

MRP marginal revenue product of some type of resource when used to produce a particular product (both the resource and the product are usually specified in a subscript)
The marginal revenue product of a particular type of resource used to produce a given product is the additional (net) revenue the producer of that good obtained by using the last unit of the relevant type of resource he used to produce that good.

$MRS_{Y/X}$ the marginal rate of substitution of Y for X
The rate at which a consumer of Y and X can substitute Y for X at the margin and remain equally well off.

$MRT_{Y/X} = MC^*_X/MC^*_Y$ the marginal rate of transformation of Y into X
The ratio of the quantity of Y the economy can produce with resources it would otherwise use to produce X to the amount of X it would have to forgo to produce the Y for marginal changes in the production of X and Y.

P — price
For the most part in this book, P stands for the per-unit price charged for a particular product. In practice, pricing may be much more complicated: a given buyer may be charged different per-unit prices for different units; different buyers may be charged different per-unit prices; buyers may be charged lump-sum fees for the right to purchase a product at a single (nonvarying) per-unit price; and the sale of one product on specified terms may be conditioned on the buyer's agreeing to purchase a second product from the seller in question or from somebody else on specified terms or on the buyer's agreeing to supply the seller of the first product with a second product on specified terms.

PB — the private benefits generated by some productive resource-use or consumption decision (often indicated by a subscript)
The private benefits a resource user (consumer) obtains by using the resource in the indicated way (by consuming the product in question). In a Pareto-imperfect world, PB will often differ from LB (see above). Thus, MRP will often differ from MLP, the MR = PB that a unit output producer secures by producing a last unit of his product will often differ from the LB that his decision to produce that unit generates (the MLV of the good *plus* any external benefits or *minus* any external costs generated directly by its production), and the PB a consumer obtains by consuming a unit of some product will differ from the LB generated by his consumption of that unit to the extent that his consumption of that unit generates external costs or benefits.

PC — the private cost someone incurs to make a specified type of resource-use decision (often indicated by a subscript)
PC may diverge from LC (see above) for one, two, or all of the following three reasons: the individual who is deciding to produce one or more units of an existing product, to create a QV investment (see below), to execute a PPR project (see below), or to use a particular known production process (rather than another) to produce some product may not have to pay anything for some of the resources his resource-use decision consumes (i.e., his resource-use choice may generate external costs), one or more nonexternality Pareto imperfections may distort the private cost to the individual in question of some or all of the resources he uses for the relevant purpose for which he does have to pay something, and/or the resource use in question may generate external benefits.

$P\pi$ — the private profits yielded by a specified resource-use choice (often indicated by a subscript)

$P\pi = PB - PC$ — the private profits yielded by any resource-use choice will diverge from the LE of that choice (see above) if the private benefits generated by the choice in question diverge from their allocative counterparts and/or the private cost of the choice diverges from its allocative counterpart unless the two divergences perfectly offset each other.

PPR production-process research

A (pure) production-process-research project is a project that is designed to discover a privately and presumptively allocatively less expensive method to produce a relevant quantity of an existing product. If a research project is designed to discover a product that is both cheaper to produce and more valuable to its consumers, it is classified as a mixed PPR and product-research project. A research project that is designed to discover a new product whose relevant average total cost of production is lower but that is less valuable to its consumers than the existing products for which it will be substituted is classified as a product-research project (which is one type of QV investment [see below]).

Q the quantity of some good that is produced

QV a modifier to the word *investment* that indicates that the investment in question is quality-or-variety-increasing.

QV investments create additional (different) or superior product variants, additional or superior distributive outlets, or additional capacity or inventory (which enable their owner to offer a greater average speed of supply throughout a fluctuating-demand cycle). Put crudely, QV investments increase the demand faced by the QV investor.

SS the supply curve of some good or input (which may be indicated by a subscript)

The supply curve for a good or input indicates the quantity of that good or input that will be supplied at different prices. The book refers to four supply curves—the supply curve of some unspecified good (SS), the supply curve of labor (SS_L), which also could be described as an average wage (AW) curve, the supply curve of subcode housing (SS_S), and the supply curve of code-quality housing (SS_C). It should be noted that when the supply curve of labor is upward sloping and the relevant employer does not engage in price discrimination when hiring labor, the MK to him of hiring an additional unit of labor will exceed the wage he pays the marginal worker—i.e., the marginal wage curve (MW) will exceed the average wage curve ($AW = SS_L$).

UO unit output

XMC external marginal cost

The portion of the allocative cost generated by the production of a marginal unit of a specified product that reflects the fact that the production of that unit consumes some resources for which the relevant producer pays nothing.

Δ a symbol for *marginal,* which always precedes another symbol that refers to a particular type of resource use

The symbol Δ indicates that the resource use in question is the marginal resource use of that type in the sense of being the least profitable but not unprofitable (in this sense, the last) resource use of that type that occurred (which may or may not be marginal in the sense of being infinitesimally small).

II. SYMBOLS AND TERMS USED EXCLUSIVELY IN DISTORTION ANALYSIS

This section lists the various distortion symbols that the book most often uses—MD, XD, MD/XD, TD, and Σ%D. Although the distortion symbols in question are freestanding in the glossary, in the book they are virtually always followed by additional symbols placed in parentheses that indicate whether the relevant distortion is in a private benefit, private cost, or profit figure. Indeed, the private benefit, cost, and profit figures in question are usually further specified by subscripts that indicate the resource use to which they relate and, when relevant, the assumption about the types of uses from which the resources used for the relevant purpose are withdrawn on which the calculation of the distortion in question is based. For example, a typical distortion symbol would be MD($P\pi_{\Delta QV}$), which stands for the distortion that imperfections in seller competition (monopoly, hence MD) would generate in an otherwise-Pareto-perfect world in the profits the creation and use of the marginal QV investment in some area of product-space confers on the investor who made it on realistic assumptions about the uses from which the resources consumed by the creation and use of the relevant marginal QV investment were withdrawn.

MD — the monopoly distortion in the private benefit, cost, or profit figure specified in parentheses that immediately follow the indicated symbol
The distortion in the figure in question—i.e., the difference between the private and allocative figure in question—that the actual imperfections in seller competition that are present in the economy would generate in an otherwise-Pareto-perfect economy.

XD — the externality distortion in the private benefit, cost, or profit figure specified in parentheses that immediately follow the indicated symbol
The distortion in the figure in question that the externalities actually generated in the economy would cause in an otherwise-Pareto-perfect economy.

MD/XD — the monopoly/externality distortion in the private benefit, cost, or profit figure specified in parentheses that immediately follow the indicated symbol
The distortion in the figure in question that the imperfections in seller competition and externalities that exist in the economy would generate in an otherwise-Pareto-perfect economy.

TD — the tax distortion in the private benefit, cost, or profit figure specified in parentheses that immediately follow the indicated symbol
The distortion in the figure in question that the taxes on the margin of income that prevail in the relevant economy would generate in an otherwise-Pareto-perfect economy.

ΣD — the aggregate distortion in the private benefit, cost, or profit figure specified in parentheses that immediately follow the indicated symbol
The aggregate distortion in the figure in question generated by the interactions of all the prevailing Pareto imperfections in the economy.

Σ%D — the aggregate percentage distortion in the private figure specified in parentheses that immediately follows the indicated symbol (in this book always $P\pi_{\Delta\ldots}$ where the ellipsis stands for some type of resource use)

The ratio of the aggregate distortion (ΣD) in the relevant profit figure to the allocative cost (LC) of the specified resource use.

Note: I recognize the problematic character of calculating the distortion that would be generated by some subset of the Pareto imperfections present in an economy on the counterfactual assumption that the economy is otherwise-Pareto-perfect (i.e., the problem caused by the fact that the imperfections that are being assumed away affect the magnitudes of the imperfections that are being considered).

Index